Rescued from Obscurity Series

Forthcoming titles in the **Rescued from Obscurity** Series, translated from the French:

D'Holbach, *Portable Theology*

D'Holbach *Critical History of Jesus Christ*

A Treatise of Three Impostors: Moses, Jesus and Muhammad (author unknown)

Geoffroy Vallée, *The Flail of Faith* and *The Art of Believing in Nothing*

Jean Meslier, *Testament for his Parishioners*

Other books form Hodgson Press:

'Lively' and Other Stories by Boris Mozhaev & a Memoir by Alexander Solzhenitsyn.

Christianity Unveiled

by

Paul-Henri Thiry Baron d'Holbach

Hodgson Press

Published in Great Britain by Hodgson Press 2008

Hodgson Press
PO Box 903ᴬ
Kingston upon Thames
Surrey
KT1 9LY
United Kingdom

enquiries@hodgsonpress.co.uk

www.hodgsonpress.co.uk

ISBN: 978-1-906164-04-1

Printed in Great Britain by Lightning Source Ltd.

Typesetting and layout by Bernard Lowe

Dedication

For our nephews—Nicholas, William, Liam and Ryan—never tempted to partake of the 'opium of the people', and thereby they offer hope for a more rational, peaceful future.

Contents

List of Illustrations

xi

Acknowledgements

Grateful thanks are due to Dr Jonathan Miller for bringing d'Holbach's work to my attention through his excellent series on BBC television, A *Brief History of Disbelief*: without this impetus, I doubt I would ever have embarked on what has turned out to be, at least for me, a most fascinating study of a giant amongst unbelievers.

I also owe a huge debt to friends who have encouraged me and provided materials for my research: my old friend since childhood, Gérard Poisson and his wife Véronique, procured for me a most valuable CD Rom, which was difficult to obtain, with the complete works of Voltaire and many other authors of the Enlightenment, which helped me to search literally hundreds of volumes of works with the greatest of ease and which would otherwise have taken years to wade through in hard copy. My grateful thanks also go to my old friend Dave Hanrahan, who painstakingly waded through my manuscript and made many valuable suggestions.

Thanks are also due in abundance to the staff of the British Library, both at the reading rooms at St Pancras and at the newspaper archive in Colindale.

Most of all, my debt to my partner Bernard Lowe is inestimable for his unflappable and unfailing patience in answer to my *cris de cœur* in the wake of computer crashes and a myriad of other technical problems, which seem at times to be sent by the unseen forces in which I do not believe in more rational and less panic–stricken moments. His eye for detail and design, and his technical expertise and good humour in the midst of the black art which is computing are a constant source of admiration and amazement to me. He has worked tirelessly on all the artwork, lay–out and typesetting of this book.

I should also like to thank the National Secular Society and the people I have come to know and admire amongst the membership. Their work in making a stand against the appalling proliferation of divisive faith schools of every type over the last few years, and many other issues of deep concern to many, is one of the few forces for a more rational and harmonious future. I urge all who can to join their voice with that of the NSS: more about their work can be accessed at www.secularism.org.uk

Figure 1: Paul-Henri Thiry Baron d'Holbach (1723—1789).

Preface

As long as organized religious belief has existed, whether an individual ascribes to the view that God or gods exist, or not, has literally been a burning issue. People have not always enjoyed the basic right openly to doubt the existence of such extra–terrestrial forces—indeed, d'Holbach did not have the right to do so, at least on paper, since virtually all his anti–religious works were published anonymously or attributed to those beyond the reach of the Church and state, i.e., they were dead. (Presumably at that point, they were at least in a position to know for sure whether there was a god or not, and God was able to deal with them personally, face to face, or at least spirit to spirit!) The Church, supported by the state, burned people at the stake for not believing, as will become clear by reading this book, and though this was not the current practice in d'Holbach's time, there were certainly those who dearly wished it were so.[1] Also, as d'Holbach points out, holding high office within the state and espousing religious belief went hand in glove, and even today it is very difficult for someone who is openly atheist to seek or hold high office in the United States of America.[2] So much for one of the great democracies of western civilization!

But much more sinister than that—somewhere on earth, someone is being tortured, maimed or killed every day, or at the very least oppressed, and often in great numbers, for either believing or not believing, in a being or beings, whose existence is scientifically utterly unprovable. The fact that a belief in unseen beings or forces, be they madonnas, gods, saints, gurus, charms, horoscopes, etc., affords personal comfort and consolation, or adds meaning for some to an otherwise meaningless or purposeless existence, is not the point: in a society claiming to be educated and democratic, these things should not be promoted and it is the view of many that they are not benign. Whilst people actually die violent, premature deaths because they either

---

[1] There is a website which lists some prominent victims of the Catholic Church, put to death on the express command of various popes down the ages: find it at http://www.lespapes.net/Qui%20les%20papes%20ont%20...htm   Unfortunately, the site is wholly in French, but it provides interesting reading.

[2] A Congressman in the USA recently admitted to the fact that he held no belief in a god of any kind and it actually hit the news as an item worthy of note. It is difficult to believe that a single, public figure saying he is an atheist should hit the headlines in this century. What is even more distressing is that his admission set in motion a smear campaign against him and the individual concerned has been described as 'crossing one of the last frontiers of politics.' See *San Francisco Chronicle*, 14 March 2007. The findings of a national survey carried out by the University of Minnesota engendered the headline, 'Atheists Identified as America's Most Distrusted Minority', which was also deemed newsworthy and featured in the headlines of many contemporary media publications.

subscribe to or reject belief systems of one kind or another, be they ever so old and bear the imprimatur of time and tradition, further goes to prove the essentially harmful nature of laying claim to absolute truth, which has no basis in fact and empirical demonstration. The good that religious belief can provide—and undoubtedly does so in certain circumstances—is no justification for us either not to enquire into it as a philosophical system, or to dismiss it as fundamentally harmless. Like many other rights we now enjoy, the right to dissent over the existence of a god or gods has been hard won and has cost lives—a fact we should not forget, and we should honour the names and memories of those who fought for this right, like every other we enjoy.

There is no area of life or knowledge, other than the sphere of religious faith, where we allow ignorance to go unchallenged or even promoted. We do not force feed people a diet of information which we know to be factually untrue—we go to great lengths to educate and encourage people to enquire as to whether something is true or false. Parents might tell their children about Santa Claus, but they capitulate when they know the game is up and the child realizes he or she has been fooled. And probably no harm is done. But the whole purpose of a formal education is to teach children and young people to question, to think rationally, to acquire factual information and proceed to form a rational judgement. Yet the law of the land in Britain still insists that prayers are offered on a daily basis in schools and that religion features on the curriculum—the only sphere of knowledge regularly peddled in schools which has no basis in fact. For many people this is just something they put up with. For the Secularist it is a significant irritation and a situation which ought to be changed and challenged, but when we call for a rethinking of this time–honoured tradition we are accused of being intolerant and militant by the Church. Furthermore, the whole issue of so–called 'faith schools', which inculcate difference and religious intolerance in children, has also become a question of the utmost importance today.

And what of AIDS in Africa? This too is a matter not only of education, but of life and death. The Catholic Church actively promotes lies and misinformation that condoms allow the deadly virus to pass through because a mere man has deemed that condoms are evil and are against God's plan, despite the fact that Jesus never pronounced on the issue, nor did anyone else in the Bible. Is that as harmless as a belief in Santa Claus or going through the motions of compulsory religious worship in schools? What arrogance that an organization claims to know without a shadow of a doubt the innermost workings of the mind of the putative Creator of the Universe!

And how can we comprehend the mind of those who, in the name of Allah—the head of a religion whose devotees tell us time without number that it is a religion of peace—are prepared to die and take many others with them for a promised existence they have never even seen with their own eyes, and the evidence for which does not exist?

As d'Holbach points out in *Christianity Unveiled*, education—not indoctrination—is the key to dispel all such folly and sheer wickedness. After the great period of the Enlightenment in Europe in the eighteenth century, against which the religious fought tooth and nail, there is no excuse even for accepting that these things are a question of faith: we have rational minds, scientific techniques, and centuries of empirical knowledge, much of which was opposed by established religion, to help us think through superstition and fantastical ideas. When we look at the sky, it really does look as though the sun and stars go round the earth—and we can forgive the ancients for believing that, though, surprisingly, not all did. Or we might be excused when, through a series of sheer, haphazard coincidences, we are struck down by a disease or ill fortune, and arrive at the conclusion that we are being punished by a divine being for something we have done wrong. Science tells us the real truth is that the earth goes round the sun and that illness is caused by microscopic viruses, rogue cells, and the like, etc. So today people really ought to know better over matters of superstition, good luck charms, horoscopes and religious dogmas. But if, when all the thinking and reflecting are done and the scientific evidence carefully considered, the enquirer still finds solace and comfort in religion, then that is their choice— but it ought not, and should not, be imposed upon others.

Hence, today religion matters and affects us all—and never more so than at the present time: for years it has not mattered and it looked as though it would just fade away. Rates of regular church attendance have fallen inexorably over the years and whether one believes in God or Allah has not been an issue in Europe for quite some time. But religious belief and the politics concomitant with it have been brought into sharp focus as never before since d'Holbach's time. Acts of terrorism and racial tensions, all of which are inseparable from the religious dimension, are now the stuff of regular headlines. Books questioning the three main world religions of Christianity, Islam and Judaism, and religious belief in general, now proliferate and regularly make the best–seller lists. Programmes on television and radio on such issues are broadcast on an almost weekly basis. Media reporting from around the globe brings these issues into our homes twenty–four hours a day, should we choose to pay attention to them.

Predictably, the religious, knowing they are cornered, hit back and desperately defend their corner, not content to let their god do his own fighting, despite his power being reputedly so great that he can create the earth and universe from nothing. They complain of a contemporary wave of 'militant secularism', but forget that it is not secularists who kill people of no faith. And we have the unedifying spectacle of believers of different

xvii

persuasions killing those whose faith they hate, just as they have done throughout history, and there seems to be no end of it today. Alister McGrath in his book *The Twilight of Atheism: The Rise and Fall of Disbelief in the Modern World*, equates the dark deeds of Stalin's and Hitler's genocide with atheism, yet he conveniently ignores, or does not know, that both these monsters were brought up in a religious environment, and that Hitler's inspiration to the end of his days was Roman Catholic hegemony.[3]

Defenders of religious faith are not just people we can glibly dismiss as 'fanatics' or 'extremists', such as those who hijack planes, wrecked the life of Salman Rushdie, or killed over a hundred and fifty people in the course of demonstrating over some cartoons in a provincial Danish newspaper. Some religious people operate on a more subtle level than that. Unelected bishops in the House of Lords and religious pressure groups ceaselessly campaign to impose their values on us all, whether the issues be abortion, euthanasia,[4] same–sex partnerships, etc., or those who secretly (or not so secretly) harbour the desire to impose Sharia law upon western democracies.

Intolerance within religious communities themselves, amongst those sharing ostensibly the same faith and god, frequently provides us with

---

[3] Alister McGrath, *The Twilight of Atheism: The Rise and Fall of Disbelief in the Modern World* (London: Rider, 2004). The author does not mention that Stalin was raised in a society which had fully embraced Orthodox Christianity in Georgia and that at school he excelled in ecclesiastical subjects, on the strength of which he won a scholarship to the Theological Seminary in Tiflis, Georgia's leading academic institution. The author shows himself to be ignorant of many other aspects of Russian history and culture, particularly on Dostoevsky and the early Bolshevik period, when the Orthodox Church was persecuted. He equates atheism with Bolshevism and draws the conclusions, partly from Russian history, that secularism wishes and seeks the demise of religious belief. He states, 'The confident secularist predictions of the demise of religion are things of the past. So if religion will not lie down and die of its own accord, can it be eliminated by other means? Yes, it can—provided the norms of civilization are totally disregarded. For the only alternative is the eradication of religion by force. The forcible suppression of religion is one of the most troubling aspects of atheism...', (p. 230). He misunderstands the point that the campaign against the Russian Orthodox Church was only part of a much bigger and more ambitious plan of social and political engineering: the Russian church merely got in the way and actively opposed Bolshevism—it was not *primarily* the direct target of an anti-religious campaign. McGrath also makes disparaging remarks against secularism and the National Secular Society (on the latter, see in particular pp. 271—72): again, his ignorance over Russian history and culture is mirrored in his lack of understanding here. Secularism stands for rationality (which he strangely denigrates along with the achievements of the Enlightenment) and liberty of conscience: no secularist wants the enforced eradication of religion—just that it be confined to the personal sphere and kept out of politics, everyday life and education.

[4] Note the activities of the Guild of Catholic Doctors and similar groups.

shocking examples of their bigotry and their brutal, uncivilized behaviour does their cause no good. We have all been shocked by events in Northern Ireland and mainland Britain with bombings and the maiming of others. But many people choose to ignore the disgusting spectacle of children on their way to school being funnelled through a police cordon, harassed by Christians of a slightly different religious hue, being spat upon and bawled at. If Christians cannot love their doctrinally near neighbour, what hope for a more universal tolerance?[5] Why are these *Christian* people spared the label of 'religious fanatics' or 'extremists' in news bulletins, whereas *Muslims* are readily labelled as such? For the sake of human happiness everywhere one wishes that such incidents were unusual or rare, but alas, they are not.

How dare the religious use the word 'atheist' and 'secularist' as labels to smear and denigrate those of us who do not share their deluded certainty that theirs is the only, single truth? And why is the term 'agnostic' much more palatable to many? Why is it frowned upon and considered bigoted to state that unless there is empirical evidence to support a premise that there is a god, one can confidently dismiss the whole idea as delusional, just as one ought to do with notions of fairies at the bottom of the garden?

Also, it is about time that the religious were a little more intellectually mature over the simplistic, infantile maxim that 'No religion = no morals'. This argument was put to bed centuries ago—and there it should remain. Yet, alas... Even recently in a House of Lords debate, the current Archbishop of York John Sentamu, quoting Lord Denning, stated that, 'Without religion, there can be no morality, there can be no law.'[6]

All these issues are modern and concern every one of us, and they can all be found in one form or another in d'Holbach's *Christianity Unveiled*, which has a resounding contemporary resonance, despite it having been written well over two centuries ago.

D'Holbach's atheism has been described as 'militant atheism'—again, the term was, and still is, intended to be derogatory—a smear, but as far as d'Holbach and his friends were concerned, it was born of a sincere desire to see mankind enlightened and freed from religious superstition and bigotry. D'Holbach felt religion oppressed people and stopped them achieving a state of real, tangible happiness, preventing them from fulfilling their true potential

---

[5] A Catholic school, the Holy Cross, was blockaded in Belfast at the end of October/beginning of November 2001 by Protestant Christians, forcing children and their parents on the way to school through a cordon, during which time they were liberally spat upon and verbally abused in a most vicious manner. Three other Catholic schools in Belfast were also subjected to the same treatment.

[6] House of Lords debate on Thursday 19 April 2007.

here on earth. Yet he was not militant in the sense that he committed acts of violence—not for him Mao's maxim that 'Political power grows out of the barrel of a gun', which today is reflected in militant Islam. He believed in the power of the written word and in the might of his arguments and rationality. He must have got something right, or at least had an important point to make, because the Catholic Church, in cahoots with the state, went to great lengths to suppress his books in France; fortunately for us they did not succeed in his case, though they did with the works of many such writers. D'Holbach's militancy sprang for an almost overwhelming sense of the all–encompassing, oppressive might of the joint forces of Church and state: he was one of a very small group of people who acted covertly, crying in the wilderness of rationality, to use a semi–biblical epithet. As will be seen from his *Christianity Unveiled*, he wanted to shake the foundations of such an unholy alliance and make people question the role of religious superstition in everyday life. Many people are still doing the same today.

While working in Bradford, I was witness to the barbarism of Salman Rushdie's *Satanic Verses* being burned in the city centre. I asked the book–burners if they had read the book: not one had. Even more shocking, they had the temerity to boast about not having read it, and they were mindlessly acting upon the instructions of one of their equally ignorant religious leaders. The incident made the front page of local and national newspapers, and as an issue it remained head–line news for many months to come.[7]

The mindless militancy of the ignorant spread as they tried to outdo the fanaticism of the book burners: just a short time later, hundreds of children were kept away from school to march on Halifax Town Hall with their

---

[7] *Telegraph and Argus*, 14 January 1989. Featured in the photograph is Councillor Mohammad Ajeeb, encouraging the whole affair: subsequently he was to become the Lord Major of Bradford, the first Asian to do so, and he was later awarded a CBE by the Queen. Councillor Ajeeb was quoted as saying, 'I am pleased that this demonstration is taking place in a peaceful manner because Islam is peace', and he pledged 'to try to persuade his fellow councillors to ban the book from Bradford libraries.' Sher Azam, president of the Bradford Council of Mosques, was quoted as saying, 'There are 65,000 Muslims in Bradford and they are angry and upset about the book. There is no doubt in our minds it should be banned.' A number of enquiries were made of the *Telegraph and Argus*, seeking permission to reproduce the photograph of the book burning and reveal the name of the photographer in order that permission be sought of the copyright holder. The newspaper was extremely reticent to provide any information once the nature of my enquiry had become known, and they ignored all communication on this matter for some time: my persistence prevailed in obtaining an eventual reply, which was a denial of all knowledge and details of the copyright holder. Part of the front page of the newspaper is reproduced here on a fair-use basis.

Telegraph & Argus

Established 1868 ONLY 18p FINAL EDITION Saturday, January 14

FURY AS BOOK IS SET ABLAZE

by STEVEN TEALE

MORE than 1,000 angry Muslims rallied in Bradford city centre today to protest about a novel which they claim attacks their faith.

They cheered and chanted as a copy of the book, The Satanic Verses, by Salman Rushdie, was burned outside police headquarters in the Tyrls.

Bradford councillor Mohammad Ajeeb told the crowd: "This gathering today is an indication of the extreme anger which the Muslim community feels about the book.

"I am pleased that this demonstration is taking place in a peaceful manner because Islam is peace."

He said he would try to persuade his fellow councillors to ban the book from Bradford libraries.

Many of the crowd waved banners and placards proclaiming "Ban Satanic Verses", "Rushdie — Eat Your Words" and "Rushdie Stinks".

More than 20 police were present, but the meeting was marshalled by dozens of Muslim officials.

Rushdie: Award

Holy

Sher Azim, president of the Bradford Council of Mosques said they object to the book because it abuses Islam and is based on distorted facts about their faith.

He said: "There are 65,000 Muslims in Bradford and they are angry and upset about the book. There is no doubt in our minds it should be banned."

The book, which has already been banned by 56 countries including India, won the 1988 Whitbread Award and almost won a Booker Prize.

Muslims claim Rushdie, an Indian author educated in Britain, challenges the authenticity of their holy book, the Koran.

The publishers have said on behalf of Rushdie that there is no chance of them banning it.

FLAMES ... Muslims burn the novel in Bradford city centre today

Figure 2: Front Page of *Telegraph & Argus*, 14 January 1989.

mothers, protesting at the outrage committed by Rushdie against Islam. Children, at their parents' behest, were deliberately deprived of a day's education at an age when they were wholly incapable of reading and understanding such a complex work of literature, and I seriously doubt whether any of their mothers had read it either.[8] Bookshops were threatened with vandalism for having the temerity to stock the book and all public libraries were urged not to make the work available for lending.[9] This was Taliban–style censorship in my native city. It was at that time I realized in a chilling way how strong the grip of superstition is on the modern mind, and on a purely intellectual level I am fascinated by the nature and substance of these ideas and the mechanism by which they operate, as one hoodwinked myself by Christianity for a short while.

D'Holbach's work came to my attention through the excellent programmes Dr Jonathan Miller presented on BBC television in 2005.[10] I had studied philosophy and the Enlightenment as part of my first degree in French and Russian at university, but the name of d'Holbach was hardly known to me. I tried to obtain a copy of his works, first in French, and then in English, but it proved difficult in both languages. The English translation, the first edition of the book I managed to buy, struck me as being hopelessly dated, and I later discovered that it was inaccurate in many instances. I also noticed while preparing this translation that whole sections had been missed out for reasons best known to the translator. Later, I read the excellent *Atheist Manifesto* by Michel Onfray, who writes of d'Holbach, 'The work of Baron d'Holbach cannot be found in the university: no scholarly or scientific edition by any philosophical publisher worthy of the name; no works, theses, or ongoing research; no paperback edition, of course (whereas editions of Rousseau, Voltaire, Kant, or Montesquieu abound); no classes or seminars devoted to analytic examination and propagation of his thinking; not one biography... Painful!'[11] With these words in mind, I hope that this volume goes some way to correcting this situation, in part at least for the English reader who does not know French. This is why the work, and many others, needs to be **rescued from obscurity**, as the title of this new series from Hodgson Press suggests.

---

[8] *Telegraph and Argus*, 3 March 1989, front–page news: the article started, 'Thousands of Muslim children were kept off school in Calderdale today as they marched with their families on Halifax Town Hall in protest over Salman Rushdie's controversial novel *The Satanic Verses*.'

[9] Reported in the *Telegraph and Argus*, 22 February 1989, p. 5.

[10] BBC TV, *A Brief History of Disbelief*, 2005 by Dr Jonathan Miller.

[11] Michel Onfray, *Atheist Manifesto: The Case against Christianity, Judaism, and Islam*, translated by Jeremy Leggatt (New York: Arcade Publishing, 2007), p. 30.

Whilst I have pinned my credentials to the mast and stated clearly that I am an atheist, I do emphasize that this work has been translated and prepared with scholarly integrity in keeping with my academic training, and I have tried to provide as much information as space will allow for the interested reader fully to appreciate the atmosphere in which d'Holbach's work was produced and what his peers had to say about it. It is hoped that this edition, therefore, will serve as a window upon a time and an era when religious belief and traditional dogmas were being challenged, as they are in our own time again.

This edition consists of a modern translation of d'Holbach's complete text of *Christianity Unveiled* with the footnotes as he saw fit to provide, together with additional footnotes of biblical passages referenced to save the reader running for his or her Bible every few pages, and I have likewise provided notes to particular events and referenced writers and philosophers mentioned by d'Holbach, in order to save the reader the trouble of constantly having to reach for an encyclopaedia.

Comments published by d'Holbach's contemporaries and extracts from Abbé Bergier's monumental refutation of *Christianity Unveiled* follow the translation of d'Holbach's work, with original and additional notes provided, as per the translation. Abbé Bergier was a Vatican 'big gun', one of the Church's most formidable intellects, commissioned expressly to launch counterattacks against all forms of religious dissent and heresy. It is my hope that the whole ensemble of documents, most of which have been translated here for the first time, will provide a window onto the character of the man and the times in which this important work was written.

An essay on the main events of church history and the development of disbelief is provided as an Appendix, in order to give the general, interested reader an overview of key events referenced in d'Holbach's and Bergier's works. On a purely practical level, this resumé has obviated the need for even lengthier footnotes. These 'extras' can either be read or ignored, depending on the level of the individual reader's interest: as Gide remarked, '*Tant pis pour le lecteur paresseux!*' {'*Too bad for the lazy reader!*'}.

If I might be so bold as to suggest a reading strategy for readers not conversant with the development of Western thought and the major rows and feuds between factions of the Christian Church (who were obviously replete with love for their neighbour and their god!), it would be a good idea to read the Appendix first, before tackling d'Holbach's text and the Refutation.

D'Holbach was a man of immense scholarship and learning, and, as a philosopher or *philosophe* very much a product of his time, he presumes a great deal of his reader: he quotes Latin sources untranslated, assuming his reading public was at ease with Latin and the classics to which he referred. I have provided a translation and notes, not having made the same assumptions! The purpose of the essay in the Appendix is to cover the essentials of what needs to be known, so as to appreciate more fully d'Holbach's text: it is not a complete survey of philosophy and church history, nor was it ever intended to be so. The issues and debates covered there have been provided more on a need–to–know basis than in any attempt to render a full account, which many others, far better qualified than me, have expertly done. The bibliography provides a list of books which point the interested reader in the direction of fuller accounts.

Names in bold type can be found in the Glossary at the end of this volume, where additional information is provided. The name appears in bold type the first time only it is used. Titles of works and foreign phrases have been translated into English and placed in braces, i.e., {}. I am deeply indebted to the *Encyclopædia Britannica 2008* on CD–Rom for much of the information in the Glossary, which has been heavily edited in the interests of space: interested readers will find much more detailed information in the original publication. I have also followed English language conventions as set out in the *Oxford Writers' Dictionary* (1990), compiled by R.E. Allen, R.M. Ritter's *Oxford Guide to Style* (2002), and *New Fowler's Modern English Usage*, revised 3rd edn. by R.W. Burchfield (OUP, 1998). Any mistakes and deviations are most likely caused by my own lack of understanding.

Further information has been provided about d'Holbach, much of which is only available in French. I hope that this edition serves to revive interest in the writing and life of a courageous man who dared to swim against the tide of the religious bigotry of his day, and whose passionate belief in education and rationality I most deeply share.

David Michael Holohan,
London 2008.

Rescued from Obscurity

A Collection of Documents on the Publication of
Christianity Unveiled

Introduction

Organized religious belief and the Church's dogmatic insistence that a monopoly of truth belongs to them has always given rise to doubters and sceptics. To appreciate fully d'Holbach's courage and that of others in his circle of friends in questioning accepted beliefs, we must look at his society and the milieu in which he was writing. It is also essential to enquire into why he even thought of challenging these *idées reçues* in print and why he bothered to swim against the powerful tide of his day, comprising the massed forces of the Catholic Church and the state. Those who questioned the cherished dogmas of the eighteenth–century French establishment seldom escaped without some cost to themselves: in writing and publishing his anti–Christian works, d'Holbach was entering into a veritable David and Goliath contest. Fortunately, d'Holbach was a man of independent means, as we shall see, and men of the upper classes could get away with more than those of a more humble birth and of limited means.

There is no complete biography of d'Holbach: information about him is to be found scattered in books now generally out of print and difficult to find outside specialized libraries, and a good deal of this literature is in French. (There is a survey of most of the literature about d'Holbach in the Bibliography.) This section aims first to collate most of the details known about him and his friends: then second, there follows a description of the society in which he wrote and published. By understanding the milieu in which he wrote, the reader will be able fully to appreciate his aims and why his work caused such a furore.

D'Holbach's Background and Early Years

Paul Thiry d'Holbach, to give him his full name, was born at Edesheim, a village near Landau, in the Rhenish Palatinate in December 1723.[1] The Palatinate (in German the area is referred to as Rheinland–pfalz) was divided into two small geographical areas, the Rhenish (or Lower Palatinate) and the Upper Palatinate. D'Holbach was born in the Rhenish Palatinate, the capital of which was Heidelberg until the eighteenth century. It is a scenic, rural area of forests and slopes where vines were tended, and the Palatinate Forest nearby is still an area of great natural beauty. Although the Palatinate

---

[1]   The generally accepted year for d'Holbach's birth is 1723, but Hubert in *D'Holbach et ses Amis* (Paris: 1928) states that his date of birth was January 1725 (p. 37). The month of his birth is also uncertain: Hibbert in *A Brief Sketch of the Life and Writings of Baron D'Holbach* (London: 1834) gives the month as 'January', (p. 1), whereas other writers claim he was born in December. The *Encyclopaedia Britannica* (2008), one of the best researched and dependable sources on these matters, gives d'Holbach's date of birth as December 1723.

remained Roman Catholic at the beginning of the Reformation (see p. 342 *et seqq.*), it adopted Calvinism in the 1560s under Elector Frederick III and the Rhenish Palatinate was devastated by Catholic troops during the Thirty Years' War. The area also suffered under French troops during the War of the Grand Alliance (1689—97), and it would be invaded again in later years: it had a long history of division and possession by foreign powers. When invaded by the troops of Louis XIV, who did his utmost to extend France's territory into the Rhineland, many native Germans emigrated and settled in America—they were the so–called 'Pennsylvania Germans'. Though Louis' expansionist efforts failed in the Palatinate, French influence was strong in the area and Louis' ambitions succeeded in neighbouring areas.

A certain Francis Adam Holbach, the son of an episcopal tax–farmer in the area,[2] moved to Paris where he made his fortune trading during the long reign of Louis XIV. It is said he was ennobled in France in 1722 and he also became a naturalized French citizen, calling himself by the more aristocratic and noble form of his name—'d'Holbach'. He had no children but his nearest family members were two sisters, both of whom suffered personal tragedy, which seemed to follow the d'Holbachs: his sister Susana became a widow early in her marriage, leaving a daughter to be raised alone, and his other sister, Paul Thiry's mother, also died leaving him an orphan at a young age. (There is no information on his father.) This was not to be the end of tragedy in Paul's life. His uncle brought Paul Thiry and his cousin to Paris and he left them his sizeable fortune when he died in 1753.[3]

Paul Thiry was baptized according to Roman Catholic rites, and by the age of twelve he was already living in Paris with his uncle: henceforth, he also was known by the less prosaic version of his name, i.e., 'd'Holbach'. At school, d'Holbach stood out from his fellow pupils by his studious habits and his remarkable memory (for which he was to become renowned amongst those who knew him later in life in academic circles). During his school career, he carried off all the prizes available to his fellow pupils through open

---

[2]   The collection of taxes was handed over to 'tax-farmers', who collected taxes and dues on behalf of the government and the Church in return for concessions for the collectors. This system significantly increased the revenues the Church and state were able to collect because the collector had a financial incentive to make sure he collected what was owed.

[3]   In his study of d'Holbach, Hubert attributes the family fortune to d'Holbach's own father, but no other evidence is given to support this. Wickwar, *Baron D'Holbach: A Prelude to the French Revolution* (London: Allen & Unwin, 1935), Appendix A, pp. 233—235, offers a brief, though inadequate, family genealogy, which is far more convincing, and he shows that it was indeed d'Holbach's uncle who made the fortune, not his father.

competition. He studied Latin and Greek (language and literature), all the sciences, and modern languages.

In 1744, d'Holbach entered the Faculty of Law at the University of Leiden, founded in 1575 by William I, Prince of Orange (1533—1584), and it was generally regarded as the 'first and foremost in all Europe', one of the oldest higher–educational institutions in Europe.[4] It had an international mix of students, amongst whom there were twenty Englishmen, several of whom would go on to great things in English society: two would become future Chancellors of the Exchequer and one would be the Lord Mayor of London, and the poet and physician **Mark Akenside** (1721—1770) studied for his doctorate there in 1744. D'Holbach socialized with many such people and in a letter of 1746 written to **John Wilkes** (1725—1797), the popular journalist and politician whom he had met at Leiden and whose friendship was to last the rest of their lives, it is obvious that d'Holbach was already writing excellent English.[5] Not only does this letter show what an accomplished linguist he was; it also shows the warmth of his character and the depth of friendship he was capable of feeling—a feature of his character which was well–known and much appreciated amongst those who came into contact with him. Later, in 1759, he would translate and publish Mark Akenside's famous poem *The Pleasures of Imagination* into French. Again, this is indicative of d'Holbach's intelligence and erudition, and significant also of his later literary activity—he would dedicate a considerable proportion of his literary efforts to the art of translation. It was by no means a trivial task to make a version in French of Akenside's poem: written in blank verse after Milton, the poem consciously emulated Virgil's *Georgics* and Horace's *Epistles*, expressing abstract philosophical thought in a lofty, high style. This work also represented d'Holbach's interest in philosophy and ideas, as well as reflecting the breadth and depth of his reading.

When the university was not in session, d'Holbach spent time on one of his uncle's estates at Heeze, near Eindhoven, in the Low Countries. He enjoyed the company of **William Dowdeswell** (1721—1775), the English politician, whom he had also met at the University of Leiden and spent the summer of 1746 with him in Heeze, from where he wrote again to Wilkes (part of the letter is cited here just as he wrote it):

---

[4] Diderot *Encyclopédie, ou Dictionnaire Raisonné des Sciences, des Arts et des Métiers.*

[5] Some of his letters, now in a British Library archive, are reproduced in Max Pearson Cushing's *Baron d'Holbach: A Study of Eighteenth Century Radicalism in France* (New York: 1914), reprinted as a Kessinger Publishing reprint, pp. 6—8. For comments on this reprinted edition see the '*Survey of Available Literature on D'Holbach—Books in English*' in the Bibliography (p. 495).

We often wished your company and made sincere libations to you with burgundy and Champaigne [sic] I had a few weeks there after I set out for Germany where I expected to spend the whole winter but the sudden death of my Uncle's steward has forced me to come back here and to put in order the affairs of this estate, I don't know how long I shall be obliged to stay in the meanwhile I act pretty well the part of a Country Squire, id est, hunting, shooting, fishing, walking every day without to lay aside the ever charming conversation of Horace Virgil Homer and all our noble friends of the Elysian fields. They are allways faithfull [sic] to me, with their aid I find very well how to employ my time, but I want in this country a true bosom friend like my dear Wilkes to converse with...[6]

The above extract shows d'Holbach to be a bon viveur and it is also indicative of his genuine love of literature and learning, and how well–connected he was from his earliest youth. As he matured and pursued his own intellectual interests, his connections with prominent men from public life grew and he regularly received men of letters and science from all over the world, from different walks of life, including even clerics. D'Holbach finished his studies at Leiden and returned to Paris, becoming a naturalized citizen in August 1749. For the rest of his life he lived in Paris and he travelled surprisingly little, which was uncommon for a man of his means, intellectual interests and age. He preferred to receive guests at home or on the family country estate of Granval at Sucy–en–Brie in the Marne Valley, to which he had access through his wife's family, and there he regularly indulged in his taste for good food, fine wine and genial company. His mother–in–law's château at Granval was a two–hour drive from Paris, where she kept open house for the baron and his friends. D'Holbach and **Diderot**, with whom had a particularly close friendship, spent many hours there, and d'Holbach found it a quiet place to work and read.

D'Holbach's elder cousin, who had been brought to Paris with him, married Nicolas d'Aîne, a wealthy man from French Flanders, whose father had made his fortune in the government under Louis XIV, and they had two daughters and a son. D'Holbach married the elder of these daughters, his second cousin Basile Geneviève Suzanne d'Aîne, who sadly died in August 1754, after only a single year of married life. This was the cause of immense grief to d'Holbach. However, he remarried two years later under rather singular circumstances: he had to obtain a special papal dispensation to marry his first wife's sister Charlotte Suzanne d'Aîne (1734—1814), by whom he was to have four children. More deaths occurred in the family and consequently he inherited fortunes from each deceased relative, making him heir to a considerable fortune.

---

[6] Quoted in Cushing, p. 9, and Wickwar, p. 19. The original letter is in a British Library archive MSS. 30867, f.18.

Figure 3: Diderot (1713—1784).

D'Holbach's first wife was highly regarded by society ladies as a woman of great integrity, warmth and hospitality herself. The memoirist **Mme D'Epinay**, quoting **Grimm**, said of her:

> 'Madame d'Holbach was the most dutiful woman I have ever known and she fulfilled her duties with the greatest of ease. This woman had no need of others to be satisfied and contented, but she neglected no detail in anything which she believed to be useful or pleasurable for her husband. It was for him that she embraced his friends. She studied their tastes; she was wholly taken up with ministering to the every need which makes their life sweeter. But it wasn't to please them that she went to so much trouble—it was so that her husband would always have his guests utterly indulged.'[7]

When she died, it was as unexpected as it was a great blow to d'Holbach. Again Grimm is quoted as saying, 'This unfortunate woman was taken from us by a dreadful illness in the fullness of her youth, at the time when we were least expecting this misfortune, and I saw my friend [i.e., d'Holbach] at the height of his prosperity suddenly plunged into the depths of despair by the death of this woman, whose whole purpose was to make him happy.'[8]

D'Holbach's second wife was equally well–admired in society and she was to have a life much longer than his. Though she hated philosophy, she entertained their erudite guests well with her charm and her accomplished lute playing. Most of d'Holbach's friends were pleased for his new–found happiness, except **Rousseau**, whose relations with d'Holbach had already cooled by this time. Rousseau, with his characteristic catty nature, was to quip:

> I haven't seen much of Mr Grimm for some time. He has hardly left the baron d'Holbach's side, who has just married the sister of his first wife, whom people say is very nice. His friends have quite rightly remarked that he is a man so keenly afflicted by the death of his first wife and so promptly consoled by the second—that does not say much for a man of sound character.[9]

Rousseau's feelings had been hurt at one of d'Holbach's dinners (of which, more below) and for that reason he had taken against d'Holbach, despite having little or no personal reason to do so. In fact, there is every reason to believe that d'Holbach had actually been very generous to Rousseau, as he

---

[7] *Mémoires et Correspondance de Madame D'Epinay*, 3 vols, (Paris, 1818), II, pp. 196—7.

[8] Ibid.

[9] Op. cit. pp. 272—273. Rousseau's letter to Mme Epinay.

was with many people and friends in need, but d'Holbach always kept his acts of charity a secret.

One example of d'Holbach's generosity is well–documented and came to light in his friend **Naigeon**'s obituary (see the translation in this volume). Naigeon, d'Holbach's close friend, collaborator and editor, tells how one of their number, a certain **Suard** (1733—1817) had appeared sad and withdrawn, and d'Holbach presumed he had money problems. D'Holbach offered him ten thousand francs, telling him that he had no use for them and hoped that his offer of help would not cause him any offence. As it happened, Suard did not take the money and the source of his chagrin turned out not to be financial, but it was characteristic of d'Holbach to act as he did. This was just one of many such acts.

This same Suard described d'Holbach's reading and erudition in his memoirs:

> He used to devour everything that came from the printing–presses of all countries, and let nothing escape from his vast memory, beyond what he wished to forget. Seneca, who likewise was a genius and a rich man, used to pay a high price for the gist of books he had no time to read: this philosopher from the land of Leibnitz used to read the books that Buffon and Diderot needed to consult, and when he had talked them over with them they were sure of knowing them better than if they had read them. Once, when he had just re–read *L'Esprit des Lois*, he analysed it so well from memory, without at all upsetting the order of the books, chapters, and ideas, that those who heard him did not hesitate to judge his analysis superior to that of d'Alembert...[10]

It must be noted that **Montesquieu**'s *L'Esprit des Lois* {*Spirit of Laws*} is over a thousand pages long, containing over 3,000 citations of closely argued political philosophy.

The **Abbé Morellet** (1727—1819) also attested to d'Holbach's erudition and character. He was a regular visitor to his house between 1760 and 1780, and witnessed his hospitality first hand:

> The Baron himself was one of the best–informed men of his age; he knew several European languages, and was not ignorant of those of antiquity; and he had a large and excellent library, a valuable collection of drawings by the best masters, excellent pictures of which he was a good judge, and a natural history cabinet. To these advantages he added extreme good breeding, and no less simplicity; his manners were easy, and his good–

---

[10] Quoted in Wickwar from D.J. Garat, *Mémoires historiques sur la vie de Monsieur Suard, sur ses écrits, et sur le 18e siècle* (Paris, 1820), pp. 206 *et seqq.*

heartedness was obvious at first sight. Small wonder that his company was courted and valued as it was.[11]

Another priest, **Abbé Galiani**, expressed his appreciation of his intellect and the generosity of his table in the pithy epithet he applied to him, saying he was '*le premier maître d'hôtel de la philosophie*'—{'the premier *maître d'hôtel* of philosophy'}.[12]

D'Holbach and his Coterie

Grimm had arrived in Paris around the end of 1748 and, through Rousseau, Diderot met the philosopher and psychologist Condillac in 1746, amongst others. These intellectual giants—writers, scientists, philosophers, etc., all sought out each other's company, as did their foreign peers when they happened to be passing through France en route to other destinations, or when they specifically went to Paris to seek out their equals and rivals in order to exchange ideas.

It is difficult to be precise about the date when d'Holbach and Diderot met for the first time: Rousseau writes that around 1751—1752, the place where Grimm and others met was at d'Holbach's house, but there is a letter from Diderot to **Voltaire** of the 11 June 1749 in which he tells him that he was in regular contact with a group of atheists and that the host has a 'taste for order, a love of the good things in life, good books and beautiful paintings, and good concerts', in fact, a place where 'nothing fine was missing'.[13] This can only be the d'Holbach household, so their friendship dated from a slightly earlier period than Rousseau had remembered.

In his memoirs, which he entitled *Confessions* (1781—1788), Rousseau described d'Holbach's regular gatherings at his house:

> Our chief meeting–place, before [Grimm] became so closely connected with Madame d'Epinay, was the Baron d'Holbach's house. This Baron was the son of a self–made man, who possessed an ample fortune, which he used nobly. He received at his house men of letters and learning, and, by his own knowledge and accomplishments, was well able to hold his own amongst them. Having been long intimate with Diderot, he had sought my acquaintance through him, even before my name became known. A natural repugnance for a long time prevented me from meeting

---

[11] Morellet, *Mémoires sur le 18e siècle et sur la Révolution* (Paris, 1821), pp. 127 *et seqq.*, (p. 129).

[12] *Correspondance inédite de l'Abbé F. Galiani pendant les années 1765 à 1783 avec Mme d'Epinay, Le Baron d'Holbach etc.*, 2 vols (1818), I, p. 36, Letter to D'Holbach written in Naples on 13 April 1770. This much-bandied-about quotation has been variously and erroneously attributed to Grimm and Diderot.

[13] Quoted in Hubert, pp. 28—29.

> his advances. One day he asked me the reason, and I said to him, 'You are too wealthy.' He persisted, and finally prevailed. My greatest misfortune has ever been inability to resist flattery, and I have always regretted yielding to it.[14]

Almost nothing is known of Naigeon's life prior to his association with the d'Holbach soirées, but we do know that Diderot met him in 1765 when he was working or studying to become a draftsman or painter.

It has been claimed that d'Holbach's idea to hold regular dinner parties at his home in Paris stemmed from his student days at Leiden, where it was fashionable to hold similar gatherings.[15] However, d'Holbach's dinners were very much a part of the general ethos of Parisian intellectual life, which revolved around various *salons*, where writers and intellectuals of every kind would meet regularly to discuss topics of interest, listen to music, read or have read to them the latest work penned by salon *habitués*. Such gatherings were in no way secret or constituted any type of clandestine society and those who 'ran' *salons* might be male or female, though many were overseen by aristocratic women, such as Mme Geoffrin. Suard, **Saurin** and **Morellet** all ran their own gatherings or *salons*. While d'Holbach's grouping was one of a number of such meeting places, his dinners were certainly the most sumptuous and possibly the most renowned. D'Holbach received men of letters, scientists, politicians and diplomats from abroad who were passing through Paris and many greatly appreciated the atmosphere of d'Holbach's coterie in particular: the philosopher **David Hume** and the writer Lawrence Sterne both visited d'Holbach in the 1760s and were taken aback by the liberal atmosphere of his circle and they delighted in it. Hume called the members of d'Holbach's dinner parties 'the sheiks of the Rue Royale', and Sterne called them 'the joyous sett'[*sic*].[16] By contrast, Horace Walpole was singularly unimpressed by the whole company, calling them all atheists, but then he did so about most people he met in Paris. He disliked philosophy and philosophers and remarked that, 'nonsense for nonsense, I like the Jesuits better than the philosophers.'[17] If he favoured the Jesuits, he was hardly likely to find kindred spirits amongst the *philosophes* at d'Holbach's table, given the fact that they had been the clerics who were directly responsible for the suspension of work on the great *Encyclopédie*, one of the most ambitious,

---

[14] J.-J. Rousseau, *The Confessions*, (un-named translator), (Wordsworth Classics, 1996), p. 360.

[15] Wattles, *Atheism in the philosophe movement from 1750 to 1775, with particular reference to Buffon, D'Alembert, Helvétius, D'Holbach and Diderot*, unpublished PhD thesis, University of Oxford, 1986, p. 180.

[16] *The Letters of David Hume*, ed. by J.Y.T. Grieg, 2 vols (Oxford: Clarendon Press, 1932), I, pp. 195—96.

[17] Horace Walpole, *Letters*, ed. by Peter Cunningham, 9 vols (London: 1880), VI, p. 370.

original and radical repositories of knowledge produced to date. Besides which, Walpole spoke French lamentably badly and he knew it, preferring not to open his mouth. On one occasion he even pretended he was deaf and gesticulated to that end to another coterie *habitué*, the historian **Raynal**, who then left him alone: when Raynal discovered Walpole's ruse, he was less than amused with him.[18]

The most prominent visitors from the British Isles, apart from those already mentioned, were **David Garrick**, **Allan Ramsay**, **Samuel Romilly**, **Edward Gibbon**, and **Joseph Priestley**. There were many other visitors from Denmark, Italy, Germany and Switzerland, comprising diplomats, scientists and all manner of other intellectuals. Benjamin Franklin also visited. However, there was a regular core membership from amongst more permanent residents of Parisian society and many were amongst the finest minds of their day. In all, the dinners took place for a period of some thirty–five years, with meetings held regularly on Thursdays and Sundays in the rue Royale in central Paris. Amongst d'Holbach's regular guests were Grimm, **Marmontel**, Raynal, **Roux**, **Saint–Lambert**, Suard, Morellet, Naigeon, Galiani, **Helvétius**, **Boulanger**, and a number of others. As a guest list, it was indeed impressive. Some attended more frequently than others because they were diplomats and occasionally they were unavailable to attend.

While d'Holbach and his coterie were trail–blazers in their own right, and d'Holbach's collaboration with Naigeon and Diderot to produce and disseminate anti–religious material was a particularly innovative feature of their friendship and regular meeting, there was a notable forerunner to them in the person of the **Count of Boulainvilliers** (1658—1722), whose protégé was **Fréret**, to whom a number of d'Holbach's works would be wrongly attributed. The Count of Boulainvilliers was a prominent figure in French society and he would read, collect, write and disseminate a huge amount of material expressing unorthodox ideas. Like d'Holbach, he was an omnivorous reader, who, also like d'Holbach,

> [...] read and took excerpts from works which might be regarded as dangerous, [and] he also wrote some himself... In dealing with his literary production, it is very difficult to determine which works he copied, which he wrote, and those which he merely inspired and encouraged. Moreover, it is highly improbable that all the works of Boulainvilliers have been mentioned in lists. [...] Fifty years before the 'Coterie Holbachique' there

---

[18] Tallentyre, Stephen G., *The Friends of Voltaire* (London: Smith, Elder, 1906), p. 129.

was a 'Coterie Boulainvilliers', which closely resembled the latter in ideas, if not in organization.[19]

As with all clubs and cliques, d'Holbach's dinner parties were not without the odd acrimonious dispute, factions and personality clashes, though these seem to have been surprisingly few—most memoirists have nothing but glowing reports to offer on these regular gatherings. The most famous contretemps involved Rousseau, who first coined the expression 'coterie holbachique' in his memoirs.

Rousseau accused d'Holbach of being rude to him, an accusation which not a single other memoirist has ever noted in d'Holbach's dealings with anyone, and one can safely assume that it was Rousseau's own paranoia, for which he was famed, which caused him to be so caustic about d'Holbach and his circle. When he made the comment about the 'coterie holbachique', he was not being complimentary. Rousseau even fell out with Mme d'Epinay, with whom he had corresponded at length and over some considerable time: he accused her, Grimm, and others of conspiring against him, just as a number of years earlier he had accused people in the d'Holbach coterie of being jealous of his success over his one–act opera, the *Devin du Village* {*The Village Soothsayer*}. He wrote:

> From the time of [the opera's] success, I no longer found in Grimm, Diderot, or, with few exceptions, in any of the men of letters with whom I was acquainted, the cordiality, the frankness, or pleasure in my society, which I believe I had hitherto found in them. As soon as I appeared at the Baron's, the conversation ceased to be general. Those present collected in small groups and whispered together, so that I was left alone, without knowing whom to speak to [sic]. For a long time I endured this mortifying neglect, and, finding that Madame d'Holbach, who was gentle and amiable, always received me kindly, I put up with her husband's rudeness as long as it was possible. One day, however, he attacked me without reason or excuse, and with such brutality—in the presence of Diderot, who never said a word, and of Margency, who has often told me since then, that he admired the gentleness and moderation of my answers—that at last, driven away by this unworthy treatment, I left his house, resolved never to enter it again.'[20]

Abbé Morellet, a more gracious and appreciative guest, again sheds light on d'Holbach's regular dinner parties:

---

[19] Ira O. Wade, *The Clandestine Organization and Diffusion of Philosophic Ideas in France from 1700 to 1750* (Princeton, New Jersey: Princeton U.P., 1938), p. 101.

[20] Ibid., pp. 375—376 or *Confessions*, Book VIII. He coined the epithet 'coterie holbachique' in Book X.

The Baron d'Holbach held two dinner parties regularly each week, on Sundays and Thursdays, where—without prejudice to the other days of the week—ten, twelve, or even fifteen or twenty, men of letters, men of the world, or foreigners, who loved and cultivated the things of the mind, were wont to meet together. There was plenty of food, and good food too; excellent wine, excellent coffee; plenty of discussions and never a quarrel; the simple manners that are suited to intelligent and educated men, yet do not degenerate into ill–breeding; gaiety without folly; and so much charm in the company there that although we arrived at two o'clock, as was then the custom, we were often nearly all still there at seven or eight in the evening. That was a place to hear the freest, most animated, the most instructive conversation that ever was—free, I mean, in regard to philosophy, religion, and government; for *les plaisanteries libres* [by which he means crude jokes and the like, *D.M.H.*] of another kind had no place there...[21] I should think there was hardly one single bold and original idea in politics or religion that was not brought forward there and discussed pro and con, nearly always with much subtlety and insight.

---

[21]   Acutally, the conversation at 'the baron's', as Diderot always referred to d'Holbach's home, was not always so sanitized: Diderot tells in a letter to his mistress Sophie Volland of an amusing incident, which typified the rather earthy sense of humour of his mother-in-law, Mme d'Aîne, who had something of a reputation for holding court in a rather lively way at Grandval. A permanent resident at Grandval was a rather dour, old Scotsman, whose real surname, ironically, was 'Hope', whom the family called 'le père Hoop' {'Old Hoop'}. By all accounts, he was always miserable and weary of life, and Mme d'Aîne always said that she had given him a bedroom which looked out onto the moat in the hope he would end it all! Diderot writes: 'The Baron is ill. He has dysentery and a fever. I came down into the drawing room where he, Old Hoop, Mme d'Aîne and Mme d'Holbach were taking tea. There sat the Baron, whose colic illness had not taken the edge off his wit, and asked, "Mother [i.e., his mother-in-law], do you know who the great Lama is?"
"Great or small, I don't know him."
"He's a Tibetan priest."
"Whether he's from Tibet or not, if he's a good priest, then I respect him."
"Once a year, when he's had a good lunch, he goes off to the toilet."
"Good for him!" she replied.
"And then... Now here comes the gross bit!"
[The mother-in-law asks:] "What do you call 'gross', if you please? It seems to me it's a need; it's quite simple, a pretty natural need, and we all have to do it... Despite your spirituality, you've got to satisfy your physical needs, just as the miller's wife does."
"Well, so be it—'gross', then... So, after the Lama has done his 'gross thing'... it's regarded as a sacred object: it's ground to a powder and sent off in little packets to all the sovereign princes, who take it as a tea on devotional days."
"What a daft thing to do!"
"Daft or not, it's a fact. Don't you think that if you got a piece of crap from Jesus Christ as a present, you'd be over the moon? Just imagine what would happen if you sent a bit of shit from the blessed deacon [of Paris] to a Jansenist... He'd put it in a gold case and how long would it be before it started performing miracles?"' Diderot, *Oeuvres complètes*, 'Letter from Grandval, 5 October 1759', XVIII, pp. 516—17.

Often one single individual would hold forth and work out his thesis quietly and without interruption. On other occasions it took the form of a duel, with the rest of the society looking on quietly—a method I have seldom come across anywhere else. [...]

It was there, if I dare mention myself alongside so many better men, that I more than once expounded my principles of public economy.

And it was there too—and one must admit it—that Diderot, Dr Roux, and the good Baron himself, used dogmatically to argue the cause of absolute atheism—as in the *Système de la Nature* {*System of Nature*}—with a persuasiveness, a good faith, and a probity that was edifying even for those who, like myself, did not share their beliefs. For it must not be thought that these ultra–liberal opinions were held by all the members of this society—full of *philosophes* as it was, in the disparaging sense of the word, which is sometimes attributed to it. A goodly number of us were theists—and not ashamed of it—and we defended ourselves vigorously against the atheists, though we loved them for being such good company.[22]

Morellet placed d'Holbach's dinner parties as the most educational of all gatherings in Paris, stating, 'But among the societies that zeal for the cause of philosophy opened up to me, I must place in the first rank that of the Baron d'Holbach for the utility, the pleasure and the instruction I gained from it.'[23]

Sometimes d'Holbach specifically brought together certain selected guests for the particular purpose of discussing a given topic: he brought the economist Adam Smith to one of his dinners in 1766 so that he might meet his French counterpart Baron Turgot (1727—1781).[24]

It is often maintained that the Holbachian coterie was a hotbed of atheism, but we know that Galiani often argued against atheism. In fact, he considered himself to be a cynical **Deist**, but in essence, that was tantamount to being little more than an atheist in terms of what he believed. However, as a term and label, 'atheist' was not one that a person would readily assume because of its wholly negative connotations, as can be seen in a letter to Mme d'Epinay: Galiani describes the atheist as a man 'impoverished of all ideas', and that all he has left in him is a 'horrible void' or 'a nothingness'.[25] The term 'atheist' was still one from which most people shied away at this time.

By contrast, in his *Memoirs* Marmontel, states that, 'God, virtue, the holy laws of natural morality were never placed in doubt, at least in my presence; to that I can attest.'[26] Certainly, Marmontel's position on religion was one of

---

[22] Morellet, op. cit., pp. 130—131.
[23] Morellet, *ibid.*
[24] Alan C. Kors, *D'Holbach's Coterie: An Enlightenment in Paris* (Princeton, New Jersey: Princeton University Press, 1976), p. 109.
[25] Galiani, *Lettres*, II, pp. 345—246.
[26] Marmontel, *Memoirs*, 19 vols, I, pp. 484—486, in *Oeuvres complètes de Marmontel*, (Paris, 1818—1920).

tolerance and it may be that in his presence no fierce debate over religion blew up.

For all his antipathy towards religion, d'Holbach happily had even men of the cloth as regular visitors to his dinners. Most notable amongst these was Abbé Bergier (1713—1790), who wrote a monumental refutation of d'Holbach's *Christianity Unveiled*—just one of a number of weighty refutations to come from his pen, and he was considered one of the Catholic Church's 'big guns', preparing ammunition to fire against its chief attackers. (For a more detailed description of Bergier's life and career, see my Foreword to his Refutation in this volume, pp. 163 *et seqq.*) Though a priest and a man of true religious conviction, he also had a warm sense of humour and expressed a gentle cynicism about the intellectual qualities of many of his ecclesiastical peers. He had a fine reputation as a scholar, church historian and classicist, and he made his name by writing refutations against major works critical of orthodox Christianity and the Catholic Church, with his books often running to several editions. Of him, Grimm stated that, 'As a defender of the Christian religion, the Abbé Bergier is certainly a cut above his brothers.'[27] Bergier's frequent appearances at d'Holbach's dinners were censured by the more intolerant and closed–minded of the faith: Diderot's brother, who was a particularly intolerant cleric, criticized Bergier for the company he kept.[28]

There were really only three members of the coterie who were outright, avowed atheists—d'Holbach, Naigeon and Diderot, and certainly Naigeon was the most vociferous of them all.

D'Holbach's views on religion were uncompromising, but his sense of refinement and his exceedingly good manners would never allow him knowingly to offend any of his guests. As far as Diderot was concerned, he was very much an atheist but he regarded many other issues as of much greater importance than the religious question. Also Diderot was acutely aware of the amount of trouble that could be caused by committing such militant views to paper, a fact attested to by d'Holbach's pseudonymous publication of so many works against religion. Even given the fact that d'Holbach was not vainglorious, no author would scratch away on paper, producing works of considerable length and remain content not to see his own name on the title page of almost any work he produced in his own lifetime, unless there was a good reason to do so. Indeed, Diderot feared for his friends who produced such atheistic works, writing in 1768, 'It's raining bombs on the house of the Lord. I go in fear and trembling lest one of these

---

[27] Grimm, *Corresp. Litt.*, VIII, p. 94.
[28] Kors, pp. 116—17.

terrible bombers gets into difficulties.'[29] He certainly had in mind his close friend d'Holbach, who was leading the bombing raid, but he wisely and cunningly published his works bearing the names of dead academics and writers, such as Boulanger. Not for d'Holbach was Voltaire's subtle approach of satirizing and ridiculing dearly held religious dogmas: d'Holbach's tone is very much that of the self–confessed, militant attacker, whom religion offends on account of its inherent anti–intellectualism and for its vice–like grip on social and political institutions. Both he and Naigeon saw religious superstition as a major weight around mankind's neck, the very thing that stood in the way of social justice and human progress, enslaving men and miring them in ignorance. D'Holbach wrote, 'As a citizen, I attack [religion] because I consider it to be harmful to the welfare of the state, because it is an enemy of human intellectual progress, and because it is opposed to sound morality, from which political interests can never be divorced.'[30] However, both d'Holbach and Naigeon knew that without a god to hope in and the comfort that such a belief can offer, the human condition was no less full of pain and insecurity: the only consolation was that at least the atheist was secure in the knowledge of not being blinded by irrational superstition and self–delusion. These issues re–emerged in the twentieth century in the stark philosophy of Sartre's existentialism: all ideas and values inherited *a priori* were jettisoned and man felt himself in a state of *angoisse* {*anguish* or *dread*}, a feeling of being *de trop* {*at a loss* or *on one's own*} to forge one's own values and meaning in life. However, for men in the Age of Enlightenment, even without God there was a general optimism—they had faith in the progress of mankind, though it was not shared by all: Grimm wrote that nature laughs at whatever system we humans devise. Of all his peers, Grimm seemed to sense the particular vulnerability of his species, stating: 'One unfortunate moment, one fire, one hurricane, one earthquake, one powerful and absurd man—a scourge more cruel than all others—is all it takes to destroy the fruits of twenty centuries of effort and genius.'[31] What a prescient resonance his words were to find in the twentieth century!

But why was Diderot so afraid for his friends and why was work on the *Encyclopédie*, that monument to rationality, stopped by the state? The next questions to consider are how free the individual was to write and publish dissenting material in France in the eighteenth century and what subjects

---

[29] Diderot, *Correspondance*, ed. by G. Roth et al., 12 vols (Paris, 1955—1970), VIII, pp. 234—235.

[30] See p. 13 of this volume.

[31] Grimm, *Corresp. Litt.*, VI, pp. 23—27, 1 July 1764: *Réflexions sur l'histoire naturelle à propos des dixième et onzième volumes de Buffon et Daubenton {Reflections on Natural History with Reference to Volumes Ten and Eleven of Buffon and Daubenton}*.

were to be avoided to be sure of not ending up in prison. One must also bear in mind that the great optimism generated by confidence in human progress and an unshakable faith in the rational, expressed in the cry of '*Liberté, Egalité, Fraternité*', was to end in the blood–bath that was the French Revolution by the end of the century.

The Period of the Encyclopédie

The *Encyclopédie, ou Dictionnaire Raisonné Des Sciences, Des Arts Et Des Métiers {Encyclopaedia, or Classified Dictionary of Sciences, Arts, and Trades}*, to give it its full title, was an eighteenth–century French encyclopaedia of monumental importance and originality, and it stands as one of the great achievements of the Age of Enlightenment: more than any other publication, it represents the voice of the age. Born of an era in which men questioned *idées reçues* in almost every sphere of knowledge, but particularly in philosophy, religion, politics, and social issues, it was a beacon of open–mindedness and tolerance. Those who contributed to it as a group were known as *philosophes*—a term which meant so much more than merely 'philosopher', its literal translation. The *philosophes* were literary men, scientists and thinkers, most were polymaths, and they were an extremely heterogeneous group, but they were united in their conviction that knowledge, learning and reason were the supreme tools by which mankind could be improved. They were fearless in challenging the might of the state and the Church: they were the intellectual *enfants terribles* of the eighteenth century, who almost did not care on whose sensibilities they trod. Those who contributed to the 72,000 articles spread over 18,000 pages of text with 3,000—4,000 plates, are known also as the *encyclopédistes* and they represented some of the finest minds in Europe. The *Encyclopédie's* political, social and intellectual repercussions went far beyond that of any other encyclopaedia ever published, appearing, as it did, just before the French Revolution. It was a truly magnificent endeavour, but it caused huge controversy and opposition, not least from the Catholic Church because of the open scepticism it expressed in many articles on religious faith. Some examples of its content have been translated as footnotes in this translation, particularly when Bergier referenced them in his refutation.

Taking as its inspiration *Ephraim Chambers' Cyclopaedia; or An Universal Dictionary of Arts and Sciences* (London, 1728), the *Encyclopédie* got off to a faltering start, but in 1747 Diderot assumed the general direction of the work, except for its sections on mathematics, which were edited by the mathematician and philosopher d'Alembert (1717—1783). Seventeen volumes were published between 1751 and 1765, and several volumes of plates were added. More volumes were added in 1776—77, including more plates and indexes. In the end, the work numbered thirty–five folio volumes.

ENCYCLOPÉDIE,

OU

DICTIONNAIRE RAISONNÉ

DES SCIENCES,

DES ARTS ET DES MÉTIERS,

PAR UNE SOCIÉTÉ DE GENS DE LETTRES.

Mis en ordre & publié par M. *DIDEROT*, de l'Académie Royale des Sciences & des Belles-Lettres de Pruffe ; & quant à la PARTIE MATHÉMATIQUE, par M. *D'ALEMBERT*, de l'Académie Royale des Sciences de Paris, de celle de Pruffe, & de la Société Royale de Londres.

Tantùm feries juncturaque pollet,
Tantùm de medio fumptis accedit honoris ! HORAT.

TOME PREMIER.

A PARIS,

Chez
{
BRIASSON, *rue Saint Jacques*, *à la Science.*
DAVID l'aîné, *rue Saint Jacques*, *à la Plume d'or.*
LE BRETON, Imprimeur ordinaire du Roy, *rue de la Harpe.*
DURAND, *rue Saint Jacques*, *à Saint Landry*, *& au Griffon.*
}

Figure 4: Frontispiece of Diderot's *Encyclopédie*.

Almost from the start, the Catholic Church and the government opposed the work: it was subjected to Jesuit censorship on both religious and political grounds, and it was formally condemned and permission was denied for further volumes in 1759, as an act of repression occasioned by the scandal caused by the radical ideas of Helvétius' treatise *De l'Esprit {On the Mind}*. The entire encyclopaedia was banned by royal decree when only the first seven volumes had been produced and work on it was officially closed down, however it continued clandestinely because it had some well–placed supporters, including Madame de Pompadour, the influential mistress of the French king Louis XV. Nevertheless, there was a constant threat of police raids hanging over its contributors, and over Diderot in particular. Some compromises were made over the content of subsequent volumes and some of the more contentious material planned was removed, unbeknown to Diderot, who was devastated when he found out. Although the *Encyclopédie* was a huge drain on Diderot's efforts and time, he produced other works of considerable note and literary value. He wrote plays, philosophical works, essays of criticism, etc., and he worked with d'Holbach and others on many projects in a redactoral capacity to bring them to publication.

Clandestine Literature in France and the Dissemination of Subversive Ideas

In 1688, the satirical French moralist and writer La Bruyère (1645—1696) had remarked, '*Les grands sujets sont défendus*' {'The big subjects [for discussion] are banned'}. As Wade has noted, between **Bayle**'s *Dictionaire historique et critique {Historical and Critical Dictionary}* of 1697 and Montesquieu's *L'Esprit des Lois {Spirit of the Laws}* of 1750, 'police censorship controlled the press to such an extent that but few works dealing with the origins and foundation of Religion, the State, and the social order found their way into print.'[32] This threat notwithstanding, there was a continuous development of free thought in France between 1700 and 1750, and in many cases, if one casts the net a little wider, one finds works beyond these two dates. Every time controversial works appeared in print, French censorship vigorously suppressed them if they dealt with 'the taboo subjects'—'*les grands sujets*'—preventing publication altogether wherever possible, and suppressing the distribution of such works post–publication, when they had slipped through the official net. However, as Russian and Soviet censorship were to discover throughout the nineteenth and twentieth centuries, the total suppression of the written word was impossible, and in France, just as in the Soviet Union much later, works were produced in small

---

[32]   Wade, p. 1.

print–runs—sometimes even in larger numbers—and sold regularly and clandestinely. Again, as under the Soviets, manuscripts were copied and recopied by hand then circulated amongst circles of intellectuals, creating a whole industry dedicated to the dissemination of banned literature. In the USSR, this cottage industry was called 'samizdat' literature, literally 'home–published' or 'self–published' literature. In France, there was no equivalent term, but the phenomenon was essentially the same.

Whilst in Russia, much of the 'suspect' or banned literature was of a political and ideological nature, which questioned the whole communist regime and the nostra of socialism, in France the banned subjects were chiefly to do with questioning the authority of the Church and state, based on and promoted directly by the monarchy. Religion was a hot topic for debate, as one case in point, and typical of its kind, illustrates:

> On 20 February, 1698, the police detained a certain Bonaventure de Fourcroy [described as] a 'man of letters, detained on suspicion'. After the usual formalities in such cases, Fourcroy was committed to St Lazare, while his papers were seized and sent to the Bastille.[33] Among the papers which are still on record in the archives of the Bastille was an incomplete work containing a short article entitled 'The Beliefs of Materialists'. The first paragraph acquaints us with Fourcroy's preoccupations: 'I am firmly persuaded that true religion is not founded on the authority of man, because men are all fallible, and that it is not founded on miracles, on martyrdom, on revelation, or on prophesies, because such proofs as these are common to all religions; and I am equally convinced that true religion is not founded either on antiquity, or on Catholicism, because it has always been impossible to cease being the idiot and because there has always been an infinitely larger number of idiots than wise men: but it is founded on reason, which is merely the right discernment between what is good and bad, and what is true and false.'[34]

It turned out that Fourcroy had been very interested in materialist ideas because he had written a treatise entitled *Doutes sur la religion proposées à Mss. les Docteurs de Sorbonne* {*Doubts on Religion set before the gentlemen Doctors of the Sorbonne*}. By attributing these ideas to the 'materialists' and merely feigning to set them before the learned doctors of the Sorbonne as ideas with which he did not necessarily agree, Fourcroy was able, in some measure, to initiate a debate while absolving himself of any close association with those concepts. However, it was this treatise which had brought him to police attention, which in turn had cause him to be a marked man and the next time he stuck his head above the parapet, he was arrested. Often the period of detention was counted in terms of months, rather than years, but

---

[33] Both of these institutions were notorious prisons.
[34] Wade, pp. 1—2, translated here from Wade's original French citation.

any length of detention is something most people would dearly wish to avoid. Small wonder, then, that d'Holbach and other thinkers like him would not put their names to contentious works and that they would even keep their authorship quiet, even amongst friends.

Wade goes on to comment on the kind of punishment meted out to such miscreants:

> To be sure, if found guilty, he will not be burned at the stake, like **Geoffroy Vallée** or **Vanini**. He may, however, spend a disagreeable time at the Bastille. To obviate this difficulty, he may easily pretend to have translated these ideas from some ancient writer, or at least to have discovered them in the papers of some unknown author, long since dead. Hence, many of these works contain a short preface, or 'avertissement', or 'avis au lecteur' {foreword}, which disclaims any intention of overthrowing accepted views and declares the complete anonymity of the work.[35]

A royal declaration of 1728 in France condemned all authors found guilty of writing 'without permission' books that raised religious 'disputes' or touched upon those already raised, that 'disturbed the tranquillity of the state', or 'corrupted morals'—all charges frequently used against the *philosophes* when caught—to be banished beyond the court's area of jurisdiction where they were tried for a first offence; for a second, they could be banished beyond the territory of France. In 1757, the *conseil d'état* {*Council of State*}[36] raised the penalty for publishing, selling, or distributing such works, including now any which 'tend to attack religion', to the death penalty, even for a first offence. There was also the possibility of being found guilty of *lèse-majesté humaine et divine* {*an offence against the sovereign*, i.e., treason, *and God*, i.e., divine treason(!)}. It is highly unlikely that even the clergy would have evoked such a law and penalty, but it was there on the statute books as a threat and in theory.[37] In practice, whilst the Church was highly exercised by subversive, atheistic works, it saw schismatics and dissenters as a greater threat to its authority, because people who remained within the general fold of the Church, yet challenged its tenets, were liable to cause terrible divisions, such as those created by the **Jansenists** and **Huguenots**.[38] Those far beyond salvation were, in many ways, a lost

---

[35] Wade, p. 3.

[36] In France, the conseil d'état [Council of State] is an organ of the French national government whose functions include assisting the executive with legal advice and being the supreme court for administrative justice. Its members are mostly senior jurists.

[37] Kors, footnote pp. 230—31.

[38] For Jansenism and Huguenots—see pp. 348 & 349, and the Glossary.

cause, but members of the clergy propagating what was regarded as an aberration of orthodox belief had a tendency to gather acolytes and sectarians and were seen as much more bothersome. To open up a debate on the basic tenets of church doctrine was to open a Pandora's Box, which the Church had learned from experience was best left closed, unless the outrage was too great to ignore.

Yet another way of dealing with contentious material was to surround it with critical silence and hope that it died a death through indifference or ignorance, i.e., to starve it of the oxygen of publicity, as the saying goes—a policy which the USSR was to adopt in the latter years of the Soviet regime.

When deluged with complaints during the period 1765—1775 from the clergy, learned bodies such as the Sorbonne and the *Parlement* (the French supreme court, heavily influenced by the Catholic Church), together with powerful private citizens, the police found it easier to move against the sellers and pedlars of such materials—these were the middlemen or colporteurs, itinerant hawkers of books and newspapers—rather than conduct lengthy investigations as to the identity of the actual author. Hence, repeated raids were made on booksellers and colporteurs, who were mostly fined or arrested for a brief period, only to resume their distributive role all over again, once in a position to do so. There was money to be made and they had no intention of letting the opportunity pass, particularly as time went on and reprisals became less severe.

The fact that many illicit and subversive works were published anonymously or posthumously has given rise to the difficulty of establishing their true authorship. However, conversations on such subjects as religious belief and the Church were commonplace when out of earshot of the police and those who might inform, and such subversive topics were widely discussed in cafés, as Wade describes in another case, that of a certain Monsieur Mathieu or Morléon, who was investigated in 1729. (The notes are filed in the Bastille archive in French and here is one translated into English.)

> 9 August 1729.
> There are in Paris certain so–called 'great minds' who speak in cafés and elsewhere of religion as a chimera. Amongst others, Monsieur Boindin has stood out more than once in the Café de Conti, on the corner of the Rue Dauphine, and if these people are not brought to book, the number of atheists or Deists will increase and lots of people will form their own kind of religion, as they have in England.
> Monsieur Mathieu or Morléon, who rents a room in a café on the corner of the Rue St Dominique, on the Charity Hospital side, produces and sells copies of several works full of disbelief and maxims contrary to the existence of God and the divinity and teaching of Jesus Christ. Loads of

people [sic], priests and others, buy copies of these works at really high prices.[39]

Free–thinking groups met regularly and the most significant of these was the '*petite société de libres chercheurs*' {*little society of free–thinkers*}, which included Fréret, Boulainvilliers, **Dumarsais**, **Mirabaud**, and **Levesque de Burigny**, who met at the home of the Duc de Noailles not only for discussion on questions of atheism, but also for the purposes of organizing and disseminating atheist literature, often in the form of a pamphlet, a full half–century before d'Holbach and Naigeon, who knew of this material and developed their ideas from similar sources.[40]

Just as cafés themselves were meeting places for exchanging views of an unorthodox and subversive nature (from the point of view of the Church and state), so areas around these same cafés were famed for being the vicinity where such materials could be bought through the services of colporteurs.

Morléon was imprisoned in the Bastille from the end of August to September 1729—not a long period of incarceration, but still an event from which most people would demur. Wade points out that, 'The years 1740—1750 saw an increased activity on the part of the police, possibly because there was also increased activity on the part of copyists and colporteurs.' He goes on to show the extent of the proliferation of such material:

> In all, we have found, by an examination of the *Catalogue général des manuscrits des bibliothèques publiques de la France* {General Catalogue of Manuscripts of the Public Libraries of France} and the Omont catalogue of the Bibliothèque Nationale {National Library}, one hundred and two different treatises which deal in an unorthodox fashion with religion, natural theology [i.e., **Deism** and **Pantheism**, q.v., Glossary], and problems of morality and politics, which were circulated during the first half of the eighteenth century.[41]

Some of the works—particularly those by, or attributed to, Fréret, Boulanger, and some pieces by Naigeon—were printed abroad, often in London or Amsterdam, but a number of these works still cannot be found and few copies exist of many. What is certain is that almost every great personal library of moneyed people like d'Holbach, who could afford to buy books regularly, contained banned books, which were often loaned to their trusted friends. A number of prominent men of the cloth were also known to possess such works, or at the very least, they read them.

---

[39] Wade, p. 5.
[40] Ibid., pp. 101 & 267.
[41] Ibid., p. 10.

Several famous works which attacked religion virulently were published anonymously and even though we do not know who the authors were today, we still have the manuscripts and so the ideas have been passed on to posterity. One such famous work is *Le Traité des Trois Imposteurs {Treatise of Three Impostors}*, the three impostors being Moses, Jesus Christ and Muhammad, though this attack on religion is more wide–ranging than just the three leaders of the world's major monotheistic religions of Judaism, Christianity and Islam. A number of the ideas expressed in works such as these are traceable in d'Holbach's *Christianity Unveiled*. It is also known that Voltaire, Diderot, Rousseau, d'Holbach and Naigeon, to mention just a few, had copies of many of these works in their personal libraries, which attests to the fact that such ideas were current, well–known, and provided the basis for subsequent works of a similar nature. Wade points out, by way of conclusion, that '[These treatises] do make plausible, however, the assumption that the gradual organization and diffusion of philosophic thought in the clandestine treatises from 1700 to 1750 established a solid foundation of liberalism upon which the writers of 1750—1789 had only to build.'[42] Many of these anti–religious books were not necessarily of an atheist persuasion: a number were deistic, such as the *Lettre de Thrasybule à Leucippe {Letter from Thrasybulus to Leucippus}*, which masqueraded as a work which had been translated from the Greek. (See below p. lxxi.) However, most of them had in common the fact that they seriously questioned the whole concept of revealed religion, rejecting biblical writings as divinely inspired, as well as Jewish and Islamic scriptures.

A considerable number of works, chiefly of a deistic nature, found their way from England to France and d'Holbach played a major role in translating these from English into French, resulting in a cross–fertilization of ideas across the Channel. D'Holbach visited England in August and September of 1765, visiting his friend David Garrick, who provided him with a good deal of deistic material which he translated and published pseudonymously. D'Holbach hated England—he found it singularly dull, yet the trip was not without its fruitful outcome since he brought back with him a variety of fresh material, some of it mere pamphlets, but other whole volumes, and the friends he had made in England kept him supplied with the latest materials of the same ilk whenever they passed through Paris.[43] English thinkers were

---

[42] Wade, p. 275.

[43] Writing to his mistress Sophie Volland from Paris on the 20 September 1765, Diderot reported that, 'The baron is back from England: he left for that country without telling anyone; he was most pleasantly received there and he was in the rudest of health while over there, but he came back disgruntled; he was unimpressed by the country and by the people as well, both of which he found less refined than reputed; he was not favourably impressed with the buildings, which he thought were almost all bizarre and

freer to express doubt in print than their French counterparts and religion was a topic of heated debate and argument, just as in France. The chief sources of anti–religious material were **John Trenchard**'s weekly newspaper the *Independent Whig*, and **John Toland**'s writing, who was also a Whig. Other works from the pen of **Anthony Collins** and **Thomas Woolston** were also sources, as were works from the much more famous David Hume, who corresponded with a number of the French *encyclopédists*. Hume's works had been translated into French and were known to the *encyclopédists* prior to his visit to Paris in 1763—65, and d'Holbach himself translated a further two short essays on suicide and the immortality of the soul for a two–volume collection of essays edited by Naigeon, and published under the title *Recueil philosophique {Philosophical Compendium}* (1770).

Even when a number of books were printed in the customary fashion with the name of the true author appended, a work could still be condemned and ordered to be burned publicly: such was the fate of many books, but some of the most blatantly critical, such as Diderot's *Pensées philosophiques {Philosophical Thoughts}* (1746), published anonymously, caused a sensation and it was condemned to be burned by an act of the Paris *Parlement* (one of a number of high or supreme courts in France) on 7 July 1746. The same fate awaited many of d'Holbach's works. D'Holbach also translated an essay by **Thomas Hobbes**—by no means a contemporary thinker of d'Holbach's time, when most of his works had already been

---

gothic; he was disaffected with the gardens, where their affectation for imitating nature is worse than the most monotonous symmetry in art; he was unenthusiastic over the mixture of tastes which cram their palaces, where the excellent, the good, the bad, and the downright horrible are all amassed together; he was dissatisfied with their entertainment, which had an air of religious ceremony about it; he was displeased with the men, whose faces showed not the slightest trace of trust, friendship, liveliness, or sociability, and which looked as though they had written all over them, *What could you and I possibly have in common?*; he was totally put off by the people of distinction who were miserable, cold, haughty, stand-offish, and vain, and the 'little people', who were dure, rude, and barbarous; he was displeased with friends' dinner parties, where each person was seated according to their rank and where each guest never let their formal and ceremonious guard down; he didn't like the meals he had out where people got served promply enough, but without a hint of good grace.' And so the list of complaints goes on! And on... in a further letter of 6 October 1765. Perhaps it was just as well that d'Holbach let the world come to him, rather than him going out to see the world. See Diderot, *Oeuvres completes*, ed. by Assézat and Tourneux, XIX, (Paris: 1876), pp. 179—180. See also the following letter in the same volume, pp. 182 *et seqq.*, where the letter develops into a description and comparison of the English and the French, particularly in relation to religious issues, and d'Holbach comes to the conclusion that, 'The Christian religion is almost defunct throughout England. It is crammed full of Deists, but there are almost no atheists, and those that are hide the fact', (p. 185).

1

translated into French; hence his ideas were well–known in France. Hobbes's essay *On Human Nature or the Fundamental Elements of Policy* dated from 1650 and ideas from it can certainly be seen in d'Holbach's own thinking and in the writing of Condillac before his translation was published in French in 1772.

French cafés from this time onwards became notorious as forums for debating and discussing unorthodox views: even in the modern era, in the twentieth century, this tradition was still extant—the Parisian café Les Deux Magots in the Saint–Germain–des–Prés area was famed for, and prided itself on, hosting the literary and intellectual élite of the city, boasting such luminaries as Simone de Beauvoir and Jean–Paul Sartre, and young foreign writers such as Ernest Hemingway. Other patrons included Albert Camus and Pablo Picasso.

D'Holbach contributed a number of articles to Diderot's *Encyclopédie* and their friendship grew to become extremely close. Diderot admired d'Holbach's depth and breadth of learning, a feature for which he was well–known and admired amongst all who came into contact with him. In all, he contributed about three hundred articles as main entries to the *Encyclopédie* on mineralogy, metallurgy, chemistry and mining, and a further hundred pieces as sub–entries. He also undertook a good number of technical translations of books on similar subjects, translating from the German into French, and it is fair to say that he played a major role in making learned scientific texts available in French which helped academics and scientists to advance French research and experimentation in these fields, as Naigeon pointed out in his obituary of d'Holbach.[44] He translated a treatise by the German scientists Kunckel and Neri, *The Art of Glass–Making* in 1752, and a similar work by Wallerius on mineralogy in two volumes, published the following year. Similar works followed by leading German academics on an almost yearly basis until around 1760. D'Holbach's major contribution to scholarship was recognized by his peers: he was made a member of learned academies in Berlin, St Petersburg and Mannheim, but it was typical of the man that he did not seek membership personally.

Diderot and d'Holbach took great delight in taking walks together in the Tuileries Gardens in Paris, during which they discussed all manner of philosophical issues and it was on one of these walks that they bumped into Mme d'Epinay, with whom he would later become friends. She mentioned this chance meeting in a letter to Grimm and also the fact that, on learning later that she wanted to find some good bottles of Bordeaux wine but had not succeed, d'Holbach sent her a case of twenty–five bottles at his own expense

---

[44]   See this volume, p. 299.

and from his own supplier, wishing as his only reward—not thanks—but simply to know that she had enjoyed the wine.[45] This act of generosity was typical of the man.

With the publication of *Christianity Unveiled* around 1766 (discussed in more detail below), d'Holbach shifted the emphasis of his academic interests into philosophy, although he did not abandon his work as a technical and scientific translator. Whether his attitude towards religious issues became more radicalized through his friendship with Diderot is a matter of conjecture, but it is highly likely. Diderot's *Lettre sur les aveugles* {*An Essay on Blindness*}, published in 1749, in which yet again he expressed his materialist, atheist views was a final straw as far as the authorities were concerned, resulting in him being arrested and imprisoned for a period of three months in Vincennes prison. To be imprisoned for expressing such views was enough to radicalize others around him and to stiffen their resolve to continue writing in this vein. Furthermore, others around d'Holbach were writing works of a similar ilk and getting into trouble for them, such as Helvétius, whose book *De l'Esprit* {*On the Mind*} (1758) also caused a scandal and was condemned to be burned publicly, and its author was forced to recant, which he did in three separate written retractions. Anyone intending to read the work was threatened with excommunication by the Cardinal Archbishop of Paris, and it was damned by no less than the Vatican itself, and the Sorbonne for good measure. It is small wonder that d'Holbach wanted to make sure that his name did not appear on the title page of his works critical of religion and the Church, and why few would know of his connection with *Christianity Unveiled*: he wanted none of the notoriety Helvétius acquired. With the ban imposed on the *Encyclopédie* in the wake of the Helvétius affair and the rough treatment his friends had received for expressing their views, discretion was certainly the better part of valour.

A personal blow to d'Holbach and his circle was the death of one of their number—the brilliant Boulanger, who died in the summer of 1759, only months after the suppression of the *Encyclopédie*. Boulanger had contributed several articles to the *Encyclopédie* on ancient tribes, some aspects of antiquity, and he had had a major input into an article on '*Déluge*', the biblical *Flood* (narrated in Genesis chapters VI–VIII involving Noah), and the mythology surrounding various other universal flood myths which are to be found in a number of ancient cultures, many of which have no obvious common cultural connection.

Boulanger had worked as a civil engineer on some of the major road–building projects in France. His views on Christianity and religion in general

---

45 *Mémoires et Correspondance de Madame D'Epinay*, II, p. 214 and pp. 360—361.

were militant and uncompromisingly atheist, and he was a regular attender at d'Holbach's dinner parties. Abbé Galiani made a pun on his name, referring to d'Holbach's house as '*la grande boulangerie*' ('the large bakery' or 'bread shop')—a pun on Boulanger's name, which means 'baker' in French. After his death, Helvétius, his closest friend and the person with whom he had sought refuge towards the end of his life when alienated from his family through disputes over religion, made sure, with d'Holbach's and Diderot's help, that his manuscripts were published.

Boulanger's article on the Flood and the universality of the legend across a wide gamut of disparate, unconnected cultures, which he described in detail and compared and contrasted, lead him to postulate that primitive man invented his religious ideas and forms of government and civilization out of a fear of such natural phenomena and catastrophes. This materialist view of man and his beliefs became a hot topic of discussion and debate at d'Holbach's dinners. In fact, Horace Walpole, on a visit to d'Holbach and having witnessed such discussions, was to quip: 'They soon turned my head with a new system of antediluvian deluges, which they have invented to prove the eternity of matter. The Baron is persuaded that Pall Mall is paved with lava or deluge stones.'[46]

Boulanger had been working on this material prior to his death, leaving a comparative study of folklore on this subject in a book entitled *Antiquité dévoilé par ses usages {Antiquity Unveiled through its Customs}* and a further manuscript which was to have been worked more fully into a history of man and society, entitled *Les Recherches sur l'Origine du Despotisme Oriental {Research into the Origin of Oriental Despotism}*. D'Holbach brought out the fragment *On Oriental Despotism* in 1761, followed by *Antiquity Unveiled* in 1765, for which he had a biographical introduction written and added by Diderot. Boulanger had also written a letter to Helvétius, stating that society had been shocked by his treatise *On the Mind* because religion had got in the way of reason, asking the rhetorical question, 'Will governments never realize that Reason, and the Law founded on Reason, ought to be the only rulers of mortal men, and that, when an established religion begins to fade and die before the enlightenment of an Age of Reason, it is to that Reason alone that one must have recourse for the maintenance of society and its preservation from anarchy? Such Reason as that ought to be almost deified, instead of being weakened and humiliated.'[47]

---

[46] H. Walpole, *Letters*, ed. Toynbee, 16 vols (Oxford: Clarendon Press, 1903—1905), VI, p. 370.

[47] Quoted in Wickwar, p. 60 and reproduced as a preface to *Oriental Despotism*, based on Boulanger's letter.

As will become clear from reading *Christianity Unveiled*, d'Holbach's sentiments coincided with those expressed by Boulanger in his *Oriental Despotism*, and the very title of his *Antiquity Unveiled* found strong echoes not only in the title of d'Holbach's work, but also in many of the thoughts expressed in it. It was also to Boulanger that the authorship of the early editions of *Christianity Unveiled* was attributed.

D'Holbach's Atheist Writing

Exactly when d'Holbach adopted an atheist stance on religious issues, as opposed to a deist or pantheist position common amongst his fellow *philosophes*, is not known. Voltaire had long been of the persuasion that the world and the universe, as it was then understood, bore too many marks of intelligent design to rule out the existence of a god and he used his famous analogy of the watchmaker: anyone looking inside a watch, he reasoned, could see how the individual parts fit together so well that it would be inconceivable to question the existence of a designer and a great mind behind the whole mechanism. The same logic was erroneously applied to nature and the world around, which, it was thought, bore all the marks of a divine designer. What they clearly rejected was all forms of divine revelation, inspiration, the miracles of Christ and many of the other supernatural and inexplicable trappings of orthodox Christianity. Of course, once all these mystical elements had been jettisoned, there was little left of the beliefs held dear by the established Church and the Christian Gospel. Faith in divine revelation was abandoned for a faith in the ability of the human mind to reason, observe, experiment and draw logical conclusions from the empirical data amassed. Critics of such a stance accused the Deists or Pantheists of making a god of human reason, which the Church had, for centuries, damned as being tainted with original sin and thereby prone to error.

These ideas have a modern resonance in proponents of theories of Intelligent Design, who reject Darwinism and hold to the watchmaker argument in much the same way as Voltaire did for most of his life: their thinking has not moved on from such an outmoded stance, despite the fact that a good deal has been written against such understandable, but erroneous, thinking. Dawkins' book, *The Blind Watchmaker*, quotes the eighteenth–century theologian William Paley, whose treatise published in 1802 stated that, were we to come across a watch without knowing exactly what it was, its precision and intricacy of design would force us to the conclusion, 'that the watch must have had a maker: that there must have existed, at some time, and at some place or other, an artificer or artificers, who formed it for the purpose which we find it actually to answer, who comprehended its construction, and designed its use.'[48]   Voltaire had stated much the same thing as early as 1734.[49]

The writer Garat stated that this was a common stance adopted on religion by intelligent, thinking men—the acceptance of a nebulous divine creator, but a rejection of virtually all other religious nostrums were also things that even d'Holbach accepted, at least early on in his life, and in this he was no exception or different from people like Voltaire:

> [D'Holbach] long adored the God whom he saw in the law and order of the universe. Toward those he loved who did not share his belief, he had the zeal of a missionary. He would pursue the unbelieving Diderot into the very workshops where the editor of the *Encyclopédie*, surrounded by machines and artisans, was making drawings of all kinds of arts and crafts for his great dictionary. Taking these very machines as his text, he would ask if he could doubt that they had been conceived and created by a mind. Yet striking as was the comparison, it touched neither the head nor the heart of Diderot. Diderot's friend fell in tears at his feet [...]: a deist he knelt down, an atheist he arose. Instead of his drawing Diderot out of the bottomless, hopeless pit of atheism, Diderot dragged him down into it.'[50]

From details of the time and place given around this incident, it is highly probable that, if this account is to be believed, it took place about 1762, when d'Holbach was about thirty–nine.

There is yet other evidence to suggest that d'Holbach was of a vague deist stance from an article he wrote for the *Encyclopédie* on 'Fer' {'Iron'} in 1756, where he states, '*Le fer étant le plus utile des métaux, la providence l'a fort abondamment répandu dans toutes les parties de notre globe*', {'As the most useful of metals, Providence has most generously distributed iron in all parts of our globe'}.[51]

Wickwar finds further evidence for a deist/pantheist outlook in d'Holbach by the fact that he translated and published Mark Akenside's *Pleasures of the Imagination* in 1759, a work redolent of ardent Pantheism, but his reasoning is weak: d'Holbach might simply have enjoyed the challenge the work presented on a purely linguistic level and there is no evidence to suggest he subscribed personally to such beliefs.

However, it may well be that because of the extensive time Diderot and d'Holbach spent together at Grandval in 1759 and 1760, his deist views took

---

[48]   Quoted in R. Dawkins, *The Blind Watchmaker* (London: Penguin, 2006), p. 4.

[49]   See footnote on p. 285.

[50]   D.J. Garat, *Mémoires historiques sur la vie de Monsieur Suard, sur ses écrits, et sur le 18e siècle* (Paris: 1820), pp. 206 *et seqq.*

[51]   *Encyclopédie*, VI, p. 493.

a more atheist turn around this time. As Wickwar points out: 'By 1763, however, when the evidence of Hume and other British visitors becomes abundant, we can be tolerably sure that open and avowed atheism and materialism was one of the distinguishing characteristics of the Baron's synagogue [i.e., his group of friends] and presumably of the Baron himself.'[52]

It is also important to differentiate between anti–clericalism, which was a commonly held position amongst many intellectuals of this time, even amongst some believers, and outright atheism—a rejection of all manifestations of religious and supernatural belief.

In his study on d'Holbach and his coterie, Hubert places the responsibility for d'Holbach's atheism and for him writing his atheistic works firmly at the feet of Diderot. However, he also mentions that in the mid–1750s, d'Holbach had been studying natural history and geological strata and the fossils found in them, which he found yielded evidence at great variance with the creation myth as expressed in Genesis, which he also considers a factor for him arriving at an atheist stance.[53] Certainly Boulanger, through his work as a structural engineer and a keen observer of geological strata, found fossils both fascinating and at odds with a creationist view of the origins of our planet, and he would have undoubtedly discussed his ideas with d'Holbach.

Yet another participant at d'Holbach's dinners, the Italian thinker Alessandro Verri, who visited Paris in October 1766, stated that he had heard that d'Holbach's atheism stemmed from the shattering experience of his first wife's death, which had destroyed his faith in God. He wrote: 'I was told that the baron's *System [of Nature]* and his passion in sustaining his views originally came from having seen his first wife die and the thought of an eternity of horrors and torments for her. This had sorely moved his heart and marked a new era for him. From that time on, he became a rabid atheist and would countenance no other opinion.'[54]

Whatever the cause, d'Holbach and some members of his coterie, but by no means all, developed a reputation for their atheism. There is a story told by a number of authorities of an incident when Hume visited one of d'Holbach's diners, at which Hume was said to have remarked: 'Atheists! [...] I don't believe there are any: I have never met one.' Apparently, this remark elicited

---

[52] Wickwar, p. 64.

[53] Hubert, pp. 34—35.

[54] Quoted in Wattles, Ch. VI, footnote No. 24; *Carteggio di Pietro e di Alessandro Verri*, I, i, p. 114f., cited in Lough, *Le Baron D'Holbach: Quelques Documents Inédits ou peu connus'*, in RHL, 1957.

a repost from d'Holbach himself: 'Then you have been somewhat unlucky. [...] Here you are at table with seventeen.'[55]

A certain missionary zeal stemmed from the *Encyclopédie*, written as it was by the finest minds of France with the express aim, clearly stated in the 'Discours Préliminare des Éditeurs' {Preliminary Discours of the Editors}, to present to the readers all facts, going back to their very origins, and thus allowing them to make up their own mind about a vast gamut of knowledge—not only the sciences and things ascertained through empirical observation and experimentation, but also on a whole range of philosophical and religious issues. Emphasis was clearly put upon the senses and empiricism, i.e., what was knowable and discoverable through observation and experimentation, and also in the (perhaps utopian) confidence that the truth liberates the mind and breaks down barriers which divide mankind into oppressors and oppressed. Like the philosophers and intellectuals of antiquity, they felt a keen sense of taking accepted, established knowledge and building upon it, preserving it for posterity and providing the basis for human knowledge to grow and flourish. They also expressed the desire to encompass the arts, language and literature, which they saw as no less important than scientific achievement.

Certainly this zeal for enlightenment found its expression in d'Holbach's philosophical works, the first of which was his *Christianity Unveiled*. As Naigeon remarks in his obituary, he was a marvellous educator with a common touch.[56] To this end, d'Holbach not only worked on the late Boulanger's works, as he did his own, but he also published them at his own expense. Boulanger's *Oriental Despotism* (1761) and his *Antiquity Unveiled* (1765) marked the first steps of what was to become a protracted campaign against religious superstition.

The Publication of Christianity Unveiled

Christianity Unveiled was one of many anti–religious works published around 1767—1770, a period which to many looked like a virulent campaign against the Church. On 22 September 1767, D'Alembert wrote to Voltaire, saying, 'We're being rained upon by countless numbers of books against the *infâme* [i.e., the Church and believers of all hues] in the form of the *Portable Theology*, the *Esprit du clergé* {Spirit of the Clergy}, the *Prêtres démasqués*

---

[55] Quoted in Wickwar, p. 39, originally recounted in S. Romilly, *Memoirs of the Life of Sir Samuel Romilly:with a selection from his correspondance, edited by his sons*, 3 vols (John Murray, 1840), I, p. 179.

[56] See p. 302.

{*Priests Unmasked*}, *The Militant Philosopher*, etc., etc., etc.[57] It appears that one has resolved to lay siege to the *infâme* in the correct form, tooth and nail, on the inside.' Also Voltaire, in a letter to the Marquis de Villevieille on 20 December 1768, remarked: 'For the last two years more than sixty volumes against the Church have been printed.'

Whether d'Holbach's attribution of the authorship of *Christianity Unveiled* to Boulanger was an act of honouring his friend, or merely a convenient cover to kick over the tracks in the sand of his own authorship and hence spare himself possible serious repercussions, is not known. Whatever the real reason, it was a little white lie he was willing to permit himself. Subsequent editions would be attributed to other writers—perhaps a taunt to the censor to discover the true identity of the author. However, d'Holbach was successful in keeping his authorship secret and even Voltaire, though not a close friend of d'Holbach, but a man very much 'in the know', was to write to Helvétius on 27 October 1766, 'Who is the author of this work attributed to Bolingbroke, Boulanger and Fréret?' And again he wrote to Falconnet on 15 May 1767, 'Could you tell me to whom *you* attribute the *Unveiled* volume? If only you knew how all the conjecture involving me makes me laugh!' Furthermore, the police inspector Hémery had noted in his journal on 5 February 1767, '...this work is attributed to Mr Boulanger, but I do not recognize his style in it, and I think it is rather from Mr Voltaire's camp.'[58]

The fact that the work's putative author Boulanger was widely regarded as correct was largely due to the similarity in titles, so many accepted that the author of *Antiquity Unveiled* was indeed the author of *Christianity Unveiled*, and scant regard was paid by many to stylistic considerations. Also the fact that such a work was rumoured to be from Voltaire's pen came as no surprise, since it was common to attribute such works to Voltaire and it was to be many years later before d'Holbach was to be universally acknowledged as the author. In the intervening years, other names were cited as being the true author, such as **Damilaville**, a friend of Voltaire's, and even when d'Holbach's name was mentioned as a possibility, a number of supposed *cognoscenti*, such as the writer and literary critic **Jean–François de la Harpe** (1739—1803), and even Voltaire himself, still refuted d'Holbach as the real author, insisting that Damilaville was the actual writer. However, it may well be that by so doing, Voltaire was not so much making a mistake, but taking

---

[57] *Esprit du clergé* {*Spirit of the Clergy*} (1767) was translated by d'Holbach from the English essay of John Toland. *Prêtres démasqués* {*Priests Unmasked*} (1768) was another of d'Holbach's translations from the English by an anonymous author.

[58] Quoted in J. Vercruysse, *Bibliographie déscriptive des écrits du baron d'Holbach* (Paris: Minard, 1971). Pages not innumerated: see under section '1756: A1. *Le Christianisme Dévoilé*'.

the heat from himself in attributing the work to yet another deceased man, viz., Damilaville, who had died in 1768. La Harpe continued to insist on the Damilaville hypothesis in his teaching at the *Lycée* (see Glossary), despite the fact that the poet, playwright and publicist **Maréchal** had correctly attributed the work to d'Holbach in his *Dictionnaire des athées anciens et modernes* {*Dictionary of Ancient and Modern Atheists*} of 1800. The French librarian and bibliographer **Barbier** (1765—1825) mentioned the various erroneous attributions in the second edition of his *Dictionnaire des ouvrages anonyms et pseudonymes* {*Dictionary of Anonymous and Pseudonymous Works*} (originally published in 1806—1808, second edition 1822) and maintained that d'Holbach was the true author, but he also stated that the original edition of *Christianity Unveiled* was published in 1761 by Leclerc in Nancy, and these details were repeated in subsequent editions.[59] All these details are correct, except for the date of 1761 (as discussed below). Abbé Morellet also confirmed d'Holbach's authorship in his *Memoirs* in 1821.[60]

D'Holbach confided the manuscript of *Christianity Unveiled* to the military officer and regular dinner guest Saint–Lambert, who took it to the publisher Leclerc in Nancy under the pretext of going there on military business. It was printed with the date 1756 and the place 'London' was falsely appended to the title page. Some copies of the printed book were sent on to Voltaire in Ferney, his home on the Swiss border, and it was he who forwarded the first two copies to Damilaville. Garrison officers stationed in Nancy brought the book in quantities to Paris, from where they were distributed further afield.

Barbier's date of 1761 is certainly in error because had *Christianity Unveiled* been published then, there would certainly have been mention of it in the works and correspondence of d'Holbach's contemporaries, and no such evidence has yet been found.

Furthermore, in an edition of the work in the Bibliothèque Nationale in Paris, a date of 'MDCCLVI', i.e., 1756, is given, but it has been *corrected* by the addition of an 'X', rendering the date 'MDCCLXVI', i.e., 1766. An argument against a date of 1756 is that the Preface of *Christianity Unveiled* is dated 'Paris, 4 May 1758'. Vercruysse has also stated that an examination of the watermark of the paper indicates dates of either 1762 or possibly 1763—the former being preferable for reasons given below.

Therefore, in the light of current scholarship, the accepted date of publication can be taken as 1766. We also know that on 1 September 1766, Sartine, lieutenant general of the Paris police, mentioned the *appearance* of

---

[59] Barbier, *Dictionnaire des ouvrages anonymes et pseudonymes* {*Dictionary of Anonymous and Pseudonymous Works*} (1806—1809), 2nd edn., I, pp. 175—176.

[60] Abbé Morellet, *Mémoires*, I, p. 133.

Christianity Unveiled to Inspector Hémery and urged him to prevent the circulation of the work by all possible means. Furthermore, there is a letter from Voltaire to his friend Damilaville of the 24 September 1766, stating, 'There is a new book, as you know, by the late Mr Boulanger. This "boulanger" [viz., "baker"—see p. liii] has kneaded a batch of dough that nobody is able to stomach.' A short time later, there is a letter from Diderot to Voltaire of the 10 October 1766, which states, 'Our friend [i.e., Damilaville] got me to read a new book. I tremble for the moment when this book will become known... If this book is known to you and you can defer all publicity over it until circumstances are more favourable, you would do well to do so.' Hence, it is quite clear that none of these perceptive, judicious men of the age were left in any doubt of the import of such a work and the dates of their remarks throw valuable light on the true date of publication.

The circulation of d'Holbach's work was slow, probably because of the heightened awareness and police vigilance in rooting out the book. This time was one of several periodic 'clamp–downs'. D'Holbach himself *mentioned* in a letter thought to be addressed to the lawyer Servan, 'From your distance in Switzerland, you probably know better than we do, how we handle with kid gloves the *Essential Compendium, Christianity Unveiled*, Fréret's *Examination*, and *The Ignorant Philosopher*, and all the other bombs which beset our ancient edifice, which has never been subjected to such forceful and repeated attacks: the second of these works has produced a prodigious and well–merited sensation, especially here.'[61]

From the point of view of the authorities, police vigilance paid off in 1768, when they arrested a certain Jean Baptiste Josserand, a young grocer's lad, who made money on the side selling second–hand books. Also arrested was another married couple—Jean Lecuyer and his wife Marie Suisse—who were caught selling *Christianity Unveiled* illegally. Their punishment was severe, as opposed to the much lighter punishments generally meted out to members of the aristocracy or to those with money. All three were sentenced to spending three days in the stocks, then they were subsequently branded, after which Josserand was condemned to spending nine years in the galleys, Lecuyer got away with 'only' five years of the same, and his wife received a

---

[61] Cited in Vercruysse in the section previously indicated. The *Essential Compendium* (*Recueil nécessaire*) was a work by Voltaire, first published in Leipzig in 1765; Nicolas Fréret, *Examen critique des apologistes de la religion chrétienne* (*Critical Examination of Apologists of the Christian Religion*) was published in 1766; Voltaire, *Le Philosophe ignorant* (*The Ignorant Philosopher*) was published in 1765. All these works attack established religion.

five–year internment.[62] Needless to say, the *philosophes* were outraged by such a harsh sentence and the whole affair became a *cause célèbre* at the time.

The '*London*' edition of *Christianity Unveiled*, actually printed in Nancy and falsely dated 1756, was condemned publicly to be torn up and burned along with other books of a similar nature by an act of the *Parlement* on 18 August 1770, and the sentence was carried out the next day.[63] However, many editions followed—five alone in 1767—and more in 1768, and editions appeared every year from 1774—1777, to mention but a few. The work was also subsequently translated into Russian in 1924 and printed in Moscow, which received the full backing of the Bolshevik government, already actively pursuing an anti–religious campaign in Russia. It was also translated into Spanish and published in 1821 under the title *El Cristianismo a descubierto*, printed in London by Davidson, and later retranslated under the more accurate, literal translation *El Cristianismo Desvelado*. It was translated for the first time into English in 1795 by W.M. Johnson, still attributed to Boulanger, who is named as the author of *Oriental Despotism* on the title page, and the work was printed in New York. This edition was subsequently printed by R. Carlile of Fleet Street in 1819, and subsequently by Gordon Press in 1974. This flawed Johnson translation has remained the only edition currently available in English until this present translation.

Christianity Unveiled was the first of a number of such works d'Holbach was to publish, mostly outside France and often printed in Amsterdam, where there was greater freedom to produce such works. Subsequently, the books were then smuggled into France and other countries as people travelled across borders with copies hidden in their trunks, sometimes in quantities, and then sold on at vastly inflated prices. Records show that everyone knew that books were smuggled into France secreted under the seats of officials, aristocrats, and figures of the court, eager to cash in on the latest literary *objet de luxe*, the 'must–have' work of the season, which could be sold at a good profit, and others simply regarded such literature as something to boast about having read. No one at the frontiers was prepared to violate the tacit privilege of such an elite, and so a blind eye was turned.[64] However, it was, of course, easier to target the poor street vendors who needed to make 'a fast buck'. It was said that Queen Christiana of Sweden was willing to pay a huge sum of money for a copy of the *Traité des Trois Imposteurs {Treatise of*

---

[62] Vercruysse, ibid. The original source is a letter from Diderot to Mlle Volland of 8 October 1768, according to Max P. Cushing, p. 29 (Kessinger Publishing Reprints edn.).

[63] 'Extraits des registres du parlement, le 18 août 1770 (Paris, 1770).

[64] Kors, p. 238.

Three Impostors} (1712), but despite her wealth, influence, and connections, she never managed to get hold of one.[65] Such was the appetite for this kind of literature.

Naigeon became d'Holbach's friend and 'partner in crime', helping him to edit and publish his own manuscripts, as well as working with him on rewriting several anti–Christian texts by other thinkers from home and abroad. Diderot also played a part in being the final arbiter in matters of style, but his input was not confined to this aspect alone. Thus began a sort of cottage industry in producing works of an anti–religious ilk and, according to Naigeon, the whole process fell into a regular pattern: d'Holbach would present a manuscript to Naigeon, who would in turn pass it on to his brother either in Paris, where his brother often visited, or in Sedan, in the Ardennes area, through a mutual friend named Bron, a tax–farmer [see p. xxviii] and the *inspecteur–général* {general inspector} of the *bureau du départ*—a sort of main post–office and warehouse, from where items would be dispatched for delivery. In Sedan, the younger Naigeon would copy d'Holbach's manuscripts and destroy the originals, then send the new manuscript 'in a package covered with two layers of wax–sealed cloth' to a certain Mme Loncin in Liège, a contact of d'Holbach's Dutch publisher Marc–Michel Rey in Amsterdam, who would then get the manuscript to him. In this way, only Naigeon was really directly involved in the publication process, and d'Holbach's name and the role of others were kept to a minimum.[66] Morellet stated in his memoirs that d'Holbach's authorship of such anti–religious works was never discussed within the coterie, even though his writing was the most scandalous of any at that time: his status as a philosopher was a well–guarded secret and most of the other members of the coterie knew him as a translator of scientific works and articles. Those who did know never discussed the matter, as Morellet states: 'We lived constantly together, and, before the Baron's death, not one of us confided to the other our knowledge of [his authorship], although each certainly thought that the other knew as well.'[67] Morellet stated that Marmontel, Saint–Lambert, Suard, Chastellux, Roux, Darcet, Raynal and Helvétius all knew the true authorship of d'Holbach's works: he goes on to say, 'The thought of the danger our friend

---

[65] *Traité des Trois Imposteurs*, edited with an introduction by Max Milo (Paris: Max Milo Editions, 2002), p. 5.

[66] Alan C. Kors, *D'Holbach's Coterie: An Enlightenment in Paris* (Princeton, New Jersey: Princeton University Press, 1976), p. 83.

[67] Morellet, *Mémoires*, I, pp. 132—134. See also Galiani, *Lettres*, I, pp. 94—96 & 110—114, and Diderot, *Correspondance*, VIII, pp. 234—235.

would have risked from an indiscretion on our part imposed a silence upon our most trusting friendship.'[68]

Though they were friends, Grimm was critical of d'Holbach's *Christianity Unveiled* from a stylistic point of view: he found it 'very badly executed... bilious... without taste', and thought that it was 'insane to risk one's peace and one's happiness for the pleasure of throwing stones at an old hovel [i.e., the Church] guarded by mastiffs who rip apart all those who do not pass without raising their eyes.'[69]

Diderot was also critical of d'Holbach's written style, complaining that it was 'too lengthy, flat and diffuse', and that 'it is fatiguing, it is boring, *and* it makes a book fall from one's hands.'[70]

The extent of the originality of d'Holbach's *Christianity Unveiled* has also been questioned. Certainly many works of a critical and clandestine nature built on those which had gone before them—a normal feature of any type of scholarship and intellectual inquiry. Wattles claims that the originality of *Christianity Unveiled* lay more in the fact that it appeared in print, rather than it being circulated in manuscript form, and that its arguments characterized a number of works of the first half of the eighteenth century and beyond. The fact that Christ is portrayed as an obscure impostor and that the early miracles are explained as charlatanism he attributes explicitly to **Fontenelle**. Wattles also attributes d'Holbach's comments on earlier cults from Fréret's *Lettre de Thrasybule à Leucippe* {*Letter from Thrasybulus to Leucippus*}, and similarly, his attack on prophesies, miracles, and martyrs he claims were taken from D'Alembert's *Eléments de Philosophie* {*Elements of Philosophy*} (1759). Furthermore, Wattles identifies d'Holbach's attack on monastic vows, chastity and obedience as having their origins in Diderot's *La Religieuse*, and he further claims that the portrayal of Christianity as a tool for suppressing self–interest and its consequences on human conduct, leading to a tragic denouement, are ideas expressed in Helvétius' work *De l'Esprit.*[71] These claims will now be examined briefly.

Fontenelle was a scientist, polymath and writer of not particularly well–received poetry and drama. However, his two essays, jointly entitled *Histoire des oracles* {*History of Oracles*} (1687) caused a considerable stir in theological and philosophical circles. In it, Fontenelle bases his comments on a lengthy work written in Latin by a Dutch medical doctor, a certain Antonius Van Dale, on the nature and role of oracles among the ancients.

---

[68] Morellet, op. cit., pp. 133—134.
[69] Quoted in Kors, p. 83 and Grimm, *Correspondance littéraire*, VII, pp. 425—426.
[70] Kors, ibid. and Diderot, *Correspondance*, XII, pp. 45—47.
[71] Wattles, Chapter VI.

Fontenelle, always eager to educate and popularize works, divests the work of its (to his mind) excessive length and linguistic inaccessibility by translating the Latin, editing passages, and providing his own commentary based on the original. By examining whether oracles 'were a trick and a ruse of pagan priests', or whether they were a genuine communication between the temporal world and the realm of the spirit, Fontenelle throws doubt upon the accepted notion that Christian scripture was truly inspired by God. He also raises questions such as, how can we know whether the oracular utterances of favoured individuals were real or a product of self–delusion, either intentional or unwitting? Furthermore, he tackles the question of whether further oracular revelations are still to be expected, or whether divine revelation has now ceased after Christ's own appearance and gospel message. The view of the Christian and Islamic religions is that God's revelation is complete and final: the writer of the last book of the New Testament, the Revelation to John or the Apocalypse of John, states clearly:

> For I testify unto every man that heareth the words of the prophecy of this book, If any man shall add unto these things, God shall add unto him the plagues that are written in this book: And if any man shall take away from the words of the book of this prophecy, God shall take away his part out of the book of life, and out of the holy city, and from the things which are written in this book. He which testifieth these things saith, Surely I come quickly. Amen. Even so, come, Lord Jesus. (Rev. 22:18—20)[72]

However, given that the Book of Revelation only just made it into the Bible, having been initially rejected as non–canonical, and the fact that, at the time it was written, the Bible as we know it had not been assembled into a canonical, coherent whole—and many would say that in its form as we know it, it is neither 'coherent' nor a 'whole'—the writer could not have known which other scriptures the Church would ultimately deem divinely inspired.[73]

---

[72] In fact, Bart Ehrman comments on this dire warning in his book *Misquoting Jesus*: he says, 'This is not a threat that the reader has to accept or believe everything written in this book of prophecy, as it is sometimes interpreted; rather, it is a typical threat to *copyists* [sic] of the book, that they are not to add to or remove any of its words.' Bart Ehrman, *Misquoting Jesus: The Story Behind Who Changed the Bible and Why* (N.Y.: HarperOne/HarperCollins, 2005), p. 54. He makes the point that copyists were so prone to altering the text they were copying—either intentionally or simply by making mistakes—that the writer of this particularl apocalypse felt the need to issue this warning.

[73] Bart D. Ehrman comments on such Christian Apocalypses: 'The coming end of all things was a source of continuous fascination for early Christians, who by and large expected that God would soon intervene in the affairs of the world to overthrow the forces of evil and establish his good kingdom, with Jesus at its head, here on earth. Some Christian authors produced prophetic accounts of what would happen at this cataclysmic end of the world as we know it. There were Jewish precedents for this

Logically, John can only have been referring to his own book when he wrote that nothing should be added or removed. It is also quite clear that there were many texts around during the period of early church history and even Eusebius did not write them off as unworthy of our attention, as he remarked in his *History of the Church*:

> Large numbers of short works composed with commendable zeal by churchmen of that early time are still preserved in many libraries. Those that I have read myself include Heraclitus on *The Epistles of Paul*; Maximus on the question so much discussed among the heretics, *The Origin of Evil* [...] and works by many other authors—lack of evidence make it impossible to give their dates or shed any light on their history. Finally, there are a number of others whom I cannot even name, whose writings have come into my hands—orthodox churchmen, as is clear from their respective interpretations of Holy Writ, but unknown to us all the same, as they are not named in their writings. (Eusebius, *History of the Church* 5: 27; Penguin edition, 1989, p. 175).

Altering the text—one might even claim 'falsifying'—was also quite common, which was again admitted by Eusebius, who states that this led to a proliferation of versions of the same work, some of which had been altered out of all recognition:

> If anyone will take the trouble to collect their several copies and compare them, he will discover frequent divergences; for example, Asclepiades' copies do not agree with Theodotus'. A large number are obtainable, thanks to the emulous energy with which disciples copied the 'emendations' or rather perversions of the text by their respective masters. Nor do these agree with Hermophilus' copies. As for Apolloniades, his cannot even be harmonized with each other; it is possible to collate the ones which his disciples made first with those that have undergone further manipulation, and to find endless discrepancies. The impertinence of this misconduct can hardly be unknown even to the copyists. Either they do not believe that the inspired Scriptures were spoken by the Holy Spirit—if so, they are unbelievers; or they imagine that they are wiser than He—if so, can they be other than possessed? (Eusebius, op. cit., pp. 177—178.)

We must also consider the fact that archaeologists and scholars have continued work on discoveries which have come to light even in the modern period, yet the Church doggedly refuses to revise any of its ideas. One

---

kind of "apocalyptic" literature, for example, in the book of Daniel in the Jewish Bible, or the book of I Enoch in the Jewish Apocrypha. Of the Christian apocalypses, one eventually came to be included in the New Testament: the Apocalypse of John. Others, including the *Apocalypse of Peter* and *The Shepherd* of Hermas, were also popular reading in a number of Christian communities in the early centuries of the church.' (Bart D. Ehrman, op. cit., p. 25.)

outstanding example is that of the discovery of the *Gospel of Judas*, the disciple of Jesus whom the Church has demonized for centuries, which was discovered as late as the 1970s.[74]

We do not know exactly when the *Gospel of Judas* was written, but the extant manuscript copy has been carbon–dated to around AD 280, making this document one of the oldest surviving original copies in existence—far older than any copies of the canonical gospels, the oldest of which is Mark's. It is thought that the original gospel was written around AD 140—160. In it, Judas's betrayal of Christ is not seen as an ignominious act, but one carried out with Christ's approval, because he acknowledged that he had to be betrayed and delivered into the hands of his enemies.

It is also the case that there are books in the New Testament which are accepted as canonical, yet they are also forgeries in the literal sense of the word: for instance, Paul's Letter to Titus is thought by scholars not to have been written by Paul at all, yet it is accepted as divinely inspired. Christians in the early church frequently forged all manner of gospels, epistles and other religious writings, most of which have been lost, but those that have come to light recently have stimulated renewed interest in them, as Bart Ehrman's books attest—see Bibliography.

The Qur'an claimed to be the final revelation of God to mankind, though it was written around five centuries after the general corpus of biblical scriptures, and the Qur'an also rejects the finality of the Christian corpus of literature, stating, 'People of the Book, why do you deny God's revelations when you can see they are true?' (Qur'an 3:70) To say the least, the situation is confusing!

---

[74] In an interview on the recent publication of a scholarly translation from the Coptic, the language in which the *Gospel of Judas* was written, a Catholic theologian and one of the Church's 'big guns' tried to dismiss the latest discovery, linking it to such light-weight works as Dan Brown's *The Da Vinci Code* and the musical *Jesus Christ Superstar*. The cleric, described as the 'Legionary Father Thomas D. Williams, Dean of Theology at the Regina Apostolorum University in Rome', relied on the old mantra that (i) no amount of proof is good enough for anyone unwilling to make a leap of faith and that (ii) everyone loves a good conspiracy theory. He concluded, 'Basically, for those who reject outright the possibility of miracles, any theory, outlandish as it may be, trumps Christian claims.' Clearly, the Church is absolutely unwilling to take seriously any new evidence or scholarship when there is the slightest chance that the *status quo* might be upset. See Catholic Online, 4/06/2006 at http://www.catholic.org/featured/headline.php?ID=3175&page=1 See also *The Gospel of Judas*, edited by R. Kasser, M. Meyer, and G. Wurst, with additional commentary by B.D. Ehrman (Washington, D.C.: The National Geographic Society, 2006). The reaction of Rowan Williams, the Archbishop of Canterbury, was similar.

Figure 5: Judas returning the thirty pieces of silver. (Source: Wikipedia.)

Judas Iscariot skulks away, having dropped the money offered to him by the priests to betray Christ. The recently published *Gospel of Judas* offers a different version of events.

By raising all these questions and others, such as the linguistic ambiguity of all prophesies, Fontenelle implies that all claims the Church might have to the absolute authority, monopoly and definitive knowledge of the divine mind, are hollow and to be viewed with the utmost suspicion. This stance is also clearly reflected in d'Holbach's *Christianity Unveiled* and in his other works, and it was a commonly held view of Deists in general, all of whom rejected the notion of the infallibility of divine revelation, whatever its source.

True to form, as will be seen in the case of *Christianity Unveiled*, the Catholic Church went into overdrive to denigrate and reply to the writer: in 1707, Baltus, a Jesuit, stated that he had caught in the work a whiff of 'detestable venom', which he further qualified, calling it 'the harmful poison of disbelief', and invited a refutation to be written and that Fontenelle further clarify his position. Fontenelle backed off, having been warned by two friends, also Jesuits, but of a less militant nature, that the knives were out and being sharpened if he ventured further to comment on the subject, and he was officially threatened that he would end up in the Bastille prison if he responded.

The fact that d'Holbach used some of Fréret's expertise on ancient cults, etc., is hardly surprising: he was an acknowledged expert in this field and he would have been the natural authority to turn to. Fréret had studied various cults from the Phoenicians and Egyptians to the Greeks, Celts, Germans, Chinese, and Indians. Indeed, it would have been foolish of d'Holbach to have disregarded his work.

Fréret's *Letter* does indeed mention ancient cults, including Jewish, and Egyptian beliefs, and those of the Chaldeans and others. His work goes into considerably more detail on these cults than d'Holbach's book, the latter preferring to make his point with a very broad brush, as befits the general ethos of the work: to have gone into the kind of detail seen in Fréret's work would have greatly enlarged the scope of d'Holbach's treatise and altered it completely. D'Holbach's *Christianity Unveiled* is intentionally more wide–ranging than Fréret's work—it is a survey which covers all the major tenets of Christian belief, including baptism and other sacraments, and draws clear social and political conclusions from such institutions. However, in Fréret's *Letter* there is not a single mention of the role played by a temporal sovereign, king or ruler, or the rule of law divested of clerical and religious interference within a state. It was d'Holbach's passionate conviction that human society needed an ethical system founded on a purely secular ethos, devoid of religious cults and superstition. He felt strongly that a symbiotic relationship between ruler/state and the Church was utterly unhealthy. In Fréret's work such ethical ramifications are not accorded the same serious, practical consideration as in d'Holbach's. In short, d'Holbach certainly drew on Fréret's expertise and knowledge, but Fréret's *Letter* is rather a detailed exposé of all the different religious systems shown to be contrary to logic and reason, and how they are apt to capture the imagination of one society or another.

Although D'Alembert's *Essay on the elements of philosophy* was published in 1759 and thereby it was probably written rather late to have specifically influenced d'Holbach's *Christianity Unveiled*, the work was a synthesis of his prior thought in a number of fields, including aesthetics, epistemology, language theory, metaphysics and science. D'Alembert's work was clearly well known to d'Holbach and, like the other *philosophes* and contributors to the *Encyclopédie*, he was a free–thinker and an opponent of religious dogma and the Church. It is difficult to single out any specific stance D'Alembert took on religious issues that was not shared by most of the members of the 'coterie holbachique', and therefore it makes little sense to look for specific borrowings. Also D'Alembert could best be described as a sceptic rather than an atheist, but he willingly supported the *philosophes'* hostility to Christianity, though he was rather more circumspect than to embrace d'Holbach's openly militant brand of aggressivity towards established belief, which could lead to a serious clash with the authorities, as already pointed out. (See also D'Alembert's comment on p. lxxvi.)

D'Holbach's attack on monastic life was certainly not new, but equally what he wrote in *Christianity Unveiled* had little to do with Diderot's novel *La Religieuse* {*The Nun*}, since it was not published until 1796, i.e., after Diderot's death and some thirty years after the publication of *Christianity Unveiled*. To be sure, the work had started out as a satire on monastic life— something of a joke—which appeared episodically between 1780 and 1782. It is also true, as has already been noted, that d'Holbach and Diderot were close friends and it is perfectly conceivable that d'Holbach knew of the content of Diderot's satire at least from conversations with him, if not from the (un)published work. Nevertheless, it seems strange to claim that d'Holbach's remarks about monastic life were in any direct way linked to Diderot's novel. Furthermore, Diderot's own work on the cloistered life was hardly original, given that there were many eighteenth–century libertine convent novels, the most famous, or infamous, being *Vénus dans le cloître* {*Venus in the Cloister*}, thought to have been written by Abbé Jean Barrin around 1680. In fact, by the end of the eighteenth century there were a couple of hundred titles of a similar nature in circulation.[75]

---

[75] Christopher Rivers, 'Safe Sex: The Prophylactic Walls of the Cloister in the French Libertine Convent Novel of the Eighteenth Century' in *Journal of the History of Sexuality*, 5, Issue: 3, 1995, pp. 381—403, (pp. 382—83).

There is certainly no doubt that there are many points of contact between d'Holbach and Helvétius, as is evident in the latter's two celebrated philosophical treatises *De l'esprit* {*On the Mind*} (1758) and *De L'homme* {*On Man*} (1772). However, d'Holbach's *Christianity Unveiled* was probably already written by the time Helvétius had officially published his first work, given the generally accepted date stated at the end of the Preface of *Christianity Unveiled*, viz., '4 May 1758', and *De L'homme* post–dates d'Holbach's work by several years. As a regular dinner guest, the views of Helvétius would have been well–known within the Holbachian coterie, but again they were certainly not exclusively his own and were shared by many of the *philosophes*. To be sure, we can identify in the work of both these philosophers anger against the Church for its intolerance of scientific experimentation and theories; a contempt for its internecine struggles, as exemplified in the battles between the Jesuits and the Jansenists; the scandals of the Church's casuistry and its contempt for human dignity and earthly happiness; the Church's political power and its meddling in secular rule; and a general, even vehement, anti–clericalism, as exemplified in the priesthood's selling favours and false hope, thus playing on the fear of the ignorant—a phenomenon which made Helvétius dub them 'vendors of hope and fear'. Many, if not most, of these views were shared by enlightened men around d'Holbach's table, and some enlightened clerics themselves sympathized with such views, so in that sense d'Holbach's work cannot be considered wholly original. However, few people, apart from those with a healthy appetite for philosophy, would be able to wade through the two treatises of Helvétius—*On the Mind* numbers some five hundred pages alone, and *On Man*, over a thousand.

Also in d'Holbach's work we find many points previously discussed by Boulainvilliers, who exposed errors in Old Testament chronology and philosophical problems associated with such ancient scriptures—biblical discrepancies in the narratives and the capricious, spiteful nature of the Almighty. He also totally rejected divine explanations for miracles. On the issue of prophesies and the ambiguous wording in which they were purposefully couched, Boulainvilliers closely followed Spinoza, with whose ideas d'Holbach was certainly very familiar, like all educated men of his era.

D'Holbach's originality, therefore, lies in the ideas he selected and the way in which he expressed and synthesized them, applying them to his subject matter so as to make them accessible to a wider reading–public. Like many philosophers, he took the ideas of others and used them as a platform to express his own and in so doing he produced a cogent, stimulating new work. He was a consummate, systematic political thinker with a common touch, being able to convey his ideas in a most accessible manner and style, even if at times he repeated himself—like many an able teacher! The fact that his

Christianity Unveiled caused such an outcry in society in general, causing it to be burned, and the fact that the Catholic Church recognized its novelty enough to commission a major refutation from one of its most formidable intellects (Bergier), attest to the work's originality within the bounds outlined above.

D'Holbach's Collaboration with Naigeon

Naigeon collaborated with d'Holbach on a number of projects, which can be summarized as follows: the latter's translation of Toland's *Letters to Serena*, originally published in 1704 and published as part of a volume entitled *Lettres philosophiques* {*Philosophical Letters*} (1768)—the volume contains a note by Naigeon, saying that the translation was done 'by a philosopher much more learned than Toland—an anonymous and pseudonymous author of several very daring works.'[76] In a note in the volume, he also states that the translator was the author of *Sacred Contagion* and an *Essay on Prejudices*. The bibliographer Barbier initially attributed the edition of *Lettres à Eugénie* {*Letters to Eugenia*} (1768) to Fréret, but in his *Dictionary* (1806) he states that the introduction and notes were by Naigeon and the translation was d'Holbach's.

The volume *Lettre de Thrasybule à Leucippe* {*Letter from Thrasybulus to Leucippus*} was a posthumous work attributed to Fréret: the first edition was undated and is presumed to date from 1765, but the reprinted volume bears the date 1768 and it was included in Fréret's collected works as his. Hubert attributes it to d'Holbach, as does Wickwar, citing Naigeon as the editor, but Vercruysse states that 'it is certainly not d'Holbach's.'[77] Generally, it is now assumed to be the work of Fréret.

According to Maréchal, Naigeon had a major hand in editing *Le Militaire philosophe* {*The Militant Philosopher*} (1768), but Galiani maintained that it was the work of d'Holbach. Barbier attributed the work to Naigeon also and stated that d'Holbach had added the final chapter which argued that 'all

---

[76] *Lettres Philosophiques sur l'Origine des Préjugés, du Dogme de l'Immortalité de l'Ame, de l'Idolâtrie & de la Superstition; sur le Système de Spinosa & sur l'origine du mouvement dans la matière*, traduites de l'Anglois [sic.] de J. Toland (Londres: MDCCLXVIII) {*Philosophical Letters on the Origin of Prejudices, On the Dogma of the Immortality of the Soul, On Idolatry & Superstition; on Spinoza's System & the Origin of the Movement of Matter*, translated from the English of J. Toland, London.}, Avertissement {Foreword}, p. 1.

[77] Hubert's work is very unreliable on bibliographical information, since he merely repeats the mistakes of commentators who went before him. Vercruysse has the last word on any matters bibliographical.

artificial religion is contrary to morality and it has absolutely nothing useful to add to it.' The edition was reprinted in 1769, 1770 and 1776.[78]

Barbier was the first person to attribute to d'Holbach the *Théologie portative, ou Dictionnaire abrégé de la religion chrétienne'* {*Portable Theology or Short Dictionary of the Christian Religion*} (there are editions of 1767 & 1768), and it is thought that most of it was indeed by him, but perhaps with some input by Naigeon.[79] (The word 'portable' was appended because it was conceived as a pocket–book, as opposed to the many weighty tomes in which most dictionaries appeared.) The name itself is somewhat reminiscent of Voltaire's *Dictionnaire Philosophique Portatif* {*Portable Philosophical Dictionary*}, which was published abroad and without the author's name in 1764 and it was also condemned by the *Parlement*, just a year later. Organizationally, the works are similar in that they provide succinct definitions of words like 'soul', 'miracle', etc. Stylistically, the *Portable Theology* has much in common with other writing which is surely by d'Holbach and we can be sure that it is his. On the title page, the work was attributed to a certain Abbé Bernier—thought to be a play on the name 'Bergier', the priest commissioned by the Vatican to write the detailed refutation of d'Holbach's *Christianity Unveiled*. The work has also been attributed to Voltaire, though this is certainly not his, and his refutation of having had any part in it (see below) can be taken at face–value. The work was so popular that in a letter to Wilkes, d'Holbach said that it was impossible to get hold of a copy in Paris and that Wilkes would have more chance of buying a copy in London.[80] This rather amusing, witty work was reprinted several times and took the form of a dictionary of definitions which ridiculed and belittled biblical stories, persons and concepts. For instance, under the heading 'Consecration', i.e., the moment when the host is pronounced holy, he wrote as a definition: 'Magical words, by the help of which a priest of the Roman Catholic Church has the power to force the god of the universe to leave his lunch in order to transform himself into bread and get bitten into himself.' And under the heading 'Jonah', he quipped, 'A cantankerous and irascible prophet. He spent three days in the belly of a whale which finally was forced to vomit him up—so difficult a morsel is a prophet to digest. God told him to lie on his behalf to the people of Nineveh, which made him bad–tempered; a prophet usually seeks only plagues and a

---

[78] Maréchal, *Dictionary*, pp. 299—301; Galiani, *Correspondance* (Paris, 1881), I, pp. 180—181; Barbier, *Dictionary*, (1806), II, p. 76.
[79] Barbier, *Dictionary*, II, p. 375.
[80] Cushing, p.56 (Kessinger reprint edn.).

rocky path.'[81] Voltaire got hold of a copy of this book and he wrote about it to Damilaville in October 1767:

> The last three months there has appeared a dozen works of an extremely liberal type, printed in Holland. *The Portable Theology* is not a bit theological: it is an endless stream of jokes arranged in alphabetical order, but it must be admitted that there are such comic features in it that even some theologians cannot refrain from laughing. Young people and women read this reckless stuff avidly. Editions of all these sorts of books simply multiply.[82]

In a letter to D'Alembert, Voltaire wrote about *The Portable Theology*, 'It is a work quite to my taste and very pleasing, but I definitely had no part in its production: it's a work I shouldn't have minded at all having done and I would have been more than pleased to have been capable of writing it.'[83]

Finally, Naigeon provided the Introduction to d'Holbach's most famous work *Système de la Nature* {*System of Nature*} (1770), which d'Holbach passed off as written by a certain 'Mr Mirabaud'.

All in all, d'Holbach and Naigeon produced some thirty works of an anti–religious nature over a ten–year period, which was punctuated by the occasional translation of a scientific work, translated by d'Holbach alone.

From about 1765, the collaboration between Naigeon and d'Holbach became particularly close, since Naigeon took up residence with the d'Holbach family and it is thought that many of the anti–religious works they published were in no small way due to his dogmatic atheism, which bordered on a missionary zeal. He was a classicist of considerable standing with an eye for detail and a devotion to pure scholarship. He loved rare books and he must have delighted in d'Holbach's extensive library. Also resident in the house was a man of a similar classical training—Lagrange (1738—1735), a young man of great erudition, whom Diderot encouraged to produce a French translation of Lucretius' *De rerum natura* {*On the Nature of Things*} and on his death he left an unfinished manuscript of Seneca translated into French, on which Diderot, d'Holbach, and Naigeon all collaborated to finish: they published it as an eight–volume edition to great critical acclaim. Lagrange worked as a tutor to d'Holbach's children. During the Revolution, Naigeon re–edited the philosophical section of Diderot's *Encyclopédie* and it was published as the *Encyclopédie méthodique*—a standard work of reference on eighteenth–century materialism. Even so, d'Holbach's work could still not

---

[81] D'Holbach, *Oeuvres philosophiques*, 5 vols, ed. Jean Pierre Jackson (Paris: Editions Alive, 1998), I, pp. 520 & 556.

[82] Voltaire, *Oeuvres complètes*, XIV, p. 406, Letter to Damilaville, 16 October 1767.

[83] Ibid., LXV, p. 453, Letter to d'Alembert, 24 May 1769.

be mentioned freely and his work was to remain highly controversial at this time.

Despite their friendship and collaboration, Naigeon did not allow his scrupulous scholarly approach to their editorial work to blind him to the fact that d'Holbach's written style, and sometimes his methodology, were not without their faults. It is quite probable that d'Holbach was acutely aware of these minor failings, particularly so given that he was writing in French, which, after all, was not his native language, even though it was of a near–native quality. D'Holbach lived in an era during which French written style was probably at its most refined and when style was as important a consideration as content. Naigeon's keen eye and punctiliousness as an editor probably did much to enhance d'Holbach's works. Later, Naigeon's younger brother was to say of d'Holbach:

> [...] although d'Holbach wrote a very clear and legible hand, and his footnotes were scrupulously exact, he called Naigeon in because he was of all his friends not only the most trustworthy and the most atheistical, but also [he was] the one who had most zeal and most talent for helping him carry out his plans, correct even his style, and prune it of false ideas; for he was sometimes so tired that he noticed neither his absurdities nor his self–contradictions nor even the most childish mistakes.[84]

It is also a mark of d'Holbach's humility as a man and a scholar that he accepted Naigeon's criticism and intervention in his own work. D'Holbach also enlisted Diderot's help in his work, providing yet another critical eye, and he frequently invited him down to Grandval, his country estate, to add his input and offer advice, which he expressed as helping him to 'wash his ragged linen'. Generally, Diderot welcomed these trips to Grandval, which he described as 'most agreeable—days divided between work, good food, walking and play', though he also hints at the occasional row with d'Holbach, probably over their work, but no details are given: he said, 'There was a dreadful scene between me and the Baron, where the fault was wholly mine.'[85] Diderot is thought to have added the biographical introduction to the Boulanger volume of *Antiquity Unveiled* and the closing chapter of d'Holbach's *System of Nature*, amongst other passages.

As far as collaborating with other members of his coterie, D'Holbach worked with Roux on a number of purely scientific translations, but these were works which did not trouble the censor or the Church.

---

[84] Quoted in Wickwar, p. 83, who claims that this was a note in the margin added by Naigeon, Jnr. in his copy of *Système de la Nature* and reproduced in a note in Damiron, *Mémoires* (1858), II, pp. 379 *et seqq.*

[85] See also Diderot, *Oeuvres complètes*, XIX, p. 340, Letter of the 20 November 1770.

D'Holbach's works got him into trouble with the authorities, the flames of whose ire were fuelled and fanned by the Catholic Church and its clergy. The four–yearly *Assemblée du clergé* {Assembly of the Clergy}, convened in Paris in 1770, happened to coincide with d'Holbach's *System of Nature* being smuggled into France and so the scene was ripe for a display of clerical might and righteous indignation. The Church went into overdrive by providing a large grant of money for the Crown to initiate a campaign against recent expressions of free–thinking in print and by funding the appointment of Abbé Bergier as canon of the Cathedral of Notre Dame, who had already written and published a refutation of d'Holbach's *Christianity Unveiled*, amongst other works. Bergier's advancement and his transfer from sleepy Besançon to Paris was made in the expectation of him producing more work of the same, and he was willing to be near libraries, publishers, booksellers and other facilities the capital had to offer, all of which would assist him in his work as chief intellectual apologist against French materialism and deist writings.[86] He was given the task of reading and judging recently published books from an orthodox, Catholic standpoint to provide ammunition to fire for the royal censor and the royal prosecutor–general, Séguier, who inveighed against the *philosophes* in a session of the Paris *Parlement* in August 1770. The consequences of the session were the condemnation and order to be burned of seven books, three of which Bergier had already refuted or for which a refutation by him was pending. The books were: d'Holbach's *Christianity Unveiled* (attributed to Boulanger), *Sacred Contagion* (1768) (accredited to Trenchard), and *System of Nature* (1770) (ostensibly by Mirabaud); Voltaire's *Dieu et les hommes* {God and Men} (1769); Levesque de Burigny's ('Fréret's') *Examen critique des apologistes de la religion chrétienne* {Critical Examination of Apologists of the Christian Religion} (published in 1766, but it is thought was composed much earlier); Woolston's *Discours sur les miracles de Jésus Christ* {Discours on the Miracles of Jesus Christ} (1769), translated by d'Holbach; and *Examen impartial des principales religions du monde* {Impartial Examination of the Principle Religions of the World}.[87] Subsequently, d'Holbach's *Portative Theology* was condemned to be torn up and burned by the public executioner in Paris

---

[86] A. J. Bingham, 'The Abbé Bergier: An Eighteenth-Century Catholic Apologist', in *Modern Language Review*, Part 3, July 1959, pp. 337—350, (p. 344).

[87] The *Impartial Examination of the Principle Religions of the World* was not listed in Barbier's *Dictionnaire des anonymes*. It appears in a catalogue of *Bulletin du bibliophile et du bibliothécaire* of the Société des amis de la Bibliothèque nationale et des grandes bibliothèques de France (1883), as item No.1122, with the place of publication (originally not stated) was Amsterdam, and the date 'around 1750'.

on 16 February 1776.[88]   All these books were condemned as 'impious, blasphemous and seditious literature, tending to destroy all idea of divinity, to rouse the people to revolt against religion and government, to overthrow all the principles of public security and uprightness, and to turn subjects away from the obedience due to their sovereign.'[89]

Despite having read these works, many *philosophes*, chief amongst whom was Voltaire, felt that only woe could ensue from attacking and questioning the very existence of God.   They were generally united in their anti–clericalism and animosity towards the Church and revealed religion, but many assumed a sceptical position on the actual existence of a deity. D'Alembert's opinion was fairly typical of many, when he pronounced on d'Holbach's *System*, 'In spite of its long–windedness, it's an awful book; yet I must confess that on the existence of God the author seems to me too rigid and dogmatic, and on this question I can see no reasonable alternative to scepticism. *What do we know about it?*'[90]

Many of the points raised in *Christianity Unveiled* were explored as individual themes at greater length and in more depth in d'Holbach's subsequent works. In his *Lettres à Eugénie {Letters to Eugenia}* (1768) the cruel nature of God is described in more detail. Similarly, in his *Histoire Critique de Jésus–Christ {Critical History of Jesus Christ}* (1770) the contradictions which exist between one gospel account and another of the same incident are examined in greater detail, just as he does over Jesus' time of death in *Christianity Unveiled*.

Though a number of his friends knew d'Holbach was responsible for such forthright atheist books, they kept their own council. Morellet assures us that those who knew beyond a shadow of a doubt d'Holbach's secret were Marmontel, Saint–Lambert, Suard, Chastellux, Roux, d'Arcet, Raynal, Helvétius, and himself, and they were willing to keep the secret for another twenty years.[91] The conscious effort to keep his authorship secret paid off, as a comment in her memoirs from the society aristocrat, the Contesse de Genlis, attests: with reference to d'Holbach's *System of Nature* she noted, 'Though not mentioned as the author, this despicable book was written by the baron d'Holbach—a fact which only came to light after his death.'[92] D'Holbach never suffered for what the state and the Church considered both

---

[88] There is a copy *in facsimile* of the order in D'Holbach, *Oeuvres*, ed. by Jackson (2001), III, pp. 733—741.
[89] Quoted in Wickwar, p. 87.
[90] Voltaire, *Oeuvres*, XLVII, Letter of 25 July 1770, p. 151.
[91] Morellet, *op. cit.*, p. 134.
[92] Contesse de Genlis, *Les Diners du Baron D'Holbach* (Paris, 1822), footnote, p. 205. {*The Dinners of Baron D'Holbach*}.

seditious and sinful activities, and he carried on his life in much the same way as he had before the publication of his scandalous works. In fact, he was to produce yet more of the same, issuing a condensed, more accessible version (from a populist point of view) of his *System*, under the title of *Le Bon–sens {Good Sense}* (1772), and translating into French, as he always had, i.e., Hobbes's *Human Nature*, which he published under the title *De la Nature humaine* (1772). In many ways, his shorter version of the *System* went some way to addressing what some critics thought was the work's chief weakness—that of *longueur*. However, from about 1773 onwards, d'Holbach turned his attention to questions of morality and eventually politics, and he did not neglect his purely scientific translating. He developed a system of morality from an atheistic starting point and he turned his attention to questions of the structure of society and its political and economic organization, and its concomitant problems. There were members of his coterie whose minds had been exercised on such matters for some time and discussions on these topics fuelled his own imagination and interest in such things. Friends such as David Hume, Adam Smith, Turgot, and Morellet had all written on economics, and despite his estrangement from the group, Rousseau's *Contract social {Social Contract}* was widely read and discussed, and there was a great deal of heated debate around contemporary issues of the monarchy and other aspects of French politics and society, as they actually unfolded in reality. There was a good deal of discussion on the subject of a constitutional monarchy and such questions of politics began to eclipse the debate on religious issues in intellectual circles.

D'Holbach's writing, editing and translating were also steering his interest into the fields of education, morality, ethics, social and political organization, etc., as he prepared for posthumous publication two manuscripts written by Helvétius, who died at the end of December 1771, and he finished off his translation of Hobbes's *Essay on Human Nature*. All these activities caused a shift in the focus of his academic interests. However, d'Holbach's writing on these matters did not capture public imagination as his onslaught on religion had done. His works on politics, morality, ethics, and social organization were full of common sense, but as such they did not cause the stir that his works on religion had generated and they did not appear as radical as a number of works written by his peers. His anti–religious writings fed a popular thirst for scandalous material which did not exist for his more sober, though no less carefully considered, later writing. The very titles of his later works indicate the direction in which his intellectual preoccupations had moved; *Politique naturelle, ou Discours sur les vrais principes du gouvernement {Natural Politics or A Discours on the True Principles of Government}* (1773); and his *Système social, ou Principes naturels de la morale et la politique, avec un examen de l'influence du gouvernement sur les mœurs* {*Social System or Natural Principles of Morality and Politics and an Examination of the Influence of Government upon Morals*} (1773), in three volumes, was placed on the Vatican *Index of Prohibited Books* on 18 August 1775; *Ethocratie, ou le Gouvernement foundé sur la morale* {*Ethnocracy, or Government Founded on Morality*} (1776); and his *La Morale universelle, ou les Devoirs de l'homme fondés sur la nature* {*Universal Morality, or the Duties of Men Founded upon Nature*} (1776), upon which Diderot is said to have collaborated closely. Notwithstanding the apparent, more staid nature of these works, they all had to be published secretly and did not bear the true author's name because they were regarded as politically dangerous.

D'Holbach's final work in this field was published posthumously by Naigeon and it was the first original work finally to bear his name on the title–page: it was his *Eléments de la morale universelle, ou Catéchisme de la nature* {*Elements of Universal Morality, or Catechism of Nature*}, published in 1790. From an analysis of the work, Naigeon's work on the manuscript was exclusively of a stylistic nature—all the ideas and reasoning remained wholly that of d'Holbach.

These works had many admirers, but they were not without their detractors, and they were an important contribution to debate in their field, as Wickwar has noted:

> However declamatory the style of these books, and however limited the circle to which they appealed, there can be no doubt whatever that they contributed to the public discussion of public matters out of which the Revolution and the political freedom of the modern world were born. And, besides this historical importance which they share with many other eighteenth–century publications, they have an importance of their own: for it is to them that we must go to find Diderot's ideas on ethics and politics, utilitarianism and secularism, worked up into a consistent system.[93]

By the age of fifty–five, i.e., around 1780, d'Holbach wrote very little else and with the death of his close friend Diderot in 1784, the liveliness seemed to fade from his famous dinners, which came to an end, and visitors—both domestic and foreign—became fewer. At the beginning of his sixty–sixth year, on 21 January 1789, he died peacefully at home on the Rue Royale and he was buried according to Catholic rites, as he had been baptized, in the parish church of St Roch. Naigeon wrote an obituary for the press (included and translated in this volume) and his books, pictures, and natural history cabinet were auctioned off. To this day, there is no plaque on the wall of the building where he lived and the whereabouts of his mortal remains are a

---

[93] Wickwar, p. 103.

mystery. Thus he died modestly, as he had lived: his lavish diner parties were not given out of a spirit of ostentation in order to flaunt his wealth, but out of a desire to surround himself with genuinely intelligent, intellectually stimulating friends, to whom he would offer the hand of friendship—and often more—even financial support when needed, with no expectation of the debt either being recorded or subsequently settled. When saving a peasant family from penury, he is said to have said to a fellow patient at a spa in the Vosges, when caught helping them, 'Don't say anything about this to anybody. Anyone would say that I am trying to play the rich benefactor and the good–natured philosopher. I am neither benefactor nor philosopher, but just a human being, and my charities are the pleasantest expense I have on these journeys.'[94]

During the Revolution, when the religious question was one of the chief issues under dispute, the time was not right to put d'Holbach's name to the subsequent editions of his works as they appeared regularly reprinted. Some of his sociological works were reissued with his name, but works like his *Good Sense* and his *System of Nature* were still dangerous books to possess, when the fate of the Revolution seemed to depend on the fate of the Christian Church. Besides, Mme d'Holbach survived until 1814 and the secret identity of the author was kept until the last survivors of the baron's generation had died, when further secrecy seemed pointless. Of all his works, d'Holbach's *System of Nature* was constantly reissued and his fame spread to Britain, America, Spain, Germany, and even Russia, where atheist materialists were all too eager to translate his works and write articles on them. The Fleet Street deist and republican Richard Carlile, who was jailed for six years in 1819 on a charge of blasphemy for republishing Tom Paine, published a translation of *Christianity Unveiled* and *Letters to Eugenia*, and he became a confirmed atheist in prison while reading a translation of the *System of Nature*. More translations into English followed of d'Holbach's minor works by Englishmen and Americans, i.e., *Christianity Unveiled* and *Good Sense*. His work was translated into German and his writings became hugely influential in his native Germany, the land of his birth.

In his work *Essai sur les préjugés ou de l'Influence des opinions sur les mœurs et sur le bonheur des hommes {Essay on Prejudices or the Influence of Opinions on Mores and on the Happiness of Men}* (1770),[95] d'Holbach states, 'Respect for accepted opinions nearly always means respect for

---

[94] Quoted in Wickwar, p. 109 and sourced in D. Hume, *Private Correspondence* (London: 1820), p. 205.

[95] The date printed on the title page of this work is given as 1770, but it was already in circulation in November 1769 and it was listed in Rey's catalogue at the end of 1769, and d'Holbach mentioned the work also in a letter at the end of the same year.

falsehood. To dissemble the truth or to hide it means helping imposture. To refuse to tell men the truth when one can is to betray the cause of mankind and fail to repay the debt one owes for one's talents.' D'Holbach sincerely believed that his writing was fulfilling his mission to tell the unvarnished truth to mankind, however uncomfortable it might be to those taken in by religious belief, hallowed by time and tradition. It is hoped that through this new translation his aim might be carried on and his influence be felt again, but in presenting other documents, notes, and supplementary material, the interested reader might gain an insight into an immensely interesting period in the history of European thought and the struggle of brave individuals who took considerable risks to further the debate on religious issues and their place in society. Their achievements and victories over religious prejudice and bigotry are enjoyed by us today, but free–thinking and secularism are yet again coming under renewed attack from many quarters.

However, we must remain optimistic, like d'Holbach, who, in his *Essay on Prejudices*, issues the exhortation:

> Scatter your truths broadcast—they will bear fruit in their season... If human nature is perfectible, if the mind of man is not meant to wander in error for ever, behold wisdom and truth become the future guides of kings, law–givers of peoples, objects of the worship of nations... Reckon on reason as a city of refuge... Truth it is that binds together all departments of human knowledge... Away all errors and obstacles that dam it in its course!

Why Another English Translation of Christianity Unveiled?

D'Holbach's *Le Christianisme Dévoilé* was first translated into English in 1795 by W.M. Johnson. This edition is still available through booksellers as a reprint of the original version, published under Gordon Press, New York, with the new date of 1974 appended. On the reverse of the title page, this edition states "Originally Published 1819", but in fact the 1819 is merely a reprint of the original 1795 translation.

One of the problems with this translation is that is contains many mistakes and a number of d'Holbach's original footnotes have been omitted. Apart from several gross mistranslations of the original French, a significant number of paragraphs have also been excised from the original text and the language of the translation is distractingly archaic to the modern ear, as one would expect—it is a product of its time.

Christianity Unveiled;

BEING

AN EXAMINATION

OF

THE PRINCIPLES AND EFFECTS

OF THE

Christian Religion.

by BARON d'HOLBACH
(Paul Henri Thiry Holbach)

———

TRANSLATED FROM THE FRENCH OF BOULANGER,

By W. M. JOHNSON.

Figure 6: Title Page of the English translation of *Christianity Unveiled*.

Whilst d'Holbach's French is generally clear and without difficulties other than those posed by the language and style typical of its era, it is somewhat male–centric, as is only to be expected from literature written at that time. Hence, d'Holbach frequently refers to '*l'homme*'—'man', when making general statements about people, along with the French equivalent of 'mankind': in more politically correct times, the translator would prefer less male–centric equivalents. Whereas it has been possible to replace 'man' with 'people' in many places, it has not always been appropriate to do so in every case and this translator hopes that the less politically correct variant will not offend the reader sensitive to such issues. D'Holbach's language was not sexist in any way: he was merely following an accepted convention and style of his day.

All d'Holbach's and Bergier's original footnotes have been translated in both works offered in this volume and reproduced in bold type: any additional clarifications to their footnotes are mine and have been rendered in ordinary type.

The notes I have provided in this edition are much more detailed than in any other. Where d'Holbach has referred to passages or verses from the Bible and has not referenced them, I have done so in order that the reader may check his information. The version of the English Bible I have used generally is the *King James Version* of 1611, but I have edited the English slightly, only to the extent of changing 'LORD' in block capitals in the original to a lower–case equivalent, i.e., 'Lord', and I have also added speech marks where appropriate and where in the original there are none: this has been done with clarity in mind. On occasions, I have had to use an English translation of the Latin *Vulgate* version of the Bible, the version which d'Holbach most surely used. I have done so only when necessary, in cases where the numbering of the Psalms or the Old Testament book differs significantly from the *King James Version*. Such instances have been clearly indicated and the equivalent passage in the *King James Version* has been given. The usual abbreviations for books of the Bible have been used throughout, as set down in the *Oxford Guide to Style*, 2002.

On the few occasions when references to the Koran have been made, I have used the following version: *The Qur'an: A New Translation by M.A.S. Abdel Haleem* (O.U.P.:2004).

Standard abbreviations have been used, such as 'O.U.P.', i.e., Oxford University Press, etc. Other traditional conventions, such as capitalizing all personal pronouns when referring to God, I have ignored. I have capitalized the word 'god' when referring directly to the Christian Divinity, but I have not done so when using the word in a more general context, i.e., 'their god', even when it is clear that the reference is to the Christian divinity. Like d'Holbach, I feel no compunction to honour the supreme being in this way.

Again, in keeping with the spirit of his age, d'Holbach included a number of quotations in Latin from Græco–Roman texts, assuming that the educated reader would have a sufficient knowledge of Latin to understand them. This cannot be assumed today and so I have translated those quotations (with expert help!) for the modern reader unfamiliar with Latin, or who has made a conscious effort to forget their school Latin. Similarly, d'Holbach assumed a knowledge of classical Roman writers and literature, together with a detailed knowledge of historical facts, people, and situations pertaining to European history: I have not made the same assumptions and I have provided notes, which I hope will prove helpful to the general reader. These notes have been kept to a minimum, but some have had to be necessarily long: they can be ignored or used as a starting point for further investigation *à volonté*.

I have kept d'Holbach italics as he used them in the original '1756' edition of his text and I have also kept his use of the capitalized form of 'Nature'. As explained earlier, d'Holbach was a materialist who used the word 'Nature' to indicate the wider concept of nature or the universe as a system, 'that vast assembly of all that exists', as he called it in his *Système de la nature* {*System of Nature*} (1770), rather than to refer to our more narrow concept of nature. For him, 'Nature' is not a living or personified force, such as 'Mother Nature', as he states clearly at the very beginning of his *System*:

> Man has always deceived himself when he abandoned experience to follow imaginary systems. He is the work of Nature. He exists in Nature. He is subject to the laws of Nature. He cannot deliver himself from them: he cannot step beyond them even in thought. He is wasting his time in trying to leap forward beyond the visible world and he will always be compelled to return to this world because he is formed by Nature and is subject to her laws. There exists nothing beyond the great whole of which he forms a part, whose influence he experiences. The beings his fancy pictures as above Nature, or those he distinguishes from her, are always chimeras formed after that which he has already seen, but of which it is utterly impossible he should ever form any complete idea, either as to the place they occupy, or their manner of acting—for there is nothing, there can be nothing out of that Nature which includes all beings. Therefore, instead of seeking out from the world he inhabits beings who can procure him a happiness denied to him by Nature, let him study Nature, learn her laws, contemplate her energies, observe the immutable rules by which she acts.[96]

It is a rational, materialistic approach to life and the world around us, based on observation, that will keep people from straying into superstitious belief of all kinds, as he states elsewhere in his *System*: 'If the ignorance of Nature gave birth to gods, the knowledge of Nature is calculated to destroy them.'

---

[96] D'Holbach, *System of Nature*, Part I.

In the same vein he has stated elsewhere: 'Theology is but the ignorance of natural causes reduced to a system.'

Hence, it is in this wider sense of 'Nature' that d'Holbach writes and for this reason I have kept his capitalization in the following translation.

I have used the older convention of 'BC' and 'AD', rather than the more fashionable and politically correct 'BCE', etc. I'm afraid old habits die hard!

On the subject of political correctness, some of d'Holbach's language, apart from the male–orientated issue already mentioned, will be regarded as perhaps a little shocking: he refers to unschooled native peoples of undeveloped countries as '*sauvages*' in French, which is translated by 'savages' or 'primitives'. I have not edited or toned down such expressions because they were a feature of the ethos of the time and I see my role as a translator, rather than a judge or censor. While one cannot rule out a certain chauvinistic attitude which is germane to such language, and it conveys not a little French moral superiority over those whom they regarded as being unfortunate not to have had a sophisticated French education, again this was a feature of an attitude of the era and I have no desire to bowdlerize the text—to some extent, the 1795 translation did just that. Similar decisions have been made over French expressions such as '*peuple grossier*'—i.e., 'the common herd' or 'common people', for which the French expression smacks a little of the derogatory expression 'the great unwashed'. To some extent I have used slightly more modern expressions to tone down some of the excesses of eighteenth–century French hauteur and sensibilities: hence, instead of 'passions' for the French word '*passions*', I have generally used 'intense emotions' or 'strong feelings', since 'passion' in English tends now to have more of a sexual nuance.

I have also made no attempt to tone down passages and references which, in these more politically correct times, may seem a little anti–Semitic. Again, this was a feature of language and thinking of the era in which this work was written and such attitudes were not confined to France: amongst the English Deists one can find a number of writings which are terribly anti–Jewish. It is hoped that readers sensitive to these issues will see them in the light of the era in which they were written and my translation in no way reflects any personal animosity towards the Jews: I have simply translated what d'Holbach wrote.

All these things are minor considerations when the work is taken as a whole: on reading d'Holbach's critique of religious belief, one cannot be other than astounded at its extraordinary contemporary resonance.

David Michael Holohan,
London, September 2008.

Christianity Unveiled

LE
CHRISTIANISME
DÉVOILÉ,
O U
EXAMEN

DES PRINCIPES ET DES EFFETS
DE LA RELIGION CHRÉTIENNE.

Par Feu M. Boulanger.

Superſtitio error inſanus eſt, amandos timet,
quos colit violat : quid enim intereſt, utrùm Deos
neges, an infames ?

Senec. Ep. 12.

A LONDRES

M. DCC. LVI.

Figure 7: Title page of the original French edition of *Christianity Unveiled.*

Christianity

Unveiled

Or

An Examination
of the Principles and Effects
of the Christian Religion

by the late Monsieur Boulanger.
(Paul-Henri Thiry Baron d'Holbach)

"Superstition is terrified of the gods, who are to be loved,
and it profanes them when it worships them, for what
difference is there between denying the existence of gods and
slandering them?"

Seneca, *Letters to Lucilius*

LONDON

1756

Preface

Letter from the Author to Mr. ******

Sir,

I am in grateful receipt of your observations, which you sent to me upon my work. Just as I am touched by the praise which you have deigned to offer me on it, and I love truth too much to allow myself to be shocked by the candour with which you have expressed your objections, I found them sufficiently serious to merit my full attention. It would be a poor philosopher who did not have the courage to listen to counter–arguments to his opinions. We are not theologians—our disputes are of the kind which end amicably, having nothing in common with those of the apostles of superstition, who seek only to catch each other out by specious arguments, and who, to the detriment of their sincerity, enter the fray only to defend the cause of their vanity and their own obstinacy. We both desire the good of mankind—we seek the truth and on that we cannot but be of one mind.

You begin by admitting the necessity of examining religion and the need to subject its opinions to the tribunal of rationality.

You admit that Christianity cannot withstand such scrutiny and that, in the eyes of common sense, it can only appear as a tissue of absurdities, of disparate fables, of preposterous dogmas, of infantile rites, of ideas borrowed from the **Chaldeans**, the Egyptians, the **Phoenicians**, the Greeks and the Romans. In brief, you admit that this religious system of belief is no more than an amorphous mass of almost all ancient superstitions created by Eastern zealotry and variously modified by circumstances, historical contexts, personal interests, whims and prejudices of those people who, since that time, have passed themselves off as mystics, as messengers of God, as interpreters of his new, divine will.

You shudder at the horrors which the Christian spirit of intolerance has caused its followers to commit whenever they have had the power to do so: you recognize that a religion founded on a bloodthirsty god can be none other than a bloody religion, and you bemoan the frenzy which, right from childhood, grips the mind of princes and peoples, consigning them to be slaves both to superstition and its priests, which stops them from understanding their true interests, turns them deaf to reason, and diverts them from the great purposes upon which they should be engaged.

You recognize that a religion founded on enthusiasm or deception cannot possibly have any sure principles and must only be a source of eternal disputes, and that it will always finish up by causing trouble, persecution and devastation, especially when political power thinks it absolutely essential to get involved in religious quarrels. You would subscribe to the idea that a good Christian, who follows literally the conduct prescribed by the gospel as the most perfect way to behave, cannot have the faintest idea of knowing on what true morality is based in this world, and that he can only be a useless misanthropist, lacking in motivation and being nothing other than a trouble-causing fanatic if his soul is on fire for God.

In the light of all this, how can you judge my work to be dangerous?

You tell me that the *wise man should think only for himself* and that a people has to have some kind of religion, whether good or bad, and that religion is a necessary restraint for those of a simple or vulgar mind who, without it, would have no further motive to hold back from crime and vice. You believe reforming religious prejudices to be an impossibility and you think that princes, who are the only ones who might achieve this, are too keen on keeping their subjects in blind ignorance, from which they benefit. So if I am not mistaken, these are the strongest objections which you can level against me and I shall try to counter them.

First of all, I do not believe that a book can be dangerous for the common people. The common people do not read any more than they think—they have neither the spare time nor the capacity to do so. On the other hand, it is not religion but the law which keeps people in check, and when a madman tells them to steal or kill, it is the gibbet which warns them not to act upon such advice. Moreover, if by chance there were a man amongst the people who were to read a work of philosophy, it is certain that such a man would be highly unlikely to turn out to be a fearful villain.

Books are written only for that section of a nation whose circumstances, education and feelings place them above criminality. That enlightened sector of society, which governs the rest of a nation, reads and deliberates over books, and if such works contain false or harmful maxims, they are quickly either condemned to oblivion or consigned to public execration. If they contain truths, then they run no danger. It is fanatics—priests and ignoramuses—who make revolutions; enlightened people, those who are objective and sensible, are always lovers of peace and quiet.

You are not, Sir, one of those pusillanimous thinkers who believes that the truth is capable of causing harm: truth is only harmful for those who hoodwink people, and mankind always needs truth. Everything must have convinced you long ago that all the evils which plague our human race have always arisen solely from our errors, from our misinterpreted interests, from our prejudices, from the false ideas we attribute to things.

In fact, if one is consistent in one's thinking, it is easy to see that it is religious prejudice in particular that has corrupted politics and morality. Is it not the ideas of a religious and supernatural nature which have caused sovereigns to be looked upon as gods?

Therefore, it is religion that kindles despots and tyrants—it is they who made bad laws;[1] it is their example that corrupted the rich and powerful; it is the rich and powerful who corrupted the common people, and these corrupted people became miserable slaves, working against their own interests to please the rich and powerful, instead of hauling themselves out of poverty. Kings were called the *images of God*; they, like him, had absolute power; they created the just and the unjust, and their will often sanctified oppression, violence and pillage, and it was through their baseness, by vice and crime, that people gained favour. Thus it was that nations became full of perverse citizens who, under leaders warped by religious ideas, continually created open or clandestine wars and had not a single motive to behave virtuously.

In societies so structured, what can religion offer? With its remote terrors or its ineffable promises, has it ever stopped man from giving vent to his powerful emotions or finding happiness in other, easier ways? Has this religion ever influenced the behaviour and life–style of sovereigns, who owe their divine power to it? Do we not see faith–fuelled princes continuously engaged in the most unjust wars, squandering in vain the blood and goods of their subjects, who snatch bread from the grip of the poor in order to fill the coffers of the insatiable rich, and who permit—yea, even give orders for— thieving, embezzling, and committing injustices? Does this kind of religion, which so many sovereigns regard as a prop to their own throne, make people more humane, more law–abiding, more sober, more innocent, and more faithful to their preaching? Alas! If we look at history, we will see sovereigns who are orthodox, zealous and religious to a scruple, yet at the same time they are betrayers, usurpers, adulterers, thieves and murderers—in fact, men who behave as though they had no fear whatsoever of God, to whom they pay lip–service.

Amongst the courtiers who surround them, we note a continuous hotch- potch of Christianity and crime, devotion and iniquity, faith and vexation, religiosity and betrayal. Amongst the priests, whose very existence is founded on a religion of a poor, crucified god, and who hold that without this religion there can be no morality, do we not see pride, avarice, lustfulness and a spirit of domination and vengeance hold sway?[2] Has their continuous

---

[1] **I put this truth in all its clarity in my work *Research into the Origin of Eastern Despotism*.**

[2] **When we complain of priests' disorderly conduct, people try to shut us up by saying that it is a case of *Do as I tell you and not as I do*. What confidence would we have in medical doctors who, when they have the same illnesses as us, would not use the same remedies as those they prescribe for others?**

preaching, reiterated down the centuries, ever had any real influence upon the behaviour and life–style of nations? Are the conversions brought about by their preaching of any practical use? Do they change the hearts of those who listen to them? Even by the very admission of the Doctors of the Church, such conversions are rare, and these Doctors always live amongst the *dregs of society*. Human perversity increases by the day and they rail against vices and crime on a daily basis, as custom demands and as the government encourages, and which finds favour with public opinion and is rewarded by those in power—all this is accomplished under the pain of being unhappy.

Hence, by the admission of its own ministers, whose religious precepts have been inculcated in people from birth and repeated interminably, religion is ineffective when it comes to people's depraved behaviour and their way of life. Mankind always side–lines religion as soon as it is at variance with their desires; they only listen to it when it favours their ardour and when it neatly accords with their temperament and what they think makes them happy. The libertine scoffs at religion when it condemns his debauchery; the ambitious person scorns it when it cramps his drive; the miser pays no heed to it when it tells him to divest himself of his riches; the courtier mocks at its simplicity when it orders him to be true and sincere.

On the other hand, the sovereign entertains religious teaching when it tells him that he is the image of the Divinity, that he has to wield absolute power like its god, and that he is the final arbiter of life and his subjects' possessions, and that he must exterminate others whose thinking does not accord with his own. The irascible man listens avidly to priestly instructions when they commanded him to hate; the vindictive person obeys religion when it permits him to take his own revenge under the pretext of avenging its god. In a word, religion changes people's basic instincts not a jot, and they only listen to it when it suits their desires. It is only upon their death–bed that religion makes people think twice, but this occurs at a time when their change of heart is useless as a universal lesson, when heaven's pardon is promised in exchange for the fruitless remorse of the dying, and it does nothing other than encourage the living to persist in their disordered ways until their very last moment.

Religion preaches virtue in vain when such virtue turns out to be contrary to people's interests or when it gets them nowhere. One cannot inculcate good behaviour in a nation whose sovereign himself is without mores and virtue, or when the rich and powerful themselves regard this virtue as a weakness, or when priests debase it through their own conduct, or when the average man in the street, in spite of the fine haranguing by its preachers, knows full well that in order to claw his way out of poverty, he has to acquiesce to the vice of those more powerful than him. In societies structured in this way, morality is no more than sterile speculation, fit only to

8

exercise the mind without impinging on anyone's conduct, apart from a small number of men, whose temperament has rendered them moderate and content with their lot. All those desirous of seeking their fortune or wishing to improve their lot will allow themselves to be swept along with the general tide, which forces them to leap over obstacles strategically placed in their way by their conscience.

So it is not the priest but the sovereign, who is best placed to establish mores in a state. He should preach by example: he ought to ward off crime by the threat of punishment; he must encourage virtue through rewards; above all, he must attend to public education in order to inculcate in his subjects' hearts only those strong urges which are useful to society.

In our society education is almost ignored by politicians. This is indicative of a most profound indifference towards a factor which is absolutely essential for the well–being of any state. In almost all modern societies public education is confined to teaching languages, which are of no use to the majority of people who learn them. Instead of teaching morality, Christians are force–fed the wondrous fables and incredible dogmas of a religion which is diametrically opposed to rationality. From the first steps a young man takes when he embarks upon his studies, he is taught to disregard the evidence of his senses, to subjugate his reason—which is portrayed as a perfidious guide—and to rely blindly on the authority of his teachers. Yet, who are these teachers?

They are priests, whose interests lie in perpetuating the universe with opinions, the fruits of which they themselves are the sole beneficiaries. These mercenary pedagogues, replete with ignorance and prejudices, are themselves rarely in tune with society. Are their contemptible, wizened souls capable of instructing their pupils in things of which they themselves are ignorant? Are these pedants, disdained even by those who entrust their children to them, really in any position to inspire in their pupils a desire for glory, noble emulation and a generosity of spirit, which are the bed–rock of all qualities beneficial to a republic? Will they teach them to value public well–being, to serve their country, to recognize their duties as a man and citizen, and as a family–man with children, and to fulfil their obligations as a master or servant? Most certainly not! One can expect only to see superstitious ignoramuses emerge from the hands of such inept, despicable guides, and pupils who, if they have absorbed anything at all from the lessons they have been taught, know nothing of the things essential for society, and they turn out to be useless members of it.

Wherever we might cast our eyes, we shall see the study of those things which are of the greatest importance to man totally neglected. The study of morality, within which I also understand politics to fall, counts for almost nothing within a European education. The only morality taught to Christians is that fanatical, impractical, contradictory, vague morality which we see exemplified in the gospels. Its effect, as I believe I have already proven, is to degrade the mind, to render virtue odious, to produce abject slaves, to quash the deepest motivations of the human spirit; and if it takes firm root in the minds of hot–heads, it turns them into the most fanatical troublemakers, capable of rocking the very foundations of society.

Despite Christianity's pointlessness and the perverse morality it teaches, its adherents dare to tell us that without it there can be no mores. But what does morality mean in Christian terms? It means endless praying, visiting places of worship, making penance, refraining from pleasures and living in a state of meditative retreat.

What good to society can be derived from these practices, which are observed without a passing reference to virtue?

If such mores lead heavenwards, then they are worthless here on earth. If virtue lies solely in those things, then one has to admit that without religion there can be no virtue. But on the other hand, one can faithfully observe all the precepts Christianity recommends without having a single virtue, which reason tells us is a necessary support for any body politic.

Hence, one must distinguish clearly between *religious* morality and *political* morality—the former makes saints, the latter makes citizens; one renders man useless, or even harmful, for the world, whereas the other must have personal development as its goal for the good of society—to form members who are useful, actively engaged, capable of service and of fulfilling their duties as spouse, father, friend and colleague, irrespective of their metaphysical outlook: despite theology's claims, religious morality is less certain by far than the immutable tenets of common sense.

In fact, it is a given that man is a social being who seeks happiness in all things, and that he does good when he find it in his interest to do so, and that he is not usually nasty because being so would be contrary to his own welfare. Taking that as read, education should teach people to come to an understanding of the social relations that exist between them and the duties which arise as a consequence of those relations, and that the government, supported by laws, rewards and penalties, confirms these lessons, delivered through education, and that helpful and virtuous behaviour are concomitant with happiness, and that shame, contempt and chastisement are the punishments for crime and vice. It is then that people will have a humanist morality, founded on their own nature, on the needs of the nation, on the interests of others and those who govern them. This morality, devoid of transcendent, theological notions, will probably have nothing at all in common with *religious* morality and society will have nothing to lose by it, as contrasted with religious morality which, as has been proven, opposes at every turn the well–being of nations, familial calm and the unity of its citizenry.

A sovereign, upon whom society has conferred supreme power, holds in his hands a great ability to motivate, which he can bring to bear upon men. He has more power than gods in moulding and reforming human behaviour and habits. His presence, his rewards, his threats... What can one say? Just a single look from him can achieve far more than all the sermonizing of priests.

The accolades, honours and riches of this world exert a much stronger influence upon even the most pious of men, than all the pompous expectations of religion. The most devout courtier fears his king more than his god. Therefore I repeat, it is the sovereign who ought to do the preaching—it behoves him to reform people's behaviour and habits. People's mores will be good, so long as the prince himself is good and virtuous, and when his citizens receive an honest education, which, by inspiring them to principles of virtue from their earliest years, will lead them to honour integrity, to detest crime, to scorn vice, and to fear infamy.

This education shall never be fruitless when continuous examples prove to citizens that it is by talent and personal merit that one is accorded honours, that one achieves a sense of well–being, distinction, esteem and favour, and that vice leads only to scorn and ignominy.

An enlightened prince at the head of a nation nurtured on such principles shall be judged truly great, powerful and respected. His preaching will be more effective than that of priests who, for centuries, have been railing against public corruption to no avail.[3]

If priests have usurped from the sovereign the right to provide public education, let him take back that right, or at least not tolerate that they enjoy the liberty of guiding the mores of nations and speaking to them on morality; let the monarch quash those priests themselves when they teach maxims which are blatantly harmful to the welfare of society. By all means let them teach that God changes into bread, but let them never teach that one can hate or destroy those who refuse to believe in this ineffable mystery. Let no mystic have the power to incite subjects against authority, to sow discord, to break the bonds which unite citizens, or to disturb public peace on account of

---

[3] **Quintilian said: '*Quidquid Principes faciunt, praecipere videntur.*'** **'Princes appear to order things to be done that they themselves do.'** The passage d'Holbach quotes is from Quintilian's *Institutio Oratoria*, Book III. (For Quintilian— see Glossary.)

mere opinions. The sovereign himself shall keep the priesthood in check as he pleases.

Fanaticism is shameful when it is unsubstantiated. Priests themselves wait upon the prince for their heart's desire and the majority of them are all too willing to sacrifice the so–called interests of religion and their conscience, when they judge this sacrifice to be expedient for their good fortune. Even when I am told that princes always believe that it is in their interests to keep a grip on religion and handle its ministers by political means, they had better think again: I reply that it is easy to convince sovereigns by a mass of examples that the Christian religion has been a hundred times more harmful to their peers, and that the priesthood has been, and always will be, a rival to their throne, and that Christian priests are, by their very nature, the least submissive of their subjects. I reply that it is easy to make every enlightened prince perceive that his real interest lies in being in control of a contented people, and that it is their well–being provided by him, upon which his own stability and elevated status depend. In a word, a prince's happiness is bound up with that of his people and he shall be stronger as the head of a nation of honest and virtuous citizens, than when leading a herd of ignorant, corrupt slaves, whom he is forced to hoodwink to keep them in check, which leads him to become mired in trickery to achieve that end.

Hence, let us not despair—one day the truth will triumph, all the way up to the throne. If the light of reason and science travails so to reach princes, it is because self–interested priests and their scrawny courtiers try to hold them back in a state of perpetual infantilism, dangling before them the power and grandeur of their mysteries, deflecting them from things essential for their true well–being.

Every sovereign who has the courage to think for himself will feel that his power will always be shaky and precarious when his only support is the phantoms of religion, the misconceptions of the common people and the whims of the priesthood. He will perceive the drawbacks resulting from a fanatical administration which, to date, has simply produced presumptuous ignoramuses, obstinate Christians who are often troublemakers, citizens incapable of service to the state and imbecilic people, gullible to the impressions of their guides who lead them astray. The sovereign will feel the immense resources for good in his hands, so long ago arrested from the nation by useless men who, under the pretext of education, hoodwink and devour them.[4]

---

[4] **Some people believed that the clergy might serve sometimes as a safeguard against despotism, but experience amply proves that this body of people has only**

A firm, wise prince will supplant religious foundations, which make good sense blush, by establishments useful to the state: these religious foundations have merely served to reward idleness, to maintain arrogance and wealth, and to further the priesthood's pride. The new state establishments will make talent spring up, will mould youth, will reward service and virtue, will offer succour to the common people and will help citizens to flourish.

I flatter myself, Sir, that these reflections will exonerate me in your eyes. I do not aspire at all to the approbation of those who think themselves interested in the ills of their fellow citizens. It is not they whom I seek to convince; one can prove nothing to men who are vicious and senseless. But I dare to hope that you will cease to regard my book as dangerous and my hopes as totally fanciful.

Many men devoid of mores have attacked religion because it thwarted their inclinations; many wise men have despised it because it appeared ridiculous to them; many people have viewed it with indifference because they did not perceived its true drawbacks. As a citizen, I attack it because I consider it to be harmful to the welfare of the state, because it is an enemy of human intellectual progress, and because it is opposed to sound morality, from which political interests can never be divorced.

It remains only for me to say to you, along with the poet who, like me, was hostile to superstition:

> Si tibi vera videntur,
> Dede manus, aut, si falsum est,
> Accingere contra.[5]

I am, etc…

Paris 4 May 1758.

---

ever feathered its own nest. **Hence, national interests and those of a sovereign have found that this group was good for absolutely nothing.**

[5]   These are lines from Lucretius *De rerum natura II*, (1042—43), which mean:
> And if you consider something to be true,
> Then consider yourself to be vanquished, but if it is false,
> Gird your loins for combat.

Titus Lucretius Carus' long, didactic poem sought to convey a moral philosophy and a knowledge of nature and the universe 'to free oneself from the unnecessary fears and suspicions which disturb the mind and preclude the attainment of happiness, especially fear of the gods and fear of death'. (W.H.D. Rouse, Introduction to *On the Nature of Things*, Loeb edition, pp. xxix-xxx: see Bibliography.) This is why D'Holbach mentions Lucretius as a fellow 'hostile' poet.

Figure 8: *Que Pico de Oro!*, from *Los Caprichos*, Goya (1799).
The Spanish title means, 'What a golden beak!' The implication is that somebody has the 'gift of the gab', preaching parrot-fashion, but without understanding to an audience of stupid people, who listen in ignorant adulation.

Chapter 1

Introduction:

On the necessity of examining religion and the obstacles encountered to this examination.

very action reasonable people take should have as its motivating force their own happiness and that of their fellows.

Everything conspires towards demonstrating to us that religion is the most important element for our temporal and eternal bliss, and that it has advantages for us not only for our passage through this world, but also in the next, in that its flattering promises offered to us will be honoured. Our duties towards the god, whom we regard as the master of our destiny, can only be founded on the benefits which we expect from him, or on the misfortunes we fear from him. Hence, it is necessary that man examine the grounds for his hopes and fears. To this end, he must have regard to his experience and reason, which are his sole guides here below.

The advantages religion procures for Christians in this visible world they inhabit are the basis on which they will be able to judge the reality of those dangled before their eyes by religion in the invisible world, towards which they are ordered to turn their gaze.

For the most part people hold to their religion only by habit. They have never seriously examined the reasons which bind them to religion or the motives for their conduct, or the foundations of their opinions. Hence, the thing which everyone regards as the most important thing in their lives has always been that which they have been most afraid of digging deeper into. People follow the paths their forbears have trodden; they believe because they have been told that they ought to do so from infancy; they hope because their ancestors hoped; they tremble because their predecessors trembled; they have almost never deigned to understand the reasons for their beliefs.

Very few people have the spare time or the ability to examine and contemplate the objects of their habitual veneration, of their such ill–considered attachment and their traditional fears. Nations are always swept along by a torrent of habits, examples and prejudices. One's upbringing habituates one's mind to the most hideous opinions, just as the body does to the most embarrassing of attitudes. Everything which has stood the test of time seems sacred to people who feel guilty if they turn their timid gaze to examine those things which bear the imprimatur of antiquity.

Predisposed towards the wisdom of their forbears, people are not so presumptuous as to examine their heritage and they do not see that mankind has always been duped by prejudices, by hopes and fears, and that the same reasons have rendered them almost always impervious to inquiry.

The common people, wrapped up in the material necessities of life, place a blind confidence in those who claim to guide them. They abdicate to them the bother of thinking for themselves, they subscribe effortlessly to all that is prescribed for them, and they believe that they will offend God if they doubted for a moment the faith of those who speak to them in his name. The rich, the great and the good of this world, find it personally advantageous to conform to received prejudices and even to maintain the *status quo*, even though they are more enlightened than the common people. Either that, or given over to indolence, to dissipation and pleasures, they are totally incapable of bothering with a religion which they always subjugate to their ardour, to their inclinations and to their desire to have a good time. In infancy we absorb all the impressions given to us, since we do not have the intellectual capacity, the experience or the courage needed to question what we are taught by those upon whom our feebleness has cast us. In adolescence our ardent passions and the constant exhilaration of our senses stop us from thinking about a religion, which is too problematic and too depressing to occupy our more agreeable moments. If, by chance, a young man looks into religion, he does so haphazardly or with bias—a mere superficial glance at such a disgusting thing soon puts him off. In our mature years, beset by different cares, with new preoccupations absorbing our attention, with ambitious plans of grandeur and power, the pursuit of wealth and the contemplation of occupations followed—all these things engross people's full attention, leaving almost no time to contemplate a religion whose depths one never had the time to plumb in the first place. In old age, with one's numbed faculties, mechanical habits and organs weakened by age and infirmity, there is no longer any opportunity to return to the source of deep–rooted opinions. Besides, with the fear of death at the forefront of a mind commonly in the grip of mortal terror, any examination of religion would appear somewhat suspicious.

Thus it is that religious opinions, once assimilated, stand their ground for centuries at a stretch. It is thus that, from age to age, nations hand down ideas that have never been properly examined. They believe that their welfare is bound to institutions, which a more mature examination would reveal them to be the source of the majority of their ills. The powers that be yet again provide support for people's prejudices and keep them from inquiry, forcing them towards ignorance, and they are always at the ready to punish whosoever might try to disabuse people of their deception.

So let us not be at all surprised if we see error almost inextricably interwoven with human–kind; everything seems to conspire to perpetuate people's blinkered state and all forces conjoin to mask the truth. Tyrants detest truth and suppress it because it dares challenge their unjust and fanciful titles; the priesthood denounces truth because it shows their lavish claims to be bogus; ignorance, passivity and people's strong emotions make accomplices of everyone in whose interest it is to blind others, to keep them under the yoke and to take advantage of their misfortunes. Thus it is that nations travail under hereditary misfortunes which they never think to remedy, either because they do not know their source or because habit accustoms them to misfortune, and it even robs them of the desire to lessen their burden.

If religion be the most important thing in our lives, if it, of necessity, influences the whole conduct of our life, and if its influence extends not only to our existence in this world, but also to the world promised to man hereafter, then undoubtedly there is nothing which demands of us a more serious examination. However, it is of all things the very issue wherein the average man–in–the–street shows the most gullibility. A person who is prepared to conduct the most meticulous examination into the least issue pertaining to their well–being will not go to the slightest trouble to ascertain the grounds for belief, or take strides to discover what it is that, by their own admission, their temporal and eternal happiness depend. People blindly rely on those whom pure chance has provided as guides; people entrust to them the bother of thinking on their behalf and they even turn their laziness and credulity into a merit. In matters of religion, mankind boasts about remaining forever in an infantilized and barbarous state.

However, in every century there have been men who, disabused of their fellow citizens' prejudices, have dared to bear witness to the truth. But what could their feeble voice do against such errors, imbibed with their mother's milk, reinforced by habit, authorized by example and shored up by a political power so often complicit in its own ruination? The stentorian uproar of trickery soon reduced to silence those who clamoured for reason. In vain did the philosopher try to inspire people to be courageous, whilst priests and kings forced them to tremble.

The surest way to hoodwink people and to perpetuate prejudices is to dupe them in infancy. Amongst almost all modern peoples upbringing and education seem to have as their only goal the production of fanatics, staunch believers and monks, that is to say people harmful or useless to society. No thought is given to forming citizens. Princes, who themselves are usually victims of a superstitious upbringing, live their entire lives in the deepest ignorance of their duties and the real interests of their states. They fancy that they have done all they can for their subjects when they have filled them full of religious ideas, which substitute for good laws and which save their masters from the tiresome bother of governing well. Religion seems to have been thought up with the sole purpose of turning sovereigns and people equally into slaves of the priesthood. The latter's sole intent is to create continuous obstacles to the welfare of nations; wherever he might reign, the sovereign's power is precarious and his subjects are bereft of useful activity, science, a loftiness of spirit and industry—in a word, of those qualities essential to sustain a society.

If, in a Christian society, there is some evidence of gainful activity, or of a scientific approach to matters, or even decent social mores—all this is produced in spite of religious opinion, because Nature, whenever possible, restores mankind to reason and forces people to work for their own well-being.

Were all Christian nations to be consistent in their principles, they would be mired in the most profound inertia and our lands would be inhabited by a small number of pious savages, who would assemble only to harm each other.

In fact, what would be the point of bothering with a world, which religion portrays to its disciples as a mere stopover? What of the assiduity of a people who are told repeatedly, on a daily basis, that their god wants them to pray, to grieve, and to live in a state of constant fear, which it laments without ceasing? How could a society survive, composed of people persuaded to be zealous for religion and convinced that they have a duty to hate and destroy their fellows on account of their opinions?

In fact, how can we expect to find humanity, justice and virtue from a crowd of fanatics, whose model is a god who is cruel, secretive and nasty, who takes delight in witnessing the tears of his unfortunate creatures, who sets traps for them and then punishes them for falling into them, and who orders theft, crime and carnage?

Such are the characteristics described by Christianity of their god, whom they inherited from the Jews. This god was a sultan, a despot, a tyrant at liberty to do anything. However, this god was portrayed as the model of perfection, and the most revolting crimes and most heinous atrocities were committed and justified in his name to support his cause, or to merit his favour.

Thus it is that the Christian religion, which boasts of lending steadfast support to morality and setting before people the strongest motivation to spur them on towards virtue, has been a source of divisions, fits of fury and crimes—all on the pretext of bringing about peace, yet it has only ever produced furious violence, hate, discord and war. Religion has given mankind a thousand ingenious motives for people to needle each other and it has lavished upon them scourges unknown to their forebears: had they known about this in advance, they would have sorely hankered after the peaceful ignorance of their idolatrous ancestors a thousand times over.

If people's mores had nothing to gain from Christianity, the power of kings, who purport to support religion, would not have derived great benefit from it. Two distinct powers were established in all states—that of religion, founded upon God himself, which almost always outshone the sovereign, and the sovereign's own power, forced into a subservient role under the priesthood, and every time he refused to bend his knee before them, he was outlawed, stripped of his rights and exterminated by subjects spurred on to revolt by religion or by its fanatics, whose hands it used to wield the knife.

Before Christianity, a sovereign of a state was also the ruler over the priesthood, but since the world has turned Christian, the sovereign is no more than the first amongst their slaves, a mere henchman carrying out their vengeful decrees.

So let us conclude that the Christian religion has no grounds whatsoever to boast of its superiority in promoting morality or a political society. Therefore, let us tear from it the **Veil** with which it has shrouded itself. Let us go back to first principles and analyse its sources. Let us follow in its footsteps and we shall find that, rooted in deception, ignorance and credulity, it has never been, and never will be, useful to society, apart from being advantageous to men who believe they have an interest in hoodwinking humankind. Religion will never cease causing the greatest misfortunes for nations, and rather than furnishing the happiness it promises, it serves only to fuel frenzied rages, to drown nations in blood, to immerse them in lunacy and crime, and make people misjudge their true interests and their most holy duties.

Figure 9: Moses receiving the Ten Commandments, from *Liber Chronicarum*, also known as *The Nuremberg Chronicle* (1493).

Chapter 2

A Short History of the Jewish People.

n a small country, almost unknown to other peoples, there lived a nation whose founders had long been slaves of the Egyptians, and who were delivered from their servitude by a priest from Heliopolis, who, by his genius and superior knowledge, knew how to gain the upper hand over them.[1]

This man, known by the name of **Moses**, had had a good education within a religion well–known for its rich supply of prodigies and for being the mother of superstitions. Moses assumed the position of leader of a hoard of fugitives, whom he persuaded that he was the interpreter of the will of their god and that he personally conversed with him, receiving his orders directly from him. He backed up his mission by works which appeared to be supernatural to men ignorant of the ways of Nature and artificial trickery. The first order he issued on behalf of God was to steal from their masters, from whom they were about to flee. When Moses had made them rich by despoiling the Egyptians, and when he was sure of their confidence in him, he led them into a desert where, for forty years, he conditioned them to total,

---

[1] Maneto and Cheremon were Egyptian historians, whose testimonies the Jew Flavius Josephus handed down to us: we learn that, in times gone by, a multitude of lepers was driven out of Egypt by King Amenophis, and that these bandit exiles elected a leader over them, a priest of Heliopolis called Moses, who made up a religion for them and gave them laws. (See *Josephus Against Apion*, Bk.I, ch.9, 11, & 12.) Diodorus Siculus also relates the history of Moses—see Volume VII of the translation by Abbé Terrasson. Be that as it may, Moses began his career by murdering an Egyptian who had quarrelled with a Hebrew man—this is even admitted in the Bible. After this, Moses ran off into Arabia, where he married the daughter of an idolatrous priest who often chided him for his cruelty. From there, this holy man returned to Egypt to foment his dissatisfied people to revolt against the king. He reigned like a tyrant: the examples of Korah, Dathan, and Abiram prove that free-thinkers had a hard time with him. He disappeared like Romulus, without anyone knowing the whereabouts of his burial place. (For Maneto, Cheremon, Josephus, Amenophis, Moses, Siculus—see Glossary.)
The reference to Korah, Dathan, and Abiram is to be found in the book of Numbers 16: Moses called these men and their families to the Tabernacle of the Lord only to have them slaughtered together with their wives and children. Although only Korah is mentioned in the following passage, it is quite clear from a previous verse (vs. 27) that they were all there, and in the extract which follows, Korah is merely representative of the whole group: 'And it came to pass, as [Moses] had made an end of speaking all these words, that the ground clave asunder that was under them: And the earth opened her mouth, and swallowed them up, and their houses, and all the men that appertained unto Korah, and all their goods. They, and all that appertained to them, went down alive into the pit, and the earth closed upon them: and they perished from among the congregation.' (Num. 16: 31—33).

blind obedience. He taught them the will of heaven, the fantastical fables of their ancestors and the bizarre ceremonies to which the Almighty linked his favours. He particularly inculcated in them the most venomous hate against the gods of other nations and the most calculated cruelty against those who adored them. By dint of carnage and rigour he turned them into biddable slaves quick to fulfil his wishes, ready to assist in his emotional outbursts and prompt to self–sacrifice to satisfy his ambitious plans. In a word, he turned the Hebrews into frenetic, ferocious monsters. After having inflamed them with this spirit of destruction, he showed them the lands and possessions of their neighbours to be a heritage, which God himself had assigned to them.

Haughty and convinced of Jehovah's protection,[2] the Hebrews marched on to victory; heaven authorized their treachery and cruelty; their religion, combined with their greed, stifled the cries of Nature in their midst and, under the leadership of their inhuman leaders, they destroyed the Canaanite nations with a barbarism revolting to any man in whom superstition has not totally annihilated reason. In their fury, dictated by heaven itself, they spared neither children at the breast, nor the feeble elderly, nor pregnant women in cities, wherever these monsters wielded their victorious arms. Upon the orders of God or his prophets, honesty was violated, justice was outraged and cruelty was carried out.[3]

---

[2] This was the ineffable name of the god of the Jews, which they dare not pronounce. His common name was Adonai, which bears the strongest possible resemblance to Adonis of the Phoenicians. (See my *Research into Oriental Despotism.*)

[3] To get an idea of the Judaic people's ferocity, read about the behaviour of Moses and Joshua, and also the orders that the god of their armies gives to Sam. in 1 Kgs. 15: 23—24, where this god commands that everyone be exterminated, without making an exception for women and children. Saul was rejected by God for having spared the blood of the king of the Amalekites. David backed up the furious actions of his god and committed an act against the Ammonites, which would revolt Nature. (See the Book of Kings 12: 31.) Nevertheless, it is this David who is set up as a model king. Despite his rebellion against Saul, his robbery, acts of adultery, and his treacherous cruelty towards Uriah, he is called *a man after god's own heart.* See Bayle's article under 'David' in his *Dictionary.* (For **Bayle** & **David**—see Glossary.)

The references which d'Holbach gives above do not correspond to the *King James Version* of the Bible because his references are to the *Vulgate* (Latin) version of the Bible, which organizes a number of the Old Testament Books differently, though not all. The book of 1 Kings is the equivalent to the First Book of Samuel in the *King James Version,* but the reference has been misprinted in any case. For the first passage to which d'Holbach refers, see Glossary under **Samuel** and for the second passage, see Glossary under **David.** For the second reference to 'The Book of Kings 12: 31', read 2 Sam. 12: 31 in the *King James Version.*

As bandits, usurpers and murderers, the Hebrews finally managed to settle in a country which was not very fertile, but which they viewed as delightful, after having come out of the desert. There, under the authority of their priests—the visible representatives of their hidden god—they founded a state which was detested by their neighbours and was a perpetual object of hate and contempt. The priesthood, under the name of a *theocracy*, governed this blind, savage people for a long time. They persuaded the common people that, by obeying them, their priests, they were obeying God himself.

Despite their superstitions, the Hebrew people, either by force of circumstances, or possibly because they were tired of the priestly yoke, finally decided that they wanted kings just like those of any other nation. However, when choosing their monarch, they felt obliged to rely on the services of a prophet. Thus began the Hebrew monarchy, whose princes were always thwarted in all their ventures by priests, mystics and ambitious prophets, who constantly put obstacles in their sovereigns' path, whom they felt were not totally subjugated to their will. The history of the Jews, in all its periods, shows us nothing but kings blindly cowered by the priesthood, or in a continuous state of war with them, forced to perish under their blows.

The ferocious and ridiculous superstitions of the Jewish people have made them the born enemy of mankind, and have turned them into an object of people's indignation and contempt. The Hebrew people were always rebellious and constantly mistreated by the conquerors of their puny country. As slaves in turn of the Egyptians, the Babylonians, and then the Greeks, they constantly experienced the harshest treatment, which they richly deserved. As a people, the Jews were often unfaithful to their god, whose cruelty, along with the tyranny of their priests, frequently disgusted them, and they were never entirely submissive to their princes, who tried to crush them with a rod of iron—to no avail: they never managed to transform the Hebrew people into loyal subjects. The Jews have always been victims and saps of mystics, and at the height of disasters their obstinate fanaticism, their insane hopes, and their indefatigable credulity sustained them against the lashes of fortune. Finally, conquered along with the rest of the world, Judea submitted to the Roman yoke.

As objects of their new masters' contempt, the Jews were harshly and arrogantly treated by men who detested their faith to the pit of their stomach. Embittered by misfortune, the Jews simply became more seditious, more fanatical, and more blinded. Proud of the promises made by their god, abounding with confidence in their oracles, which time after time foretold a state of well–being but which constantly eluded them, incited by fanatics and impostors who successively scoffed at their credulity, the Jewish nation waited for a messiah, a monarch, a liberator, who would free them from the yoke under which they travailed, to raise them up to reign over all nations of the universe.

Figure 10: *The Nativity.* **Plate from** *The Holy Bible,* *with Illustrations by Gustave Doré* **(1870).**

Chapter 3

A Short History of Christianity

It was in the midst of this nation, so predisposed to feed on hopes and idle fantasies, that a new visionary appeared, whose followers managed to change the face of the earth. He was a poor Jew who claimed to have hailed from the royal blood of David[1] and he remained unknown for a long time in his own country, only suddenly to emerge from obscurity in order to make proselytes for himself. He found candidates amidst a most ignorant rabble. So he preached his doctrine, persuaded them that he was the Son of God, the liberator of his oppressed nation and the Messiah announced by their prophets. His disciples, either impostors or simple saps, bore startling witness to his power: they claimed that his mission had been proven by countless miracles.

The only miracle of which he was capable was to convince the Jews, who, far from being touched by his beneficent, supernatural acts, put him to death by an abominable form of torture.

Thus the Son of God died in full view of the whole of Jerusalem. However, his adherents maintained that he was secretly resurrected three days after his death. Visible only to them and invisible to the nation to whom he had come to enlighten and convert to his doctrine, the resurrected Jesus, it is claimed, conversed for a while with his disciples, after which he ascended back into heaven where, having become God, like his father, he shares with him the adoration and homage of those who follow his law.

His followers, by accumulating superstitions, conjuring up impostors, concocting dogmas and amassing mysteries, contrived a religious system little by little, which was ill–defined and disjointed, and was called Christianity, after its founder—Christ. The different nations, to whom the Jews had been respectively subjugated, had infected them with a multitude of dogmas borrowed from paganism: thus the Judaic religion, which is Egyptian

---

[1] **The Jews maintain that Jesus was the son of a soldier called Pandira, or Panther, who seduced Mary, a hairdresser, and married to a man called Jochanan. Alternatively, according to other authorities, Pandira enjoyed relations with her several times, whilst she thought that she was having relations with her husband. Hence she fell pregnant and her sorrowful husband made himself scarce to Babylon. Yet others maintain that Jesus had learned magic in Egypt, and that he came to Galilee to exercise his art, where he was ultimately put to death. See Pfeiffer, *Theologica Judaïcæ et Mahomedicae, et principia Lypsiae, 1687*. Others attest that Jesus was a crook and a self-appointed leader of a band of robbers. See the Gemara.** (For further information on **Mary**—see Glossary.)

in origin, adopted rites, ideas and a proportion of its notions from peoples with whom the Jews had associated.[2]

It should not surprise us at all, therefore, when we see the Jews and the Christians who succeed them, imbued with notions drawn from the Phoenicians, from the Magi or Persians, or from the Greeks and Romans.

In matters of religion, men's errors have a general, mutual resemblance; they differ only in their permutations. The trading conducted by the Jews and Christians with the Greeks led them, above all, to a knowledge of **Plato**, which was analogous to the fanciful mind of Orientals and thereby it was in keeping with the spirit of a religion, which has made it its duty to become inaccessible to reason.[3] Paul, the most ambitious and enthusiastic of Jesus' disciples, then took his doctrine, laced with elements of the sublime and the fantastical, to the peoples of Greece, Asia and even to the Romans themselves. He had his followers, just as any other man who appeals to the imagination of ignorant, unschooled people, and this active apostle passes, quite understandably, for the founder of a religion which, without him, would never have spread on account of his ignorant colleagues' lack of knowledge, from whom he did not tarry to separate himself, in order to assume the leadership of his sect.[4]

Be that as it may, at its inception the Christian religion was forced to restrict itself to the masses; it was embraced only by the most contemptible men amongst the Jews and pagans. It is amongst men of this kind that the fantastical takes the strongest hold.[5] As a hapless god, the innocent victim of

---

[2] An interesting and very accessible book on Egyptian and other origins of the Christian religion is Gary Greenberg, *101 Myths of the Bible: How Ancient Scribes Invented Biblical History* (Sourcebooks Inc.: Illinois, 2002).

[3] **Origen says that Celsus criticized Jesus Christ for having borrowed several maxims from Plato. See Origen, *Against Celsus*, I. St Augustin admits that he found in Plato the beginning of the Gospel of John. See Augustin, *Confessions*, Bk. VII, Chs. 9, 10 & 20. The concepts of the 'Word' [*logos*] are obviously borrowed from Plato; the Church has since found the way to lift a very sizeable part of Plato's philosophy, as will be demonstrated hereafter. (For Celsus and Augustin, St—see Glossary.)**

[4] **The Ebionites, or first Christians, regarded St Paul as an apostate and a heretic, because he totally rejected the Law of Moses, which the other apostles merely wanted to reform. (For Ebionite—see Glosary.)**

[5] **The first Christians were contemptuously called Ebionites, which means 'beggars' or 'villains'. See Origen, *Against Celsus*, Books I & II. See also Eusebius, *Ecclesiastical History*, Bk. III, ch. 37. Ebion in Hebrew means 'poor'. The term 'Ebion' has since been personalized and it means 'heretic', or 'leader of a sect'. Be that as it may, the Christian religion was to appeal mainly to slaves, who were excluded from sacred things, as people who were regarded as barely human: as a religion, it convinced them that one day their time would come and**

maliciousness, enemy of the rich and the powerful, Jesus Christ had to console himself with the poor and needy.

Having an austere life–style and a contempt for wealth, the first gospel preachers ministered to others who were disinterested in their appearance, and whose ambition was confined to holding sway over souls, establishing an equality which their religion engendered, holding goods in common and offering mutual help to members of their sect—these were precisely the things which would appeal to the aspirations of the poor, and in this way, their number as Christians multiplied. A sense of bonding, harmony and mutual affection towards which the early Christians were all constantly urged, was bound to seduce people's honest souls. The Christians' submission to the powers that be, a long–suffering spirit, poverty and living in obscurity, made the nascent sect regarded as being of little danger to a government used to tolerating all manner of splinter groups. Thus, the founders of Christianity had many adherents amongst the people and had but a few detractors or enemies—just a few idolatrous priests or Jews interested in sustaining the established religions. Little by little, under the cover of obscurity and shrouded in mysteries promoted by its adherents, this new cult put down extremely deep roots and became too wide–spread to be suppressed. Too late did the Roman government notice the progress of this despised association. Christians in their numbers dared to challenge the pagan gods all the way to their temples. Concerned emperors and magistrates wanted to stamp out this sect, which they found offensive: they persecuted those whom they could not win over by milder means and those whose fanaticism made them obstinate. However, their torture worked in the Christians' favour—all persecution did was multiply the number of their friends. Eventually, their fortitude in torture appeared supernatural and divine to those who watched on. Their enthusiasm was infectious and all tyranny did was to procure new defenders of the very sect they were trying to stamp out.

Therefore, let Christians cease singing the praises of the wondrous progress of their faith. It was a religion of the poor and it heralded a poor god. It was preached by the poor to the ignorant poor, and it consoled them in their wretched state. Its gloomy concepts themselves were analogous to the unfortunate and poverty–stricken position of the common people. Their close bond and harmony, so admired amongst the early Christians, is no more miraculous: a nascent and oppressed sect sticks together and fears its interests might dissipate. In those early times, how could its priests, who were

---

that in the after-life, they would be happier than their masters. (For **Eusebius**— see Glossary.)

themselves persecuted and treated as subversives, dare preach intolerance and persecution?

Ultimately, the severity brought to bear upon the early Christians could not make them change their minds, because tyranny annoys people, and their mind is indomitable when it has to do with opinions on which they believe their salvation depends. Such is the inevitable effect of persecution. Nonetheless, Christians, for whom the example of their own sect should have made them think twice, have proved unable to get over their own mania for persecuting, even up to the present time.

Roman emperors became Christians themselves, that is to say, having been dragged along by a current which became a general phenomenon, they were obliged to avail themselves of the support of such a powerful sect, and so they put Christianity on a pedestal. They protected the Church and its ministers, they wanted their courtiers to adopt its ideas, they looked unfavourably upon those who remained attached to the traditional Roman paganism and, little by little, they arrived at the point of ultimately banning it upon pain of death. They mercilessly persecuted those who held fast to the cult of their forbears. Christians paid the pagans back with interest for all the ills they had suffered. The Roman Empire became a hotbed of sedition, caused by the frenzied zeal of its sovereigns and its peace–loving priests, who, just a short time previously, desired only mercy and tolerance. Emperors, either as politicians or simply as superstitious believers, heaped favours and benefits upon the priesthood, who were frequently misinterpreted—they used them to establish their authority. Then the power they themselves had created was honoured and pronounced divine. The priests were relieved from all civil functions, in order that nothing should detract them from their sacred ministry.[6] Hence, the pontiffs of a sect, who were once oppressed and had to bow and scrape, were now independent.

At last, having become more powerful than kings themselves, the priesthood soon assumed the right to take command over them. These priests, serving a god of peace, yet forever at odds with each other, communicated their manias and outbursts of rage to the people as the astonished universe stood witness under the law of grace to quarrels and misfortunes, never experienced before under more peaceful divinities, who partook of mortal adoration without any disputes.

---

[6] See Tillemont, *The Life of Constantine*, IV, article 32, p. 148. (For **Tillemont**—see Glossary.)

Such was the relentless march of a superstition, innocent at its inception, but subsequently far from bringing happiness to mankind, and it became a bone of contention and an infinite source of calamities.

'Peace on earth and goodwill to all men'—that's how the gospel was presented to men, which has cost the human race more spilt blood than all other religions of the world put together.[7] 'Love the Lord thy God with all thy strength and thy neighbour as thyself.'[8] That, according to the lawgiver and god of the Christians, is the sum of their duties. However, we see Christians in an impossible situation—they have to love and adore this god who is hostile, harsh and capricious. On the other hand, we see them eternally engaged in tormenting, persecuting and destroying their neighbour and their brothers. What kind of a reversal is it, that a religion which spouts only mercy, harmony, humility, pardon for sins, and submission to sovereigns, has become a thousand times the signal for discord, fury, revolt, war and the blackest of crimes? How have priests of a god of peace managed to use his name as a pretext to disrupt society, to alienate humanity, to authorize the most incredible infamies, to set citizens at odds with each other, and to assassinate their sovereigns?

In order to explain all these contradictions, one has only to cast one's eyes upon the Christian god inherited from the Jews. Not content with the appalling colours with which Moses painted his god, Christians went on further to disfigure the picture. The fleeting chastisements of this life are the only ones mentioned by the Hebrew lawgiver: the Christian sees his barbarous god pouring forth unbounded vengeance for time without end. In a word, Christian fanaticism feeds upon the revolting idea of a hell, where their god, transformed into a torturer, as unjust as he is implacable, will slake his thirst with the tears of his unfortunate creatures, whose existence he will perpetuate in order to make them eternally miserable. There, engrossed in vengeance, he will delight in tormenting the sinner and he will listen with rapture to the vain howling from his dungeon, whose flames he stokes. The hope of seeing an end to his punishments will not allow for a moment's respite between bouts of torture.[9]

---

[7]   '"Glory to God in the highest, and on earth peace, good will toward men",' (Luke 2: 14) was how the angel of the Lord announced the birth of Christ: d'Holbach's phrase is a paraphrase from the Gospel.

[8]   This is also a paraphrase of a verse in Luke's Gospel: 'And he answering said, "Thou shalt love the Lord thy God with all thy heart, and with all thy soul, and with all thy strength, and with all thy mind; and thy neighbour as thyself",' (Luke 10: 27).

[9]   Similar sentiments were expressed by John Stuart Mill (1806—1873), son of the famous Scottish philosopher James Mill (1773—1836), who, writing of his father, stated: 'As it was, his aversion to religion, in the sense usually attached to the term,

In a word, by adopting the terrible god of the Jews, Christianity went over and beyond his cruelty: Christianity represents God as the most crazed of tyrants, the most treacherous, the most cruel the human mind could possibly come up with. Christianity supposes that God treats his subjects with the injustice and barbarism truly worthy of a demon. In order to persuade ourselves of this truth, let us become familiar with the tableau of Judaic mythology, adopted and made even more outrageous by Christians.

---

was the same kind with that of Lucretius: he regarded it with the feelings due not to a mere mental delusion, but to a great moral evil. He looked upon it as the greatest enemy of morality: first, by setting up factitious excellencies,—belief in creeds, devotional feelings, and ceremonies, not connected with the good of human kind,— and causing these to be accepted as substitutes for genuine virtues: but above all, by radically vitiating the standard of morals; making it consist in doing the will of a being, on whom it lavishes indeed all the phrases of adulation, but whom in sober truth it depicts as eminently hateful. I have a hundred times heard him say, that all ages and nations have represented their gods as wicked, in a constantly increasing progression; that mankind have gone on adding trait after trait till they reach the most perfect conception of wickedness which the human mind could devise, and have called this God, and prostrated themselves before it. This *ne plus ultra* of wickedness he considered to be embodied in what is commonly presented to mankind as the creed of Christianity. Think (he used to say) of a being who would make a Hell—who would create the human race with the infallible foreknowledge, and therefore with the intention, that the great majority of them were to be consigned to horrible and everlasting torment. The time, I believe, is drawing near when this dreadful conception of an object of worship will be no longer identified with Christianity; and when all persons, with any sense of moral good and evil, will look upon it with the same indignation with which my father regarded it.' (Quoted in Christopher Hitchens, *The Portable Atheist: Essential Readings for the Nonbeliever* [Philadelphia: Da Capo Press, 2007], pp. 58—59.)

Figure 11: *Hell*, **Dieric the Elder (1450).**

Figure 12: *Adam and Eve Driven Out of Eden.* **Plate from** *The Holy Bible, with Illustrations by Gustave Doré* (1870).

Chapter 4

Of Christian Mythology or the Christian Ideas of God and His Behaviour.

God, by an inconceivable act of his own omnipotence, created the universe out of nothing.[1] He created the world as a dwelling place for man, whom he made in his own image. Hardly had man, this unique object of God's handiwork, seen the light of day, when his creator set a trap for him, into which God undoubtedly knew he would fall. A talking serpent seduced a woman, who was not taken aback by this phenomenon in the least. She, in turn, was persuaded by the serpent to encourage her husband to eat a fruit forbidden by God himself.[2] By this minor slip–up, Adam, the father of the human race, brought upon himself and upon the whole of innocent posterity a myriad of misfortunes, the consequences of which were death. But it does not end there... Through the transgression of a single man the entire human race becomes the object of celestial ire: mankind is punished for an act of unintentional blindness by a universal

---

[1]   For the ancient philosophers, it was axiomatic that 'nothing comes of nothing'—*ex nihilo nihil fit*. The creation, as told by Christians today, that is to say, the creation of all things from nothing, is a fairly modern theological invention. The word '*Barah*', which is used in Genesis, means *to make, compose, or dispose of already existent matter*. In Greenberg, *101 Myths of the Bible*, there is a detailed analysis of the language of the original Hebrew text and its meaning as used in the creation myth, and the author makes a convincing case for the author of Genesis sticking close to Egyptian myths (see pp. 11—33).

[2]   Greenberg states, 'Genesis modeled [*sic*] the clever serpent after the Egyptian God Set, who took the serpent form of Aphophis, enemy of Re', and notes also that the act of eating of the fruit of the Tree of Knowledge 'represents the Egyptian concept of Ma'at (i.e., moral order) and eating of it gives one eternal life', (p. 64 & Bibliography)—yet God's punishment for snacking on the fruit was the depravation of eternal life and mortal death, as well as banishment from the Garden of Eden and a whole host of further calamities from which mankind would never be free ever again. In fact, God planted two trees in the Garden of Eden—the Tree of Life (about which God said nothing) and the Tree of Knowledge. Greenberg states that, 'These two special trees symbolically represented the Egyptian deities Shu and Tefnut', (p. 48). Furthermore, God had warned that, 'But of the tree of the knowledge of good and evil, thou shalt not eat of it: for in the day that thou eatest thereof thou shalt surely die', Gen. 2: 17: however, they did not die on that day. Greenberg has a great deal of interesting things to say about the serpent and Egyptian mythology and concludes that, 'the purpose of this story is to condemn the Egyptian idea that knowledge of moral order would lead to Eternal Life, which conflicted with Hebrew monotheistic teachings', (p. 51: see also pp. 48—54).

flood. God repents of having populated the earth:[3] he finds it easier to drown and destroy the human race, rather than change mankind's heart.

However, a small number of righteous people escape from this scourge. But even when the earth had been flooded and the human race annihilated, that was still not enough for God's implacable vengeance. A new race emerged, but despite it having emanated from God's friends, i.e., those whom he saved from the wreckage of the world, this race also began to irritate him again by committing new crimes—the Almighty can never manage to get his creatures to be the kind of people he wants them to be. A new wave of corruption gripped the nation and produced a fresh fit of pique in Jehovah.[4]

In the end, biased in his mercy and preferential treatment, he turns his gaze upon an idolatrous Assyrian: he forms an alliance with him, promising that his race, having multiplied like the stars in the sky, or like the grains of sand

---

[3] 'And Noah built an altar unto the Lord; and took of every clean beast, and of every clean fowl, and offered burnt offerings on the altar. And the Lord smelled a sweet savour; and the Lord said in his heart, "I will not again curse the ground any more for man's sake; for the imagination of man's heart is evil from his youth; neither will I again smite any more every thing living, as I have done. While the earth remaineth, seedtime and harvest, and cold and heat, and summer and winter, and day and night shall not cease",' (Gen. 8: 20—22). There are other passages of the Bible which state that God repented of his ire and actions: viz., 'And God sent an angel unto Jerusalem to destroy it: and as he was destroying, the Lord beheld, and he repented him of the evil, and said to the angel that destroyed, "It is enough, stay now thine hand." And the angel of the Lord stood by the threshingfloor of Ornan the Jebusite.' (1 Chr. 21: 15) 'The Lord repented for this: "This also shall not be," saith the Lord God.' (Amos 7: 6) 'And God saw their works, that they turned from their evil way; and God repented of the evil, that he had said that he would do unto them; and he did it not.' (Jonah 3: 10) How can a perfect, all-powerful, all-knowing god make a mistake from which he has to repent? Clearly this kind of language has been changed: the English Standard Version has for 1 Chr. 21: 15 'And God sent the angel to Jerusalem to destroy it, but as he was about to destroy it, the Lord saw, and he *relented* [*my emphasis, D.M.H.*] from the calamity. And he said to the angel who was working destruction, "It is enough; now stay your hand." And the angel of the Lord was standing by the threshing floor of Ornan the Jebusite.' Amos 7: 6 in the English Standard Version— same translation, 'The Lord relented concerning this; "This also shall not be," said the Lord God.' There is surely a big difference between '*relenting*' and '*repenting*' in the original: the two concepts are not interchangeable.

[4] Greenberg notes that, 'After the flood, Genesis tells of the repopulation of the earth and the origins of nations. These genealogical histories actually reflect political events of the early to middle first millennium B.C., showing the artificial and late origin of these stories. They date to a time after Israel arrived in Canaan, and again demonstrate the literary genius of the biblical redactors, who can take myths and legends from a variety of sources and different time frames and integrate them, almost flawlessly, into a long continuous narrative. But the task was difficult and contradictions seeped in. Occasionally, we even find the equivalent of typos in the textual transmission', (op. cit., p. 10).

in the sea, will find favour with his god for ever.[5] It is to this chosen race that God reveals his will and it is for them that he upsets a hundred fold the order of Nature, which he had already established: it is for them that he is unjust, that he destroys entire nations. However, this favoured race was not particularly any happier, nor were the people any more attached to their god than before: they constantly flee into the arms of alien gods, from whom they seek help, since it was previously denied to them by their own god, and so they outrage their god, who is perfectly capable of exterminating them.

Sometimes their god punishes them, sometimes he consoles them, sometimes he hates them without reason, and sometimes he loves them for no more reason. Finally, being in the impossible situation of not being able to bring to heel this perverse people, whom he doggedly cherishes, he sends down his own son. This son is also not listened to. What can I say? This cherished son, equal to God his father, is put to death by a people who are the object of his obstinate tenderness, but God is powerless to save the human race without sacrificing his own offspring. Thus an innocent god becomes the victim of a just god, by whom he is also loved. Both of them consent to this strange sacrifice, judged necessary by a god who knows that it will be to no avail for a hard–hearted nation, whom nothing will change. Will the death of a god, who proved to become superfluous for Israel, at least be of use to atone for the sins of the human race generally? Despite the eternal nature of the alliance, sworn with all solemnity by God the Almighty and renewed so many times with their descendants, the favoured nation finally found itself abandoned by its god, who could not bring them to heel. The merits of suffering and God's son's death are now open to nations previously excluded from his bounteousness: these peoples are now reconciled to heaven, which henceforth assumes an aura of greater justice in this regard. The human race is returned to a state of grace. However, despite the deity's efforts, his favours are as nought: men continue sinning and they incessantly fuel his celestial ire and render themselves fit only for eternal punishments, which await the vast majority of them.

This is an accurate history of the god upon whom Christianity is founded. After such strange, such cruel behaviour, so alien to all rational thinking, is it at all surprising to observe those who adore this god having no idea of their social responsibilities, failing to recognize justice, trampling on the toes of

---

[5] "'I will surely bless you and make your descendants as numerous as the stars in the sky and as the sand on the seashore. Your descendants will take possession of the cities of their enemies...',' (Gen. 22: 17). He is referring to Abraham, whose loyalty God tried by asking him to sacrifice his own son as a test, stopping him at the last minute from killing him. As a consequence of Abraham's near infanticide, God made this promise to him: it is a strange basis on which to found a covenant.

35

humanity, and making every effort in their fervour to assimilate the barbarous divinity, whom they adore and nominate as their model? What leniency is man entitled to expect from a god who did not spare his own son? What mercy can the Christian man, persuaded of this fable, show towards his fellow man? Is he not bound to think that the surest way to please his god is to be as bloodthirsty as him?[6] Is it not at least obvious that the followers of such a god are bound to be of a dubious morality, that their principles are mercurial?

Actually, this god is not always unjust and cruel—his conduct is variable. Sometimes he appears to have created all nature for man alone, but at other times he seems to have created mankind merely as a target, upon whom to exert his arbitrary rages. Yet on other occasions, he cherishes man for all his faults, only to condemn the human race to misery, just for an apple.

In short, this immutable god is agitated in turn by love and anger, by vengeance and pity, by benevolence and regret: he has never displayed that consistency of behaviour that characterizes wisdom. Partisan in his affections for a single nation, contemptible and cruel without grounds for the rest of humanity, he decrees fraud, theft and murder, and imposes on his cherished people the duty to commit the most atrocious crimes without a second thought, urging them to betray honesty and despise the rights of other peoples.

On other occasions, we see God defending these same crimes, ordering justice and telling men to abstain from things which disrupt the social order. This god, who is called equally, the *God of Vengeance*, the *God of Mercy*, the *God of Armies* and the *God of Peace*, blows continuously hot and cold. Consequently, he leaves each of his worshippers to be the arbiter of their own conduct and hence his morality becomes arbitrary. Is it at all surprising, therefore, that up until now, Christians have never been able to agree amongst themselves whether it is more fitting in their god's eyes to show mercy towards men, or exterminate them for their opinions?

In brief, they find it a problem to know whether it is more expedient to cut the throat and kill those who do not think at all like them, or to allow them to live in peace and show them humanity.

---

[6] **The death of the Son of God is offered as indubitable proof of God's kindness. But is it not rather an indubitable proof of God's ferocity, of his implacable vengeance and cruelty? Upon his death-bed, a good Christian said: 'He had never understood how a good god could put an innocent god to death to appease a just god.'**

It is not known whom d'Holbach had in mind by this quotation: there is no known or obvious source.

Christians never fail to justify their god's strange and often iniquitous behaviour, attributed to him in their sacred books. This god, they say, as the absolute master of his creatures, can dispose of them at will, without him being accused of injustice or being asked to justify his actions: his justice is not like man's justice and man has no right to blame him. It is easy to see the inadequacy of this reply. In fact, by saying that their god is just, men's concept of this virtue can only be based on a supposition that it resembles the effects of this justice as exhibited amongst their fellow men. If God's behaviour is not just, as we understand it in human terms, then we cannot have any idea of what God's justice is like, since we attribute a quality to him of which we have no knowledge ourselves. If, as is said, God owes his creatures nothing, we may assume that he is a tyrant whose only precept is caprice, and consequently he cannot be the model for our concept of justice or our guiding light for anything else, given that he has no bond with us, for all mutual dealings must be reciprocal. If God owes his creatures nothing, how can they owe him anything? If, as we are constantly told, men are to God as clay to the potter, there can be no moral relationship between us and him.[7] Nevertheless, it is upon such relationships that every religion is founded. Hence, to say that God owes nothing to his creatures and that his justice is not at all like that of men is to undermine the foundations of all justice and all religions, which suppose that God must reward men for good and punish them for evil.

It is constantly stated that it is in another life that God's justice will be demonstrated, but in that case, we cannot call him just in this world, especially since we so often witness virtue oppressed and vice rewarded. For as long as this is the state of affairs, we cannot even come within striking distance of calling such a god 'just', since he indulges in committing fleeting injustices, (at least in *this* life—and this is the *only* life by which we might judge him), which we assume he is disposed to put right at some future time.

But isn't all this mere gratuitous speculation? If God were capable of being unjust only for a moment, why do we flatter ourselves that he might not be so again at some later juncture? Furthermore, how can we reconcile his particular fallible brand of justice with his so–called immutability?

---

7 '"But now, O Lord, thou art our father; we are the clay, and thou our potter; and we all are the work of thy hand",' (Isa.64: 8). '"O house of Israel, cannot I do with you as this potter?" saith the Lord. "Behold, as the clay is in the potter's hand, so are ye in mine hand, O house of Israel",' (Jer. 18: 6). '"The precious sons of Zion, comparable to fine gold, how are they esteemed as earthen pitchers, the work of the hands of the potter!",' (Lam. 4: 2). 'Hath not the potter power over the clay, of the same lump to make one vessel unto honour, and another unto dishonour?' (Rom. 9: 21). These are just a few of a number of similar verses in both the Old and New Testaments.

And what has just been stated about God's justice can also be levelled at his so–called goodness, which is the basis for men's obligations towards him. In fact, if God is all–powerful, if he is the author of everything, if nothing is done but by his order, how can we attribute goodness to him in a world where his creatures are exposed to continuous misfortunes, to cruel illnesses, to physical and moral revolutions, and finally, to death? People can only attribute benevolence to God in so far as they receive blessings at his hand: as soon as they experience pain and suffering from him, this god can no longer be considered a good god to them.

Theologians safeguard their god's benevolence by denying that he is the author of evil, which they attribute to an evil genie borrowed from magic, who is perpetually engaged on harming the human race and frustrating the good intentions that providence bestows upon men.

God, we are told by those Doctors of the Church, is in no way the author of evil—he merely permits it. Can they not see that to permit evil is tantamount to committing evil for an all–powerful agent who has it in his power to prevent it?[8] In any case, if God's beneficence proves to be fallible on just one occasion, what assurance is there that it will not always fail?

In fact, within the Christian system of belief, how can God's benevolence or his wisdom be reconciled with his conduct, which is often barbarous, and with his orders, which are so often bloodthirsty, just as the holy books narrate?

How can a Christian attribute compassion to a god who has created the majority of men merely to be eternally damned?

The reply will be, without a doubt, that God's behaviour is an impenetrable mystery for man, which we have no right to scrutinize, and that our feeble reasoning would lead us astray each time we would sound the depths of divine wisdom;[9] that we have to adore him in silence and submit ourselves with fear and trembling[10] to the oracles of a god, who has made his own will

---

[8]   This is a philosophical point famed for being stated by Epicurus: see p. 312 and footnote № 9 on that page of this volume.

[9]   'O the depth of the riches both of the wisdom and knowledge of God! how unsearchable are his judgments, and his ways past finding out!' (Rom. 11: 33). 'Where is the wise? Where is the scribe? Where is the disputer of this world? Hath not God made foolish the wisdom of this world?' (1 Cor. 1: 20 and 3: 19). 'Nay but, O man, who art thou that repliest against God? Shall the thing formed say to him that formed it, "Why hast thou made me thus?",' (Rom. 9: 20).

[10] This epithet is used frequently in the New Testament: 'And his inward affection is more abundant toward you, whilst he remembereth the obedience of you all, how with fear and trembling ye received him', (2 Cor. 7: 15). 'Servants, be obedient to them that are your masters according to the flesh, with fear and trembling, in singleness of

known. Hence our lips have been sealed by having been told that the divinity has revealed himself to mankind.

Figure 13: *Tower of Bable*, **Lucas van Valckenborch (1594). (Source: Wikipedia.)**

your heart, as unto Christ...' (Eph. 6: 5). 'Wherefore, my beloved, as ye have always obeyed, not as in my presence only, but now much more in my absence, work out your own salvation with fear and trembling', (Phil. 2: 12).

**Figure 14: The first chapter of *B'reshit*, or the Book of Genesis.
Exhibit in the Jerusalem Museum. (Source: Wikipedia.)**

Chapter 5

On Revelation.

ow can we know without recourse to reason if it is true that the divinity has spoken? Yet on the other hand, has the Christian religion not outlawed reason? Has it not forbidden our use of reason to examine the miraculous dogmas it presents to us? Does it not continuously rail against our *profane reason*, which it accuses of being inadequate for the task and which it often regards as an outrage against Heaven?

Before being in a position to judge divine revelation, we should have an accurate idea of the divinity. But from where are we to derive this idea other than from revelation itself, since our powers of reasoning are too meagre to aspire to a knowledge of the Supreme Being?

So revelation itself is our proof of its own authority. Despite this vicious circle, let us open the books which ought to enlighten us and surrender our reason to them, as we must. Shall we find there specific concepts about the god, whose oracles have been communicated to us? Shall we discover there God's attributes, so that we know exactly with whom we are dealing? But is this god not just a mass of contradictory qualities, which only add up to an inexplicable enigma?

If, as is supposed, this revelation has come from God himself, how can we trust the Christian god who portrays himself as so unjust, so false, and so deceitful that he sets traps for people, delights in enticing them, blinds them to the truth, hardens their hearts, plants false signs to trick them, and spreads amongst them a spirit of confusion and falsehood?[1]

---

[1] **In Scripture and in the writing of the Fathers of the Church, God is always represented as a tempter. He allowed Eve to be tempted by a serpent; he hardened Pharaoh's heart; Jesus Christ himself is a '*stumbling stone*'. These are the various points of view offered us of the Divinity.**
The Exodus account of Moses repeatedly returning to Pharaoh, asking him to allow the Children of Israel to go free, firmly places the responsibility for Pharaoh's recalcitrance upon God himself: we read repeatedly, 'But the Lord hardened Pharaoh's heart, so that he would not let the children of Israel go', (Exod. 10: 20). Christ is described in the New Testament as a 'stumbling block', as d'Holbach points out: 'Wherefore also it is contained in the scripture, "Behold, I lay in Sion a chief corner stone, elect, precious: and he that believeth on him shall not be confounded. Unto you therefore which believe he is precious: but unto them which be disobedient, the stone which the builders disallowed, the same is made the head of the corner, And a stone of stumbling, and a rock of offence, even to them which stumble at the word, being disobedient: whereunto also they were appointed",' (1 Pet. 2: 6—8).

Hence, from the first steps man takes into an enquiry of the Christian revelation, he is cast into suspicion and confusion: he does not know whether this god who has spoken to him has it in mind to trick him, just as he has duped so many others by his own admission.[2] In any case, is man not bound to think that way when he sees the interminable squabbles amongst God's holy guides, who have never been able to concur on the right way to understand the Divinity's specific oracles as revealed by him personally?

Is it not the case that the sincere enquirer into God's revelation, as espoused by Christians, experiences incertitude and fear, which redoubles on reading that this God has aspired to make himself known only to a very few favoured beings, whilst wanting to remain hidden from the rest of humanity, for whom, however, this revelation was equally essential? How is the enquirer to be sure that he was not one of those people from whom this partisan god had wanted to remain hidden? Ought this man's heart not be troubled by the spectacle of a god who agrees to reveal himself and announce his decrees, but only to a very small number of men, when compared with the totality of mankind?

Is the inquirer not tempted to accuse this god of the blackest of malice, seeing that, by not having revealed himself to many nations, he has caused their inevitable damnation right down the centuries? What image can one form of a god who punishes millions of men for having been unaware of his secret laws, which he has himself made public knowledge, but only on the sly and in an obscure, unknown corner of Asia?

Hence, when the Christian consults revealed literature, everything ought to conspire to set people on their guard against the god talking to them. Everything arouses one's suspicion against God's moral character, everything appears uncertain: the Christians' god, in cahoots with the

---

[2] 'He hath blinded their eyes, and hardened their heart; that they should not see with their eyes, nor understand with their heart, and be converted, and I should heal them', (John 12: 40). 'And if by grace, then is it no more of works: otherwise grace is no more grace. But if it be of works, then it is no more grace: otherwise work is no more work. What then? Israel hath not obtained that which he seeketh for; but the election hath obtained it, and the rest were blinded. (According as it is written, God hath given them the spirit of slumber, eyes that they should not see, and ears that they should not hear;) unto this day.' And David saith, "Let their table be made a snare, and a trap, and a stumblingblock, and a recompence unto them: Let their eyes be darkened, that they may not see, and bow down their back alway." I say then, "Have they stumbled that they should fall?" God forbid: but rather through their fall salvation is come unto the Gentiles, for to provoke them to jealousy', (Rom. 11: 6—11). 'Therefore thus saith the Lord, "Behold, I will lay stumblingblocks before this people, and the fathers and the sons together shall fall upon them; the neighbour and his friend shall perish",' (Jer.6: 21).

interpreters of his so–called will, seems to have put together a plan to redouble the depths of our ignorance. In fact, to compound our doubts, we are told that God's revealed will is all mystery, that is to say there are things which are inaccessible to human understanding. So what was the point of mentioning them in the first place? Should a god not reveal himself to people for the express purpose of being understood? Is this conduct not as ridiculous as it is insane? To say that God has made his revelation only to announce mysteries is like saying that God has only revealed himself to remain unknown to us, to hide his ways from us, to throw us off the right track, to intensify our ignorance and incertitude.

A revelation which is true, which emanates from a good and just god, which is essential for all mankind, ought be clear enough to be heard by the whole human race.[3]

Is the revelation on which Judaism and Christianity are founded of this kind?

Euclid's *Elements* are intelligible to all who wish to hear them: this work does not cause any controversy amongst geometricians. But is the Bible just as clear, so that revealed truths cause no arguments at all amongst the theologians who pronounce on them? By what mischance need the Scriptures, revealed by the divinity himself, require further commentary and yet more elucidation from above in order for them to be believed and understood? Is it not astounding that that which ought to serve as a guide for all men is understood by not a single one of them? Is it not cruel that that which is vital for them should be the least understood?

All is mystery, darkness, incertitude and controversy in a religion proclaimed by the Almighty in order to enlighten the human race. The Old and New Testaments contain essential truths for men, despite the fact that no

---

[3]   This also begs the question why many Muslims are against the Koran being translated into other languages? If God or Allah is an Arabic speaker only, then how can Muslims claim that Islam is a universal religion? And what of those who are mentally incapable of learning Arabic and praying in it, or simply do not have the opportunity? When imams preach in languages other than Arabic, can Allah understand what they are saying, and indeed, does he inspire the imam in Arabic or in another language, which he might not understand? Ought something as simple as language, which is an accident of birth and upbringing and something the whole of mankind has to put up with, be a barrier to something as mighty as the salvation of a human soul, created by God in the first place? Ought one's native tongue, over which one has no control, stand between eternal damnation and eternal bliss to a god who is all-merciful and all-powerful? Furthermore, it was God who created diverse languages, as we read in the Bible in the story of the Tower of Babel—see Gen. 11: 1 *et seqq.*, which makes it clear that different languages were sent by God to cause confusion: God has maliciously made communication difficult between peoples and him.

one can understand them and each one can be understood differently, and theologians are never in agreement about how they are to be interpreted. Little satisfied by the mysteries contained in their sacred books, Christian priests throughout the centuries have invented what their followers ought to believe, despite the fact that their founder and god has never spoken on such issues.

No Christian may question the mysteries of the Trinity, the Incarnation, or the efficacy of the sacraments, and yet Jesus Christ never set out his thoughts on these matters. In the Christian religion everything seems to have been left to the imagination, to whims and to the arbitrary decisions of its ministers, who seize the sole right to conjure up mysteries and articles of faith as their own interests require. It is thus that this revelation is perpetuated by the Church, which claims to be divinely inspired and, far from enlightening the minds of its children, it conspires merely to confuse and plunge them into a sea of incertitudes.

Such are the effects of this revelation which serves as the bedrock of Christianity, whose reality it is not open to question. God, we are told, has spoken to mankind, but when did he speak? He spoke thousands of years ago to a chosen group of men, whom he used as his mouthpiece. But how can one be sure that God has truly spoken, apart from relying on the testimony of those men who claim to have received his orders in the first place?

Those interpreters of the divine will are mere men themselves, and are men not prone to making mistakes and misleading others? Therefore, how can one know whether to trust the testimony that Heaven's mouthpieces have given? How can we know whether they themselves were not the dupes of an overactive imagination or of some kind of illusion? How can we discover today if it is really true that Moses did in fact converse with his god thousands of years ago and that he was the vessel of Jewish law?[4] What was

---

[4] For more information on **Moses**—see Glossary. 'And the Lord said unto Moses, "Write thou these words: for after the tenor of these words I have made a covenant with thee and with Israel." And he was there with the Lord forty days and forty nights; he did neither eat bread, nor drink water. And he wrote upon the tables the words of the covenant, the ten commandments. And it came to pass, when Moses came down from mount Sinai with the two tables of testimony in Moses' hand, when he came down from the mount, that Moses wist not that the skin of his face shone while he talked with him', (Exod. 34: 27—29). 'And the Lord spake unto you out of the midst of the fire: "Ye heard the voice of the words, but saw no similitude; only ye heard a voice. And he declared unto you his covenant, which he commanded you to perform, even ten commandments; and he wrote them upon two tables of stone. And the Lord commanded me at that time to teach you statutes and judgments, that ye might do them in the land whither ye go over to possess it",' (Deut. 4: 12—14).

Moses' character like? Was he calm and cool or excitable, sincere or deceitful, ambitious or selfless, truthful or duplicitous?

How can we relate to the testimony of a man who, after having performed so many miracles, never managed to disabuse his people of their idolatry and who, having caused forty–seven thousand Israelites to die by the sword, had the audacity to proclaim that he was the 'mildest of men'?[5] Are the books, whose authorship is attributed to this Moses and which report so many incidents that occurred after his death, really authentic?

What ultimate proof do we have of Moses' mission, apart from the testimony of six hundred thousand unsophisticated, superstitious, ignorant and credulous Israelites, who were perhaps dupes of a fury–driven lawgiver, ever–ready to exterminate them, or who never knew what they ought to write afterwards about this infamous legislator?

And what proof does the Christian religion offer us of the mission of Jesus Christ? What do we know of his character and temperament?

What degree of faith can we add to the testimony of his disciples who, by their own admission, were unsophisticated, unschooled men, and thereby they were consequently prone to being hoodwinked by the tricks of a deft impostor?

---

[5] While Moses was talking to God, receiving his commandments, the people of Israel made images of other gods and worshipped them. When Moses discovered this, he instructed the sons of Levi to smite their own relatives, as recounted in the Book of Exodus: 'Then Moses stood in the gate of the camp, and said, "Who is on the Lord's side? Let him come unto me." And all the sons of Levi gathered themselves together unto him. And he said unto them, "Thus saith the Lord God of Israel, Put every man his sword by his side, and go in and out from gate to gate throughout the camp, and slay every man his brother, and every man his companion, and every man his neighbour." And the children of Levi did according to the word of Moses: and there fell of the people that day about three thousand men', (Exod. 32: 26—28). Like the fall of Adam and Eve from God's grace, this sin, committed by the Israelites, was to be felt by subsequent generations who had nothing to do with this incident and who were themselves innocent of breaking God's law, as another passage of Exodus confirms: 'And the Lord passed by before him, and proclaimed, "The Lord, the Lord God, merciful and gracious, longsuffering, and abundant in goodness and truth, keeping mercy for thousands, forgiving iniquity and transgression and sin, and that will by no means clear the guilty; visiting the iniquity of the fathers upon the children, and upon the children's children, unto the third and to the fourth generation." And Moses made haste, and bowed his head toward the earth, and worshipped', (Exod. 34: 6—8). The origin of this figure of 47,000 is not known, but when all the casualties of all such killing sprees in the Old Testament are added up, the total is close to that figure.

45

Ought not the testimony of the most learned scholars of Jerusalem hold greater weight than that of a few ignorant men, who are usually the dupes of those who would deceive them? This actually leads us on to an examination of the proofs on which Christianity is founded.

Figure 15: Title page of a manuscript of the *Prose Edda*, depicting Odin and other figures from Norse mythology. (Source: Wikipedia.)

Chapter 6

On Proofs of the Christian Religion, Miracles, Prophecies and Martyrs.

In the preceding chapters we saw legitimate reasons why we should question the revelation made to the Jews and Christians. In any case, Christianity in this regard has no advantage above any other world religion, since all of them claim to have emanated from a divine source and maintain that they have an exclusive right to their god's favours, despite the divergence of all faiths.

The Indians assure us that **Brahma** himself is the originator of his cult. The Scandinavians maintain that their cult comes from the fearsome **Odin**. Likewise the Jews and the Christians got their cult from Jehovah through the ministry of Moses and Jesus, and the Muhammadans assure us that they got theirs through their prophet, inspired by the same god.

Hence all religions claim to have emanated from heaven; all of them forbid the use of reason to examine their sacred credentials; all claim to be true to the exclusion of all others; all threaten divine wrath against those who refuse to submit to their authority. In fact, because of the obvious contradictions with which they are replete, and because of their half–baked, obscure and frequently odious ideas about the divinity and his bizarre laws, and because of the disputes which they cause among their followers—all have an air of falseness about them.

In a word, all religions on earth show us nothing more than a mass of deception and delusions which are equally revolting to reason. Hence, as far as its claims are concerned, Christianity has no advantage over all the other religions which have infected the world, and its celestial origin is challenged by all other belief systems with just as much justification as it throws doubt on the others.

Therefore, what makes it possible to decide in Christianity's favour? How can the benevolence of its claims be proved? Has it superior qualities which favour it, and if so, which? Does it give us a greater insight into the essence and nature of the divine? Alas! It merely looks even more inconceivable than all other religions; it simply appears to personify a capricious tyrant whose whims are sometimes favourable, but more often harmful, for the human race. Does Christianity improve people? Alas! It is evident everywhere that it divides people, setting them at odds with each other, making them intolerant and forcing them to become their brothers' butcher.

Does Christianity make empires flourish and grow powerful? Wherever it reigns, do we not see servile people, devoid of vigour, energy and activity, wallowing in shameful lethargy, having not a single idea of true morality?

So what are the distinguishing features which compel us to recognize the superiority of the Christian faith above all others?

We are told that it is by its miracles, its prophecies and its martyrs. But I can see miracles, prophecies and martyrs in all other world religions.

There are cases everywhere in the world of men more artful and more educated than the herd, who dupe people with spells and dazzle them by acts they believe to be supernatural because they are ignorant of the knack of pulling them off and of the secrets of Nature.

If the Jew cites the miracles of Moses to me, I see these so–called wonders performed before the eyes of a most ignorant and stupid, credulous and contemptible people, whose testimony bears no weight for me. Besides, I have a suspicion that accounts of these miracles were inserted into the Hebrew sacred texts long after the death of those who might have been able to refute them.

If the Christian cites Jerusalem and the testimony of the whole of Galilee to convince me of the miracles of Jesus Christ, I merely see yet again an ignorant people who vouch for them, or I ask how was it possible that an entire people witnessed the Messiah's miracles and yet consented to his death—they even demanded it vigorously? Would the people of London or Paris allow a man to be put to death before their very eyes, who had brought the dead back to life, restored sight to the blind, made the lame to walk, and cured the paralysed? If the Jews demanded the death of Jesus, all his miracles are negated for every uninformed person.

On the other hand, could one not contrast the miracles of Moses, and likewise those of Jesus, with those performed by Muhammad before the eyes of all the assembled people of Mecca and Arabia? At least Muhammad's miracles were enough to convince the Arabs that he was divine.[1]   The

---

[1]   It is not clear what d'Holbach means by this statement because Muhammad is not reputed to have performed any miracles like those supernatural acts attributed to Moses and Jesus Christ. Muhammad's reputation as a prophet and God's messenger stems from his own personal standing and character, and his success as a military commander and tactician, but more specifically upon the prophecies he made, which Muslims claim were proved to be accurate and true by history. In fact, according to the Koran, many people encouraged Muhammad to perform miracles like Jesus to prove his special status as a prophet from God: however, Muhammad refused, as is clearly stated: '[this Koran] is a revelation that is clear to the hearts of those endowed with knowledge. Only the evildoers refuse to acknowledge Our revelations. They say, "Why have no miracles been sent to him by his Lord?" Say, "Miracles lie in God's hands; I am simply here to warn you plainly." Do they not think it is enough that We have sent down to you the Scripture that is recited to them', (29: 49—52). There are a number of similar passages stated in the Koran.

miracles of Jesus convinced no one of his mission. **Saint Paul** himself, who became his most ardent disciple, was not at all convinced by Jesus' miracles, despite the existence of so many eye–witnesses at that time; Saint Paul needed a new miracle to change his mind. Why should we believe today in miracles which were not thought convincing at the time of the Apostles themselves, that is to say—a short time after they were performed?

Also, let it not be said that the miracles of Jesus Christ are just as well attested as any facts of secular history, and that to doubt them is as ridiculous as doubting the existence of Scipio or Caesar, in whom we believe solely through reports made by historians. The existence of a man, an army general, or a hero, is not beyond belief, but neither is it a miracle.[2] We can give credence to plausible facts reported by **Livy**, whilst contemptuously rejecting the miracles he narrates. Men often combine the most foolish credulity with the most distinguished of talents and Christianity itself provides us with innumerable examples of this. In matters of religion, all evidence is suspect and even a most enlightened man's vision of events is seriously distorted when he is in the grip of enthusiasm, intoxicated with fanaticism, or seduced by his own imagination. A miracle is an impossible thing: God could not be immutable if he altered the natural order.

One might say perhaps that, without changing the natural order, God, or his chosen ones, could find the resources in Nature unknown to other men, but then their works would not be supernatural and would have nothing miraculous about them. In fact, a miracle is contrary to the constant laws of Nature, so consequently God himself cannot perform miracles without undermining his wisdom. Upon seeing a miracle, a wise man would be quite right to doubt what he had really seen: he should examine it to see whether the extraordinary effect, which he does not understand, might not be due to some other natural cause, whose workings he does not comprehend.

But let us suppose for a moment that miracles are possible and that those performed by Jesus were really genuine, or at least, that they were not inserted into the gospels long after the event. Those who bore witness to them—the Apostles who saw them—were they really trustworthy, and is their testimony not subject to be challenged at all? Were these witnesses well–educated?

---

[2] **A supernatural event requires much stronger evidence than a fact that does not go beyond the boundaries of the plausible. It is easy to believe that Apollonius of Tyana existed because the evidence of Philostratus can be relied upon and there is nothing in that to offend reason, but when Philostratus claims that Apollonius performed miracles, it is then that I stop believing in his 'evidence'. I believe that Jesus Christ died, but I do not believe that he rose from the dead.** (For **Apollonius** and **Philostratus**—see Glossary.)

By the Christians' own admission, these witnesses were men without learning, plucked from the dregs of humanity and consequently they were credulous and incapable of examining the facts. And were these witnesses impartial? No! Without a doubt, they had a vested interest in supporting these miraculous deeds which proved their master's divinity and the veracity of the religion they wanted to establish. Were these same deeds corroborated by contemporary historians? Not a single one of them has mentioned them, and in a city as superstitious as Jerusalem, no one—not a single Jew or a solitary pagan—had heard speak of the most extraordinary and prolific deeds that History has ever reported. It is only ever Christians who testify to the miracles of Christ.[3]

We are required to believe that upon the death of the Son of God, the earth trembled, there was an eclipse of the sun and the dead arose from their tombs.[4] How is it that such extraordinary events were noticed only by a few Christians? Were they the only people to witness them? We are expected to believe that Christ was resurrected: we are told the witnesses were the Apostles, some women and some disciples. But would not a formal appearance in a public square have been more convincing than all the secret appearances made to men motivated by forming a new sect?

---

[3] For ancient historians writing around the time of Christ and subsequent centuries—see Glossary under **Pliny** (the Elder), **Pliny** (the Younger), **Seneca, Suetonius, Tacitus, Plutarch, Celsus, Philo** of Alexandria, **Justus** of Tiberias, and **Josephus**.

[4] Details of the supernatural events and consequences surrounding the crucifixion of Christ vary in the four gospel accounts: they are by no means consistent. The Gospel of Matthew states: 'Now from the sixth hour there was darkness over all the land unto the ninth hour', (Matt. 27: 45). And subsequently: 'Jesus, when he had cried again with a loud voice, yielded up the ghost. And, behold, the veil of the temple was rent in twain from the top to the bottom; and the earth did quake, and the rocks rent; and the graves were opened; and many bodies of the saints which slept arose, and came out of the graves after his resurrection, and went into the holy city, and appeared unto many. Now when the centurion, and they that were with him, watching Jesus, saw the earthquake, and those things that were done, they feared greatly, saying, "Truly this was the Son of God",' (Matt. 27: 50—54). However, Mark's Gospel differs in the detail—no mention is made of the earthquake, the eclipse or the resurrection of the dead: 'And it was the third hour, and they crucified him', (Mark 15: 25). The narrative continues: 'And when the sixth hour was come, there was darkness over the whole land until the ninth hour', (Mark 15: 33). 'And Jesus cried with a loud voice, and gave up the ghost. And the veil of the temple was rent in twain from the top to the bottom', (vv.37—38). One would have thought that such momentous, cosmic events would have been of more historical note than a mere veil being torn in two. There is also no mention of any earthquake, the veil ripping, the eclipse, or the resurrection of the dead in John's Gospel. Luke's Gospel mentions the veil being rent: 'And the sun was darkened, and the veil of the temple was rent in the midst', (Luke 23: 45). However, again there is no mention of the other supernatural events.

Figure 16: *Deposition*, **Albrecht Dürer (1497—1500).**

51

According to St. Paul, the Christian faith is founded on the resurrection of Jesus Christ: should it not, therefore, be a fact that is proven to nations in the clearest and most indubitable way possible?[5] Could one not accuse the Saviour of the world of spitefulness for only having shown himself to his disciples and his chosen ones? Did he not want the whole world to believe in him? The Jews, we are told, deserved to be blinded for putting Christ to death. So why, in that case, did the Apostles preach the gospel to them? Did they believe that a personal testimony would receive more credence than the evidence of their own eyes?

As for the rest, the accounts of the miracles seem to have been invented merely to compensate for a lack of rationality: truth and evidence have no need of miracles to be accepted. Is it not rather surprising that the divinity finds it easier to interfere with the laws of Nature than to teach men clear truths, capable of convincing them and forcing their assent?

Miracles were invented merely to convince men of things impossible to believe in; there would be no need of miracles if one appealed to reason. Hence, one set of unbelievable things serve to prove other incredible things. Almost all impostors who have introduced religion to people have proclaimed improbable things; then they performed miracles to make them believe in what they told them. They said, 'You cannot understand what I am telling you, but I shall prove to you that I am speaking the truth by doing things before your eyes that you cannot comprehend.' The people paid for that by their reason: their mania for marvels has always stopped them from thinking. They could not see at all that miracles are no explanation for the impossible, nor do they change the essential truth.

Whatever miracles a man might perform, or, if you like, a god himself might execute, they will never prove that two and two no longer make four, and that three is really only one, and that a non–incarnate being, devoid of internal organs, could have spoken to man, and that a wise, just and good being was capable of ordering foolish things, injustices and acts of cruelty, etc. From all this it is obvious that miracles prove nothing, apart from the dexterity and deception of those who wish to hoodwink mankind to back up the lies they tell, and the stupid credulity of those whom these impostors seek to seduce. The latter have always begun by lying, by giving false ideas of the

---

[5]   **The Bazilidians and the Cerinthians were heretical Christian sects dating back to the origins of Christianity and they maintained that Jesus never died and that Simon the Cyrenian was crucified in his place. See St Epiphanius** *Haer.* **[***Against Heresies* **or** *Panarion***], ch. 28. So we see that from the very inception of the Church, men have doubted the death and consequently the resurrection of Jesus Christ—and the Church wants us to believe in it today! (For Bazilidians, Cerinthians, Epiphanius—see Glossary.)**

divinity and by claiming to have done a private deal with their god, and to prove their incredible claims they performed incredible deeds, which they attributed to the omnipotence of the being who sent them.

Any man who performs miracles has no truth to prove—only lies. Truth is simple and clear, but the miraculous always heralds duplicity. Nature is always true—it operates within immutable laws. To say that God performs miracles is to say that God contradicts himself, that he countermands the laws of Nature which he set down and that he renders pointless human rationality, of which he is the author. It is only impostors who tell us to disregard our experience and alienate our reason.

Thus, the so–called miracles recounted to us by Christianity, just like all those of every other religion, are rooted in nothing more than people's credulity, in their enthusiasm, their ignorance, and in the impostors' guile. We can say just the same about their prophecies. Men have always been curious to know about the future and consequently they have always found men well–disposed to serve them. We see charmers, soothsayers and prophets in all nations of the world. In this regard, the Jews were no more favoured than the Tartars, Negros, primitives, and all the other people of the world—all had their impostors ready to dupe them for material rewards. These miracle–workers must have soon felt the need for their oracles to be vague and ambiguous, so as not to be found wanting. Therefore, it should come as no surprise that Judaic prophecies are sufficiently obscure and ambiguous so as to find in them anything one wishes. Those prophecies which Christians attribute to Jesus Christ are not interpreted in the same light by Jews, who are still waiting for the Messiah, whom the former believe arrived eighteen centuries ago.

Judaic prophets have prophesized a liberator from time immemorial to a nation perturbed and dissatisfied with its lot—a deliverer who was expected equally by the Romans and by almost all other nations of the world.

All men have a natural propensity to hope for an end to their misfortunes and believe that Providence will not duck its obligation to give them a more charmed life.

The Jews, a more superstitious people than any other, have always expected a conqueror or a monarch, based on the promises of their god, who would change their lot and drag them out of their pit of shame. But how can we see a liberator in the person of Jesus? He was a destroyer, not a restorer, for the Hebrew nation, and since him the Jews have enjoyed no share at all of the favours of their god.

There is no shortage of people who say that the destruction of the Jewish people and their dispersion were foretold, and they provide convincing proof

53

of Christian prophecies. I reply that it was easy to predict the dispersion and destruction of a people who have been constantly anxious, restless and rebellious towards their masters, endlessly riven by internecine divisions. Furthermore, this people was often conquered and scattered: the temple was destroyed by **Titus**, but it had previously suffered the same fate under **Nebuchadnezzar**, who led captive tribes into Assyria and distributed them amongst his states.[6] We are aware of the dispersion of the Jews and not of that of other conquered nations because, after a certain time, conquered nations become subsumed within the conquering nation, whereas the Jews never mixed with those amongst whom they lived, always leading separate and distinct lives. Is it not the same with the **Guebres** (or the Parsees) of Persia and of **Hindustan**, just as with the **Armenians**, who live in the land of the Muhammadans? The Jews remained dispersed because they are unsociable, intolerant and blindly attached to their superstitions.[7]

Thus, Christians have not a single reason for singing the praises of prophecies contained in the Hebrews' books, never mind laying claim to prophecies in their own religious books: they regard the Hebrews as custodians of a religion which they abhor.

All down the ages, Judea was subservient to priests who were hugely influential in affairs of state and got involved in politics and in predicting fortunate or unfortunate events, which they had good reason to expect.

No country contained a greater number of visionaries; we see prophets in charge of public schools where they inculcated the mysteries of their art into those whom they judged worthy, or who wished, by fooling a credulous

---

[6] The Nebuchadnezzar referred to here is, in fact, **Nebuchadnezzar II**—see Glossary.

[7] **The Acts of the Apostles evidently prove that, before the time of Jesus Christ, the Jews were dispersed: they came from Greece, Persia, Arabia, etc., to Jerusalem for the feast of Pentecost. See Acts 2: 8. Also, after Jesus, it was only the inhabitants of Judea who were scattered by the Romans.**
The passage to which d'Holbach refers is the following: 'And there were dwelling at Jerusalem Jews, devout men, out of every nation under heaven. Now when this was noised abroad, the multitude came together, and were confounded, because that every man heard them speak in his own language. And they were all amazed and marvelled, saying one to another, "Behold, are not all these which speak Galilaeans? And how hear we every man in our own tongue, wherein we were born?" Parthians, and Medes, and Elamites, and the dwellers in Mesopotamia, and in Judaea, and Cappadocia, in Pontus, and Asia, Phrygia, and Pamphylia, in Egypt, and in the parts of Libya about Cyrene, and strangers of Rome, Jews and proselytes, Cretes and Arabians, we do hear them speak in our tongues the wonderful works of God', (Acts 2: 5—11).

people, to gain their respect and to procure the means to live at their expense.[8]

Therefore the art of prophesying was a trade in every sense of the word, or, if you like, an extremely useful and lucrative branch of commerce in a poor nation persuaded that their god was constantly active solely on their behalf. The great profits which resulted from this fraudulent peddling must have created divisions between Jewish prophets; we also note that they decried each other, each one denigrating his rival as a *false prophet* and claiming that he had been inspired by an evil spirit.

There were constant quarrels between these impostors to decide to whom the privilege fell to hoodwink their fellow citizens.

In fact if we examine the conduct of these prophets, so lauded in the Old Testament, we find them to be anything but virtuous people. We see arrogant priests perpetually occupied by affairs of state, which they always knew how to entangle in religious affairs. We see the seditious subjects that they are, continuously engaged in intrigues against a sovereign who had not fully bowed his knee to them, cutting across his plans, whipping up the people against him, often managing to destroy him, thus fulfilling the disastrous predictions they had made against him.

Amidst the majority of prophets who played a role in Jewish history we see rebels determined to overthrowing the state, to incite trouble and fight against civil authority, of which priests were always enemies when they did not find it sufficiently compliant or suitably submissive to their own interests.[9]

---

[8] St Jerome maintains that the Sadducees did not adopt the prophets, preferring to limit themselves to the five books of Moses. Dodwell says, in his *De jure laïcorum*, that the prophets prepared themselves for prophesy by drinking wine. (See op. cit., p. 259.) It transpires that there were jugglers, dancers, poets and musicians who belonged to the ranks of prophets. (For Dodwell—see Glossary.)

[9] The prophet Samuel, who was displeased with Saul and who refused to support his cruelty, declared that he had forfeited the crown and created a rival to him in the person of David. Elijah appears to have been nothing other than a seditious subject who, finding himself the underdog in disputes with his sovereign, had to make a quick getaway to escape punishments rightly due to him. Jeremiah himself gives us to believe that he was a traitor in that he entered into an alliance with the Assyrians against his besieged native country: he seems to have spent every last effort in sapping his fellow citizens of the courage and will to defend themselves. He bought a plot of land from his relatives at the very time he proclaimed that his compatriots were to be dispersed and taken away into captivity. The King of Assyria commended this prophet to his general Nabuzardan and told him to take great care of him. See *Jeremiah*. (For **Samuel, Saul, David, Elijah**, and **Jeremiah**—see Glossary.)

Be that as it may, the carefully contrived textual obscurities of those prophecies pertaining to the Messiah—or liberator of Israel—can be applied to any particular man, or to any fanatic or prophet who happens to turn up in Jerusalem or Judea.

Christians, whose minds were fired by the concept of their Christ, believed that they saw him everywhere, or that they distinctly saw him in the most obscure passages of the Old Testament: by the use of allegories, subtleties, commentaries and forced interpretations, they finally managed to fool themselves into finding categorical predictions amidst the most disjointed daydreaming, in vague oracles, and in the most bizarre hotchpotch of sayings pronounced by the prophets.[10]

---

[10] It is easy to see anything in the Bible, as St Augustine did, by imagining that he saw the whole of the New Testament in the Old. According to him, the sacrificing of Abel is symbolic of that of Jesus Christ; Abraham's two wives are symbolic of the synagogue and the church; a thread of red silk shown by a harlot who betrayed Jericho signifies the blood of Christ; the lamb, the goat and the lion are all figures of Jesus Christ; the bronze snake represents the sacrifice of the cross. Even the mysteries of Christianity are foretold in the Old Testament—manna prefigures the Eucharist, etc. See St Augustin, Sermon 78, and his Epistle № 157. How can any sensible man possibly see in the Emmanuel of Isaiah the Messiah, who was subsequently dubbed Jesus? See Isa. 7: 14. How can one see in this obscure Jew, who was put to death, a leader who would govern the people of Israel? How can we see a liberator king, a restorer of the Jewish nation, in a man who, far from having delivered his fellow citizens, has come to destroy Jewish law, and then after his coming, his country is desolated by the Romans? One needs to be totally blind to see the fulfilment of these predictions in the Messiah. Jesus himself does not seem to have been clearer or happier in his own prophecies. In the Gospel of Luke chapter 21 he clearly announces the Last Judgement; he speaks of angels who, at the sound of the trumpet, will assemble mankind to give an account of their lives before him. He adds, 'Verily I say unto you that this generation shall not pass until these predictions are fulfilled.' However, the world continues its existence and Christians have been waiting for eighteen hundred years for the Last Judgement.

St Augustine's sermon as referred to in d'Holbach's note reads: 'Is not Christ called "the Lamb"? Is not Christ "the Lion" too? Among wild beasts, and cattle, a lamb is simply a lamb, and a lion, a lion: but Christ is both. The first are respectively what they are in propriety of expression; the Latter both together in a figurative sense. Nay much more; besides this it may happen that under a figure, things very different from one another may be called by one and the same name. For what is so different as Christ and the devil? Yet both Christ and the devil are called "a lion". Christ is called "a lion": "The Lion hath prevailed of the tribe of Judah"; and the devil is called a lion: "Know ye not that your adversary the Devil walketh about as a roaring lion, seeking whom he may devour?" Both the one and the other then is a lion; the one a lion by reason of His strength; the other for his savageness; the one a lion for His "prevailing"; the other for his injuring. The devil again is a serpent, "that old serpent"; are we commanded then to imitate the devil, when our Shepherd told us, "Be ye wise as

Men do not turn out to be so difficult over things which fit in with their views. When we care to consider Hebrew prophecies without bias, we see them merely as amorphous rhapsodies which are simply the outcome of fanaticism and raving; we find these prophecies to be obscure, enigmatic and just like pagan oracles; in fact everything proves to us that these so–called divine oracles are nothing more than the delusions and trickery of a few men accustomed to taking advantage of the credulity of a superstitious people who give credence to illusions, visions, apparitions and spells, and who were avidly susceptible to all the daydreaming that was churned out for them, so long as they were embellished with the fantastical. Wherever ignorant men are to be found, there will be prophets, visionaries and miracle–workers; this twin–armed business will diminish proportionately as nations become more enlightened.

Finally, Christianity authenticates its dogmas by a large number of martyrs, who have sealed with their blood the truth of religious opinions they embraced. There is no religion on earth which has not had its ardent defenders ready to sacrifice their life for ideas on which they have been persuaded that their eternal happiness depended. The superstitious and ignorant man is obstinate in his prejudices and his credulity stops him from suspecting that his spiritual guides might have fooled him, and his vanity makes him believe that he himself could not have been duped. In fact, if his imagination is strong enough to see heavens' gates open and the divinity ready to reward his courage, then there is no torture that he will not brave or endure. In his state of emotional intoxication, he will despise short–lived torments and he will laugh amidst his torturers, and his lunatic mind will even make him insensitive to pain. Pity melts spectators' hearts; they admire the martyr's miraculous firm resolve and his enthusiasm captivates them; they believe his cause is just and his courage, which seems to have an air of the supernatural and divine about it, becomes an incontrovertible proof that his opinions are true. Thus it is that, like an infectious disease, the enthusiasm of faith is passed on.

Man is always drawn to those who show the greatest resolve and tyranny attracts supporters through all those it persecutes. Thus, the early Christians' steadfastness was bound naturally to produce followers, so martyrs prove

---

serpents, and simple as doves"?' (vv. 5—9.) Isa. 7: 14 reads: 'Therefore the Lord himself shall give you a sign; Behold, a virgin shall conceive, and bear a son, and shall call his name Immanuel.' Luke 21: 32—33 predicts: 'Verily I say unto you, this generation shall not pass away, till all be fulfilled. Heaven and earth shall pass away: but my words shall not pass away.' This whole chapter of Luke is full of prophecies which have not yet come to pass: it is more than a generation since Christ uttered his prophesy and we are still all waiting!

nothing, save the intensity of their fanaticism, the depth of their blindness, the obstinacy that superstition can produce, and the cruel insanity of all those who persecute their fellow men for their religious opinions.

All fanatical emotions produce their martyrs; pride, vanity, prejudices, love, an enthusiasm for public good, even crime itself—all make martyrs on a daily basis, or at least intoxicate people, making them turn a blind eye to the dangers involved.

Is it surprising, therefore, that enthusiasm and fanaticism, people's most potent emotions, have so often made them confront death when intoxicated by the hope offered to them?

In any case, just as Christianity has its martyrs in which it glories, does Judaism not also have its own? The hapless Jews, whom the inquisition condemned to the flames, are they not also martyrs to their religion, whose constancy in their own faith proves just as much about their religion as Christian martyrs prove about theirs? If martyrs prove the authenticity of a religion, then there is no religion or sect which could be regarded as untrue.

In fact, amongst the (possibly exaggerated) number of martyrs upon whom Christianity prides itself, there are many who were rather more victims of ill–considered zeal, of a revolutionary spirit and of a seditious mindset, which is the religious mindset. The Church itself dares not justify those whose reckless ardour has sometimes pushed them to the point of breaching public order by smashing idols and ransacking pagan temples. If men of this kind were to be regarded as martyrs, then all rebels, all subversive elements in society would have the right to this title when brought to justice.

Figure 17: *Martyrdom of the Ten Thousand,* **Albrecht Dürer (*c.* 1498).**

Figure 18: *The Trinity*, Andrei Rublev (*c.* 1410). (Source: Wikipedia.)

Chapter 7

On the Mysteries of the Christian Religion.

To reveal something to someone is to uncover secrets previously not known to them.[1]

If one were to ask Christians which important secrets were absolutely essential that God himself had to take the trouble to reveal, they would say that the greatest of these secrets, the most vital for mankind, is that of the unity of the divinity—a secret which, according to them, people would never have been capable of discovering by themselves. But are we not within our rights to ask if this assertion is really true? There can be no doubt that Moses proclaimed a single god to the Hebrews and that he brought all his strength to bear to make them enemies of the idolatry and polytheism of other nations, whose beliefs and religious practices he denounced as abominable in the eyes of the celestial monarch who had delivered them out of Egypt. But without the assistance of Judaic revelation, had not a great number of pagan sages discovered a god who was supreme master over all other gods?

Furthermore, was not Fate, to which all other pagan gods were subordinate, a single god to whom the whole of nature subjected its sovereign law? As regards the traits which Moses depicted of the divinity, neither the Jews nor the Christians had the right to glory in them. We see God solely as a bizarre despot, irritable, brimming with cruelty, injustice and partiality, full of malice, quick to throw all men cursed by him into the most appalling perplexity. And what does he become if one adds for good measure some of the inconceivable attributes which Christian theology endeavours to attribute to him? Do we come to know the divinity better when he is described as *pure spirit*, as a *non–material* being, unlike anything our senses have ever known before? Is the human mind not confused by such negative attributes as *infinity*, *immensity*, *eternity*, *omnipotence*, and *omniscience*, etc., with which this god has been adorned merely to render him more inconceivable? How can we reconcile other moral qualities attributed to this god, such as wisdom, benevolence and justice, with his strange and often atrocious conduct as described on every page of the Christian and Hebrew books? Would it not have been better to have left people in total ignorance of this divinity than to reveal a god replete with contradictions, who gives constant

---

[1] In pagan religions mysteries were revealed to initiates: they were instructed in things they did not know. In the Christian religion people are taught what they must have faith in the trinity, the incarnation, the resurrection, etc., that is to say in things they do not understand even after they have been revealed, and thus they are cast into even greater ignorance than before these revelations were even disclosed.

rise to disputes and serves as a pretext for disturbing people's peace of mind? To reveal such a god to us has nothing to do with enlightenment—it merely throws people into the greatest confusion and provokes them to argue and harm each other, making them miserable.

Be that as it may, is it really true that Christianity confesses a single god, the same one as that of Moses? Do we not see Christians adoring a triple divinity under the name of a *Trinity*? The supreme god brought out from all eternity a son equal to himself; from these two comes a third god, equal to the first two; these three gods, equal in their divinity, perfection and power, nevertheless form a single god. Is it not enough then to set out this concept to show how absurd it is? So is that why the divinity went to all the trouble of enlightening mankind, to reveal similar mysteries? Have even the most ignorant and primitive of nations brought forth any opinions more monstrous and more likely to disconcert reason?[2]

However, there is nothing in the writings of Moses which gives rise to such a strange construct: it is only by assembling the most convoluted exegesis that one can claim to find a doctrine such as the Trinity in the Bible. As for the Jews, they are quite content with the single god proclaimed to them by their lawgiver, and it has never entered their head to triple him.

---

[2] **The dogma of the Trinity is obviously borrowed from the musings of Plato, or possibly from allegories under which this romantic philosopher chose to conceal his doctrine. It would appear that it is to him that Christianity is indebted for the majority of its dogmas. Plato acknowledged three *hypostases* or modes of being of the divinity. The first constituted the *Supreme Being*; the second—the *Logos*, or the 'Word'—divine intelligence, which emanated from the first god; the third is *Spirit* or the Soul of the World. The early Christian doctors of the Church seem to have been Platonists: their religious enthusiasm doubtlessly found an analogous doctrine in Plato. Had they been truly grateful, they would have made Plato into one of their prophets or one of the Founding Fathers of the Church. Jesuit missionaries in Tibet found a divinity almost identical to that in our country, and the Tartars' god is called 'Kon-sio-sik', or 'Single God', and 'Kon-sio-fum', which means 'Triple God'. They say the words om, ha, hum, to their rosary beads, which mean 'intelligence', 'might' (or 'power' or 'word'), and 'heart' and 'love'. These three words are one set of names for the divinity. See *Lettres édifiantes* {Edifying Letters}, XV. The number three was always revered by the ancients because in eastern languages the word *salom* meant 'three', and also 'health' or 'salvation'.**

The *Lettres édifiantes* (full title *Lettres édifiantes et curieuses*) to which d'Holbach refers were written by a French Jesuit called Charles le Gobien (1671—1708). He was a professor of philosophy and he was also in charge of a Franco-Chinese mission to eastern Asia, where missionaries were sent to convert the indigenous population to Christianity. His *Letters*, published in 1703, were an attempt to inform the public about the heathen practices of Asiatic peoples and presumably to convince them of the need for sending out missionaries. They have not all been translated into English.

The second of these gods, or in Christian parlance, the *second person of the trinity*, took on human nature, became incarnate in the womb of a virgin and, renouncing his divinity, he endured all our human weaknesses and he even suffered an ignominious death to expiate the sins of the world. That is what Christianity calls the *mystery of the incarnation*. Who cannot see that these absurd notions were simply borrowed from the Egyptians, Indians and Greeks, whose ridiculous myths imagine gods clothed in human form, susceptible to human infirmities like men?[3]

So Christianity commands us to believe that a god transforms into a man without detriment to his divinity and that he should suffer and die, offering himself as a sacrifice, and that he could not escape from such bizarre conduct in order to appease his own ire. That is what Christians call the mystery of the *redemption* of mankind.

It is true that this dead god was resurrected, similar to **Adonis** of the Phoenicians, **Osiris** of the Egyptians, and **Attis** of Phrygia, who were, in times gone by, the symbols of Nature which periodically dies and is reborn, but the god of the Christians spurns his ashes and emerges triumphant from the tomb.

Such are the supernatural secrets, or sublime mysteries, the Christian religion reveals to its disciples; such are the ideas—sometimes lofty, sometimes abject—but always inconceivable, that we are given of the divinity; such is the enlightenment that revelation has given our minds! It seems that the revelation adopted by the Christian revelation was offered merely to increase two–fold the clouds that veil the divine essence from men's eyes.

We are told that God wanted to make things appear ridiculous to confound the curiosity of those whom he wanted to enlighten—apparently—by his special grace. But what can one make of a revelation which, far from teaching us anything, takes delight in confusing the clearest of concepts?

Hence, despite the revelation so trumpeted by Christians, their mind has not the slightest insight into the being who is at the very foundation of their entire religion; on the contrary, this famous revelation serves only to confuse all concepts we might form of it.

---

[3] **The Egyptians seem to have been the first to maintain that their gods had taken on human flesh. Foë, the god of the Chinese, was born of a virgin impregnated by a ray of the sun. In Hindustan the incarnations of Vishnu are universally accepted. It seems that theologians of all nations, despairing of not being able to elevate themselves to the level of a god, had no other choice than to bring them down to their level.**

Holy Scripture calls the divinity a hidden god.[4] David tells us that *he set his hiding place in the shadows, where he stirred up waters and the clouds form a canopy to hide him.*[5]

Ultimately, Christians enlightened by God himself have only contradictory ideas and incompatible notions of him, which render his existence doubtful or even impossible in the eyes of anyone who has recourse to reason.[6]

In fact how can one conceive of a god who, having created the world solely for the happiness of man, still allows the greatest majority of the human race to be wretched in this world and the next? How can a god who enjoys supreme bliss possibly take offence at the actions of his creatures? Such a god, then, is sensitive to pain and he is apt to become upset, therefore he is subordinate to his subjects, who can delight or wound him at will.

How can a powerful god afford his creatures such baleful liberty, which they can misuse both to offend him and cause their very own perdition? How can a god turn into a man, and how can the creator of life and Nature die

---

[4] The New Testament openly admits that its teachings are a mystery and, despite revelation, they remain hidden: 'But we speak the wisdom of God in a mystery, even the hidden wisdom, which God ordained before the world unto our glory', (1 Cor. 2: 7). Promises of full understanding are made only when the Messiah makes his next appearance: 'Therefore judge nothing before the time, until the Lord come, who both will bring to light the hidden things of darkness, and will make manifest the counsels of the hearts: and then shall every man have praise of God', (1 Cor. 4: 5).

[5] The verse the writer has in mind is found in 2 Samuel: King David describes the hiding place or the temple God has made for himself thus: 'And he made darkness pavilions round about him, dark waters, and thick clouds of the skies', (2 Sam. 22: 12).

[6] **A Father of the Church said: *Tunc Deum maxime cognoscimus, cum ignorare eum cognoscimus.***
The Latin means: 'Now we have maximum knowledge of God by not knowing who God is', i.e., by knowing that we cannot know God, we have already reached the limits of what is knowable about him. It appears from the quotation below that d'Holbach attributes this to St Denis. D'Holbach also quoted this Latin maxim in his *Système de la Nature {System of Nature}*, volume II, originally published in 1770: 'I find, in the work of Doctor Clarke, a passage of Melchoir Canus, bishop of the Canaries, which could be opposed to all the theologians in the world, and all their arguments: Puderet me dicere non me intelligere, si ipsi intelligerent qui tractarunt. Heraclitus said, if it were demanded of a blind man what sight was, he would reply that it was blindness. St. Paul announced his God to the Athenians as being precisely the *unknown* God to whom they had raised an altar. St. Denis, the areopagite, says, it is when they acknowledge they do not know God, that they know him best. Tunc deum maxime cognoscimus, cum ignorare eum cognoscimus. It is upon this *unknown*. God that all theology is founded! It is upon this *unknown* God that they reason unceasingly!! It is for the honour of this *unknown* God, that they cut the throats of men!!!' (*The System of Nature or Laws of the Moral and Physical World by Baron d'Holbach, with notes by Diderot*' translated by H.D. Robinson and originally published in 1868 [republished by Batocle Books, Kitchener, 2001], p. 196.)

himself? How can a single god become a triple god without undermining his singularity? We are told that these things are mysteries, but these mysteries destroy the very existence of God.

Would it not be more logical to concede, along with **Zoroaster** or **Mani**, that there are two principles or opposing forces in nature, than to admit, along with Christianity, that an omnipotent god does not have the power to prevent evil; that a just god is yet partisan; that a merciful god is yet implacable, who will punish a fleeting crime throughout all eternity; that he is a single god who triples himself; and that the creator god of all beings consented to die, being unable to satisfy his own divine justice in any other way?

If two contrary elements cannot coexist in the same being at the same time, then the existence of the Jewish and Christian god is, without doubt, impossible. Hence, one is forced to conclude that the Doctors of the Church, rather than revealing the divinity to us, have done nothing other than destroy him, or at least they have rendered him unrecognizable through all the attributes that they have used to embellish, or rather to disfigure, their divinity.

It is thus that divine revelation, by dint of fables and mysteries, has merely clouded man's reason and made him uncertain of forming the simplest concepts of that essential being, who governs Nature by immutable laws.[7]

If one cannot deny the existence of a god, it is at least certain that one cannot acknowledge the one whom Christians adore, and whose religion they maintain reveals his conduct, his orders and his qualities.

If being an atheist is to have no idea of the divinity, Christian theology cannot be regarded as anything other than a scheme which shatters the existence of the Supreme Being.[8]

---

[7] There are many verses in the Bible which openly state that God has actively and purposefully confused men's minds, yet he punishes them for their confusion: see Gen. 11: 7; 'Go to, let us go down, and there confound their language, that they may not understand one another's speech.' Also, 'Therefore, behold, the days come, that I will do judgment upon the graven images of Babylon: and her whole land shall be confounded, and all her slain shall fall in the midst of her', (Jer. 51: 47).

[8] **Christian theologians have never been able to agree amongst themselves about the proofs of the existence of a god. They have called each other atheists because their 'proofs' have never been coherent. There are very few people amongst Christians who have written about the existence of God without having been accused of being an atheist. Descartes, Clarke, Pascal, Arnauld and Nicole have all been regarded as atheists. The reason is very simple: it is totally impossible to prove the existence of a god who is so bizarre as the one that Christianity has embraced. No doubt we shall be told that man does not have the capacity to judge the divinity, and that his mind is too limited to conceive of him. If that be**

PUNCH, OR THE LONDON CHARIVARI.—September 29, 1860.

A GOOD OFFER.

GARIBALDI. "TAKE TO THIS CAP, PAPA PIUS. YOU WILL FIND IT MORE COMFORTABLE THAN YOUR OWN."

Figure 19: *A Good Offer.* Illustration from *Punch, or the London Charivari,* 29 September 1860.

so, then why engage in endless reasoning? Why attribute qualities to him that are mutually contradictory? Why tell stories about him? Why bicker and slit each other's throats over how we might interpret the fantasies churned out about him?

(For **Descartes, Clarke, Pascal, Arnauld,** and **Nicole**—see Glossary.)

Chapter 8

Other Mysteries and Dogmas of Christianity.

ittle content with the veil of mysterious clouds with which Christianity enveloped the divinity and the Judaic fables adopted on his behalf, the Christian Doctors of the Church seem totally obsessed with proliferating mysteries and increasingly thwarting their disciples' rational thinking.

Religion was intended to enlighten nations, but it is nothing but a tissue of riddles and a maze from which it is impossible to extricate oneself by common sense. The most inconceivable things believed within ancient superstitions were bound to find a niche within a religious system which, as a matter of principle, imposed an eternal silence upon rationality. Greek fatalism was transformed into the doctrine of *predestination* at the hands of Christian priests.

According to this tyrannical dogma, the God of Mercy predestines the vast majority of unfortunate mortals to eternal torment, since he only puts them in this world for a certain time in order that they abuse their abilities and liberty, which in turn makes them worthy of the implacable ire of their creator.

As a god fully equipped with foresight and kindness, this god gives people *free will*, which he knows very well they will abuse, ultimately only to earn them eternal damnation.[1]

Thus the Divinity brings into the world the vast majority of people, to whom he does not give the inclinations essential for their happiness, nor does he allow them to behave in any way other than to give him the pleasure of plunging them into hell. There is nothing more frightening than the paintings which Christianity has produced of this sojourn, destined for the greatest part of the human race. The God of Mercy will drink the tears of such miserable wretches throughout eternity, whom he caused to be born and remain in sorrow. The sinner, shut up in his dark dungeon, shall be eternally consigned to be devoured by flames with the vaults of his prison resounding only with the gnashing of teeth and howling.[2] The totality of his torments, prolonged

---

[1] See p. 345.

[2] Little is said in the Bible about what heaven will be like, but hell is described with a good deal of consistency: a verse in Matthew's Gospel is typical—'But the children of the kingdom shall be cast out into outer darkness: there shall be weeping and gnashing of teeth', (Matt. 8: 12). There are a number of similar verses in the Bible, especially in Matthew's Gospel, who seemed to have something of a fixation for this concept: see Matt. 13:42 & 50; 22: 13; 24: 51, and 25: 30. Luke expresses similar sentiments in Luke 13: 28. The Book of Revelation is full of similar and more gruesome passages.

over millions of centuries, will be but a beginning of them, and the hope and consolation of seeing an end to them will be non–existent and it will delight God. In a word, God, through an act of his omnipotence, will make people eligible to suffer without interruption and without end, and his justice will allow him to punish crimes which are over and forgotten and of but a moment's duration, by torturing people for an infinite period, that is—for all eternity.

Such is the concept of the Christians' god who demands their love. This tyrant created people only to make them miserable; he gave them the power of reason only to dupe them, inclinations only to lead them astray, liberty only to spur them on to do actions which must damn them for all eternity: in fact, he has favoured mankind with advantages not granted to animals, in order to give him the chance to subject human beings to torments, from which animals and inanimate objects are exempt. The doctrine of predestination makes man's fate much more lamentable than that of stones and beasts.[3]

It is true that Christianity promises a blissful sojourn to those whom the divinity singles out as the targets of his love, but this place is reserved only for a small number of his elect, who, through no merit of their own, will nevertheless have rights to the goodness of their god who is partial to them, but cruel towards the rest of humanity. Thus it is that *Tartarus* and *Elysium* of pagan mythology, thought up by impostors who wanted either to make men tremble with fear or win them over, found a place in the Christian religious system, their names having been changed to *Hell* and *Paradise*.

We are constantly told that the dogma of rewards and punishments in another life is beneficial for people who, in the absence of that, would surrender themselves without fear to great excesses. By way of reply I would say that the Jewish lawgiver had carefully hidden this so–called mystery, and the dogma of a future life was part of a secret which, in Greek mythology, was revealed only to initiates. This dogma was unknown to the common

---

[3] **The doctrine of gratuitous predestination is the basis of the Judaic religion. In the writings of Moses we see a partisan god biased towards his chosen people, but unjust for all other nations. In Greek theology and history we see men everywhere punished by gods for inevitable crimes predicted in oracles. We have examples in Orestes, Œdipus, Ajax, etc. Throughout time, men have always made God out to be the most unjust of all beings. In our society, according to Jansenists, God grants his grace to whomever he pleases, without any regard to merit, which is much closer to Judaic, Christian and pagan fatalism than the doctrine of the Molinists, who believe that God grants his grace to anyone who merits or asks for it. It is certain that a fair number of Christians are real fatalists. They get out of all this by saying that the ways of God are mysterious, but if they are so, why do they always quibble about them?**

herd and society did not allow it to survive. In any case, it is not the threat of future terrors which present passions always disdain, or at least make them appear an issue in an effort to restrain men—it is good laws which do that, it is an education based on reason, on honest principles.

If sovereigns governed wisely and fairly, they would have no need of dogmas of rewards and punishments to keep people in check. People will always be more taken with present advantages and with visible punishments than with pleasures and torments promised in another life. The fear of Hell will not hold back criminals, whom the fear of their fellows' contempt, infamy and the gibbet are incapable of restraining. Are Christian nations not full of criminals who constantly defy the threat of Hell, whose existence they have never doubted?

Be that as it may, the dogma of a future life supposes that man will live on in an after–life, or that at least after his death he will be eligible for the rewards and punishments which religion has in store for him.

According to Christianity, one day the dead shall take on their mortal bodies.[4] By a miracle of omnipotence, the dissolved and dispersed molecules, of which their bodies are composed, will be reconstituted and they shall be reunited with their immortal souls—such are the fantastical ideas which the doctrine of the *Resurrection* conveys.

The Jews, whose lawgiver never spoke of this strange phenomenon, seem to have dug up this doctrine from Magi during their time in captivity in Babylonia. However, the doctrine was not universally accepted amongst them. The **Pharisees** accepted the resurrection of the dead, but the **Sadducees** rejected it. Today this teaching is one of the fundamental tenets of the Christian religion.[5]

---

[4] There are a number of biblical passages which refer to the resurrection of the dead: one of the most comprehensive references is to be found in 1 Cor. 15: 19—54: 'In a moment, in the twinkling of an eye, at the last trump: for the trumpet shall sound, and the dead shall be raised incorruptible, and we shall be changed. For this corruptible must put on incorruption, and this mortal must put on immortality. So when this corruptible shall have put on incorruption, and this mortal shall have put on immortality, then shall be brought to pass the saying that is written, "Death is swallowed up in victory",' (vv. 52—54). Of course, the Book of Revelation contains a number of passages about this teaching.

[5] **The writer of Ecclesiastes (ch. 3: 19) compares the death of man with that of animals and seems to query the doctrine of the immortality of the soul. In the Gospels we do not see Jesus Christ reproaching the Sadducees for denying the resurrection. However, this article of faith merited a mention a good number of times by a god who had just revealed so many singular truths to men and who, in any case, would have to resurrect himself. It is true that in the Gospels, Jesus**

Followers of Christianity believe firmly that they will be resurrected one day and that this resurrection will be followed by a universal judgement and the end of the world.

According to them God, who knows everything right down to man's most secret thoughts, shall arrive on clouds to make men give an exact account of their behaviour. He will judge them with the greatest pomp and ceremony and after this judgement their lot will be irrevocably decided: the just will be given entry to their blissful sojourn which the divinity reserves for his elect and his angels, and the wicked shall be hurled into the flames reserved for demons, the enemies of God, and all other people.

In fact, Christianity acknowledges invisible beings whose nature is different from that of humans, some of whom carry out the will of the Almighty, but others of whom are perpetually engaged in thwarting God's plans. The former are known by the name of *angels*, or 'messengers', subordinate to God. It is claimed that God uses them to watch over the administration of the universe and, above all, for the preservation of mankind. These benevolent beings are, according to Christians, *pure spirit*, but they have the power to make themselves detectable by taking on human form. The sacred books of the Jews and Christians are full of appearances of these miraculous beings, whom the divinity sends to favoured people as guides, protectors and guardians. From this we can see that good angels in Christians' imagination are just like nymphs, **Lares** and **Penates**, who populated pagan imagination, just as **fairies** did for writers of romantic stories.

The invisible beings of the second type come under the general term of *demons*, *devils* and *evil spirits*. They are regarded as enemies of mankind, tempters of men, seducers, who are perpetually engaged in trying to make people fall into sin. Christians attribute to them extraordinary powers, such as the ability to perform miracles similar to those of God Almighty, and particularly a power which rivals his, to the extent of thwarting his plans

---

says that God is not a 'God of the dead': but that alone does not prove the resurrection—that rather proves that Abraham, Isaac and Jacob are not dead, given that these patriarchs have not yet been resurrected. At least Scripture does not tell us that.

The verse in Ecclesiastes reads: 'For that which befalleth the sons of men befalleth beasts; even one thing befalleth them: as the one dieth, so dieth the other; yea, they have all one breath; so that a man hath no preeminence above a beast: for all is vanity.' The other verse to which d'Holbach alludes is: 'I am the God of Abraham, and the God of Isaac, and the God of Jacob? God is not the God of the dead, but of the living', (Matt. 22: 32).

Figure 20: *The Punishment of Gluttony.* Illustration to Dante's *Purgatory*,
Gustave Doré (1870).

The narrator of Dante's *Divine Comedy* is guided through the underworld by Aeneas who had
already visited the underworld himself as narrated in Book VI of Virgil's epic poem *Aeneid.*

completely.[6] In fact, although the Christian religion does not formally attribute to the Devil the same magnitude of power as God's own, it maintains, nevertheless, that this malicious spirit stops people from arriving at a state of happiness, which the benevolent divinity has in store for them, and that he leads the vast majority of human beings to perdition. In a word, according to the ideas of Christianity, the Devil's empire is even more extensive than that of the Supreme Being—the latter only just manages to save a few elected members, whilst the Devil leads to damnation an immense crowd of those who do not have the strength to resist his dangerous promptings. Who cannot see that Satan—the Devil—an object of terror for Christians, is borrowed from the dualistic concept believed in long ago in Egypt and throughout the whole of the Orient? **Osiris** and **Typhon** of the Egyptians, **Ormazd** and **Aharimane** of the Persians and **Chaldeans** were the source of a continuous war, which now lives on between the god of the Christians and his redoubtable adversary. It is on the basis of this system of thought that people believed they could come to terms with all the good and the ill that befell them. An all–powerful Devil allows people to absolve the Divinity of the responsibility for all the unmerited misfortunes that necessarily afflict the human race. Such are the frightening and mysterious dogmas on which Christians agree, but there are many more, specific to particular sects. Similarly, a large sect of Christianity proclaims an intermediate place, masquerading under the name of *Purgatory*, where the lesser criminal souls, who do not merit Hell, are confined for a time to expiate the faults they committed in this life through a rigorous series of torture, after which they are admitted into eternal bliss.

---

[6] Apart from Genesis—the Garden of Eden incident, when Satan addresses Eve in the form of a serpent, and a single mention of Satan in I Chron. 21: 1, plus Satan's pestering Job—most verses relating to the Devil or the Evil One, portraying him as an evil force who works against God, are to be found in the New Testament. The Devil famously tempts even the Messiah Himself, as narrated in Matthew's Gospel, chapter 4. Casting out devils was one of the chief ways the Gospel writers had of 'proving' that Christ was who he claimed to be, because his power was greater than that of the devils, as Jesus said to a crowd of doubters, 'But if I cast out devils by the Spirit of God, then the kingdom of God is come unto you', (Matt. 12: 28). Also note the number of incidents in the Gospels where disease and illness are attributed to the manifestation of demonic presence: Matt. 12: 22 is a good example, 'Then was brought unto him one possessed with a devil, blind, and dumb: and he healed him, insomuch that the blind and dumb both spake and saw.' Note also Mark 1: 34: 'And he healed many that were sick of divers diseases, and cast out many devils; and suffered not the devils to speak, because they knew him.' The New Testament sees the Devil as aggressive and always out to trip man up: 'Be sober, be vigilant; because your adversary the devil, as a roaring lion, walketh about, seeking whom he may devour', (1 Pet. 5: 8). There are over a hundred such verses in the New Testament.

This dogma, obviously borrowed from Plato's musings, is a source of inexhaustible riches at the hands of priests of the Roman Church, given that they have usurped the power to open Purgatory's gates and they maintain that their powerful prayers are capable of moderating the rigour of divine decrees by shortening the duration of torture which souls, whom a just god has condemned to a period of misery, have to endure.[7]

All the above proves to us that the Christian religion has not left its followers without a good number of things to keep them in awe and trembling. And it is by making people shake in their boots that they are subjugated and kept in a state of mental anxiety.[8]

---

[7] It is obvious that it is to Plato that the Roman Catholics are indebted for their concept of *Purgatory*. This exalted philosopher divides the souls of men into categories of *pure, curable,* and *incurable*. The first type belongs to the just who return by remerging with the universal soul of the world, that is to say to the divinity, whence they emanated. The second type goes to hell, where they undergo a yearly review before the judges of this shady empire: the latter allows those souls who have sufficiently expiated their sins to return to the light. The third group, the 'incurables', remains in Tartarus, where they are tortured for evermore. Plato, just like the Casuist Christians, shows how crimes and misdemeanours merit varying degrees of punishment. Protestant Doctors of the Church, doubtlessly jealous of the riches of Catholic clergy, were imprudent enough to reject the doctrine of *Purgatory* and in so doing, they have significantly diminished their own income. It might have been wiser to have banished the doctrine of *Hell*, from where nothing can help those souls escape, rather than *Purgatory*, which is a good deal less revolting and from which priests have the ability to free souls for money.

[8] Muhammad felt the need to frighten men in order to establish a hold over believers, just like Doctors of the Church. The Koran says, 'Those who do not believe shall be clothed in a garment of fire: boiling water will be poured on their heads; their entrails and their skin will be dissolved and they shall be flogged with iron clubs. Each time they try to leave hell to extricate themselves from their torture, they shall be dragged back by demons, who will say to them, "Taste the pain of flames".' See *Alcoran*, ch.8. [This is a possible allusion to the sura 'Sad', XXXVIII, vs. 57 of *Koran*: "They will savour boiling and stinking water, and all manner of similar things." Cf. Jacques Berque, *The Koran: An Attempt at a Translation* (Albin Michel), p. 491.]
The Koran has a great deal to say about Hell, as opposed to what it reveals about Paradise, and the description of the torments and punishments for disbelief and unbelievers, etc., are particularly graphic. The passages d'Holbach quotes above are as follows, from a modern translation in English: 'If only you [Prophet] could see, when the angels take the souls of the disbelievers, how they strike their faces and backs: it will be said, "Taste the punishment of the Fire. This is caused by what your own hands have stored up for you: God is never unjust to His creatures",' (8: 50—51). 'But the evildoers will have the worst place to return to: Hell to burn in, an evil place to stay—all this will be theirs: let them taste it—a scalding, dark, foul fluid, and other such torments', (38: 55—58).

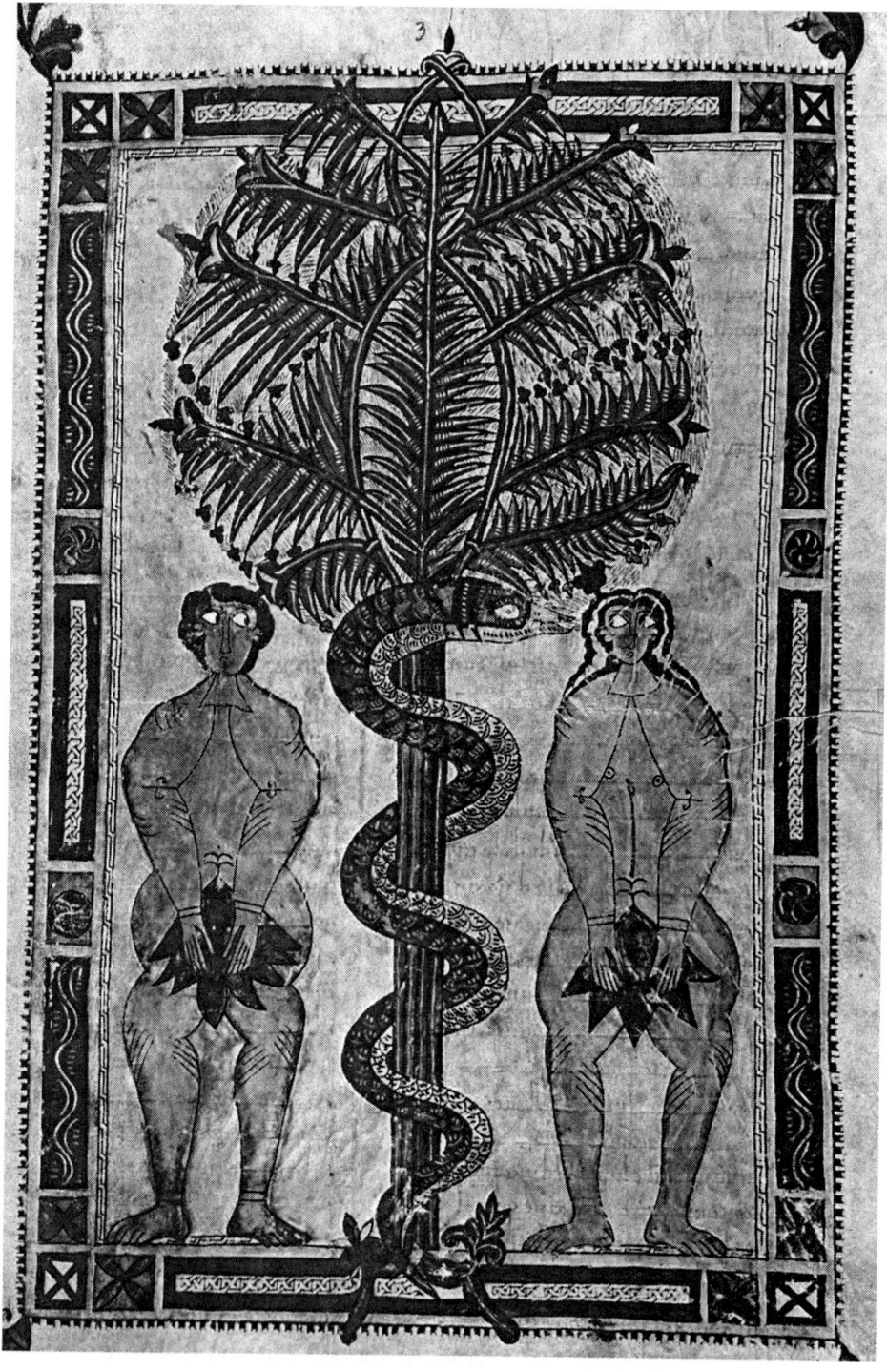

Figure 21: *Original Sin.* Illuminated parchment (*c.* 950—955). (Source: Wikipedia.)

Chapter 9

On Rites and the Mysterious Ceremonies, or on Christian Theurgy.[1]

iven that the dogmas taught by the Christian religion are mysteries inaccessible to human rationality, and that the god they proclaim is an unknowable god, it should not surprise us that its unintelligible, mysterious tone extends to its rites and ceremonies. Under a god who has revealed himself only to confound human reasoning, everything must be incomprehensible and make common sense appear wrong.

The most important Christian ceremony and the one without which no man can be saved is called *baptism*: it consists of pouring water on the head of a child or an adult whilst invoking the Trinity. By the mysterious virtue of this water and the words accompanying it, man is spiritually *regenerated*: he is washed clean of the stains of sin handed down from race to race, from the time of the first father of the human race. In a word, he becomes a Child of God and thereby he is capable of entering into glory when he leaves this world. However, according to Christians, people die only as a consequence of Adam's sin, and if this sin is washed away through baptism, how is it then that Christians still succumb to death? We may well be told that it is a spiritual death, not a physical one, from which Jesus Christ has delivered mankind. However, this spiritual death is nothing other than sin, and so in that case, how is it that Christians continue to sin as if they had never been redeemed and delivered from it? From this we see that baptism is a mystery which defies reason and which experience proves to be ineffective.[2] In some

---

[1] **Theurgy is the kind of magic which was performed by the help of benevolent spirits.**
Theurgy is: 'a system of magic, originally practised by the Egyptian Platonists, to procure communication with beneficent spirits, and by their aid produce miraculous effects; in later times [it is] distinguished as 'white magic' from goety or 'black magic'. Or: [it is] the operation of a divine or supernatural agency in human affairs; the effects produced among men by direct divine or spiritual action.' (*The Oxford English Dictionary* [O.U.P., 2002].)

[2] **The baptismal ceremony was practised as part of the mysteries of Mythras: initiates were regenerated through it. Mythras was also a mediator. Although Christian Doctors of the Church regard baptism as essential for salvation, we note that St Paul did not want to baptize the Corinthians. We also see that he circumcised Timothy. (For Mythras—see Glossary.)**
With reference to Paul not baptising, but simply preaching the Gospel, it is stated in 2 Corinthians: 'For Christ sent me not to baptize, but to preach the gospel: not with wisdom of words, lest the cross of Christ should be made of none effect', (2 Cor. 1: 17). With reference to Timothy: 'Then came he to Derbe and Lystra: and, behold, a certain disciple was there, named Timotheus, the son of a certain woman, which was a Jewess, and believed; but his father was a Greek: Which was well reported of by the

Christian sects, a bishop or a pontiff, on pronouncing some words and applying a little oil to the forehead, makes the Holy Spirit descend upon an infant or upon a young man: through this ceremony, the Christian is *confirmed* in the faith and he receives—invisibly—a whole host of blessing from the Most High. Of all Christians there are some who, having most completely abandoned their reason and entered most fully into the inconceivable ethos of their religion and not being content with the mysteries they share with the other sects, they give credence to a particular belief, which is bound to cause the strangest of surprises—it is the doctrine of *transubstantiation*. At the awesome voice of a priest, the Lord of the Universe is forced to descend from his glorious dwelling–place to change into bread; this 'bread–become–God' is an object of veneration by a people who boast that they detest idolatry.[3]

In such puerile ceremonies, to which these enthusiastic Christians attach the greatest value, one cannot but notice the pronounced vestiges of *theurgy* practised amongst peoples of the East. The divinity, forced by the power of a few magical words which accompany their ceremonies, obeys the voice of his priests or of those who know the secret of how to trigger this sorcery, and God performs miracles at their bidding. This sort of *magic* is perpetually practised by Christian priests: they make their disciples believe that these set phrases, handed down by tradition, and these arbitrary acts and movements of

---

brethren that were at Lystra and Iconium. Him would Paul have to go forth with him; and took and circumcised him because of the Jews which were in those quarters: for they knew all that his father was a Greek. And as they went through the cities, they delivered them the decrees for to keep, that were ordained of the apostles and elders which were at Jerusalem. And so were the churches established in the faith, and increased in number daily', (Acts 16: 1—5).

[3] **The Brahmins of Hindustan distribute rice in their pagodas: this distribution is called *Prajadam*, or Eucharist. Mexicans believe in a transubstantiative power. Father Acosta mentions this in Book V, ch. 24 of his *Travels*. Thus, it is not just the Roman Catholics who have gone in for this extravagant notion. Cicero believed that the human mind was incapable of being pushed so far into a delirious state so as to eat its own god. See *De Divinatione*, Book II. Protestant believers were courageous enough to reject this mystery, even though it was formally established by Jesus Christ, who stated quite clearly, 'Take, eat, this is my body.' Averroës said; 'Anima mea sit cum Philosophis, non vero cum Christianis, gente stolidissima, qui Deum faciunt et comedunt.' Peruvians had a passover during which they sacrificed a lamb, whose blood they mixed with flour and distributed it amongst the people. See *Alnetane quaest.*, Bk. II, ch. 20, § 5. (For Acosta, Averroës, Cicero—see Glossary. For transubstantiation—see p. 329.)** In fact, the Latin should read 'Sit anima mea cum Philosophis...' and it means 'I would really much prefer my mind to be on the side of the philosophers, rather than with the Christians, who are a most stupid people as what they make into a god, they eat.'

their bodies, are all capable of forcing the God of Nature to suspend his laws, to fall in with their wishes and pour out his grace.

Thus, in this religion the priest acquires the right to command God himself: this is how he uses his power over his God and it is on the basis of this actual theurgy, or upon this mysterious deal made between heaven and earth, that the puerile and ridiculous ceremonies, which Christians call sacraments, are founded.

We have already seen this theurgy in baptism, in confirmation, and in the Eucharist; we find it again in the act of *penitence*, that is the power which priests of some sects take upon themselves to pardon sins confessed to them in the name of Heaven. The same theurgy is at work in those who have taken religious orders and it is played out in ceremonies which impart to a few men a holy character and distinguishes them from lay mortals. The same theurgy is at work in the functions and rites which plague the last moments of the dying man, and even in marriage, when the Christian supposes that this natural union could not be approved of by Heaven unless validated by the ministry of a priest who obtains the Almighty's approbation for the couple.[4]

In a word, we see this white magic, or theurgy, in *prayers*, in set phrases, in liturgy and in all Christian ceremonies: we find it in their belief that words, when arranged in a certain manner, can alter the will of their god and force him to change his immutable decrees. Its efficacy can be witnessed in *exorcisms*, that is to say, in ceremonies, through which, with the help of magical water and a few words, they believe they can cast out evil spirits who infest humankind. *Holy water*, which amongst Christians has taken the place of the Romans' *lustral water*, possesses, according to them, the most astonishing virtues: it turns places and objects, previously considered profane, into sacred things.

Christian theurgy, when used by a pontiff in a royal rite, contributes to making heads of nations more respectable in the people's eyes and imparts a wholly divine character upon them.

Hence, all is mystery, all is magic, all is incomprehensible in these dogmas, as everything else is in a religious cult revealed by a deity, whose purpose was to deliver humanity from its blindness.

---

[4] **Roman Catholics believe in seven sacraments, which is a cabbalistic, magical, mystical number.** (For **Cabbala**—see Glossary.)

Figure 22: Holy Water containers at Lourdes, France.
Photo by Jean-Noël Lafargue. (Source Wikipedia under Copyleft Licence.)

Chapter 10

On Christian Holy Books.

To convince us of its celestial origins, the Christian religion bases its credentials on books which it regards as sacred and inspired by God himself. So let us now look and examine whether these works really are founded on, and bear the real marks of, wisdom and omniscience—all qualities which we attribute to the Divinity.

The *Bible*, the object of Christian veneration in which there is not a single word that has not been inspired by God, consists of an incongruous hotchpotch of sacred Hebrew books, known under the name of the *Old Testament*, combined with more recent works, equally inspired by the founder of Christianity, known under the name of the *New Testament*. At the beginning of this collection, which serves as the Christian religion's foundation and code of law, are five books attributed to Moses, who, we are told, was no more than the divinity's secretary while he wrote them. Moses goes back to the origin of things: he wants to initiate us into the mystery of the world's creation, despite his having only the vaguest, confused idea about what he is writing, betraying at every turn a profound ignorance of the laws of physics. God creates the sun, which is the light–source for our planetary system, several days after he has created light itself.[1] God, who himself

---

[1]   It is not commonly known or admitted by Christian apologists that there are in fact two contradictory accounts of the creation of the world. In fact, scholars have found so many variations and mutually contradictory passages within just the first eleven chapters of Genesis that this has led them to conclude that the first part of the book is an amalgamation of two separate sources which developed independently of each other, and have been rather clumsily spliced together. This hypothesis, which can be applied to the whole of the Pentateuch—the first five books of the Bible attributed to Moses—is set out in detail in Greenberg's book *101 Myths of the Bible* (see Bibliography). Of the two creation accounts he writes: 'Genesis begins with two separate and contradictory stories about Creation. The first, in Genesis 1—2: 3 and attributed to the priestly source P, presents the familiar account of the seven days of Creation , in which the process unfolds in an orderly and structured sequence of events from the formation of heaven and earth to the production of vegetation, animal life, and humanity. Contrary to popular belief, the first Creation story makes no mention of Adam and Eve being created in the image of God. The only reference to humanity is to an entity created on the sixth day that is described as both male and female, and it is this collective entity, male and female, that is created in God's image. The second account, in Genesis 2 and attributed to the Yahwist source J, serves as an introduction to the story of Adam and Eve and their children. This version of Creation is less complete than the priestly version. The two stories differ in many details. Each provides a different order of Creation and different explanations as to how things came about. Perhaps the most significant difference deals with the question of morality. The first Creation features no talk about moral principles. The second, which serves

cannot be represented by any image, creates man after his own image: he creates *male* and *female* and, soon forgetting what he had created, he creates woman from the man's rib. In a word, from the very first pages of the Bible we see only ignorance and contradictions.[2] All this proves to us that Hebrew cosmology is but a tissue of fables and allegories incapable of giving us any idea of things, fit only to appeal to a primitive people who are ignorant and unschooled, strangers to science and rational thinking.

In the rest of the books attributed to Moses we see a mass of improbable, fantastical stories and a stack of ridiculous, arbitrary laws. In fact, the author concludes by reporting his own death.[3] The books after Moses are no less replete with ignorance: Joshua stops the sun in its rotation;[4] **Samson**, the **Hercules** of the Jews, has the strength to topple a temple... One could endlessly point out all the blunders and fables that all passages of this work contain, which Christians have the nerve to attribute to the Holy Spirit. The whole history of the Hebrews merely presents us with a mass of tales unworthy to be considered seriously as history and as a reflection of the majesty of the Divinity: ridiculous when viewed rationally, it seems to have been invented only to pander to the credulity of an infantile, stupid people.

---

as an introduction to the stories of Adam and Eve and their children Cain and Abel, deals primarily with issues of moral concern. In it, we have commandments by God about proper behaviour, tales of sin, murder, and punishment, and something known as the Tree of Knowledge of Good and Evil. The second Creation story introduces some of the central moral principles of Western Civilization, such as original sin, moral accountability for one's actions, being our brother's keeper, and the role of marriage. In addition, the two versions present different images of the deity. The P source portrays an all-powerful disembodied spirit who can summon forth elements of the universe with a word, wink, or snap of the fingers. The deity in J has corporal form, likes to putter around in the garden, bake animal crackers, sculpt little figurines, go for strolls, and oversee the help as they take care of the house, like a dilettante managing the country estate.' (Gary Greenberg, *101 Myths of the Bible: How Ancient Scribes Invented Biblical History* [Illinois: Sourcebooks, Inc., 2002], pp. 7—8.)

[2] **St Augustin confesses that there is no way of holding to the literal sense of the first three chapters of Genesis without wronging religion and attributing things to God which are unworthy of him, thus forcing the believer to have recourse to allegory. See St Augustine, *De Genesi, conta Manichaeos*, Book I, ch. 2. Origen also agrees that if we take the biblical account of creation literally, it is absurd and contradictory. See *Philos.*, p. 12. (For Augustin, St, and Origen—see Glossary.)**

[3] See **Moses** in the Glossary.

[4] 'Then spake Joshua to the Lord in the day when the Lord delivered up the Amorites before the children of Israel, and he said in the sight of Israel, "Sun, stand thou still upon Gibeon; and thou, Moon, in the valley of Ajalon." And the sun stood still, and the moon stayed, until the people had avenged themselves upon their enemies. Is not this written in the book of Jasher? So the sun stood still in the midst of heaven, and hasted not to go down about a whole day', (Josh.10: 12—13).

This amorphous compilation is interposed with obscure and incoherent oracles, by which various visionaries or prophets have successively satiated Jewish superstition. In a word, everything in the Old Testament exudes enthusiasm, fanaticism, and ranting and raving, often couched in pompous language: there is everything there, apart from common sense, clear logic and rationality, which seem to have been doggedly excluded from the book—and all this serves as the Hebrews' and Christians' guide to life.

The abject and frequently absurd ideas which this book conveys about the Divinity have already been pointed out: God seems ridiculous in all his behaviour, blowing hot and cold, contradicting himself at every turn, acting unwisely, repenting for having done what he has done, building up with one hand only to destroy with the other, retracting through the voice of one prophet that which had already been announced by another. At one turn God punishes by death the whole human race for a sin committed by a single man, only to announce through Ezekiel that he is just and does not hold children responsible for the sins of their fathers.[5] The Divinity orders the Israelites through Moses to plunder the Egyptians, yet in the *Ten Commandments*, issued as part of the Law of Moses, it is forbidden to steal and kill. In a word, Jehovah is constantly in a state of self–contradiction in the book inspired by his own Holy Spirit—he changes with the wind, never

---

[5]   The writer is probably referring to a passage in Ezekiel, which expresses the Covenant which God made with the Children of David, i.e., the Israelites, where it appears that God is saying that, despite the waywardness of his chosen people, he is willing to forgive past sins and continue to bless Israel as a nation. 'And David my servant shall be king over them; and they all shall have one shepherd: they shall also walk in my judgments, and observe my statutes, and do them. And they shall dwell in the land that I have given unto Jacob my servant, wherein your fathers have dwelt; and they shall dwell therein, even they, and their children, and their children's children for ever: and my servant David shall be their prince for ever. Moreover I will make a covenant of peace with them; it shall be an everlasting covenant with them: and I will place them, and multiply them, and will set my sanctuary in the midst of them for evermore', (Ezek. 37: 24—26). As d'Holbach points out elsewhere, David is a strange choice for king, given that he is a murderer and double adulterer. Be that as it may, previous promises made to the Israelites have not been so generous, and there are a number of texts in which God promises to keep on exacting punishment, generation after generation, for misdemeanours committed by former generations. See 'Thou shalt not bow down thyself to them, nor serve them: for I the Lord thy God am a jealous God, visiting the iniquity of the fathers upon the children unto the third and fourth generation of them that hate me', (Exod. 20: .5). 'Keeping mercy for thousands, forgiving iniquity and transgression and sin, and that will by no means clear the guilty; visiting the iniquity of the fathers upon the children, and upon the children's children, unto the third and to the fourth generation', (Exod. 34: 7). Clearly there is a great lack of consistency in the way God behaves, just as d'Holbach points out.

maintaining any uniformity of conduct, and he often paints himself in tyrannical colours, enough to make the most hardened criminal blush.

Likewise, if we cast our eyes over the New Testament we shall see nothing indicative of the spirit of truth, which reputedly dictated this work. Four historians, or fabulists, wrote a fantastical story about the Messiah with little agreement between themselves on the details of his life, sometimes contradicting each other in the most glaringly obvious way. The genealogy of Christ as set down by Matthew does not resemble that of Luke; one gospel writer has Christ make a trip to Egypt, but another makes not a mention of this flight;[6] one writer has Christ's mission last three years, another claims it was only three months.[7] Nor do we see any more consistency over events recorded by several writers: St Mark says that Jesus died at the third hour, that is, at nine o'clock in the morning, whereas St John says that he died at the sixth hour, which is midday.[8] According to SS Matthew and Mark, the women who visited Jesus' tomb after his death saw only a single angel, but in

---

[6]   The genealogy of Christ is outlined in the Gospel of Matthew 1 and again in Luke's Gospel (ch. 3); the two versions are radically different. This is an old chestnut which Christian apologists have tried to explain away down the ages and a fact that non-believers have made much of because it would appear to show clearly that the Scriptures are neither infallible nor divinely inspired. Eusebius (AD c. 260—339) offers a rather rambling explanation for this anomaly in his *History of the Church*, Bk. I, §7, which some readers may find convincing: see Eusebius, *The History of the Church* (Penguin Classics, 1989), pp. 20—23, and Glossary and Bibliography in this volume. The Gospel of Matthew mentions the flight into Egypt in Matthew 2, but none of the other gospel writers mention this trip.

[7]   The length of Jesus' ministry is not clear, as d'Holbach states: the Apostle John mentions three Passovers (John 2: 13; 6: 4, and 13: 1), which would indicate a three-year period, but Christ's ministry had not started at the period in time of John ch. 2, because Jesus was still gathering his disciples. In the Gospels of Matthew, Mark and Luke, Jesus is baptised, then he is led into the wilderness for forty days and he subsequently disappears for nine months, which would appear to indicate that a two-year ministry (plus a few months) is more likely. Some believe that his ministry was only one year in duration, but others estimate the time to be but a few months. Many scholars have tried to make a detailed chronology of the life of Christ and few manage to agree with each other, proving the point d'Holbach makes here. What is clear is that the Bible does not state categorically how long Christ's ministry was, which is strange—one would have thought this to be a vital piece of information, especially when the Gospels purport to present a detailed account of his life and teaching.

[8]   'And it was the third hour, and they crucified him', (Mark 15: 25). 'And it was the preparation of the passover, and about the sixth hour: and he saith unto the Jews, "Behold your King!" But they cried out, "Away with him, away with him, crucify him." Pilate saith unto them, "Shall I crucify your King?" The chief priests answered, "We have no king but Caesar." Then delivered he him therefore unto them to be crucified. And they took Jesus, and led him away', (John 19: 14—16). Even allowing for a delay between the pronouncement of the sentence of crucifixion and the actual carrying out of the act, there is a considerable discrepancy in time.

the account of SS Luke and John they saw two angels.[9] These angels were outside the tomb according to some gospel writers, but inside, according to others. Several miracles of Jesus are even more diversely reported by the evangelist witnesses, or by mystics, and the case is the same with his appearances after his resurrection. Do not all these things make us doubt the infallibility of the evangelists' accounts and the reality of their divine inspiration? What can we say of the false and dreamt–up prophecies attributed to Jesus in the gospels? For example, St Matthew claims that Jeremiah predicted that *Christ would be betrayed for thirty pieces of silver*, but this prophecy is nowhere to be found in Jeremiah.[10] Nothing is more confusing than the way in which the Christian Doctors of the Church extract

---

[9] 'In the end of the sabbath, as it began to dawn toward the first day of the week, came Mary Magdalene and the other Mary to see the sepulchre. And, behold, there was a great earthquake: for the angel of the Lord descended from heaven, and came and rolled back the stone from the door, and sat upon it. His countenance was like lightning, and his raiment white as snow: and for fear of him the keepers did shake, and became as dead men. And the angel answered and said unto the women, "Fear not ye: for I know that ye seek Jesus, which was crucified",,' (Matt. 28: 1—5). However, Mark 16: 4—7 states: 'And when they looked, they saw that the stone was rolled away: for it was very great. And entering into the sepulchre, they saw a young man sitting on the right side, clothed in a long white garment; and they were affrighted. And he saith unto them, "Be not affrighted: Ye seek Jesus of Nazareth, which was crucified: he is risen; he is not here: behold the place where they laid him. But go your way, tell his disciples and Peter that he goeth before you into Galilee: there shall ye see him, as he said unto you".' In the Matthew account the angel is sitting outside the tomb, but in the Mark account, he is inside. There is also a disparity when the women arrived at the tomb: in the Matthew version, they actually see the stone being rolled away, but in the Mark version, the tomb is already open when they get there. The St Luke account has: 'And they found the stone rolled away from the sepulchre. And they entered in, and found not the body of the Lord Jesus. And it came to pass, as they were much perplexed thereabout, behold, two men stood by them in shining garments: And as they were afraid, and bowed down their faces to the earth, they said unto them, "Why seek ye the living among the dead?",' (Luke 24: 2—5). St John writes: 'But Mary stood without at the sepulchre weeping: and as she wept, she stooped down, and looked into the sepulchre, and seeth two angels in white sitting, the one at the head, and the other at the feet, where the body of Jesus had lain. And they say unto her, "Woman, why weepest thou?" She saith unto them, "Because they have taken away my Lord, and I know not where they have laid him",' (John 20: 11—13).

[10] 'Wherefore that field was called, the field of blood, unto this day. Then was fulfilled that which was spoken by Jeremy the prophet, saying, And they took the thirty pieces of silver, the price of him that was valued, whom they of the children of Israel did value; And gave them for the potter's field, as the Lord appointed me', (Matt. 27: 5—10). D'Holbach is correct in saying there is no such prophesy recorded in Jeremiah.

83

themselves from these difficulties. Their answers are made only for men who have made it their duty to remain in a state of blindness.[11]

---

[11] **Theophylactus says that nothing proves more surely the true faith of the Evangelists than the fact that they do not agree on all points, '[...] for without these differences, one might suspect that they had conspired to write their accounts.' See *Theophylactus premium in Matthaeum*. St Jerome himself says that the quotations of St Matthew do not agree with the Greek version of the Bible: 'Quanta fit inter Matthaem et Septuaginta, verborum, ordinisque discordia, sic admiraberis, si Hebraïcum videas, sensusque contrarius est.' See Hieronymus, *De opto genere interpretationis*. Erasmus is forced to admit that the Holy Spirit allowed the Apostles to stray from the right path: 'Spiritus ille divinus, mentium apostolicarum moderator, passus est suos ignorare quaedam, & labi, etc.' In *Matthaeu*, Bk II, ch.6. In general, one has to have a robust faith if reading St Jerome is not enough to debunk the Holy Scriptures.** (For Theophylactus and Jerome/Hieronymus/Sophronius—see Glossary.) The first Latin quotation means, 'However great the disparity is between Mathew and the Septuagint, both in terms of vocabulary and word order, you would be amazed if you were to see the Hebrew and the sense were the opposite.' (Hieronymus, *On the Best Type of Translator*.) The second Latin quotation means, 'The Holy Spirit, the controller of the apostles' minds, suffered his own men to ignore certain things and to slip up.' It would have been impossible, in any case, for the gospel writers to confer, given that the four gospels were written at different times: Mark's gospel is generally accepted to be the earliest of the four accounts, being the shortest and presumably written during the decade preceding the destruction of Jerusalem in AD 70, i.e., many years after Christ's death, which alone raises a number of problems. Most scholars agree that it was used by Matthew and Luke in composing their accounts; more than 90 percent of the content of Mark's Gospel appears in Matthew's, and more than 50 percent in the Gospel of Luke. It appears that Mark's account has also been subject to editing and additions: 'The final passage in Mark (16: 9—20) is omitted in some manuscripts, including the two oldest, and a shorter passage is substituted in others. Many scholars believe that these last verses were not written by Mark, at least not at the same time as the balance of the Gospel, but were added later to account for the Resurrection. Mark's Gospel stresses the deeds, strength, and determination of Jesus in overcoming evil forces and defying the power of imperial Rome. Mark also emphasizes the Passion, predicting it as early as chapter 8 and devoting the final third of his Gospel (11—16) to the last week of Jesus' life. One of the most striking elements in the Gospel is Mark's characterization of Jesus as reluctant to reveal himself as the Messiah. Jesus refers to himself only as the Son of Man, and while tacitly acknowledging Peter's declaration that Jesus is the Christ, he nevertheless cautions his followers not to tell anyone about him', (*Britannica, 2008*). One can find such discrepancies and changes of emphasis in all the gospel accounts. For example, 'there has been considerable discussion of the actual identity of the author [of John's gospel]. The language of the Gospel and its well-developed theology suggest that the author may have lived later than John and based his writing on John's teachings and testimonies. Moreover, the facts that several episodes in the life of Jesus are recounted out of sequence with the Synoptics and the final chapter appears to be a later addition suggest that the text may be a composite. The Gospel's place and date of composition are also uncertain; many scholars suggest that it was written at Ephesus, in Asia

Any thinking man will be aware that all the ingenuity of sophistry could never reconcile such glaring contradictions and the strained efforts of interpreters will only prove the weakness of their cause. Is it by subterfuge, subtleties and lies that one might serve the Divinity?

We find the same contradictions and the same errors in the pompous gibberish attributed to St Paul. This man, filled with the Spirit of God, merely shows in his discourses and epistles the enthusiasm of a maniac. The most carefully studied commentaries cannot make us understand or reconcile the contradictions, the enigmas and the doubtful concepts with which all his works are full, nor his dubious behaviour, which is sometimes pro– and at other times anti–Judaism.[12] One cannot get any further enlightenment from any other works attributed to the Apostles. It would seem that these people, inspired by the Divinity, have come upon the earth merely to stop their disciples understanding anything about the doctrine they wanted to be taught about.

Minor, in about AD 100 for the purpose of communicating the truths about Christ to Christians of Hellenistic background', (*Britannica, 2008*).

[12] **St Paul tells us himself that he was caught up in a state of rapture. How? Why? And what did he learn? 'Ineffable things which man cannot understand.' In that case, what good purpose did this miraculous trip serve? But how can we rely on St Paul telling the truth when, in the Acts of the Apostles, he incriminates himself by lying before the High Priest saying he is being persecuted *because he is a Pharisee and because of the resurrection of the dead*: there are two untruths here—(i) because St Paul at this time was the most zealous apostle of Christianity and consequently he was a Christian and (ii) because the grievances held against him had not the slightest thing to do with the resurrection. See Acts of the Apostles 23: 6. If the apostles lie, how can we rely on their testimony? On the other hand, we see this great apostle changing his opinions and behaviour at every turn. At the Council of Jerusalem he goes head to head against St Peter, whose opinions favoured Judaism, whilst later on he himself conformed to Jewish rites. In fact he continuously goes along with the crowd, being all things to all men. He seems to have been an example to the Jesuits, whose behaviour was criticized in the Indies over their treatment of idolaters, whose cult they allied to that of Jesus Christ's.**

The passage to which d'Holbach refers is as follows: 'But when Paul perceived that the one part were Sadducees, and the other Pharisees, he cried out in the council, "Men and brethren, I am a Pharisee, the son of a Pharisee: of the hope and resurrection of the dead I am called in question." And when he had so said, there arose a dissension between the Pharisees and the Sadducees: and the multitude was divided. For the Sadducees say that there is no resurrection, neither angel, nor spirit: but the Pharisees confess both', (Acts 23: 6—8).

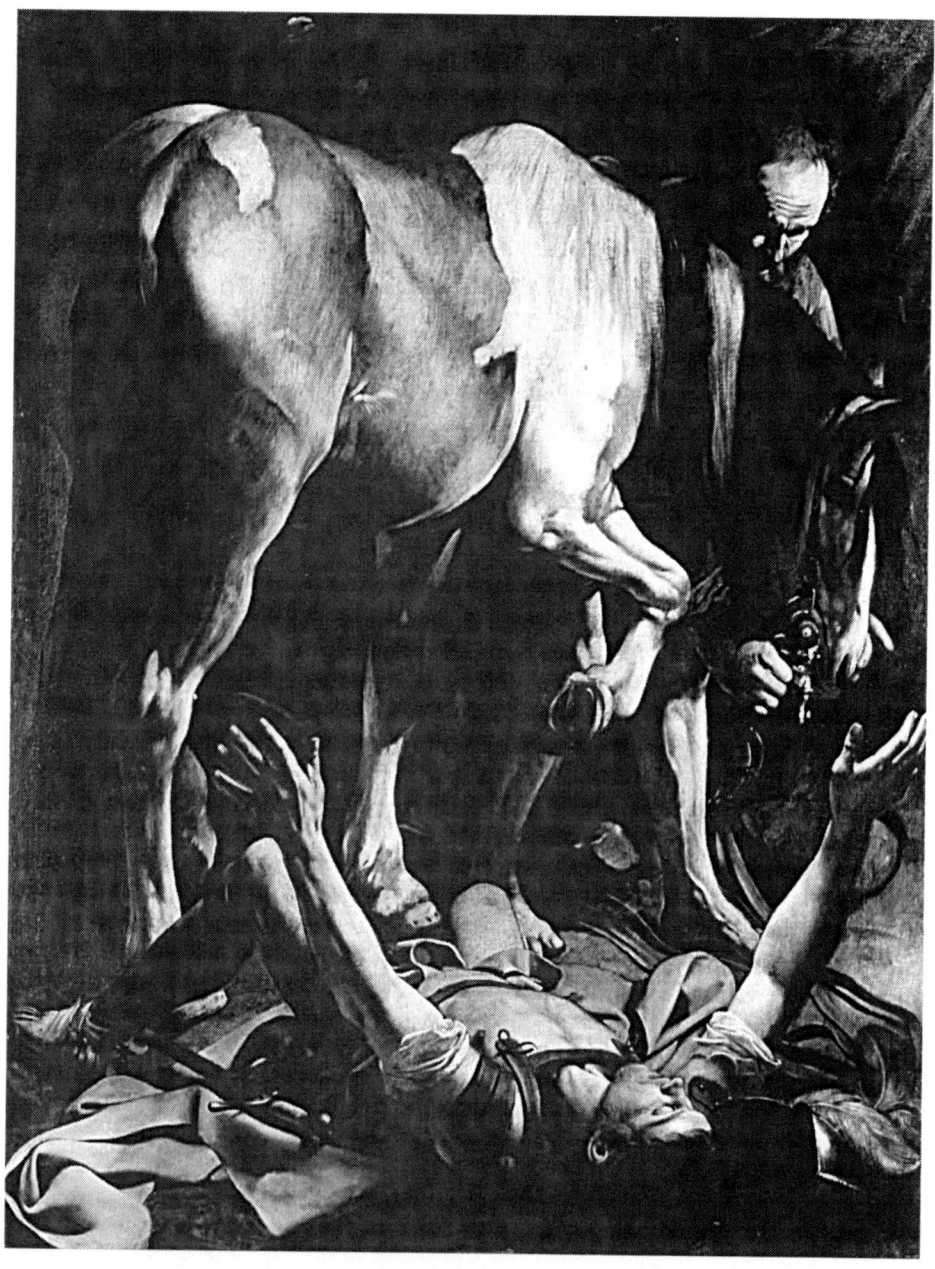

Figure 23: *The Conversion of Saint Paul,* Caravaggio (1601).

Finally, the collection of books which comprises the *New Testament* concludes with a mystical book, known under the name of the *Book of Revelation of St John*—an unintelligible work, by which the author wanted to outdo all the other gloomy, calamitous ideas contained in the Bible. In it John shows to an aggrieved human race the future outlook of a world bound to perish. He fills the imagination of Christians with terrible ideas, just ripe to make them tremble and to put them off their perishable life, rendering them useless or harmful to society.

This is how fanaticism crowns this compilation, revered by Christians but ridiculous and contemptible for anyone with an ounce of common sense. It is unworthy of a god full of wisdom and goodness, and detestable for anyone who considers all the ills that it has brought upon the world.

Ultimately Christians have never known where they stand because they have embraced a book such as the Bible as a rule–book for their behaviour and opinions—a work replete with terrifying fables and dreadful ideas about the Divinity, full of striking contradictions: they have never been able to agree on just how they are to interpret the whims of a changing and capricious god, and they have never known precisely what it is that God requires of them.

Hence this obscure book has been a bone of contention for Christians, an inexhaustible source of quarrels, and an arsenal in which the most fiercely opposed parties have equipped themselves equally with arms. Geometricians do not have a single dispute on the fundamental principles of their science. What is it that has made the Christians' revealed book, containing the fundamentals of their divine religion on which their eternal happiness depends, so unintelligible and subject to disputes, which have so often bathed the earth in blood?

Judging by the effects it has had, shouldn't such a book rather be regarded as the work of an evil spirit, of a lying and dark spirit, rather than that of a god who is interested in the preservation and well–being of mankind, and who wants to enlighten them?

Figure 24: *Hell*, Folio 108r from the fifteenth–century *Book of Hours: Très Riches Heures du duc de Berry.*

Chapter 11

On Christian Morality.

If we go by what the Christian Doctors of the Church say, it would appear that before the arrival of the founder of their sect there was no real morality on earth: they depict the whole world plunged in darkness and crime. However, men have always required morality—a society without morality cannot survive. Before the advent of Jesus Christ, we see nations flourishing and enlightened philosophers continuously calling men to fulfil their duties. In a word, we find in Socrates, in Confucius, in the **gymnosophists** of India, maxims which are in no way inferior to those of the Christian Messiah. In paganism we find examples of fair–mindedness, humanity, patriotism, temperance, selflessness, patience and tenderness, which openly belie the claims of Christianity and which prove that before their founder there existed virtues far more real than those Christ came to teach us.

Did it take a supernatural revelation for men to realize that justice is necessary to maintain a society and that injustice only brings them closer to enemies who would harm them? Was it necessary for a god to speak to demonstrate to a community that they need to care for each other and offer mutual support? Did people need help from on high to discover that vengeance is an evil, that it is an outrage against the laws of the land, which, when they are just, exact retribution themselves on behalf of the citizen? Is pardon for offences not a consequence of this principle and do acts of hatred not drag on when people want to exact their own implacable vengeance? Is forgiving an enemy not the outcome of a grandeur of spirit which gives us the upper hand over those who offend us? Do we not gain the moral high ground by doing a good turn to our enemies? Does this kind of conduct not fit us for making friends of our enemies? Does anyone who wants to survive not perceive that vice, intemperance and voluptuous pleasure threaten longevity? And finally, has experience not proven to all thinking people that crime is an object of one's fellows' hatred, that vice is injurious to those same people who are infected by it, and that virtue attracts respect and love for those who cultivate it?

People have only to think about who they are, what their real interests are, and what the aim of society is, to understand that they are mutually dependent upon each other. Good laws will force them to be prudent and they will have no need of invoking rules from heaven, required for their preservation and happiness. Reason suffices to teach us our duties towards others of our species. What benefit can be derived from a religion, which continuously contradicts and degrades rationality?

Doubtless people will say that religion, far from contradicting morality, serves as a support for it and renders its obligations more sacred by giving it divine sanction. I reply that the Christian religion, far from supporting morality, makes it shaky and uncertain. It is impossible to provide a solid foundation for morality through the positive will of a changeable god who is partisan, capricious and orders justice and injustice, harmony and carnage, tolerance and persecution, from the same lips. I say that it is hopeless to follow the precepts of a rational morality under the influence of a religion which makes a merit out of zealotry, vehemence, and the most destructive fanaticism. I say that a religion which orders us to mimic a despot who delights in setting traps for his subjects, whose vengeance is implacable and who wills us to exterminate all those who have the misfortune to displease him, is incompatible with any moral code. The crimes with which Christianity, above all other religions, is sullied have as their only pretext the placating of a savage god, inherited from the Jews. The moral character of this god must necessarily govern the conduct of those who adore him.[1] If this god is changeable, those who adore him will be unpredictable and their morality will be arbitrary, along with their temperament.

All this is indicative of the source of uncertainty in which Christians find themselves when it comes to examining whether it is more in keeping with the spirit of their religion to *tolerate*, or to *persecute*, people of different opinions. Both parties find equally in the Bible the precise orders of the Divinity who authorizes such diametrically opposed conduct. Sometimes *Jehovah* declares that he hates idolatrous people and that they must be wiped out:[2] sometimes Moses forbids *damning the gods of other nations.*[3]

---

[1] **The good king St Louis remarked to his friend Joinville that, 'When a layman hears his Christian religion being maligned, he should defend it not merely by words but with *a good, sharp sword*, by striking the slanderer and unbeliever across the body, until the point penetrates.' See *Joinville*, published by Ducange, p. 2.** (For **Louis** and **Joinville**—see Glossary.)

[2] There are many verses in the Bible, particularly in the Old Testament, which express God's hate of other deities: 'And I will destroy your high places, and cut down your images, and cast your carcases upon the carcases of your idols, and my soul shall abhor you', (Lev. 26: 30). However, at another point in his dealings with the Israelites, God tells them that it is up to them whether they follow another religion, represented by idols, or Him; within the terms of the Old Testament it is unusual for God to offer such a choice: 'As for you, O house of Israel, thus saith the Lord God; "Go ye, serve ye every one his idols, and hereafter also, if ye will not hearken unto me: but pollute ye my holy name no more with your gifts, and with your idols",' (Ezek. 20: 39). Moses yet again gives the people of Israel a choice as to which religion they might follow: 'And the Lord shall scatter you among the nations, and ye shall be left few in number among the heathen, whither the Lord shall lead you. And there ye shall serve gods, the work of men's hands, wood and stone, which neither see, nor hear, nor eat, nor smell. But if from thence thou shalt seek the Lord thy God, thou

Sometimes the Son of God forbids persecution, but then afterwards he said himself that men should be *forced to enter into his kingdom*.[4] However, with the idea of a severe, cruel god deeply ingrained in their psyche and always at the forefront of their minds, rather than the concept of an easy–going god, true Christians have always believed that they were forced to show great zeal against those they believed to be God's enemies. They imagined that it was impossible to offend him by overindulging in fierceness for his cause. Notwithstanding God's orders elsewhere, Christians have almost always felt on sure ground when persecuting, tormenting and exterminating those whom they regarded as objects of celestial ire. Tolerance has only ever been a feature of cowardly Christians and those lacking in zeal—a temperament which has little in common with the god whom they serve.

Do true Christians not feel the need to be ferocious and bloodthirsty when the examples they have been set are 'saints' and 'heroes' of the *Old Testament*? Do they not find grounds to be cruel in the conduct of Moses, the lawgiver, who not once, but twice caused the blood of the Israelites to flow, who killed more than forty thousand victims for his god?[5] Do Christians not find justification for their own brutality in the treacherous barbarity of **Phineas**, of **Jael**, and of **Judith**? Do Christians not see in that perfect model of a king, **David**, a monster of barbarity, infamies, adulteries and mutiny, which in no way seemed to stop him from being 'a man after God's own heart'? In a word, everything in the Bible seems to proclaim to the Christian that it is by furious zeal one pleases the Divinity, and that this zeal is sufficient to cover all crimes in his eyes.

---

shalt find him, if thou seek him with all thy heart and with all thy soul', (Deut. 4: 27—29).

3   The verse d'Holbach is thinking of is possibly the following: 'Thou shalt not revile the gods, nor curse the ruler of thy people', (Exod. 22: 28).

4   'But I say unto you, Love your enemies, bless them that curse you, do good to them that hate you, and pray for them which despitefully use you, and persecute you', (Matt. 5: 44). Which verse d'Holbach had in mind when he writes about forcing people into the Kingdom of God is not clear: perhaps he refers to Jesus' parable about the man who had prepared a great feast, but no guests turned up, so he forced passers-by to come and take part in the banquet—Luke 14: 15—24. It is clear from Christ's comments that the parable is to do with entering God's Kingdom and there is an element of compulsion in the parable.

5   There are numerous incidents when people fall by the hundreds, and often by the thousands, in the books of Exodus and Numbers, which are glibly narrated: e.g., 'And the children of Levi did according to the word of Moses: and there fell of the people that day about three thousand men', (Exod. 32: 28). However, there is a veritable orgy of killing ordered by Moses, acting on the instructions of God, in the book of Numbers, when many thousand people are killed: 14,700 in Num. 16: 49; 24,000 in Num. 25: 9, and two further groups of 250 in Num. 16: 35 and Num. 26: 10. These victims of God's orders number in excess of forty thousand, as d'Holbach points out.

Figure 25: *David and Bathsheba*, Jan Massys (1562).
(Source: Wikipedia.)

Therefore, it comes as no surprise to see Christians mercilessly persecuting each other. When they have appeared at all tolerant, it was only because they were themselves persecuted or were too feeble to persecute someone else in return: as soon as they had the power, they made sure that they let the full force of it be known to all those who did not share the same opinions on all points of their religion. Since the foundation of Christianity we have seen different sects at loggerheads: we see Christians hating each other, dividing from each other, harming each other and treating each other with the choicest cruelty. We see sovereigns, imitators of David, supporting the fury of their squabbling priests and serving the Divinity by fire and the sword: we see kings themselves becoming victims of religious fanaticism, since Christians are respecters of none when they believe that they are obeying their god.

In a word, the Christian religion, which boasts of harmony and peace, has for centuries caused more devastation and bloodshed than all the superstitions of paganism taken together. It has built a wall of division between citizens of the same state, and unity and tenderness have been banished from families.[6] Being unjust and inhuman has become a duty. Under a pretty, iniquitous God, offended by man's errors, each person became iniquitous; under a vindictive, jealous god, each person felt obliged to enter into quarrels to avenge wrongs done to him; and ultimately, under a bloodthirsty God, the shedding of human blood became a merit.

These are the important services that the Christian religion has offered to morality. Let it not be said that it is through a shameful abuse of religion that these horrors have been wrought. A spirit of persecution and intolerance emanates directly from a religious ethos, whose source it believes is a god jealous of his power, who has formally issued orders for murder, whose devotees have been inhumane persecutors, and who, in a fit of anger, did not spare his own son. When serving a god with this kind of awful character, one is much surer of pleasing him by exterminating his enemies, than by leaving them to their own devices to offend their creator. Such a divinity of necessity serves as a pretext for the most injurious excesses: fervency for his glory serves as a veil, covering the zeal of all manner of impostors and fanatics who claim to be interpreters of heaven's will; a sovereign may believe that he might give himself over to the most heinous crimes, thinking that he can wash them in the blood of his god's enemies.

A natural consequence of the same principles means that an intolerant religion can only be conditionally submissive to the authority of temporal sovereigns. A Jew or a Christian may obey a head of a society only when his orders coincide with the arbitrary, and often insane, whims of his god. But who shall decide if a sovereign's orders, which are most advantageous to society, coincide with the whims of this god? It will doubtlessly be ministers of the Divinity, the interpreters of his oracles, the confidents of his secrets.

---

[6] In fact, Christ Himself admitted that his preaching would set familial members at odds with one another: "'But when they shall lead you, and deliver you up, take no thought beforehand what ye shall speak, neither do ye premeditate: but whatsoever shall be given you in that hour, that speak ye: for it is not ye that speak, but the Holy Ghost. Now the brother shall betray the brother to death, and the father the son; and children shall rise up against their parents, and shall cause them to be put to death. And ye shall be hated of all men for my name's sake: but he that shall endure unto the end, the same shall be saved",' (Mark 13: 11—13). Note also: "'The father shall be divided against the son, and the son against the father; the mother against the daughter, and the daughter against the mother; the mother in law against her daughter in law, and the daughter in law against her mother in law",' (Luke 12: 53).

Thus in a Christian state subjects must defer more to priests, rather than to their sovereign;[7] and all the more so if the sovereign offends the Lord, if he neglects his worship, if he refuses to accept God's dogmas, if he does not defer to the priests—then he must lose his right to govern the people, whose religion he endangers. What shall I say? If the life of such a sovereign is a stumbling block to his subjects, to God's reign, and to the Church's prosperity, he must be removed from among the living as soon as the priests give the order. A host of examples prove to us that Christians have often followed these detestable maxims: fanaticism has spurred subjects to take up arms against their legitimate sovereign a hundred times and has caused trouble in society. Under Christianity, priests were always the arbiters of kings' fates: it counted as little to these priests that everything on earth was overthrown, so long as religion was respected. Nations have been unwilling to serve their sovereign every time they were persuaded that their sovereign was unwilling to serve God. Sedition and regicide take on an aura of legitimacy to zealous Christians, whose duty is to obey god rather than men, and who could not, without risk to their eternal well–being, weigh up the pros and cons between the eternal and the temporal monarch.[8]

By following these disastrous maxims, stemming from the principles of Christianity since its foundation in Europe, it is not surprising that we often witness peoples in revolt and sovereigns so shamefully debased under priestly authority, and monarchs deposed by priests with armed fanatics rising up against temporal power and, ultimately, princes whose throats have been slit. And do Christian priests not find in the *Old Testament* their seditious views authorized by example? Does the example of David not justify the actions of rebels against a monarch? Usurping power, acts of violence and treachery, the most glaring manifestations of violations of human and natural rights—were not all these things legitimized by god's people and his leaders?

---

[7] There is no Christian who has not been taught from the cradle that *it is better to obey God than man*. But obeying God is nothing other than obeying his priests. God no longer speaks for himself—it is the Church which speaks on his behalf; and the Church is a corps of priests who can often find in the Bible that the sovereign is wrong, that laws are criminal, that the most sensible institutions are irreligious, and that tolerance is a crime.

[8] Enemies of the Jesuits have always maintained that they see the killing of a tyrant as a praiseworthy and legitimate action: it does not take much thought to decide whether Ehud did the right thing, or whether Jacobus Clemens [i.e., Jacques Clément] was a criminal or not, or whether Ravaillac was merely following the dictates of his conscience. St Thomas Aquinas formally preached regicide. See *Les coups d'Etat*, II, p. 33. Christian princes ought to tremble when thinking about the consequences of the principles of their religion. (For Ehud, Clément, Ravaillac, and Aquinas—see Glossary.)

So that is the support religion has lent to morality: the supreme principle of Christianity is to acknowledge the god of the Jews, that is to say a tyrant, whose supernatural whims destroy at every turn the rules required to sustain society. This god creates the just and the unjust, and his supreme will changes evil into good, crime into virtue; his whim overturns his own laws of Nature; he destroys human relations at his pleasure and, having jettisoned all obligations towards his creation, he seems to allow men not to follow any specific laws, apart from those he prescribes in differing circumstances through the voices of his interpreters and visionaries. These people preach nothing but submission when they are the bosses, but when they believe themselves wronged, they preach only revolt. Are they ever so weak? Then they preach tolerance, patience and tenderness. Are they ever so strong? Then they preach persecution, vengeance, pillaging and cruelty. They continuously find things in their holy books to authorize the contradictory maxims which they churn out: they can find commands diametrically opposed to each other in the oracles of their changeable, immoral god.

To found a moral code upon such a god, or equally upon books which contain contradictory laws, is to provide morality with an uncertain basis, by making it dependent upon the whims of those who speak in God's name and upon the temperament of each one of his worshippers.

Morality should be rooted in unchanging laws; a god who destroys these laws destroys his own handiwork. If this god is the progenitor of mankind, if he wants happiness for his creatures, if he is concerned for the conservation of our species, then he should want people to be just, human and beneficent: he should not wish for people to be unjust, fanatical or cruel.

All the above tells us what we should think of those Doctors of the Church who maintain that, without Christianity, no man can have either morality or virtue.[9] The very opposite is certainly more true and one might suggest that any Christian who would imitate his god and put into practice the often unjust and destructive orders having emanated from his mouth, must, of necessity, be wicked. Were we to be told that his orders are not always unjust and that frequently Holy Writ exudes beneficence, harmony and fairness, I should say that Christians must have an inconsistent moral code, which at one turn will be good, and at another—evil, according to their personal interest and disposition. From this it can be seen that by following their religious ideas, Christians cannot have espoused a true morality and they must continuously ebb and flow between criminality and virtue.

---

[9] See my comments on p. vi in the Preface on remarks made by the current Archbishop of York. Who says d'Holbach's work is dated?!

On the other hand, is there not a danger in allying morality to religion? Instead of shoring up morality, is lending it religion's support not to render it feeble and ruinous? In reality, religion does not stand up to scrutiny and any man who discovers the weakness and the falseness of its fundamental evidence will be tempted to believe that this morality is just as much a chimera as is the religion on which it is based.

Thus it is that often, after having thrown off the yoke of religion, we see perverse men abandoning themselves to debauchery, intemperance and crime. When breaking the bonds of superstition, they fall into complete anarchy and believe that all is permissible because they have discovered that religion was but a fable.[10]

Unfortunately, this is why the words *unbeliever* and *libertine* have become synonymous. We would never have fallen into this danger if, instead of teaching a theological morality, we were to teach a natural morality. Instead of forbidding debauchery, crime and vice because God and religion forbid these faults, we should teach that all forms of excess are harmful for the preservation of mankind and make people contemptible in society's eyes, and that reason forbids it because it wants to sustain humanity, and that Nature prohibits it because it works for man's durable happiness.

In a word, notwithstanding God's desires, and independent of the rewards and punishments promised by religion in another life, it is easy to prove to anyone that it is in their interest in this world to take care of their health, to respect the mores of others, to gain respect from one's fellow human beings, and ultimately to be modest, temperate and virtuous.

---

[10] These sentiments can be found in many places in Dostoevsky's *œuvre*, for example in his novel *The Brothers Karamazov*, where Ivan Fyodorovich Karamazov is reported to have said, '...for every separate person, like ourselves for instance, who believes neither in God nor in his own immortality, the moral law of nature ought to change immediately into the exact opposite of the former religious law, and that egoism, even to the point of evildoing, should not only be permitted to man but should be acknowledged as the necessary, the most reasonable, and all but the noblest result of his situation.' (Part I, Book II, Chapter 6). The sentiments are repeated: 'Evildoing should not only be permitted but even should be acknowledged as the most necessary and most intelligent solution for the situation of every godless person!' Later in the novel, the famous axiom is expressed that, 'If God does not exist, then all is permitted.' The existentialist thinker Sartre took up this idea and it has been a platform for many twentieth-century ideologies. Of course, Dostoevsky was writing from a Christian standpoint and he equated socialism—especially in the form that it was expressed in Russia, in Bolshevism—with virtual nihilism and widespread destruction.

Those whose passions stop them from hearing such clear principles based on reason will not prove to be any more obedient to the voice of religion, which they will cease to believe in as soon as it proves to be at variance with their unregulated desires.

So let the boasting stop about the alleged advantages the Christian religion brings to bear upon morality. The principles which it draws upon from Holy Writ tend towards destroying morality; morality's alliance with religion only serves to weaken the former. Besides, experience shows us that Christian nations often have more corrupt mores than those which they call infidel and savage: the former are more subject to religious fanaticism and passion, fit only to banish justice and social virtue from society. For every credulous mortal whom religion holds in check, it pushes thousands of people into crime; for every man it makes chaste, it makes a hundred fanatics, a hundred persecutors, a hundred intolerant people—all much more harmful to society than the most imprudent debauchees, who only harm themselves.

At the very least, it is certain that the most Christian nations of Europe are not best known for being the places where morality is most manifest and observed. In Spain, Portugal and Italy, where the most superstitious sect of all Christianity has made it seat, people live in the most shameful ignorance of their social obligations: theft, murder, persecution and debauchery are all there in full measure; the superstitious abound and one sees very few virtuous men, and religion itself, complicit in crime, provides refuge for criminals and the easy means to make their peace with the divinity. Prayers, religious practices and ceremonies seem to relieve men of their duty of displaying virtue.

In countries which boast of possessing Christianity in all its purity, religion has so totally hijacked its followers' attention that they are entirely unaware of morality and believe that they have fulfilled all their social duties as soon as they show a scrupulous attachment to religious minutiae, which are totally at odds with what is needed for a healthy society.

Figure 26: *The Last Judgement.* Plate from *The Doré Gallery of Bible Illustrations* (1870)

Chapter 12

On Christian Virtues.

What has been noted already shows us what we ought to think of Christian morality. If we examine the virtues proposed by Christianity, we find that they bear the stamp of devotion, but they are not really appropriate for mankind in that they detract man's attention from the important things in life and they are of no practical use for society—indeed, they often have dangerous consequences for it.

In fact, in the precepts or advice that Jesus Christ came down to give us, we find merely extravagant, impossibly impracticable maxims, just rules which, if followed to the letter, would harm society: and in those precepts which might actually be practicable, we find nothing that was known any better by sages of antiquity, who did perfectly well without the aid of revelation.

The entire message of the Messiah, his whole law for us to follow, could be summed up as *love God above all else and one's neighbour as oneself.* Is this precept possible? Imagine loving an angry, capricious, unjust god, the god of the Jews! Are we to love an unjust, implacable god, who is cruel enough to condemn his creatures to eternal damnation?! Fancy loving the most fearsome object that the human mind has ever managed to dream up! Is such an object intended to evoke affection in the heart of man? How can one love that which one fears? How can one cherish a god under whose rod we are forced to tremble? Are we not kidding ourselves when we try to convince ourselves to love such a terrible, revolting being?[1] And is loving our neighbour as ourselves any more feasible? Every man, by his very nature, loves himself in preference to all others; he loves others only in so far as they contribute to his personal happiness; he becomes virtuous as soon as he does something good for his neighbour; he shows a generosity of spirit when he sacrifices his love of self for that of another; but he never loves his neighbour

---

[1] Seneca says quite rightly that a wise man cannot fear the gods, given that a person cannot love the object of his fears: *Deos nemo fanus timet, furor enim est metuere salutaria, nec quisquam amat quos timet. De beneficiis, 4.* The Bible tells us: *Initium sapientae, timor Domini* (Fear of the Lord is the beginning of wisdom). Should that not really be, 'the beginning of folly'? (For **Seneca**—see Glossary.) The first Latin quotation reads: 'No sane man fears there are gods for it is madness to fear that which is so much to our benefit and advantage, nor does anyone love that which he fears.' (*On Benefits*). The biblical reference is found in two verses, expressing similar sentiments: 'The fear of the Lord is the beginning of wisdom: a good understanding have all they that do his commandments: his praise endureth for ever', (Psalm 111: 10), and 'The fear of the Lord is the beginning of wisdom: and the knowledge of the holy is understanding', (Prov. 9: 10).

other than for the advantageous qualities he finds in him; he cannot love his fellow until he is acquainted with him, and the love he has for him is bound to be in keeping with what he gets out of him.

So to love one's enemies is an impossible precept. One can abstain from harming those who harm us; but love is a heart–felt emotion, stimulated within us only when we see something advantageous for ourselves. Just laws amongst a civilized people have always forbidden the taking of personal vengeance or taking the law into one's own hands; a spirit of magnanimity, a generosity of spirit, a courageous spirit, can all bring us to do good to those who offend us; at that moment we can become more magnanimous than our offender and we can even make such people have a change of heart. Hence, without having recourse to a supernatural moral code, we feel that suppressing vengeance in ourselves works towards our personal advantage.

So let Christians cease extolling the virtues of pardoning sins that only a god can grant and which proves the divine nature of his moral code. Long before the Messiah, **Pythagoras** said, 'We take revenge on our enemies by trying to make friends of them',[2] and **Socrates** says in his *Crito*, 'An offended man is not permitted to take revenge by committing another offence.'[3]

---

[2] In the writing of Diogenes Laertius on Pythagoras, we read: 'Another of his rules was that men should honour the Gods above the daemones, heroes above men; and of all men parents were entitled to the highest degree of reverence. Another, that people should associate with one another in such a way as not to make their friends enemies, but to render their enemies friends.' (From Diogenes Laertius, *Vitae philosophorum*, VIII, written around AD 200, section XIX, in *The Lives and Opinion of Eminent Philosophers by Diogenes Laertius: The Life of Pythagoras*, transl. by C.D. Yonge [London: Henry G. Bohn, 1853].)

[3] In *Crito* there are two general themes: (i) how one should repay evil or a wrong done to one, and (ii) the standing of a citizen *vis-à-vis* the state, and that of the slave to his master. In the end, Socrates decides to submit to his fate—the death sentence facing him. The work is written in a typical Socratic dialogue form, between Socrates and Crito:

Socrates: Then we must do no wrong?
Crito: Certainly not.
Socrates: Nor when the injured injure in return, as the many imagine; for we must injure no one at all?
Crito: Clearly not.
Socrates: Again, Crito, may we do evil?
Crito: Surely not, Socrates.
Socrates: And what of doing evil in return for evil, which is the morality of the many—is that just or not?
Crito: Not just.
Socrates: For doing evil to another is the same as injuring him?
Crito: Very true.

Undoubtedly, Jesus forgot that he was speaking to men when, in order to lead them to perfection, he told them to abandon their possessions to the greed of the first abductor who came along and to offer the other cheek to receive a further outrage, and not to resist even the most unjust violence, and to forego the perishable riches of this world, and to leave one's home, goods, parents and friends, in order to follow him, and to abstain from even the most innocent of pleasures.[4] Who does not see in this sublime council the language of fanaticism and hyperbole? Are these magical exhortations not made to discourage people and throw them into the depths of despair? Would not the literal implementation of these commands be destructive for society? What shall we say of such a moral code which orders the heart to disassociate itself from the objects that reason commands us to love? By refusing the benefits that Nature offers us, are we not spurning gifts granted to us by the Divinity? What real benefits can be derived for society from these cruel, melancholic virtues which Christians regards as perfection? Does a person really become of benefit to society when one's mind is perpetually troubled by imaginary terrors, by gloomy thoughts, by black anxieties, which prevent one from attending to what one owes to the family, to one's own country and to those around? Were people to fall in with these sad principles, would they not become as insufferable to themselves as they would be to others? It is generally agreed that fanaticism and obsession are at the root of Christ's morality. The virtues which he commends to us tend to isolate people, plunging them into a sombre mood and often render them harmful to their fellows. Here on earth we need human virtues, but Christians only see their advantages beyond our present reality; society needs

---

Socrates: Then we ought not to retaliate or render evil for evil to any one, whatever evil we may have suffered from him.
(Plato, *The Trial and Death of Socrates: Four Dialogues*, translated from the Greek by Benjamin Jowett [N.Y.: Dover Thrift Editions, 1992], p. 49. The full text can also be found on the Project Gutenberg website.)

[4] 'Jesus said unto him, "If thou wilt be perfect, go and sell that thou hast, and give to the poor, and thou shalt have treasure in heaven: and come and follow me",' (Matt. 19: 21). The command is repeated in other gospels: 'But I say unto you, That ye resist not evil: but whosoever shall smite thee on thy right cheek, turn to him the other also', (Matt. 5: 39), and again in Luke 6: 29. The command to follow unconditionally is also stated: 'And another also said, "Lord, I will follow thee; but let me first go bid them farewell, which are at home at my house." And Jesus said unto him, "No man, having put his hand to the plough, and looking back, is fit for the kingdom of God",' (Luke 9: 61—62); 'And every one that hath forsaken houses, or brethren, or sisters, or father, or mother, or wife, or children, or lands, for my name's sake, shall receive an hundredfold, and shall inherit everlasting life', (Matt. 19: 29). The would-be follower also has to abjure earthly delights: 'And that which fell among thorns are they, which, when they have heard, go forth, and are choked with cares and riches and pleasures of this life, and bring no fruit to perfection', (Luke 8: 14).

real virtues for its preservation, to give people energy and vitality; families need vigilance, affection and work; all people of the human race need the desire to obtain legitimate pleasures and add to the totality of their happiness.

Christianity is perpetually obsessed either by degrading people through paralyzing terrors, or by intoxicating them with frivolous hopes—both feelings are equally likely to distract them from their real duties. If Christians followed their law–giver's principles to the letter, they would always be useless or harmful members of society.[5] In fact, what advantages

---

[5] **Despite the praises which Christians heap upon their divine master's precepts, we find plenty of them which are totally contrary to fairness and right thinking. In fact, when Jesus said, 'Make for yourselves friends in heaven with riches you have acquired unjustly', does he not imply quite directly that it is all very well to steal from others to give alms to the poor? His spokesmen will no doubt tell us that he is speaking in parables, but it is easy to perceive the real sense. What is more, Christians often carry out their god's advice: many of them steal throughout their lives to afford themselves the pleasure of making donations upon their death to monasteries and hospitals. In another incident in the Bible, the Messiah treated his mother very badly when she was looking for him. He ordered his disciples to purloin an ass. He caused a herd of swine to be drowned, etc. In truth, none of these actions sit well with a good moral code.**

The biblical references to which d'Holbach refers are as follows: "'And I say unto you, make to yourselves friends of the mammon of unrighteousness; that, when ye fail, they may receive you into everlasting habitations",' (Luke 16: 9). As regards Christ's mistreatment of his mother, d'Holbach refers to the incident in Mark's Gospel when Christ was teaching in the synagogue at a very young age, while his parents were worried as to his whereabouts: 'There came then his brethren and his mother, and, standing without, sent unto him, calling him. And the multitude sat about him, and they said unto him, "Behold, thy mother and thy brethren without seek for thee." And he answered them, saying, "Who is my mother, or my brethren?" And he looked round about on them which sat about him, and said, "Behold my mother and my brethren! For whosoever shall do the will of God, the same is my brother, and my sister, and mother",' (Mark 3: 31—35). Christ's order to take possession of an ass or a donkey is narrated in Matthew's Gospel: 'And when they drew nigh unto Jerusalem, and were come to Bethphage, unto the mount of Olives, then sent Jesus two disciples, saying unto them, "Go into the village over against you, and straightway ye shall find an ass tied, and a colt with her: loose them, and bring them unto me. And if any man say ought unto you, ye shall say, 'The Lord hath need of them'; and straightway he will send them",' (Matt. 21: 1—3). The incident with the herd of pigs is narrated in the gospels of Matthew, Mark and Luke, when Jesus cast out an evil spirit and sent it into a herd of pigs, which promptly went and jumped off a cliff. Not surprisingly, the locals did not want Jesus hanging around any longer, given the damage he had done to the farmer's livestock. 'And when he was come to the other side into the country of the Gergesenes, there met him two possessed with devils, coming out of the tombs, exceeding fierce, so that no man might pass by that way. And, behold, they cried out, saying, "What have we to do with thee, Jesus, thou Son of God? Art thou come hither to torment us before the time?" And there was a good way off from them an herd of many swine feeding. So the devils besought him, saying, "If thou cast us out, suffer us

can mankind derive from these ideal virtues which Christians call *evangelical*, *divine* and *theological*, which they prefer to real, humane social virtues, since, without the former, they maintain that one cannot please God or enter into his glory?

Let us examine these much–vaunted virtues in detail and let us see what benefit they are to society, whether they really merit taking precidence over those which reason inspires in us as essential for the well–being of mankind.

The first of the Christian virtues is *faith*, which is fundamental to all the others, and it consists of an impossible conviction in revealed dogmas and absurd fables which Christianity commands its disciples to believe in.

Hence we see that this virtue demands a total renunciation of common sense, an impossible acceptance of improbable facts, a blind submission to the authority of priests as the sole guarantors of the veracity of the dogmas and marvels in which all Christians must believe, on pain of eternal damnation.

Although essential for everyone, this virtue is, however, a gift from Heaven—the fruit of special grace, and it forbids doubt and scrutiny, depriving people of the faculty to exercise reason and the freedom to think, and it reduces them to the mindless state of beasts on matters which are essential for eternal happiness. From this we can see that faith is a virtue invented by men who fear the light of reason, who wanted to hoodwink their fellows and subjugate them to their own authority, and who sought to degrade them to hold total sway over them.[6] If faith be a virtue, it is assuredly beneficial only to the spiritual guides of Christians, who are the sole beneficiaries of its fruits. This virtue can be nothing other than

---

to go away into the herd of swine." And he said unto them, "Go." And when they were come out, they went into the herd of swine: and, behold, the whole herd of swine ran violently down a steep place into the sea, and perished in the waters. And they that kept them fled, and went their ways into the city, and told every thing, and what was befallen to the possessed of the devils. And, behold, the whole city came out to meet Jesus: and when they saw him, they besought him that he would depart out of their coasts.' (Matt. 8: 28—34). In fact, Mark's gospel tells us that the pigs numbered about two thousand—no wonder the farmer asked Jesus to make himself scarce: see Mark 5: 13. Why could he not have simply destroyed the evil spirits without vandalizing the livestock? Having said that, as a Jew, Jesus would not have been fond of pork!

6   **St Paul said: '*Fides ex auditu*' ['faith from hearing'] which means that one must believe on the basis of *hearsay*. Faith is never anything other than adhering to priests' opinions. Faith is pious pigheadedness, which makes it unimaginable that priests might have fooled themselves and doubt that they could ever want to fool others. Faith has to be founded entirely on the good opinion we have of the priests' own enlightenment.** The verse referred to is, 'So then faith cometh by hearing, and hearing by the word of God', (Romans 10: 17).

disastrous for all other people whom it teaches to despise reason, which is that which distinguishes us from the animals and which can be our only sure guide through this world. In fact, Christianity represents our capacity for reasoning as perverted, as an unreliable guide, as an apparent acknowledgement that it was never made for thinking beings. However, should we not ask the Christian Doctors of the Church to what extent we should renounce our reason? Do they themselves not have recourse to it in certain cases? Is it not to this same reason that they appeal when trying to prove the existence of God? If this reason is perverted, how can they rely on it in a matter as important as being able to ascertain the existence of God?

Be that as it may, to claim that one believes in something one cannot conceive of is obviously a lie; to believe in something without being able to understand what it is that one believes in is an absurdity. Therefore, we need to weigh up our motives for believing. But what are the Christian's motives? It is his confidence in the guides who instruct him. But on what is this confidence founded? On revelation. But on what is this revelation itself founded? On the authority of spiritual guides. Such is the way in which Christians reason. Their arguments in favour of faith boil down to saying: *in order to believe in religion one has to have faith, and in order to have faith one has to believe in religion*; or, one needs to have faith already in order to believe in the necessity for faith.[7] Faith evaporates as soon as we engage our reason; as a virtue, faith does not stand up to sober scrutiny, and that is what makes Christian priests turn into the enemies of science. The founder of Christianity himself declared that faith was intended only for simple people and children.[8] Faith is the consequence of grace, which God never grants to enlightened people or to those accustomed to using their common sense; faith

---

[7] Several theologians have held the view in their works that faith alone is sufficient for salvation. Generally this is the virtue that priests most commonly advocate. At least, it is the one they rely on most for their own existence. Therefore, it is not surprising that they have sought to establish this virtue by fire and the sword. It was to promote faith that heretics and Jews were burned during the Inquisition; it was to lead people back to faith that kings and priests persecuted people; it was to reinforce faith that Christians exterminated all non-believers. Oh, what a wonderful virtue worthy of a god of grace! And his ministers punish mankind when they refuse his graces.

[8] 'And [Jesus] said, "Verily I say unto you, except ye be converted, and become as little children, ye shall not enter into the kingdom of heaven",' (Matt. 18: 3). 'At that time Jesus answered and said, "I thank thee, O Father, Lord of heaven and earth, because thou hast hid these things from the wise and prudent, and hast revealed them unto babes",' (Matt. 11: 25). 'In that hour Jesus rejoiced in spirit, and said, "I thank thee, O Father, Lord of heaven and earth, that thou hast hid these things from the wise and prudent, and hast revealed them unto babes: even so, Father; for so it seemed good in thy sight",' (Luke 10: 21).

is made only for people incapable of thinking, or for souls intoxicated by fanaticism, or for people irresistibly attached to the prejudices of their childhood. Science has been, and always will be, the target of hatred for the Christian Doctors of the Church, and they would be enemies of themselves if they liked scientists.[9]

A second Christian virtue—an extension of the first—is *hope*. Founded on the flattering promises Christianity makes to those who make themselves miserable in this world, *hope* nourishes their fanaticism and makes them lose sight of their earthly happiness, rendering them useless to society; it convinces them that God will reward in Heaven their uselessness, their black mood, their hate of pleasures, their senseless mortifications, their prayers and their inactivity. How can people, intoxicated with these pompous hopes, possibly apply themselves to the actual well–being of those around them, when they are indifferent to their own well–being? Do people not think that by making themselves miserable in this world they hope to please God? In fact, as flattering as the Christian concept of the future is, religion sours it by their jealous god's threats: he wants people to work out their own salvation with fear and trembling,[10] and would punish their presumptuousness and damn them unmercifully if they had the frailty of being human for a single moment in their life.

The third of the Christian virtues is *charity*, which consists of loving God and one's neighbour. We have already seen how difficult, if not impossible, it is to feel tenderness for any being whom we fear.

No doubt Christians would tell us that this fear is a *filial fear*,[11] but these words change nothing in essence: fear is an intense feeling totally opposed to love. A son who fears his father, who has good reason to dread his anger and who shudders at his whims, will never love him sincerely.

Therefore the love a Christian has for God can never be true; they will hardly want to respond to the tenderness of an ogre who surely strikes fear in their heart; they will never love him for anything other than because he is a tyrant to whom they have to pay respectful lip–service, which is not heart–felt. The staunch believer is not being honest with himself when he pretends to cherish his god; his tenderness is but a feigned tribute, like that people offer to inhuman despots who, even though they bring sorrow upon their

---

[9]   See pp. 323 *et seqq.* See also **Hypatia** in the Glossary.

[10] 'Wherefore, my beloved, as ye have always obeyed, not as in my presence only, but now much more in my absence, work out your own salvation with fear and trembling', (Phil. 2: 12).

[11] 'Like as a father pitieth his children, so the Lord pitieth them that fear him', (Ps.103: 13).

subjects, demand the outward signs of affection. If some tender souls, by dint of illusion, manage to whip up their emotions into a state of divine love, then it is the product of a mystical, romantic passion, produced by a frenetic state of mind through an over–active imagination, which makes these souls consider their god only from a most ridiculous aspect, by choosing to close their eyes to his real faults.[12]

A love of God is not the most inconceivable mystery of our religion.

The virtue *charity*, considered to be the love of our neighbour, is a virtuous and essential disposition of the mind. It is, however, no more than that tender humanity which those of our species share, which inclines us to offer help to those to whom we are attached. But then how can we reconcile this attachment with a jealous god's command that we should love only him, who came to separate the son from the father and friend from friend?[13] According to the maxims of the gospels, it would be a crime to offer to God a heart shared by another earthly object; it would be idolatry to allow that creature to compete with its creator.

In any case, how can one love beings who continually offend the Divinity, or those who represent a continuous threat of offending him? How can one love sinners?

Experience also shows us that religious bigots, obliged on principle to hate themselves, are not at all inclined to treat others better than themselves, to make life easier for others or to show any indulgence to anyone.

Those who treat people in that way have not arrived at a state of perfection in divine love. In a word, we see that those who make out that they love the Creator most ardently are not the same people who show the greatest sympathy for the wretchedness of their fellow creatures. On the contrary, we see them routinely pouring forth bile upon everything around them, sourly picking out mistakes amongst their peers and turning indulgence towards

---

[12] **Mystical devotion is the product of an ardent and impressionable temperament. Women who suffer from hysterics are frequently those who love God most keenly; they love him feverishly, as they might love a man. St Thésèse, Madeleine de Pazzi, Marie Alacoque, and almost all the most devoted nuns fall into this category. Their imagination makes them lose their reason and they surrender themselves to God, whom they depict with the most charming traits and with the affection which they are not allowed to offer to members of our species. Strong imagination is required to fall in love with an invisible object, and something much stronger still is required to love an object which has not the slightest loveable features; one really has to be mad to love something hateful. (For St Thérèse, Marie-Madeleine de Pazzi and Marie Alacoque—see Glossary.)**

[13] See footnote № 4, p. 101.

human frailty into a crime.[14] In fact, a sincere love for the Divinity must be accompanied by zeal. A true Christian has to become annoyed when he sees his god offended and he must arm himself with a just and righteous cruelty to repress the guilty, having, of necessity, an ardent desire to make religion reign supreme. It is this zeal, derived from a love of the Divine, which is the source of the persecution and fury which Christianity has so many times been guilty of using; it is a zeal characteristic of executioners and martyrs. It is the same zeal which makes the intolerant grasp the Almighty's thunderbolt from his very hands under the pretext of avenging his insults.

It is this kind of zeal which makes members of the same family and citizens of the same state hate each other, torment each other for their opinions and often over puerile ceremonies, which fanaticism makes them regard as of paramount importance.

It is such zeal which has kindled in our own continent of Europe a thousand religious wars, noted for their atrocity.

And finally, it is religious zeal which justified slander, treason and carnage—in a word, the most catastrophic disorders for society. It has always been permissible to employ trickery, treachery and lying, so long as it was to uphold God's cause.[15]

The most irascible men, the most quick–tempered and corrupt of men, are usually the most zealous; they hope that, as a reward for their zeal, Heaven will pardon the perversity of their ways and all their other forms of dissoluteness.

---

[14] In the most Christian of countries, religious bigots are usually regarded as the scourge of society: good company fears them as kill-joys, just like bores. A sanctimonious wife rarely has the talent to cope with loving her husband, children and others around her. Such a dreary, melancholic religion cannot have amiable disciples. A miserable god is bound to make miserable devotees. Christian Doctors of the Church have judiciously remarked that 'Jesus Christ cried, but he did not laugh'.

[15] The Ecumenical Council of Constance had Jan Hus and Jerome of Prague burned despite the Emperor's guarantee of safe-conduct. Several Christians have taught that one should never keep faith with heretics. Popes have issued a hundred sermons and oaths against the heterodox. Accounts of religious wars amongst Christians tell us of treachery, cruelty and perfidy without parallel example in other wars. All is permissible when fighting God's cause. In these wars we see nothing but children crushed against city walls, pregnant women disembowelled, young women raped and massacred. In the end, religious fanaticism brings out the inventive genius in man's savagery. (For **Jan Hus** and **Jerome of Prague**—see Glossary and also pp. 344 *et seqq.*)

Figure 27: Enraptured Nun - Natacha Trouhanowa in the play *Miracle*, E.O. Hoppé (1911).

It is as a consequence of this same zeal that we see fanatical Christians cross continents and seas in order to extend God's kingdom, to make proselytes for him and to acquire new minions. Similarly spurred on by the same zeal, missionaries believe they have an obligation to disturb the peace in states which they regard as infidel, whilst at the same time they would find it very odd if missionaries came into their country to declare a different law.[16]

---

[16] **Kamhi, Emperor of China, asked some Jesuit missionaries in Pekin, 'What would you say if I sent missionaries to your country?' We know all about the revolts Jesuits started in Japan and Ethiopia, which resulted in Christianity being completely banned. A holy missionary said: 'Missionaries without muskets were not up to making proselytes.'**
There is a problem with this footnote: even given the notorious difficulties of transliterating Chinese proper names across different languages, there was no Chinese emperor with a name remotely like Kamhi or Camhi, as it appears in the original text. There is also no mention of this emperor in the *Encyclopédie*, though the subject of Christian missionaries in China is explored: one emperor of China is reported as saying, 'If a knowledge of Jesus Christ was essential for our salvation and God truly wanted to save us, why has he left it so long to drag us out of our error?' (*Encyclopédie*, under the entry 'Philosophy of the Chinese' [Chinois, Philosophie des], III, p. 341.) D'Holbach is probably referring to Xu Guangqi (also known as Hsū-Kuang-ch'i), who lived in 1562—1633. He was not the emperor of China, but he rose to great heights within the royal court in China and it was he who invited Jesuit missionaries to China, not the emperor himself. The first Jesuits arrived in Shanghai in 1608 under the leadership of Lazzaro Cattaneo, an Italian Jesuit and Xu Guangqi fell under their influence and converted to Catholicism. He became the first of his countrymen to translate European books into the Chinese language, translating with Matteo Ricci, a Jesuit scholar of some note, Western books on mathematics, hydraulics, and geography. Their most famous translation was Euclid's *Elements* (*Chi-ho yüan-pen*), which exerted a great influence on Chinese mathematics. (See *China Heritage Quartely*, Dec. 2006, No.8. See also *Britannica*.) Christian Jesuit missionaries first arrived in Japan in 1549, through the influence and person of the Jesuit Francis Xavier, sponsored primarily by Portugal and Spain. Although there was a strong proselytizing element to the mission, there was always a serious commercial incentive—the Christian Church has never been slow to cash in on both the spiritual, as well as temporal, economic advantages. The writer of the very informative Wikipedia article on missionaries in Japan writes, 'Missionaries were not reluctant to take a military action if they considered it an effective way to Christianize Japan', and indeed they did take up arms and intervene in internal struggles in Japan. (See Wikipedia under the entry 'Kirishitan'.) In the *Encyclopédie*, under the entry 'Japon' [Japan], VIII, p. 453, the writer notes that the interference of Christian missionaries in Asia caused a great deal of unrest between the indigenous population and the adherents of their native religious belief, 'So the secular emperor of Japan banned Christianity in 1586 and forbade the practice of it on pain of death. However, trading with the Portugese and Spanish continued to be allowed, but missionaries carried on making proselites who were subjected to torture when discovered. The monarch forbade all subjects to harbour any Christian priests in the country, but the Govenor of the Phillipines introduced Cordeliers [Franciscan monks] as an ambassarodial mission

As soon as these propagandists of faith had power in their hands, they fomented the most appalling revolts, or else they committed violence upon subjugated peoples in conquered territories, resulting in making their Divinity absolutely hated. No doubt they believed that foreigners, having lived for such a long time without a knowledge of their god, could be nothing more than animals on whom they had the right to execute the greatest cruelty. For a Christian, an infidel was never anything more than a dog.

It would seem to be a consequence of Judaic ideas that Christian nations usurped the possessions of the inhabitants of the New World. Apparently, the Castilians and Portuguese had exactly the same right to commandeer America and Africa as the Hebrews had to make themselves masters over Chaldean territory, either to exterminate the inhabitants there, or turn them into slaves. Did a pontiff of the God of Justice and Peace not assume the right to share out distant empires to European monarchs, whom he wanted to favour? These obvious violations of Natural law and nations seemed legitimate to Christian princes, for whom religion sanctified avarice, cruelty and usurpation.[17]

---

to the emperor of Japan. These monks started to build a public chapel in the capital city, but they were hounded out and the persecution of Christians redoubled. This culminated in a Christian armed uprising in 1637 [...] and a total of 37,000 people were massacred, which came to an end in 1638, in the reign of the Empress Mikaddo. The revolt was finally quashed and as a consequence Christianity was completely banished from Japan, which had been introduced initially in 1549.' As far as Ethiopia is concerned, a reliable website bears the following information: 'In the rural plateaux of northern Ethiopia, one can still find scattered ruins of monumental buildings alien to the country's ancient architectural tradition. This little-known and rarely studied architectural heritage bears silent witness to a fascinating, if equivocal, cultural encounter that took place in the 16th–17th centuries between Orthodox Ethiopians and Catholic Europeans. The Indigenous and the Foreign explores the enduring impact of the encounter on the religious, political and artistic life of Christian Ethiopia, one not readily acknowledged, not least because the public conversion of the early 17th-century King Susenyos to Catholicism resulted in a bloody civil war, enveloped in religious intolerance.' (See THE INDIGENOUS & THE FOREIGN: The Jesuit Presence in 17th Century Ethiopia at http://pwp.netcabo.pt/patrimonio.sgl/sitebuild/index.htm)

[17] **St Augustine teaches that 'all things belong to the just by divine right', a maxim which itself is based on a passage in the Psalms which says that, 'the righteous shall eat of the fruit of the labour of the unrighteous'. See St Augustine, *Epistle* 93. We know that the Pope, in a papal bull issued for the benefit of the kings of Castile, Aragon and Portugal, drew a line of demarcation which settled conquests made by each of them over the infidels. Going by such principles, does the whole universe not become prey to Christian banditry?**
The passage to which d'Holbach refers in St Augustine's *Epistle* [Letter] is reproduced below. Note that the maxim on which the passage is based is not a *Psalm*, but a *Proverb*. 'Listen to the testimony which through me is addressed to you by those who

Finally, Christianity regards *humility* as a sublime virtue; it attaches the greatest value to it. No doubt divine and supernatural enlightenment were not needed to perceive that pride offends people and makes those who show it to others appear unpleasant. It does not take much thinking to convince ourselves that arrogance, presumptuousness and vanity are unpleasant, contemptible qualities. But Christian humility has to go much further still: one has to abandon reason, one must mistrust one's virtues, one has to refuse to reward good actions with fairness, and one even has to lose one's justly merited self–respect.

From this we can see that this so–called virtue is apt only to degrade people, to shame them in their own eyes, to stifle all energy and desire to make themselves useful to society. To deny people their self–esteem and not appreciate that of others is to crush the keenest motivation which carries people on to greater actions, to study and to innovation. It seems that Christianity offers merely to turn its followers into the most abject slaves of

---

are the Lord's wheat, suffering meanwhile until the final winnowing, among the chaff in the Lord's threshing-floor, i.e., throughout the whole world, because "God has called the earth from the rising of the sun unto the going down thereof," and throughout the same wide field the "children praise Him". We disapprove of everyone who, taking advantage of this imperial edict, persecutes you, not with loving concern for your correction, but with the malice of an enemy. Moreover, although, since every earthly possession can be rightly retained only on the ground either of divine right, according to which all things belong to the righteous, or of human right, which is in the jurisdiction of the kings of the earth, you are mistaken in calling those things yours which you do not possess as righteous persons, and which you have forfeited by the laws of earthly sovereigns, and plead in vain, "We have laboured to gather them", seeing that you may read what is written, "The wealth of the sinner is laid up for the just"; [Prov. 13: 22] nevertheless we disapprove of anyone who, availing himself of this law which the kings of the earth, doing homage to Christ, have published in order to correct your impiety, covetously seeks to possess himself of your property. Also we disapprove of anyone who, on the ground not of justice, but of avarice, seizes and retains the provision pertaining to the poor, or the chapels in which you meet for worship, which you once occupied in the name of the Church, and which are by all means the rightful property only of that Church which is the true Church of Christ. We disapprove of anyone who receives a person that has been expelled by you for some disgraceful action or crime, on the same terms on which those are received who have lived among you chargeable with no other crime beyond the error through which you are separated from us. But these are things which you cannot easily prove; and although you can prove them, we bear with some whom we are unable to correct or even to punish; and we do not quit the Lord's threshing-floor because of the chaff which is there, nor break the Lord's net because of bad fishes enclosed therein, nor desert the Lord's flock because of goats which are to be in the end separated from it, nor go forth from the Lord's house because in it there are vessels destined to dishonour.' St Augustine, *Epistles*, № 93, ch. 12. See: http://www.newadvent.org/fathers/1102093.htm

111

no use to the world, and their blind submission to their priests is a substitute for all manner of virtues.

Let us not kid ourselves: a religion which prides itself on being supernatural must of necessity try to denature man. In fact, in a delusional state of enthusiasm, it forbids people to love themselves, it orders them to hate pleasures and to cherish pain, and it makes a merit of chance ills which befall them.

From all this austerity stem those penances so destructive to health, those extravagant mortifications of the flesh, cruel privations, senseless practices, and ultimately slow suicides, through which the most fanatical Christians believe they merit Heaven.

It is true that all Christians do not feel themselves capable of miraculous perfection, but everyone believes that in order to save themselves they are obliged at least to mortify their senses, to renounce blessings which a good god offers them because they suppose that this god would become vexed if they made use of them, and that God only offers his blessings in order that one should abstain from going anywhere near them. How could reason approve of virtues which are destructive to ourselves? How could common sense accept a god whose intention is to make us unhappy and who delights in thinking up torments to inflict upon his creatures? What fruit can society reap from these virtues, which make people gloomy, miserable and incapable of being useful to their fatherland?

Without recourse to superstition, are reason and experience not sufficient to prove to us that passions and pleasures, when pushed to excess, rebound on us, and that abusing the best things in life is a veritable evil? Does our nature not force us to moderation and to shun things harmful to us?

In a word, should our self–preservation not moderate our cravings and make us flee from that which would lead to our destruction?[18] It is evident that Christianity authorizes suicide—at least indirectly.

---

[18] **The harmful idea that man has had a sense of the divine from time immemorial, allied to a desire to distinguish oneself from the crowd through extraordinary acts, is the real source of the concept of penance, which we see exercised in all parts of the world. There is nothing more astonishing than the penances done by Indian yogis, with whom Christian penitents hardly compare. Priests of Astarte in Syria and of Sibyl in Phrygia became eunuchs; the Pythagoreans were the enemies of pleasure; and the Romans had vestal virgins, similar to our nuns. Perhaps the idea of being obliged to offer penance in order to appease a divinity is derived from former times, when people were convinced that God wanted the sacrifice of human blood. There is no doubt that that was the basic motivation for Jesus Christ's sacrifice, which strictly speaking was a *suicide*. The Christian**

It was as a consequence of these fanatical ideas, particularly in the early years of Christianity, that deserts and forests became populated by perfect Christians who, by cutting themselves off from the world, deprived their family of support and their country of citizens, in order to give themselves over to a life of futility and contemplation.

This is why there are legions of monks and **cœnobites** who, rallied under the ensign of various enthusiasts, are enlisted in armies of people, useless or harmful to the state. They believed that they deserved Heaven by burying their talents, which were much needed by their fellow citizens, and by making a vow to inertia and celibacy.

Thus it is that in countries where Christians are more devoted to their religion, a host of people commit themselves piously to live their whole life as useless, miserable people. What heart is so barbarous so as not to shed tears over the fate of these victims, plucked from that enchanting sex which Nature destined to be a joy for the males of our species! As unfortunate dupes of youthful enthusiasm or forced by an imperious family with ulterior motives, these women are forever banished from the world. Rash oaths bind them forever to a life of boredom, solitude, slavery and poverty. A pledge contrary to Nature forces them to a state of perpetual virginity. Even a more mature frame of mind cannot reclaim them when, sooner or later, it makes them bitterly regret their imprudent vows, because society consigns them to oblivion on account of their pointless lives and their voluntary sterility. Cut off from their families, they slip into boredom, bitterness and tears, wallowing in a life perpetually frustrated by troublesome, despotic jailors.

Finally, isolated and without support, bereft of family ties, all they have left is the dreadful consolation of seducing other victims to share the boredom of their solitude and their torture, which for them is no solace. In a word, Christianity seems to have taken upon itself the task of going against Nature and reason in all things. When it acknowledges some virtues approved of by good sense, it always wants to go one step too far; it never keeps to that happy medium, which is the point of perfection. Pleasures of the flesh, dissoluteness and adultery, in brief—illicit, shameful pleasures—are evidently things which any man, eager for his own self–preservation and his fellow citizens' esteem, should resist. Pagans have realized and taught this

religion, by acknowledging such a god as a model for emulation, proclaims to its followers that they must self-destruct in order to make a hasty exit from this perverse world. In the majority of cases, martyrs were really suicide victims. Trappist monks and those of Septfonds were equally guilty of this. (For Astarte, Sibyl, Pythagoreans, Trappist monks, Septfonds monks—see Glossary.)

113

PUNCH, OR THE LONDON CHARIVARI.—June 30, 1860.

ALL SORTS OF JUGGLING TRICKS

MASKS OF ALL KINDS

TOY M   RY

KIDNAPPING.

Figure 28: *Kidnapping.* A print from *Punch, or the London Charivari*, 30 June 1860.

truth, despite the extreme immoral behaviour for which Christianity reproaches them.[19]

The Christian religion, little concerned with such reasonable maxims, recommends *celibacy* as a state of perfection; the perfectly legitimate marriage bond is an imperfection in their eyes. God, the Father of the Christians, had declared in Genesis: 'It is not good that man should be alone.'[20] He had formally ordered all his creatures to 'increase and multiply'.[21] His Son in the gospels came to revoke this command; he claimed that to be perfect one had to renounce marriage, to resist one of the strongest desires that Nature inspires in man, i.e., to die without descendants, to deny the State its supply of citizens and support in their old age.[22] If we

---

[19] **Aristotle and Epictetus recommended purity in speech. Menander said that a good man could never consent to corrupting a virgin or to committing adultery. Tibullus said, 'casta placent superis'. Mark Anthony thanked the gods for having preserved his chastity in his youth. Romans had laws against adultery. Father Tachard said that the Siamese people had a moral code which forbade not only dishonest actions, but also even having impure thoughts and desires. From this we observe that chastity and pure mores were highly valued by nations, even before the inception of Christianity, or even before people had heard about it.** The Latin quotation reads: 'Chaste things please the gods.' Presumably Tibullus was not terribly bothered about pleasing the gods because he carried on an illicit, adulterous affair for years with a woman called Delia! (For **Aristotle, Epictetus, Menander, Tibullus, Anthony [Mark]**, and **Tachard**—see Glossary.)

[20] 'And the Lord God said, "It is not good that the man should be alone; I will make him an help meet for him",' (Gen. 2: 18).

[21] 'And God blessed them, and God said unto them, "Be fruitful, and multiply, and replenish the earth, and subdue it: and have dominion over the fish of the sea, and over the fowl of the air, and over every living thing that moveth upon the earth",' (Gen.1: 28).

[22] 'His disciples say unto him, "If the case of the man be so with his wife, it is not good to marry." But he said unto them, "All men cannot receive this saying, save they to whom it is given. For there are some eunuchs, which were so born from their mother's womb: and there are some eunuchs, which were made eunuchs of men: and there be eunuchs, which have made themselves eunuchs for the kingdom of heaven's sake. He that is able to receive it, let him receive it",' (Matt. 19: 10—12). 'And every one that hath forsaken houses, or brethren, or sisters, or father, or mother, or wife, or children, or lands, for my name's sake, shall receive an hundredfold, and shall inherit everlasting life', (Matt. 19: 29). Similar sentiments are stated in Mark 10: 28—30. In Luke's gospel, the sentiment of indifference to, or abandonment of, the family and wife is actually transformed into outright hostility towards them: 'If any man come to me, and hate not his father, and mother, and wife, and children, and brethren, and sisters, yea, and his own life also, he cannot be my disciple', (Luke 14: 26). In the New Testament, marriage is clearly seen as a safety valve for sexual incontinence, to be indulged in when all else fails. The author of the Epistle to the Corinthians is the misogynist St Paul: 'Now concerning the things whereof ye wrote unto me: It is good for a man not to touch a woman. Nevertheless, to avoid fornication, let every man

consult our reason, we shall find that the pleasures of love are harmful when taken to excess, and that they are crimes when they harm others. We know that to corrupt a young woman is to condemn her to shame and infamy, and it is to destroy her chances in society.[23] We shall find that adultery is an invasion of the rights of another, which destroys the union between spouses and, at the very least, separates hearts that were made to love each other. We conclude from these things that marriage, being the only means of satisfying honestly and legitimately a need of Nature, to propagate society and to provide support, is a state much more respectable and far more sacred than destructive celibacy—that voluntary castration—which Christianity has the cheek to turn into a virtue. Nature, or the author of Nature, invites men to multiply by appealing to our sense of pleasure and God openly declared that woman was necessary for man.

Experience has given us to understand that people should form a society not only to enjoy fleeting pleasures, but also to provide mutual help through life's bitter moments, to bring up children, to turn them into worthy citizens, and to find a support in them in our old age.

By giving man superior strength to that of his female companion, Nature intended man to work to support his family. By giving women companions weaker organs, Nature fit them for less onerous, but no less essential, tasks. By giving them a more sensitive, softer soul, Nature intended women to offer a tender quality, to be offered most particularly for her weaker children.

---

have his own wife, and let every woman have her own husband. Let the husband render unto the wife due benevolence: and likewise also the wife unto the husband. The wife hath not power of her own body, but the husband: and likewise also the husband hath not power of his own body, but the wife. Defraud ye not one the other, except it be with consent for a time, that ye may give yourselves to fasting and prayer; and come together again, that Satan tempt you not for your incontinency. But I speak this by permission, and not of commandment. For I would that all men were even as I myself. But every man hath his proper gift of God, one after this manner, and another after that. I say therefore to the unmarried and widows, it is good for them if they abide even as I. But if they cannot contain, let them marry: for it is better to marry than to burn', (1 Cor. 7: 1—9).

[23] The Koran is less squeamish about sexual relations outside marriage with unmarried women or girls: it sanctions sex with slave girls and women prisoners of war: 'The believers will succeed: those who pray humbly, who shun idle talk, who pay the prescribed alms, who guard their chastity except with their spouses or their slaves—with these they are not to blame...', (4: 1—6), and,'Prophet, We have made lawful for you the wives whose dowries you have paid, and any slaves God has assigned to you through war...', (33: 50). There are other references of this ilk also in the Hadith, which contain the sayings and teaching of the Prophet Muhammad—a book which is regarded as holy by Muslims and second in authority only to the Koran.

These are the happy ties which Christianity would keep us from forming;[24] these are the plans which it endeavours to cut across by proposing celibacy as a state of perfection, which leads to the depopulation of society, contradicts Nature, leaves men open to debauchery, isolating them and advantageous only to the odious policies of priests of several Christian sects, who have made it their duty to cut themselves off from their fellow citizenry, having formed a cohort doomed to drag on without posterity. *'Gens æterna, in qua nemo nascitur.'*[25]   And to those of its followers who dared not, or could not, aim at perfection, Christianity granted the indulgence of marriage, but it

---

[24] It is clear that within the Christian religion marriage is regarded as an imperfect state. This stems, perhaps, from the fact that Jesus Christ was a member of the Essene sect who, similar to contemporary monks, renounced marriage in favour of celibacy. In all likelihood, these ideas were adopted by the early Christians who, expecting the world to end at any moment according to Christ's prophecies, felt that it was pointless having children and proliferating ties to a world on the brink of annihilation. That said, St Paul said *'it is better to marry than burn'*. Jesus himself spoke in glowing terms of those who *'made eunuchs of themselves for the kingdom of heaven'*. Origen followed this advice or precept to the letter. St Justin the martyr said that God *'wanted to be born of a virgin so as to evade an ordinary genesis, which is the fruit of an illegitimate desire'*. The elevation of celibacy to a state of perfection was one of the main reasons why Christianity was banned in China. St Edward the Confessor abstained from his wife throughout his whole life. The idea of perfection bound up with chastity caused the demise of the Saxon royal families' line of succession in England. The monk St Augustine, apostle to the English, asked St Gregory the pope, *'How much time should elapse before a man, who had had sexual relations with his wife, could enter into the Church and be admitted to the communion of the faithful?'* (For Essene, Origen, Justin, Edward, Augustine, and Gregory—see Glossary.)

[25] Celibacy prescribed for the priests of Rome seems to be the consequence of a highly refined policy amongst pontiffs who subjugate the priesthood to this law. Firstly, celibacy was intended to increase popular veneration, to make people believe that their priests were not made of flesh and bone, like all other men. Second, by forbidding marriage to priests, the Church broke ties which bound them to their families and to the state, to adjoin them solely to the Church, whose *property would thus never be shared and would remain wholly in tact within the Church*. It is through celibacy that the priests of Rome have become such powerful, yet such bad, citizens. Celibacy gives them a sort of independence: they never have to think of posterity. A family man has needs unknown to the celibate, who sees everything finishing with him. The most ambitious popes have been the greatest promoters of priestly celibacy. It was Pope Gregory VII who toiled passionately to establish it. Were priests allowed to marry, kings and princes would soon become priests and the sovereign pontiff would no longer find them to be docile subjects. It is to celibacy that harshness, inhumanity, stubbornness and rumbustiousness are all due, of which Catholic clergy have always been accused. The Latin reads, 'An eternal people amongst whom no one is born.'

PUNCH, OR THE LONDON CHARIVARI.—August 28, 1858.

DANGEROUS FLIRTATION, OR SAM AND THE SCARLET LADY.

Figure 29: *Dangerous Flirtation, or Sam and the Scarlet Lady. A print from Punch, or the London Charivari,* 28 August 1858.

appears to punish them by placing awkward hindrances to this bond. Hence divorce is forbidden by the Christian religion. The marital ties of the most ill–matched couples have become indissoluble: once married, the partners are forced to languish for ever as a result of their imprudence, even though marriage, which has only goodness, tenderness and affection as its basis and goal, will become for them a source of discord, bitterness and pain.

This is how the law, in keeping with cruel religion, conspires to prevent an unhappy pair from breaking the chains that bind them. It appears that Christianity has done all in its power to put people off marriage in favour of celibacy, which is bound to lead to debauchery, adultery and dissoluteness.[26]

However, the God of the Jews allowed divorce and we do not see at all by what right his son, who had come to fulfil the Law of Moses, revoked such a wise dispensation.[27]

We shall not speak here of other obstacles which, since its foundation, the Church has put before marriage.[28]

---

[26] **Nature always holds sway: celibates have needs, just as any other men. They can find their outlet solely in prostitution and adultery, or in other ways which decency forbids to mention. In Spain, Portugal and Italy, monks and priests are monsters of lust: debauchery, pederasty and adultery are absolutely commonplace in those countries on account of celibacy. Secular vices would also become less common if marriage were not indissoluble.** Divorce first became legal in France on 20 September 1792. It was abolished in 1816, and despite divorce bills presented by legislators in the 1830s and in 1848, it was only re-established in 1884 under the Third Republic. Throughout this period, France's political climate shaped its divorce laws; divorce was regarded as a republican, even a revolutionary, institution throughout the nineteenth century. [Source: *Encyclopedia of 1848 Revolutions*, available on the internet.]

[27] 'When a man hath taken a wife, and married her, and it come to pass that she find no favour in his eyes, because he hath found some uncleanness in her: then let him write her a bill of divorcement, and give it in her hand, and send her out of his house', (Deut. 24: 1). There are other verses of a similar ilk. However, as d'Holbach points out, Christ's line on divorce in the Gospels is quite different: 'They [i.e. the Pharisees] say unto him, "Why did Moses then command to give a writing of divorcement, and to put her away?" He saith unto them, "Moses because of the hardness of your hearts suffered you to put away your wives: but from the beginning it was not so. And I say unto you, whosoever shall put away his wife, except it be for fornication, and shall marry another, committeth adultery: and whoso marrieth her which is put away doth commit adultery",' (Matt. 19: 7—9). Similar sentiments are repeated by Christ earlier in the same Gospel; see Matt. 5: 31—2. The same incident is related in Mark's Gospel, but Christ takes a harder line still by not adding the proviso about fornication; see Mark 10: 1—12.

[28] **The sovereign pontiffs of Rome must have a great laugh when they see kings pleading for their marriage to be dissolved. From the earliest of times, it is obvious that marriage between relatives was not permitted by civil law; princes**

By outlawing marriages between relatives, does it not seem to have forbidden marriage to those who wanted to be united, who knew each other perfectly well and loved each other so tenderly?

Such are the perfections that Christianity puts before its children; these are the virtues it prefers to those which it condescendingly dubs *human virtues*. What is more, Christianity rejects and repudiates the latter, calling them false and illegitimate, because those who possess them have no faith.

What?! Those heroic virtues of Greece and Rome, held in such great esteem, yet deemed not real virtues! If the fairness, humanity, generosity, temperance and patience of these pagans were not considered *virtues*, then what can we call them?

Is it not a travesty of all ideas of morality to maintain that the justice of pagans is not real justice, that their kindness is not genuine kindness, and that their benevolence is akin to a crime? Are the true virtues of **Socrates, Cato, Epictetus** and **Antonine** not preferable to the zeal of **Cyril**, the obstinacy of **Athanasius**, the uselessness of **Anthony**, the disavowing of **Chrysostom**, the

---

and emperors, even Christian ones, defended and permitted this sort of marriage at the beginning. See the *Codex Theodosianus* [Theodosian Code], Art. 12, law 3, and in the Code, law 5, Art. 8, para. 10, and also in op. cit., Arts. 8, 9, 37. The kings of France have exercised the same right. Pierre de Marca has formally stated: '*Pars illa juris tunc erat pene Principes, fine ulla controversia.*' See de Marca, *De Concordia sacerdotii et imperii*. However, little by little the Church has usurped this right of princes and it is the popes who hold sway over, and have the last word, on the conjugal bond, and there was a time when it was impossible to know whether one had made a good or a bad marriage: the Church forbade marriage to relatives so distant that it was impossible to recognise them as relatives. *Familial affinity* became an obstacle: *spiritual affinities* were invented—godfathers and godmothers were unable to marry each other, and in this way popes became the arbiters of the fate of kings and their subjects. Under the pretext of *incestuous marriage*, the pope meddled in affairs of the state hundreds of times by excommunicating sovereigns and declaring their children illegitimate; thus he dictated the line of succession to the throne. However, according to the Bible, it is an indubitable fact that the children of Adam must have married their sisters. Theologians banned marriage between relatives for a reason very much worthy of them: they claimed that, 'These marriages are criminal because if conjugal affection were added to a union between relatives in which love already exists, it is feared that the love the spouses would have for each other would be too great.'
The Latin quotation reads: 'That part of the law was then within the emperor's compass, without any dispute', which is from *On the Concord of the Priesthood and the State*. (For **Codex Theodosianus** and **Marca**—see Glossary.)

Figure 30: St John Chrysostom (347—407). (Source: Wikipedia.)

St John Chrysostom's sobriquet was 'Golden Mouth'.

ferocity of **Dominic**, and the abject humility of the soul of **Francis**?[29]

All the virtues that Christianity admires are both excessive and fanatical, or they have as their sole aim to make man timid, abject and unhappy. If they give people courage, they soon become obstinate, haughty, cruel and harmful to society in the eyes of the Church. But this is how people have to behave to stand against the views of a religion which scorns the Earth, which does not balk at causing trouble, so long as its jealous god triumphs over his enemies.

No true morality can be compatible with such a religion as Christianity.

---

[29] We know that St Cyril, abetted by a group of monks, attempted to assassinate Orestes, the governor of Alexandra, but he merely succeeded in killing the beautiful, knowledgeable and virtuous Hypatia in a most barbarous fashion. All the saints revered by the Roman Church have been either rebels who usurped power, or fanatics who fought for their own ambitious ends, or imbeciles showered with riches, or madmen, or visionaries who caused their own downfall. (For **Hypatia**—see Glossary.)

Chapter 13

On the Practices and Duties of the Christian Religion.

ust as Christian virtues have nothing solid and real to recommend them and they serve no purpose for which reason might justify them, so logic will see no point in a whole host of annoying practices which are irrelevant and sometimes even dangerous, which Christianity insists are duties to be observed by its staunch followers, and which shows them sure ways of appeasing the divinity, of obtaining his grace and meriting his ineffable rewards.

The first and most essential of the Christian duties is *prayer*. The Christian's happiness is bound up with continuous prayer. His god, who is reputedly full of goodness, wants to be begged to pour out his grace; he only dispenses it when importuned. Susceptible to flattery like any other earthly king, he insists on a specific etiquette, so he only listens favourably to voices when wishes are presented to Him in due form. What can we say of a father who, knowing his children's needs, would not agree to give them the food they needed unless they made a bid for it through fervent supplication, which often goes unheeded?

On the other hand, is it not mistrustful of god's wisdom to prescribe rules for his behaviour? Is it not to call into question his immutability to believe that his creatures can force him to change his decrees? If God knows everything, does he really need to be constantly pestered by his subjects' heart's desires and wishes? If he is omnipotent, how could he be flattered by his subjects' respect or by their repeated supplications and their prostration at his feet?

In a word, prayer suggests a capricious God with a faulty memory, susceptible to praises, flattered to see his subjects humiliated before him, and eager at every moment to receive the repeated tokens of their subjugation.

Can these ideas, borrowed from earthly princes, really be effectively applied to an all–powerful being who created the universe solely for mankind and desirous only for his creatures' happiness? Can one suppose that an omnipotent being without equal or rival could be envious of his own glory? Does this glorify a being who is incomparable in every way? Do Christians not see that by wanting to exult and honour their god, what they are really doing is debasing and shaming him?

It is also a feature of the Christian religion that prayers offered by one group can be effective for others. God is rather partial to his favourites and can only take requests from them, heeding solely his people's supplications when offered up by their ministers. Hence, God becomes a sultan, accessible only to his ministers, his viziers, his eunuchs and the ladies of his harem.

This is the origin of the *raison d'être* of the innumerable horde of priests, cœnobites, monks and nuns, who have no other function than to raise their idle hands heavenwards in prayer night and day to obtain his favours for society. Nations pay dearly for these important services and the idle pious live in splendour, whilst real merit, hard work and industry go largely poorly rewarded.[1] On the pretext of attending to their prayers and ceremonies of their cult, the Christian, especially in some of the more superstitious sects, is obliged to remain idle with his arms crossed for a large part of the year; he is convinced that he is honouring his god by this lack of productivity; feast days, proliferated by priests' interests and people's credulity, lay off millions of pairs of hands; instead of cultivating his fields, the working man goes off to pray in a temple and there he feasts his eyes on puerile ceremonies and his ears are crammed with fables and dogmas, of which he can understand nothing.[2] A tyrannical religion accuses the artisan or cultivator of sin when, during those days consecrated to idleness, he dares busy himself with caring and providing for his numerous and impoverished family; and, in cahoots with religion, the government punishes those who have the audacity to earn their crust, instead of saying their prayers or sitting with their arms crossed.[3]

Can reason sanction the bizarre obligation of refraining from eating meat and other foods, which certain Christian sects impose? As a result of this rule, working people are forced to make do for long periods of time with expensive, unwholesome food, inappropriate for them to regain their strength.

---

[1] An emperor (Justin, if I am not mistaken) asked for god's pardon, having qualms about the amount of time he was giving to administering state affairs which distracted him from his prayers.

[2] There is a passage in Diderot's novel *The Nun*, in which a nun herself questions the whole institution of her calling: 'Are convents so essential to the constitution of a state? Did Jesus Christ institute monks and nuns? Can the Church really not do without them? What need has the bridegroom of so many foolish virgins, and what need has the human race of so many victims? Will the need never be felt to narrow the opening to these chasms in which future generations will be lost? Are the routine prayers which are said there worth as much as the penny that charity gives to the poor? Does God, who created man as a social being, approve of him locking himself away?' (Diderot, *The Nun*, translated by R. Goulbourne [Oxford: O.U.P, Oxford World Classics Series, 2005], p. 74.)

[3] In his capacity as emperor, Constantine issued a decree in AD 321 that all work of the judiciary, professions, and ordinary urban occupations cease on Sundays. Work in the countryside and agriculture was exempt. These measures were at least more reasonable than those which exist nowadays, especially in Roman Catholic families. Now it is the pope and bishops who dictate feast days and force people to be idle. See Tillemont, *Vie de Constantin* {*Life of Constantine*}, article 15, p. 180. (For **Constantine** and **Tillemont**—see Glossary.)

What despicable, ridiculous ideas must these crackpots have of God, who believe that he gets annoyed by the quality of the dishes that go into the stomachs of his creatures? However, for the right price, heaven becomes more accommodating. Christian priests have ceaselessly harassed their credulous followers to force them to transgress, and all this for the opportunity to make them atone for their alleged transgressions at great cost. Everything in Christianity, right down to sins, is turned to priestly profit.[4]

No other cult has ever put its adherents in such a position of total, continuous dependence upon its priests as Christianity has. They never lost sight of their prey; they took just enough measures to enslave men and to make them contribute to their power, riches and their kingdom. As mediators between the Celestial Monarch and his subjects, these priests were viewed as paid courtiers, like ministers authorized to exercise power in his name, as his favourites, to whom the divinity can deny nothing. Thus the ministers of the Almighty became the absolute masters of the Christians' lot; they held these slaves in their grip for life, subjugated them by fear and prejudices; they grabbed them for themselves and made them their own by a host of practices and duties as puerile as they are bizarre, taking the trouble to make them understand that they were indispensable for their salvation. They turned any failure to perform these duties into a crime more grave than the obvious violation of the rules of morality and reason. It is not at all surprising that in the most Christian of sects, that is to say, the most superstitious ones, we see man perpetually beset by priests. Hardly has a child emerged from a mother's womb, than his priest baptizes him for money on the pretext of washing away a so-called *original stain of sin*, which reconciles him with a

---

[4] **The Greeks and Eastern Christians observe more Lenten and ordinary fast days with greater strictness. In Spain and Portugal, permission is bought to eat meat on days when it is forbidden; people are obliged to pay taxes or a 'crusade bull', even when they have conformed to Church commandments, without which no absolution is granted. The habit of fasting and refraining from eating certain foods has come down from the Egyptians to the Jews, whence they were passed on to Christians and Muhammadans. The powers Roman Catholics regard as heretical are about the only ones who profit from abstaining from eating meat: they are the English who sell cod, and the Dutch—herrings. Is it not rather odd that Christians abstain from eating meat, which is not prescribed anywhere in the New Testament, whereas they do not demure at all from blood, i.e., black pudding, or the meat of animals which have been strangled, which are absolutely forbidden by the Apostles in terms no less strong than fornication. See Acts of the Apostles 15: 8.**
The verse in Acts is actually 15: 20, which states: 'But that we write unto them, that they abstain from pollutions of idols, and from fornication, and from things strangled, and from blood.'

god whom he has not yet had the chance to offend and, with the help of words and incantations, the priest tears him away from the Devil's clutches.

From his earliest childhood, the Christian's education is usually entrusted to priests, whose principal aim right from the start is to inculcate in him the prejudices essential to coincide with their views. They inspire terrors in them which will increase throughout the rest of their lives, stuffing them full of fables, senseless dogmas and the incomprehensible mysteries of a magical religion.

In a word, they turn children into superstitious Christians, but never into useful citizens or enlightened people.[5] There is only one thing that priests teach them as essential—that they are to be devotedly obedient to that religion. They are told, 'Be devout, be blind, despise your reason, think only about Heaven and neglect your earthly existence—that is all that God asks of you to lead you to happiness.'

To keep the Christian mired in the despicable, fanatical ideas with which their childhood years are imbued, priests in several sects order them to come often to them to off–load onto their bosom their most secret faults, their most hidden actions, their most confidential thoughts; they force them to come and humiliate themselves at their feet and pay homage to their power; they scare the guilty and, if they judge them worthy, then they reconcile them with the divinity who, at the order of his ministers, sets aside the sins which defiled them.

The Christian sects which indulge in this practice boast that it is an extremely effective rein on people's behaviour and highly useful for containing men's passions; but experience proves to us that in the countries where this custom is most faithfully observed, far from having mores purer than any others, they are far more wanton. These easy expiations merely embolden people to commit more sins.

The life of the Christian is a cycle of dissoluteness and periodic confession. The priesthood alone profits from this custom which puts them in reach of wielding absolute power over people's conscience. How extensive the power of this corps of men is, who can open and close Heaven's gates at their will and have access to family secrets, and who can light the fires of fanaticism in people's minds at their behest! Without the priests' consent, Christians cannot engage in sacred mysteries because they have the right to exclude

---

5   **Throughout most of the world, men's education is entrusted to priests. Therefore, it should come as no surprise that ignorance, superstition and fanaticism still linger on. It is the same in Protestant countries as well as in Catholic ones—universities are purely priestly establishments. It would appear that Europeans only want to create monks.**

them. They might get over this so–called privation, but the anathemas or excommunication the priests can pronounce are everywhere a real threat for them. Spiritual punishments produce temporal consequences and any citizen who incurs the Church's disfavour is in danger of incurring that of the government and becoming a hate–figure by his fellow citizens. We have already seen that ministers of religion have meddled in marital matters. Likewise, without priestly consent, a Christian cannot officially be a father; he has to submit to the capricious conventions of religion. Without their consent, official policy, in cahoots with religion, would exclude children from the ranks of citizenry.[6] Throughout the whole course of their lives, Christians are obliged to attend the ceremonies of their cult on priests' instructions, on pain of incurring guilt.

As soon Christians faithfully fulfil this important duty, they believe themselves to be favoured by God and are persuaded that they no longer owe anything further to society. It is in this way that these useless practices substitute for morality, which becomes subordinated to religion everywhere it falls under its control. When a person's term of life comes to an end and they are lying on their bed, Christians are yet again assailed by priests during their last moments. In some Christian sects, religion seems to be so designed as to make people's death a thousand times more bitter. A quiet priest comes to bring anxiety to the very litter of the dying: under the pretext of reconciling them with their God, he comes to make them savour the spectacle of their end.[7] Whilst this habit is detrimental to the citizen on the receiving end, it is, to say the least, extremely profitable for the priesthood, who owes a large part of their riches to the salutary terrors they inspire in their rich, dying Christians. Morality does not yield the same fruits: experience shows us that the majority of Christians living safely in excess or in crime take the trouble to reconcile themselves with God at the point of death. With the help of a last–minute act of repentance and a generous helping of money for the clergy, priests expiate people's faults, permitting them to hope that Heaven confines to oblivion the plundering, the injustices and the crimes they have

---

[6] If one reads history, one finds that Christian priests have desired to meddle in all affairs: the Church, like a fussy mother, has got involved in hairstyles, clothing, and children's footwear. In the fifteenth century, the Church was vexed with pointed shoes, which were named '*souliers à la poulaine*' {'long pointed shoes'}. In his day, St Paul decried curled hair.

[7] There is nothing more barbarous than the customary practices offered to the dying by the Roman Church. The sacraments make more people die than illnesses and doctors: fright can only cause unfortunate turmoil to an already enfeebled body. However, official policy conspires with religion to maintain these cruel customs: in Paris, once a doctor has already made three visits to a sick person, regulations state that the last rites must be administered.

committed during the whole course of a life which has harmed their fellows. Even death does not put an end to the sway the priesthood has over some Christian sects: priests make profit out of the body. For the right price, one can acquire the right to have one's mortal remains deposited in a temple, which spreads vile infections and illnesses in towns and cities. What can I say? The power of the priesthood extends even to the life beyond the boundaries of death. Prayers can be bought from the Church at great cost to deliver the souls of the dead from the alleged agonies in store in the next world and to expiate all sin. Blessed are the rich in a religion where, at a price, one can interest God's favoured people to pray to set aside eternal damnation, which his immutable justice would have inflicted upon them![8]

Such are the principal duties Christianity prescribes as essential and the observation of these things is crucial to one's salvation. Such are the arbitrary, ridiculous, harmful practices it often dares to prescribe as a substitute for people's duties towards society. We shall not countermand the different superstitious practices accepted by some sects, but rejected by others, such as the honours paid to the memory of those pious fanatics, those heroes of zealotry, those obscure contemplators, whom the Roman pontiff places among the number of saints.[9] We shall not mention pilgrimages, which superstitious people make such a fuss over, or indulgences, through which sins are forgiven. We shall just confine ourselves to say that these things are more commonly respected by people than is generally admitted and that rules of morality are often totally ignored. It costs people a good deal less to conform to rites, ceremonies and practices, than to be virtuous. A good Christian is a person who conforms exactly to priestly demands. These people are required to be blind, liberal and submissive—qualities which substitute for all virtues.

---

[8] **Through the dogma of Purgatory and the power of the Church's prayers the Roman Church has often managed to fleece families of their richest inheritances. Christians often disinherit their family members in favour of the Church: this is termed 'to bequeath one's soul'. At the Council of Basle in 1443, Franciscans tried to have the following proposal adopted: 'Beatus Franciscus, ex divino privilegio, quot annis in Purgatorium descendit, suosque omnes in coelum deducit.' However, this dogma was weighted too much in Franciscan friars' favour and it was rejected by the bishops. The opinion of the Catholic Church is that prayers for the deceased are given over to the masses: that way, the richest people fund them—and rightly so.**

The Latin quotation means: 'Blessed Francis, of divine privilege, descends into Purgatory every year to lead all his own kind up to heaven.' (For the **Council of Basle**—see Glossary.)

[9] **We know that the *dairi*—or Japanese popes—had the right to canonize or make saints, just like their Roman counterparts. These saints were known as *kami* in Japan. (For Kami—see Glossary.)**

Chapter 14

On the Political Effects of the Christian Religion.

After having examined the uselessness, even the danger, of the goals of Christian perfection and the virtues and duties the Christian religion sets before us, let us see if it has any happier influence on politics, or if it is of any real benefit to the nations in which this religion has been established and faithfully observed.

First, we find that wherever Christianity is confessed, it establishes two sets of laws, each mutually at odds with the other. Politics are intended to maintain union and harmony between citizens. The Christian religion, despite preaching that people should love one another and live in peace, soon destroys this precept by the inevitable divisions which always arise amongst its followers, who are bound to hear its ambiguous oracles differently through its Holy Books. Robust debates between the Doctors of the Church right from the inception of Christianity are plain for all to see.[1]

From then onwards, we find schisms in every century, heresies followed by persecutions and fights—all meet for destroying the harmony of which Christianity boasts and which is rendered impossible by a religion in which everything is abstruse. In all religious disputes both parties believe they have God on their side—consequently, they are obstinate. How can they behave in any other way, since they confuse *God's cause* with their *own vanity*?

Thus, little disposed to give an inch on either side, they fight each other, torment each other, tear each other apart, until brute force wins the argument and common sense never occurs to them. In fact in all dissentions which have cropped up amongst Christians, political authority has always had to intervene. Sovereigns have taken part in priests' frivolous disputes, which they viewed as issues of paramount importance. In a religion established by God himself there is no such thing as triviality. Consequently, princes armed themselves against one group of their subjects: the royal court's way of thinking decided on its subjects' matters of belief and faith; the opinions they pushed were the only true ones; their advisors were the guardians of orthodoxy and all others were deemed heretics and rebels, whom the former made it their duty to exterminate.[2]

---

[1] From the very first time that the Apostles gathered together at the Council of Jerusalem, we see St Paul quarrelling with St Peter over whether Judaic rites should be observed or renounced. Even men who had first-hand knowledge of the faith could not get on, and things have not changed for the better since.

[2] A thinking man said that in each state, orthodox religion was like a henchman. In fact if one looks closely at it, one would come to the conclusion that it is kings

Princes' prejudices, or their mistaken policies, have always made them regard those of their subjects who did not share their opinions on religion as bad citizens, dangerous for the State and as enemies of their power. Had they left it to the priests to settle their own impertinent disputes, they would not have harassed people to lend weight to their arguments and their quarrels would have fizzled out of their own accord, or at least they would not have affected the public peace. If impartial kings had rewarded good people and punished the bad without having regard to their speculations, their cult, or their ceremonies, they would not have forced a great number of their subjects to become their sworn enemies, born of a power that oppressed them. It is by dint of injustices, of violence and persecution, that Christian princes have tried to bring back heretics into the fold at every turn. Should common sense not have shown them that this kind of conduct was ripe only for making hypocrites and hidden enemies of people, and even for fermenting revolt?[3]

But these considerations are not for princes upon whom Christianity works from childhood onwards, filling them with fanaticism and prejudices. It nurtures in them a powerful, obstinate attachment to trivia, an impetuous ardour for dogmas alien to the good of the State, an anger brought to bear against all those who refuse to submit to their despotic opinions. From the point when sovereigns find it quicker to destroy than to lure people back tenderly to the fold, their arrogant despotism does not stoop to reason. Their religion persuades them that tyranny is legitimate and that cruelty is commendable, so long as it is linked to Heaven's cause.

In practice, Christianity has always turned sovereigns into despots and tyrants when they showed special favour to it: it represented them as divinities on Earth and it lent respectability to their whims, as if they were the will of Heaven itself; it delivered people into their hands like a herd of slaves, to do with them as they willed. As a mark of gratitude for their religious zeal Christianity often pardoned sovereigns' most perverse injustices, acts of violence and crimes, and also, on pain of irritating the Almighty, Christianity commanded nations to languish without complaint under the sword, which struck them instead of protecting them. Therefore, it comes as no surprise that since the establishment of Christianity we see so many nations groaning

---

and soldiers who have established all Christian dogmas. If Louis XIV had lived, the *Unigenitus* constitution would have become an article of faith in our country. (For **Unigenitus**—see Glossary.)

[3] After the revocation of the Edict of Nantes, Louis XIV tormented the Hugenots, as we know, and at the same time forbade them to leave France. This kind of behaviour seems about as sensible as that of children who torment caged birds and then cry when they drop dead. (For **Edict of Nantes** and **Hugenot**—see Glossary: see also p. 349.)

under deeply religious tyrants, who had no other merit than a blind attachment to religion and who, into the bargain, indulged in the most revolting crimes, the most appalling tyranny, the most shameful extreme behaviour and the most unbridled licence. Whenever there have been injustices, oppression and pillaging by sovereigns—either religious or hypocritical—the priests have always made a point of repressing their subjects.

Furthermore, it should not amaze us to see so many incompetent or evil princes supporting the interests of religion because they need its mistaken policies as a prop for their own authority. Kings would have no need of superstition to govern their people if they showed equity and enlightened virtues, if they understood and put into practice their real duties, if they truly concerned themselves with the happiness of their subjects; but since it is easier to conform to rites rather than to have real talent or behave virtuously, Christianity all too often has found support in princes, themselves disposed to support it and even its henchmen, eager to be of service to both.

Ministers of religion have not shown the same accommodating attitude towards sovereigns who refused to enter into a common cause with them, to embrace their quarrels and serve their zealous aims. They rose against rulers who opposed them, punished them for their excesses, brought them to reason, moderated their ambitious claims and encroached upon their *immunities*.

On such occasions as those, priests cried *impiety, sacrilege*; they maintained that the sovereign had *usurped the censer*, that he was usurping rights granted to him by God himself. In a word, they tried to raise the people up against a perfectly legitimate authority by arming fanatics against sovereigns, whom they misrepresented as tyrants for not having submitted to the Church. Heaven has always been ready to avenge injustices committed against its ministers; these people themselves never cowered and they only preached submission to others when allowed to share in authority, or when they were too feeble to resist it. That is why at the dawn of Christianity we see powerless apostles preaching submission; as soon as they perceived a power base, they preached persecution; as soon as they discerned the strength of their position, they preached revolt, disposed kings and ordered their throats to be cut.

In all political societies where Christianity has had its seat, two rival powers exist in a state of constant, mutual struggle, and this kind of strife usually tears the kingdom apart. Subjects join in the fray with one group fighting for their sovereign and the other fighting for God, or believing that they are doing so. The latter must always carry the day, since it is down to the priesthood to poison people's mind with fanaticism and prejudice. It is by educating subjects that they will be prevented from yielding to fanaticism;

in any country where there is ignorance and intellectual darkness, the authority of the priesthood has to be reduced to set subjects free little by little from the yoke of superstition, otherwise it will always be limitless and more powerful than the king's own sovereignty.

But the majority of sovereigns fear educated people. They join forces in cahoots with the priesthood to stifle reason and to persecute all those who have the courage to proclaim it. Blind to their own interests and to those of their nation, rulers seek to be in command over mere slaves, whom priests infantilize at will.

In countries where Christianity wields its most absolute domination there is widespread, shameful ignorance and utter despondency: sovereigns in league with priests appear to plot the downfall of science, the arts and innovation, which are the fruits of free thought.

Amongst Christian nations, the least religious are the freest, the most powerful and the happiest. In countries where spiritual despotism goes hand in glove with temporal despotism, people stagnate in sloth, laziness and torpor. The peoples of Europe who boast of having the purest faith are certainly not the most flourishing, nor are they the strongest nations: sovereigns, slaves themselves to religion, merely command other slaves, who do not have sufficient energy and courage to enrich themselves and work for the benefit of the State. In these sorts of countries priests alone are opulent and everyone else languishes in abject poverty.

But what do power and national prosperity mean for a religion which wants its followers to neglect their earthly contentment, which regards wealth as harmful, which preaches a poor god who commends utter poverty of spirit and mortification of the senses to its followers?

Without doubt, it is by forcing people to practise these maxims that, in many Christian states, the priesthood has grabbed most of the nation's wealth for themselves and live in splendour, whilst the rest of the population bows their head to them in penury.[4]

---

[4] For those who care to calculate, it is obvious that in Italy, Spain, Portugal and Germany, church revenue exceeds not only that of the sovereign, but also that of all its citizens. It is claimed that Spain alone has more than 500,000 priests, who enjoy immense incomes. The King of Spain certainly has not a sixth of their income at his disposal to defend the whole state. If monks and priests be essential to a country, one must conclude that Heaven makes a country pay a pretty price for their prayers. The expulsion of the Moors ruined Spain: it is only by ridding the country of monks that its fortunes might be restored. However, such an operation would demand a great deal of shrewdness: a king who tried to do that too suddenly would be dethroned at a stroke by people who would not

These are the advantages which the Christian religion provides for political societies: they form an independent state with a state, with religion turning people into slaves and favouring the sovereign's tyranny when they prove to be compliant, but it turns subjects into rebels and fanatics when their sovereign lacks such co–operation. When Christianity is at one with politics it crushes, debases and impoverishes nations, depriving them of science and innovation. When it stands independent of politics it makes its citizens unsociable, disruptive, intolerant and rebellious.

If we examine in detail this religion's precepts and the maxims which emanate from it, we see that it deprives a state of everything that makes it prosperous.

We have already noted the concept of imperfection which Christianity attributes to the state of marriage and the esteem in which it holds celibacy: these ideas are not to the advantage of a nation's population, which is unquestionably the premier source of power for a state.

Commerce is also no less at odds with Christian religious views, whose founder pronounced anathema on wealth and excluded it from the Heavenly Kingdom. All industry is equally forbidden for the perfect Christian, who lives a temporary life on this earth and who must never concern himself with tomorrow.[5] Also, should a Christian not be so foolhardy and reckless as to agree to serve in the armed forces? Given that a man never has the right to assume that he pleases his god or is *in a permanent state of grace*, would it not be foolish to expose himself to eternal damnation? And what about a

---

understand that he wanted to do so for their own good. Spain must be educated at all costs and the people rendered content with their master. (For **Moor**—see Glossary.)

[5] **St John Chrysostom said, '*A merchant can never please his god, and a Christian can never be a merchant, who must be driven out of the church.*' He bases this on a passage in Psalm 70, which says, '*I have never known trading.*' If this principle be true, then the whole of the rue Saint Honoré is damned.** (For **Chrysostom** [St John]—see Glossary.)

To which verse and Psalm d'Holbach is referring here is a mystery: even given that the numbering of Psalms frequently differs between English and foreign versions of the Bible, there is no verse in the Book of Psalms which corresponds to this quotation. In both the *Bible de Louvain* (1550) and the *Bible de Sacy* (also known as the *Bible de Mons*) (1659), there is no corresponding verse in Psalm 70, nor in the Latin *Vulgate* edition. Furthermore, the original phrase d'Holbach quotes—'Je n'ai connu le négoce'—appears nowhere in French versions of the Book of Psalms, either ancient or modern.

The rue Saint Honoré in Paris was noted for its affluence from the seventeenth century onwards: its grand buildings were constructed and financed by rich financiers and bankers as a monument to their wealth. Today the street and area around it are still noted for exclusive shops and expensive retail outlets.

133

Christian who is charitable to his neighbour and ought to love his enemies—does he not become guilty of the gravest of crimes when he causes a man to die whose spiritual state he does not know, and whom, therefore, he might suddenly confine to Hell?[6] A soldier is a monster in Christianity, unless he is fighting for his god. If he dies, then he becomes a martyr. Christianity always declared war on science and the humanities, which they regarded as an obstacle to salvation: '*knowledge puffs up*', said an apostle.[7] Men who must subjugate their reason to the yoke of faith need neither rationality, nor learning. By Christians' own admission, the founders of their religion were ignorant, unschooled men: it is essential that their disciples be no more educated than they in order that they give credence to the fables and delusions these ignorant, revered people handed down to them. It has always been obvious that the most educated men commonly make the worst Christians. Education, quite independent of faith, undermines Christianity and turns the religious away from the *Book of Salvation*, which is considered their only essential book. Just as learning is beneficial for political society, ignorance is much more advantageous for religion and its ministers. Centuries bereft of learning and innovation were a golden era for the Church of Jesus Christ. It was then that kings were most subjugated, and it was then that its ministers grabbed all society's wealth. Priests of a very large Christian sect want people to be so submissive to them that they want to keep them in ignorance of the contents of their Holy Books, which contain the rules they must follow.[8] Their conduct is doubtless very wise because

---

[6] **Lactantius said, 'A Christian can be neither a soldier nor an accuser.' See I, p. 137. Quakers and Mennonites never bear arms: they are more consistent than other Christians.** (For **Lactantius, Quaker,** and **Mennonite**—see Glossary.)

[7] D'Holbach refers to the Apostle Paul, who wrote, 'Now as touching things offered unto idols, we know that we all have knowledge. Knowledge puffeth up, but charity edifieth', (1 Cor. 8: 1).

[8] D'Holbach is referring to the Catholic Church and, to some extent, the Protestant Church because for a long time there was no readily available English translation of the Bible, which was commonly to be found only in Latin. Priests in the Catholic Church said the mass in Latin, a language that few people understood. Translations of the Bible into other European languages came after the English translation. The first scholarly translation of the Bible to be made available in English was in 1611, the version now known as the *Authorized Version* or the *King James Version*. An English translation of the Latin *Vulgate* (itself a translation of the original texts) was the only version acceptable to the Catholic Church until well into the twentieth century, though with revisions: however, it was a translation of a translation, which is bound to contain textual differences in emphasis. Notwithstanding this, the Church was not eager to allow its followers to read its sacred texts: see pp. 346 *et seqq*.

reading the Bible is the surest way of all to disabuse Christians of their respect for the Scriptures.[9]

In a word, by following Christian maxims rigorously, no political society could survive. If there were any doubt about this assertion, just listen what the early Doctors of the Church had to say: one will see that their morality is totally incompatible with the maintenance and strength of the state. One will see that, according to **Lactantius**, no man can become a soldier; that according to **St Justin**, no man should marry; that according to **Tertullian**,[10]

---

[9] **Pope St Gregory in his time had a very large number of pagan books burned. From the inception of Christianity we know that St Paul had books brought to him to be burned—a practice which is still carried out by the Church. The founders of Christianity were to forbid people to learn how to read upon pain of death. The Roman Catholic Church wisely took holy books from the hands of the common man. As soon as people started to read them in the sixteenth century, religion became replete with heresies and revolts against priests. The happiest time for the Church was when only monks knew how to read and write, and when they appointed themselves keepers of books! If anyone were in any doubt about the hate and contempt the Fathers of the Church showed for learning, they only have to look at the following passages: St Jerome said: '*Geometria, arithmetica, musica, habent in sua scientia veritatem, sed non ex scientia illa, scientia pietatis. Scientia pietatis est noscere scripturas, et intellegere prophetas, evangelia credere, apostolas non ignorare.*' See Hieronymus {St Jerome's} '*Commentary on the Epistle of Timothy*'. St Ambrose said, '*Quid tam absurdum quim de astronomia et geometria tractare, et profunda aërispatia metiri, relinquere causas salutis, errores quaerere.*' See St Ambrose *De Officiis*, Book I. St Augustine said: '*Astrologia et geometria, et alia eiusmodi, ideo despecta sunt a nostris, quia nihil ad salutem pertinent.*' See St Augustine *De ordinis disciplina*, 'For the exactness which geometry gives to the mind, it ought to be banned in all Christian states'.**
The Latin inscriptions above read respectively: 'Geometry, arithmetic and music have truth in each of their disciplines, but the knowledge of devotion does not come from those disciplines. The knowledge of devotion comes from understanding the scriptures and the prophets, a faith in the Gospels and familiarity with the Apostles.'
'What can be more absurd than to treat the subjects of astronomy and geometry, and to measure the depths of space, while we abandon the causes of our salvation and seek after error.'
'Astrology, geometry and other such things, are contemptible in our eyes, for they have nothing to do with salvation.'

[10] For fuller remarks on **Tertullian**—see Glossary. The passage d'Holbach is referring to is perhaps the following: 'Let even this fact help to remind you that all the powers and dignities of this world are not only alien to, but enemies of, God; that through them punishments have been determined against God's servants; through them, too, penalties prepared for the impious are ignored. But both your birth and your substance are troublesome to you in resisting idolatry. For avoiding it, remedies cannot be lacking; since, even if they be lacking, there remains that one by which you will be made a happier magistrate, not in the earth, but in the heavens.' (From Tertullian *On Idolatry*, ch. XVIII.)

no man can be a magistrate; that according to St Chrysostom,[11] no man should engage in commerce; and that according to a large number of them, no one should study.

Finally, by combining the above maxims with those of the Saviour of the World, one has to conclude that a Christian's duty is his own perfection, and so he is a most useless member of society as far as his country, his family and those around him are concerned: he is an idle meditator who thinks only about the next life, who has nothing to offer in terms of benefits to this world, and who has nothing more pressing than seeking a rapid exit from the here–and–now.[12]

To see if the Christian is a real fanatic or not, from whom society can derive not a single advantage, let us listen to **Eusebius** of Caesarea: 'The kind of life recommended by the Christian Church surpasses our present nature and communal life; in the Christian life, we search neither for marriage, nor children, nor riches; in fact, it is totally alien to normal life; it allies itself solely with the cult of the divine; it is given over uniquely to an immense love of heavenly things. Those who follow it in that way, almost detached from mortal life and having only their body bound to earth, are totally elevated in spirit to Heaven and dwell there already like pure, celestial spirits;[13] they hold the life of other men in utter contempt.'[14]

A man who is totally convinced of the truths of Christianity cannot apply himself to anything here below: everything for him is an opportunity to fall; everything is a distraction from his salvation. If Christians, by some happy chance, were not inconsistent and did not continuously deviate from their sublime speculations, and did not renounce their fanatical perfection, no Christian society could ever survive and nations enlightened by the gospels would regress to a state of savagery. One would only see feral beings for whom social ties would be totally broken, who would only pray and groan in this valley of tears and would be engaged upon making themselves and everyone else miserable, in order to become worthy of Heaven's blessings.

---

[11] For fuller remarks on **Chrysostom**—see Glossary.

[12] **Tertullian said: '*Nil nostra a refert in hoc aevo, nisi de eo celeriter recedere.*' Lactantius makes the observation that the idea of the imminent end of the world was one of the principal causes of the propagation of Christianity.**
      The Latin reads: 'Nothing is of importance in this age, except to flee from it quickly.'

[13] The word d'Holbach uses in this quotation in the original is *intelligences*, a feminine plural noun which now generally means 'intelligence', though it is rarely used in the plural. In the seventeenth century this word could also mean 'spirit' or 'angel', as the *Dictionnaire de l'Académie Française*, 1st edn. (1694) states, 'On appelle les Anges, *Les Intelligences celestes*' {'*Angles are called* "Celestial intelligences"'}. Hence, the word here could be translated as 'spirits' or 'angels'.

[14] **See Eusebius *Ecclesiastical History*, II, p. 29.**

Figure 31: Eusebius of Caesarea (*c.* 263—339). (Source: Wikipedia.)

137

Finally, a religion whose maxims tend to make men intolerant, which turns sovereigns into persecutors, which renders subjects either slaves or rebels, whose obscure dogmas are the subject of endless disputes and whose precepts oppress men by turning them away from thinking about their real interests—such a religion, I say, is destructive for every society.

Figure 32: *A Cardinal's Pets. (c. 1850).*

Chapter 15

On the Church or the Christian Priesthood

There have always been men who knew how to exploit the foolishness of people on earth. Priests of all religions have found a way of establishing their power, their wealth and glory, based on the fears of commoners, but no religion had so many reasons as Christianity to enslave people to the priesthood. The first preachers of the gospel—the Apostles—are depicted as truly divine men, inspired by the Spirit of God and sharing his omnipotence. Although each of their successors did not enjoy the same prerogatives in the opinion of some Christians, the corps of the priesthood (or the Church) is continuously enlightened by the Holy Spirit, who never ever abandons them. The Church basks in a collective infallibility and consequently decisions become just as sacred as those of the Divinity himself—it is in a state of perpetual revelation.

According to the lofty notions Christianity conveys to us of its clerics, the priesthood must, by virtue of the rights which Jesus Christ himself held, command nations, encounter no obstacle to its will, and even make kings themselves bow to their authority. So then, it comes as no surprise that Christian priests have wielded immense power for such a long time in this world. Their dominion had to be unlimited, since it was founded on the authority of the Almighty; it had to be despotic because men have no right to restrict divine power; and it was bound to degenerate into abuse because priests who commanded such power were men, intoxicated and corrupted by impunity.

At the outset of Christianity, the Apostles, by virtue of Jesus Christ's mission, preached the gospel to the Jews and the Gentiles. As we have seen, the novelty of their doctrine attracted proselytes from amongst the common people. These new Christians, full of fervour with their new–found opinions, formed their own distinctive congregations in each town, which were governed by men appointed by the Apostles. The latter, having received the faith at first hand, kept a watchful eye on the diverse, established Christian groups.

This seems to be the origin of *bishops* or *inspectors* in the Church, who have come down to us today in this guise, in which princes, now overseeing the priests in modern Christianity, now glory.[1] We know that all the

---

[1] **St Jerome highly disapproved of the distinction between bishops, priests and parish priests. He held the view that *priests and bishops*, according to the teaching of St Paul, were the same thing at the inception of the Church; he said that *distinctions arose in religion at the instigation of Satan*. Nowadays, bishops—**

members of this nascent sect held all their possessions in common. It appears that this duty was rigorously enforced since, on the order of St Paul, two new Christians were struck down dead for having kept back a part of their own property.[2] Funds from this community were at the Apostles' disposal, and after them this right fell to the *inspectors* or *bishops*, or *priests*, who replaced them. And since priests had to make their living at the altar, it is perfectly credible that these bishops helped themselves liberally to the public purse for their instruction. Those who successfully tempted new spiritual conquests doubtlessly had to content themselves with the voluntary contributions given by new converts. Be that as it may, treasures amassed by the credulous piety of the faithful became an object of priestly greed and caused discord amongst them: each one of them wanted to govern and dispose of community funds. From there, intrigues and factions arose which could be seen springing up all over within God's church.[3] Priests were always the first to cast aside their religious fervour, since sooner or later ambition and greed were sure to disabuse them of the maxims of disinterestedness which they preached.

For as long as Christianity was humiliated and persecuted, bishops and priests fought each other behind closed doors and their quarrels never spilled over into the public arena.

---

who are good for nothing—enjoy huge incomes, while the large cohort of parish priests—who do all the work—are dying of hunger.

[2] The passage d'Holbach refers to is found in Acts 5: 1—11: 'But a certain man named Ananias, with Sapphira his wife, sold a possession, and kept back part of the price, his wife also being privy to it, and brought a certain part, and laid it at the apostles' feet. But Peter said, "Ananias, why hath Satan filled thine heart to lie to the Holy Ghost, and to keep back part of the price of the land? Whilst it remained, was it not thine own? And after it was sold, was it not in thine own power? Why hast thou conceived this thing in thine heart? Thou hast not lied unto men, but unto God." And Ananias hearing these words fell down, and gave up the ghost: and great fear came on all them that heard these things. And the young men arose, wound him up, and carried him out, and buried him. And it was about the space of three hours after, when his wife, not knowing what was done, came in. And Peter answered unto her, "Tell me whether ye sold the land for so much?" And she said, "Yea, for so much." Then Peter said unto her, "How is it that ye have agreed together to tempt the Spirit of the Lord? Behold, the feet of them which have buried thy husband are at the door, and shall carry thee out." Then fell she down straightway at his feet, and yielded up the ghost: and the young men came in, and found her dead, and, carrying her forth, buried her by her husband. And great fear came upon all the church, and upon as many as heard these things.'

[3] **Blood was often shed over the elections of bishops. Prétextat said: 'Let me be made Bishop of Rome and I shall become a Christian.'** (For **Prétextat**—see Glossary.)

A ROW AMONG "THE POPE'S BRASS BAND."

(SEE THE PARLIAMENTARY DEBATES.)

Figure 33: *A Row Among "The Pope's Brass Band"*. A print from
Punch, or the London Charivari, **21 May 1853**.

141

But when Constantine wanted to strengthen his position by enlisting the help of a group of people who had already managed to grow great in number by virtue of their obscurity, everything changed the face of the Church. Those in charge of the Christians, who had become seduced by authority and turned into courtiers, started to fight each other openly.[4] They engaged sovereigns in their quarrels, persecuted their rivals, and, having had honours and riches heaped upon them little by little, they were no longer recognizable as the successors of those poor Apostles or *messengers*, whom Jesus had sent out to preach. They became princes who, defended by the weapons of opinion, were in a position to dictate the law to sovereigns themselves and to set the world alight.

The office of Pontiff was separated from the Empire under Constantine by regrettable foolhardiness. Emperors would soon have reason to rue the day they did this. In fact, the Bishop of Rome, from that city which has long been master of the world and whose very name alone impressed nations, knew how to profit skilfully from the troubles within the Empire—from barbarian invasions and from the emperors' weaknesses, being too far removed to watch over their conduct. And thus, by dint of machinations and intrigues, the Roman Pontiff came to ascend the throne of the cæsars. It was for him that military leaders like Aemelian and Scipio fought.[5] He was regarded in the East as the monarch of the Church, as the universal Bishop, as the Vicar of Christ on earth—in fact, he became the infallible organ of the Divinity.[6]

---

[4] By 'courtier', d'Holbach means that group of men who surrounded the sovereign, paid lip-service to him and his policies, but who were always on the look out to feather their own nest and pursue their own interests, i.e., they were royal toadies, of whom Jonathan Swift said, 'The two maxims of any great man at court are, always to keep his countenance, and never keep his word'. (Swift, *Thoughts on Various Subjects*.)

[5] D'Holbach cannot have intended for his readers to take this statement literally, because the great military general Scipio fought against Hannibal in the Second Punic War in around 200 BC, well before Christianity and the papacy had even been founded. He simply cites these two military leaders as examples of men through whose efforts the Roman Empire had expanded in Africa (Tunis) and in Europe, thus almost handing an empire on a plate to the future Roman Pontiff, who eagerly annexed and built his own empire on that which had already been laid down by former generals and Roman emperors. In this sense the pope became a latter-day cæsar, who readily ascended to the Roman 'throne' and ruled as if it were his by right.

[6] **We know that the pre-eminence of the pope, which was always contested by the patriarchs of Alexandria, Constantinople and Jerusalem, is founded on a dubious passage in the *New Testament*. The pope claims to be St Peter's successor, to whom Jesus had said: 'You are Peter and on this stone I shall found my church.' But the best commentators deny that St Peter had ever been to Rome. As regards the pope's infallibility, although many Christians have enough strength of mind to deny it, if one counts up those who subscribe to this incontestable truth, one**

Though these lofty titles were rejected by the Eastern Church, the Roman Pontiff reigned without rival over the vast majority of the Christian world. He was a god on earth. He became the arbiter of their destiny through the imbecility of sovereigns. He founded a *theocracy*, or a divine government, of which he was head and the kings were his lieutenants. He dethroned them and he incited people against them when they had the audacity to resist him.

In a word, for centuries spiritual arms were stronger than temporal arms: it was within the pope's authority to hand out crowns and he was always obeyed by stupefied nations: he divided princes in order to reign over them, and even today his empire would still be standing had the progress of the Enlightenment—against which sovereigns seemed to be such enemies—not relieved them little by little of their power, or had these sovereigns, regardless of their religious convictions, not listened to the call of ambition, rather than to the call of duty.[7] In fact, given these ministers of the Church receive their power directly from Jesus Christ Himself, it is tantamount to revolting against him to resist these representatives of his on earth. Kings, just like their subjects, cannot elude the authority of God without committing a crime: spiritual authority emanating from the Celestial Monarch must prevail over the temporal authority of men. A prince who is truly Christian must be the servant of the Church, as the primary slave of the priests.

It comes as no surprise then that during centuries when ignorance reigned, priests were more powerful than kings, and they were always obeyed by the people in preference, since they were more attached to the interests of Heaven than to those of earth.[8] Amongst superstitious nations, the voice of

---

finds among them the Spanish, Italians, Portuguese, Germans and the Flemish, and even the majority of the French. Bellarmine states that the pope has the right to commit injustices: '*Fure potest contra jus decernere.*' (For **Bellarmine**—see Glossary.)

The New Testament verse to which d'Holbach refers is to be found in Matthew's Gospel: 'And I say also unto thee, that thou art Peter, and upon this rock I will build my church; and the gates of hell shall not prevail against it', (Matt.16: 18). This sounds like a rather flimsy pretext for the sophisticated and powerful organization that has become the Vatican and the papacy. The Latin reads: 'Theft can strive against justice.'

[7] It is ambition and the desire to usurp others' possessions that gave the popes their great influence in Europe. Sovereigns, instead of uniting against them as they ought to have done, did nothing other than court them onto their side to receive honours, in order to get their hands on goods that excited their desires.

[8] It is obvious that during periods of great ignorance, Christians made more of their priests than their kings. In Saxon England the penalty fixed by law for the murder of the Archbishop of Canterbury was greater than that payable for the life of the monarch.

the Most High and his interpreters must be heeded more than the voice of duty, justice and reason.

Good Christians who are submissive to the Church must be blind and bereft of rationality every time the Church orders them to be so: it has the right to render men absurd and the power to command us to commit crimes.

On the other hand, men whose power on earth comes from God cannot be answerable to any power: hence the independence of the Christian priesthood is founded on the principles of their religion and they always knew how to take full advantage of this. It is not surprising then that Christian priests, made rich and financed by the generosity of kings and the people, failed to recognize the real source of their opulence and privileges. Men can take away what men have given by stealth or imprudence. Nations, disabused of their prejudices, could one day demand back their donations, extorted from them by fear, stealth or deception.

Priests knew all these drawbacks; they maintained that they only had what God alone had granted them through men's offerings and, by an amazing miracle, they were taken at their word.[9]

There is a great deal of truth in the point d'Holbach makes in this footnote, as the historian M.T. Clanchy states: 'In 1139 [King] Stephen took an even more radical action by arresting Roger bishop of Salisbury and his nephews, Alexander bishop of Lincoln and Nigel bishop of Ely. This should have won Stephen control of the administration, as Roger and his nephews had been the principal officers in the Exchequer and Chancery since Henry I's reign. But this resolute action merely enabled Henry of Blois to demonstrate his new powers as papal legate by summoning Stephen to Winchester to answer for the crime of imprisoning bishops. Henry reminded his brother that *it was the favour of the Church and not the prowess of knights which had raised him to the throne.*' (My italics, D.M.H.) (See M.T. Clanchy, *Early Medieval England* [London: The Folio Society, 1997], p. 86.)

[9] **Divine rights or ecclesiastical immunities granted to priests date far back in history. Isis, who was a goddess, gave a third of her kingdom to the priests of Egypt in order to enlist them to convey divine honours to Osiris, her husband, after her death. See Diodorus Siculus, Bk. II, ch. 1. Egyptian priests always received tithes at the very least, and they were exempt from paying all public duties. Moses, who was an Egyptian and hailed from the tribe of Levi, just like the god of the Jews, seemed wholly occupied with making sure that priests were well catered for through sacrifices and tithes, which were granted to them. Christian priests also indubitably inherited these rights from Jewish priests; from this it is obvious that it would be a great sin not to pay tithes to the Church and that it would be a great crime to want to submit them to ordinary taxation. In Genesis 47: 26, we read that, *'the land of priests pays nothing to the king.'* According to Leviticus (27: 21 & 18) *'the goods of priests cannot be bought back'.* Christian priests, as can be seen, have held to Judaic law where goods are concerned. (For Diodorus and Osiris—see Glossary.) The verses quoted by d'Holbach are as follows: 'And Joseph made it a law over the land of Egypt unto this**

144

Thus the interests of the priesthood were separated from those of society. Men devoted to God and chosen to be his ministers were no longer citizens; they were no longer associated with profane subjects; laws and civil tribunals had no more power over them; they were judged only by men of their own kind. That is why their greatest excesses often went unpunished; their person, under God's submission, was inviolable and sacred.[10] Sovereigns were obliged to defend the possessions of the priesthood and to protect them without any contribution to the public charges, or at least they contributed as much as they judged was in their interests to do so. In a word, these revered men were harmful and nasty for societies, and they lived in it merely to devour it, under the pretext of feeding them instructions and praying for them—but they were untouchable.

---

day, that Pharaoh should have the fifth part, except the land of the priests only, which became not Pharaoh's', (Gen. 47: 26). Leviticus ch. 27 deals with all manner of tithes and gifts to priests, etc., 'And if a man shall sanctify unto the Lord some part of a field of his possession, then thy estimation shall be according to the seed thereof: an homer of barley seed shall be valued at fifty shekels of silver. If he sanctify his field from the year of jubile, according to thy estimation it shall stand. But if he sanctify his field after the jubile, then the priest shall reckon unto him the money according to the years that remain, even unto the year of the jubile, and it shall be abated from thy estimation. And if he that sanctified the field will in any wise redeem it, then he shall add the fifth part of the money of thy estimation unto it, and it shall be assured to him. And if he will not redeem the field, or if he have sold the field to another man, it shall not be redeemed any more. But the field, when it goeth out in the jubile, shall be holy unto the Lord, as a field devoted; the possession thereof shall be the priest's. And if a man sanctify unto the Lord a field which he hath bought, which is not of the fields of his possession; Then the priest shall reckon unto him the worth of thy estimation, even unto the year of the jubile: and he shall give thine estimation in that day, as a holy thing unto the Lord', (Lev. 27: 16—23).

[10] **Henry II, king of England, fell foul of the Archbishop of Canterbury (Thomas à Becket) because he wanted to punish ecclesiastics for murders and crimes they had committed. Finally, the King of Portugal was forced to solicit permission in vain to censure Jesuits accused of the crime of *lèse-majesté* against his person. The church does not willingly allow its ministers to be punished: that is when it abhors the spilling of blood. However, it is not so fussy when it comes to spilling that of others.** Even today the Catholic Church negociates special privileges with regard to taxation and the (non-) payment of duties through Concordats, agreed between the Vatican and sovereign states. Also, in similar vein, the Vatican has negociated special immunities from prosecution for priests who might be accused of crimes or fall foul of aspects of the criminal law. The Vatican also has the power over its own followers, priests and laity, to silence them and prevent them from giving evidence against one of their own, not to mention the special right to withhold any evidence divulged in the confessional. Clearly these are all special rights which have been granted to the Church, from which ordinary citizens are exempt. For details on Concordats and other agreements concluded with the Vatican, see http://www.concordatwatch.eu /

In fact, for eighteen centuries, what fruit have nations garnered from their teaching? Have these infallible men been able to agree amongst themselves the essential points their religion revealed to them by the Divinity? What kind of strange revelation is it that needs continuous commentaries and interpretation? What are we to think of these divine Scriptures, which each sect interprets in such a different way?

Though people have been nourished endlessly on teaching by so many pastors, people enlightened by the light of the gospel are no more virtuous or more educated on the matter which is of the utmost importance to them. They are told to submit to the Church, but the Church can never agree on anything amongst themselves. In every century it has been busy reforming, explaining, destroying and re–establishing its heavenly doctrine; whenever necessary its ministers create new dogmas, unrecognizable to the church founders. Each age sees the birth of new mysteries, new ways and new articles of faith. Despite the Holy Spirit's inspiration, Christianity has never managed to reach a clarity, simplicity and consistency of teaching, which are the undisputable proofs of a proven system. Neither *councils*, nor *canon law*, or a host of *decrees* and laws which form the Church's code have been able to lay down the definitive objects of the Church's faith up to now.

If a rational pagan wanted to embrace the Christian faith, he would be thrown into the greatest perplexity from his very first steps at the sight of so many multiple sects, each of which claims to lead along the surest path to salvation and stick closest to the Word of God. Which of these sects should he decide upon, seeing how they regard each other with horror, and several of the sects damn some more mercilessly than others? Instead of tolerating each other, why do they torment and persecute one another, and why do those who have power inflict upon their rivals the most well–considered cruelties and the utmost fury, which wreck peace within society? Let us not kid ourselves—Christianity, little content with doing violence against men to subjugate them outwardly to its cult—has invented the art of terrorizing free–thought and tormenting consciences, an art which was unknown to all pagan superstitions. The zeal of church ministers does not confine itself to the exterior—they rummage around in the recesses of the heart, they insolently violate its impenetrable sanctuary, they justify their sacrilegious acts and ingenious cruelty by the great interest they take in the salvation of souls.

Such are the effects which necessarily result from the principles of a religion which believes that an error is a crime worthy of the anger of its god. It is as a result of these ideas that priests, with the consent of sovereigns, are given the duty in certain countries of maintaining the faith in all its purity. As judges of their own cause, they condemn to the flames those whose opinions appear dangerous to them.[11] Surrounded by informers, they spy on citizens' actions and conversations, and sacrifice all offenders in order to secure their own position. It is on the basis of these abominable premises that the *Inquisition* was founded; it wanted to find people guilty and just the very act of existing was enough to give rise to their suspicions. These were the principles of a bloodthirsty tribunal which perpetuated ignorance and numbed people's minds wherever the mistaken policies of kings allowed them to exercise their wrath.

In countries where people believe they are more enlightened and freer we see bishops, who have shamelessly written statements and professions of faith signed by those who are dependent upon them, asking them misleading questions. What can I say? Even women are not exempt from their investigations; a prelate wants to know their feelings on unintelligible subtleties for the very things they themselves invented.

Disputes between Christian priests gave rise to animosity, hate and heresies. We have seen this since the birth of the Church. A system founded on miracles, fables and obscure oracles is bound to be a rich source of quarrelling.

Instead of spending their time on useful knowledge, theologians never concern themselves with anything other than their dogmas; instead of studying real morality and teaching people their true duties, they strive to recruit new converts. Christian priests fritter away their idle time in useless speculation on a barbarous and mystifying discipline, which, under the name of a 'knowledge of God', or 'theology', attracts the respect of the common man.   This system of presumptuous ignorance, obstinate and derived according to the nature of its god, is as incomprehensible as he is. Hence, disputes arose out of disputes.

Often the greatest geniuses and those whose minds were unworthy of frittering their time away on puerile subtleties of idle questions and arbitrary

---

[11] Civil tribunals, when they operate justly, follow the maxim that every avenue should be explored that helps the defence of the accused: tribunals during the Inquisition took the completely opposite approach.   The accused was never informed of the reason for their detention and witnesses were never brought forth; even if ignorant of their crime, people had to admit it—these were the maxims Christian priests worked to.   It is true that the Inquisition did not condemn a person to death: priests could not personally spill blood.   This function was kept in reserve for its secular arm and its treacherous members made out that they were interceding for the accused, but naturally, they were not listened to. What can one say? They would have made a fine rumpus had the magistrate taken them at their word. This kind of behaviour is well suited to men whose aim it is to stifle humanity, sincerity and decency.

opinions merely served to create friction, instead of being useful to society. People entered into quarrels which they had never understood, and princes leapt to the defence of priests to whom they wanted to show their favour. They decided orthodoxy at the thrust of the sword and the group they chose overwhelmed all others, because sovereigns always feel obliged to get involved in theological arguments. They do not see that by involving themselves in them, they accord them importance and gravitas, and Christian priests have always called upon human help to support opinions which they believed God had guaranteed as having an eternal quality. Heroes in church annals turn out to be merely obstinate fanatics, victims of their own foolish ideas or raging persecutors, who treated their adversaries with the greatest inhumanity, or they turn out to be troublemakers who stir up national dissent. The world of our fathers was decimated by defending extravagant ideas which proved risible to posterity, but which is no less insane than them.

In almost every century complaints have been voiced openly about abuses by the Church and there has always been talk of reformation. But despite this so-called reform *amongst those in charge and members of the Church,* corruption always reigns. Priests who are greedy, troublemakers and seditious made nations groan under the weight of their vices, and princes were too feeble to bring them to their senses. It was only these tyrants' own divisions and quarrels that diminished the weight of the yoke the people and sovereigns alike had to bear. The empire of the Roman Pontiff, after having lasted a good number of centuries, was finally undermined by irate enthusiasts, by rebellious subjects who dared challenge this redoubtable despot's rights. Several princes, weary of their bondage and poverty, embraced opinions which placed them within reach of being able to grab the clergy's booty. Thus the unity of the Church was destroyed, sects multiplied, and each one of them fought to defend their own system of belief.

Founders of this new sect, which the Roman Pontiff dubbed *innovators,* *heretics* and *impious,* in truth renounced some of their former opinions. But satisfied with having made a few steps towards reason, they never dared shake off the yoke of superstition fully: they continued to respect Christian Holy Books, which they regarded as the only guide for the faithful, and they claimed to have found in them their own guiding principles.

Finally, they delivered these obscure books (in which anyone can easily find anything they want to find and in which the Divinity often speaks in contradictory terms) into the hands of their followers who, soon having lost their way in the tortuous labyrinth of these texts, caused new sects to burgeon.

Thus the heads of sects, the so-called reformers of the Church, merely caught a glimpse of the truth, or merely latched on to its minutiae. They continued to respect the Christian sacred oracles and to recognize the cruel, bizarre God in them, admiring their extravagant mythology and their anti–rational dogmas. They ended up adopting its most incomprehensible mysteries, whilst balking, however, at other difficult ones.[12]

Therefore, it is not surprising that despite all reforms, fanaticism, disputes, persecution and wars spread like wildfire all over Europe. The dreaming of innovators only resulted in plunging Europe into new misfortunes, as blood flowed everywhere and people became no more reasonable, or any happier.

Priests of all sects continually wanted to dominate and make their decisions appear infallible and sacred. They persecuted people every time they had the power to do so and nations always consented to their manias, whilst states continued to be toppled by their calamitous opinions.

Intolerance and a spirit of persecution are the essence of every sect which has Christianity as its foundation: a cruel, partisan God, who gets irritated at men's opinions, cannot accommodate a religion which is gentle and humane.[13]

In fact, in every Christian sect the priest will always exercise power, which can be disastrous for a state: each sect has its enthusiasts, mystics and fanatics who will ferment trouble every time they are told that *God's cause* demands it, that the *Church is in danger*, and that it is a case of fighting for the *glory* of the Almighty.

In Christian countries we also see temporal powers servilely subjugated to the priesthood, ready to do their bidding, to exterminate their enemies, to work for their grandeur, to maintain their rights, their wealth and their immunities. In almost all nations in the grip of the gospel, the laziest men, the most seditious, the most useless and the most dangerous are the most honoured and the best rewarded. People's superstition makes them believe

---

[12] **By what right do Protestants, who give credence to the doctrines of the Trinity, the Incarnation, Baptism, etc., reject the mystery of transubstantiation? When one goes so far down the road to admit one absurdity, why stop half-way?** (For transubstantiation—see p. 329.)

[13] **Calvin had Servetus burned in Geneva. Although Protestant priests allowed their followers the right to question them, they punished them when the outcome of their examination did not accord with their own ideas. Protestant churches do not boast that they are infallible, but they want their opinions to be followed as if they were. It was over religious quarrels and a lack of tolerance that Charles I was forced to lose his head. Although Protestant nations boast of being tolerant, religious differences place a great barrier between citizens: Calvinists, Lutherans and Anglicans hate and despise the papacy, just as the pope consigns them to eternal damnation. Everywhere the dominant sect makes all the others feel its cruel superiority.** (For **Calvin** and **Servetus**—see Glossary.)

that no effort should be spared for the ministers of their God. These sentiments are the same in all sects.[14] Wherever priests impose their ideas upon sovereigns they force them to skew their policies in favour of their religion and they oppose those institutions which are most advantageous for the state.

Everywhere priests become teachers of the young, whose minds they fill with their sorrowful prejudices from childhood onwards.

However, the priesthood has always enjoyed the highest degree of wealth and power in those countries under the submission of the Roman Pontiff. Credulity subjugated even kings to the priesthood; kings were mere executors of their will—so often cruel—and they have been ready to wield the sword whenever priests gave the order.[15]

Monarchs of the Roman sect, who are more blind than all others, had a foolish confidence in the ministers of the Church and this was the reason they fell in so readily with their personal interests. This sect made all others pale into insignificance in terms of their intolerant rages and their atrocious persecution. Its unruly, cruel mood made it justifiably hateful to other, less unreasonable nations, that is to say, to the less Christian ones.[16] It is not at all surprising that the Roman religion was invented purely to make the priesthood all–powerful. Its priests had the knack of identifying themselves with the Divinity; their cause was always his cause, their glory became a matter of God's glory, their decisions were his divine oracles, and their treasures belonged to his Heavenly Kingdom. Their pride, avarice, and

---

[14] However, I make an exception for the Quakers or Shakers, who have the good sense not to want any priests in their sects. (For **Quaker** and **Shaker**—see Glossary.)

[15] 'Ad nutum sacerdotis', as the mild St Bernard remarked.
The Latin means, 'At the nod of the priest'. (For **Bernard**—see Glossary.)

[16] God rejects the lukewarm. Every Christian must be full of zeal since he has to love his god tenderly. A truly Christian king must exterminate everything, rather than allow his subjects to offend his god. Philip II and Louis XIV were truly Christian kings. The English and the Dutch are lukewarm, cowardly Christians, who prefer the prosperity of the state and commerce to religious interests. In Christianity, tolerance and indifference towards religion have become synonymous. How can one adopt a tolerant attitude towards a religion whose founder declared, 'Who is not for me is against me'? (For **Philip II** and **Louis XIV**—see Glossary.)
The Biblical quotation, uttered by Jesus, is found in Matthew's Gospel: 'He that is not with me is against me; and he that gathereth not with me scattereth abroad.' (Matt. 12: 30). (Luke 11: 23 expresses the same sentiments.) On the subject of being 'lukewarm', the Bible also has this remark—a criticism levelled at the church at Laodicea at the beginning of the Book of Revelation: 'So then because thou art lukewarm, and neither cold nor hot, I will spue thee out of my mouth', (Rev. 3: 16).

cruelty were legitimized in the interests of the Celestial Master. And what is more, in this sect the priest saw his sovereign at his feet, making a humble confession of his sins and asking him to reconcile him with his God. It is rare that one sees a priest using his holy ministry for the happiness of the people. It has never entered into his head to reproach monarchs for abusing their power, for the poverty of their subjects, or for the tears of the oppressed; too timid, or too much of a good courtier to bellow the truth in their ears, they never speak of any bad treatment under which nations groan, or of onerous taxes which overwhelm them, or of the futile wars which destroy them, or of the perpetual infringements of their rights as citizens. These issues do not interest the Church at all—if they did, it would at least make priests of some use in exerting their influence to apply a brake to the excesses of superstitious tyrants.[17]

The terrors of the other world would be pardonable lies if they served to make kings tremble. But that has never been the goal of ministers of religion: they have never stipulated the interests of the people, they lavished their incense upon monarchs' tyranny, they received indulgences for their real crimes, they supplied monarchs with easy pardons for sins, and they promised them Heavenly pardon if they entered into their quarrels with gusto.

Thus, in the Roman religion the priesthood reigned over kings and consequently they were assured of ruling over their subjects. Religious superstition and despotism made an eternal alliance and united their efforts to make people miserable slaves.

Priests subjugated subjects by religious terror so that the sovereign might devour them; he, in turn, rewarded the priests with free licence, opulence and grandeur, and enlisted them to destroy all his enemies.[18]

---

[17] **Marshal de D** remarked to Louis XIV: 'I can well conceive that Your Majesty finds a confessor who, in order to curry favour, gives him absolution, but I cannot understand how the priest Father Le Tellier can find anyone to grant him his own absolution.'** (For **Le Tellier**—see Glossary.)

[18] **Catholic nations are the most ignorant and enslaved in Europe: religious slavery brings in its wake political slavery. Priests of the Roman Church seem to have offered sovereigns the same pact that the Devil offered Jesus Christ when he tempted him in the wilderness: 'Haec omnia tibi dabo, si cadens adoraveris me.' In other words, 'We shall deliver unto you all your subjects, bound hand and foot, if you submit yourself to our fantasies.'**
The Latin reads: 'All this shall be yours if you fall down at my feet and worship.' The quotation is from Matthew's Gospel: 'Again, the devil taketh him up into an exceeding high mountain, and sheweth him all the kingdoms of the world, and the glory of them; and saith unto him, "All these things will I give thee, if thou wilt fall down and worship me",' (Matt. 4: 8—9).

What shall we say of these Doctors of the Church, whom Christians call *casuists*, of these so–called moralists, who wanted to assess just how far the creature might go towards offending his Creator without risking his salvation?

These profound men have enriched Christian morality by a ridiculous tariff of sins: they know the degree of anger that each sin provokes in the splenetic Supreme Being. True morality has only one standard by which to judge men's faults: the worst 'sins' are those which harm society most. Behaviour which harms us is imprudent and foolish, but that which harms others is unjust and criminal.

Everything, right down to idleness itself, is rewarded in Christian priests. Ridiculous foundations subsidize a whole crowd of idlers who live a life of ease and devour society without lifting a finger for it.

People already crippled with taxes are further tormented by leeches who make them pay dearly for useless prayers offered up negligently, whereas talented men—the innovative scientist and the courageous serviceman—languish in poverty or have just enough to get by, while idle monks and lazy priests enjoy a shameful abundance in states which tolerate them.[19]

In a word, Christianity makes societies complacent to all the ills that ministers of divinity cause them. Neither the uselessness of their prayers—proven by experience to be so throughout the centuries—nor the bloody outcomes of their disastrous disputes, or even their wild excesses, have managed to disabuse nations of these holy men, upon whom people are simple–minded enough to believe that their eternal salvation depends.

---

[19] **The most biting satire ever written about Christian priests has already been written in St Matthew's Gospel, chapter 23. Everything that Christ said about the scribes and Pharisees pertains exactly to our priests. In the parable of the Good Samaritan Jesus Christ informs us that of all men priests are the most inhuman. It is rare in our society that beggars ever turn for help to an ecclesiastic.**

The parable of the Good Samaritan, who helped a man who had been robbed and gave money to have him looked after, when religious men had walked on by, is told in Luke 10: 25—37. It is cited by Christ as an act of genuine altruism to a stranger, whom religious men had not considered to be their 'neighbour', and thereby they had not observed the commandment to 'love thy neighbour as thyself'.

Chapter 16—The Final Chapter

Conclusion

All that has been said thus far proves in the clearest possible way that the Christian religion is contrary to the prudent running and well–being of nations. Christianity can only prove to be advantageous for princes who lack education and virtue, who believe that it is their duty to reign over slaves, rob them blind and tyrannize them with impunity to join forces with the priesthood, whose function has always been to hoodwink people in the name of Heaven.

But these imprudent princes must remember that to succeed in their plans they cannot escape from being servile to priests themselves, who turn their sacred arms against them every time they fail to submit to their whim or refuse to serve their mania.

We have seen above that the Christian religion, by its fanatical virtues, its senseless striving for perfection and its zeal, is no less harmful to sound morality, to right reasoning, to the benefit of the individual and family harmony. It is easy to see that a Christian who lays claim to a gloomy God and promotes suffering as a model must be in a constant state of depression and self–inflicted misery.

If this world is no more than a fleeting event, if this life is merely a pilgrimage, it stands to reason that it would be foolish to get involved with anything here below.

If their God is offended either by the actions or opinions of fellow believers, he ought to punish them himself most severely, if he has the power to do so; without that, there would be a lack of zeal and affection for this god. A good Christian ought either to flee this world or make it uncomfortable for himself and for others.

These thoughts should satisfy those who hold that Christianity is useful for politics and morality, and that without religion man cannot be virtuous nor be a good citizen.

The inverse of this proposition is surely much more the case, and one can be sure that a perfect Christian who keeps faithfully to his religious principles, who would like faithfully to imitate the holy men his religion holds up as models, who would practise austerity, live in solitude and would infect society with their enthusiasm, their fanaticism and their obstinacy—

such a man, I say, has no real virtue and would be a useless member of a state or an impractical, dangerous citizen.[1]

Were to believe the supporters of Christianity, there is apparently no morality in any country where this religion has not gained a foothold. However, a superficial glance at the world suffices to prove to us that there is virtue everywhere—no political society could survive without it. Doubtlessly there exist amongst the Chinese, the Indians and the Muhammadans good fathers, good husbands, obedient and grateful children, and subjects who are faithful to their princes; and there would be good people in great numbers, just as amongst us, and even more so, were they to be well governed and if, instead of them being taught senseless religious dogmas from their earliest childhood, there were a wise political structure and fair laws to teach them a pure form of morality, not perverted by fanaticism, which invited them to do the right thing through rewards and deterred them from crime by sensible forms of punishment.

I repeat—wherever we look it seems that religion has been invented only to spare sovereigns the bother of being just and of making good laws and governing well.

Religion is the art of intoxicating men with fanaticism to stop them getting up to all manner of wickedness, heaped upon them here below by those who govern them.

Invisible forces have been dreamt up to threaten people who are forced to suffer in silence the miseries they have caused, and they are made to hope that if they agree to be miserable in this world, they will be happier in the next.

---

[1] **Our priests never cease to grouse and grumble against non-believers and philosophers, whom they call *dangerous subjects*. However, if one considers history, one would find that a philosopher had never caused revolutions in a state. On the other hand, not a single revolution has taken place without religious people being up to their necks in it. The Dominican who poisoned Emperor Henry VI with a host, Jacques Clément, and Ravaillac were not unbelievers. It was not philosophers, but Christian fanatics, who put Charles I on the gallows. It was the minister Gomarus and not Spinoza who set Holland on fire, etc, etc, etc. (For Clément, Ravaillac, Gomarus, Spinoza, Charles I—see Glossary.)**

D'Holbach is either mistaken or there is a misprint here: as Voltaire points out, the note should read 'Henry VII': see p. 292. The reference is to Henry VII of Luxembourg who was crowned in Rome. Pope Clement V was alarmed by Henry's preparations to invade the kingdom of Naples, a papal fiefdom, and threatened excommunication. A Dominican monk, Bernardo da Montepulciano, was reputed to have killed the king by giving him a poisoned host for communion during the ceremony in 1313, but a subsequent trial found him innocent.

This is the way that religion has become the mainspring for unjust and cowardly policies perpetrated by rulers who believed men had to be hoodwinked in order to govern them more easily.

Enlightened and virtuous princes are far from using such base methods of control: let them learn what is in their true interest, let them know that their lot is linked to that of their subjects, let them understand that they cannot be truly powerful themselves if they are not served by citizens who are themselves courageous, actively engaged, industrious and virtuous, and possess a sense of belonging to their masters.

And let these masters know that their subjects' sense of belonging can only be based on the happiness which it brings. If kings were convinced of these important truths, they would have no need of religion or priests to govern a nation.

Let them be just, let them be fair, let them be rigorous in rewarding talent and virtue, and in discouraging unproductivity, vice and crime, and soon their states will be full of useful citizens who will feel that their own interests lie in serving and defending their country, and in cherishing their leader, who is the source of their happiness. Then they will have no need of revelation, mysteries, Paradise, or Hell to fulfil their duties.

Morality will always be hollow if it is not applied by a higher authority. It is the sovereign who must be the chief pontiff of his own people. It is down to him alone to teach morality, to encourage virtue, to insist on justice, to provide a good example and punish abuses and vice. He weakens his power the moment he allows a power to arise within his state, whose interests diverge from his own, whose morality has nothing in common with that which his subjects require, and whose principles are diametrically opposed to those which are useful to society.

Christian princes have relied on zealous, fanatical priests to provide education in their states and they have produced a whole mass of superstitious people, having no other virtue than blind faith, militant zeal and blinkered submission to puerile ceremonies; in a word, they have equipped them with bizarre notions which have no influence on their conduct or work, and have done nothing to improve them.

In fact, despite the alleged good influence of Christianity, do we see more virtue in those who profess religion than in those who pay no heed to it? Are men who have been redeemed by the blood of God himself more just, more law–abiding, and more honest than others?

Could there possibly be any evidence at all of oppression, any plundering, any fornication or adultery amongst these Christians, so convinced of their religious dogmas? Could there possibly be any intrigues, any acts of treachery or liable amongst those faith–filled courtiers? And amongst its priests, who proclaim awe–inspiring dogmas and terrible punishments to others, is there the slightest possibility at all of discovering any injustice, vice or dark deeds? Surely not! And finally, are there amongst them any non–believers or *rational minds*, those unfortunate people who are taken away to be executed through an excess of religious zeal on a daily basis? Surely not!

All these men are Christians, for whom religion acts not at all as a restraint: they continuously violate their most obvious moral duties, they consciously offend a God whom they are conscious of having irritated, and yet they flatter themselves that at their death they will be able to make a last–minute act of repentance to appease a heavenly Deity, whom they have outraged during the course of their whole lives.

We will not deny, however, that the Christian religion can sometimes be a restraining influence for some timorous souls who do not have either the ardour, or the unfortunate urge to commit big crimes, or the hard–heartedness that a habit of vice leads them to develop. However, these timorous souls would have been honest people even without religion. The fear of becoming hateful in the eyes of their fellows, of incurring their contempt, and of losing their good reputation, would have been enough to restrain them from incurring such censure. Those who are blind enough to ride roughshod over these sensibilities would have had equal contempt for them anyway, despite of all religion's threats.

One cannot deny either that the fear of a God, who sees all men's innermost secret thoughts, acts as a deterrent for a good many people; but this deterrent is ineffectual for strong passions, whose distinctive feature is to make people blind to all that is harmful in society.

On the other hand, people who are habitually honest have no need of being spied upon to do good: they fear succumbing to their own self–loathing and self–hate, and to feeling remorse—these are terrible feelings for anyone whose heart has not been hardened by wrong–doing.

Let no one say that without a fear of God one cannot feel remorse. Anyone who has been brought up honestly is bound to feel within themselves a sense of pain mixed with shame and fear every time they contemplate dishonourable actions which might sully them. Often one will judge oneself more harshly than one's fellows might and dread the gaze of one's peers, preferring to flee from oneself—that is what constitutes remorse.

Figure 34: Reading the bawdy prose of Rabelais.
The Sketch—Literary Supplement, **1893.**

157

In a word, it is not religion which acts as a deterrent to people's strong inclinations, so much as reason, education and sound morality, which can be much more effective. If wicked people expected to be punished every time they thought about committing a dishonest act, they would be forced to desist.

In a well–ordered society contempt ought always to accompany vice and punishment always follow a crime. Education, guided by public interest, should always teach people to cherish their own self–esteem, to dread the contempt of others and to fear infamy more than death.

But this morality cannot sit happily with a religion which instructs people to despise themselves, to hate themselves, to shun the respect of others and seeks only to please a god, whose own conduct is accountable to none.

Finally, if the Christian religion constrains people's hidden urges, as is claimed, if it exerts a beneficial effect on some individuals, these advantages are so rare, so feeble and so dubious, that how can they be compared to the obvious ills this religion has caused and *still* causes on earth, which are wholly tangible and legion? Can a few vague, predictable sins, or a few conversions useless to society, or a few sterile, tardy acts of repentance, or some futile restitutions—can all these things be weighed in the balance against continuous dissention, bloody wars, dreadful massacres, persecution, and incredible acts of cruelty, all of which the Christian religion has been the cause and pretext since its very foundation? Christianity arms whole nations for mutual destruction and seeks to stifle secret thoughts. It inflames the hearts of millions of fanatics and causes trouble in families and states, and it bathes the earth with tears and blood.

Let common sense decide ultimately what advantages the *Good News* brings to Christians, which their God came down to announce.

Many honest people and those convinced of the ills Christianity brings upon nations still continue to regard it as a necessary evil, and that it would be dangerous to try to uproot it. People, they say, are superstitious and need chimeras: they get angry when one wants to take them away. But I reply that people are superstitious only because everything has conspired to make them so from childhood. They expect their happiness to come from these fantasies because the government all too often refuses to give them tangible things. They would never get angry with leaders who benefited them; such sovereigns would be much stronger than priests and God.

In fact, it is the sovereign alone who can lead people back to reason. He would have to gain their confidence and their affection by providing them with benefits and, little by little, he would disabuse them of their fantasies, which he himself would have to see through. He would stop superstition from being harmful by heaping contempt upon it, by never getting involved in its futile quarrels, by dividing it, by forcing tolerance upon different sects who fight each other, and by unmasking its adherents, making them look mutually ridiculous. When a prince permitted reason to combat foolishness by giving back liberty to people's minds, then superstition would finally fall by the wayside of its own accord.

True tolerance and freedom of thought are the real counterbalances to religious fanaticism. By promoting these things a prince will always be master of his own state; he will never share his power with seditious priests who have no power over an enlightened, firm and virtuous prince. Deception is timid and arms will fall from priests' hands at the sight of a monarch who dares to despise religion, who is supported by the people's affection and the power of truth.

Just as criminal and ignorant policies have used religion almost everywhere to enslave people and make them miserable, virtuous and enlightened policies weaken and destroy religion little by little in order to make nations happy. Just as education up to now has served only to produce maniacs and fanatics, a more enlightened education would form good citizens. Just as a morality propped up by marvels and founded on future promises has not been capable of bridling people's excesses, so a morality established on the real and actual needs of the human race proves that, in a well–ordered society, happiness is always a reward for virtue. Shame, contempt and punishments are the wages of vice and the companions of crime.

Hence, let sovereigns have no fear of disabusing their subjects of a superstition which has reduced them to slavery and has stood against the well–being of states for centuries.

If error be an evil, then let truth stand against it. If fanaticism be harmful, then let it be fought against by the sword of reason; let them relegate to Asia a religion brought forth by the ardent imagination of Eastern peoples; let our Europe be reasonable, happy and free; let mores, industry, a grandeur of spirit, innovation, conviviality and peace be seen to reign here; let the sovereign command and the subject obey under the umbrella of the law, and let us all enjoy its unchanging durability.

Might we hope that one day reason will be permitted to pour out its power, long since usurped by error, illusions and magic? Will nations ever turn from their mythical hopes to contemplate their real interests? Will nations ever throw off the yoke of these haughty priests, those holy tyrants who are only ever interested terrestrial faults?

Let us harbour the hope that truth will ultimately triumph over lies. Princes and people, weary of their credulity, will rush back to the truth. Reason will break their chains, the shackles of superstition will shatter at its sovereign voice, and rationality, destined to be our guiding light, will share its power with none other.

Amen.

A Controversy in Documents

Foreword to Bergier's Refutation

Abbé Nicolas–Sylvain Bergier was considered to be the most formidable theological opponent of the *Encyclopédists* and defender of Roman Catholic orthodoxy in his day. He was born of a humble family, one of four children, on 31 December 1718 at Darney in Franche–Comté, which was a stronghold of conservative Roman Catholic tradition. He was educated in Besançon at the *collège*, seminary and university there, and he eventually gained a doctorate in theology, graduating in 1744; afterwards he was ordained as a priest in the Church. His education was as deep as it was wide, including Greek, Latin and Hebrew, Roman canonical law, jurisprudence, medicine, geography, history, and theology as interpreted by SS Augustine, Bonaventure, and Thomas Aquinas.[1] He refused a university professorship in theology at the University of Besançon, preferring instead to pursue courses of further study in Paris from 1745 to 1748. In addition to studying, he was called upon to preach and lecture around the capital, where he was invited to remain, but being still under the jurisdiction of the Archbishop of Besançon, he was called back to assume parish duties in the vicinity, where he remained for some twenty years. Despite his prodigious intellectual capabilities, he worked diligently with his parishioners and he did not consider himself above helping the peasants of his parish with their agricultural activities in due season. However, he did not neglect his studies and to his already impressive range of ancient languages, he added English, as well as taking a keen interest in physics and natural history. He was a voracious reader and, like d'Holbach, he had an excellent memory: he could quote from memory 'virtually all important and secondary authors of antiquity.'[2]

Bergier's writing career started in 1753, when he won two gold medals as first prizes against stiff competition from the Academy of Besançon for an historical and oratorical essay. Later that year, he published an essay on a linguistic topic, comparing the roots of words from ancient Greek, Latin, Hebrew and French, which drew praise from Grimm. This was followed by a further work entitled *Origine des dieux du paganisme* {*The Origin of Pagan Gods*}, which attracted some attention from the *Encyclopédists*.

Bergier's first of many polemical works was a refutation—a genre of writing to which he would dedicate virtually the rest of his life; it was an attack on Rousseau's treatise on education (*Emile*, 1762) and on his religious

---

[1] One of the best and most detailed sources of Bergier's life and writing, upon which this resumé of his career is based, is to be found in the article by Alfred J. Bingham, 'The Abbé Bergier: An Eighteenth-Century Catholic Apologist', in *Modern Language Review*, 3 (July) 1959, pp. 337—350.

[2] Bingham, p. 338.

views, entitled *Le Deism réfuté par lui–même* {*Deism Refuted by Itself* } (1765), which was lauded by Grimm and others as the best and most compelling attack on Rousseau's philosophy. The work was edited and purged of the latest unfashionably unorthodox ideas of Catholic dogma at that time, then it was translated into Italian and a dedication to Pope Clement XIV was added: this work brought him to the attention of the Church's grandees and it became a 'best–seller', running to several editions.

Buoyed up by the success of his *Deism Refuted*, though he had not cared for the editing to which it had been subjected, he published his *Certitude des preuves du christianisme, ou Réfutation de l'Examen critique des apologistes de la religion chrétienne* {*Certainty of the Proofs of Christianity, or Refutation of the Critical Examination of the Apologists of the Christian Religion* } in April 1767, a work ostensibly directed against Fréret, to whom the *Critical Examination* was attributed, but whose actual author is now known to be **Levesque de Burigny**. Though praised by interested parties, this work did not enjoy the same success in terms of volume of books sold as his *Deism Refuted*, because the general reading public had more of a taste for the scandalous and outrageous, than for such a serious refutation of religious ideas under attack.

However, the writing of Rousseau, Fréret and de Burigny seemed tame by comparison with the books d'Holbach and Voltaire were starting to produce, though, of course, no one knew outside his circle that d'Holbach was the true author of such trenchant, anti–religious material. From June 1766 to November 1767, and again in 1769, Bergier attacked forty–seven major articles from Voltaire's *Dictionnaire philosophique portatif* {*Portable Philosophical Dictionary*} (1764), and by mid–March of 1768, he was ready to send off the weighty manuscript (in terms of length and content) to the printer in Paris against d'Holbach's *Christianity Unveiled*. Bergier went to Paris and he even struck up a friendship with the 'coterie holbachique', which was not that unusual, given that he was not the only *abbé* on the guest list; however, he certainly did not know how close he was sitting to the author of the work on which he had just written his refutation. His *Apologie de la religion chrétienne, contre l'auteur du Christianisme dévoilé et contre quelques autres critiques* {*Apology of the Christian Religion Against the Author of Christianity Unveiled and Against Certain Other Critics*} was published in December 1768, and as the title suggests, Bergier had turned the work into a multi–targeted attack on Fréret, Bolingbroke, Voltaire, Boulanger and Naigeon, etc., though he did not always know that these people were the authors of the works he was criticizing because some had been published anonymously or attributed to other writers. Most of this refutation is directed against d'Holbach's work, though the works of the other writers indicated are mentioned when their ideas coincide or express similar criticisms of Christianity as those in *Christianity Unveiled.*

The papal nuncio sent copies of Bergier's refutation to Pope Clement XIII, who dispatched a commendation by return, and when he died shortly after that, the nuncio went through the same process, which also elicited a blessing from the new pope, Clement XIV.

In 1770 d'Holbach published his *System of Nature*—anonymously, as was his wont—and this was quickly followed by yet another refutation from Bergier's pen, this one entitled *Examen du matérialisme, ou Réfutation du Système de la nature, par Mirabeau* [sic] {*An Examination of Materialism, or Refutation of the System of Nature by Mirabeau*} (1771), a two–volume work against Mr Mirabaud (the correct spelling of the name), the reputed author of the work.

For a few years before his *Examination of Materialism* appeared, a tussle had been going on for Bergier's services between the Archbishop of Besançon and the Bishop of Arras, both of whom wanted him to assume duties within their jurisdiction. In the end, the desire to be near good academic facilities such as libraries, bookshops and publishers, made Bergier decide to take up the offer of a post in the cathedral of Notre Dame de Paris, and confessional duties to the royal household were later added to his remit. In his article, Bingham states that, 'Records show that [Bergier] harboured few ambitions and fewer illusions about advancement in a hierarchy then dominated by aristocratic families'.[3] For these services, Bergier received pensions and payments in the expectation that he would produce much more of the same kind of writing in defence of the Church, which enabled him to support an ailing sister and a feckless brother back home: after all, he had come from a poor background and, from his family's point of view, he had done well for himself in the capital, and as a celibate priest he had no immediate family dependents of his own in Paris. During the ensuing period he did not match the publishing pace of his former years, though by 1773 he had completed the initial draft of the first part of his *Traité historique et dogmatique de la vraie religion* {*Historical and Dogmatic Treatise of the True Religion*}, a work which was to grow to a massive twelve volumes, which was finally published in September 1780, followed by a second edition four years later.

In the mean time, Bergier compiled his own *Dictionnaire de théologie* {*Dictionary of Theology*}, which he completed by the end of 1788. Before it was finished, Bergier was approached to revise and write articles for a new

---

[3]   Bingham, op. cit., p. 344.

supplement to the *Encyclopédie* by the publisher Charles–Joseph Panckoucke. It was natural that such an expert as Bergier be asked to contribute to what was one of the world's most widely consulted works of reference, but the encyclopædia's association with such anti–religious thinkers and attitudes horrified some of the more conservative members of the Catholic Church. Bergier agreed, but he was severely criticized for his association with the work, which eventually emerged as a four–volume supplement in 1776—77, which Diderot refused to edit.

After this, Bergier produced little and his *Dictionary* was met with critical silence from some quarters, by colleagues who could not forgive the fact that one of their own, who had received a papal blessing no less, could possibly have collaborated with the *Encyclopédists*: Catholics were urged to spurn the *Encyclopédie* and the supplement as a '*vaste collection d'erreurs pernicieuses*' {'*a vast collection of pernicious errors*'}. Bergier was accused of having lost his way and his mission. Though not a view endorsed by everyone, the Church had—quite typically—turned on one of its own, the very person who had done more to defend the faith against 'the bombs raining on the house of the Lord', as Diderot had described the *encyclopédists*' salvo on religious dogma. (See p. xl.)

In January 1790, Bergier caught a cold and he wrote to an old friend that he had not left his room in three months, save to attend mass, as his cold was getting worse. By early April his lungs were so congested that he succumbed to the infection and he died on 10 April 1790.

During the early part of the nineteenth century, which saw a Catholic revival, theologians revisited his works, in particular his *Historical Treatise* and his *Dictionary*: they were revised and edited, and ran into many editions—the former work was reprinted at least fifteen times, and the latter—thirty–eight times before 1883, including the translations made into Italian, Spanish and German. Though he never knew it, this was a fitting testament to Bergier's erudition and industry.

Translator's Note

The following translation comprises extracts from Bergier's refutation of d'Holbach's *Christianity Unveiled*. The original numbering of the sections in Bergier's work has been kept and, as with the previous translation, the original footnotes are printed in bold type. Further elucidation has been added as judged necessary. I have retained the old–fashioned way of referring to Islam as a religion and as it was accepted in Bergier's time—viz., 'Muhammadanism'. Sections where other works, apart from *Christianity Unveiled*, are refuted in detail have been omitted for the sake of space, in order to make available as many as possible of Bergier's specific comments on d'Holbach's work. I have merely chosen those passages which struck me as the most interesting, since much, of necessity, has had to be missed out: Bergier's original refutation runs to almost eight hundred pages. As with the translation of d'Holbach's original work, any (proper) nouns which appear in bold type in the text can be looked up in the Glossary for further elucidation: these nouns appear in bold type only the first time they occur.

Bergier's *Apologie* follows the order of d'Holbach's original work from the preface onwards, confronting his ideas a chapter at a time, and generally using d'Holbach's chapter headings. The exceptions are—Chapter IV, where d'Holbach has '*De la mythologie chrétienne*' {'*On Christian Mythology*'}, Bergier uses the less pejorative title of '*De la Théologie Chrétienne*' {'*On Christian Theology*'}; Holbach's Chapter VI—'*Des preuves de la religion chrétienne, des miracles, des prophéties, des martyrs*' {'*On Proofs of the Christian Religion, Miracles, Prophesies, and Martyrs*'}, in Bergier's work has been changed by him to '*Des preuves de la Révélation*' {'*On the Proofs of Revelation*'}, and then he treats '*Des Miracles*' {'*On Miracles*'}, '*Des Prophéties*' {'*On Prophesies*'}, and '*Des Martyrs*' {'*On Martyrs*'}, as separate subsections.

Where sections have been curtailed, this has been indicated by an ellipsis in square brackets, viz., [...]. I have also kept Bergier's original italics, but I have provided cross–references to d'Holbach's original text in translation to enable the reader to place his citations in context.

APOLOGIE

DE

LA RELIGION

CHRÉTIENNE,

Contre l'Auteur du Chriſtianiſme dévoilé,
& contre quelques autres Critiques.

Par M. BERGiER, Docteur en Théologie, Aſſocié
à l'Académie des Sciences, Felles-Lettres & Arts de
Beſançon, & Correſpondant de l'Académie Royale des
Inſcriptions & Belles-Lettres.

Jaɕent ſe in ſui eloquii vanitate, & de argumentationum ſua-
rum verſutia, quæ inimica eſt fidei, glorientur; nolis placet Apoſ-
toli obedire præceptis, dicentis: VILETE NE QUIS VOS DECI-
PIAT PER PHILOSOPHIAM. S. Leo, Epiſt. 131, cap. 2.

Deux Volumes in-12 reliés, 6 livres.

TOME PREMIER.

A PARIS,

Chez HUMBLOT, Libraire, rue S. Jacques, entre la
rue du Plâtre & celle des Noyers, près S. Ives.

M. DCC. LXIX.
Avec Approbation & Privilége du Roi.

Figure 35: Title page of Bergier's refutation (1769).

Apology
of
The Christian Religion

Against the Author of *Christianity Unveiled,*
And Against Other Critics
by
Monsieur Bergier, Doctor of Theology,
Associate of the Academy of Science,
Literature and the Arts, Besançon, and
Corresponding Member of the *Académie
des Inscriptions et Belles-Lettres*

*Let them boast in the emptiness of their eloquence and
brag about the cunning of their proofs, which are hostile
to the faith; we take delight in obeying the directions of
the Apostle, who says, 'See that no one deceives you
through philosophy'.*
Letter from Pope Leo I to the Emperor Leo, Letter 132.

Two Volumes in 12mo bound, Six Books

Volume One

Paris

*Humblot Publisher and Bookshop,
St Jacques Street, between Plâtre St. and Noyers St.,
Near St Ives.*

1769 By Royal Approval

The *Académie des Inscriptions et Belles-Lettres* was one of five learned academies founded in 1663 and this one was dedicated to the promotion of the humanities: it was originally founded under another name under Louis XIV and then its name was changed to that cited here and it became an official state institution by royal decree in 1701.

Papal Greeting and Blessing from Clement XIII[1]

Our Dear Son,

Greetings and Apostolic Blessing be upon you!

We have been given a book by you in two volumes, through which you have undertaken to defend the Christian religion against the pernicious writings of present–day libertines. We would never have believed that impiety could have reached such a pitch of fury as it has, had it not been made known to us through your book, at the beginning of which you expose the principal points of the insane doctrines which the unfortunate author, whose refutation you have undertaken, seems to have claimed in the first place. Up to the present time, the blasphemies uttered, despite their bias against the teaching of the gospel, at least admitted that the laws of Christian morality were commended by their sanctity; we were seized with horror at the spectacle of such monstrous, glaring errors of a writer who, through an unprecedented blasphemy, has dared to assert that these laws are pernicious to states, contrary to sound morality, opposed to the progress of the human mind, and that they ought absolutely to be abandoned. So, Our Dear Son, you have rendered an essential service to Christian society through your book by refuting this impious doctrine, its contrived calumnies, the worthless opinions of an impious author, who is ridiculously infatuated by the superiority of his genius: his opinions contradict and shock common sense. We also note that you refer the reader to two other works of yours already published and we regret not having seen them: whoever reads your *Apology* will be unable to resist reading these two other works.[2] Furthermore, we hold

---

[1] **Pope Clement XIII** (born 7 March 1693 in Venice, and died 2 February 1769 in Rome), whose original name was Carlo Rezzonico, was pope from 1758 to 1769, having been elected pope on 6 July 1758, at a time when anti-Romanism amid European princes was revealed most explicitly in the Bourbons' plan to destroy the Society of Jesus, then at the peak of its influence. The Jesuit issue dominated Clement's pontificate and that of his successor, Clement XIV. In January 1769, the ambassadors of Spain, Naples and France personally demanded that Clement completely suppress the Society of Jesus throughout the world. He refused, despite their threat to form national churches independent of Rome, and shortly after he suffered a stroke and died. **Pope Clement XIV** (born 31 October 1705, near Rimini, and died 22 September 1774, in Rome), had the original name of Giovanni Vincenzo Antonio Ganganelli, and the Franciscan name of Lorenzo, was pope from 1769 to 1774. Bergier's work occurred at the time of the end of one papacy and the beginning of the next, hence the two papal blessings issued.

[2] These works are *Le Déisme réfuté par lui-même* {*Deism Refuted by Itself*} and *La Certitude des Preuves du Christianisme* {*The Certainty of the Proofs of Christianity*}, both published by Humblot, the publisher who published his *Apology of the Christian Religion against the Author of Christianity Unveiled*.

fast in our hearts, and, so to speak, before our eyes, the testimony to your piety and the zeal which has fired you to defend our holy religion, and we thank you for your gift to us in doing so. We pray to God that he will confer upon you life and strength, so that you may continue to use your efforts for the benefit of the Catholic Church, to which we see you have consecrated all your natural and acquired talents, and we give you, Our Dear Son, an Apostolic Blessing with the affection of a paternal heart.

Granted in Rome at Santa Maria Maggiore with the seal of the Chancery,[3] 31 January 1769, the eleventh year of our Pontificate, M.A. Arch. De Chalcédoine, Pope Clement XIII.

---

[3] The 'seal of the Chancery' literally translated is 'under the ring of the Fisherman', because the papal seal was made by a special ring known as the 'Fisherman's ring', because it bore the image of St Peter, said to be the founding and first pope of the Catholic Church who, according to the Gospel, was a fisherman.

Papal Brief of Our Holy Father, Pope Clement XIV.

Our Dear Son,

Greetings and Apostolic Blessing be upon you!

The felicitations which you offered me for my elevation to Sovereign Pontiff were made all the more agreeable by the proofs you proffered through the submission of your books, written in defence of our religion. We were delighted to receive these—a testament of your faith, your piety, and your erudition; we whole–heartedly applaud your work, which is so helpful in repelling the attacks of non–believers and for affirming the beliefs of the faithful. We exhort you, Our Dear Son, to look upon the honour these books do you not as a reward for your studies and for your vigilance, but as the motivation to undertake your work anew, to continue to render service to the Catholic Church, to use for the honour and glory of God the talents which you have received from Him. We assure you, then, that we shall always feel a sincere sense of gratitude towards you and an affection equal to that of Clement XIII, our predecessor of sacred memory, and as a token of our paternal benevolence, we grant you, Our Dear Son, an Apostolic Blessing with singular affection.

Granted in Rome, in Santa Maria Maggiore, with the seal of the Chancery, 5 July 1769, the first year of our Pontificate.

Benoît Stay.[4]

An expression of royal approbation from Riballier, Royal Censor, and a note from King Louis XV are appended also to our Dear Son Bergier, Priest and Doctor of Theology

---

[4] Papal secretary to several popes.

Reflections on the Preface and the Work of the Author of *Christianity Unveiled*, on the Noticeable Progress of Unbelief amongst Philosophers, and on their Contradictions.

§1

If ever there were an enterprise capable of shocking us it is that produced by the author of this book, which we now embark upon examining here. For the one thousand seven hundred years that Christianity has been established, there is plenty of scope to assume that this religion has been thoroughly examined: amongst those who have professed it and have been capable of grasping its spirit and principles and able to weigh up its proofs, there would be presumably at least one from amongst the great number of philosophers who have attacked it, there would have been some fairly perceptive geniuses who had noticed its real faults. After so many books have been published for and against it, we really ought to look at a writer who promises to '*unveil*' Christianity, who undertakes to convince us that, either amongst its readers, or amongst the enemies of the gospel, he is the one person to appear with a true idea of its faults.

So as not to leave us in any doubt of his aim, the writer announces clearly at the end of his preface that '*Many men devoid of mores have attacked religion because it thwarted their inclinations; many wise men have despised it because it appeared ridiculous to them; many people have viewed it with indifference because they did not perceived its true drawbacks. As a citizen, I attack it because I consider it to be harmful to the welfare of the state, because it is an enemy of human intellectual progress, and because it is opposed to sound morality, from which political interests can never be divorced.*'[1] This undertaking is as unconvincing as it is rash; we are in no doubt curious to see how a writer, whose talents might seem nothing less than sublime, might execute such a task.

He attacks religion as a citizen, and as citizens we believe we must defend it: the author himself invites us to do so at the end of his *Preface*. We willingly accept this sort of challenge: we shall apply ourselves to showing that Christianity is necessary for the good of states, that it facilitates the progress of the human mind, and that it is a unique force of true morality and sensible politics. The intensified efforts made to destroy the principal source of so much good ought to make religion even dearer to us.

---

[1] See p. 13.

§2

Let us observe first of all the progress our adversaries have made; once rather modest, their claims did not get them very far. They were fairly ready to admit that, of all the other world religions, Christianity was the purest, wisest and the most useful; at its most basic level, the moral level, there was no one who would refuse to pay it homage and it was futile to search for any other form of support for it in the miraculous deeds which served as its foundation. Today the philosophical mind has progressed: it has discovered that this morality, which was so blatantly obvious, is not what it has appeared to be hitherto, and that it is now deemed to be directly opposed to the enlightenment of reason, to the well–being of states and to rational politics. Consequently, the greatest service that one could render the human race is to rid us of it, once and for all. In a word, to make men wise and happy, no religion is required any longer.

We saw the consequences of this long ago and the ultimate end to which the enemies of religion wanted to lead us; we must be grateful to them for justifying our predictions. The person to whom we shall reply has not *unveiled* Christianity—he has distorted it, but he has shown us several mysteries of the new way of thinking, which is useful for us to know.

He has exposed the consequences of the principles of non–belief and the end to which they must inevitably lead; he has revealed the train of thought that one follows of necessity when one abandons the rule of faith; he has shown us the alternative wherein all men find themselves, who know either how to reason be a Catholic Christian, or a **Pyrrhonian** without religion.

Until now, our most famous philosophers have restricted themselves to establishing Deism or natural religion, and they have concentrated all their attacks against the proofs of revelation. All contend that revelation was not needed, since several nations know nothing of it yet, and that it has served no purpose, since those who do know of it have become neither wiser, nor more virtuous, and that it has even proved to be pernicious, since it has created divisions amongst men.

The same objections to their arguments as were made against natural religion, whose defenders they claim to be, have been set before them—that Christianity, essential for mankind, has been misunderstood and distorted amongst all peoples who have not been enlightened by revelation, and natural religion has not been sufficiently powerful to safeguard them from idolatry or from the most revolting disorders, and if they have conserved the slightest idea of revealed Christianity, it serves merely to make them all the more guilty.

The author of *Christianity Unveiled*, convinced that there is no point to this corollary, has opted to overstep the mark and maintain his steady position—that of the pointlessness of all religion, and that the foundations of morality and society should rest solely on civil laws. He is a philosopher pushed to the limit and disconcerted, who has felt that Deism is not a position that he could maintain for very long, and he believes himself to be either more sincere or more consistent than any other philosophers who haughtily preach a total absence of religion.

It is pointless to ask him if he believes in any god and what he understands by that name, or whether there is any such thing as Providence, or whether we have a soul and what its nature and destiny might be. It would be of no avail to ask him if there is a future life, or whether he professes to be ignorant of all these things, as if they were a mere superfluity, dangerous even to engage upon, and whether we have any need of such dogmas to be virtuous. Civil laws, temporal interests, the tribulations and rewards of this life—all that, according to him, is the only motivation capable of making people wise and happy.

We must presume that this is the final frontier for the philosopher and that he can go no further. O that Heaven might show the abyss into which this philosophy casts people and that ultimately they might take fright and turn back in their tracks!

§3

Christianity Unveiled fully exposes the real thinking of our adversaries and the sentiments which enflame them. Many of them had taken cover under a carapace of moderation, harbouring rancour and hate in their hearts, which they had sworn against religion. This assailant, less circumspect than his peers, has spoken the true language of impiety and has adopted a tone that suits him well. He rails, he piles on the abuse, he calumnies without any sense of decency or restraint, and his gloomy character makes him see everything as black. Everything connected with religion he finds odious; its teaching, worship, morality, discipline, ministers—nothing is spared. Even sovereigns are not beyond the reach of his outrage; as soon as they protect religion, they are, according to him, unworthy of governing. His book would be much better entitled *Irreligion Unveiled*; he sets before us principles which lead to disbelief, its ultimate outcome, and the sentiments it inspires.

Can we sufficiently admire what heights philosophy has scaled nowadays and the scope of its enlightening discoveries? In the *Letter from Thrasybulus to Leucippus*, atheism has been taught without beating about the bush;[2] in *On*

---

[2]   See Introduction p. xlix and Fréret in the Glossary.

the Mind we have pure materialism;[3] in *Philosophical Essays Concerning Human Understanding*—there is wholesale scepticism;[4] in the *Philosophical Dictionary*—nothing but sheer fatalism:[5] and in the *Discourse on Inequality*—the teaching that man's natural state is that of brutal beasts;[6] and finally, in *Christianity Unveiled*, it is brought home to us the pointlessness and danger of having any religion at all. I am not speaking of the secondary writers who have copied, commented on or developed all these marvellous principles: I pass over in silence the obscenities with which several of these weighty writers have sullied their pen: assuredly posterity owes altars to those masters who have taught mankind so well.

Such are the immortal monuments of philosophy's sublime discoveries. If its followers are really jealous of its glory, it is here that this ignominy is best made good. They ought to be keenly aware that their prejudice, as shown in such monstrous works, has caused them to stray: they were bound to take vengeance upon the dogmas of natural religion by using the weapon of reason alone, which has so shamefully betrayed them and laid bare that meagre resource within them, which society can clearly perceive when their most cherished interests are in danger, and right–thinking souls are justly reassured in their fear of philosophy, that by striking at the very foundations of religion, it might overturn the foundations of civil life by the same blow.

Our so–called citizens shall not prevail—that we can predict, and likewise anyone else who attacks religion. Be they atheist, sceptic, materialist, fatalist or cynic—it is all the same to them, and provided that Christianity perishes, all will be well. That is the only end to which these Apostles of Natural Religion aspire.[7]

§4

It is not difficult to work out that the author of *Christianity Unveiled* borrowed his system from Hobbes, which was reworked by Bayle, who from him also were derived most of the sophisms with which the author has attempted to back up his opinions. For some time now the writings of this foolhardy critic of religion have been the source whence non–believers have dug up their doctrine: not one of them has resisted copying him. In his *Thoughts on the Comet*, Bayle tried his utmost to prove that an atheist society could exist, observe laws and practise social virtues without having any

---

[3] See Introduction pp. xliv & lii and Helvétius in the Glossary.
[4] See Hume in the Glossary.
[5] See Voltaire in the Glossary.
[6] See Rousseau in the Glossary.
[7] By 'Apostles of Natural Religion' Bergier means Deists, whom he had refuted in *Deism Refuted by Itself* (1765).

knowledge whatsoever of the Divine, without any form of religion: he maintained that Paganism, far from acting as a rein on human emotions, has merely served to foment them and that religion in general has been used to justify all crimes. However, he conceded that an understanding of the true God and the Christian religion are a very powerful deterrent to repress all vices, to strengthen societal ties and the foundations of states.[8] Our author, who is even more daring, maintains that the Christian religion itself can produce no benefit—on the contrary, it does more harm than good for the cause of true morality and sensible politics. To prove this, he turns against Christianity all the objections Bayle had made against idolatry and he concludes that the neatest and best thing to do is to ban all forms of religion. Such is the natural progression of this kind of error.

§5

Let us establish briefly the principles on which we shall oppose him and we can develop them further in the course of this work.

(i) Wherever laws go unsupported by religion and are reduced merely to a coactive force, they have to be severe to the point of excess and multiplied *ad infinitum*: it is then, under such circumstances, that a government becomes despotic and its people reduced to slaves. This point shall be proven by fact and by observations taken from the *Spirit of Laws*.[9] In this way, whilst railing against the despotism of sovereigns and the enslavement of peoples within our current political system, which is guided by religious laws, the writer strives with all his might to establish the one and the other through civil laws; all he does is transpose our so–called tyranny onto civil laws, for which he wholly reproaches religion: that is his first contradiction.

(ii) Far from weakening human motivation, which leads towards social virtues, self–interest, a love of keeping a tight grip upon ourselves, and the fear of temporal penalties and infamy, etc., all these things are strengthened by religious faith, to which it lends its full support: in fact rather than destroying anything, it supplies an even stronger and more compelling motivation. It is absurd to propose that without religion these natural motives would be enhanced. Is it not absurd to maintain that two forces pulling man along in tandem, in the same direction, would be less effective were one to be removed?

Bayle and his imitators complain continuously to us that, despite the sense of morality and the enlightenment of reason, despite the authority of civil laws and the watchful eye of the police, despite the restraint provided by

---

[8] **Addendum to *Pensées diverses*, chapter 4.**
[9] See Montesqieu in the Glossary.

religion and a fear of the life to come, man is constantly bad; but by a crude contradiction they maintain that without this latter motivation, man can be virtuous.

(iii) The indispensability of religion for refining mores and for supporting the government is demonstrated by experience and by incontestable fact. In all nations of the world not guided by this powerful, motivating force we find no pure mores, or social virtues, or wise laws, or moderate government: the states of such peoples are either entirely barbarous, or infinitely beneath ours. Enemies of religion would be well–punished were they to be reduced to living amongst these peoples, who know nothing of these things. Now, when it comes to morality and politics, to deny one's experience is shocking to common sense.

(iv) It is equally certain that it is religion which had a civilizing effect on all formerly barbarous peoples, and that religion everywhere has been the forerunner of establishing laws and society, and that all the first legislators had recourse to religion to sanction and strengthen their laws. Not a single legislator has ever thought that purely temporal motives were powerful enough to strengthen social bonds. Is it not tantamount to dragging mankind back to their former condition, to return people to a barbarous, savage state by wanting to maintain the handiwork of these early lawgivers, yet destroy the very foundation on which it has stood?

(v) Even amongst civilized peoples, civil laws are powerless without mores: Horace said, 'Quid vanæ sine moribus leges proficient?',[10] and all wise men have repeated this subsequently. To build a moral edifice solely upon human laws is to claim that the weakest will support the strongest, and it is to take away from all corrupt nations all means and all hope of reform. On this issue one can consult the excellent chapter 'On Mores' in *The Friend of Man*,[11] where our author's system is already refuted.

(vi) His system of thought has been refuted by the most famous philosophers, ancient and modern; it is fairly unusual that a writer, whose authority is rather weak anyway, today claims to put them all right. Cicero, after having established the important dogma of the existence of a god who scrutinizes men's hearts, expresses himself thus: 'Can one deny that such

---

[10] Horace, *Odes*, Bk.III, № XXIV 'Intactis opulentior' {'The Need for Moral Restraint'}. The actual line from Horace should read, '*Quid leges sine moribus vanae proficiunt*', which means '*What use are laws, vain as they are without morals...*'

[11] **Second Part, ch. 4, p. 148.** *L'Ami des Hommes, ou Traité de la population* (1756—58) {*The Friend of Man, or Treatise on Population*} was written by Mirabeau, marquis de (aka Victor Riquetti), (1715—1789). It was one of the most popular works of political economy of its time.

sentiments are of great use when one sees on how many occasions one's oath is the seal of one's word, and to what extent religion plays a part in our faith in treaties, and how many crimes the fear of divine punishment has warded off, and how pious a society is, which is persuaded that they have in their midst, as their judge and witness, the Divinity himself?'[12]

'Without piety', Cicero says again, 'there will be neither godliness nor religion, and thence what disorder, what trouble will there be amongst us? I have my doubts that, we were to quash piety towards the gods, it would lead to the annihilation of good faith, civil society, and the principal virtue, which is justice.'[13]

---

[12] *De Legibus* I, 2, № 7. The reference is to Cicero, *On Laws*, Book II. 'As the beings furnished with reason are incomparably superior to those who want it, and we cannot say, without impiety, that any thing transcends the universal Nature, we must therefore confess that divine reason is contained within her. Who will dispute the utility of these sentiments, when he shall reflect how many cases of the greatest importance are decided by oaths; how much the sacred rites performed in making treaties tend to assure peace and tranquillity; also, what numbers the fear of divine punishment has reclaimed from a vicious course of life; and how sacred the social rights must be in a society where a firm persuasion obtains of the immediate intervention of the immortal gods, both as witnesses and judges of our actions? Such is the "preamble of the law," to use the expression of Plato.' (See *The Political Works of Marcus Tullius Cicero: Comprising his Treatise on the Commonwealth; and his Treatise on the Laws.* Translated from the original, with Dissertations and Notes in Two Volumes. by Francis Barham, Esq. [London: Edmund Spettigue, 1841—42], II.)

[13] *De Nat. Deor.* I, I, n. 2. Cicero, *De Natura Deorum* {*On the Nature of the Gods*}, Book I, Section ii. A longer extract is provided below to appreciate the context of the quotation. 'For there are and have been philosophers who hold that the gods exercise no control over human affairs whatever. But if their opinion is the true one, how can piety, reverence or religion exist? For all these are tributes which it is our duty to render in purity and holiness to the divine powers solely on the assumption that they take no notice of them, and that some service has been rendered by the immortal gods to the race of men. But if on the contrary the gods have neither the power nor the will to aid us, if they pay no heed to us at all and take no notice of our actions, if they can exert no possible influence upon the life of men, what ground have we for rendering any sort of worship, honour or prayer to the immortal gods? Piety, however, like the rest of the virtues, cannot exist in mere outward show and pretence; and, with piety, reverence and religion must likewise disappear. And when these are gone, life soon becomes a welter of disorder and confusion; and in all probability the disappearance of piety towards the gods will entail the disappearance of loyalty and social union among men as well, and of justice itself, the queen of all the virtues.' (Cicero, *Nature of the Gods & Academics*, translated by H. Rackham [Cambridge, Mass.: Harvard U.P., Loeb Classical Library, 2000], pp. 5—7.)

Plutarch observes that one will find not a single city anywhere without a knowledge of a god and of a religion; he even adds that to found a republic without any religious cult would be to build a city in the clouds.[14]

The ancients had more respect for idolatry than philosophers have nowadays for the holiest of religions. Neither Epicurus nor his followers ever publicly declaimed against pagan gods, against their worship, or against their ministers. Plato was convinced of the falsity of the religious belief of the masses, but he did not want to lay a finger on popular religion.[15] In Cicero, Academician Cotta maintains that on the subject of religion, one has to keep to the priests' instructions without consulting the philosophers.[16] The

---

[14] Plutarch, *Reply to Colotes*. Colotes was one of Epicurus' favourite disciples. The text to which Bergier refers reads: 'No, I think a city might rather be formed without the ground it stands on than a government, once you remove all religion from under it, get itself established or once established survive. Now it is this belief, the underpinning and base that holds all society and legislation together, that the Epicureans, not by encirclement or covertly in riddles, but by launching against it the first of their most Cardinal Tenets, proceed directly to demolish. Then as if driven by some vengeful Fury they confess that in upsetting established observances and sweeping aside the ordinances of the laws they are committing a grave offence, as if on purpose to make it impossible to pardon them. For to be wrong in a belief is a failing, if not of sages, yet of men; but to accuse others of doing what you are guilty of yourselves—how is that to be described without a generous expenditure of the strong language that it deserves?' (Plutarch, *Moralia*, XIV, translated by B. Einarson & P.H. De Lacy [Cambridge, Mass.: Harvard U.P., Loeb Classical Library, 2004], pp. 301—303.)

[15] **In his *Timaeus*.**
Plato, *Timaeus*, 'If then, Socrates, in many respects concerning many things—the gods and the generation of the universe—we prove unable to render an account at all points entirely consistent with itself and exact, you must not be surprised. If we can furnish accounts no less likely than any other, we must be content, remembering that I who speak and you my judges are only human, and consequently it is fitting that we should, in these matters, accept the likely story and look for nothing further.' (Francis M. Cornford, *Plato's Cosmology: The* Timaeus *of Plato* [Indianapolis/Cambridge: Hackett Publishing Company, 1997], p. 23.) Plato's *Timaeus* was a work written late in his life, thought to have been written probably around 360 BC, but no exact date is known. It is the most complete statement of his cosmology.

[16] *De Nat. Deor*. I, 3, n. 4. *De Natura Deorum*: '"Very well", rejoined Cotta, "let us then proceed as the argument itself may lead us. But before we come to the subject, let me say a few words about myself. I am considerably influenced by your authority, Balbus, and by the plea that you put forward at the conclusion of your discourse, when you exhorted me to remember that I am both a Cotta and a pontiff. This no doubt meant that I ought to uphold the belief about the immortal gods which have come down to us from our ancestors, and the rites and ceremonies and duties of religion. For my part I always shall uphold them and always have done so, and no eloquence of anybody, learned or unlearned, shall ever dislodge me from the belief as to the worship of the immortal gods which I have inherited from our forefathers. But on any question of religion I am guided by the high pontiffs, Titus Coruncanius, Publius Scipio and Publius Scaevola, not by Zeno or Cleanthes or Chrysippus; and I have

Stoic Balbus recognizes that it is a pernicious and impious custom to argue against the gods, whether one does it though conviction or for amusement's sake.[17] These philosophers did not follow their own advice on this principle, but they provided a lesson for our present–day philosophers, who have not derived any benefit from it.

Although the majority of philosophers, intoxicated by the principles of erroneous metaphysics, did not believe in the penalties or rewards of a future life, they all however recognize the need of this dogma to maintain social stability. When they spoke as legislators, they reasoned quite differently from what they taught in schools.[18] It is thus that philosophy always made a profession of faith and contradicted itself, and it often paid lip–service to religion.

(vii) When writing against religion, the most avowed atheists have not admitted its usefulness when they looked upon it as a political weapon for keeping the people's nose to the grindstone, but they have rendered homage to it, even while calumnying it. Whilst calling religion a fable, they concede that the beauty of virtue can at best make an impression on philosophers and on men of a naturally fortunate disposition, but it is religion alone that can

---

Gaius Laelius, who was both an augur and a philosopher, to whose discourse upon religion, in his famous oration, I would rather listen than to any leader of the Stoics. The religion of the Roman people comprises ritual, auspices, and the third additional division consisting of all such prophetic warnings as the interpreters of the Sybil or the soothsayers have derived from portents and prodigies. Well, I have always thought that none of these departments of religion was to be despised, and I have held the conviction that Romulus by his auspices and Numa by his establishment of our ritual laid the foundation of our state, which assuredly could never have been as great as it is had not the fullest measure of divine favour been obtained for it. There, Balbus, is the opinion of a Cotta and a pontiff; now oblige me by letting me know yours. You are a philosopher, and I ought to receive from you a proof of your religion, whereas I must believe the word of our ancestors even without proof".' (Cicero, *Nature of the Gods & Academics*, translated by H. Rackham [Cambridge, Mass.: Harvard U.P., Loeb Classical Library, 2000], pp. 289—291.)
This extract comes from Book III, Section ii of *De Natura Deorum*.

[17] *Ibid.,* **I, 2, in fine.** "'These are more or less the things that occurred to me which I thought proper to be said upon the subject of the nature of the gods. And for your part, Cotta, would you but listen to me, you would plead the same cause, and reflect that you are a leading citizen and pontiff, and you would take advantage both *pro* and *contra* to choose to espouse my side, and preferably to devote to this purpose those powers of eloquence which your rhetorical exercises have bestowed upon you and which the Academy has fostered. For the habit of arguing in support of atheism, whether it be done from conviction or in pretence, is a wicked and an impious practice.'" (See end of Book II of *De Natura Deorum*, op. cit., pp. 283—285.)

[18] **Warburton, *Dissertations*, № 8.** (For **Warburton**—see Glossary.)

have an effect on most other people.[19] For everyone believing in a god, to recognize the necessity of religion is to confess the truth; God could not link order and the happiness of mankind with error.

(viii) Despite our beautiful, modern minds' bias against religion, not every philosopher has adopted Bayle's paradox; several have even refuted it. The most famous of our writers says, 'Such is the weakness of mankind; such is man's perversity, that for them it is doubtless better to be subjugated by all possible superstitions, as long as they are not lethal, than to live without religion. Man has always needed a restraint; and although it is ridiculous to sacrifice to fauns, sylvans and nymphs, it was a good deal more useful to adore images of the Divinity than to give oneself over to atheism. An atheist who would be a thinker, violent and powerful, would be just as dreadful a scourge as a superstitious, bloodthirsty being... Wherever there is an established society, there is a need for religion. Laws keep watch over public crimes and religion keeps watch over secret crimes.'[20]

We shall see elsewhere that the writer of *The Spirit of Laws* established the same truth. The author of *Emile* refuted Bayle even more forcefully.[21] This question was examined carefully in the *Encyclopédie* and a conclusion was reached in favour of religion.[22] In *Philosophical Essays on Human Understanding*, all are called bad citizens and bad politicians who work to disabuse man of religious persuasions.[23] In a *Letter to Dr Swift*, Lord Bolingbroke speaks just as advantageously of it.[24] Woolaston recognized that without religious habits, men would soon give up altogether on all virtues and would revert to being feral and untamed.[25]

(ix) Bayle himself, when in a more moderate mood and not carried away by his own vanity in defending a foolish system, refuted his own principles, saying, 'If one did not associate future benefits, as promised in Scripture to the faithful, with practising virtue, then one could consign virtue and innocence to the number of things that Solomon pronounced in his definitive judgement, "Vanity of vanities, all is vanity."'[26] So then it is settled, that

---

[19] **Ibid., First Dissertation.**
[20] *Traité sur la Tolérance*, **ch. 20.** {*Treatise on Tolerance*}. By 'The most famous of our writers...' Bergier clearly means Voltaire. (For Voltaire—see Glossary.)
[21] *Emile*, **III, pp. 181** *et seqq.* (See Rousseau in the Glossary.)
[22] **See the articles on 'probity', 'society', and 'virtue'.**
[23] *Essais Philosophiques sur l'entendement humain* {*Philosophical Essays on Human Understanding*}, **Essay No. 11 in** *Essays*, **II, p. 114.** (See Hume in the Glossary.)
[24] **Helvétius in** *Mercure de France*, **May 1767, p. 521.**
[25] **Warburton, *Dissertations*, № 15, p. 273.**
[26] *Critical Dictionary*, **article on Brutus, note F.**
   Available on the internet at http://humanities.uchicago.edu/orgs/ARTFL/

within the atheistic, non–believing system of thought, there is not a single motive for urging men towards virtuous behaviour.

Bayle also said, 'Speaking generally, the real, principal force of religion, as far as the practice of virtue is concerned, lies in the belief of the existence of an eternity of punishments and rewards, but by destroying the dogma of the immortality of the soul, one destroys the deepest motivating forces of religious belief'.[27]

Once having made such a formal acknowledgement, one can go on to write that morality has no need of being buoyed up by the penalties and rewards of the life to come, and that states and nations would be far better governed by the sole force of civil laws, rather than by religious laws; the author shows no shame in presenting a system known by him to be false.

(x) So then, let us just concede to our adversaries for a moment more than what they have a right to claim and more than that which they will ever convincingly prove, namely, that religion is absolutely useless for supporting morality and the foundations of society; but does it necessarily follow from there that Christianity should be eradicated? I maintain that there is even more reason to preserve it. Atheism, or non–belief, is not at all a natural state for man: to be an atheist one has either to have been brain–washed to the point of stupidity, or to have been led astray by philosophy. In civilized states, people are neither the one nor the other. If the true religion is not to be found there, a false one, of necessity, is bound to be invented: this is proven by the way all nations of the world are run. The author himself made this very point and there is no denying it.[28] Before deciding to destroy Christianity, it is essential to begin by proving that it is the worst of all possible religions and nominate one that would be to the greater advantage of people.

---

[27] *Ibid.* **Article on Sadducees, note F.**
Bayle, under the article heading 'Sadducees', referenced his own work on *Diverse Thoughts on Comets*, noting that the Sadducees were a Jewish sect '[...] who quite openly denied the immortality of the soul'. He goes on to say, again quoting himself from his *Diverse Thoughts*, 'I cannot see that, even holding such a dreadful opinion, they led a life which was any more corrupt than the rest of the Jews, and that, on the contrary, it was highly likely that they were a much more honest people than the Pharisees, who prided themselves on a close observation of the Law of God'. The comment such as 'dreadful opinion' is typical of the tongue-in-cheek style in which the whole dictionary was written and this style was adopted specifically to subvert accepted religious dogmas of the day. It is a tactic and style that Diderot adopted later in his *Encyclopédie*, which also incurred the wrath of the Church.
[28] **The Preface, p. iv.** (See p. 6 of this edition.)

Is the author advocating Deism or the religion of China? Such a religion, so extolled today, satisfies neither the people nor philosophers. In China, several men of letters are atheists and materialists, just as in our country, and the people, without exception, are idolaters.[29] This fact confirms what we have just stated.

So what is the goal of these enemies of Christianity? Let them be atheists if they wish, that is their business: but in order to turn whole nations into what they are one would have to begin by brain–washing them. That is the only extravagant *modus operandi* of this new philosophy.

§6

Unfortunately, from the very outset of the Preface, the advocate of this new approach trips himself up at the very first hurdle. As a self–styled censor of his own work, he is forced to admit that everything is already proven and unquestionable: he is reduced to concede that '*Christianity is a tissue of absurdities*' and '*an amorphous mass of almost all ancient superstitions*' that it is '*a bloody religion*', which changes kings into tyrants and people into slaves; that '*a good Christian [...] cannot have the faintest idea of knowing [...] true morality*' and that '*he can only be a useless misanthropist [...] or a trouble–causing fanatic.*'[30] Thus, in three pages, or rather in three words, religion's case is tried and judged without right of appeal: this is the tone which persists throughout the work. We shall show in detail the falsity and absurdity of these rantings, which persist at every turn.

Nevertheless, he *maintains* that his book would not be dangerous for people to read: ordinary people, he says, are incapable of reading and making rational judgements: '*When a madman tells them to steal or kill, it is the gibbet which warns them not to act upon such advice. Moreover, if by chance there were a man amongst the people who were to read a work of philosophy, it is certain that such a man would be highly unlikely to turn out to be a fearful villain.*' He insists that truth can never cause any harm in any case.[31]

What follows from the author's reasoning here is clear for all to see; (i) anyone cunning enough to keep their crimes from public knowledge or adept enough to extricate themselves from death by the gibbet might simply be a thief or killer who gets off scot–free—then they would have nothing to dread either in this world, or the next; (ii) there are no torments to fear from a whole host of crimes against which civil law has instituted no penalties and

---

[29] **Duhalde, *Description of China*, III, pp. 31 & 46.**
[30] **The Preface, pp. ii, iii, & iv.** (See pp. 5—6 of this edition.)
[31] **Ibid., p. v.** (Ibid., p. 6.)

185

which would no longer fill us with horror—crimes such as breaking one's word without the slightest scruple, or betraying a friend, or breaking a sworn oath, the seduction of innocence, breaking up family ties, etc. According to our critic, such edifying morality might be recommended to the general populous without so much as a second thought.

Seemingly the ordinary man–in–the–street is not capable of reading a work of philosophy, but he is quite capable of listening to the language and maxims of *Christianity Unveiled*, such as the allegation that religion is '*a tissue of absurdities*' and superstitions, and that '*we [...] see faith–fuelled princes continuously engaged in the most unjust wars, squandering in vain the blood and goods of their subjects, who snatch bread from the grip of the poor in order to fill the coffers of the insatiable rich, and who permit—yea, even give orders for—thieving, embezzling, and committing injustices*', and that, '*Amongst the priests [...] we [...] see pride, avarice, lustfulness, and a spirit of domination and vengeance*'.[32]

These rantings are repeated a thousand times in the book and are unworthy of comment: without being philosophers, people will easily recognize that it is par for the course to lay into priests and princes, to want to destroy the priesthood and royalty.

A person capable of reading philosophy '*would be highly unlikely to turn out to be a fearful villain.*' He might be highly unlikely, but he might just turn out to be so: amongst the ranks of men of letters there are still black–hearted men. In a century in which everyone prides themselves on how much they know, can we really rely on run–of–the–mill knowledge to act as a restraining influence on criminality? If *Christianity Unveiled* ever perverted a single person, would that not be sufficient grounds on which to outlaw the book and make us detest its author?

'*The truth can never cause any harm*', but it is precisely that which proves that the thought–process advocated here is not the truth.

§7

If our wise critic is to be believed, that '[...] *it is religion that kindles despots and tyrants [...] Kings were called the images of God; they, like him, had absolute power; they created the just and the unjust and their will often sanctified oppression, [...]*' etc.[33] This is just the kind of mayhem that the

---

[32] **The Preface, pp. ix & x.** (This edition, p. 7.)
[33] **The Preface, p. xxi.** Ibid.

THE BIBLE AND THE MONK. BY J. PETTIE IN THE WINTER EXHIBITION. SUFFOLK STREET.—SEE PRECEDING PAGE.

Figure 36: *The Bible and The Monk.* **A print by J. Pettie from** *The Illustrated London News*, **1865.**
The monk is confiscating a copy of the Bible, possession by the masses of which was proclaimed a sin by the Catholic Church.

author wants to establish by destroying religion: he maintains that the will of the prince is the only supreme law and that there are no other punishments to fear than those he might inflict, or any rewards to hope for, other than those which depend on him. Is it not a fact that sovereigns are absolute rulers, like God, and that in reality they are the only terrestrial gods?

He says, '*A sovereign, upon whom society has conferred supreme power, holds in his hands a great ability to motivate, which he can bring to bear upon men. He has more power than gods in moulding and reforming human behaviour and habits. His presence, his rewards, his threats... What can one say? Just a single look from him can achieve far more than all the sermonizing of priests. The accolades, honours and riches of this world exert a much stronger influence upon even the most pious of men than all the pompous expectations of religion. The most devout courtier fears his king more than his god.*'[34]

This language, borrowed from Bayle, is a masterpiece of absurdity.[35] On the one hand, the author opposes the despotism of kings, on the other he makes them the sole arbiters of men's destiny and he accuses them of having created the just and the unjust, and he does not recognize any rule other than the law which has emanated from their authority in order to distinguish criminality from virtue. He reproaches them for playing god and he attributes to them more power than to god: he blames them for misusing religion to subjugate people to their will, yet he wants to destroy religion, which is the only barrier that can be used to oppose their abuse of power.

According to him it is the sovereign's duty to '*mould and reform human behaviour and habits*', and he states that, '*People's mores will be good so long as the prince himself is good and virtuous.*'[36] But if he happens to be depraved, then what will become of mores, the law, the state and the people's destiny? Would it not be the case then, that '*his will would often sanctify oppression, violence and pillage*'? If everything be dependent upon the sovereign's behaviour and character, what guarantee is there that he would respond to our needs as soon as there were no more religion and he knew nothing of God?

Here we see the sum total of the wisdom of the philosophical mind, which seeks only to destroy and triumphs solely in setting forth objections to religion. Is it a question of substituting a more rational system? Our learned critics fall at the first hurdle and all their principles are mere contradictions.

---

[34] **The Preface, p. xx.** (This edition, p. 11.)
[35] **See his *Diverse Thoughts*, para. 138.**
[36] **Preface, p. xxi.** (This edition, pp. 11 & 7.)

§8

The author is at his most eloquent when he is declaiming on the pointlessness of religion. He says, '*Mankind always side–lines religion as soon as it is at variance with their desires; they only listen to it when it favours their ardour and when it neatly accords with their temperament and what they think makes them happy.*'[37] Here he paints the behaviour of sovereigns, priests, the people, and that of the good and the great, in the blackest of colours.

For a moment, let us indulge him in his rancorous censure: so what are the consequences of all this? Religion does not quash extreme behaviour completely, yet he insists faith has to be abolished. By the same token, civil laws do not stop all forms of crime, so logically they too ought to be suppressed. '*To say that religion does not act as a deterrent because it does not always restrain people is to claim that civil laws do not act as a deterrent either.*' So the author of *The Spirit of Laws* argues against Bayle.[38]

To free men's excesses from religion's yoke and replace it with the bridle of the law is like loosening a wild animal's chain to replace it with a piece of string. The more laws are tightened up and proliferated, the more they become ineffectual: the greater the number of laws, the more decadent the behaviour. *Corruptissima Respublica, plurimæ leges.*[39]

But the author of *Christianity Unveiled* does not stop at saying that religion is pointless: he maintains that it is pernicious and he levels against it all the calumnies of its enemies, both ancient and modern.[40] So what follows from this? (i) Montesquieu has observed that, 'It is improper to argue against religion in a weighty tome and provide a long list of all the ills which it has caused unless one also makes a list of all the good things it has done. Were I to recount all the ills the world had suffered at the hand of civil law, the monarchy and republican government, I should put down the most appalling blunders.'[41] (ii) Let us go along with the author's principle for a moment, that all religions, without exception, are pernicious. However, notwithstanding philosophy, man is absolutely determined to invent a religion for himself, since there is no society without a religion. Hence, one

---

[37] **Preface, p. ix** *et seqq.* (This edition, p. 8.)
[38] *L'Esprit des Loix* {*The Spirit of Laws*}, **Book 24, ch. 2.** (For Montesquieu—see Glossary.)
[39] The Latin means, 'The more corrupt the Republic, the more laws abound.' Though Bergier does not attribute this phrase to any classical author, it is generally accepted to have been written by Tacitus.
[40] **Preface, p. xvii.** (This edition, pp. xli & 13.)
[41] *L'Esprit des Loix* {*The Spirit of Laws*}, **I, Book 24, ch. 2.**

must choose the least harmful of any religions, and will the author refuse Christianity this privilege? (iii) We shall demonstrate that Christianity has never done anything evil and that, thanks to the gospel, we are better off than infidel nations in all regards. Therefore the destruction or weakening of religious belief amongst us would lead to calamitous misfortune.

§9

Our zealous citizen complains that our pupils' education is neglected with regard to politics: he maintains that the teaching of religious morality renders people useless and harmful for the rest of the world, and that it is up to the government and politics to form good citizens. So, he wants '*the government, supported by laws, rewards, and penalties,* [to] *confirm these lessons, delivered through education, and* [ensure that] *helpful and virtuous behaviour are concomitant with happiness,* [so that] *shame, contempt and chastisement are the punishments for crime and vice.*'[42]

Nice idea in theory and worthy of Plato's *Republic*! But can this be put into practice without religion? This philosopher would never think so. In an atheist nation, were such a thing to exist, would those in charge have sufficiently strong motivation to dedicate their efforts to the public good, and would the people be sufficiently compliant to accommodate their particular zeal and interests, and submit to the yoke of authority? That is what we must examine first of all.

It would be good for us to know the fundamentals of this new sort of morality, given that it will be based entirely on politics and having nothing to do with religion, and what clear and certain concepts one might invent when dealing with vice and virtue, and what rule one might create to distinguish good laws from bad.

Then we would have to discover in detail how a system of temporal rewards could be drawn up for all laudable actions, and what sensible punishments there would be for actions which reason condemns—but all that is impracticable. In order to punish crime we do not need to examine what motivated it; it is sufficient to know that it is injurious to society. However, to reward a virtuous action, one has to know the real motivation behind it to understand wherein the merit lies; but who is able to see into the depths of a man's soul? Where would we find the resources ample enough to reward every action that appears laudable? No legislator has ever followed such a plan, nor would he ever attempt to do so.[43]

---

[42] **Preface, p. xvii.** (This edition, p. 10.)
[43] **See Warburton *Dissertations*, № 1, pp. 39 *et seqq.***

Had the author thought this through, one might have dispensed with a detailed refutation, but the mere proposal of his system is blatantly absurd. He has not given these matters due consideration—he has merely heaped insult upon insult against religion, running through a whole gamut of points without developing a single one: he puts forward all manner of objections without substantiating any of them, he cites facts and embellishes them, he quotes passages from the Bible and usually twists them, and if one were to cut out his repetitions, his book would be half its length and it would be reduced to a few commonplace objections, found in all unbelievers' writing.

However, since he has singled out Christian morality and the public expression of its worship, these two points appear to merit closer discussion. The main point of my two works published recently was to set out the proofs of our religion and I merely touched upon issues concerning Christian morality, worship, discipline and their consequences. Now this refutation of *Christianity Unveiled* will serve as a substantial supplement to both my former works.[44] Whenever points raised here have already been dealt with in my other works, references are provided for the reader.

§10

[...]

I shall follow the same order as *Christianity Unveiled,* despite it being extremely unsystematic and the fact that the author repeats himself endlessly: I shall even keep the same chapter headings,[45] omitting nothing, especially if anything appears to present the slightest impression of difficulty: however, I shall not respond with the same indecent invective, which is its own refutation and needs no further comment. If I appear sometimes to repeat the same thoughts and answers, the fault is not mine, but that of the author.

It may be that I am blamed often for paying undue attention to what appears to be frivolous points and to mere speculation, devoid of proofs: but in an era when all books against religion are written and avidly read, and when the slightest sophisms are trumpeted as irrefutable arguments, and when even the most absurd systems of thought might really catch on, or at the very least seduce an infinite number of readers, if only for a fleeting moment, it seemed necessary for me to leave no stone unturned. I prefer to err on the side of overzealousness rather than to skip over the slightest point that might be taken as a *coup* against the cause I seek to uphold and allow the slightest blot to remain upon the truth.

---

[44] *Le Déisme refute par lui-même* {*Deism Refuted by Itself*} **and** *La Certitude des preuves du Christianisme* {*The Certainty of the Proofs of Christianity*}.

[45] This is not entirely true: see p. 167.

Hence, it was impossible to write a shorter refutation. In order to substantiate the falsity of such dangerous speculation, it has often proved necessary to refer back to history to clarify facts, to explain properly a fundamental tenet of our faith, and to muster all the proofs. If our pathway is less fraught than that of our critic, whose deviations we are obliged to follow, it will prove to be sounder and will lead the reader more surely to a knowledge of the truth.

My task is no less fraught to furnish an interesting response to the difficulties raised, which amount to nothing when they are stripped of the pustulous rantings which festoon his style: the reader might well be bored to death to hear endless repetitions of '*this is false*', or '*the author takes liberties*', or '*the writer slanders...*' However, should the risk of being less widely read discourage us from not doing full justice to respond to our critics for the sake of our religion? The enemies of religion show no fear in revolting reasonable minds with their furious, obscene attacks: and so should we fear putting the public off by offering them a cold, insipid defence? So long as they are sound and convincing, I shall resist making my arguments populist: such serious debate is not meant for the amusement of frivolous minds and I shall leave stylistic stunts to charlatans, whose purpose is to hoodwink the public.

When replying to a writer who forgets himself and flies into a rage at every turn, it is terribly tempting to adopt a bitter tone, but I shall try to avoid that as much as possible. I shall answer his biased, bilious language in an innocent, upright and truthful tone. I shall also abstain from naming the author because he is either no more, or he is possibly using a pseudonym: I have no grudge against him—it is to the book alone that I address myself.

[...]

Chapter 1

On the Necessity of Examining Religion and the Obstacles Encountered to this Examination.

§1

The Doctors of the Christian religion have never aspired to forbid anyone the freedom to examine the proofs of religious faith:[46] that is a right that would be unjust to take away from any people, but furthermore, it is an obligation germane to their preaching. Far from imposing the yoke of blind faith upon its followers, as its enemies have always held,[47] Christianity, on the contrary, commands them to be 'always ready to justify faith through reason'.[48] Faith is not an obstinate system of belief but a 'submission to reason'.[49] The vast number of works written, especially in recent times, to expound principles, proofs, dogmas and Christian morality, and to reply to the criticisms of those who have attacked them, are clear testimony to the spirit which inspires ministers of the Christian faith and to the sincere zeal with which they are imbued to educate people.

It is empty rhetoric to claim that: '*For the most part, people hold to their religion only by habit; [...] they have been most afraid of digging deeper into*

---

[46] This is clearly not the case, since the Catholic Church fought hard to keep the Scriptures from being translated into any popular vernacular, and in England at least, reading the Scriptures was punishable by death: see p. 336.

[47] **Orig. contr. Cels. I, i, Cambrige** [sic] **edn., p. 8.** {Origen, *Contra Celsum* [*Against Celsus*]}. (For Origen—see Glossary.)

[48] **I Petri, 3, 15.**
There is an obvious difference in emphasis within the translations: Bergier quotes this verse in French, but the reference is the *Vulgate* version of the Bible, which states, '*Dominum autem Christum sanctificate in cordibus vestris parati semper ad satisfactionem omni poscenti vos rationem de ea quae in vobis est spe*', which is rendered in the *King James Version* of the Bible, 'But sanctify the Lord God in your hearts: and be ready always to give an answer to every man that asketh you a reason of the hope that is in you with meekness and fear', (1 Pet. 3: 15).

[49] **Rom. 12, 1.**
The verse states, 'I beseech you therefore, brethren, by the mercies of God, that ye present your bodies a living sacrifice, holy, acceptable unto God, which is your reasonable service,' which in the *Vulgate* is '*obsecro itaque vos fratres per misericordiam Dei ut exhibeatis corpora vestra hostiam viventem sanctam Deo placentem rationabile obsequium vestrum.*' There is an obvious disparity within the translations, as the preceding footnote shows, with inevitable shifts in emphases and style of language. This clearly demonstrates the foolishness of Christian fundamentalists who insist that every word of the Bible was inspired by God and know the Scriptures only through the medium of English, and who place great emphasis on specific turns of phrase and individual words.

it; [...] *they have almost never deigned to understand the reasons for their beliefs*,[50] and to continue in this tone for the rest of this chapter. This criticism may well be true with regard to people brought up in error, in idolatry and in Muhammadanism—peoples who have not the slightest smattering of a knowledge of the humanities or science, but it is absolutely inapplicable to Christians: and it is even more so in an era and amongst people of a nation, where studying and enlightenment are even more wide–spread and are more advanced than anywhere else.

Never before have we enjoyed such liberty to write about religion, or to put it even plainer—such licence—as now. If this liberty were ill–founded and if the veracity of religious proofs had been so doubted, they would have been destroyed ages ago by incontrovertible arguments; our faith has been the target of philosophers' concerted efforts to destroy it and subjected to rancorous bile distilled from their pens. Their books are in everyone's hands and their philosophical zeal has spread them throughout the whole of Europe. If ever there were a time for turning the spotlight on these matters—it is now. This is not the time to complain that Christianity has not been fully examined.

After so many discussions, endless arguing and such a furore, has the world been disabused of religion and have Christian apologists been confounded? What success have the Apostles of non–belief enjoyed? Their victories are plain to see. They have seduced foolish young things who wanted all too readily to read objections to the faith before having studied its proofs; their nascent impetuosity got the better of them before examining the issues and they drew hasty conclusions. Enemies of the faith managed to throw sand in some ill–informed readers' eyes, who had never reflected on how our faith had become established, and disbelief had already become entrenched in their warped minds, in which libertinism had long ago effaced religious principles. For those who have bothered to study it carefully, who are free of phobias and prejudices, and are capable of making an impartial examination of Christianity, what fruit have they gleaned from reading the writings of our detractors? Indignation or pity—that's what! Some less well–informed readers were initially blinded and their faith was temporarily shaken, but they have soon been disabused of these ideas by reading the books of our apologists and their faith has even redoubled. Therefore, it is not those who remain attached to their religious faith that one must accuse of credulity, prejudice and blindness: it is rather those who have abandoned their faith without an intimate knowledge of it in the first place.

---

[50] *Christianity Unveiled,* p. 2. (This edition, p. 15.) *Important Examination of Lord Bolingbroke,* **Preface,** p. 2. This work was, in fact by Voltaire—see Glossary. *The Militant Philosopher,* Ch. 4. For *The Militant Philosopher,* see pp. lviii, lxxi, & 443.

There is an essential difference between the way the defenders of religion write and its detractors. The former approach it methodically and calmly, setting forth principles and drawing inferences, citing evidence from works of monumental importance: they bring forth their adversaries' objections in all good faith and they answer them, they posit a logical system, measured and supported by evidence, which satisfies the mind. The critics of religion tackle things quite differently: they stack up queries and endlessly reiterate them, copying from each other, yet they maintain a profound silence on the basic proofs and on answers provided a hundred times to their criticisms: they crack jokes and pile on the abuse, but they prove nothing. Their hate, mockery and frequent obscenities are substitutes for reasoning and comprise their strongest arguments. Their works, read avidly by the intellectually shallow, are always trumpeted with pomposity as novelties, as a *tour de force* to which theologians will never find an answer, but in essence they are merely rehashed works.[51] These writings are the booty of Hobbes, Spinoza, and Bayle, or extracts cobbled together from works in English. There is not a single one which is essentially nothing other than insincerity and spite. Such writers as this are highly unsuited to getting down to the truth and they are even less likely to be able to demonstrate it to others.

To cast aspersions on all those who write in defence of religion, the author of the *Important Examination* states that they have '*closed minds and are obsessed with a desire to show off*':[52] doubtless, those philosophers are exempt from all that. They are above human fanaticism and are never in the grip of a closed mind or a desire to blow their own trumpet, and their written style is proof positive of their soul's candour and their honourable intentions.

That same author reels off the yarn of one Jean Mélier [sic], an alleged priest, who, on his death bed, asked God to forgive him for having taught Christianity.[53] He would be a unique example of a kind. However, many philosophers have asked for God's forgiveness on their death–bed for having attacked religion through their libertinism and who, after having lived an ungodly life, wanted to die as Christians: do they not constitute a violent prejudice against the sincerity of others? They are fearless in rude health, but

---

[51] **See the Editor's Note in *Important Examination*.**

[52] **Page 2.**

[53] *Important Examination*, **p. 11.** This is a reference to Jean Meslier (1664–1729): note the correct spelling. Bergier is wrong to dismiss him and his circumstances as a 'yarn': he was a real person and very much a member of the cloth. (For Meslier—see Glossary.)

it only takes a fever to upset all their outbursts. Bayle, who must have known them well, was the first to mock them.[54]

§2

The author of *Christianity Unveiled* deplores the misfortune of the human race in pathetic tones. He remarks: '*everything seems to conspire to perpetuate man's blinkered state and all forces conjoin to mask the truth. Tyrants detest truth and suppress it because it dares challenge their unjust and fanciful titles; the priesthood denounces truth because it shows their lavish claims to be bogus.*'[55] This is sheer pomposity and not at all the language of reason. So truth, according to him, consists of questioning sovereigns' titles and claims made by the priesthood. In fact, this is the twin purpose of his work. In it sovereigns share the same unworthiness as ministers of religion: rights to the throne are treated equally disparagingly as

---

[54] *Reply to the Provincial Man*, **chapter 21; and** *Dictionary*, **article by Desbarreaux, Remark F.** (For *Reply to the Provincial Man* & *Dictionary*, see under Bayle in the Glossary.)
The reference to the 'Desbarreaux case' is amusing and worthy of a substantial footnote here. According to the article referenced above, Desbarreaux (or Des-Barreaux, as it is printed in Bayle's *Dictionary*, II, pp. 279—280) was born in Paris in 1602 of a noble family. He was educated by the Jesuits and showed great promise. He wrote a number of poems in Latin and French. However, he was generally infamous for his libertine life-style, including a homosexual liaison with a young, handsome lad called Théophile, who, it is said, had fallen in love with him. However, the dictionary article states that 'Desbarreaux died a good Christian in 1674'. The 'Remark F' in the reference above is a quotation from a sonnet by Desbarreaux, expressing his repentance and the *Dictionary* states that this sonnet 'was known by everybody' and that his death-bed repentance became something of a *cause célèbre*. The extract from the sonnet is as follows, translated below into (non-rhyming, non-scanning) English—it is quite a death-bed prayer!

Great God, your judgements are full of fairness,
And you always take pleasure in looking upon us favourably:
However, I have sinned so much that your goodness
Could never pardon me all my sins without shocking your sense of justice.
Yes, My God, the enormity of my impiety
Leaves your power the only option to torment me for all eternity:
Your interest must go against my bliss;
And even your clemency expects my perdition.
May your will be done, as is your glory;
May you take exception to the tears that flow from my eyes;
Fulminate, smite me, it is high time for you to render war for war:
As I perish, I adore the reason which has made you so bitter:
But on what shall your damnation fall
That is not all covered by the blood of Jesus Christ?

[55] *Christianity Unveiled*, **p. 7.** (This edition, p. 16.)

those of the Church. He proposes not only to wipe out all religion, but also all authority and subordination. This is what he calls 'revealing the truth to the human race.'

'The priesthood denounces truth', he says. Not at all! On the contrary, the priesthood invites all those who are capable of researching to do so, but to do it in good faith, to study religion from its sources before reading things which merely inspire prejudice against it. It forbids only those who are not sufficiently well–versed in its teachings from reading its enemies' books.[56] It permits anyone sufficiently schooled in the faith to read anything, so as not to risk being taken in. Religion approves of all polemical works where issues are discussed with exactitude and impartiality: in fact, it even complains that such works are not read enough.

Our adversaries' complaining about this is no more than a ruse to lure everyone to read their works, but this insidious trick does not work too well.[57] These books, ever presented in various guises, but in essence they are just the same, are in the hands of young people and women. It is to be hoped that their very multiplicity will prove to discredit them: the cloak–and–dagger way in which they circulated is often their greatest allure. The public ends up by reading the same sophisms repeatedly, echoed twenty times over by different people. After having devoured so many pamphlets in which the same criticisms of religion are endlessly made, people might turn out to be curious as to how we might respond, and so things end up turning full circle.

It is not true, at least in our country, that 'the average man–in–the–street [...] blindly relies on those whom pure chance has provided as guides.'[58] I shall show presently that in the bosom of the Catholic Church, the docility of the common man towards their pastors' teaching is not blind acceptance: the faithful listen to their voices because they reveal the genuine claims of their mission; these claims, by their very nature, justify and reassure the most unschooled man in his faith, just as they do the most well–informed.[59] If the author's criticisms find any currency amongst other sects or even amongst infidels, then that is up to them to reply; we cannot vouch for what has nothing to do with us.

The author adds: 'However, in every century there have been men who, disabused of their fellow citizens' prejudices, have dared to bear witness to

---

[56] This is a covert reference to the *Index of Prohibited Books*—see Glossary. This is yet another example of the Catholic Church keeping dissenting views away from the faithful so as to 'protect' their thinking, like reading the Bible.

[57] *Important Examination*, **p. 8.**

[58] *Christ. Unveil.*, **p. 9.** (This edition, p. 17.) *Important Exam.*, **p. 2.**

[59] See *The Certainty of the Proofs of Christianity*, **chapter 12, § 1.**

the truth.' But priests and kings have joined forces to impose silence upon them.[60] It would have been appropriate for him to have informed us who these great men were who, throughout the centuries, have taught the truth—by which he means atheism and disbelief. This uncommon teaching does not have a long tradition in our country: in centuries gone by, its followers were less common than nowadays. Anyway, despite the authority of kings and priests, works of those sublime geniuses have come down to us: the writings of **Vanini, Pomponazzi**, Hobbes, Spinoza, and many others who have copied them—all have survived. We are well–placed to know their views, just as they were heard themselves, and we know the kind of proofs they have propounded, masquerading under what they call the 'truth'. These kinds of writers are even less timid nowadays than they were and they pontificate fairly publicly—their voices resound throughout Europe and by examining their books we can judge how dreadful their ideas are. In vain do they pride themselves on being more successful than their predecessors: their writings are a little more comprehensible, without being any less emotional, which is why they will be despised even more readily. Their predecessors were refuted dispassionately, which was not at all difficult, and these modern writers will be refuted in their turn and fall into the same oblivion.

According to our author, it is not by habit or by example, it is not prejudice or politics, it is *'the stentorian clamour of trickery'*[61] that has supported religion up to now, despite the clamour of unbelievers. We know perfectly well by experience the advantages Christianity provides, founded as it is on solid proofs; there is a striking comparison between Christian and infidel nations and the absurdity of all other systems which people have wanted to replace it, and the trouble its adversaries have always taken in despising and hating each other, and the refutations they have made against one another. Amongst those so–called adherents of the truth, can one single out two who have been in perfect unison with each other and have agreed upon the same principles? The author of *Important Examination* seems to want to establish Deism and he advises us to adore God through reason.[62] However, by comparison, the writer of *Christianity Unveiled* leaves aside the question of God's existence and does not even want to speak of him.[63]

[...]

---

[60] *Christ. Unveil.*, **p. 9.** (This edition, p. 17.) *Militant Philosopher*, **ch. 1, p. 23.**
[61] See p. 17.
[62] **Page 2.**
[63] **Chapter 7, pp. 102 & 103.**

Chapter 2

A Short History of the Jewish People

[...]

§6

According to the author of *Christianity Unveiled*, the Hebrews '*had long been slaves of the Egyptians and were delivered from their servitude by a priest from Heliopolis, who by his genius and superior knowledge knew how to get the upper hand over them.*'[64] How did this priest manage to deliver them out of slavery? That is what the author does not tell us. [...]

In a footnote the author accuses Moses of killing an Egyptian. The Bible only justifies this crime because of Moses' extraordinary mission—a mission proven by the events which follow in the narrative. Our author also accuses him of having married an idolatrous priest's daughter.[65] Nowhere does it state that Jethro or his daughter were idol–worshippers: on the contrary, the story of Moses testifies to the fact that Jethro knew and worshipped the true god.[66] The author also states that Moses returned to Egypt to raise up the dissatisfied Hebrew nation against the king. This begs the question, does an alienated nation, reduced to a state of slavery, violate justice by wanting to come out of a country in which they are oppressed? In fact he adds that Moses reigned tyrannically because Korah, Dathan and Abiram were punished for having revolted against him.[67] History states that they were swallowed up alive into the bowels of the earth. But was it Moses that was responsible for such a supernatural and miraculous punishment?[68]

If we are to believe our critic, Moses '*persuaded* [the Hebrews] *that he was the interpreter of the will of their god* [...]. *He backed up his mission by works which appeared to be supernatural to men ignorant of the ways of*

---

[64] **Page 16.** (This edition, p. 21.)

[65] See footnote, p. 21. Moses' marriage to the daughter of Jethro is at the end of Exodus ch. 2 and the beginning of ch. 3.

[66] **Exodus 18 vs. 10.** The whole passage of this incident reads: 'And Moses told his father-in-law all that the Lord had done unto Pharaoh and to the Egyptians for Israel's sake, and all the travail that had come upon them by the way, and how the Lord delivered them. And Jethro rejoiced for all the goodness which the Lord had done to Israel, whom he had delivered out of the hand of the Egyptians. And Jethro said, "Blessed be the Lord, who hath delivered you out of the hand of the Egyptians, and out of the hand of Pharaoh, who hath delivered the people from under the hand of the Egyptians. Now I know that the Lord is greater than all gods: for in the thing wherein they dealt proudly he was above them",' (Exod. 18: 8—11).

[67] This incident occurs in Numbers 16.

[68] See the footnote, p. 21 for details.

Nature and artificial trickery.'[69] It would have been good he had explained to us:

(i) How Moses, having beguiled the Hebrews, was able to win over the Egyptians to part with this people, whom they retained as slaves and whose services they found most useful.

(ii) What were these 'works', regarded as supernatural by the Hebrews in their ignorance? All the waters of the Nile were changed into blood; all Egypt was over–run with insects and harmful animals; the whole country was ravaged by hail and pestilence, then shrouded in darkness, and the word of a single man delivered them from all these plagues. All the first–born of Egypt were killed in a single night; the waters of the Red Sea were parted on the left and the right to give safe passage to the entire Hebrew nation; a pillar of cloud went on ahead during the day and became luminous at night—are these 'works' those of an impostor, able to manipulate natural forces or even trick people?

Our censor also observes: *'The first order he issued on behalf of God was to steal from their masters, from whom they were about to flee.'*[70] It is untrue that the Hebrews stole from the Egyptians: they asked them for their most precious goods, which they gave them in order to hasten their departure, fearing they would perish if they held them back any longer.[71] The Egyptians knew that the Hebrews were never coming back.[72] God, as sovereign arbiter of the rights of two peoples, made the final decision to give the Egyptians' valuables to the Hebrews as a just recompense for the services the Hebrews had rendered them during their time of slavery.

(iii) If the Egyptians looked upon the Hebrews as fugitives and thieves, what would have stopped them from pursuing this hoard of slaves, taking back the booty they had purloined and killing them all off? These are points the author has not deemed appropriate to elucidate.

---

[69] *Christ. Unveil.*, p. 17. (This edition, p. 21.)

[70] *Christ. Unveil.*, p. 18. (Ibid.) *Important Exam.*, Ch. 7, p. 36. *Militant Philosopher,* ch. 20, pp. 156 & 160.

[71] See Exod. 11: 1—2: 'And the Lord said unto Moses, "Yet will I bring one plague more upon Pharaoh, and upon Egypt; afterwards he will let you go hence: when he shall let you go, he shall surely thrust you out hence altogether. Speak now in the ears of the people, and let every man borrow of his neighbour, and every woman of her neighbour, jewels of silver and jewels of gold".' For 'borrow' read 'purloin'!

[72] **Exod. 12: 33.** 'And the Egyptians were urgent upon the people, that they might send them out of the land in haste; for they said, "We be all dead men".'

§ 7

The author continues: '*When* [Moses] *was sure of their confidence in him, he led them* [i.e., the Hebrews] *into a desert where, for forty years, he conditioned them to total, blind obedience. He taught them the will of heaven, the fantastical fables of their ancestors and the bizarre ceremonies to which the Almighty linked his favours. He particularly inculcated in them the most venomous hate against the gods of other nations and the most calculated cruelty against those who adored them. By dint of carnage and rigour, he turned them into biddable slaves, quick to fulfil his wishes, ready to assist in his emotional outbursts, and prompt to self–sacrifice to satisfy his ambitious plans. In a word, he turned the Hebrews into frenetic, ferocious monsters.*'[73] This vehement, ranting tone is not at all that of reason or truth: there are as many paradoxes here as there are words. Either Moses was an ordinary man, thrown upon his own natural resources and ingenuity, or he was the minister of God's will, armed with powers superior to those of Nature. If the latter, then his behaviour is entirely justifiable and to question his behaviour is to take issue with Heaven itself.

In the former case, his behaviour is incredible. How did he manage to get his people to eke out an existence in an awful desert, amidst arid, burning sand, where nothing grows and where there is not even any water? And how did such a people resolve to follow him as their leader? How is it that this wild, indomitable people did not abandon their 'mad leader' at the very outset? How come they did not take out their despair and fury upon him? I maintain that this fact alone is more incredible than all the miracles Moses wrought.

The author of *Christianity Unveiled* states with regard to the Hebrews, '*he turned them into biddable slaves, quick to fulfil his wishes.*'[74] But do slaves withstand hunger and the constant threat of death? Moses and his people were either mad and frenetic, or they were driven by the hand of God: there is no in–between. A bout of frenzy does not last forty years.

Again, he states that Moses '*taught them* [...] *the fantastical fables of their ancestors*', etc. What fable? He taught them about the early history of the world, about the genealogy of the Patriarchs from whom they were descended. If the Hebrews had never heard speak of this, if this tradition had not survived amongst them, how could they have believed in it? He taught them about the arrival of their forefathers in Egypt, the story of Joseph and their servitude; if all that were but a fiction, Moses would have had as many

---

[73] *Christ. Unveil.*, p. 18. (This edition, p. 21.) *Military Phil.*, ch. 20, pp. 156 & 160.
[74] See p. 22 also.

witnesses to contest it as he had listeners—there would have been no shortage of old men who were in a position to contradict him.

Moses taught them the promises made to Abraham and his heirs to give them the land of the Canaanites. Apparently our critic considered this to be another careless mistake—he should have taken them straight there or kept quiet about the promise altogether.

There is more to follow: '*Moses taught them* [...] *the bizarre ceremonies to which the Almighty linked his favours*': but if the ceremonies were that bizarre, the Hebrews would have resisted submitting themselves to them. A lawgiver does not deliberately embark upon changing people's mores, ideas and customs, and at a stroke turn them into the enemy of another nation. Once again, there is no half–way stage: either Moses was guided by enlightened ideas from a higher source, or he was the most reckless of men. The author of *Important Examination* decided that Moses was a fool.[75] That is not the opinion of **Strabo**, nor of **Diodorus Siculus**, or of **Longinus**.[76] The author of *Christianity Unveiled* says that Moses, '*knew how to get the upper hand over* [the Hebrews]' by his '*genius and superior knowledge*'. He paints him as a furious madman who, '*by dint of carnage and rigour*', turned them into stupid slaves and into '*into frenetic, ferocious monsters*'. He could not be more revoltingly at variance with the real image of Moses. But is his portrayal of his people any more reasonable than that of their leader?

§ 8

The Hebrews marched against their neighbours to invade their territories and take their possessions, and '*heaven authorized their treachery and cruelty; their religion, combined with their greed, stifled the cries of Nature in their midst, and, under the leadership of their inhuman leaders, they destroyed the Canaanite nations with barbarism revolting to any man in whom superstition has not totally annihilated reason.*'[77] In order to appreciate the ridiculousness of this invective, let us enter into the spirit of the epoch of that story. Amongst all ancient peoples, and particularly amongst the semi–civilized, the rule of war was cruel and inhuman: it is still so today amongst the savages of America. They knew nothing of the reasonableness of conquest, which consists of sparing defeated people in order to make new subjects of them. This method, less barbarous than outright war, was introduced only during the time when great empires were

---

[75] *Important Examination*, **ch. 4, p. 29.**

[76] *Treatise on the Sublime* [Longinus]. What Diodorus Siculus wrote about Moses is hardly an endorsement of him: see the Glossary for what these historians said about Moses.

[77] *Christ. Unveil.*, **p. 19.** (This edition, p. 22.) *Important Exam.*, **ch. 7, pp. 36** *et seqq.*

being established and when there were sovereigns around who were eager to extend their dominion by pushing back the borders of their states. Amongst civilized peoples, war is waged between armies and ordinary citizens take no part in it. In antiquity, as amongst savages now, every man was a soldier and war was carried on between individuals with fury being a personal matter: people sought not only to conquer, but also to pillage and destroy, to reduce everything to nothing by burning and shedding blood.

We cannot deny that the Hebrews waged war according to this cruel method, but did other nations behave any differently? Can one state that, when taking enemy cities, the Hebrews employed more revolting barbarism than the Greeks when they sacked Troy, or during the **Peloponnesian War**, or even more than **Nebuchadrezzar**'s generals when taking Jerusalem,[78] or than the Romans on their expedition to **Epirus**, or during the siege of **Numantia**, or throughout the destruction of **Corinth** and **Carthage**? Is he asserting that Greek heroes such as **Hercules**, **Theseus**, **Achilles** and **Ulysses**, who are set on a pedestal, were any more humane, virtuous individuals than the leaders of the Jewish nation? As a famous philosopher has remarked: *'What was it about that period that it was called "heroic times"? They were times when one got one's throat cut for a well or a cistern, just as happens nowadays for an entire province.'*[79]

---

[78] See Glossary under **Nebuchadrezzar II** for details of him and his attack on Jerusalem.

[79] *Sequel to Miscellany of Literature, History and Philosophy*, **ch. 70, III, p. 232**. This is a reference to an edition of Voltaire's collected works. Eleven volumes of Voltaire's collected works (XX—XXXII of the Garnier 1883 edn., in 54 vols.) are called '*Mélanges*' [*Miscellany*]. In fact, this quotation comes from a pot-pourri of remarks on the Koran, entitled 'Alcoran ou plutôt Le Koran' {'The Alcoran or rather the Koran'}, from Section II. It appeared in 1784 in Volume IV of the *Œuvres de Voltaire*, at the end of his tragedy *Mohamet* {*Muhammad*}. In 1756 it became part of Volume IV, under '*Suite des Mélanges. B.*' The context is interesting because it shows what Voltaire thought about Islam and the reference is translated below. The term 'Alcoran' was a popular term of reference for the Koran (or Qur'an as it is preferred nowadays) in many European countries.

After having gone through a long list of rules, regulations and requirements relating to the observance of Islam, Voltaire comes to the conclusion that, whilst a number of its precepts are fine and laudable in terms of social morality, there are so many restrictions and impositions within the Islamic faith that, as a system of belief, he describes it as 'dreadful', and he concludes that it is 'treacherous and murderous'. However, he goes on to say:

'How much more preferable is a man like Confucius, the chief among mortals, who experienced no kind of revelation: he relied solely upon reason and not upon lying or the sword. As viceroy of a large province, he made morality and the law flourish. Though disgraced and poverty-stricken, he taught his precepts both in a state of ennoblement and in penury: he made virtue attractive and he had as his disciples the oldest and wisest of peoples. The Count of Boulainviliers, who was rather taken with

The Hebrews often used betrayal and treachery, they often violated justice and good faith—it was a general maxim accepted by all peoples: *Dolus an virtus quis in hoste requirat?*[80] The Greeks, the Carthaginians, and even the Romans during the heyday of the Republic, were all no less religious. The Hebrews, who are depicted as so perfidious, nevertheless kept the oath which they had sworn to the Gibeonites when caught unaware:[81] they never treated their slaves as they themselves had been treated in Egypt, and never did they

---

Muhammadanism, tried hard to sing the Arabs' praises to me and he wouldn't have it that they were just a bunch of crooks: they used to steal before they got Islam while they still worshipped the stars, and subsequently they thieved under Mohammed in the name of God. It was said that they had retained their simple outlook from heroic times, but what was it about that period that it was called "heroic times"? They were times when one got one's throat cut for a well or a cistern, just as happens nowadays for an entire province. The first Muslims were fired by Mohammed with a maniacal keenness. Nothing is more terrible than a people who, having nothing to lose, fight jointly in a spirit of pillage and religion.'

[80] *'Guile or valour—of what importance are they to an enemy?'* This is a quotation from Virgil's *Aeneid*, Bk. II, 390. The sense being, 'What does it matter how one overcomes an enemy—by guile or valour?' The inferance being that any way will do, so long as one overcomes an enemy.

[81] **Joshua ch. 9.** Having destroyed the city of Ai (a Canaanite city) and slaughtered its inhabitants on God's express instructions, Joshua's reputation spread to a near-by group of people called the Gibeonites who, afraid they might be next in line for annihilation, pretended to be a people from distant parts who had come to conclude a peace treaty with the Israelites. This was accomplished according to plan and an entente was sworn on oath. However, Joshua later learned of the deception, yet he decided to keep the sworn oath, but the entire people were reduced to being the Israelites' slaves, serving them as woodcutters and water carriers for the rest of time. The story is intended to show how merciful the Israelites could be. The ferocity to which the city of Ai was subjected is narrated in Joshua Chs. 7—8, and the concluding sack of Ai is particularly brutal: 'And when Joshua and all Israel saw that the ambush had taken the city, and that the smoke of the city ascended, then they turned again, and slew the men of Ai. And the other issued out of the city against them; so they were in the midst of Israel, some on this side, and some on that side: and they smote them, so that they let none of them remain or escape. And the king of Ai they took alive, and brought him to Joshua. And it came to pass, when Israel had made an end of slaying all the inhabitants of Ai in the field, in the wilderness wherein they chased them, and when they were all fallen on the edge of the sword, until they were consumed, that all the Israelites returned unto Ai, and smote it with the edge of the sword. And so it was, that all that fell that day, both of men and women, were twelve thousand, even all the men of Ai. For Joshua drew not his hand back, wherewith he stretched out the spear, until he had utterly destroyed all the inhabitants of Ai. Only the cattle and the spoil of that city Israel took for a prey unto themselves, according unto the word of the Lord which he commanded Joshua. And Joshua burnt Ai, and made it an heap for ever, even a desolation unto this day. And the king of Ai he hanged on a tree until eventide: and as soon as the sun was down, Joshua commanded that they should take his carcase down from the tree, and cast it at the entering of the gate of the city, and raise thereon a great heap of stones, that remaineth unto this day. (Josh. 8: 21—29.)

act, treat perfidiously or cruelly the vanquished, as one might reproach the **Lacedemonians** with regard to the **Helots**.[82] Ought we to be so unjust as to judge the Jews according to a law unknown to people at that time, and to whom we owe a debt for the enlightenment and morality we have received from the gospel?

We might excuse other peoples' crimes committed through the ignorance and depravity to which God had abandoned them, but it was God himself who inspired the Hebrews, who issued them with orders, who authorized them to act—that is what revolts the mind and reason in this case.

Of course, God could have undoubtedly enlightened, converted, and reformed the Hebrews, refashioned their mores and character to make them models of justice and humanity for the centuries during which they existed; but would this moral miracle—a phenomenon far more incredible than all the physical miracles—have had to be part of Wisdom's divine plan of necessity? That is the point that our philosophers ought to begin by addressing. God wanted to punish the Canaanites, who were an abominable people: he wanted to use the Hebrews to exterminate them. Can we accuse Him of going too far in meting out their punishment? God led the Hebrews by his special providence, but he governed them according to the spirit, the mores and the political ethos of the time, common amongst all nations. Whilst the Hebrews' crimes cause us to question this special providence, those very crimes, and some even worse which are prevalent amongst all peoples, do not appear any less to go against his general providence. Should the fact that men have always been bad make us doubt that God created man and that he governs the world?

Furthermore, I maintain that had the Jewish nation had more gentle mores, they would not have survived amongst the peoples where they lived. Can a weaker nation surrounded by savage and barbarous peoples possibly live safely if it does not wage war like the rest, and if it does not become just as fearsome towards their neighbours as they are to them? Can such a nation afford to be humane towards its enemies, who know nothing other than the

---

[82] See *The Origin of Laws*, etc., **Part III, I, Bk. 6, ch. 3, Art. i.** Bergier is referring to Goguet, Antoine Yves (1716—1758) *De l'origine des loix, des arts, et des sciences ; et de leurs progrès chez les anciens peuples* (1758) {*On the Origin of Laws, of Arts, and of Sciences, and their progress amongst Ancient Peoples*}. This is a serious philosophical treatise and yet, amusingly, it starts with a section entitled 'De l'état du Genre Humain au sortir du déluge' {'On the State of Mankind at the End of the Flood'}, an examination of man just after the Universal Flood and Noah's family, as if this were an established, historical fact:. (For Lacedemonians and Helots—see Glossary.)

rule of might, without risking becoming victims themselves? Despite the meekness of our French mores, when it came to making war against the savages of America, were we not forced to use the cruellest reprisals in order to intimidate them? Their ferocity made any clemency shown towards them when defeated appear as a mark of weakness, and this would have done nothing other than instigate yet further insults on their part.

By making himself known to the Hebrew people, God saved them from polytheism and idolatry, from all the dreadful disorders that were common amongst all other nations: He gave them wise laws proportionate to the crudeness and the uncouthness of their incipient, emerging human condition—that is St Paul's reflection on this issue.[83] Divine Wisdom kept a purer morality, a more holy religion for happier centuries yet to come.

Solon was fêted for having given the Athenians the best possible laws, but they were the best they could bear at the time. Montesquieu remarked, '*That is the sponge one must apply to wipe away all the difficulties raised over the laws of Moses.*'[84] What did the bogus Bolingbroke say about this remark, which is replete with good sense? He exclaimed it was blasphemy. He said, '*What?! Does God act proportionally? Proportionate to whom? To the thieving Jews?! God is even more crude than they are!*'[85] Calm yourself, religious philosopher! When Solon acted proportionate to the spirit of the times in the Athenians' interest, he was not being 'more crude' than they: he was acting much more wisely than they.

---

[83] **Gal. 3: 21 and Heb. 7: 19.** These verses say respectively:
'Is the law then against the promises of God? God forbid: for if there had been a law given which could have given life, verily righteousness should have been by the law.'
'For the law made nothing perfect, but the bringing in of a better hope did; by the which we draw nigh unto God.'

[84] *Spirit of Laws*, I, 14, ch. 21. The remark comes from the section entitled 'Chapitre {Chapter} XXI: 'Comment les lois doivent être relatives aux mœurs et aux manières' {How Laws Must Relate to Mores and Manners'}. Montesquieu quotes Plutarch's *The Life of Solon*, Ch. IX, saying, 'Solon was asked if the laws he had given the Athenians were the best. He replied: "I've given them the best they could tolerate." A fine sentiment which should be understood by all lawgivers. As far as Divine Wisdom goes, the Jews were told, "I've given you precepts which are not good", which means they had a relative goodness. That is the sponge one must apply to wipe away all the difficulties raised over the laws of Moses.'

[85] *Import. Exam.*, ch. 3, p. 24.

Chapter 3

A Short History of Christianity

§ 2

The author of *Christianity Unveiled* states that: '*It was in the midst of this nation, so predisposed to feed on hopes and idle fantasies, that a new visionary appeared, whose followers managed to change the face of the earth.*'[86] These carefully chosen words are enough to expose the author as not recognizing anything supernatural about the establishment of Christianity. Does it not fly in the face of so many circumstances, absolutely contrary to the natural course of things, that a nation as ill–educated as the Jews produced the wisest and most enlightened law–giver of all time; that without any education or any other form of human resource he formulated a plan to change the face of the earth; that to do so he began not by pandering to the fanciful hopes of his people, but by directly overturning all their preconceptions, and that this was achieved through the ministry of twelve poor fishermen?

Before and after Jesus Christ, several people tried to pass themselves off as the Messiah, but they were promptly abandoned and scorned: their failure only emphasizes the supernatural nature of Jesus Christ's own mission.

The author of *Important Examination* felt the gravity of these observations and in order to get round them, he had recourse to a particular expedient—he issued a formal denial of **Tacitus** and **Suetonius**. He said: '*No one spoke of waiting for the appearance of the Messiah… It is certain that no Jew hoped for it, wanted it, or proclaimed it during the time of Herod the Great.*'[87] But, ever prone to contradicting himself, he admits in the same work that, '*There was a party, a sect, which recognized Herod as sent by God.*' It is quite certain, therefore, that people were waiting for someone sent from God and that Tacitus and Suetonius had not just dreamt it up. If Herod himself had not been persuaded of this argument, why did he have so many innocent children killed? This horrible act of cruelty was preserved in the memoirs of a Roman writer, as well as in the gospel.[88]

---

[86] **Page 24.** (This edition, p. 25.)

[87] *Import. Exam.*, ch. 11, pp. **56**—**57.**

[88] **Macrobius, *Saturnalia*, I, 2, ch. 4.** Macrobius offers no real evidence or historical sources for the incident when Herod allegedly killed the children, as recounted in the Gospel of Matthew, ch. 2. Macrobius writes: 'A certain Vettius had ploughed up a memorial to his father, whereupon Augustus remarked, "This is indeed cultivating your father's memory." When he heard that Herod, King of the Jews, had ordered boys in Syria under the age of two years to be put to death and that the king's son was

It is very useful to note the different obscure and isolated sects which were around at the time and all of them, without exception, were quickly crushed: only Christianity managed to captivate the whole world.[89]

§ 3

I do not blush to repeat our critics' calumnies against our Saviour, by which the Jews tried to blacken the circumstances of his birth and life. The Jews maintained that Jesus was born of Mary who had been seduced by a soldier and that he had learned how to do magic tricks in Egypt, and that he was the leader of a gang of thieves. However, the Jews only dared write these lies several centuries after the birth of Christianity: they kept them under wraps for a long time and the books containing these allegations are full of errors, anachronisms and childish accusations, which the enemies of our religion have not dared to use until now. Even in the *Philosophical Dictionary* these things are mentioned with the utmost scorn.[90]

---

among those killed, he said, "I'd rather be Herod's pig than Herod's son".' (Macrobius, *Saturnalia*, translated with an introduction and notes by Percival Vaughan Davies [N.Y.: Columbia U.P., 1969], p. 171.) In his introduction, the translator notes, 'Although the works of Macrobius contain no reference to Christianity, he may have been a Christian...' (op. cit., p. 1.) Again, this is thin 'evidence' indeed to assert that this incident actually took place. (See Glossary also.)

[89] *Important Exam., ibid.*

[90] *Phil. Dict.* **under the article 'Messiah'.** The article referred to in Voltaire's *Philosophical Dictionary* contains the following passage about the Messiah's background. It must be born in mind that Voltaire, in keeping with many sceptics of his time, wrote in tones of feigned horror at the impiety of some of their sources in order to get their work past the censor and to bring information into the public arena without offending the Church more than was absolutely necessary. Of course, this was not always possible, but they were often successful. Voltaire repeated these allegations on more than one occasion, and to what extent he either approved or disapproved of this story is difficult to judge. 'Just as the Jews have contested the Messianic qualities of Jesus Christ, they have also left no stone unturned in reducing him to a contemptible level by surrounding his birth, life and death with all the ridicule and opprobrium that their criminal determination could muster. Of all works that this form of Jewish blindness has produced, there is none more hateful and extravagant than an ancient book entitled *Sepher Toldoth Jeschut*, [or for 'Jeshut' read 'Jeshu'] unearthed from the depths by Mr Wagenseil, in the second volume of his work entitled *Tela ignea Satanae*, etc. It is in the *Sepher Toldoth Jeschut* that one reads an appalling story from the life of our Saviour, trumped up with all possible passionate hate for our faith. Hence, for example, he dared to write that a certain man named Panther or Pandera, an inhabitant of Bethlehem, took a fancy to a young, married woman who was married in Jokanan. The product of this unholy union was a son called Jesua or Jesu. The father of this child was forced to make himself scarce and went off to Babylon. As for this young child Jesu, he was sent to various schools but, the author adds, he was insolent enough to look up and uncover his head in the presence of the Jewish High Priests, instead of bowing his head and covering his face as was the

It was left to the mendacious Bolingbroke to inform us that the details of Jesus' life, as published by the Jews, were by his own admission from '*an extravagant book*', which reported '*many things which were much more plausible than the gospels.*'[91] I invite the reader to read extracts from these 'life–stories' in Mr **Bullet**'s *History of the Establishment of Christianity*, in which the merit and wisdom of our opposing critic can be assessed.[92]

It is pointless to refer our author to such an authoritative work because he maintains that **Celsus**' history of the life of Christ is as old as the gospels: but Celsus cited this book in the second century. Hence, his allegation is false. In fact, Celsus himself referred to this Jewish author who accused Jesus of being born of an adulterous relationship;[93] however, there is no such allegation made against Jesus' birth cited from any Jewish sources. This can be proven to our great advantage in that the Jews formally recognized in this work the reality of Jesus Christ's miracles.[94] So, Jesus Christ's mission was proven by his miracles, quite apart from the circumstances of his birth.

It is untrue that the narrative of Jesus' life as told by the Jews was subsequently corrupted and that '*a number of bland fables were added*', including irrelevant miracles, and that '*this book has come down to us in an extremely distorted form.*'[95] We have this book and it has come down to us just as the Jews wrote it: they kept it secret for as long as they could and Christians heard about it only in the last few centuries.

Not content with casting doubt on the miraculous conception of Jesus in Mary's womb, the enemies of Christianity have once again set about

---

custom, and for this audacious act he was roundly scolded: this incident gave rise to the priests looking into his background and finding out that he was impure, which led to his public disgrace. The detestable book *Sepher Toldoth Jeschut* has been known from the second century and Celsus cited it with complete trust, but Origen refuted it in his ninth chapter. There is also another book entitled *Toldoth Jeschut*, published in 1705 by Mr Huldric, which follows the Gospel account of Christ's life in the greatest detail from his childhood onwards, but which is replete at every stage with the grossest of anachronisms: he has Jesus Christ being born and dying under the reign of Herod the Great, and he claims that it was to this prince that allegations of adultery against Panther and Mary, the mother of Jesus, were made.' The work *Toldoth Jeshu* {תולדות ישו ספר} is an actual book by Johann Christoph Wagenseil (1633—1705), written in Hebrew and Latin and published in 1681. There is a copy in the British Library. (For Voltaire—see Glossary.)

[91] *Import. Exam.*, ch. 11, p. 60.

[92] See p. 75.

[93] **Orig. contr. Cels. l, i, Cantabr. edn., pp. 24, 26, 54.** In fact Celsus provided a full reference to the work to which he refers and which Bergier denies. (For Celsus— see Glossary.)

[94] *History* by Mr. Bullet, p. 92.

[95] *Import. Exam.*, p. 62.

spreading a ridiculous falsity and in doing so, they have had recourse to their usual weapons of obscenity and calumny. They have suggested that Saint Augustine, in his *Twenty–Second Sermon*, stated, when speaking of the angel: '*imprægnavit Mariam per aurem*.'[96] This is absolutely fraudulent: there is nothing of this kind in Saint Augustine.[97] Sanchez has been accused of speaking of the same mystery in terms which would set modesty a quiver.[98] In fact, Sanchez does not express himself in these terms and this represents yet another of the author's errors.[99] Although the way he expresses himself does not represent a danger for theologians who read his work with a chaste heart and for a legitimate understanding, I abstain from reporting what he has written here: it would only serve as more poison for the perverse minds of philosophers.

---

[96] *Le Dîner du Comte Boulainvilliers*, **p. 33.** This was a work (dated 1767) by Voltaire and can be found in his *Œuvres complètes*, XXIV, in the volume 'Mélanges V'. The Latin reads, '[he] impregnated Mary through her ear.'

[97] Though this idea does not occur in St Augustin's sermon, as Bergier states, it was a concept which was sufficiently widely believed that an early polemic against this rumour was published; it is described in an article by Sebastian Brock, 'Passover, Annunciation and Epiclesis: Some Remarks on the Term *Aggen* in the Syriac Versions of Lk. 1:35' in *Novum Testamentum*, XXIV, Fasc. 3 (Jul., 1982), pp. 222—233.

[98] *Import. Exam.*, **ch. 1, p. 63.** *L'Homme aux Quarante Ecus*, **p. 59.** '*L'Homme aux Quarante Ecus*' {'*The Man of Forty Ecus*'} (1768) is a satirical novel by Voltaire, the forty *écus* (an old unit of currency) of the title being the sum of the man's annual salary. In Chapter VII of the novel, the Forty-Ecus man gets married and discovers that his wife has soon become pregnant. Unsure how this has come about, he asks a land surveyor, the epitome of an educated man, who tells him what Hippocrates and Sanchez stated on the subject, the latter having written a book entitled *Matrimonio*: the land surveyor uses the religious context of Mary becoming pregnant, who 'emitted seminal fluid which, when mixed with that of the Holy Spirit' had produced the child. The two men are both disgusted by this method of reproduction. The spraying of semen is cited as common amongst aquatic life, which leads on to a discussion about various other methods of insemination, not only in the animal kingdom, but also amongst humans. The question of Mary becoming inseminated via the ear canal occurs in Voltaire's *Les Questions de Zapata, Traduites par le Sieur Tamponet, Docteur de Sorbonne* {*Zapata's Questions, translated by Mr Tamponet, Dr of the Sorbonne*} (1767)—Question №. 50. In fact Thomas Sanchez (1550—1610) was a real person and not just a figment of Voltaire's imagination in his satirical work. He was a Jesuite priest whose book *Matrimonio*, to which Voltaire alludes, was in fact entitled *Disputationes de sancti matrimonii sacramento* (1602) {'*Questions on the Sacrament of Holy Matrimony*'}, one volume of which ironically found its way onto the Catholic Index of banned books for not being in keeping with some points of Catholic teaching on marriage at the time. The *Catholic Encyclopaedia*, XIII of 1912 hints that the language used by Sanchez in this work was more candid than propriety of the era would allow, and it was another reason for it being banned and for him being accused of immorality.

[99] **Sanchez, I, 2, *Disputationes*, 21, № 11.**

I agree with the author of *Christianity Unveiled* that Jesus was *'a poor Jew, who claimed to have hailed from the royal blood of David.'*[100] The truth of this claim is proven by his authentic genealogy, derived from the very archives of a nation, which always took particular care in maintaining genealogies in order to be able to justify the birth of the Messiah when he appeared on earth. Jesus' poverty, far from making his mission suspect, on the contrary serves to raise the profile of his virtues: a Saviour who came to teach men to be indifferent to worldly riches had to start by giving them a personal example. A God, a friend of the poor, might outrage the haughty, voluptuous philosophers, but it is not from them that we ought to learn the pinnacles of Divine Wisdom.

§ 4

It is slanderous to suggest that Jesus Christ *'made proselytes for himself [...] amidst the most ignorant rabble'* and to repeat time and again that *'at its inception the Christian religion was forced to restrict itself to the masses; it was embraced only by the most contemptible men amongst the Jews and pagans.'*[101] In another work I have shown that during his life, Jesus Christ had followers amongst the Jews who were distinguished—they were doctors of law, and that the disciples converted wise men and philosophers in great numbers.[102] It is not necessary to repeat these proofs here and our detractors will never manage to disparage them.

There is also a further mark of their dishonesty in the way in which the author of *Important Examination* treated the miracles, the behaviour and the teaching of Jesus Christ, presuming that his readers were not familiar with the gospels.[103]

[...]

---

[100] **Christ. *Unveil.*, p. 24.** (This edition, p. 25.)

[101] *Ibid.*, **pp. 25 & 29.** (This edition, pp. 24—26.) *Import. Exam.*, **ch.14, p.87.**

[102] ***Certitude of the Proofs of Christianity*, ch. 6, § 1.**

[103] *Import. Exam.*, **ch. 11, p. 63. *Letters on the Miracles*—the first and fourteenth letters. *Question of Zapata*, №s. 4, 55, & 56. *Dinner of the Count of Boulainvilliers*, p. 28.**
Voltaire published anonymously a *Collection des Lettres sur les Miracles* in Geneva in 1767 {*'Collection of Letters on the Miracles'*}, a series of twenty letters, which are to be found under *Miscellany IV (1763—1766)* (*Mélanges IV*) of Voltaire's *Collected Works*, XXV. The *Letters* were actually written in 1765. *Letter* № 1 questions Christ's miraculous birth, and *Letter* № 14 is more wide-ranging in terms of its subject matter: it deals with general disputes over theological issues with specific reference to the credibility of miracles in general, and it also mentions conflicts which have escalated into civil and international wars, engendered by religious questions.

§5

The author of *Christianity Unveiled* states that, '[Jesus'] *disciples, [as] either impostors or simple saps, bore startling witness to his power: they claimed that his mission had been proven by countless miracles.*'[104] Here are new issues to examine. Were the disciples of Jesus Christ impostors, or simply hoodwinked? Were they the only people to have borne witness to the miracles of their master? The glibness with which the author of *Christianity Unveiled* passes over the miracles shows that he has not studied the material in depth.

If Christ's disciples had been hoodwinked, it is doubtless because of their nation's hopes, which the author dismisses as a fanciful dream, and that Jesus arrived at a time when the Jewish people were in a state of anticipation, waiting for a messiah for whom Jesus passed himself off. '*But we trusted that it had been he which should have redeemed Israel.*'[105] They latched on to him because he promised them that he would grant them a great place in his kingdom. However, his ultimate, ignominious death must have disabused them of this. To remain attached to a master who had tricked them and exposed them to the scorn and hate of their own nation, to continue come what may to preach his resurrection and divinity, despite possible ill–will directed towards them, to face torture and death for the sake of an impostor who had played on their credulity—does all this seem normal human behaviour? Would the human heart countenance such things? One might concede that they had been duped up to the time of Jesus' death, but to have persisted in blind faith despite his death and the apparent emptiness of his promises, and notwithstanding the danger their preaching exposed them to— that is something that is beyond comprehension. Therefore we must conclude that Jesus was true to his promises when he appeared before them in his resurrected form and that they were neither deceitful nor impostors.

Might they have been? First of all, they do not force upon us certain facts about Jesus, commonly held by our enemies in the hope of scoring such points, regarding his poverty, the obscurity in which he lived until the age of thirty, his preaching, his death and the ignorance of most of his followers: any impostor wanting to dazzle and fool the world would not have begun by admitting to all these things. Be that as it may, the disciples made known their master's miracles, his resurrection and ascension into heaven—it is these things that they set before us and it is for our enemies to prove all this to the contrary.

---

[104] *Christ. Unveil.*, **p. 25.** (This edition, p. 25.)
[105] **Luke 24: 21.**

§6

(i) What might the disciples have hoped to gain from the fable that they concocted? They themselves declared that Jesus had predicted that they would be *'hated, despised, persecuted, and counted as nought for his name.'*[106] An impostor would have patted himself on the back for his success in advance, he would promise victories and a wonderful outcome. Never have we seen anyone formulate such a daring plan, only to succumb and fall victim to it for the sheer pleasure of doing so.

(ii) Were the disciples looking to derive some personal advantage out of all this for themselves? They worked for the sole glory of their master and everything they did was in his name: they did not attribute any miracles they performed to their own power, or the message they preached.[107] The author of *Christianity Unveiled* contends that, *'their ambition was confined to holding sway over souls'*.[108] In other words, they were happy to remain poor, to be consumed by work, to sacrifice their own lives, to shed their own blood, so long as the gospel was preached and they stated and acted according to this plan.[109] So selfless were these impostors!

(iii) Is deception compatible with their character, their doctrine, or their behaviour? They are criticized for being simple, crude, lacking in erudition, from which they do not defend themselves at all. Would a plan to convert the world even occur naturally to men such as these? They preached only sincerity, uprightness, charity, tenderness and patience: and they went one better—they practised it. And our author soon accedes this point to them. Would such simple, guileless men become martyrs for a fallacy? Would such rogues turn into apostles of virtue? Faithful and intrepid in their cause, they said the same things in the presence of their disciples and their enemies: they neither avoided persecution nor interrogation; they were fearless and never retracted what they said, or contradicted each other either in private or in groups. They preached the same things in the three parts of the known world and they were the same on their travels, in their homeland and in

---

[106] **John 15 & 16, et al.** This 'quotation' is a composite of several verses stated in the chapters of John's Gospel as referenced by Bergier.

[107] **Acts 3: 12.** The context of the passage is: 'And as the lame man which was healed held Peter and John, all the people ran together unto them in the porch that is called Solomon's, greatly wondering. And when Peter saw it, he answered unto the people, "Ye men of Israel, why marvel ye at this or why look ye so earnestly on us, as though by our own power or holiness we had made this man to walk? The God of Abraham, and of Isaac, and of Jacob, the God of our fathers, hath glorified his Son Jesus...",' (Acts 3: 11—13).

[108] **Page 30.** (This edition, p. 27.)

[109] **II Cor. 12: 15.** 'And I will very gladly spend and be spent for you; though the more abundantly I love you, the less I be loved.'

foreign lands, whether in prisons or on the scaffold. What unknown power could maintain this sort of consistency amongst them in the teeth of the impact of all human emotions? By contrast, two individual philosophers cannot agree on a single system of disbelief, but the so–called 'fable of Christianity' was able to unite a hundred or so preachers early on.

(iv) The disciples could not have set about substantiating these 'fables' in a worse way. The apostles did not try to publicize their master's miracles and his resurrection in foreign lands. They did so in Jerusalem under the very noses of those who had crucified him: they called upon the people of Jerusalem as witnesses and they dared use this public knowledge as evidence: they did not wait ten or twenty years after the event: they preached fifty days after the death of Jesus Christ, right at the time when the number of people gathered in Jerusalem was at its greatest, when the assembled witnesses from different areas of Judea were all together. They were listened to and they persuaded people: eight thousand people became Christians after they preached on two occasions. Could such an act of deception, able to have been disproved on the spot and against which an entire town was in a position to testify, possibly grip the minds of eight thousand people in so few days?

(v) If the apostles were impostors, then the behaviour of the Jews is inexplicable. How could the Council of Jerusalem, so aggressive and furious against the Master, show such patient indulgence towards his disciples? It was important for these magistrates to justify their behaviour with regard to Jesus Christ and to oppose the apostles' preaching to all the world about the truth of these events, and to send well–substantiated, well–authenticated information to the synagogues, and particularly to Rome, about the false doctrines of the 'crimes'—real or supposed—of Jesus Christ, about the 'tricks' by which he had hoodwinked the people, about the 'false reports' of his resurrection, and about the audacity and dissimulation of the disciples. But these Pharisees, known for being such zealous priests, remained in a state of jealous inactivity. Instead of publicly unmasking these new impostors, they merely imprisoned them for a few days and threatened them, but they did not disabuse anyone of their message. In almost all towns in which St Paul took the gospel he made proselytes amongst even the leaders of the synagogues. The fact that the power of the truth sealed the mouths and tied the hands of members of the Jewish Council is not at all miraculous: but that trickery should have prospered so easily will never ever be understood.

Let it be repeated: our adversaries disdainfully reject the miracles of Jesus Christ and the apostles because they depart from the earth's laws of physics, and yet they readily admit to even greater miraculous events in the moral sphere, which are even more incredible and which worked no less against the natural order. At least they all agree with each other on this.   [...]

§8

According to the author of *Christianity Unveiled*, '*The only miracle of which* [Jesus] *was capable was to convince the Jews, who, far from being touched by his beneficent, supernatural acts, put him to death by an abominable form of torture.*'[110]

This objection, made on another occasion by the Emperor **Julian**, ought to appear sublimely ridiculous at the pen of our critic.

(i) After having railed against the Jews' fanaticism, blindness and obstinacy, and against the vain hope with which they deluded themselves that a powerful king would make his appearance—a triumphant Messiah to deliver them—how can he be surprised that Jesus Christ, with all his miracles and virtues, did not finally manage to convince the whole Jewish nation? A single Jew converted by a poor Messiah is a miracle, so mass incredulity, especially amongst the leaders of the nation, should not surprise anyone.

(ii) Philosophers in general do not accede to any miracles to back up a doctrine which they just cannot swallow: were the miracles to be a hundred times clearer and better proven, their disbelief would still be the same. If the Jews had thought as they do, how would the miracles of Jesus Christ have managed to convert them?

(iii) It is not true that Jesus Christ never touched or converted a single Jew. Apart from the twelve apostles and seventy–two disciples, whom we already know about, he had a very large number of followers—both open and secret—although they were not attached to him and did not follow him around like the former. His apostles were the first to convert several thousand Jews and the number increased daily. He was condemned and put to death by the Jewish nation's leaders, in whose interest it was to stifle his doctrine through their false, religious zeal; but Judea was full of people convinced of Jesus' holiness and the veracity of his miracles, who recognized him as the Messiah and the Son of God. It could only be because the Jews feared a general uprising in the light of the evidence of recent events that restrained them from dealing as violently with the apostles as they had with Jesus.

(iv) In fact, the Jewish sacred books foretold that the Messiah would be rejected by his own people;[111] that his miracles would be attributed to magic

---

[110] *Christ. Unveil.*, **p. 25.** (This edition, p. 25.)

[111] **Dan. 9: 26.** The verse cited by Bergier states: 'And after threescore and two weeks shall Messiah be cut off, but not for himself: and the people of the prince that shall come shall destroy the city and the sanctuary; and the end thereof shall be with a flood,

by mischief–makers, and that he would be put to death and rise again. This tradition still exists in the books of their Church Doctors.[112] Given that all these things came to pass as predicted, the Jewish leaders' incredulity cannot be considered as a refutation of our position, but as a proof against that of our adversaries.

§9

Our critics' voice clamour as one to point out that Jesus Christ died '*in full view of the whole of Jerusalem*', whereas his disciples assure us that '*he was secretly resurrected*', and that he was '*visible only to them and invisible to the nation to whom he had come to enlighten and convert to his doctrine.*'[113]

It is untrue that Jesus Christ was resurrected in secret: he was brought back to life in the presence of the soldiers who were guarding his tomb, and he showed himself to over five hundred of his assembled disciples:[114] he chatted informally with them for forty hours. He was never invisible to the whole nation, since this multitude of his disciples were part of it and an appearance to such a great number was enough to convince all those right–thinking Jews. It is irrelevant to speculate whether Jesus Christ could have proved his resurrection in a more flamboyant or convincing way, since we consider that he did so sufficiently and effectively for any reasonable person.[115] Were Jesus Christ to have revealed himself to the whole of Jerusalem in broad daylight, our adversaries would still say, as they already have, that this proof would have been sufficient for those who had seen him, but insufficient for those who had not.

Jesus Christ died in full view of the whole of Jerusalem, but did he die as an ordinary man? The words he spoke on the cross, the cry that he uttered immediately prior to expiring, the earth' shaking, the solar eclipse, the opening up of tombs and the appearance of the dead—were these marvels yet too weak to touch people capable of opening their eyes to the light? The Roman officer present at Calvary was frightened by these events and confessed to the divinity of Christ. Many people changed their lives, beat

---

and unto the end of the war desolations are determined.' These are hardly the circumstances of Jesus' fate!

[112] Bullet, *History of the Establishment of Christianity*, **pp. 102 & 117.** (For Bullet—see Glossary.)

[113] *Christ. Unveil.* **p. 26.** (This edition, p. 25.) *Import. Exam.*, ch. 11.

[114] **I Corinthians 15: 6.** The verse states, 'After that, he was seen of above five hundred brethren at once; of whom the greater part remain unto this present, but some are fallen asleep.' If this striking event were true, then why do none of the Gospels mention such an amazing fact?

[115] **See Ditton's book.** (For Ditton—see Glossary.)

Figure 37: *Resurrection*, Albrecht Dürer (1510).

their breast and were touched to the point of repentance.[116] Did those who persevered in their blindness merit being witnesses to the resurrection of Jesus Christ and observe further miracles? Our philosophers' principle is strange: the more stubborn and obstinate a person is in resisting the known truth and being unworthy of heaven's grace, the more God is expected to produce miracles in order to make people believe. So is divine power at the beck and call of the foolish? We are astonished at the Jews' refusal to believe and they did not believe because they were philosophers.

[...]

§11

Our critics regard St Paul as the true founder of our religion, as the author of *Christianity Unveiled* states that, '*without him, [Christianity] would never have spread because of his ignorant colleagues' lack of knowledge*', and that this apostle '*took his doctrine, laced with elements of the sublime and the fantastical, to the peoples of Greece, Asia and even to the Romans themselves. He had his followers, just as any man who appeals to the imagination of ignorant, unschooled people.*'[117]

There are only three mistakes in this allegation. The first is that without the efforts of St Paul, Christianity would not have spread. However, this apostle did not preach in Egypt, Africa, Persia, India, or in Gaul, but Christianity became established from the earliest times in those places nonetheless, just as in other places. The second mistake is that St Paul's colleagues were ignorant: they were so when Jesus Christ first chose them to follow him, but through his divine education and because of the descent of the Holy Spirit, they became cleverer than all the world's sages. The writings of St Peter, St John the Evangelist, St John the Divine and St Jude exude nothing but wisdom and understanding of the things of God. It is indubitably astonishing that these men, so unschooled in worldly knowledge, could have so perfectly enlightened men more than all the pompous Greek schools of learning. The third error is that St Paul spoke to the imagination

---

[116] **Matt. 27 & Luke 23.** The verse in Matthew is vs. 54: 'Now when the centurion, and they that were with him, watching Jesus, saw the earthquake, and those things that were done, they feared greatly, saying, "Truly this was the Son of God".' Luke's Gospel states: 'Now when the centurion saw what was done, he glorified God, saying, "Certainly this was a righteous man",' (Luke 23: 47). What Bergier does not tackle here is the issue of the disparity between the details of Christ's crucifixion as reported by the various Gospel writers. D'Holbach mentions this in his Chapter VI and extracts of Bergier's refutation which deal with these points are included later.

[117] *Christ. Unveil.*, **p. 28.** (This edition, p. 26.) *Import. Exam.*, **ch. 12, p. 70.**

of unschooled people. Our teaching, our mysteries, our hopes do not appeal at all to the imagination—on the contrary, they revolt it. It is paganism that appeals to man's imagination. How could a doctrine that one can describe as *'laced with elements of the sublime and the fantastical'* possibly appeal to those who do not understand it at all? It appears that our adversaries have so studied each other's writing that they write rubbish.

It is even more untrue that St Paul set himself apart from the other apostles *'in order to assume the leadership of his sect'*.[118] The writings of St Paul do not contain any doctrine contrary to that of the other apostles: he himself declares that he went to Jerusalem expressly to confer with the other apostles to see if his version of the gospel was any different from theirs.[119] St Peter, far from accusing this apostle of preaching his own gospel, praises his wisdom and calls him his own, very dear brother.[120]

It is a pathetic argument to fling the same reproach at St Paul as the **Ebionites** did, that he had a different attitude to the Law of Moses from the rest of his colleagues. We know that the Ebionites were semi–Christian Jews who were infatuated with the continuing tradition of the so–called Law of Moses, to which they wanted to submit converted pagans: this was an error which was condemned not only by St Paul, but also by all the apostles assembled at the Council of Jerusalem.[121]

Finally, it is sheer fancy to state that the Ebionites, who rejected St Paul, were the first Christians: I agree that the name 'Ebionite' (meaning 'poor') was given by the Jews to those amongst their number who embraced Christianity, but it is no less a fact that this name was retained by those who insisted on retaining their Jewish faith alongside a faith in Jesus Christ. The

---

[118] *Christ. Unveil.*, p. 28. (This edition, p. 26.) *Import. Exam.*, ch. 12, p. 72.

[119] **Gal. 2: 2.** 'And I went up by revelation, and communicated unto them that gospel which I preach among the Gentiles, but privately to them which were of reputation, lest by any means I should run, or had run, in vain.' What Bergier does not mention here is that in the very same chapter of Galatians there is a major doctrinal dispute reported between SS Paul and Peter over whether it was essential for new Christian converts to be circumcised or not, as the Jews had to be. Clearly there were doctrinal disputes within the early church and as the summary of church history section in this volume makes it painfully obvious, disputes arose (and continue to arise) thick and fast, which were and are of a sufficiently serious character to cause bitter rifts and schisms. The world Anglican Communion is deeply divided over the issues of homosexuality and female bishops, which are highly likely to lead to a major schism in the future.

[120] **2 Pet. 3: 15.** 'And account that the longsuffering of our Lord is salvation; even as our beloved brother Paul also according to the wisdom given unto him hath written unto you…'

[121] **Acts ch. 15.** Again, this dispute revolves around the issue of the necessity of being circumcised, as noted above.

author of *Christianity Unveiled*, who cited Origen's second book against Celsus, need only have looked also at his fifth book to recognize his error.[122] Had he also read **Eusebius** more carefully, whom he also cites against us, he would have found precisely the contrary of what he has said.[123]

[...]

§ 21

Not a single enemy of ours has exceeded the hate for our religion beyond that of our 'unveiler'. According to him, it is fruitless for our religion to order us to love God in everything and our neighbour as ourselves: he writes, '*We see Christians in an impossible situation—they have to love and adore this god who is hostile, harsh and capricious. On the other hand, we see them eternally engaged in tormenting, persecuting and destroying their neighbour and their brothers.*'[124] This criticism seems so completely justified to him that he repeats it ten times altogether throughout his work. I shall reply to this in Chapter 12, §1.[125]

Suffice it to say here that he paints an imaginary god and that he has never known the God we adore. Faith portrays him as goodness and holiness itself:

---

[122] **See the Cambrige [sic] edition, p. 272.**

[123] *Hist. Eccl.* **I, 3, ch. 27.** Bergier is referring to Eusebius' *Historia Ecclesiastica* {*Ecclesiastical History* or *History of the Church*}—see Glossary. The passage Bergier has in mind from Eusebius is: 'There were others whom the evil demon, unable to shake their devotion to the Christ of God, caught in a different trap and made his own. Ebionites they were appropriately named by the first Christians, in view of the poor and mean opinions they held about Christ. They regarded Him as plain and ordinary, a man esteemed as righteous through growth of character and nothing more, the child of a normal union between a man and Mary; and they held that they must observe every detail of the Law—by faith in Christ alone, and a life built upon that faith, they would never win salvation.' (Penguin, revised edition, 1989, p. 90.) The editor of the revised Penguin translation comments in a note: 'The word [Ebionite] is derived from a Hebrew word meaning "poor": this may indicate that the original Ebionites were materially poor, or that they thought of themselves as the "poor ones" who depend utterly on the grace of God [...]. The derivations Eusebius gives (both derived from Origen)—that they have a poor or mean idea of Christ in thinking him merely a man, or display poverty of intelligence in rejecting the pre-existence of the Reason (or Word) of God—are both derogatory. They seem to have been Jewish Christians, who respected Christ, but could not conceive of his relationship with God as anything other than that of a man inspired by God (like one of the prophets). Eusebius is scornful of Jewish Christianity, and knows little about it anyway: it seems to have been much more important in the early centuries of Christianity than appears from *The History of the Church*,' op. cit., p. 366.

[124] *Christ. Unveil.* **p. 36.** (This edition, p. 29.)

[125] See pp. 268 *et seqq.* of this edition.

it teaches us to love him as our father, our benefactor, and our saviour: it continuously reminds us of his benefits; it sets before our eyes eternal happiness which he prepares for us; it exhorts us to throw ourselves into the arms of his divine mercy. If it invites us to fear his justice, it is because, unfortunately, this fear is necessary to turn us away from evil. Reason makes us understand his justice in all its forms: the philosophy of the ancients has anticipated all these ideas and there is not a single professing atheist who could disapprove of them.

Going by the portrait the writer has painted of Christian malice, one is tempted to ask him amongst which people he has been living, to which acts of cruelty he has been witness, and of which massacres has he been a victim? Would he have led the tranquil life he has led, had religious zeal been as ardent as he represents it? Now, in an era wherein minds are calmer, where is the wisdom in raking over memories of times which might enflame them afresh?

However many times without number it is pointed out to us that our conduct sits ill with our belief, this unfortunate trait is also common amongst philosophers. Is there a single one of them who, in practice, faithfully follows the beautiful, moral maxims which they so vaunt before us in their books? Cicero has already reproached them for this.[126] All that need be done to confound them is to direct the same reply that Jesus Christ did to the

---

[126] *Tuscul. quest.* **1, 2, № 11.** The reference is to Cicero's work *Tusculan Disputations* {*Tusculanae disputationes*, also known as *Tusculanae Quaestiones*}, thought to have been written around 45 BC. They examine the Stoic principles or paradoxes that moral worth is the only good; virtue is sufficient for happiness; all sins and virtues are equal; every fool is insane; only the wise man is really free; only the wise man is really rich. The aim of this book is to show that death should not be feared. The following passage is from the *Disputation* cited by Bergier, though in context it refers more to poets than to philosophers, so in this respect Bergier has not been entirely honest in quoting this source:
'But do you not see how much harm is done by poets? They introduce the bravest men lamenting over their misfortunes: they soften our minds; and they are, besides, so entertaining, that we do not only read them, but get them by heart. Thus the influence of the poets is added to our want of discipline at home, and our tender and delicate manner of living, so that between them they have deprived virtue of all its vigour and energy. Plato, therefore, was right in banishing them from his commonwealth, where he required the best morals, and the best form of government. But we, who have all our learning from Greece, read and learn these works of theirs from our childhood; and look on this as a liberal and learned education.' (Cited from the edition on www.gutenberg.net)

221

Pharisees: '*Let him who is without sin amongst you cast the stone*' against religion.[127]

Let us leave aside the bitter, insulting reproaches levelled against us: the wrath, the revolt, the wars, the murders and the persecution that priests are charged with—we shall come on to those later. Crimes are committed despite religion and in spite of civil laws, the voice of reason and the maxims of philosophers: so religion, laws, reason and philosophy are all sources of ill for mankind. Sophism is ridiculous: one ought to be ashamed to resort to it again.

However, it is religion which has served '*as a pretext to disrupt society*'.[128] Fair enough. But has it not done so as a pretext to maintain the law, to establish the authority of government, to avenge natural equity, and to safeguard the people's interests? For this is it necessary to remove these different motives, which human passions are always ready to abuse, and do so every day?

Without a doubt, it was priests or followers of Christianity who massacred twenty–eight Roman emperors in less than a century, who caused twenty–two general revolutions in China, who strangled a dozen or so sultans, and who have often bathed the Persian and Indian thrones in blood. But listening to our critics, one would think that all crimes have been committed by Christians, and that there has not been a single infidel people, whom we might reproach for atrocities in even greater number.

§ 22

However, that is the substance of our author's gloating and upon which he unfolds his eloquence—in fact, to tell the truth that is the substance of his whole work, repeated at least a dozen times. First, he maintains that the outcome of all this is to be found in the contradiction between our mores and our faith, based on our ideas of God and justice. He says, '*the Christian sees his barbarous god pouring forth unbounded vengeance for time without end.*'[129] I shall not reproduce the rest of the passage, which is expressed in fanatical invective and makes us shudder with horror. In a word, he claims

---

[127] The reference is to the New Testament incident when a woman, having been caught committing an act of adultery, was brought before Christ, who restrained the crowd from stoning her to death: 'So when they continued asking him, he lifted up himself, and said unto them, "He that is without sin among you, let him first cast a stone at her",' (John 8: 7). Regarding this story in the New Testament, Bart Ehrman points out that, '[...] it was not originally in the Gospel of John. In fact, it was not originally part of any of the Gospels. It was added by later scribes.' (*Misquoting Jesus*, pp. 63—65.)

[128] See, p. 29.

[129] **Christ. Unveil. pp. 37, 43, 138, etc.** (This edition, p. 29.)

that we adore a cruel God and that is why we ourselves are the same. That is the sum total of what we may glean from this chapter.

However, all philosophers admit to a natural religion and believe in punishments and rewards in this life, and many ancient philosophers have believed them to be eternal and just, as we do, and so we must conclude that this opinion made them just as cruel as us.[130]

In the second place, if the idea we have of God is the cause of our crimes, then all peoples who have a different idea of God must have been paragons of gentleness and humanity. Now without mentioning any other ancient or modern acts of cruelty, how is it that pagans, who do not believe in the Jewish or Christian God, have treated others with equal barbarity? How is it that there is cannibalism amongst the savages? Must we abjure our religion and go off to eat our enemies' flesh with these benign peoples?

With our feeble reasoning we do not begin to concede to the teaching of eternal damnation, described by the author in such horrible terms. Faith teaches us to accept it and ancient philosophers did not find it at all incredible. It is mere slander poured forth by the author of the *Philosophical Dictionary* that many Church Fathers did not believe in this doctrine.[131] We

---

[130] **See passages of Plato, Celsus and Virgil in Warburton** *Dissertations*, № 11, II, p. 115.

[131] *Philosophical Dictionary*, **the article 'Hell'.** Voltaire's article referenced here is both interesting and amusing and it merits a detailed footnote. Voltaire starts the article by listing the many peoples and cultures in which a similar concept to that of the Christian Hell has been invented: he mentions the Indians, Japanese, Koreans, Chinese and Tartars, before going on to the Greco-Roman concepts of hell and stating that many ancient poets and philosophers ridiculed it. He then notes: 'Finally the Pharisees and the Essenians amongst the Jews admired the idea of a hell and created their own version of it: they took the concept from the Greeks and Romans and then the Christians adopted it. Many Fathers of the Church have never believed in eternal damnation: they found the idea of a poor man burning in hell for all eternity for having stolen a goat an absurdity. Virgil was right when he said in his sixth book of the *Aeneid* (verses 617 & 618):

> Sedet aeternumque sedebit
> Infelix Theseus.

> [Hapless Theseus sits
> And evermore shall sit {in hell}]'

The rest of the passage is worth quoting to make Voltaire's point: '...and Phlegyas, most unblest, gives warning to all and with loud voice bears witness amid the gloom: "Be warned; learn ye to be just and not to slight the gods!"' (Virgil, *Aeneid*, transl. by H.R. Fairclough, revised by G.P. Goold [Cambridge, Mass.:Harvard U.P.: Loeb Classical Library, 1999], p. 575.) Clearly the people in hell, whom Aeneas comes

err badly when we try to integrate the prerogatives of infinite justice with the demands of human justice: all that is infinite surpasses our natural understanding. We do not find it in the least strange when, throughout all eternity, God's goodness recompenses obedience to him, which has lasted for but a few moments, and so is it all that much more difficult to accept that he punishes momentary disobedience or, in particular, persistent criminality to the point of death, by a method of torture which will never cease? We do not condemn human justice when it punishes a momentary crime by death because its limited duration is not what has caused the enormity of the crime. Therefore, it is foolhardy to get worked up against divine revelation when it teaches us that God will avenge the same kind of crime by eternal punishment. This dogma causes virtuous men no grief—it revolts only the wicked. But since this does not suffice as a deterrent, what rein could be imposed upon men were this to be removed?

A belief in this truth, far from inculcating cruelty, persecution and a seditious spirit in Christians, would on the contrary serve as the best deterrent, were human passions capable of serious reflection. Jesus Christ threatened all who lacked charity towards their brothers with the fires of hell.[132] So the thinking of the author of *Christianity Unveiled* is utterly

---

across, are meant as a warning to all who step out of line. Voltaire's article continues: 'He maintains in vain that Theseus sits on a chair for all eternity and that this posture is his torment. Other ancients believed that Theseus was a hero who did not sit in hell and that he was to be found in the Elysian Fields. It was only recently that a Calvinist theologian named Petit-Pierre preached and wrote that the damned would one day receive divine grace. Other ministers told him that they would not. The dispute hotted up and it was said that the king, their sovereign, instructed them that since he was consigned to hell with no hope of escaping, he found this situation good and that they were to join the fray. The damned by the Church of Neufchâtel got rid of the poor little Petit-Pierre, who had mistaken hell for purgatory. It is said that one of them wrote, "My friend, I do not believe in eternal hell any more than you do, but you must realize that it is good that your servant, your tailor, and particularly that your public prosecutor, all do." [...] We constantly have to deal with rogues and hoards of people who are of limited means, are brutal, or drunks and thieves. Preach to them, if you will, that there is no hell and that the soul is moral. As for me, I shall scream in their ears that they shall be damned to hell if they rob me. I shall imitate the rural priest who, having been outrageously fleeced by his flock, said to them in his Sunday sermon, "I don't know what Jesus Christ was thinking of to die for a bunch of crooks like you lot!"'

[132] **Matt. 25: 41.** The context is important and verse 41 is indicated in bold type below: 'Then shall the King say unto them on his right hand, "Come, ye blessed of my Father, inherit the kingdom prepared for you from the foundation of the world: For I was an hungred, and ye gave me meat: I was thirsty, and ye gave me drink: I was a stranger, and ye took me in: Naked, and ye clothed me: I was sick, and ye visited me: I was in prison, and ye came unto me." Then shall the righteous answer him, saying, "Lord, when saw we thee an hungred, and fed thee? Or thirsty, and gave thee drink? When

ridiculous and the more he repeats himself, the more he proves his blind prejudice.

---

saw we thee a stranger, and took thee in? Or naked, and clothed thee? Or when saw we thee sick, or in prison, and came unto thee?" And the King shall answer and say unto them, "Verily I say unto you, Inasmuch as ye have done it unto one of the least of these my brethren, ye have done it unto me." **Then shall he say also unto them on the left hand, "Depart from me, ye cursed, into everlasting fire, prepared for the devil and his angels:** For I was an hungred, and ye gave me no meat: I was thirsty, and ye gave me no drink: I was a stranger, and ye took me not in: naked, and ye clothed me not: sick, and in prison, and ye visited me not." Then shall they also answer him, saying, "Lord, when saw we thee an hungred, or athirst, or a stranger, or naked, or sick, or in prison, and did not minister unto thee?" Then shall he answer them, saying, "Verily I say unto you, Inasmuch as ye did it not to one of the least of these, ye did it not to me." And these shall go away into everlasting punishment: but the righteous into life eternal', (Matt. 25: 34—46).

Figure 38: *Lucifer.* Blake's illustration to Dante's *Inferno*, Canto XXXIV (*c.* 1825).

Chapter 4

On Christian Theology, or the Ideas which Christianity Gives us of God and His Behaviour.[133]

§ 2

According to our Scriptures God brought the world forth from nothing: grievance number one. This act of creation is incomprehensible: nothing comes from nothing—that is an axiom of ancient philosophy. In any case, the Greek word *barah* means merely 'to make' or 'to arrange'. The sense that we give this word today is a fairly modern invention of theology.[134]

Since ancient philosophy had no idea about creation and had Holy Scripture also said nothing about it, how could the idea of it have occurred to theologians?[135] That is what we must first try to explain. Suppose that the Hebrew term does not always signify creation in the real sense, what is the sense of the term as used by Moses? *'God said, "Let there be light", and there was light.'*[136] As the psalmist says, *'The Lord spoke and all was created: he commanded and all was created'*—they both say absolutely the same thing.[137] Could human speech possibly provide any more emphatic an expression to describe the act of creation?

This act of creation is incomprehensible: let us assume that again. Are such things as an eternal world and eternal matter comprehensible? These things contain a contradiction: creation has nothing contradictory about it. An eternal world and eternal matter would be just as independent and just as immutable as God: divine omnipotence would have had no effect on them. Had the teaching of creation, as we believe it, been suggested to the wisest men amongst the ancient philosophers, they would have preferred it to all the absurd hypotheses that they had thought up.

The author of *Christianity Unveiled* also objects to our Holy Book, pointing out that just after having created man, *'his creator set a trap for him,*

---

[133] Note Bergier has changed the subtitle of this chapter: d'Holbach's original title states 'On Christian Mythology or the Christian Ideas of God and His Behaviour.'

[134] *Certainty of the Proofs of Christianity*, ch. 11.

[135] One of the most famous creation myths of classical antiquity is that expressed by Plato in his *Timaeus*. (For Plato—see Glossary.)

[136] Gen. 1: 3.

[137] There is no Psalm in an English or French translation of the Bible which fits this quotation. The nearest psalm to fit the context states, 'Let them praise the name of the Lord: for he commanded, and **they were created**.' (Ps. 148: 5) The French Bible follows this translation closely. Bergier has clearly altered the text for his own purposes, since the French he quotes specifically states 'tout a été créé'—{*everything was created*}.

into which God undoubtedly knew he would fall.'[138] So issuing a command to man is akin to setting a trap for him, is it? This is a new idea worthy of our modern philosophy. Did God not create man free, subject to his laws and obedience? We all carry within us the reply to this question. Did God do a disservice to a free man by putting his destiny in his own hands? I appeal to common sense.

The serpent which speaks and seduces the woman is a new monster in the eyes of our philosopher, but neither Jews nor Christians are ever mistaken about that. The Devil or the Evil One made use of this creature: almost at the inception of creation, the first woman had not had enough experience to be either surprised or frightened by this phenomenon.

That the whole human race is punished for the mistake of the first man is an injustice which we cannot attribute to God, according to our censors. They would think differently if they had paid closer attention to the nature of the punishment. Because of the sin of the first man, God was justifiably able to strip him and his descendants of all the totally free privileges he had granted them. Immortality, absolute control over one's emotions and the right to supernatural bliss were by no means the essential prerogatives of humanity. A king may strip a gentleman of his nobility to punish him: his children, although innocent of their father's fault, share in his punishment without having any scope to complain. I have dealt with this question in greater length in another work.[139]

§ 3

The author finds it really strange that God inundated the earth in a universal flood and that '*God repents of having populated the earth and he finds it easier to drown and destroy the human race, rather than change mankind's heart.*'[140] Everything is equally easy for God who is omnipotent: when it pleases him he may change sinners' hearts, but to lead them upon the right path he may use laws, punishments and rewards, because these are the means which best suit the nature of free, intelligent beings. The author of *Christianity Unveiled* should not disapprove of these methods, since he would have no rein on mankind other than civil laws, punishments and earthly rewards. What greater, more fitting monument is there to make sinners tremble down the ages, than the traces of a universal flood over the entire face of the earth?

---

[138] See p. 33.
[139] *Deism Refuted*, Letter № 7.
[140] *Christ. Unveil.* **p. 40.** (This edition, p. 34.)

When Scripture attributes to God human emotions, actions or human fervour such as hate, anger or repentance, these expressions can lead us into error over the divine nature. We are told in other passages that God is pure spirit, eternal, immutable, utterly perfect. Our Holy Books are written in popular language because they must have a universal appeal—to the ignorant, as well as to the more literate. Were all philosophers of the world to unite in explaining to us the nature and ways of God, they would find it impossible to find expressions in human language suitable to describe the infinite and distinguish his ways from those of his creatures.

As far as our critics are concerned, God's providence is condemned for the pointlessness of the flood because the human race reverted to sinning all over again: '*the Almighty can never manage to get his creatures to be the kind of people he wants them to be.*'[141] Just because men have not paid due regard to God's punishments, does it follow that his justice should never have taken disciplinary measures? Many people have been affected by his chastisements down the ages and without these outbursts disorder would have been all the greater. Civil laws and torture do not put a stop to all heinous crimes and one does not dare conclude that these things must be aborted. God is infinitely powerful, but he is infinitely just and wise, and the least honour we can offer him is to trust that he had his good reasons for doing what he did.

---

[141] See p. 34.

Chapter 5

On Revelation

§ 2

According to our same critic, we have to open *'the books which ought to enlighten us and surrender our reason to them, as we must [...]*. But they *'do not give us specific concepts about God, who is [...] a mass of contradictory qualities which form an inexplicable enigma. [...] God [...] portrays himself as so unjust, so false, and so deceitful that he sets traps for people, delights in enticing them, blinds them to the truth, and hardens their hearts, plants false signs to trick them, and spreads amongst them a spirit of confusion and falsehood. [...] Hence, from the first steps man takes [...] he is cast into suspicion and confusion: he does not know whether this god who has spoken to him has it in mind to trick him, just as he has duped so many others by his own admission.'*[142]

Never before has the author reasoned with such confidence and made false suppositions and allegations. First, he supposes—wrongly—that our Holy Books are meant to instruct us without further help. The text of these books alone does not suffice to establish a true understanding of God without the teaching of the Church. In Holy Scripture there are obscure expressions which could give us a false idea of God's attributes and his behaviour: but apart from these, there are other passages which explain them, and it is from the Church that we must derive our understanding, because the Church would never mislead us.

Second, it is not true that God is portrayed in the Holy Books in such hateful terms as our author is pleased to amass: these books do give us totally contradictory ideas. They teach us that God is not only good and merciful but, according to the words of the prophet, he is the God of Truth;[143] he is not like man—he is incapable of lying;[144] all his judgements are justice itself;[145] he is faithful to all his words and holy in all his deeds.[146] Jesus Christ

---

[142] *Christ. Unveil.*, p. 53. (This edition, pp. 41 *et seqq.*)

[143] **Exod. 34: 6.** 'And the Lord passed by before him, and proclaimed, "The Lord, The Lord God, merciful and gracious, longsuffering, and abundant in goodness and truth".'

[144] **Num. 23: 19.** 'God is not a man, that he should lie; neither the son of man, that he should repent: hath he said, and shall he not do it? Or hath he spoken, and shall he not make it good?'

[145] **Deut. 32: 4.** 'He is the Rock, his work is perfect: for all his ways are judgment: a God of truth and without iniquity, just and right is he.'

[146] Bergier gives as his reference for this point Ps. 144: 13: *'mem regnum tuum regnum omnium saeculorum et potestas tua in omni generatione et generatione* {Thy kingdom is a kingdom of all ages: and thy dominion endureth throughout all generations. The

repeated the same things in the gospel and our reason alone makes us perceive the truth of what he says.

In vain the author tries to prove his assertion in a footnote,[147] stating that '*God allowed Eve to be tempted by a serpent*'. The question is whether God had given Eve the knowledge and strength sufficient to resist this temptation and whether she voluntarily did not take advantage of these resources. I suggest that was the case and had she resisted, God would never have punished her.

The author also points out that '*God hardened pharaoh's heart*', but it is written also that it was pharaoh himself who hardened his own heart by resisting the miraculous events God performed in order to touch him. We say the same thing of a father who has lost his family and allowed his children to sink into debauchery, having done nothing to stop them.

In the gospel Jesus Christ is called a stumbling–block and he has only been so for the Jews through their own malicious obstinacy: Jesus reproaches them for '*this people's heart is waxed gross, and their ears are dull of hearing, and their eyes they have closed; lest at any time they should see with their eyes and hear with their ears, and should understand with their heart, and should be converted, and I should heal them.*'[148] All such passages should arouse people's suspicion, not of God, but with regard to human beings themselves.

It is also pointless for the author to say that the Christian should be alarmed '*when he sees the interminable squabbles amongst God's holy guides, who have never been able to concur on the right way to understand the Divinity's specific oracles, as revealed by him.*'[149] The main body of priests do not argue at all over the dogmas of our faith: the Church's teaching is constant, uniform, perpetual and universal. If certain individuals have stirred up disputes and formed sects, it is because they have forgotten the rule that Jesus Christ established in order to maintain a unity of faith: it is they who wanted to extend revelation not along church lines, but in their own way, and their own error proves the necessity for the rules that Jesus Christ established, and not the fact that his way is false or open to doubt. Heretics are men who want to bring into religious matters the nitpicking, obstinate spirit of philosophers.

Is it fitting to blame us for the disputes of these men? Is there a single dogma derived from instinctive knowledge over which they argue amongst

---

Lord is faithful in all his words: and holy in all his works}, *Vulgate*. This reference does not correspond to the *King James Version*.

[147] **Page 53.** (This edition, p. 41.)

[148] **Matt. 13: 15.**

[149] *Christ. Unveil.*, **p. 54.** (This edition, p. 42.)

themselves? Is there a single teaching against which they have not written a book? The simple believer, whom they would arrest from their 'sacred guides', would have their faith confirmed many fold, were they to listen to the lessons these enemies of religion pour forth.

§ 3

It is no easy task counting up all the lies that the author of *Christianity Unveiled* amassed in order to support his paradox.

(i) It is a lie that '*this God has aspired to make himself known only to a very few favoured beings, whilst wanting to remain hidden from the rest of humanity, for whom, however, this revelation was equally essential.*'[150] God does not want to be hidden from anyone: on the contrary, '*he wants all men to be saved, and to come unto the knowledge of the truth.*'[151] To some he gives more abilities and help to acquire this knowledge than others, but he does not want a single person to be deprived of it.

(ii) It is also a lie that God, '*by not having revealed himself to many nations [...] has caused their inevitable damnation right down the centuries*'.[152] God has never failed to manifest himself to more or less all nations: we are told about this by Saint Paul.[153] If they go astray, it is their own fault for not having taken advantage of the knowledge God had provided for them.

(iii) It is a falsehood that '*God punishes millions of men for having been unaware of his secret laws, which he has himself made public knowledge, but only on the sly and in an obscure and unknown corner of Asia.*'[154] God never punishes unintentional ignorance and he will never condemn to hell any man for having been ignorant of the gospel, unless this man has had the means to become acquainted with it.

---

[150] See p. 42.

[151] **1 Tim. 2: 4.**

[152] See pp. 42 *et seqq.*

[153] **Acts 14: 16.** The context of this verse is important: St Paul and some of his other followers were distressed to find out that a number of people had turned to idolatrous religions and they remonstrated with them. However, the text clearly says that God allowed this to happen—one might even say 'abandoned' them to go their own sweet way: he withheld his grace from them, a point for which neither Bergier nor any other Christian apologist has a logical and suitable reply. Verse 16 is indicated by bold script: 'And saying, "Sirs, why do ye these things? We also are men of like passions with you, and preach unto you that ye should turn from these vanities unto the living God, which made heaven, and earth, and the sea, and all things that are therein: **Who in times past suffered all nations to walk in their own ways.** Nevertheless he left not himself without witness, in that he did good, and gave us rain from heaven, and fruitful seasons, filling our hearts with food and gladness",' (Acts 14: 15—17).

[154] See p. 42.

Do justice, humanity and good faith allow a writer to charge Christianity with all the things that every good Christian condemns and detests, and that no Catholic theologian would ever support? What idea can we possibly conceive of our enemies when they behave in such a way? What ill has this divine religion done to them for them to calumny it with the fury that they do?

Therefore, it is not true that when a Christian consults the books revealed to us everything should put us on our guard against a God who has spoken to us: it is simply not true that God, together with the interpreters of his so–called will, appear to have conspired to obfuscate and increase the darkness of people's ignorance.

Translator's Note

The following chapter {the sixth of Bergier's refutation}—'*On Proofs of the Christian Religion, Miracles, Prophecies and Martyrs*'—strikes me as one of the most interesting of the whole work and for that reason I have dealt with it in some detail: after all, if there are credible historical sources outside the New Testament canon which attest to the existence of a real person called Jesus Christ, who actually performed miracles, then we ought to look at the evidence carefully. Naturally, the Church has tried hard to produce this kind of evidence and many of the references Bergier uses are well–known and have been so for many years. However, scholarship has moved on and what follows constitutes an interesting discussion on the historicity of Christ.

Chapter 6

On Proofs of the Christian Religion, Miracles, Prophecies and Martyrs.

Article I—Miracles

§ 5

Our author writes, '*I ask how it was possible that an entire people witnessed the Messiah's miracles and yet consented to his death—they even demanded it vigorously?*'[155] He is the last person to ask this question when everywhere in his work he paints the Jews as '*frenetic, ferocious monsters*'[156] and refers to them as '*this blind, savage people*',[157] who have '*ferocious and ridiculous superstitions*'[158] and '*obstinate fanaticism and insane hopes.*'[159] He also portrays them as seditious and blind; so is it proper that he asks how this people behaved, given the character traits he attributes to them?

The Jews, who were witnesses to the Messiah's miracles, called for his death because the leaders of the nation had persuaded them that if they had let him live any longer, the Romans would have swooped down on Jerusalem and destroyed the town and the temple, exterminating them as a race.[160]

---

[155] This edition, p. 48.
[156] **Page 18.** Ibid., p. 22.
[157] **Page 21.** Ibid., p. 23.
[158] **Page 22.** Ibid.
[159] **Page 23.** Ibid., p. 23.
[160] **John 11: 49.** The context needs to be seen: 'Then many of the Jews which came to Mary, and had seen the things which Jesus did, believed on him. But some of them went their ways to the Pharisees, and told them what things Jesus had done. Then

But the author persists: '*Would the people of London or Paris allow a man to be put to death before their very eyes, who had brought the dead back to life, restored sight to the blind, made the lame to walk and cured the paralysed?*'[161] I would reply that the people of London and Paris are not at all the kind of people whom the author depicts the Jews to be. I would also add that in Paris and London one might even demand the death of a just man who had performed miracles, were one persuaded, for good or ill, that the well–being of the state depended upon it. Since the time when the Athenians demanded Socrates' death, nothing comes as a surprise.[162]

Therefore, it is really wrong to conclude, as it is to state, that '*If the Jews demanded the death of Jesus, all his miracles are negated for every uninformed man.*'[163] Those same Jews, who demanded the death of Jesus, repented of this and they were converted in large numbers, going on to adore him as the Messiah and the Son of God. By doing so, they went on to pay homage to his miracles in the most authentic and least suspicious way.

§ 8

Before going on to examine the author's objections to the plausibility of the miracles, it is fitting that I conclude my remarks on criticisms levelled against those who conveyed the certainty of them and were witnesses to them. In vain does the author impute ignorance, credulity and abject stupidity to these witnesses.

The author asks, '*And were these witnesses impartial? No! Without a doubt, they had a vested interest in supporting these miraculous deeds which proved their master's divinity and the veracity of the religion they wanted to*

---

gathered the chief priests and the Pharisees a council, and said, "What do we? For this man doeth many miracles. If we let him thus alone, all men will believe on him: and the Romans shall come and take away both our place and nation." And one of them, named Caiaphas, being the high priest that same year, said unto them, "Ye know nothing at all, nor consider that it is expedient for us, that one man should die for the people, and that the whole nation perish not." And this spake he not of himself: but being high priest that year, he prophesied that Jesus should die for that nation; And not for that nation only, but that also he should gather together in one the children of God that were scattered abroad. Then from that day forth they took counsel together for to put him to death', (John 11: 45—53).

[161] See p. 48.

[162] See ***Lettre au P. Berthier sur le Matérialisme*, p. 4.** This reference is to a work by Coyer, Gabriel François, entitled *Lettre au Père Berthier sur le matérialisme* (Geneva, 1759) {*Letter to Father Berthier on Materialism*}. Berthier, Guillaume François (1704—1782) is the putative author of this work, which is sometimes attributed also to Diderot.

[163] See p. 48.

235

establish.'[164]   Short of being blind, is it impossible to overlook the absurdity of this supposition? This is the ridiculous, incredible, appalling scenario that he is proposing as regards Jesus Christ's followers: that they were ignorant men, unschooled, scraped up from the dregs of humanity, who formulate the boldest, the most dangerous plan ever to have entered into an ambitious mind, a plan to establish a new religion; that they were a group of superstitious Jews, blindly attached to their laws and their form of worship; that they harboured the hope of a liberator to come; that without rhyme or reason, or motives with common interests, they formed a plot between them to abolish their laws and to change the outlook of an entire nation! Furthermore, he alleges that they were shamefully tricked by a fanatical, sham leader and believed that it was in their interest to dedicate themselves to his glory, to support his divinity at a cost to their own peace of mind and life itself!

Apostles interested in supporting miraculous deeds! Wherein did this interest lie? They exposed themselves to the fury of the Jews, the contempt of pagan believers and Roman suspicion because of their political outlook, and ultimately they ran the risk of the same fate as their master—that was the sum total of their personal interest! There is only a single interest that could have put them above all ordinary human fears—that of truth and virtue.

§ 9

Our author continues: *'Were these same deeds corroborated by contemporary historians? Not a single one of them has mentioned them, and in a city as superstitious as Jerusalem, no one—not a single Jew or a solitary pagan—had heard speak of the most extraordinary and prolific deeds that History has ever reported.'*[165]   Is all this true? We must first ask our well–read critic who these historians are, who might have made mention of the miracles of Jesus Christ. We only know of three Jewish writers of that time: **Josephus**, **Philo**, and **Justus of Tiberias**—and the works of the latter have not survived. I maintain that the first writer did speak of them, but even if he had said nothing of them, his silence would have been as eloquent for us as his witness.[166]   Philo was not a historian but a philosopher, and so he did not write about past events. Nevertheless, he knew of Christ and his miracles. Anastasius Sinaita, the Partiarch of Antioch in the sixth century, relates that according to **Ammonius**, a philosopher of Alexandria who lived in the third

---

[164]   **Page 70.** (This edition, p. 50.)
[165]   Ibid.
[166]   *Certitude of the Proofs of Christianity*, ch. 2, § 8.

century,[167] Philo wrote a work against Mnason, a disciple of the apostles who had denied the divinity of Jesus Christ, but he did not deny that he had spoken of his humanity.[168] He asserted that his miracles were insufficient to prove his divinity and that his suffering and ignominious death were not in keeping with his status as a god.[169] In other works written by Jews against Jesus Christ, the precise dates of which are not known, they formally all agree on the miracles of Christ.[170]

As far as the pagans were concerned, in Rome and throughout Greece there was a profound ignorance of anything that was going on in Judea at the time. As soon as the existence of Christians began to be known, they were slandered and persecuted and things were written against them, but no writer at the time dared put forward any false challenge against the miracles of Jesus Christ—not one of them dared cite any Jewish sources to prove that he was an impostor.[171]

---

[167] There are at least two philosophers called Ammonius, but a certain Ammonius Saccas was a Greek philosopher from Alexandria who flourished in the third century AD, and who was often referred to as one of the founders of Neoplatonism. See Glossary.

[168] Mnason was an early convert to Christianity, from Cyprus, and he is mentioned in Acts 21: 16. Apart from these facts, there seems to be little known about him.

[169] **See a book entitled *Ho degos*, ch. 14, pp. 24 & 25, in Gresset, *Works*, XIV.** This footnote is something of a puzzle: Gresset, Jean-Baptiste-Louis (1709—1777) was a French poet and dramatist who received immediate and lasting acclaim for his irreverently comic narrative poem 'Vert-Vert' {*Vert-Vert, or the Nunnery Parrot*}, (1734), a play on the French word for 'green'—describing with wit, tinged with malice, the adventures of a parrot who attempts to maintain his decorous convent background while on a visit to another convent. Brought up by Jesuits, Gresset was a brilliant pupil and, after entering the Jesuit order in 1726, he continued his education in Paris before returning to teach in Amiens and Tours. 'Vert-Vert', which was circulated privately and printed without the author's permission, brought him instant success in Parisian circles, where the literati were astounded that such a refined wit could come from within the Catholic Church. The parrot became the inspiration for a comic opera by Offenbach and a canvass in oils by the painter Millet. It was also the inspiration for a bright-green mousse called 'le gâteau Vert-Vert'. Spurred on by the success of this work, Grasset carried on writing works which showed great wit, but which were interpreted by the Church as anti-clerical, leading to him being banned from the order. In 1759 Gresset wrote *Lettre sur la comédie* {*Letter on Comedy*}, in which he renounced all his previous poetic and dramatic works as irreligious. It is curious that Gresset's '*Works Volume 14*' should be cited, because Gresset's literary output was not so voluminous; most editions of his *complete works* being only two or three volumes, at the most. It might be that there is a misprint in the text. I have not been able to trace the work *Ho degos*.

[170] **See previous chapter 3, § 3.** (This edition, pp. 208 *et seqq.*)

[171] *Certainty of Proofs*, **ch. 4 and ch. 3, § 3 above in this work.**

It is therefore absolutely contrary to the truth that there was not a single Jew or pagan who had not heard of the miracles of Jesus Christ.[172]

Our author continues, '*It is only ever Christians who testify to the miracles of Christ.*'[173] The very opposite has been proven: however, let us go with that for a moment. I maintain that Christians ought to be heard on these events and that their witness is undeniable; that the disbelief of those who have no regard for them proves nothing.

Who are these Christians? They are Jews or pagans who were converted through miracles. Therefore, these are men who have examined these things at close quarters and the weight of factual evidence has overcome their prejudices, their self–interest, their fear and reluctance to judge others. The truth has exerted more influence upon them than human emotions and a natural squeamishness at changing their religion, and they made themselves vulnerable to the point of death in order to uphold the reality of what they had seen. What could be more compelling evidence?

On the other hand, who are they who were not touched by these miracles? They are men who spurned verifying them or who, despite being persuaded of their reality, tried to explain them away for good or ill and have not recognized the consequences which compelled them to become Christians because they dreaded the repercussions of such a dangerous step. But does their disbelief or indifference diminish the evidence of these events?

What is being demanded of us when we are asked to provide evidence from authors who were their contemporaries, yet they never became Christians? We are required to provide witnesses who paid homage to the truth but spurned it, who were both enlightened yet disbelieved, and who were fair–minded towards Christianity and still were its enemies—in a word, witnesses who were not at one with themselves. There is one such person—it is **Josephus**: quite predictably, our adversaries reject him because he is precisely the kind of person required. They say that it is impossible that Josephus recognized the miracles of Jesus Christ as sufficiently authentic and carried on with his Jewish faith. And to think that they persist in requiring witnesses who were not Christians!

---

[172] This is a gross exaggeration on Bergier's part, who deals with this whole question inadequately, like so many apologists for Christ with regard to concrete historical evidence of Christ's existence from sources other than the New Testament canon. Evidence for the very existence of Jesus Christ as an actual historically verifiable person does not exist, apart from one instance in the writing of Josephus, which was probably a late scribe's addition. (For Josephus—see Glossary.)

[173] *Christ. Unveil.*, **p. 71.** (This edition, p. 50.)

§10

The author of *Christianity Unveiled* finds it very strange that pagan authorities are silent on the earthquake, the solar eclipse and the resurrection of the dead and of Jesus Christ himself. The author of the *Philosophical Dictionary* has also made the same observation.[174] But both of them take this silence to be misplaced. **Phlegon** in his *History of the Olympiads* in the fourth year of the second century, which is the eighteenth year of Tiberius and that of the date of Jesus Christ's death, attested to these things:[175] **Thallus** in his *Syrian Histories*, which is no longer extant, wrote of these events also.[176] **Tertullian**, in his *Apologeticum*, calls upon Roman senators as witnesses to the effect that these miracles were recorded in their annals.[177]

And there is more: **Chalcidius**, a pagan philosopher of the third century, knew of our gospels, and far from treating them as fanciful stories, as the sharp minds of our day do, he called them '*a holy and venerable history*':[178] he cited the adoration of Jesus by the Magi. It is absolutely untrue that pagan authors never spoke of the events which prove our religion to be true.

Our disbeliever would want further witnesses of the resurrection of Jesus Christ, other than his apostles and his disciples: he says, '*But would not a formal appearance in a public square have been more convincing than all the secret appearances made to men motivated by forming a new sect?*'[179] I shall not go back over for a second time the imputed interest the apostles had in

---

[174] **See the article on *Christianity*.**

[175] In fact, very little is known about this work and writer: some chapters have been preserved in Eusebius' *Chronicle*, but the work is largely lost and Eusebius is hardly an independent source. Furthermore, Phlegon wrote in all seriousness on marvels, zombies and ghosts, so we might not want to take him too seriously as an independent witness. See Glossary.

[176] **Eusabius, *Chronicle*. Origen, *Against Celsus*, Bk. I, 2, p. 80.** (For **Eusabius, Origen** and **Celsus**—see Glossary.) Irrespective of the source of 'evidence' or eye-witness reports of eclipses, the gospels of Matthew, Mark and Luke concur that the solar eclipse lasted three hours, i.e., 'from the sixth to the ninth hour'—see Matt. 27: 45 & 51—54; Mark 15: 33 and Luke 23: 44—45. This is an astronomical impossibility—eclipses of the sun last minutes not hours: in fact they last for only about eight minutes at most. Furthermore, Christ's crucifixion took place around the period of the Passover when, traditionally, there was a full moon: a solar eclipse could not have taken place at the time of a full moon because the moon and the sun are in the wrong positions. All attempts by astronomers to establish a solar eclipse around the time of Christ's crucifixion in AD 32 have failed—they simply could not have taken place during that year. There are also no records of earthquakes in Jerusalem at that time.

[177] **Chapter 21.**

[178] **See his commentary on *Timeus*, p. 219.**

[179] See p. 50.

forming a new sect, but I maintain that, according to the way our adversaries think and reason, a formal public appearance by Jesus Christ would not have proved to be any more decisive than the evidence we already have. How could we be certain of such an appearance? Through the testimony of witnesses. Now, we began by setting down as a principle that when it comes to miracles, all testimony is suspect. The resurrection of Jesus Christ is proven already, but those disbelievers are so totally convinced of the contrary that they will never believe it anyway.

I concur that Christ's resurrection ought to be *proven to nations in the clearest and most indubitable way possible*:[180] and I also maintain that it was so. The witnesses who promulgated it were many in number, worthy of our trust and irreproachable. They saw and touched Christ: they drank, ate and conversed with the resurrected Christ: they were men of good faith, of a character far beyond all dissimulation and devoid of any combined, common interest.

[...]

§11

But what is the point in providing proofs of the miracles when people maintain that they are impossible in the first place? That is the opinion philosophers hold and it is on this basis that the author of *Christianity Unveiled* sets out his fundamental position: '*A miracle is an impossible thing: God could not be immutable if he altered the natural order.*'[181] In the first place, I cite the opinion of another philosopher on this—Jean–Jacques Rousseau, who asks, '*Can God perform miracles, that is to say can he act against the laws he has established? Were this question to be treated seriously it would be impious, if not absurd. It would be to accord too much honour to him who resolved it in a negative way, than to punish him: it would be sufficient to lock him away. But also, what man has ever denied that God was capable of performing miracles? One would have to be a Hebrew to ask if God were able to set out tables in the desert.*'[182]

---

[180] See p. 52.

[181] *Christ. Unveil.* p. 69. (This edition, p. 49.)

[182] *Lettres écrites de la Montagne* {*Letters Written from the Mountains*}, **Letter № 3, p. 87.** In Rousseau's *Lettres écrites de la Montagne* (1764), the whole of Letter № 3 is a continuation of a discussion on miracles started in Letter № 1. The biblical reference is to the Israelites doubting their God while Moses was away, up the mountain, receiving the ten commandments: 'Furthermore the Lord spake unto me, saying, "I have seen this people, and, behold, it is a stiffnecked people: Let me alone, that I may destroy them, and blot out their name from under heaven: and I will make of thee a nation mightier and greater than they." So I turned and came down from the mount, and the mount burned with fire: and the two tables of the covenant were in my two

The author of the *Philosophical Dictionary*, a profound metaphysician if ever there was one, maintains the same position, that miracles are impossible.[183] In another work, this doctrine is handed down to us as a result of the thinking of Hobbes, Collins and Bolingbroke, and one could also add Spinoza.[184] Thus Jean–Jacques Rousseau confines that lot to the madhouse!

For us, who are less severe, we shall listen to their reasoning.

They say, '*A miracle is a violation of the laws of mathematics, which are divine, immutable and eternal. On this account alone a miracle is a contradiction in terms.*'[185] This is clear: there is no further point in seeing if the account is true.

'*A miracle is a violation of the laws of mathematics.*' This either makes no sense or it means that when God performs a miracle, two and two cease to make four. The author of the *Philosophical Dictionary* ought to do himself and his masters the honour of explaining properly the connection between these two ideas. Up to now, we have been told that a miracle is a violation of the laws of physics, but now it is a violation of mathematics. Whether it is a violation of the laws of mathematics has never entered into the heads of any of these philosophers.

That a miracle is a '*violation of divine laws*' needs further explanation. It is a violation of these laws for but a few moments, at a particular time and place, and it in no way interferes with the operation of these laws anywhere else in the world. When Jesus Christ walked on water, this did not work against the laws of gravity for all other bodies.

That a miracle is a '*violation of immutable laws*' means that these laws are immutable for creatures who cannot change them, but they are not immutable for God, who made them in the first place. Is it not up to God, as the Creator and Sovereign Lord of the universe, to suspend these laws whenever he wants?

[...]

---

hands. And I looked, and, behold, ye had sinned against the Lord your God, and had made you a molten calf: ye had turned aside quickly out of the way which the Lord had commanded you. And I took the two tables, and cast them out of my two hands, and brake them before your eyes', (Deut. 9: 13—17).

[183] *Philosophical Dictionary*, see under article 'Miracles'.

[184] *Letters Written from the Mountains*, Letter № 2. See also the *Philosophy of History*, ch. 33.

[185] *Philosophical Dictionary*, article on 'Miracles'. *Letters Written from the Mountains*, Letter № 2.

Article II—Prophesies

§ 13

Enemies of revealed scripture speak no more sense on the subject of prophesies than they do about miracles. They maintain that there are prophets in all nations of the world: the Jews were no more favoured in this regard than were the Egyptians, Chaldeans, Tartars, Negroes, savages, or any other peoples of the earth. It would have been fitting to have produced a complete body of prophesies gathered from the Egyptians, the Chaldeans, or from savages in order to juxtapose them with those of the Jews. Then we would have seen if they bore the same kind of authenticity and if they formed a sequel of predictions which in every point conformed to the events and history of a people, and if there were any whose fulfilment we could verify, as we can with the Judaic prophesies. This is the basis on which their merit ought to be judged.

The author of *Christianity Unveiled* claims that the Jewish prophesies are so obscure that one can read into them what one will. To test this assertion he ought to have tried to set out a secular history of our century and provide a running commentary alongside it. That would be an interesting work! **Porphyry** thought quite differently: he found the prophesies of Daniel so perfectly clear that he maintained they had been fabricated before the event.

The author of *Important Examination* appears to have been of the same opinion when it comes to the books attributed to Daniel, David, Solomon and to other prophesies made in Alexandria.[186]

If our critics had taken more care over reconciling their diverse opinions, it would have been easier to have replied to them: their error is never uniform.

In the first place, if the prophesies had been invented by the Alexandrian Jews, they would have been written in a Syrian dialect which was in common usage amongst them, rather than their having being written in Hebrew, and it would also not have been necessary to make Chaldean paraphrases of them.

Second—the prophesies were already spoken of in books which existed and were known amongst the Jews—in the last Books of Kings and in the **Paralipomenon**—now these books predate the foundation of Alexandria.

Third—the Jews of this town, who were taught by the Greeks in commerce, would have written in a much simpler style—the prophesies of Isaiah, Jeremiah, Ezekiel and others, bear the imprint of a time more ancient than the Second **Book of Machabees**.

---

[186] *Important Exam*, chapter 10, p. 54.

Figure 39: *The Tiburnine Sibyl.* **Illustration from the**
Nuremberg Chronicle **(1493).**

Fourth—any forger who predicted events after they had happened would have made their prophesies clearer in order to give them more authority, so their obscurity—a criticism levelled against them—is a mark of their antiquity.

Fifth—were falsifiers to have been as adept as is suggested, they would never have been able to link so perfectly the sequence of their predictions with the chain of events as they affected the Jews, the Chaldeans and the Persians, and have kept to an exact chronological order, and have made the prophets speak as fittingly to the differing circumstances as they found themselves in. Christians and pagans, both enemies of the Jews, would have soon discovered the assumptions made, just as the falsity of the Sibylline Oracles has been proven.

Jewish writers are constantly portrayed as mindless fanatics, and thereby it is assumed that they were more adept deceivers than everyone else in the world.

The objection that, *'those prophecies which Christians attribute to Jesus Christ are not interpreted in the same light by Jews, who are still waiting for the Messiah, whom the former believe arrived eighteen centuries ago.'*[187] I shall answer this point when I reply to the allegation made against the Church Fathers, that they have misused the prophesies of the Old Testament.[188]

§ 16

In concluding his summary of Judaic prophesies, the writer of *Christianity Unveiled* calls them disjointed daydreaming, a bizarre hotchpotch, formless ramblings, works of fanaticism and delirium, vague, obscure, enigmatic oracles, like those of the pagans, in which the Jews found everything they wanted to see, and in which the Christian mind, obsessed with the idea of a Christ, believed they had seen everywhere they looked. He might have expressed himself more decorously and more wisely, like a philosopher.

Instead of replying in the same tone, I shall restrict myself to tackling just a few of the clearer, more detailed points, so that the reader may judge whether they merit the epithets he lavished upon them.

God promised Abraham that through his children, Ishmael and Isaac, he would make him the father of Nations.[189] As a token of his promise, he ordered him to change his name and practise circumcision within his family, and he pledged to give to the descendants of Isaac the land of the Chaldeans

---

[187] *Christ. Unveil.*, p. 77. (This edition, p. 53.)
[188] See § 17 *et seqq.*
[189] Genesis Chapters 16, 17 *et seqq.*

and to bless all nations after him.[190] He predicted that Ishmael would be a proud, wild man, that he would raise his hand against everyone and that everyone would raise theirs against him, and that he would set his standard amongst his brethren.[191]

We are witnesses to the fulfilment of this prophesy. Even today, Asia is populated by nations who confess the name of Ishmael and Abraham as their real forefathers and the descendants of Isaac are dispersed throughout the world. The Ishmaelites are circumcised in their fourteenth year, whereas the Jews, descended from Isaac, are circumcised on the eighth day: both keep to their traditions as a mark of their origins. The race of Isaac have possessed the lands of the Chaldeans for the last 1,400 years, and this is proven by the genealogy of the Saviour, who descended from this Patriarch through his forebears and he united all these rights in his person and it is through him that all nations were blessed.[192]

---

[190] The reason given in the Bible for changing the name to Isaac was because it meant 'he laughed', because the promise of this son was made to Abraham and his wife Sarah when they were very old and way past the age to reproduce. However, the real reason for the change of name was 'because his original name recalled his connection to Osiris, the Egyptian god who granted eternal life', (Greenberg, *101 Myths of the Bible*, pp. 156—157). As with many changes of this kind made, the biblical redactors combined the multiple sources of this story very clumsily, as Greenberg points out: on at least two occasions 'Fear of Isaac' appears as an alternative name for the God of Israel and to render this as 'Fear of He Laughed' would not strike terror in the heart of anyone! Greenberg points out many early borrowings in the Old Testament from Egyptian myth, which later editors of the scriptures wanted to edit out 'to discredit the theology associated with Osiris.'

[191] Gen. 16: 11—12. 'And the angel of the Lord said unto her, "Behold, thou art with child and shalt bear a son, and shalt call his name Ishmael; because the Lord hath heard thy affliction. And he will be a wild man; his hand will be against every man, and every man's hand against him; and he shall dwell in the presence of all his brethren".' There is a linguistic problem with this verse: the phrase 'in the presence of all his brethren' could also be translated as 'to the east of his brethren'—compare the *King James Version* with the New International Version of Gen. 16: 12. If the Ishmaelites are to be found throughout Asia, they cannot all be living to the east of all their brethren, although in the Old Testament the decendants of Ishmael are associated with the Midianites (Judges 7 and 8: 24), who were broadly a Bedouin people who lived in the desert region to the east of the Jordan. The vagueness of this prophecy exemplifies d'Holbach's point, rather than Bergier's, and it is also indicative of the linguistic and archeological problems which beset much of the Old Testamtent.

[192] As with many other Old Testament myths, there are many conflicting details, as Greenberg points out: 'The founders of ancient Israel were Abraham, his son Isaac, and Isaac's son Jacob, collectively know as the Patriarchs. Jacob, who on two occasions changed his name to Israel, had twelve male children, the most important of whom were Joseph and Judah, and each of the sons founded one of the Twelve Tribes of Israel. [...] While Genesis frequently says or implies that the covenant passed from

On his death–bed Jacob predicted to Judah, his son, that his family would maintain a pre–eminence over all the other nations until God's messenger came, to whom all would render their obeisance,[193] and the tribe of Judah upheld their position as first amongst the Jews until the advent of Jesus Christ, according to the gospel prediction.[194]

Jeremiah foretold that the Jewish nation would be taken into captivity to **Babylon** and that their captivity would last for seventy years, after which

---

Jacob to Joseph, and then from Joseph to his son Ephraim, in a portion of the story known as the Blessing of Jacob, there is an indication that the covenant passed into the hands of Judah. This inconsistency, one of many, shows how the later feuds between the kingdom of Israel (under the leadership of Ephraim) and the kingdom of Judah heavily influenced the telling of patriarchal history', (Greenberg, *101 Myths*, p. 107). There is a detailed analysis of this whole issue on pp. 107—114 in Greenberg. He also points out in his Conclusion that many changes were made to Old Testament accounts to show that 'Egypt was an evil nation that persecuted the Hebrews before the Exodus with the contrasting view that Babylonian was the most sophisticated and respected cultural force in the Near East of the late first millennium B.C. This resulted in the alteration of early stories about Israel's origins in Egypt. False genealogies and backgrounds were created to give the Hebrew ancestors and their relatives a Babylonian or non-Egyptian background', (ibid., p. 297). Clearly, these details cannot be taken as either faithful to history, or as the definitive word of God.

[193] **Gen. 49.** The passage is as follows: 'Judah, thou art he whom thy brethren shall praise: thy hand shall be in the neck of thine enemies; thy father's children shall bow down before thee. Judah is a lion's whelp: from the prey, my son, thou art gone up: he stooped down, he couched as a lion, and as an old lion; who shall rouse him up? The sceptre shall not depart from Judah, nor a lawgiver from between his feet, until Shiloh come; and unto him shall the gathering of the people be. Binding his foal unto the vine, and his ass's colt unto the choice vine; he washed his garments in wine, and his clothes in the blood of grapes: His eyes shall be red with wine, and his teeth white with milk', (Gen. 49: 8—12). Since there is no agreement on what 'Shiloh' actually means, Bergier's 'evidence' holds little water: the name can mean anything from an actual place, i.e., it is proper noun, or it can mean 'peace'. In this context, some authorities think it means 'the peaceful one', yet Christ's advent heralded anything but peace, as he himself said, 'And Jesus said, For judgment I am come into this world, that they which see not might see; and that they which see might be made blind.' (John 9: 39).

[194] Gen. 49: 8—10 indicates that 'the sceptre', i.e., the symbol of kingship, shall pass to the tribe of Judah, and Greenberg notes: '[...] not surprisingly, David and Solomon came from the tribe of Judah. But Israel didn't have a king for hundreds of years after the Exodus, and a significant faction of the Israelites objected to the institution of kingship. While the prophecy says that the sceptre shall not depart from Judah, according to the Bible, the first king, Saul, came from the tribe of Benjamin. The sceptre had departed from Judah. When Saul died, his son, also a Benjaminite, succeeded him, while David only ruled in Judah. It was not until two years after Saul's death that David became king over all Israel', (Greenberg, op. cit., p. 167).

time they would return to their homeland.[195]   Isaiah, who lived more than a century before, added that Cyrus would be the liberator of this nation and that he would have Jerusalem and the Temple rebuilt:[196] this event was exact in every detail to the prophecy.

That same Isaiah, more than six hundred years before the ruin of Babylon, predicted that it would never again be inhabited for centuries and that it would be wiped out to the extent that not a single trace would be left of it.[197] We know today that the oracle was perfectly fulfilled and that there are hardly any traces of this famous city remaining.

Ezekiel prophesied that Egypt would be devastated and that in the future no prince of Egyptian origin would rule it.[198]   Now Egypt has been successively conquered by the Persians, the Greeks, the Romans and by the Turks, and has always been under foreign domination.

Daniel announced to Nebuchadnezzar that his reign would be succeeded by the Medes and the Persians, and that they would be overturned by the Greeks, and that the first king of that nation would be more powerful than his successors, and that he would form four kingdoms out of the ruins of his empire, and that the latter would fall under the yoke of an even more

---

[195] **Jer., chs. 25 & 29.** There was a forced detention of the Jews in Babylonia following the latter's conquest of the kingdom of Judah in 598/7 and 587/6 BC. The exile formally ended in 538 BC, when the Persian conqueror of Babylonia, Cyrus the Great, gave the Jews permission to return to Palestine. Historians agree that several deportations took place (each the result of uprisings in Palestine), that not all Jews were forced to leave their homeland, that returning Jews left Babylonia at various times, and that some Jews chose to remain in Babylonia—thus constituting the first of numerous Jewish communities living permanently in the Diaspora. Many scholars cite 597 BC as the date of the first deportation, for in that year King Jehoiachin was deposed and apparently sent into exile with his family, his court and thousands of workers. Others say the first deportation followed the destruction of Jerusalem by Nebuchadrezzar in 586; if so, the Jews were held in Babylonian captivity for forty-eight years, and not seventy.

[196] **Isa., chs. 44 & 45.** 'That saith of Cyrus, "He is my shepherd, and shall perform all my pleasure": even saying to Jerusalem, "Thou shalt be built"; and to the temple, "Thy foundation shall be laid",' (Isa. 44: 28).

[197] **Isa., chs. 13 & 14.**

[198] **Ezek. 30:13.** The full prophesy regarding Egypt is: 'Thus saith the Lord God; "I will also make the multitude of Egypt to cease by the hand of Nebuchadrezzar king of Babylon. He and his people with him, the terrible of the nations, shall be brought to destroy the land: and they shall draw their swords against Egypt, and fill the land with the slain. And I will make the rivers dry, and sell the land into the hand of the wicked: and I will make the land waste, and all that is therein, by the hand of strangers: I the Lord have spoken it." Thus saith the Lord God; "I will also destroy the idols, and I will cause their images to cease out of Noph; and there shall be no more a prince of the land of Egypt: and I will put a fear in the land of Egypt",' (Ezek. 30: 10—13).

formidable power and under this one, the kingdom of God would be born to exist for all time.[199] History teaches us that, in fact, the empire of the Assyrians did indeed make way for that of the Medes and the Persians, and that the latter were subjugated by Alexander, and that the states of this conqueror formed four kingdoms: thereafter the Romans became the masters and that it was under the reign of Augustus that the Saviour of the world was born. We have already noted that Porphyry found this prophesy so clear that he believed it had been written after the event.[200]

Isaiah predicted the birth of the Messiah and the attendant circumstances: he said he would be born of a virgin and of the royal blood of David. Another prophet named the place of birth as Bethlehem and others announced that it would take place during the period of the second temple. When Jesus was born, the anticipation of the advent of the redeemer was not only wide–spread amongst the Jews, but throughout the Orient, as Tacitus and Suetonius attest. Herod's alarm and the massacre of the first–born, known to the Romans, was a terrible monument to these events.[201]

---

[199] **Dan., chs. 2, 7 & 8.**

[200] In fact, Porphyry did not know how accurate he was by making this statement—or did he? Greenberg states, 'The predictions attributed to Daniel were written after the occurrence of the events described', (op. cit., p. 287). The gift of prophecy and dream interpretation were given to Daniel by God as a form of blessing and this skill was to earn him a high position of authority when brought to Babylon in about 587 BC after Nebuchadnezzar had conquered Judah and removed the Hebrews from Canaan. Nebuchadnezzar had a series of dreams which Daniel interpreted with startling accuracy, but the book of Daniel 'describes the succession of several kings during the lifetime of Daniel and the sequence is substantially inaccurate', (Greenberg, p. 288). Other predictions made about Nebuchadnezzar actually refer to events in the life of another king, Nabonidus, the fourth in succession **after** Nebuchadnezzar, leading Greenberg to conclude that 'Daniel appears to be a prophet who has a better grasp on the future than the present, which leads to the conclusion that the predictions were written after the fact, when the later events were well known but the earlier history was a bit fuzzy', (op. cit., pp. 288—289).

[201] **Macrobius, *Saturnalia*, I, 2, ch. 4.** There is a reference to Herod killing the first-born, as related in Matt. 2: 16, but no authorities are cited and it is reported as a rumour, which is typical of the whole work, full as it is of tittle-tattle and remarks on astrology, the zodiac and pagan gods. There are no direct references to Christianity in the work. (For Tacitus and Suetonius—see Glossary.) In his detailed description of Herod's rule over several books of the *Jewish Antiquities*, Josephus makes not a single mention of the 'Killing of the Innocents', as the Catholic Church refers to the massacre of the first-born. In fact, Josephus mentions many acts of cruelty committed by Herod, from single individuals to whole groups, whom he believed were plotting against him, but there is no reported massacre of children. It is inconceivable that Josephus would have 'overlooked' such an incident, had it been based in historical fact. On the contrary, Josephus relates a prophesy an Essene makes of Herod, saying that he was blessed by God: 'There was a certain Essene named Manaemus, whose virtue was

Chapter 53 of Isaiah describes the death of the Messiah in the same details as the gospel writers and one can compare them: the Chaldean paraphraser of this prophet heard about the death of Christ, the Messiah, as we did. David had already predicted all the details of the Messiah's death in Psalm 21.[202] Jesus Christ himself, when about to expire on the cross, pronounced the first words of this psalm to demonstrate that all predictions had come to pass in him. Was it, then, pure hazard that made the Jews do all they did down to the

---

attested in his whole conduct of life and especially in his having from God a foreknowledge of the future. This man had (once) observed Herod, then still a boy, going to his teacher, and greeting him as "King of the Jews." Thereupon Herod, who thought that the man either did not know who he was, or was teasing him, reminded him that he was only a private citizen. Manaemus, however, gently smiled and slapped him on the backside, saying, "Nevertheless, you will be king and you will rule the realm happily, for you have been found worthy of this by God.' (Josephus, *Jewish Antiquities*, Book XV, 373—374, translated by R. Marcus and A. Wikgren (Harvard, Mass.: Harvard U.P., Loeb Classical Library, reprinted 2004), pp. 437—439. Clearly, Bergier is picking and choosing his ancient sources, as is typical of all Christian apologists. For **Macrobius**—see Glossary. Eusebius describes Herod's gruesome end in his *History*, citing the *Jewish Antiquities* of Josephus, relishing that 'God struck Herod and drove him to death' as a punishment for his 'plot against our Saviour and the other helpless infants'; 'He had an overpowering desire for food, which it was impossible to satisfy, ulceration of the intestines with agonizing pains in the lower bowel, and a clammy transparent humour covering the feet. The abdomen was in the same miserable state, and in the genitals mortification set in, breeding worms', (Eusebius, *History*, Penguin revised edition, 1989, p. 24, from Josephus, *Jewish Antiquities*, Book XVII, section vi, 5—Loeb edn. [1998], p. 243). A more prosaic and historically accurate version is that Herod's estranged son, Antipater (*c.* 46—4 BC) tried to poison his father and from the description of Josephus some experts have concluded that Herod died of chronic kidney disease, complicated by Fournier's gangrene.

[202] Isaiah's prophecy is couched in general terms and some of the details are quite simply wrong when compared with the gospel accounts: Is. 53: 7 describes the Messiah's demeanour 'as a sheep before her shearers is dumb, so he openeth not his mouth,' yet we know he had a conversation with Pilate, albeit brief. Bergier's reference to Psalm 21 is to the Latin *Vulgate* Version, which is actually Psalm 22 in the *King James Version*, which opens with the words, "My God, my God, why hast thou forsaken me?" These are the words attributed to Christ on the cross just before his death, see Mark 15: 34 and Matt. 27: 46. Luke has Christ say something different: 'And when Jesus had cried with a loud voice, he said, "Father, into thy hands I commend my spirit": and having said thus, he gave up the ghost', (Luke 23: 46). John's Gospel has Christ address his mother and complain that he was thirsty: he does not address God in this version. This point proves nothing from the point of view of prophesy: Christ, as a Jew, would have a good knowledge of the Old Testament scriptures and if he really was delusional enough to believe he was the Messiah, he may well have uttered the words of the psalmist as part of his scheming to convince people he was the messiah and acted according the the prediction in Isaiah.

Figure 40: *Massacre of the Innocents*, Giotto di Bondone (*c.* 1305).

last detail, just as their prophets had predicted of the Messiah? And were these *'vague'*, *'obscure oracles'* in which one can read into them *'anything one wishes'*?[203]

§ 17

Our critics accuse Jesus Christ of having been no clearer or happier in his prophesies.[204] I shall cite only a single one of them: he predicted that the Temple of Jerusalem would be destroyed from top to bottom and that not a single stone would be left of it.[205] The emperor Julian, who had resolved to prove this prophecy false, invited the Jews from all provinces of the empire to rebuild the Temple. The governor of Palestine, on Julian's orders, spared no attention, expenses, or effort. Hardly had the first foundations of the building been dug than balls of fire came out of the earth and overturned all the work done, burning the workers, rendering the site inaccessible, and forcing them to abandon the enterprise. It was **Ammianus Marcellinus**, an officer in Julian's militia, a contemporary writer, and incidentally a shrewd historian, who recounted this fact.[206] His account has been confirmed not only by the evidence of several ecclesiastic writers, of whom several were eye–witnesses, but further in two letters from Julian himself.[207]

---

[203] See p. 53.

[204] *Christ. Unveil.*, **p. 85.** *Import. Exam.*, **ch. 16, p. 97.**

[205] **Matt. 24: 2 and Luke 19: 44.** The reference to Matthew states: 'And Jesus said unto them [i.e., his disciples], "See ye not all these things? Verily I say unto you, There shall not be left here one stone upon another, that shall not be thrown down".' Luke has: '"For the days shall come upon thee, that thine enemies shall cast a trench about thee, and compass thee round, and keep thee in on every side, And shall lay thee even with the ground, and thy children within thee; and they shall not leave in thee one stone upon another; because thou knewest not the time of thy visitation",' (Luke 19: 43—44).

[206] **Amm. Marcell. I, 23,** *ab initio.* This reference is to Ammianus Marcellinus' *History.* (For Marcellinus, Ammianus—see Glossary.) The passage to which Bergier refers is as follows: '...eager to extend the memory of his reign by great works, he [i.e., Julianus Augustus] planned at vast cost to restore the once splendid temple at Jerusalem, which after many mortal combats during the siege by Vespagian and later by Titus, had barely been stormed. He had entrusted the speedy performance of this work to Alypius of Antioch, who had once been vice-prefect of Britain. But, though this Alypius pushed the work on with vigour, aided by the governor of the province, terrifying balls of flame kept bursting forth near the foundations of the temple, and made the place inaccessible to the workmen, some of whom were burned to death; and since in this way the element persistently repelled them, the enterprise halted.' (Ammianus Marcellinus, *History*, translated by John C. Rolfe [Cambridge, Massachusetts: Harvard University Press, Loeb Classical Library, 2006, reprint], II [Book XXIII], p. 311.)

[207] **See *History* by Mr. Bullet, № 104** *et seqq.* (For Bullet—see Glossary.)

Up until now, our adversaries have not dared to say what they think of this singular event: the author of *Miscellany of Literature, History and Philosophy* in 8vo dismissed it plain and simple: he issued a denial against Ammianus Marcellinus and all the others, and treated his account with ridicule.[208] So that's how the history of philosophy is written, then!

---

[208] *Miscell.,* **III, chapter 63, p. 52.** Voltaire provided a general introduction and some notes by way of a commentary to a new translation into French of Marcellinus' *Chronicles of Events*. In the general introduction, Voltaire points out that two esteemed scholars, Pierre Pithou and Claude Chifflet, maintained that Ammianus Marcellinus was a Christian and therefore tried to portray any events pertinent to Christianity in a favourable light. But then Voltaire points out there are other passages which show that his sympathies were more pagan. Rolfe, Marcellinus' translator for the scholarly Loeb edition, states: 'That Ammianus was not a Christian is evident from many of his utterances, for he speaks of Christian rites, ceremonies, and officials in a way which shows a lack of familiarity with them. At the same time he was liberal in his attitude towards the Church: he twice censures the closing of the schools of rhetoric to Christian teachers, praises the simple life of the provincial bishops, and in general favours absolute religious toleration. [...] He indicates a belief in astrology, divination, dreams, and other superstitions of his time, and he speaks of *Fortuna* [chance, fate] and *fatum* ['divine will' or the 'will of a god'] as controlling powers, but shows that they may be overcome or influenced by man's courage and resourcefulness.' (Introduction in *op. cit.,* pp. xiv-xv.) While admitting that, generally, Marcellinus is a worthy historian, Voltaire concurs with Rolfe, pointing out that there are passages in his narrative where 'he stoops to the level of the most ignorant when it comes to superstition,' by which Voltaire means all kinds of supernatural events and belief in gods of every description, and he cites the passage about the rebuilding of the Temple as a prime example of his superstitious nature. In his notes specific to this passage, Voltaire remarks: 'Defenders of the faith have rejoiced in this miraculous event and particularly so because it is the disinterested testimony of a pagan who reports the event simply, without any commentary. However, the sincerity of history does not permit us to cover up the fact that St Jerome, who was also a contemporary and lived near to the theatre of this event, makes not a single mention of it. Furthermore, this is what the sceptic Gibbon says on this issue: "Such an authority (i.e., that of Ammianus) is sure to satisfy the believer and astonish the disbeliever, but a philosopher will ask for more authentic evidence from an intelligent and impartial eye-witness. In the midst of this important crisis, all singular natural phenomena would appear to be, and produce the effects of, a miraculous event. The devout trickery of the Jerusalem clergy and popular credulity would not hold back in embellishing and exaggerating this glorious deliverance; and twenty years after a historian of the empire, who had not a thought for theologians' disputes, now manages to embellish his work with such a specious and dazzling miracle." Be that as it may, enlightened Christianity can take any proof derived from this miracle with a pinch of salt, because the fact of its fulfilment is firmly established. Despite the will of a powerful person, the Temple has never been rebuilt: the mysterious survival of the Jew and his religious cult, notwithstanding their dispersion as a people which happened so many centuries ago, speaks volumes by comparison with all forms of supernatural testimony confirmed by Scripture.' (From Voltaire's introduction and notes in, *Ammien Marcellin, Journadès. Frontin, Végéce, Modestus,*

It is falsely alleged that Jesus Christ foretold the Last Judgement in the Gospel of Luke, chapter 21. He predicted the ruination of Jerusalem and the Jewish nation, but in the lively, bold, figurative language of an Oriental style.[209] One can compare this chapter with that of the capture of Babylon in Isaiah, the defeat of the King of Egypt in Ezekiel, the ruin of Tyre and Sidon in Joel's prophesy, and one will see the same images and expressions. Mr Fréret has already written his critique on this and I have pointed out that he is in error.[210] What is the point of going over them all again?[211]

[...]

The reproach made against the Church Fathers that '*It is easy to see anything in the Bible, as St Augustine did, by imagining that he saw the whole of the New Testament in the Old*', is even more ill–founded.[212] In order to convert the Jews and to convince them through their scriptures, they had to be explained in the manner used by the Doctors of the Church and in the way they were accustomed to do so. Now it is certain, as we can see in the works of Philo and in the commentaries of the most ancient rabbis, that they had a predominant penchant for allegories. When the author of *Important Examination* admits that, '*this style contributed more than*

---

published under the direction of de Nisard [Paris: Firmin-Didot, 1869], III, pp. ii and p. 396.)

[209] The passage to which Bergier refers is really the entire chapter 21 of Luke, but these are the salient points: 'And as some spake of the temple, how it was adorned with goodly stones and gifts, he said, "As for these things which ye behold, the days will come, in the which there shall not be left one stone upon another, that shall not be thrown down." And they asked him, saying, "Master, but when shall these things be and what sign will there be when these things shall come to pass?" And he said, "Take heed that ye be not deceived: for many shall come in my name, saying, I am Christ; and the time draweth near: go ye not therefore after them. But when ye shall hear of wars and commotions, be not terrified: for these things must first come to pass; but the end is not by and by." Then said he unto them, "Nation shall rise against nation, and kingdom against kingdom: And great earthquakes shall be in divers places, and famines, and pestilences; and fearful sights and great signs shall there be from heaven. But before all these, they shall lay their hands on you, and persecute you, delivering you up to the synagogues, and into prisons, being brought before kings and rulers for my name's sake",' (Luke 21: 5—12). He goes on to paint a picture of carnage and genocide, the destruction of Jerusalem by a foreign enemy, and the usual supernatural phenomena such as 'signs in the sun, and in the moon, and in the stars; and upon the earth distress of nations, with perplexity; the sea and the waves roaring...' (vs. 25). Finally, he predicts his own return in glory, 'And then shall they see the Son of man coming in a cloud with power and great glory', (vs. 27).

[210] *Certit. Of Proofs of Christ.*, ch. 11, § 10.

[211] *Import. Exam.*, chapter 16, p. 97. *Questions of Zapata*, № 53. *Dinner of the Count of Boulainvilliers*, p. 24.

[212] See footnote, p. 56.

anything else to the propagation of Christianity', he discredits his own argument. This methodology was used particularly for the Jews, since it was very much to their taste, so how could one say, therefore, that Christians could not prevail against the Jews, as they could against the Gentiles?[213] If there were fewer Jews converted than Gentiles it is because the former were few in number outside Palestine in each province of the empire by comparison with the Gentiles.

§ 22.

It is stated as a form of criticism against Christianity that it was certain that the Romans tolerated all religions, but why would they not tolerate Christianity unless they wanted to destroy paganism? We must clear up this point and turn it against our adversaries as a proof.

Paganism, whose maxim was to accept any number of gods, had no right or any interest in condemning the gods of another people: each nation was permitted to have their own particular gods and the worship of one group did not demean the other, and the pagans had neither apostles nor missionaries.

Judaism was regarded by the Jewish nation itself as being a religion just for their nation, which had been given only to the descendants of Abraham, and so the Jews had no interest in looking to make proselytes. Content to follow their own laws in freedom and to surrender nothing of them to pagan practices, they never preached Judaism to the Gentiles.

The apostles were ordered by Jesus Christ to preach the gospel to all nations,[214] declaring themselves, above all, to be sent by God to all people to make them pay obeisance to the faith in the name of God.[215] They proved their mission through miracles, preaching everywhere the unity of the Godhead and the falsity of paganism, the futility and superstition of their cult, and the disciples spoke and behaved the same in Rome as elsewhere:[216] it was not difficult to see that if Christianity were to become established, paganism would soon be wiped out.

The pagans doubtless understood this and that is why they found Christianity odious as soon as it was introduced to them. Also we maintain that this could not have been otherwise and that, as soon as it was noticed in

---

[213] *Import. Exam.*, **p. 92.**

[214] **Matt. 28: 19.** 'Go ye therefore, and teach all nations, baptizing them in the name of the Father, and of the Son, and of the Holy Ghost.'

[215] **Rom. 1: 5.** 'By whom [i.e., the Son of God] we have received grace and apostleship, for obedience to the faith among all nations, for his name...'

[216] **Mark 16: 20.** 'And they went forth, and preached every where, the Lord working with them, and confirming the word with signs following.'

Rome that Christianity was making real progress, it became of the utmost importance to get rid of it.

If by preaching the cult of a single God to the exclusion of all others one is preaching against *tolerance*, then we admit that Christianity was essentially *intolerant* and that for the only true religion it could not be otherwise.

Spreading the gospel in Rome as a supernatural mission that had been proven and authenticated was regarded as an act of sedition, an attempt on the law, a crime worthy of death, and so it is clear that all the preachers of the gospel were seditious people who ought to be put to death. But it must also be pointed out at the same time that idolatry was enshrined in Roman law, so God could not give anyone a mission to disabuse people of it.

But were the first Christians *intolerant* in the odious sense that our adversaries intend? That is to say, did they believe they had a right to disrupt pagan worship, their feast days, their pagan ceremonies, to cause insult in the temples of the gods and to their ministers and worshippers? Assuredly not: it is a lie to suggest that the fervour of Christians alone made enemies of Christianity.

I admit that in the fourth century, or towards the end of the third, there was some over–zealous behaviour on the part of some individuals, but this was only after the emperors had already issued edicts in favour of the Christian religion. When these edicts were revoked, the two religions were set at loggerheads, so to speak, and Christians were often pushed to the limit by the continuous snubs of the pagans. Hence, they allowed themselves to indulge in some repressive measures, but they were far less excessive and far less extensive than our adversaries maintain.

'*Christianity*', they say, '*wanted to crush all other religions*'.[217] If one means by this that Christianity wanted to convert all peoples and by doing so they would topple other cults, nothing could be truer: but if one means that Christians undertook to destroy other cults by violent means, that is another lie.

Is it not strange that Roman toleration is thrown in our faces? Romans had become philosophers and they were as tolerant as those of today are.[218] These people willingly put up with paganism, Muhammadanism, the religion of the Brahmins and the Lamas, and even atheism itself. But as for Christianity, they never tolerated it and they swore an everlasting hate for it, and they resolved to destroy it or perish.

---

[217] *Import. Exam.*, ch. 26, p. 143.
[218] *Philosophical Dict.*, see under the article '*Atheists*'.

After having seen their best shot against the proofs of revelation, we might venture to ask further: Is there anywhere in the world a religion which can demonstrate a continuous succession of prophesies as authentic, as clear, and as so obviously verified as those of the Old and the New Testaments? Is there any other religion based on so many miracles that are so prolific, so striking and so incontestable, as those of Moses, of the prophets, of Jesus Christ's and his apostles, like those of the founding faithful and eye–witnesses, who spilt their blood to testify to the truth? Let us be shown any such religion, let a religion equal to Christianity be raised aloft for all to see.

God has deigned to speak to mankind, and could he have accompanied his revelation with signs more obvious, more easily recognizable, more infallible and more fitting, to stop people in their tracks? How could any reasonable mind refuse to pay homage to teaching so replete with external signs and which presents the sublime nature of its truths, the purity of its morality, the sanctity and usefulness of its worship, and all the marks of wisdom and divine goodness? Now these are the doctrines of Christianity which we shall offer by way of justification against our enemies' lies.

Chapter 8

Other Mysteries and Dogmas of Christianity

§ 1

In this chapter the author of *Christianity Unveiled* continues in the same vein as he did in the preceding chapter: he twists and distorts the Christian faith, making it appear odious: he thinks up fallacies in order to have the pleasure of railing against them. Whilst it is extremely tiring to have to refute these lies, nevertheless it behoves us to put the facts straight.

Is it not a crying injustice to impute for a second time to the Christian faith the doctrine of *absolute predestination*, which is one of the most awful teachings of Calvinism? God takes no delight in any Catholic Christian thinking that '*the God of Mercy predestines the vast majority of unfortunate mortals to eternal torment.*'[219] Neither does God give people a free will merely so that '*they abuse their abilities and liberty* [...] *to give him the pleasure of plunging them into hell.*' We detest all these blasphemies and we believe the contrary, that God '*will have all men to be saved, and to come unto the knowledge of the truth*',[220] and that Jesus Christ '*died for all*'[221] without exception, and that He is '*the Saviour of all men, especially of those that believe.*'[222] By virtue of divine will and redemption through Jesus Christ, God gives to all men, without a single exception, more or less the most abundant, efficacious means, but always sufficient for knowing and practising what is good, and that these means leave man with the full scope of his free will and that no one is damned, other than by his own fault.

We believe in an eternity of punishments and rewards because Jesus Christ taught us about them,[223] and we maintain that this dogma contains nothing contrary to the infinite justice of God. It is a vain sophism to say that there is no sense of proportion between a momentary sin and torture which will last for all eternity. It is not the duration of the crime which constitutes its scale: the justice of men condemns to death or to perpetual banishment a criminal on a daily basis, whose crime lasted but a moment.

In vain does the author of the *Philosophical Dictionary* state that several Church Fathers did not believe in eternal punishment. Origen was the only

---

[219] *Christ. Unveil.*, p. 104. (This edition, p. 67.) *Militant Phil.*, ch. 10, p. 159.
[220] 1 Tim. 2: 4.
[221] 2 Cor. 5: 15.
[222] 1 Tim. 4: 10.
[223] *Phil. Dict.* Art. 'Hell', p. 287.

Figure 41: *The Stygian Lake, with the Ireful Sinners Fighting.* **Blake's illustration to Dante's** *Inferno*, **Canto VII (*c.* 1825).**

258

one who was reproached for attacking this constant and universal article ofthe Church's faith: once again the proofs against this accusation remain without comment here, since Origen had plenty of learned apologists to refute him. The controversy which has recently blown up again between Swiss Protestant ministers is absolutely alien to the Catholic Church and merits no attention whatsoever. There is nothing weaker or less well–reasoned than the writing of Petit–Pierre against eternal punishments in hell.[224]

Once again, this blasphemer says that God *'caused [man] to be born and remain in sorrow'* and that *'he gave [people] the power of reason only to dupe them, inclinations only to lead them astray, liberty only to spur them on to do actions which must damn them for all eternity.'*[225] The horrors that these errors inspire can only come back upon the head of the author who thought them up.

It is a gross abuse of the term to maintain that the teaching of *free predestination* is at the basis of the Judaic religion. The choice God made in choosing the Hebrew people to give them his law was not an absolute predestination for eternal life: by choosing this people, he did not condemn other peoples to eternal damnation; he allowed them the means sufficient to acquire knowledge of him and serve him. Therefore, there was no partiality or injustice in this choice. When God gives a man more intellect or innate talents, or a temperament and character which are more felicitous than that of another, can one accuse him of partiality and injustice? Just because he does not distribute his gifts freely, can one deny his providence? If God may, without injustice, introduce some inequality within his natural gifts, why can he not do the same in the way he distributes his supernatural benefits?

The purpose of my work is not to discuss the opinions of those whom the author calls Jansenists or Molinists, whose ideas he sets out very badly:[226] being sincerely attached to the Church, I do not approve of any of the belief systems that the Church has condemned. It is a lie that true Christians must *ipso facto* be *'real fatalists'*:[227] in order to maintain this error one has to renounce all Christian principles—it is the philosophers of today who have chosen to revive this monstrous, fatalistic doctrine, as I have already pointed out.[228]

---

[224] See footnote № 131 above.
[225] *Christ. Unveil.*, **p. 106.** (This edition, p. 68.)
[226] *Christ. Unveil.*, **p. 107.** (This edition, footnote p. 68.)
[227] Ibid.
[228] See pp. 345 *et seqq.*, which refer to Calvin's ideas, to which this is a reference.

Chapter 9

On Rites and Ceremonies of the Christian Religion[229]

§ 3

Experience teaches us that pageant is necessary to capture people's attention: a religion stripped of all outward expression can neither attract nor instruct. Protestants are all too well aware of that today and only now do they see the disadvantages of a cult divested of pomp,[230] and according to the judicious remark in *The Friend of Man*, any religion reduced to the purely spiritual is soon '*consigned to the back of beyond*'.[231] Suppose instead of the scandalous nudity of Greek dancing and games—the folly and indecency that dishonour pagan festivals—religion were to grip people in place of the circus and barbarity of the amphitheatre through its ceremonies, which are full of gravity and decorum, fitting to inspire gentle and pure mores in people: malcontent philosophers would still blame them, yet what is it to them whether people are wise or deprived of good sense, whether they are civilized or infantilized?

The indecency of the author's language in *Christianity Unveiled* is plain to see and who fails to blush at his comparison of Christian ceremonies with pagan theurgy, by which is meant the superstitious and absurd practices through which certain philosophers, who are just as blind as the common people, maintain they have dealings with spirits, which are common throughout nature and adored as gods?[232] What positive relevance do these

---

[229] Note that Bergier has changed the title of d'Holbach's original chapter: as will be seen by reading this section, Bergier is offended by the word 'theurgy'.

[230] **See *The Spirit of Laws*, I, 25, ch. 2.**

[231] **Second Part, ch. 4, pp. 169 & 235.** The reference is to the Marquis de Mirabeau's work, *L'Ami des Hommes* {*The Friend of Man*}, see footnote № 11 above. Writing about personal freedom in a chapter on 'Mores', Mirabeau asks whether people should be forced to comply with certain expectations of society: 'Should we force people to go to mass, for example?' and 'Should the government or the police interrogate people over the content of their conversations and habits?' etc. He concludes, 'It is of little importance to the government whether you go to mass on days of obligation or not, as long as you behave yourself and do so quietly...' (op. cit. edn. published 1758, Avignon), p. 88. But ultimately, he sees religious non-observance as the thin end of the wedge: 'And since appearance is and always will be everything to the common people, and since transgressions go hand in hand with observances, disdain, or at least discussions, on the Church's orders will enter people's heads. When a spirit of regularity is lost and all religion is reduced to the spiritual level, it is soon consigned to the back of beyond', ibid., p. 89.

[232] **See Julian, Porphyry, Iamblichus, etc.** Bergier most likely means 'Julian the Apostate'. (For all these philosophers—see Glossary.)

bizarre ceremonies have for society? We are indignant when we hear the sacraments likened to '*magic*', or dubbed '*puerile*' and '*ridiculous ceremonies*'. It is hard to imagine how a writer can come to such a conclusion so imperiously and be so badly informed.

According to him, it is wrong to believe that baptism washes away original sin, since the effects of this sin continue to exist, given our continuing inclination to do evil and the inevitable necessity of death. He concludes that baptism is a mystery impenetrable to reason, which experience tells us belies its efficacy.[233]

But for us to be able to say truthfully that baptism washes away original sin, is it necessary that it removes all the consequences of sin? It takes away the principle and the worst of the consequences, which is eternal damnation. The other consequences exist, because for the Christian they serve as a test and a reward for they contribute to eternal salvation.

It is also a lie to say that St Paul did not want to baptize the Corinthians: he did not baptize them himself because he was mainly occupied with preaching the gospel, but he had them baptized by his disciples,[234] just as he had the Ephesians baptized.[235]

What does it matter if a kind of baptism was practised within the rites of **Mithras**?[236] Baptisms or purification by water have been used among all peoples because it is a powerful and natural symbol, but it can produce no effect unless performed amongst the worshippers of the true God.

In order to ridicule the mystery of the Eucharist, the author has recourse to his usual methodology: he distorts it and imbues it with a belief which I detest. It is not true that at the awesome voice of a priest the God of the universe *is forced* to descend from his glorious abode in order to '*change into bread*', nor is it true that we adore this bread.[237] Jesus Christ is present in the Eucharist without leaving his glorious abode and he is not forced to do so, but he wants to, and the bread is not God because it is no longer bread. Before picking an argument with our faith it behoves the author to read our Catechism at least.

It is not at all surprising to find that there is a kind of Eucharist amongst the Indians, Mexicans and Peruvians. The outward show of religious practices of eating victims or offerings made to a divinity as a sign of having received

---

[233] *Christ. Unveil.*, **p. 119.** (This edition, p. 75.)
[234] **1 Cor. 1: 17.** 'For Christ sent me not to baptize, but to preach the gospel...'
[235] **Acts 19: 5.** 'When they heard this, they were baptized in the name of the Lord Jesus.'
[236] See p. 75 and Glossary.
[237] See p. 76.

grace and a testimony of kinship is a habit that has been dominant amongst many peoples. The divine Christian lawgiver did not go off to the Indies or to America in order to find this symbol: he drew upon it from nature and he wisely distanced it from anything that might defile it.

Figure 42: Baptism in the River Jordan at Kinneret, Palestine.
Photo by Bantosh. (Source: Wikipedia.)

Chapter 10

On Christian Holy Books

§ 12

In *Christianity Unveiled* the author speaks of the books of the New Testament in his customary style. He says, '*Four historians, or fabulists, wrote a fantastical story about the Messiah with little agreement between themselves on the details of his life, sometimes contradicting each other in the most glaringly obvious way.*'[238] I shall examine these so–called contradictions carefully. However, the reader is asked to bear in mind the remarks already made about the gospels at the beginning of Chapter 3: he will know if these '*stories*' can be treated as fables by a man of good sense.

Let us just suppose for a moment that the gospel writers are in '*little agreement between themselves on the details*' over the life of Jesus Christ. They are chiefly in agreement over the principal events of his birth, his preaching, his miracles, his death, his resurrection, his ascension and on the doctrines he taught. Would the accounts of several secular historians who agreed perfectly on a series of public events not vary between themselves on minor details of time, place and the way events developed, and would that be grounds on which to doubt their narrative and to treat it as a fable?

But the gospel writers contradict each other! It is a question of proving this. This is the great objection of our philosophers—the genealogy of Jesus Christ as recorded by Matthew is very different from that set down by Luke.[239] By the way they speak about this, one would think that there were no explanations for this fact. A moment's reflection is all it takes to deal with this.

St Matthew sets out to prove that Christ descended from David through his paternal side, through Joseph his legal father, through the branch of the family that leads back to King David. St Luke traces Jesus Christ's lineage through the descendants of Mary and the branch of her younger siblings. When the two family branches are compared, they concur with Zerubbabel, and with Matthat or Mathan, the great–grandfather of Jesus: this Matthat (or Matthan) was the son of Eleazar and the son–in–law of Levi, just as Joseph was the son of Jacob and the son–in–law of Heli, and so, consequently, Joseph and Mary were first cousins and they had to marry according to the

---

[238] **Page 131. (This edition, p. 82.)** *Dinner of the Count of Boulainvilliers, p. 7.*
[239] *Christ. Unveil.*, **p. 131.** *Important Exam.*, **ch. 13, p. 78.** *Phil. Dict.*, **I, Art. on** 'Christianity', **p. 206.** *Questions of Zapata*, **№ 50.** *Treatise on Tolerance*, **ch. 11, p. 99.** *Second Letter on the Miracles*, **p. 353, and** *Letter* **№ 20, p. 195.**

law, as written in the last chapter of the Book of Numbers. The alleged contradiction shows that Jesus Christ combined in his person all the rights of the blood–line of David and the Patriarchs and all the characteristics of the Messiah. We shall not go into other difficulties and details that arise from the genealogies—one can find the solution to these problems in **Dom Calmet** and in other interpreters' works.[240]

It is stated in Luke that Jesus was born under the reign of Cyrinus or Cyrenius, when the Emperor Augustus ordered a census of the whole empire: however, there never was such a census and no author speaks of it, and Cyrenius was only the governor of Syria ten years after the birth of Jesus.[241]

Our philosophers, who have copied this objection from Dom Calmet, should at least have looked at his reply which exposes the error. This commentator has pointed out with several examples that the Greek text of Luke's could be literally translated as follows: '*This census was carried out before **Cyrenius** was governor of Syria.*' So the so–called chronological fault absolutely does not exist. One might add that the census was started under Quintilius Varus before the birth of Jesus Christ, and it was only completed under Cyrenius, which is why the gospel attributes it to him. There is nothing extraordinary in all this.

Our critics tell us that there never was a census. But what do they know about it? They know that not a single secular writer spoke of it. So that's the sum total of their proof. But how many other historical events do we know of through the sole testimony of a single writer? We do not have an exact historical account of the period of Augustus' reign and we have very few Roman historians whose work has come down to us complete, and yet they are arguing over the silence of historians. Censuses, of which St Luke speaks, were a constant fact of life in the first few centuries, and **St Justin** in his *Second Apology*, and **Tertullian** in his *Apologeticum*, refer the Romans to their archives in order to convince themselves of this.[242]

Our New Testament critics have dreamt up a marvellous expedient to find yet more contradictions. If one Evangelist relates one incident upon which the others are silent he is instantly accused of contradicting the others. St Matthew has Jesus travel to Egypt—a fact not mentioned by the other gospel

---

[240] See footnote, p. 82.

[241] *Import. Exam.*, ch. 13, pp. 85—6. *Questions of Zapata*, № 51. *Letter on Miracles*, **p. 183.**

[242] In fact, one historian Bergier does not mention in this connection is the writer Flavius Josephus, who mentions some of these details in his *Antiquities*, but scholars agree that, as a historian, he is not always reliable. See *Antiquities*, XVII, (viii, 1); XVII, (xiii, 2 & 5), and XVIII, (i, 1).

writers. The author of *Important Examination* concludes that, according to one Evangelist, Jesus was brought up in Egypt, but according to another he was raised in Bethlehem.[243] St Matthew tells of the adoration of the Magi and the massacre of the babies, but the other gospel writers are silent on these events—therefore, yet more contradictions. One of the Evangelists writes of three trips to Jerusalem by Jesus after his baptism, while another mentions only a single journey. They conclude that the first writer has Jesus Christ's mission last for three years, whilst the second for only three months. More contradictions are assumed.[244]

If we followed his method we would also have grounds on which to accuse our critics of a good number of contradictions. One argues against the text of St Matthew, the other against that of St Luke, saying nothing of the first. Another attacks the Gospel of St John, but says nothing of the others, and so he supposes that only John is in the wrong and that the others are correct. If we were to think like that, would anyone deign to listen to us?

Have two authors who have not copied from each other—even contemporaries—ever been noted for reporting the same historical account, exact in all details and circumstances? A writer who wants to give an exact historical account of a century or a memorable event begins by assembling the diverse memoirs of his contemporaries: so long as these different memories come from educated and sincere people, we do not make any more special claims and we do not suspect their truthfulness if one is more detailed than the other, and if there is some variation in the narrative; one can reconcile them, as far as possible, and make sense of them by cross–referencing the one with the other: that is how our best histories are composed. When it is the facts of the gospels at stake, our philosopher friends do not seem to approve of this method and they reject everything that is not to their liking.

In order to show us real contradictions, they ought to have cited passages of the gospels where it said that Jesus Christ *had always been brought up in Bethlehem*, or they should have told us some fact which contradicted the event of the adoration of the Magi, or the massacre of the babies, or that it was absolutely stated clearly that Jesus Christ had only made one, single journey to Jerusalem since his baptism, or that *his mission lasted only three months*. That would have been difficult to do since that would involve just as many false and erroneous statements.

---

[243] *Import. Exam.*, ch. 13, p. 78.
[244] *Phil. Dict.*, I, p. 206. *Questions of Zapata*, Nºs 52 & 53. *Second Letter on the Miracles*, p. 36. *Eighteenth Letter*, p. 184. *Twentieth Letter*, p. 195.

The author of *Christianity Unveiled* believes that he has uncovered yet more glaring contradictions. He says, '*St Mark says that Jesus died at the third hour, that is, at nine o'clock in the morning, whereas St John says that he died at the sixth hour, which is midday.*'[245] That is totally wrong: the author has not read the gospel. St Mark says that it was the third hour when Jesus was led to Calvary to be crucified and that at the sixth hour, a shadow fell over Judea and Jesus died at the ninth hour, or at three o'clock in the afternoon.[246] SS Matthew and Luke relate exactly the same thing.[247] St John says that when Pilate released Jesus to the Jews to be crucified, it was not the sixth hour but *about* the sixth hour—*hora quasi sexta*.[248] Hence, the time given is less precise than the other Evangelists, but it does not contradict them.

The author also points out that: '*According to SS Matthew and Mark, the women who visited Jesus' tomb after his death saw only a single angel, but in the account of SS Luke and John they saw two angels. These angels were outside the tomb according to some gospel writers, but inside according to others.*'[249] The reconciliation of these two accounts is very simple when we compare the different texts of the Evangelists. On arrival at the tomb, the holy ladies first of all saw an angel sitting outside, who invited them into it to see that the body of Jesus was no longer there.[250] They went into it and were astonished not to find the body, but they also noticed two further angels placed one at the head and the other at the feet, in the place where the body of

---

[245] ***Christ. Unveil.*, p. 132.** (This edition, p. 82.)

[246] **Mark 15: 25, 33, & 34.** The entire passage is reproduced here to enable the reader to assess the relevant section: '[25]And it was the third hour, and they crucified him. [26]And the superscription of his accusation was written over, THE KING OF THE JEWS. [27]And with him they crucify two thieves; the one on his right hand, and the other on his left. [28]And the scripture was fulfilled, which saith, "And he was numbered with the transgressors." [29]And they that passed by railed on him, wagging their heads, and saying, "Ah, thou that destroyest the temple, and buildest it in three days, [30]Save thyself, and come down from the cross." [31]Likewise also the chief priests mocking said among themselves with the scribes, "He saved others; himself he cannot save. [32]Let Christ the King of Israel descend now from the cross, that we may see and believe." And they that were crucified with him reviled him. [33]And when the sixth hour was come, there was darkness over the whole land until the ninth hour. [34]And at the ninth hour Jesus cried with a loud voice, saying, "Eloi, Eloi, lama sabachthani?" which is, being interpreted, "My God, my God, why hast thou forsaken me?"'

[247] **Matt. 17 & Luke 23.**

[248] **John 19: 14.** 'And it was the preparation of the passover, and about the sixth hour: and he saith unto the Jews, "Behold your King!"'

[249] See p. 82.

[250] **Matt. 28 & Mark 16.**

Jesus had been laid to rest.[251] Mary Magdalene in particular saw them in the same way.[252] There is no contradiction here.

Nor are there any other contradictions in the way in which the Evangelists report the various miracles of their Master and his appearances after his resurrection. Biblical interpreters have shown a hundred times their solutions to these objections and they are neither strange nor contrived in order to please the blind: it is our critics who blind themselves and try to do the same to others.

[...]

---

[251] **Luke 24.**

[252] **John 20.** '[11]But Mary stood without at the sepulchre weeping: and as she wept, she stooped down, and looked into the sepulchre, [12]And seeth two angels in white sitting, the one at the head, and the other at the feet, where the body of Jesus had lain.'

Chapter 12

§1

On Christian Virtues

In order to speak rationally about Christian morality, one has to have practised it; in order to make a fair judgement upon the virtues it inspires, one has to have had direct experience of them. Our adversaries have only ever contemplated these virtues with a defensive, critical eye, and the author of *Christianity Unveiled* is a prime example of this.

He intends to show that these Christian virtues are not meant for men, that they are pointless and often pernicious to society, as are the precepts and admonitions of the gospels: the few that he does admit as having some merit, he believes have been much better taught by the sages of antiquity.

First, he maintains that charity is impracticable and that it is impossible to love God as religion portrays him—angry, unjust and full of implacable vengeance. He repeats this insult at least four times. For our author, fear and love are two incompatible concepts: the fear of the Lord is for him far from being '*the beginning of wisdom*'—it is the height of foolishness.[253]

The *Militant Philosopher* goes one step further with this image of God, suggesting that Jupiter was a more valuable god than the Christian God on this level because, according to him, '*Jupiter seemed like a chaste and sober monarch, yet he burned alive almost all his subjects on a mere whim, without any regard for their merit, their vices or their virtues.*'

We concur that it is impossible to love God such as our critics portray him: but the colours in which they paint him are not taken from our religion. A Christian who is better informed than our philosopher knows that God is not only our Master, but he is also our Father, and that he loves us more tenderly than even the most affectionate mother.[254] The Christian also knows that God's love for us pours forth continuously in blessings;[255] that all we are and have, and all we are able to do, comes to us as gifts from His goodness;[256]

---

[253] **Page 162.** (This edition, pp. 29 & 38.) *Milit. Phil.*, **ch.1, pp. 31 & 32, etc.** *Letter to Eugenia*, **p. 20.** The quotation is from Ps. 111: 10; 'The fear of the Lord is the beginning of wisdom.'

[254] **Isa. 49: 15.** 'Can a woman forget her infant, so as not to have pity on the son of her womb? And if she should forget, yet will not I forget thee.'

[255] **Ps. 144: 9.** 'The Lord is sweet to all: and his tender mercies are over all his works.'

[256] **Ps. 8: 6.** 'Thou hast made [man] a little less than the angels, thou hast crowned him with glory and honour'

and that he cannot hate his creation because he is patient, merciful, and all–powerful;[257] and whenever God becomes irritated by his creation, he remembers that he is merciful.[258] God does not treat us according to our sins, but he takes pity upon us as a father takes pity on his own child, because he knows our frail nature.[259] When he punishes us, he does so with a heavy heart and only to make us wiser.[260] He only consigns to eternal punishment those who have always rejected the pardon he offers to them.[261] These are the loving character traits of God that the Old Testament portrays for us: the ones depicted in the New Testament are even more touching.

How can anyone have the temerity to juxtapose this view of God with the traits of the mythological gods such as Jupiter, whom poets describe? This so–called 'god' was not only a *fickle* god, and a *drunkard* and a *debauched individual*—he was a monster, besmirched with all manner of crimes, as the *Militant Philosopher* agrees: he was an unnatural son who dethroned and maimed his father, an incestuous brother who abused his own sister, an unfaithful husband who had committed over a hundred acts of adultery and crimes against nature, an unjust and bizarre master who entertained mortals

---

[257] **Sap. 11: 24.** The reference is to the Latin (*Vulgate*) version of the Bible, to the Book of Wisdom or *Sapientia*, which has 'But thou hast mercy upon all, because thou canst do all things.' The Book of Wisdom is one of seven so-called 'Sapiential', or 'wisdom books' of the Septuagint Old Testament, which include Job, Psalms, Proverbs, Ecclesiastes, Song of Solomon and Ecclesiasticus (Sirach). The Book of Wisdom is non-canonical for Protestants and Jews. In the book, Wisdom is depicted as a feminine personification of an attribute of God, i.e., Sophia; she is 'a breath of the power of God, and a clear effluence of the glory of the Almighty.' The text of the Book of Wisdom can be read in *Cambridge Annotated Study Apocrypha*, ed. by Howard Clarke Kee (Cambridge: CUP, 1989), pp. 38—58.

[258] **Hab. 3: 2.** The reference is to the Prophesy of Habakkuk (or Habacuc), or The Book of Habakkuk, 'O Lord, I have heard thy hearing, and was afraid. O Lord, thy work, in the midst of the years bring it to life: In the midst of the years thou shalt make it known: when thou art angry, thou wilt remember mercy.' (For Habakkuk—see Glossary.)

[259] **Ps. 102: 10 & 13.** 'He hath not dealt with us according to our sins: nor rewarded us according to our iniquities.' 'As a father hath compassion on his children, so hath the Lord compassion on them that fear him.' (*Vulgate*)

[260] **Sap. 12: 2.** Again, this is a reference to the Book of Wisdom (Sapientia): 'And therefore thou chastisest them that err, by little and little: and admonishest them, and speakest to them, concerning the things wherein they offend: that leaving their wickedness, they may believe in thee, O Lord.'

[261] **Sap. 27.** This reference is clearly a misprint because there are not 27 books in the Book of Wisdom. The verse to which Bergier referred is likely to have been ch. 3 vs.10 'But the wicked shall be punished according to their own devices: who have neglected the just, and have revolted from the Lord,' or 3: 11—'For he that rejecteth wisdom, and discipline, is unhappy: and their hope is vain, and their labours without fruit, and their works unprofitable.'

or punished them without any regard to their virtues or crimes. He would cast down bolts of lightning for no other reason than to satisfy his vengeance and he placed so–called heroes in heaven who were burdened with labours, and he subjected himself to the laws of blind destiny, which he could not obey himself.

It is pointless to go over again the dogma of predestination which renders God a tyrant, who has destined the human race for horrible torment and from whom only a small number of his elect people will be spared through his absolute will.[262] We have already pointed out that no Catholic Christian has ever believed or preached this mindless dogma. Faith teaches us that God has placed our salvation into our own hands and that our vocation and the choice God makes for us are assured through our good works.

It is an error to say that fear is incompatible with love: the more a child loves his father tenderly, the more he fears displeasing him and the more he dreads his indignation. It is not surprising that a philosopher, who doubts the existence of God and Providence, has trouble in conceiving how one could love him. The righteous alone are worthy of enjoying the charms of this virtue and it is through their faithfulness in observing the Lord's law that they bear testimony to their love for him.

It is another error to posit that it is impossible to love one's neighbour as oneself, and that one can only love him in proportion to the advantages one derives from this relationship, and that it is impossible to love one's enemies. By maintaining these paradoxes, the author of *Christianity Unveiled* does not do justice to the feelings of his heart. Fortunately he contradicts himself when he says, '*Man becomes virtuous as soon as he does something good for his neighbour; he shows a generosity of spirit when he sacrifices his love of self for that of another.*'[263] When one sacrifices one's self–interest and love of self in favour of another, is that not the same as loving one's neighbour as oneself? Cicero, a more rational thinker than our critic, did not recognize friendship in a man who loved himself more than he loved his friend:[264] he

---

[262] See pp. 67 *et seqq.*

[263] See p. 99.

[264] *De Legibus*, I, 1, n. 34. Cicero, *Of Laws*: 'It is to this essential union between the naturally honorable, and the politically expedient, that this sentence of Pythagoras refers:—"Love is universal: let its benefits be universal likewise." From whence it appears that when a wise man is attached to a good man by that friendship whose rights are so extensive, that phenomenon takes place which is altogether incredible to worldlings, and yet it is a necessary consequence, that he loves himself not more dearly than he loves his friend. For how can a difference of interests arise where all interests are similar? If there could be such a difference of interests, however minute, it would be no longer a true friendship, which vanishes immediately when, for the sake of our own benefit, we would sacrifice that of our friend.'

said that to seek our own advantage and not that of others is not friendship, but a base trade–off of interests.[265]

On commanding us to love our enemies, Jesus Christ explained what it meant: wishing them well and doing them a good turn, and praying for those who persecute and slander us.[266] He showed us by his own personal example that this is not an impossible precept and his disciples practised it to the letter. The philosophers' morality confines itself to forbidding vengeance, but the gospel permits neither hate nor resentment. Pagan sages singled out beneficence as a mark of a generous spirit: Jesus Christ commands it as a means of pleasing God and showing ourselves to be like him. So let it be said which of these things is the most perfect.

[...]

---

[265] *De Nat. Deor.*, **I, 1, n.123**. Cicero, *De Natura Deorum* {*On the Nature of Gods*}: 'If we base our friendship on its profit to ourselves, and not on its advantage to those whom we love, it will not be friendship at all, but a mere bartering of selfish interests. That is our standard of value for meadows and fields and herds of cattle: we esteem them for the profits that we derive from them; but affection and friendship between men is disinterested; how much more so therefore is that of the gods, who, although in need of nothing, yet both love each other and care for the interest of men.' In fact, the correct reference should read 'Book I, Section 122' and not '123'. (See Cicero, *Nature of the Gods & Academics*, translated by H. Rackham [Cambridge, Mass.: Harvard University Press—Loeb Classical Library, 2000], p. 119.)

[266] **Matt. 5: 44 & Luke 6: 27**. 'But I say unto you, Love your enemies, bless them that curse you, do good to them that hate you, and pray for them which despitefully use you, and persecute you,' and 'But I say unto you which hear, Love your enemies, do good to them which hate you.'

Chapter 16

Conclusion

§ 11

The author of *Christianity Unveiled*, state–appointed advisor to sovereigns, enjoins them to despise religion and to establish an atmosphere of tolerance and freedom of thought.[267] He says, '*By promoting these things a prince will always be master of his own state.*' That is by no means assured and experience has shown us to the contrary. Supporters of free–thinking are even more covetous of the right to freedom of action and this claim may have far–reaching consequences. Always ready to discuss the rights of sovereigns, they are never so submissive as when they are weakened.

Not content with just wishing the revolution well, for which he has already drawn up a plan, our critic, suddenly elevated to the status of prophet, dares to announce its fulfilment. After having demanded that we '*relegate to Asia a religion brought forth by the ardent imagination of Eastern peoples*', he announces that one happy day Europe will become rational and free, and that '*truth will ultimately triumph over lies*'.[268] That's what we hope, but in a different sense. Europe, disabused of false and murderous principles which for more than a century have been forced upon people and infected them through religious disbelief, is already rendering its just deserts to its imperious masters. Europe knows that these philosophers do not toil to make nations rational, but to intoxicate them with philosophical fanaticism, which is a thousand times more dangerous than religious fanaticism, and that their plan is not to make men more free, but to bind them to the yoke of foolish ideas: they think less about allowing social virtues to reign, but to strike at the very foundations of virtue and society itself. One can sense that philosophical pride and disdainfulness are not appropriate for forming good citizens and that they turn people into cynics and madmen, and that in former times the predecessors of these superb doctors were the object of scorn and public derision—a fate no more honourable these people merit today. For its part the government has no difficulty in seeing that, under the particular pretext of establishing sovereign authority upon the ruins of religion, these dangerous policies merely lead towards shaking off the yoke of all authority, and that, in essence, these philosophers preach the despotism of religion as a ploy to establish anarchy.

---

[267] *Christ. Unveil.*, **p. 292.** (This edition, p. 159.) *Letter to Eugenia*, **p. 68.**
[268] See p. 159.

The philosophers have expended all that they know and hate to inspire people against religion; henceforth their eloquence is arid and all that is left for them is servile repetition. Their readers, eager at first for something novel, have now begun to weary of their jejune repetitions; all the philosophical brochures they churn out daily will soon be consigned to oblivion; those who supported the same cause a century ago are already less well–known and less sought–after now. It is now fifty years since England was the grand theatre of all these anti–religious arguments and English philosophers, just as formidable as ours, had hatched a plan to wipe out Christianity in their country, but now they are fully refuted, exposed and silenced. With commendable emulation, French philosophers have stepped into the abandoned breach and today we have the glorious pleasure of sending back to the English their philosophical debris, disguised *à la française*. Just as fashions are of short duration in our country, the fad of disbelief will soon pass like all the rest. The sickness we caught from our neighbours will soon run its course, like leprosy or St Anthony's fire.[269]

We have a sure guarantee of our hopes while the august blood of Blessed Louis shall remain on the throne and we shall have no fear of revolutions either in religion, or in politics.[270] The Christian religion, founded on the Word of God, has always been victorious when blows have smitten it throughout the centuries and it has always been strengthened by the buffeting which seemed to have shaken it, and it will triumph once again over these new philosophers, just as it triumphed over those of the ancients. Its proofs, when better studied, will deal the final *coup de grâce* to all minds through its brilliance, and its morality shall endure to touch all hearts even more effectively, and its worship, purged of all foreign taint, shall appear even more worthy of respect; its ministers, ever under the scrutiny of jealous enemies, shall take stock of themselves and become irreproachable, and the philosophers themselves shall increase in wisdom and blush at their excesses, and they will learn to respect a religion whose benefits they so unjustly do

---

[269] 'St Anthony's fire is a name given to ergotism, i.e., the illness caused by eating the diseased transformation of the seed of rye and other grasses, such as wheat, which is really the sclerotium or hardened mycelium of a fungus (Claviceps purpurea), in colour dark-violet, and in form resembling a cock's spur. Eating this mould can produce hallucinations, but it can also produce a burning heat or fever, and it can cause inflammation. It is also a disease viewed as a consuming agency. St Anthony's fire is a name for one or more inflammatory or gangrenous diseases of the skin, variously identified with erysipelas, ergotism, etc.,' (OED, CD-Rom, 2004.)

[270] Clearly, this is a reference to Louis XV, whose sobriquet was ironically 'Louis le Bien-Aimé' {'Louis the Well-beloved'}: his ineffectual rule contributed to the decline of royal authority which led to the outbreak of the French Revolution in 1789. Louis died in 1774.

273

not recognize. God, who watches over his handiwork, has no need of our feeble hands to sustain him, but by consecrating ourselves to the service of this holy religion, we have dedicated to him our watchfulness and our travails; sometimes the humblest of his instruments are used by him to accomplish his designs. '*The Lord bringeth the counsel of the heathen to nought: he maketh the devices of the people of none effect. The counsel of the Lord standeth for ever, the thoughts of his heart to all generations*', (Ps. 32: 10—11).

Figure 43: *Lying in State of the Late Pope Pius IX.* **Kissing the Pope's feet: an illustration from** *The Graphic,* **23 February 1878.**

Figure 44: Benedictine Nun (*c.* 1846).

Figure 45: Friedrich Melchior, Baron von Grimm (1723—1807).

'Letter to Sophie or Reproaches Addressed to a Young Philosopher'

By Grimm[1]

Sophie, whence comes this passion of yours for philosophy, unknown in people of your sex and age? How is it that in the flower of your youth, possessed, along with your girl–friends as you ought, of such a hunger for pleasure and absorbed with looking your best, you either know nothing of those things or you neglect your natural advantages by giving yourself over to meditation and study? If what **Tronchin** says is true, that in forming you, nature delighted in placing the soul of an eagle in a house of gossamer, then at least bear in mind that first amongst your duties is to cherish this unique handiwork.

Is it that you are exercised by the principle of so many of the contradictions found in man which, since time began, has always been the source of wonder and the object of philosophical enquiry? Man, so physically feeble yet so intellectually intrepid, audacious at times yet timorous, proud but retiring, who assesses time and space in the batting of an eyelid, and yet knows not how to quell the emotions in his blood. He is given life but for a moment, still he sets himself up as arbiter of the blind and inflexible laws of necessity, which are ever ready to carry him away. Through unrelenting reasoning he enervates his delicate, frail constitution, he assails his life to its very foundations when all around urges him simply to revel in it. Illusion is the force of its sweetest pleasures, error and lies beset it on all sides, and man

---

[1] This is a translation of Grimm's Letter to Sophie Volland in which he discusses *Christianity Unveiled*. The letter was dated 15 August 1763 and the original can be found in Grimm, Friedrich Melchior, von Baron, *Correspondance littéraire, philosophique et critique addressée à un souverain d'Allemagne, 1753—1769*, 16 vols (Paris: Lonchamps, 1813), V, pp. 367 *et seqq.* (For Volland, Sophie—see Glossary.) The style is florid, lofty and complex, and Grimm's sentences are a mass of subordinate clauses which can be achieved with greater economy and neatness in French than in English, for reasons of grammar. There is also not a little hint of intellectual smugness and haughtiness about it, characteristic of the age and milieu in which it was written. I have made little attempt to neutralize or tone down the masculo-centric nature of the piece by using the more gender-inclusive terms 'people' or 'one'—the original is elliptical enough, as already explained, and such padding would make it sound clumsy and render it even more verbose than it already is in translation. However, it is an interesting piece and attests to the fact that Grimm did not know who the author of *Christianity Unveiled* was at the time of writing, although he came to discover this later, and he perceptively spotted that the style was certainly not that of Voltaire, as was rumoured.

travails tirelessly to dispel them. Truth reveals only doubts and uncertainties and man burns to find out life's secrets: the vanity of having dared contemplate it seems to be his consolation and the fruit of his searching, but it yields also the fatal knowledge of its emptiness.

Sophie, the imagination is a source of such grandeur, but also of so much misery. This quality, which is man's crown, is at once so sublime, yet so lugubrious, and it constantly confounds the order and harmony of his constitution. The more vivid and forceful it is, the more easily his delicate, supple organs are troubled, and he is given over to the force of external objects, rendering him the play thing of all extraneous impressions. It is she, the imagination, Sophie, that has turned us into liars and poets, has taught us to exaggerate all our ideas and change their whole constitution. It is she that has created this phantasmagoria of illusionary, chimerical beings, through which she established connections with us: she has attributed supernatural and mythical causes to all physical and unavoidable misfortunes, and when man's duty comes down to being happy, just and beneficent, it is she who formed a bizarre code of imaginary, artificial duties, perverting the goal of our existence, corrupting our nature, turning us into cruel, religious and absurd beings, set against the whole earth.

Man's wayward ways therefore are grounded in the same principle which has also immortalized his genius through so many of his masterpieces. A being endowed with imagination should have substituted reality for chimeras, simple facts for systems of lies and fables. The delicate nature of our organs, without which imagination has neither leeway nor strength, made us feeble, thoughtless, fearful and perturbed, and instead of trying to get to the bottom of the true, physical causes of so many diverse impressions—so hidden and so reluctant to reveal themselves—our taste for fiction has everywhere substituted moral and imaginary causes. Just consider, Sophie, those massive edifices that error has always elevated alongside immutable truth, and you will find, perhaps, that man's genius in his waywardness is no less fecund, no less varied, than is evident in the products of his handiwork, and that to think up such absurdities and chimeras cost him more effort than he would have expended in accounting for and finding out the immutable, eternal laws of the universe.

You who like going back to fundamental principles and possess a brilliant, lively imagination to uncover the different forms and transformations through which mankind, at the dawn of comprehending our history, must have passed to date, you can see amongst all peoples the ancient vestiges of religious faith—sometimes simple and crude, and so closely resembling the rustic naïveté of primitive mores—and sometimes sophisticated and unintelligible, and as such, all the more revered—but they are all always based on deception and on man's insurmountable penchant for looking for supernatural causes to explain physical phenomena. This is the way fables of the existence of invisible beings, of the non–material, of the immortality of souls—conceived by the most spiritual of people and imbued with a fertile mythology in poetry and images—were passed on to the most vulgar nations: for these people do not possess sufficient imagination to invent their own myths, yet they had the wherewithal to delight in the lies they were offered, and if simple right–thinking can satisfy a few wise men, absurd, extravagant beliefs ought to exert a general and absolute power over those people who know of no other, more pressing, need, or of more delightful pleasures than that of being moved by unseen, mysterious causes, or being transported by images.

It is a lofty and philosophical outlook which attributes the first religious ideas of ancient peoples to the physical revolutions of our globe. The first glimpses we cast upon the history of nature prove to us both the antiquity of the earth and the distress that it must have felt. Man, in the grip of great physical calamities, was bound to look for unknown causal powers; he was bound to have created gods for himself and render himself the object of their love or their hate. Animals, having escaped danger, soon lose all memory of it until it is revived again when beset by, and in the grip of, a fresh peril; but man's imagination, assailed by perils which threaten his existence and shaken by nature's great phenomena, must soon have created a system of punishments and rewards concomitant with the myth of a vengeful god, angered by the foibles of human frailty. Despite attributes of goodness, justice and beneficence, with which we have a mind to embellish the Divinity, you will find, Sophie, that in all he says and does, the God of Nations is a capricious, cruel, bizarre, vindictive and ferocious being: amongst whichever people he finds himself, he seeks to drag and immire them in crimes for the sole, barbarous pleasure of punishing them and exacting his vengeance upon them. Such is the god of the Jews, whom Christians, notwithstanding all their metaphysical subtleties, have never managed to render truly just and benevolent towards humanity; such is blind, implacable Destiny amongst almost all nations, which decides the happiness and virtue of mortals in the course of their inescapable fate. One was right to say that, without the fear of a vengeful, pernicious force, the idea of God would never have entered into men's heads.

Quite by chance the other day I found a copy of *Moral and Philosophical Epistles* by an English poet whose name I do not know.[2] Quite unintentionally I opened this collection, which has only just come out, and I found in it an engraving which struck me as being quite wonderful. It was a

---

2   It is not known to which volume Grimm refers here: the editors of Grimm's *Correspondance* have been unable to trace any such work.

picture of a wood carver, busy finishing off a figure of a crane on his workbench. Whilst he was working on carving the legs, which had not yet fully taken on their finished form, his wife was already prostrate before the crane, teaching her child to worship it. It was the words of Lucretius writ large:

Quod finxere timent.[3]

Sophie, such is the genius of man: as soon as he invents his ghosts, he takes fright of them himself.

I am giving your messenger a copy of *Research into the Origin of Oriental Despotism*, which you requested of me. You will find some of these ideas developed in there. It is the work of a bold and a rather rough–and–ready philosopher. He does not try to ease you into the truth little by little, but he unceremoniously rips off the blindfold of one's misconceptions straight away. You might forgive me such audacity; you would desire in your guide at least that charm which seduces and captivates the mind, that which beautifies the most severe truth. A pure and readable style, a gentle, nuanced, friendly approach make philosophy touching and inspires in us confidence and passion for the medium. The Greeks taught us to love grace combined with forcefulness; let those who would seek to enlighten and instruct us imitate the manner of our masters' style.

You spurn systems and reckless assertions of all kinds and will perhaps reproach the philosopher for your reading something that sets out his opinions too forcefully and for having given you something already proven and wholly plausible. You want, Sophie, that the person to whom you wish to entrust your teaching should give no greater weight to his ideas by way of evidence than you can give to them yourself; you want him to involve you in his work and research, something that does not reveal all at a stroke to you, leaving you nothing to think about and puzzle over yourself. People need clear truths to share in common, and usefulness and honesty can have only one sense in any language, and morality should not be a theoretical discipline; but the philosopher who deals with fundamental issues, who goes back to first principles, who seeks to fathom the genius of nature and man, should only write for minds practised in the art of meditation. The more the questions he broaches are shrouded in doubt and obscurity, the less he should allow himself to be carried away, infatuated by his own ideas, and the less importance he attaches to them, the more one will be disposed to find meaning in them. A lofty, sublime overview, a profound and illuminating

---

[3]   'Men fear what they fashion.'

idea, carelessly dashed down on paper, will capture your attention more surely than a truth which has been laboriously unfolded by a dogmatic writer.

Let us banish, Sophie, banish for ever from our own research that sad, sterile methodology, whose least mistake is to have taught ordinary minds to encroach upon the language and rights of men of genius. The march of truth is like lightening sent forth from the firmament, which flares up in a moment and illuminates everything. You will notice its effect in an instant, and such a fleeting moment is sufficient for minds such as yours: the minds of others are like children, whom the charlatan entertains by faking meteors in the sky; there are those who, the more they are blinded, the happier they are. Let us leave the charlatans to their work and not waste our time with them.

The philosopher sends his greetings and misses you.[4] He has caused me grief these last few days because he knew the day of the month and the week, but he maintains that it is your absence which is the cause of his negligence. Sophie, if he never learns to date his letters, just put it down to his happiness and genius. Come back home so that he will not be in your debt to this miserable science [i.e., letter–writing]. We are counting the minutes, waiting for you to be brought back to the bosom of friendship and philosophy. We take walks in the evening on the terrace by the quiet banks of the Seine, but our conversations are less lively and your shouts of indiscrete joy do not penetrate the night's silence. As for other matters, we constantly discuss the power of truth. He constantly sees truth and virtue as two great statues, towering over the surface of the earth, motionless in the midst of the ravages and ruins of all that is around. For my part, I also see those statues, but on a pedestal which, for me, seems beset by errors and prejudices, encircled by a blundering herd of simpletons who are unable to raise their eyes above the dais on which they stand, or if amongst them there are a few favoured beings who possess the penetrating eye of an eagle with which they manage to pierce the clouds obscuring those grand figures, they quickly become the objects of hate and persecution by a small, vicious crowd, who are full of presumptuousness and stupidity. What does it matter that these two statues are eternal and immobile, if there is no one to contemplate them, or if the fate of him who notices them does not differ from that of the blind man walking in darkness? The philosopher assures me that the moment will come when the clouds will open up and men will prostrate themselves before it, and they will see the truth and render homage to virtue. That moment, Sophie, shall resemble the moment when the Son of God shall descend amidst the clouds. We beseech you that your return to us will be less distant in time.

---

[4] Grimm is referring to Diderot.

Notes added by Grimm.

The *Research into the Origin of Oriental Despotism*, mentioned above, was printed in Geneva about a year ago, but very few copies have found their way into France. It is a posthumous work by the late Monsieur Boulanger, inspector of bridges and highways. His profession often involved him in examining strata of earth and he dedicated himself to studying natural history, and since the initial stages of his scientific studies convinced him of the necessity of going right back into distant antiquity, he applied himself with ever greater ardour to studying ancient languages—Hebrew in particular. He rapidly made great strides in this, as his *Research into the Origin of Oriental Despotism* bears testimony. He died four years ago in the prime of life, not being, I believe, more than thirty–six years old. He was just as already noted—a little rough–and–ready as a philosopher, but the audacity of his views is sometimes astonishing, though he has the propensity of repeating himself all too often. Were his book to be shorter generally, and his ideas delivered in a less dogmatic tone, then it would have a far greater impact. At the beginning of this *Research* is a letter addressed to Monsieur Helvétius at the time of the great uproar caused by his book *On The Mind*.[5] This piece is better written than Monsieur Boulanger's work itself. This author had also left several other manuscripts which are to be found in the libraries of people curious about such matters, but death interrupted him from putting the finishing touches to any of these works.

Christianity Unveiled

There is a book entitled *Christianity Unveiled, or An Examination of the Principles and the Effects of the Christian Religion*, by the late Monsieur Boulanger, a volume in–8°. First, one notes that it has been given this title to match the volume *Antiquity Unveiled*: however, it does not take much to recognize that these two works have not come from the same pen. It is also equally certain that the provenance of the work in question is not Ferney at all,[6] because I rather think that the patriarch[7] would have moved heaven and earth to distribute it—that would have been a less impossible task than for him to have abandoned his form and style so completely, so there is not a

---

[5]   This is a reference to Helvétius' book *On the Mind*—see Introduction, pp. xliv & lii.
[6]   Ferney was the place in France, close to the Swiss border and near Geneva, where Voltaire built his chateau so that he would be able to escape quickly abroad, should the need arise on account of his writing and publishing contentious material.
[7]   I.e., Voltaire.

single trace of him in it. For the same reason I do not think that this is a work of any philosopher known to us, because I can detect nothing of any of their written styles in it. So whence does it hail? I certainly wouldn't mind knowing and I think that the author has done right not to have let anyone in on his secret. It is the most daring and most shocking book that has ever appeared anywhere in the world. The preface consists of a letter wherein the author examines whether religion is really necessary either as a mere useful means for maintaining law and order, or for policing empires, and as such, whether it merits any respect at all. As he establishes his opinion in the negative, consequently he undertakes to prove throughout the work the absurdity and incoherence of Christian dogma and the mythology that stems from it, and its absurd influence upon people's hearts and minds. In the second part he examines Christian morality and he maintains that its general principles hold no advantage over any other moral code anywhere else in the world, because justice and kindness are features of all world catechisms, and that not a single people, be they ever so barbarous, has ever taught the necessity of being unjust and wicked. As far as Christianity's singular moral features go, the author asserts that they are fit only for extremists who are rather unsuitable for duties within the world's societies. In the third part, he undertakes to prove that the Christian religion has had the most sinister and disastrous political effects, and that the human race owes to Christianity all the misfortunes that have assailed it for the last fifteen to eighteen centuries, and that there is still no end of it in sight. This book is written with more vehemence than real eloquence: it also drags on somewhat. His style is polished and correct, although it is a little harsh and dry, and his tone is solemn and sustained. There is nothing original in it, and yet it grips the reader's interest. Despite his unbelievable temerity, there is no denying that the author is an upright man who passionately has the prosperity and welfare of society at heart. Having said that, I think that his good intentions would prove to be a rather feeble excuse were a compulsory judicial writ, or an indictment, to be served upon him.

Figure 46: Voltaire (1694—1778). (Source: Wikipedia.)

Letter No. 6613—To Madame de Saint–Julien from Voltaire on *Christianity Unveiled.*

15 December[1]

Most charming butterfly of philosophy, of society, and of love! I would have been enchanted to have seen you honour my confinement again with one of your appearances—you would even have been my first doctor, since it is about two months since I left my bed at all.

Do you know, Madame, that I have some very serious things to say in response to the highly moral, but undated, letter you wrote to me? You inform me that in your social circles, *Christianity Unveiled*, by the late Monsieur Boulanger, is being attributed to me, but I can assure you that in fact people do not attribute this work to me at all. I share your view that there is a good deal of clarity and warmth, and sometimes even eloquence, in the writing. However, it is full of repetitions, oversights and linguistic slips, and were I to have written it, I should have deeply regretted it, not only as an academician, but also as a philosopher, and even more so as a citizen.

The book is diametrically opposed to my principles. This book leads to atheism, which I absolutely detest. I have always regarded atheism as the gravest of rational errors because it is ridiculous to say that the composition of the world belies a supreme Craftsman, and that it would be impudent to say that a watch denies the existence of a watchmaker.[2]

---

[1] Voltaire, *Œuvres Complètes*, XLIV (Paris: Garnier, 1881), pp. 534—535.

[2] Voltaire had already expressed this view in 1734: see *Œuvres Complètes*, XXII, p. 194. He had also stated the same idea in some satirical verses entitled *Cabals* (see Volume X), composed in 1772, and translated below without any attempt to reflect the poetic style:

[...]

> It is true I mocked Saint-Médard and the papal bull;
> But I still have some qualms about nature.
> The universe perplexes me, and for me it is unthinkable
> That this watch exists, yet without a watchmaker.

Thirty years later, Voltaire argued with Pierre Louis Moreau de Maupertuis (1698—1759), a mathematician, on the very same issue and he used the same argument.

The papal bull referred to in Voltaire's poem is the '*Unigenitus Dei Filius*', issued by Pope Clement XI on Sept. 8, 1713, which condemned the doctrines of Jansenism (essentially Calvinism with a twist), a dissident religious movement within the French Catholic Church. The publication of the bull began a doctrinal controversy in France that lasted throughout much of the eighteenth century. One of the chief opponents of the bull was Francis of Paris, who died and was buried in the cemetery of Saint-

Nor do I condemn this book any less as a citizen: the author seems to be too much of an enemy of the powers that be. Men who think like him would only form an anarchic clique, and I can see to what extent anarchy is to be feared by the example of Geneva.[3]

It is my custom to write my thoughts in the margins of my books and you will see, when you come to Ferney, the margins of my copy of *Christianity Unveiled* bursting with notes, which show that the author is wrong on so many of the most essential facts.

I find it painful, Madame, that the malice and the casualness of those butterflies in your area, who have neither your intellect nor your grace, continuously put down to me works like these, that are sufficient to be the ruination of those so imputed.

As regards the Maréchal de Richelieu, I am not at all surprised that he did not have time to speak to the Count of Saint–Florentin about the unfortunate family which had aroused your compassion—he was about to go off to Bordeaux. Your kind soul did all it could. Through your kind offices this family is already getting an allowance at his expense—funds that are being squeezed out of him for having given supper to a fool of a heretic priest twenty–six years ago. When I have a favour to ask on behalf of some poor unfortunates, I shall ask for a good word from you, Madame, when I seek help from the Duke of Choiseul. I have importuned him several times with my indiscrete requests and he has always deigned to grant me what I took the liberty of asking him for. I fear I might exhaust his kind offices, were it not for knowing through you the extent of his largess.

Come to Ferney, Madame. We shall sing its praises and yours, as a prologue for an opera *Pandora's Box*, and you shall be my Pandora, but you won't open the box.

Please accept, Madame, the respect and affection of an old recluse.

Médard, and his followers claimed that his grave in the cemetery was the site of a number of miracles.

3   The reference to Geneva is to the fact that, as a city, it had got rid of its Catholic bishop and declared itself an independent state in the sixteenth century, and it was also the city in which Calvin made his home for a time—one of the pivotal figures in the theological upheavals of the Reformation, which split the church in Europe for ever. Geneva in the eighteenth century was at the zenith of its prosperity. Material wealth stimulated a burst of culture and artistic creativity. As the birthplace of Rousseau and the sanctuary of Voltaire, Geneva attracted the elite of the Enlightenment and helped to foster the development of the new political science, derived from natural law.

Remarks
On

Christianity Unveiled, or An Examination of the Principles and the Effects of the Christian Religion[1]

Title: *Christianity Unveiled.*

This work is more full of rhetoric than methodology. The author repeats and contradicts himself sometimes. People will say that it is 'irreligiosity unveiled'.

Preface: *'In a word, religion changes people's basic instincts not a jot and they only listen to it when it suits their desires.'[2]*

What does he mean by '*suits*'? That is a really strange turn of phrase nowadays.

'Despite Christianity's pointlessness and the perverse morality it teaches, its adherents dare to tell us that without it, there can be no mores.'[3]

Can one call Jesus Christ's morality 'perverse'?

Chapter I: *'If people's mores had nothing to gain from Christianity, the power of kings, who purport to support religion, would not have derived great benefit from it.'*

What? Would it have been better to sacrifice men to Teutates?[4]

Chapter II: *'This man, known by the name of Moses, had had a good education in a religion[5] well–known for its rich supply of prodigies and for*

---

[1]   From Voltaire, *Œuvres Compètes* (Paris: Garnier, 1880), XXXI, pp.129—133.
[2]   In fact, Voltaire misquotes d'Holbach's text: he writes the word 'duties', not 'desires'. Voltaire, op.cit., p. 129. (This edition, p. 8.)
[3]   Ibid., p. 10.
[4]   Ibid., p. 19. Teutates is an ancient Celtic god who was worshipped especially in Gaul. He is the god of war, fertility and wealth. His name means 'the god of the tribe', from the Gallic *touta* which means 'tribe' or 'people' (similar to the Celtic *tuatha*). Teutates is also known under the names of Albiorix ('king of the world') and Caturix ('king of the battle'). Human sacrifices were made to appease him. He is the equivalent of the Roman god Mars.
[5]   In fact, Voltaire uses the word 'region' not 'religion'. (This edition, p. 21.)

being the mother of superstitions. Moses assumed the position of leader of a hoard of fugitives, whom he persuaded that he was the interpreter of the will of their god, [and that he personally conversed with him],[6] *receiving his orders directly from him.'*

So does the author admit, then, the authenticity of the books of Moses?

'[...] *the Jewish nation waited for a messiah, a monarch, a liberator, who would free them from the yoke under which they travailed, to raise them up to reign over all nations of the universe.'*[7]

Not as far as their prosperity went, because the Jews had no need of one at that time.

Chapter III: '"Peace on earth and goodwill to all men"—*that's how the gospel was presented to men, which has cost the human race more spilt blood than all other religions of the world put together.'*[8]

This is not an accurate quotation.

'*The fleeting chastisements of this life are the only ones mentioned by the Hebrew lawgiver: the Christian sees his barbarous god pouring forth unbounded vengeance for time without end. In a word, Christian fanaticism feeds upon the revolting idea of a hell...'*[9]

The author forgets that other religions included a hell long before Christianity.

Chapter IV: '*It is constantly stated that it is in another life that God's justice will be demonstrated, but in that case, we cannot call him just in this world, especially since we so often witness virtue oppressed and vice rewarded.'* [10]

This can be said of all other religions which lay claim to an afterlife, just as well as it can be levelled against Christianity.

---

[6] This passage is omitted in Voltaire's original text: he may have been using an earlier edition.

[7] This edition, p. 24.

[8] Ibid., p. 29.

[9] Ibid.

[10] Voltaire's text has 'crime'. This edition, p. 37.

Chapter V: '*Before being in a position to judge divine revelation, we should have an accurate idea of the divinity.*'[11]

Not at all, if one wants to find out if there are any proofs.

'*Is it not the case that the sincere enquirer into God's revelation, as espoused by Christians, experiences incertitude and fear, which redoubles on reading that this god has aspired to make himself known only to a very few favoured beings, whilst wanting to remain hidden from the rest of humanity [...]?*'[12]

This is not true. The apostles claimed to be sent throughout the whole earth. The author continuously confuses the Mosaic and Christian religions.

'*What was Moses' character like?*'[13]

What does it matter?

'*What ultimate proof do we have of Moses' mission, apart from the testimony of six hundred thousand unsophisticated, superstitious, ignorant, credulous Israelites [...]?*'[14]

If the author gives credence to this testimony, he contradicts himself.

Chapter VI: '*Hence, as far as its claims are concerned, Christianity has no advantage over all other religions which have infected the world.*'[15]

There is no superstitious religious belief amongst the sect of Chinese scholars.

'*Wherever it [i.e., Christianity] reigns, do we not see servile people, devoid of vigour, energy, and activity, wallowing in shameful lethargy and having not a single idea of true morality?*'[16]

Exaggeration!

---

[11]   This edition, p. 41.
[12]   Ibid., p. 42.
[13]   Ibid., p. 45.
[14]   Ibid.
[15]   Ibid., p. 47.
[16]   Ibid.

'At least Muhammad's miracles were enough to convince the Arabs that he was divine.'[17]

Muhammad did not perform any miracles. The only miracle in the Koran is that of the journey from Mecca to Jerusalem in one night.

Chapter VII: *'There can be no doubt that Moses proclaimed a single god to the Hebrews.'*

The author keeps on going against his own principles by attributing the *Pentateuch* to Moses.[18]

'Do we come to know better the divinity when he is described as pure spirit, *as a* non–material being *unlike anything our senses have ever known before? Is the human mind not confused by such negative attributes as* infinity, immensity, eternity, omnipotence, and omniscience, *etc.'*[19]

The author is barking up the wrong tree by countering this idea of God, which is not only a Christian idea, but a universal one.

'How can we reconcile other moral qualities attributed to this god, such as wisdom, benevolence and justice, with his strange and often atrocious conduct as described on every page of the Christian and Hebrew books? Would it not have been better to have left man in total ignorance of this divinity than to reveal a god replete with contradictions […]?'[20]

The ancients gave God the same attributions without revelation or contradictions.

'[…] *the Tartars' god is called* 'Kon–sio–sik', *or* 'single god', *and* 'Kon–sio–fum', *which means* 'triple god'. *They say the words* om, ha, hum, *to their rosary beads, which mean* 'intelligence', 'might', *and* 'power' *or* 'word', 'heart' *and* 'love'.'[21]

The word *oum* [sic] comes from the Brahmins.

---

[17] This edition, p. 48.
[18] Ibid., p. 61.
[19] Ibid.
[20] Ibid.
[21] Ibid., p. 62, footnote.

Chapter VIII: '*We are constantly told that the dogma of rewards and punishments in another life is beneficial for people who, in the absence of that, would surrender themselves without fear to great excesses. By way of reply, I would say that the Jewish lawgiver* [i.e., Moses] *had carefully hidden this so–called mystery, and the dogma of a future life was part of a secret which, in Greek mythology, was revealed to initiates. This dogma was unknown to the common herd* [...]'[22]

> Not so. The idea of a future existence was a common dogma. It was the unity of God that was a secret dogma.

'*If sovereigns governed wisely and fairly, they would have no need of dogmas of rewards and punishments to keep people in check.*'[23]

> All Greek republics admired this dogma.

'*In fact, Christianity acknowledges invisible beings whose nature is different from that of humans...*'[24]

> And Gentiles as well.

Chapter IX: 'Holy water, *which, amongst Christians has taken the place of the Romans' lustral water...*'[25]

> It should say '*amongst Catholics*'.

'*The books after Moses are no less replete with ignorance: Joshua stops the sun in its rotation.*'

> It turns on its axis. It should say, *which does not continue to rotate around the earth.*'[26]

Chapter XI: '*Instead of forbidding debauchery, crime, and vice because God and religion forbid these faults, we should teach that all forms of excess are harmful for the preservation of mankind and make men contemptible in*

---

[22] This edition, p. 69.
[23] Ibid.
[24] Ibid., p. 70.
[25] Ibid., p. 77.
[26] Clearly, Voltaire has not taken Galileo fully into account! See, p. 80.

society's eyes, and that reason forbids it because it wants to sustain humanity, and that Nature prohibits it because it works for man's durable happiness. In a word, notwithstanding God's desires, and independent of the rewards and punishments promised by religion in another life, it is easy to prove to anyone that it is in their interest in this world to take care of their health, to respect the mores of others...'[27]

Why take away from men the restraining influence that a fear of the Divinity gives them? All philosophers, except Epicureans, maintain that one must be just to please God.

'*In countries which boast of possessing Christianity in all its purity, religion has so totally hijacked its followers' attention that they are entirely unaware of morality and believe that they have fulfilled all their social duties as soon as they show a scrupulous attachment to religious minutiae, which are totally at odds with what is needed for a healthy society.*'[28]

This is an abuse of religion—it is not religion.

Chapter XII: '*The entire message of the Messiah, his whole law for us to follow could be summed up as* love God above all else and one's neighbour as oneself.'[29]

And to follow Moses.

Chapter XVI: [From a footnote] '*The Dominican who poisoned Emperor Henry VI...*'[30]

It should read 'Henry VII'.

End of my remarks on *Christianity Unveiled*.

---

[27] This edition p. 96.
[28] Ibid., p. 97.
[29] Ibid., p. 99.
[30] Ibid., p. 154.

Portrait of Baron d'Holbach by Grimm

I saw Monsieur the Baron d'Holbach only during the last years of his life, but in order to know him, to share those feelings of esteem and veneration which all his friends vowed to him, and whose soul and mind could not fail to inspire their characteristic features in all those who came across him, one did not have to have a close and long–standing relationship with him. I shall try to paint his character as it appeared in my eyes, and I dare say that if his spirit could hear me now, I would like to think that the frankness and simplicity of my homage to him would not displease it.[1]

I have never met a more erudite man of letters or anyone who was as universally well–read as Monsieur d'Holbach, and I have never seen a man of his intellectual stature with so little aspiration to be so, or to appear so. One would never have discovered the secret of his vast erudition were it not for the fact that he took a sincere interest in all advances being made in all fields of knowledge and enlightenment, and had he not had a burning desire to pass on to others everything that he thought would be useful for them to know. His fount of knowledge was just like his personal fortune—it was not just at his personal disposal; it was equally available to others, and neither was held just for show... and one would never have suspected him of possessing either, were he to have been able to forego the sheer joy he derived from making these things accessible to his friends, as to himself.

The rapid progress made in natural history and chemistry in our country over the last thirty years is due largely to him: it is he who translated the finest work published by German scholars in these scientific fields, which were almost unknown in France, or at least, they were badly neglected. His translations were richly endowed with excellent notes, which people found so useful, without knowing then to whom they owed their debt—and even today, few actually know.

It is not indiscrete now to admit that he was the author of that infamous book *System of Nature*, which caused such a stir in Europe eighteen or twenty years ago.[2] The whole furore caused by this work did not for a moment tempt him to be arrogant and even though he was fortunate enough to remain out of the limelight of suspicion, it was rather his modesty that served him

---

[1] The original of this piece can be found in Grimm, *Correspondance littéraire*, XIV (1788—1789), pp. 286—293. It was written in March 1789, following d'Holbach's death earlier that year and the obituary published in the *Journal de Paris*, written by Naigeon. Grimm's 'Portrait of Baron d'Holbach' is followed in the volume cited here by an extensive bibliography of his works (pp. 293—297). Grimm's original footnotes have been reproduced here in bold text.

[2] *System of Nature* was published in 1770.

even better in this regard than all his friends' caution. I cannot assent to the doctrine taught in this work with his degree of fanaticism, audacity and verbosity: but all those who knew the author consider it only fair to admit that no self–seeking or personal goal lay behind his attachment to this sorry system of thought. He became a devotee of it with the purest of intentions and with such a degree of self–denial that his depth of faith in it would have honoured an apostle of the holiest of religions.

His *Social System* and *Universal Morality* caused much less of a sensation than his *System of Nature*, but these two works equally demonstrate that, after having desired to overthrow the old barriers that human weakness had believed ought to stand as bulwarks against the vices and passions which dishonour it, the author felt even more keenly that new safeguards ought to be put in their place: these were his faith in a mind illuminated by a good education and by good laws, and in these he fancied he had found the resources which could support a reign of virtue, and, thanks to its happy influence, it would procure for us all the calm and benefits to which our nature is responsive.

Is the remarkable difference between the success of these last two works, as opposed to the notoriety of the first, not enough to show our objection to his system as a whole, and to its impact on morals in particular? The more one limits oneself to destroying the principles which have long served to constrain men's habits and excesses, the easier it is to appeal to them successfully: but when one attempts to substitute different principles for those principles which have doubtlessly been over–exploited, the task becomes incomparably more difficult, and one soon runs the risk of losing all favour gained in the first place.

Besides, it will be agreed that the latter two works differ considerably from the first in terms of their subject matter, but they do not differ less in terms of their talent. The *System of Nature* is extremely unevenly written, crammed full of boring repetitions and pointless declamations; nonetheless there is in it a generally enthusiastic tone and quite an impressive eloquence and philosophical erudition. There are pages in it, in fact a good many pages, in which one readily recognizes the hand of a superior writer, and that is easily understandable because these are the pages written by Diderot. There were many fewer pages in his *Social System* and *Universal Morality*, where one finds that same verbosity as in his *System of Nature*, and there are many excellent principles, but also many places with a common, tendentious methodology, little stylistic dynamism, and a lack of variation in the ideas, as there is also in the way in which they are expressed.

As a fellow citizen and childhood friend of the famous **Lavater**, I might be forgiven, perhaps, for sharing my thoughts to some extent on the Baron's physiognomy: I have always been struck by the connection between his facial characteristics and those of his mind. He had all the normal, regular features which were fairly handsome, yet he was not an attractive man. His large, protruding forehead, just like Diderot's, bore the marks of a vast, extensive mind, but being less convoluted, less rounded, it did not evince the same warmth or the same energy or the same fecundity; his facial expression did not portray the tenderness and the habitual serenity of his soul.

Monsieur the Baron d'Holbach came to believe with the greatest of ease in the power of reason because his fervour (and ours too, by which we always judge that of our equals), was precisely what was necessary to assert the influence of good principles. He loved women and he was extremely partial to the pleasures of the table, without being a slave to either. He was incapable of hating anyone: however, it was not without effort that he feigned a natural horror for priests and for all supporters of despotism and religious superstition. When speaking of them, his gentleness wore thin in spite of himself, and his geniality often became bitter and provocative. One of the most uncontrollable obsessions which consumed him all his life, and particularly so in his twilight years, was an acute sense of curiosity: he loved new discoveries like a child adores toys, and as a consequence he had a kind of blindness—a natural, enthusiastic addiction—which meant that he applied very little discernment to all things good or bad, true or false, and there was nothing that did not hold some kind of fascination for him, in which he was prepared to believe. It really seemed as though all the credulity he spurned with regard to curiosities from the other world, he kept entirely in reserve for those in newspapers and cafés. It amused him to recount in the most glorious detail a 'fact', which all attendant circumstances blatantly announced to be false. 'Do you know the story about what happened yesterday?' 'No.' 'It's simply unbelievable.' 'Oh, well tell us anyway...' How many times he became angry with Monsieur de **Meister**[3] who, by a single word at dinner, shot to pieces a story in which he had taken such a delight in telling that morning under the arches of the Palais–Royal! 'That's just typical of you', he would say with genial irritation; 'You never say anything and you never want to believe in anything.'

Monsieur d'Holbach counted amongst his friends the most famous people of this country—such people as Helvétius, Diderot, d'Alembert, Condillac, Turgot, Buffon, Rousseau, and also many foreigners of worthy note, such as Hume, Garrick, Abbé Galiani, etc.[4] Just as he took delight in such

---

[3] This name has been added by the editor of the piece: originally the name printed in the text was 'Grimm', but it was tought to be a misprint.

[4] **For a long time his house was one of the most favoured haunts of contributors to the *Encyclopédie* and their most famous synagogue. It is all too true that it lost**

distinguished company, who had the ability to lend his mind more power and more scope, one could note that, by the same token, there was not a single one of those illustrious men who had not learned many useful and fascinating things from him. He possessed a magnificent library and the scope of his memory was sufficient unto all the subjects by which his studies had enriched it: he remembered things effortlessly, including all manner of things worthy and unworthy of being retained. 'Whatever system my imagination might come up with', Monsieur Diderot said to me on more than one occasion, 'I am sure that my friend d'Holbach would come up with facts and authorities, by which I might substantiate it.'

Mme Geoffrin would often say of him with the good sense so characteristic her sound judgement: 'I have never seen a more unpretentiously unpretentious man.'

One of the most estimable traits of Monsieur d'Holbach's character was his beneficence; one could not add a more touching example of this than that which Monsieur Naigeon recounted in the *Journal de Paris*: and we shall constrain ourselves to copying that case here.

'Monsieur d'Holbach had in his social circle a man of letters,[5] who for some time seemed pre–occupied, quite and profoundly depressed. Upset by the state in which he saw his friend, he ran round to see him and said, "I do not want to pre–empt any confidence which you feel you ought not to confide in me: I respect your secret, but I see you sad, suffering, and your situation worries and troubles me greatly. I know how little money you have and you could have needs, about which I know nothing. I have brought you ten thousand francs that I have no call for: if you have any friendship for me, do not refuse to accept them, and you can give me them back in a little while, a bit later when your good fortune returns." This friend was touched, moved as one might expect, and he assured him that he had no need of money and that his sadness was due to something else, and so he did not accept this favour offered to him; but he never forgot it and it is from him directly that I got this information.'[6]

Paul Thiry, baron d'Holbach, member of the Academies of St Petersburg, Manheim and Berlin, and born in the Palatinate. He was brought up from his tenderest years in France, where he spent most of his life and died in Paris on

---

some of its former favour when M. d'Holbach's children became established there because he had to cut back on its culinary budget. (Author's Note.)

[5] The name given by the author in a footnote is **Suard** (see Glossary).

[6] See pp. 301.

21 January 1789, aged sixty–six.[7] Having lost his first wife, Mademoiselle d'Aîne, at a very early age, he obtained permission from the Court of Rome to marry her sister, who survived her. He leaves behind him two sons and two daughters, one of whom married the Marquis of Châtenay, and the other married the Count of Nolivos.

---

[7] Here is yet another example of the many men of virtue who have no belief in God whatsoever, but have a firm belief in morality, and for whom their atheism is the foundation of all their ethics. Despite being a Deist, it is the person of d'Holbach that Rousseau portrayed so warmly and so faithfully in the character of Wolmar in his novel *La Nouvelle Héloïse* and it is of him that Julie says, '*He is so benevolent without expecting any sort of reward; he is more virtuous and selfless than us.*' We are going to add this judicious observation as a note in Diderot, *Works*, Volume XII, p. 115 (Paris, 1821). The author of this piece would like to announce that he has long been engaged in collecting materials which will avenge the outrages committed against d'Holbach, this beneficient philosopher, who has been their target. We now believe that the moment has finally come when we can publish, without danger, a list of the works already published [anonymously or pseudonymously] to rehabilitate the memory of this philosopher, who was the most unbelieving and most beneficent man of his century. This list of d'Holbach's works has been compiled according to the most authoritative sources: we believe it to be useful to put these references into the public arena, because it is evident that society attaches as much interest and importance to religious issues as ever, as it strives to reform itself on information commonly put out which all positive minds ruthlessly reject; and we look to the time when society will finally come of age as the prejudices which have beset us since childhood will finally be snuffed out.
There then follow several pages of bibliographical information listing d'Holbach's works, several of them being marked by asterisks to indicate the sentence pronounced on them by the *Parlement* on 18 August 1770 and 16 February 1776, condemning them to be burned by the public executioner. Much of this information would have come as a surprise, if not a shock, to the readers of the journal. Some of this information has been superseded by the monumental research done by Vercruysse (see Bibliography).

Numéro 40.   171

JOURNAL DE PARIS.

Lundi 9 Février 1789, de la Lune le 15

Le Soleil se leve à 7 heur. 5 minut. , & se couche à 4 heur. 55 minut.

La Lune se leve à 4 heur. 33 min. du soir , & se couche à 6 h. 38 m. après minuit.

Rapport du Tems vrai au Tems moyen. Au midi du soleil, la pendule doit marq. 0 h. 14 m. 39 s.

Hauteur de la Rivière. Le 7 à 4 p. 6 p. , & le 8 à 4 p. 6 p. (haut. moyenne 5 pieds.)

Réverbères. Non allumés jusqu'au 10.

	Époques.	Thermom.	Baromèt.	Vent.	État du Ciel & Remarques.
Observations Météorologiques du Sam. 7 Fév.	A 7 h. m.	+ 4, 2	27. 6, 7	O. fort.	Couvert & grand vent toute la journée , petite pluie par intervalle.
	A 10 m.	+ 5, 5	27. 7, 6		
	A 11 ¼ s.	+ 3, 8	27. 10, 1		

NÉCROLOGIE.

Lettre sur la mort de M. le Baron d'Holbach.

Non hoc præcipuum amicorum munus est prosequi defunctum ignavo questu. Tacit. (1)

Permettez-moi , Messieurs , de consacrer dans votre Journal quelques lignes à la mémoire d'un homme dont la perte irréparable excite aujourd'hui les justes regrets de ses amis , de ceux qui le connoissoient à peine , & plonge sa famille dans une douleur aussi touchante que vraie. La pratique habituelle & constante de toutes les vertus qui font le plus d'honneur à la nature humaine , lui avoit mérité l'estime publique , & cette espèce de vénération dont les ames honnêtes se sentent naturellement pénétrées pour tout ce qui leur offre l'image de la perfection morale & le spectacle si doux , si consolant d'un homme de bien.

Si on en excepte les Mathématiques , dont M. le Baron *d'Holbach* savoit néanmoins autant qu'un bon esprit en doit apprendre , lorsqu'il n'en veut pas faire son étude particulière , on peut dire qu'il avoit cultivé avec succès toutes les sciences , & qu'il a même

---

(1) Le principal devoir d'un ami n'est pas d'honorer par de stériles larmes la mémoire de celui qu'il a perdu.

reculé les bornes de plusieurs , telles que la philosophie spéculative & purement rationelle , la politique & la morale ; c'est à lui que l'on doit en grande partie les progrès rapides que l'Histoire naturelle & la Chymie ont faits il y a environ 30 ans parmi nous ; c'est lui qui en a inspiré le goût & même la passion ; c'est lui qui a traduit les excellens Ouvrages que les Allemands avoient publiés sur ces Sciences presqu'ignorées alors , où du moins très négligées ; & ces traductions sont enrichies d'excellentes notes , soit pour éclaircir , soit pour rectifier le texte.

Personne n'étoit plus communicatif que M. le Baron *d'Holbach* ; personne ne prenoit aux progrès de la raison un intérêt plus vif , plus sincère , & ne s'occupoit avec plus de zéle & d'activité des moyens de les accélérer. Il prêtoit facilement ses livres , & les donnoit même souvent à ceux en qui il reconnoissoit les talens nécessaires pour s'en servir utilement. « Je suis riche , me disoit-il , & » je m'estime heureux d'avoir conçu de bonne » heure qu'une grande aisance ne devoit être » qu'un instrument de plus pour opérer le » bien plus efficacement , pour le rendre du- » rable , & , selon son expression énergique » & hardie , *pour l'enflammer.* »

Egalement versé dans la plupart des ma-

Obituary

Letter on the Death of Monsieur the Baron d'Holbach.[1]

Non hoc præcipuum amicorum munus est prosequi defunctum ignavo questu.
Tacitus.[2]

Sirs, permit me to devote a few lines in your Journal to the memory of a man whose irreparable loss today provokes the just regrets of his friends and even of those who hardly knew him, and plunges his family into a state of grief, which is as touching as it is heart–felt. His habitual and constant practice of every virtue, which is human nature's greatest honour, earned him public esteem, and this type of respect naturally grips all honest souls when they see an image of moral perfection and gentleness, which good men find so consoling.

Although Monsieur the Baron d'Holbach had acquired a knowledge of Mathematics [sic] to the level that any well–educated person ought to have reached, except for those people who want to make of it a special study, one can say that he had cultivated a profound knowledge of all the sciences and that he had even pushed back the boundaries of several branches of science, such as the speculative sciences and pure reason, politics and ethics; it is to him that we owe, in large measure, the rapid progress made in natural history and chemistry over the last thirty years; it is he who inspired a taste, even a passion, for these subjects; it is he who translated excellent works published by German scientists, which were almost unknown in France, or at the very least they were terribly neglected up to that time, and his translations were enriched with excellent notes, either by way of further explanations or corrections to the text.

No one was more communicative than Monsieur the Baron d'Holbach; no one took a livelier, more sincere interest in the progress of reason, or applied himself with more zeal and industry to ways of promoting knowledge. He freely lent his books and he even gave them often to those in whom he recognized the talent necessary to make good use of them. 'I am rich', he would say to me, 'and I count myself lucky to have understood early that great affluence ought to be nothing other than just another tool to facilitate good more easily, to make it durable, and, in accordance with its vigorous, bold expression, *to anoint it with sweet scent.*'

---

[1] *Journal de Paris*, 9 February 1789, pp. 175—177.
[2] 'It is not the chief duty of friends to follow the dead with unprofitable laments.' Naigeon does not reference this quotation: in fact, it is from Tacitus, *Annals*, Book II, 71.

Equally well–versed in the majority of subjects he considered of the utmost importance and of which men of reason ought to have a firm command, he brought to discussions on such subjects a sound judgement, a strict logic, and a precise, punctilious, analytical approach. He was not a man who had everything worked out correctly in his head, but he was one of those people who got things wrong the least; that is a rare quality even amongst people with minds on a par with his and of that same, special character as his. Whatever the object of his discussions with friends, or even with those indifferent to him, which more or less all societies contain, he effortlessly filled those who listened to him with inspiration for the art or the science on which he was discoursing; and no one ever took their leave of him without regretting that they had not cultivated that branch of knowledge, which had been the substance of their conversation, without wanting to be better informed and more enlightened, and particularly, without admiring the clarity, the accuracy, and the orderliness of his mind, with which he knew how to present his ideas.

He was known and admired by all the scholars of Europe. Foreigners of fame desired to be admitted into his company. Many people of higher rank in Germany and England were flattered to be acquainted with him and were eager to honour publicly his merit and virtue; I do not make that remark to suggest that this is Monsieur d'Holbach's crowning achievement, but merely to indicate the difference in education between grand lords and those who are destined to command others in different countries.

When Voltaire came back to Paris in 1778, Monsieur d'Holbach wanted to see him and observe at close quarters this great man, the author of so many masterpieces in all genres. He was introduced to Voltaire, who came before him and said with all the vivacity he put into everything he found interesting, 'I am charmed, Monsieur, to see you. I have known you by reputation for some time and you are one of the men whose respect and friendship I have most coveted.'

With the exception of Voltaire, Fontenelle and Montesquieu, whom Monsieur d'Holbach knew little and with whom circumstances had not allowed him to have closer ties, he counted amongst his friends the most celebrated men of his century—such men as Helvétius, Diderot, d'Alembert, Condillac, Turgot, Buffon and Rousseau, and if, as a result of imparting some knowledge, or during a clash of ideas and opinions, he sometimes had cause to learn from these interlocutors, who lent greater impetus and scope to his already innately accurate, contemplative mind, one can say in all honesty that there was not a single one of those illustrious men cited, who had not learned many useful things from him and whose ideas he had, in many respects, enhanced and extended.

To his fine mental precision—a quality so rare and so essential in everyday life, and on which one is reliant more than is supposed—he added a constant correctness of conduct, the most respectable social virtues, unaffected manners—patriarchal qualities of the old school. It was of him that Mme Geoffrin said with her customary originality and good sense that he was 'the most unpretentiously unpretentious man', and nothing could characterize him better.

Perhaps this would be the appropriate place to speak of his beneficence, but I shall only cite this trait in the lines of the inimitable poet:

> What a sweet thing a true friend is!
> He seeks your needs in the depths of your heart;
> He is tactful enough to spare you the need of having to disclose them yourself.[3]

Monsieur d'Holbach had in his social circle a man of letters, who for some time seemed pre–occupied, quite, and profoundly depressed. Upset by the state in which he saw his friend, he ran round to see him, and said, 'I do not want to pre–empt any confidence which you feel you ought not to confide in me: I respect your secret, but I see you sad, suffering, and your situation worries and troubles me greatly. I know how little money you have and you could have needs about which I know nothing. I have brought you ten thousand francs that I have no call for: if you have any friendship for me, do not refuse to accept them, and you can give me them back in a little while, a bit later when your good fortune returns.' This friend was touched, moved as one might expect, and he assured him that he had no need of money and that his sadness was due to something else, and so he did not accept this favour offered to him; but he never forgot it and it is from him directly that I got this information, which he was happy to tell me and of which Monsieur d'Holbach never spoke, nor did he of many other similar incidents, which do him no less honour. He took delight in finding the reward for such good deeds deep within his own heart. Nevertheless, he had an aversion to ungrateful people and I remember him pronouncing on this one day, saying to me, 'As a man, I am happy to play the simple part of a benefactor when driven to do so: I don't run after my money, but I get pleasure from a little bit of gratitude, when all that's needed is to see others as I wish to see them.'

---

[3] Naigeon does not attribute this poem, but it is from a fable of the famous fabulist poet La Fontaine (1621—1695), entitled 'Les Deux Amis' (Two Friends), Fable № XI, Book VIII.

I have never known a man whose cheerfulness was more attractive, more natural, or more genuine, and whose joking was more biting or more original, resembling that which the English call 'humour'. His expressions themselves, sometimes translated, and, so to speak, coined from Latin, further added to the originality of his ideas and to the playfulness of his conversation.

Like Diderot, who readily and instinctively surrendered his mind, his imagination and his knowledge to those with whom he had dealings, and presumed that all men had and lived by such principles of integrity as he did, Monsieur d'Holbach would say to him, 'You are the most fortunate man I know; you have never come across either a fool or a rogue, and you have never read a bad book, because as you read it, you rewrite it.'

One day, when Mme Geoffrin strongly reprimanded a man of letters in whom she took an interest and who justified himself with the same vivacity and fervour over the careless thinking for which he was being reproached, Monsieur d'Holbach, who listened to them in silence, went up to them and asked them with a smile, 'You don't happen secretly to be married, do you?'

He brought to society this spirit of keen observation, which habitual contemplation does not always produce, but which renders it more precise, more useful, and without which one only recognizes man in the abstract and in the ideal, but not in the particular. He knew that there was a special art in doing good and, above all, in turning it into something of a general, constant usefulness. Experience and reflection had taught him that the choice of the most suitable means to effect a great revolution in ideas and in the speculative principles of men was not a matter of indifference, and that one misses the mark every time that one targets it before the mind is adequately prepared. This is what made him say in the vernacular, a style permissible in conversation, to a famous man highly placed, whose inflexibility and rectitude had often stopped him from adapting to the irresistible constraints of circumstances: 'You are an excellent carrier and you handle your cart well, but you have forgotten that little knob of lard that greases the axles.'

Several years ago the Empress of Russia took steps to enquire of him his ideas on legislation;[4] he hastened to reply to this mark of honour shown him by that august Sovereign, and she had the good grace to let him know that she had put his work right next to that of Montesquieu.

He provided the learned editors of the first *Encyclopédie* with a large number of excellent articles on natural history, politics and philosophy.

---

[4] This is a reference to Catherine the Great (Catherine II) of Russia (1729—1796).

I had the opportunity to observe elsewhere with what exactitude Monsieur d'Holbach fulfilled his duties as a father, and the care that he took over his children's upbringing; I shall add here that he was a good husband, a good parent and a good citizen. I lived around him for twenty–four years, enjoying his trust and his intimate, tenderest and most constant friendship. I loved him, respected him, and weep for him as for my own father: he will always be in my thoughts, always dear to my heart, and the time I spent at his house and in the bosom of his family, so justly cherished and revered, will be the moments I shall delight most in remembering, and my memories of him today are mixed with bitterness and pain, but they will fill the last years of my life with tenderness.

Paul Thiry Baron d'Holbach, Member of the Academies of St Petersburg, Manheim, and Berlin, was born in the Palatinate and died in Paris on the 21 January last, aged sixty–six. I have the honour of being, etc…

Signed Naigeon.

Appendix

A Brief Survey of the Development of Philosophical and Christian Thought and Some Essential Points of Church History

The purpose of this essay is to provide a survey of the most important issues in the development of philosophical thought and its interaction with the Christian Church. This is not a complete account either of the history of philosophy, or the Church, and the explanations of events offered here are provided to obviate the need for long footnotes in the translations and to save the reader from having to reach constantly for the encyclopaedia. The information given here has been provided on a need–to–know–basis and, when read in conjunction with the Glossary, it is hoped that it will enhance the reader's appreciation of the issues raised in the translations and offer an overview of the historical tradition and development of thought.

Until Christianity arrived, philosophical reasoning was the established intellectual force of western culture which developed over centuries, chiefly in Greece and Rome. Philosophers turned their attention to a wide range of subjects, from the immediate issues such as politics and the social organization of society, to more abstract issues such as ethics, and to topics which we would now regard as scientific, based on the detailed observation of the world around them: they wanted to know and speculated on how the world was ordered, and so they inquired into mathematics, astronomy, anatomy, medicine, and many other spheres of knowledge, not to mention the arts and literature—poetry, prose, rhetoric, and the theatre, etc. We are fortunate to have access to these philosophers' and writers' thoughts through a vast library of their works, many of which have survived the ravages of time, though sadly a huge corpus of written material has been lost.

Early philosophical speculation flourished, generally free from the strictures of religious dogma until the foundation of the Christian Church: the Greeks and Romans had their gods, but to a large extent the established religion of the state—paganism—did not impinge upon the development of ideas and scientific speculation, and their moral codes were governed by how one acted and behaved in society and in public life, with little care being expressed for what went on as private behaviour: they had no specific concept of sin—all morality was based on mutual respect and the fulfilling of one's duties as a citizen, soldier, or public figure—generally the darkest recesses of the human heart or mind were a private matter, or perhaps a matter for philosophical speculation. The Græco–Roman gods had left no prescriptive, revealed way of behaving and thinking: one's peers and the law were the arbiters of good or bad behaviour. In any case, judging by the

305

behaviour of the gods, they were certainly not to be emulated or seen as role models, given the many myths of incest, regicide, bestiality, and the like.

It was Christianity that set at odds reason and faith, rational thought and superstitious belief, largely because it claimed to have a divinely revealed body of 'sacred texts', which prescribed in great detail how one had to work, think and even eat. These commandments and mind–set were inherited from Judaism, whose god had issued an incredibly detailed set of precepts, which had to be observed. The books of Leviticus and Deuteronomy gave detailed orders on issues which today many find ridiculous to observe, such as not wearing garments made of mixed fibres, or not sowing more than one crop on a patch of land, etc.: '*Ye shall keep my statutes. Thou shalt not let thy cattle gender with a diverse kind: thou shalt not sow thy field with mingled seed: neither shall a garment mingled of linen and woollen come upon thee*', (Lev. 19: 19). Certainly these same books laid down many other quite reasonable rules governing inter–personal relationships—'*Ye shall not steal, neither deal falsely, neither lie one to another*', (Lev. 19: 11). Fundamentalist Christians still quote from these books when it suits them, i.e., to condemn those people they do not like, such as homosexuals, yet they glibly disregard these other, out–moded commands, which, in context, ought to be given just the same weight and emphasis as the rules on eating shell–fish. After all, the penalties for wearing garments of mixed fibres is stoning to death.

One of the chief differences between Christian and pagan belief in antiquity was that, generally speaking, there was no body of sacred texts or corpus of divine revelation, save for a few pagan oracles. Stories of the Greek gods were passed down orally and even when they were written down, they were never invested with the kind of divine authority Judaism, Christianity, and latterly Islam, attributed to their scriptures. The fact that the Greeks had no such religious canon did not detract from their possessing a powerful sense of the divine and sacred, and despite their scattered geographical settlements, their beliefs helped maintain a surprisingly uniform sense of culture through religious festivals, which were often accompanied with physical competitions in the form of games and public events: the latter took the form of animal sacrifices, aimed at mediating between the gods and man.

Two fundamental strands of thinking emerged from antiquity—the Aristotelian and Platonic, the very bedrock of modern philosophical thought. Though it is ludicrous to attempt to summarize both branches of philosophy in a few lines when whole volumes have been written about each, it is nevertheless essential that some basic tenets be grasped to understand how the Christian Church reacted to this corpus of knowledge, which in turn led to the closing of the western mind to rationality.

Hon. John Collier   "WAITING FOR THE ACCUSED"   Royal Academy

Figure 48: *Waiting for the Accused,* Hon. John Collier, Royal Academy Exhibition of 1891.

The original exhibition notes stated, 'Interior of a torture chamber [...]. Three Dominicans, who form the court, sit at a table draped in black, waiting for the arrival of the accused.'

Although it is generally accepted that the rational, empirical scientific method began with Aristotle (384—322 BC), nevertheless the philosopher and scientist Thales of Miletus (who flourished in the sixth century BC) correctly predicted an eclipse of the sun, as well as discovering five geometric theorems. The influence of Aristotle cannot be overstated and every scientist to date is indebted to him for his method of reasoning: this starts from a proposition or premise, and works through to a syllogism. Hence one can state:

> Every Greek is human. Every human is mortal. Therefore every Greek is mortal.

Although examples of this kind of thinking seem almost puerile today because we have become so accustomed to such rationality, it represented a huge leap forward in developing a system of logic. Aristotle went on to define abstract terms now in common use in logical argument and the vocabulary to express grammatical analysis, as well as making amazingly detailed observations in the fields of biology, botany, chemistry, zoology and many other branches of science. As knowledge grew through observation and understanding, the Greek philosophers believed less and less that the gods were interfering in human affairs and reliance was increasingly placed on an understanding of the natural causes of phenomena such as earthquakes, eclipses, etc., though it often did not stop poets and the general populous anthropomorphizing them. Of crucial importance for the advancement of human knowledge was the fact that Aristotle believed that knowledge was cumulative, growing from generation to generation, and that the accepted corpus of knowledge from a previous generation was always open to challenge, scrutiny, further investigation and verification by experiments or logic. Hence, the Greeks examined Egyptian and Babylonian wisdom to reassess it, often developing it further. This attitude fostered an enquiring mind that took nothing on faith or at face value, subjecting everything to rational, empirical scrutiny. Thus the body of knowledge in many fields grew in complexity and it also fostered a humility that not everything was known or even knowable: the only absolutes were those things which could be discerned through observation, logic and mathematics.

Ancient philosophers also recognized the public role faith could play in society, as a force for national cohesion, identity and stability. Aristotle was of the opinion that, 'Men create gods after their own image, not only with regard to their form, but with regard to their mode of life.' He perceptively noted also that, 'A tyrant must put on the appearance of uncommon devotion to religion. Subjects are less apprehensive of illegal treatment from a ruler whom they consider god–fearing and pious. On the other hand, they do less easily move against him, believing that he has the gods on his side.'[1] Hence, it was recognized that religious faith could be used as a form of repression, coercion, control and manipulation. D'Holbach also makes the point forcibly that, from ancient times to the present era, rulers have understood that by ignoring logic and rationality, and appealing to established religious organizations, upon which favours are heaped to curry support, people can be ruled and made to do almost anything.

This has a chilling contemporary corollary, as Hitler also understood and noted:

> For how shall we fill people with blind faith in the correctness of a doctrine, if we ourselves spread uncertainty and doubt by constant changes in its outward structure? [...] Here, too, we can learn by the example of the Catholic Church. Though its doctrinal edifice, and in part quite superfluously, comes into collision with exact science and research, it is nonetheless unwilling to sacrifice so much as one little syllable of its dogmas; [...] it is only such dogmas which lend to the whole body the character of a faith.[2]

He also said:

> The Catholic Church is a model above all in its uncommonly clever tactics and its knowledge of human nature, and in its wise policy of taking account of human weaknesses in its guidance of the faithful. I have followed it in giving our party program the character of unalterable finality, like the Creed. The Church has never allowed the Creed to be interfered with. It is fifteen hundred years since it was formulated, but every suggestion for its amendment, every logical criticism or attack on it, has been rejected. The Church has realized that anything and everything can be built up on a document of that sort, no matter how contradictory or irreconcilable with it. The faithful will swallow it whole, so long as logical reasoning is never allowed to be brought to bear on it. But if there is one thing that will perplex and demoralize the flock of believers it is an alteration of a solemn confession of faith, no matter how remote it may have become from practical realities, no matter if it has become simply a venerable ancient monument.[3]

---

[1] Aristotle, *Politics*, V. 1314b39. The former saying is unsourced.

[2] Adolf Hitler, *Mein Kampf*, II, chapter 5.

[3] Hitler, quoted by H. Rauschning, *The Voice of Destruction* (New York: Puttnam, 1940), pp. 239—40. Hermann Rauschning (1887—1982) was a German conservative who joined the Nazi Party and rose hight in the ranks, but then he fled Germany and turned against Hitler and his politics. He wrote a number of books quoting conversations with Hitler and this quotation is from his book *Gespräche mit Hitler* (Zürich-New York: Europa Verlag, 1940). It was published in an English translation,

It is also worth noting here that the Vatican never put a single work of Adolf Hitler's on the ***Index of Prohibited Books*** (q.v. Glossary).

By contrast with Aristotle, Plato (428/427—348/347 BC), though also a rationalist, had a metaphysical side to his philosophy which at times bordered on the mystical. He was of the opinion that the world as we perceive it is not the ultimate reality, but a shadowy image of a reality beyond our perception.[4] Some ancient philosophers also tackled the subject of the origin of the universe and man himself, as d'Holbach notes at the beginning of chapter 4 of *Christianity Unveiled* (see p. 33). The axiom '*ex nihilo nihil fit*' is not attributed to any one particular philosopher, but Plato came up with a creator figure, whom he called Demiurge. Clearly if 'nothing came from nothing', an explanation for our existence had to be sought. He believed that the Demiurge was akin to a craftsman, having an image in mind of the object he intended to create, which he fashioned according to that design, much as a joiner would make a chair or table from an idea of the finished object in his head. Though the concept was abstract, the finished product, i.e., the table, was tangible and real. However, Plato's Demiurge should not be equated with the creator god of the Bible and he never intended that this creator should be the object of worship: he is not even credited with meddling in human affairs.[5] Plato's more metaphysical outlook can be seen in another dialogue, *Phaedo*, during which he discusses the existence and nature of a 'soul'.

Hence, Plato went beyond the observable world of the senses, speculating on a theory of Forms which underpin the universe: these include abstract concepts such as 'Beauty', 'Justice', etc., but for all his rather esoteric mode of thinking, he was deeply concerned for the quality of human life—an integral part of which were his ethics and politics, believing that life comprised unchanging and eternal realities laying at the very foundations of our existence, constants in the midst of the changing, transient nature of people's life.

---

entitled *Hitler Speaks: Interviews with Hitler*, (London: Thorton Butterworth, 1939). In America, the title was changed to that cited above. It must be noted that some historians have expressed serious doubts over Rauschning's reliability as a memoirist.

[4] Strange as it may seem, some elements of Platonic thought permeated early Christian thinking, as we read in St Paul's Epistle to the Corinthians, 'For now we see through a glass, darkly; but then [i.e., in the next world] face to face: now I know in part; but then shall I know even as also I am known', I Cor. 13:12.

[5] Plato expresses these ideas and many more on scientific issues in his dialogue *Timaeus*, 20D—30C. It is not known exactly when Plato wrote this work, but it is thought the date of composition is somewhere between 361—347 BC.

It is easy to see how the Judeo–Christian idea of a creator god has many points of contact with Plato's idea, but these creation myths are only two amongst many. It is estimated that the book of Genesis, which contains the Judeo–Christian creation myth, might have been written down as early as approximately 950 BC. Plato's work dates from perhaps 347 BC. There are many cultures with older writing systems than that of the Hebrews, and given that most cultures seem to have a creation myth, the one described in Genesis can probably be viewed as only one amongst many and equals. Sumerian culture and writing seems to have thrived in the third millennium BC and there is evidence of a number of creation stories from that tradition.

Greek learning and culture were preserved through a vast library at Alexandria, which was more than a repository of knowledge—it was also an academy where research was carried out; it had a huge museum and it was a teaching centre. The library contained many translations of works from other Mediterranean countries, including works from the Middle East and India. It was destroyed during a civil war in the late third century BC, and its sister library was destroyed by Christians in AD 391, partly because it was housed in a former pagan temple.[6]

Two other important strands of philosophy must be mentioned here because they are of direct relevance to the translations in this edition: they are the schools of Epicureanism and Stoicism.

Epicurus (341—270 BC) wrote mainly on physics—amazingly on atoms and particles which, of course, he could not see, but which science has subsequently proven to be true—and on astronomy, natural phenomena (earthquakes, etc.), and ethics: it is for his ethics that he is mentioned here. The aim of Epicurus' teaching was to make men free, not in a political sense or even to free them from moral obligations. He wanted to invest them with a sense of personal freedom. He believed that the ultimate aim of life was to be happy, by which he intended 'free from pain in the body and from trouble in the mind'. To this end, Epicurus believed in withdrawing from society to pursue personal happiness. He was of the opinion that there are two things which are obvious obstacles to mankind achieving happiness—they are fear and the existence of evil. Fear can take many forms, i.e., fear of personal injury and safety, etc., but he believed the fear of death could be overcome through logic:

> Therefore, foolish is the man who says that he fears death, not because it will cause pain when it arrives, but because anticipation of it is painful.

---

[6] Reliable historical details as to who fully destroyed the Alexandrian library and when are hard to come by, and various people from Julius Cæsar to the Moslem Caliph Omar have been blamed for different stages of its destruction.

> What is no trouble when it arrives is an idle worry in anticipation. Death, therefore—the most dreadful of evils—is nothing to us, since while we exist, death is not present, and whenever death is present, we do not exist. It is nothing either to the living or the dead, since it does not exist for the living, and the dead no longer are.[7]

It can be seen here that Epicurus rejects the idea of an afterlife. For passages like this, along with many others, Epicurus has been called an atheist, but that is a misreading of his philosophy. He believed in the existence of gods: 'For the gods exist; of them we have distinct knowledge. But they are not such as the majority think them to be.'[8] However, Epicurus made a clear distinction between what he understood to be 'the gods' on the one hand, and 'false religions' on the other, which insisted that the gods govern the world and intervened directly in human affairs, to which Epicurus did not give credence.

Epicurus made a series of statements on the thorny problem of the existence of evil within the jurisdiction of a benevolent god, and to this day his argument has never been satisfactorily answered by Christian apologists: it is the problem of the existence of evil and the absolute of an almighty, omnipotent, and supposedly good god. Epicurus deduced that the existence of evil is incompatible with the existence of a supreme being, who has a care for mankind and is powerful enough to intervene to stop the devastating effects of evil, assuming that god knows about it taking place. Many Greeks believed that the gods were good, as Plato states in *Timaeus*: 'Why did the Creator make the world? He was good, and therefore not jealous, and being free from jealousy he desired that all things should be like himself.'[9] But it is to Epicurus that the following argument is attributed:

> Either God wants to abolish evil and cannot; or he can but does not want to. If he wants to but cannot, he is impotent. If he can but does not want to, he is wicked. If God can abolish evil and really wants to do so, then why is there evil in the world?[10]

---

[7] Epicurus, *Letter to Menoeceus*.

[8] Ibid.

[9] Plato, *Timaeus*, Part I, 29D–30C.

[10] Sentiments based on this statement can be found in Lucretius, *De rerum natura* (*On the Nature of Things*), but this passage does not appear verbatim or *in toto*: it was cited and attributed to Epicurus by the Christian theologian Lactantius, whom d'Holbach quotes in his *Christianity Unveiled*. Lactantius attributes it to Epicurus in his *Treatise on the Anger of God* (1632), and he tries to deal with the import of it: 'God either wishes to take away evils and is unable; or He is able and is unwilling; or He is neither willing nor able, or He is both willing and able. If He is willing and is unable, He is feeble, which is not in accordance with the character of God; if He is able and

D'Holbach drew attention to these thoughts in his work *Le Bon–sens {Good Sense}* (1772), a condensed version of his *System of Nature* (1770), in which he states: 'For more than two thousand years honest minds have waited for a rational solution of these difficulties; our theologians teach us that they will not be revealed to us until the future life.'[11]

One other philosophical school which must be considered for the purposes of this book is that of Stoicism. This is a belief founded by Zeno of Citium around the middle of the fourth century BC, but added to and changed by numerous thinkers. The Stoic mentality (as suggested by the English word 'stoical', derived from it) stresses the importance of exercising personal virtue—the only true virtue, which involves disregarding riches, poverty, health, and even death itself. Self–control and self–knowledge are essential components to making up one's mind as to how to choose the right course of action in any given situation. Passions of every kind are to be viewed with the utmost suspicion as they are bound to mislead. The Stoics believed that the world was governed by order and the ability to perceive this order and live in harmony with it, i.e., to live in accordance with nature, was the true expression of virtue. Unlike the Epicureans, the Stoics believed that man should take an active part in public life and the affairs of state in order to improve the lot of everyone in society. Hence, Stoics commonly occupied

---

unwilling, He is envious, which is equally at variance with God; if He is neither willing nor able, He is both envious and feeble, and therefore not God; if He is both willing and able, which alone is suitable to God, from what source then are evils? Or why does He not remove them? I know that many of the philosophers, who defend providence, are accustomed to be disturbed by this argument, and are almost driven against their will to admit that God takes no interest in anything, which Epicurus especially aims at; but having examined the matter, we easily do away with this formidable argument. For God is able to do whatever He wishes, and there is no weakness or envy in God. He is able, therefore, to take away evils; but He does not wish to do so, and yet He is not on that account envious. For on this account He does not take them away, because He at the same time gives wisdom, as I have shown; and there is more of goodness and pleasure in wisdom than of annoyance in evils. For wisdom causes us even to know God, and by that knowledge to attain to immortality, which is the chief good. Therefore, unless we first know evil, we shall be unable to know good. But Epicurus did not see this, nor did any other, that if evils are taken away, wisdom is in like manner taken away; and that no traces of virtue remain in man, the nature of which consists in enduring and overcoming the bitterness of evils. And thus, for the sake of a slight gain in the taking away of evils, we should be deprived of a good, which is very great, and true, and peculiar to us. It is plain, therefore, that all things are proposed for the sake of man, as well evils as also goods.' This text can be accessed on the internet at http://en.wikisource.org/wiki/Ante-Nicene_Fathers/Volume_VII/Lactantius/A_Treatise_on_the_Anger_of_God_Addresse d_to_Donatus/Chap._XIII

[11] D'Holbach, *Good Sense*, translated by Anna Knoop (New York: Prometheus Books, 2004), p. 52.

posts in Roman government and they made dutiful soldiers. It is not difficult to see that there are elements in Stoicism which were to appeal greatly to the early Christian church—especially the concept of eschewing earthly possessions and riches, and having a squeamish attitude towards 'passions', especially those of a sexual nature.

There were thinkers from the earliest times, even from about the fifth century BC, who expressed doubts that any knowledge could be known with any certainty. Given that the world was in a constant state of flux, they wondered how it was possible to be sure of anything. These philosophers were known as Sceptics (or Skeptics), from the Greek verb meaning 'I enquire'. Although as a philosophy it went through many transformations and had many proponents, such an attitude has continued into the modern era: it was embraced as a spring–board by Descartes (1596—1650) for his system of thought, when he famously wrote 'Je pense, donc je suis' {I think, therefore I am}, better known in Latin as 'Cogito ergo sum', (though it was originally written in French), and it was subsequently reiterated from Locke to Hume, through to Kant and beyond. In antiquity, Sceptics set themselves up as direct opponents of Epicureanism and Stoicism.

Greek culture declined and the influence of Rome grew, but the two cultures still had many points of contact: there was also a huge cross–fertilization of ideas. In fact, Greek and Roman culture had more elements in common than they had differences. Many Roman writers relied heavily upon gods from the Greek tradition, which often corresponded to their own, and Latin names were assigned to Greek deities who were almost identical to their Roman counterparts: hence Zeus becomes Jupiter, Poseidon—Neptune, etc. The poet Ovid managed to mix the two cultures easily during the first century BC and not only the cultural icons were adopted, but so also were Greek literary forms, such as the dialogue, political treatises, the epic, etc.

Stoicism was adopted and promoted chiefly through the works of Cicero and he wrote an extremely interesting treatise *On the Nature of the Gods*, revealing that doubters were not uncommon among the ancients:

> There are a number of branches of philosophy that have not as yet been by any means adequately explored; but the inquiry into the nature of the gods, which is both highly interesting in relation to the theory of the soul, and fundamentally important for the regulation of religion, is one of special difficulty and obscurity [...] The multiplicity and variety of the opinions held upon this subject by eminent scholars are bound to constitute a strong argument for the view that philosophy has its origin and starting–point in ignorance, and that the Academic School were well–advised in 'withholding assent' from beliefs that are uncertain [...] As regards the present subject, for example, most thinkers have affirmed that the gods exist, and this is the most probable view and the one to which we are all led by nature's guidance; but Protagoras declared himself uncertain, and

Diagoras of Melos and Theodorus of Cyrene held that there are no gods at all. Moreover, the upholders of the divine existence differ and disagree so widely, that it would be a troublesome task to recount their opinions. Many views are put forward about the outward form of the gods, their dwelling–places and abodes, and mode of life, and these topics are debated with the widest variety of opinion among philosophers; but as to the question upon which the whole issue of the dispute principally turns, whether the gods are entirely idle and inactive, taking no part at all in the direction and government of the world, or whether on the contrary all things both were created and ordered by them in the beginning and are controlled and kept in motion by them throughout eternity, here there is the greatest disagreement of all.[12]

Plus ça change!

From what Cicero says in this work, there was obviously a lively, on–going debate amongst philosophers as to whether gods existed or not. Cicero goes through many questions which are still asked today, such as to how we might discern whether god or gods exist, the *appearance* of intelligent design in the universe, etc., but he comes up against the old question of whether the gods created evil—since evil exists—and whether they created the universe imperfect—since imperfections are obvious. In his long treatise, Cicero fails to come to any convincing conclusion, but he is willing to give the gods the benefit of the doubt.

For the writer, philosopher and statesman Seneca (4 BC—AD 65), another Stoic, religion was a tool used by rulers to keep order in society: 'Religion is regarded by the common people as true, by the wise as false, and by rulers as useful.' D'Holbach makes exactly the same point in his *Christianity Unveiled* and thus we see here, as in other instances above, d'Holbach's treatise against the Church was not entirely original: he was using arguments which had long been rehearsed in classical literature, but his merit lay in the way he collated these arguments and developed them further, to say nothing of his courage in doing so in the face of opposition from the Church and state.

Christianity as the Established Religion

There is every evidence to suggest that the first Roman emperor to confess Christianity—Constantine I (AD 280?—337), also called 'The Great'—knew very little about the Christian faith or even attended public acts of Christian worship but, shrewd politician that he was, he used it to support his imperial rule, whilst at the same time taking care to maintain the support of pagans as

---

[12] Cicero, *Nature of the Gods*, translated by H. Rackham (Cambridge, Mass.: Harvard U.P./Loeb Classical Library, 2000), pp. 3—5.

well. After Diocletian's, his predecessor's, persecution of Christians, which was the last major period of persecution under the Romans, Constantine took a much more favourable attitude towards Christians. According to his panegyrist Lactantius, Constantine had a vision of God which led to his conversion and he favoured the Church by a number of measures and gifts: he gave the bishop of Rome the Lateran palace as a gift, a property which had belonged to the wealthy Laterano family, which subsequently became the Palace of the Popes. He also granted the Church fiscal and legal privileges and immunities from civic burdens, which in effect freed the clergy from any obligations to serve the state so as not to detract them from their divine offices. The Church was also granted the right to inherit property. Typical of his pragmatism, Constantine pronounced Sunday to be under the protection of the state, granting the Christian Church a special day free from work as the Jews had, but he made sure that it coincided with the pagan day of rest, i.e., Sunday or the 'day of the Sun', the day officially designated for worshipping that celestial body. It is abundantly clear from this that our Sunday is emphatically not the Sabbath day of Judaism and the Bible, though it quickly became associated with it as such.

Constantine also extended the legal jurisdiction of bishops, involving them to a much greater extent in the administration of civil justice. This marked an extension of ecclesiastical power in state affairs and civil society, exercised through the clergy, although these powers were later reduced under subsequent rulers. However, the Church has never been reticent in insinuating itself into state affairs, a phenomenon which is severely criticized by d'Holbach in *Christianity Unveiled* and in other works, and this uneasy Church/State pact and struggle for power was dramatically played out during the reign of Henry VIII. The Catholic Church in particular, but not exclusively, has constantly striven to acquire for itself special privileges and concessions to augment its influence and protect its interests—both ideological and pecuniary—and this kind of wheeling and dealing has continued into the modern period through Concordats or special agreements, negotiated between the Vatican and individual sovereign states.[13]

It is certain that Constantine I did not favour the Church solely for his own political ends, since it is clear from a series of letters which have survived, written between AD 313 to the early 320s, that his faith was more genuine than has often been admitted. It must be said that he was more broadminded than some rulers who would follow on after him in history, because he issued an edict of religious tolerance in AD 313, granting Christians religious

---

[13] Much to the chagrin of the Catholic Church, these semi-secret deals are being documented and translated into English so that they can be accessed more widely: see the Concordat Watch site at http://www.concordatwatch.eu/

freedom, while still allowing pagans to worship their gods. He did, however, suppress divination, as a number of emperors had tried to do before him. The Romans showed less tolerance to the Jews, outraging them by entering their temples and in particular by going into the Holy of Holies in Jerusalem, closed even to ordinary Jews. As procurator of Judea, Pontius Pilate so angered the local Jewish believers that they revolted against Roman rule, and tensions between the occupying Romans and the Jews is often referred to in the New Testament. This kind of opposition was frequently met with violent suppression.

Whatever his personal commitment to Christianity, Constantine used it to establish and maintain stability within his empire. He tried to maintain a multi–faith society by allowing Christianity and paganism to co–exist. However, one of the things which horrified Constantine was the schismatic nature of the Christian Church.

The Problem of Forming a Canon, a Creed and Schisms

Believers of all three monotheistic religions—Judaism, Christianity and Islam—have made wild, glib claims for their holy books, which they have all dubbed '*The* Word of God'. Despite each of these world religions laying claim to the same deity and the considerable shared cultural heritage and borrowings, their texts are widely different, notwithstanding a modicum of mutual acceptance and respect of each other's books. All fundamentalist believers of each faith show the same simplistic thinking by claiming that they have *the singular truth*, revealed in the hotchpotch of their sacred texts, collected over a protracted period of time and often written by very different writers (except in the case of Islam), and they appear to believe that their god had delivered their texts from heaven 'hot off the press', in a form collated as we know them today. They never consider the huge implications of this kind of thinking and there are many complex issues at stake: whoever god's secretary or scribe was, be he Moses, Muhammad, Matthew, Mark, Luke or John—none of them wrote down the substance of their divine revelation during the lifetime of their particular prophet or messenger from god. Moses could not have written down Yahweh's law because the Hebrew script did not even exit then. None of the New Testament gospel writers knew Jesus personally and the earliest account recorded in writing—that of Mark—was probably written at the earliest in AD 70, i.e., decades after Jesus had existed (if he existed at all). The other 'gospels' (the word is derived from the Anglo–Saxon meaning 'good story'!) were written relying very heavily upon Mark's version, the implication being that all his mistakes and misinterpretations were copied over into their own work. Muhammad himself wrote not a single line of the Koran because, apart from anything else, he was illiterate, and the Koran did not exist in written form until twenty–five years after the prophet's death: the Islamic second holy book, the *Hadith*, was not formed until two centuries after Muhammad. Furthermore, the sacred texts of the Christians initially had little to do with the ancient Jewish books which form the Old Testament of the Bible: both the Old and New Testaments come from different traditions and it was the early, founding Fathers of the Christian Church who went to exhaustive lengths to cross–reference these books, expending inordinate efforts in voluminous exegesis to try and prove that the New Testament was the fulfilment and perfect compliment of the Old. The Jewish prophecies of the Hebrew scriptures have been used to show that Jesus Christ was the fulfilment of predictions and to support claims that these texts were divine, evinced by their 'accurate' foretelling of the future.

Fundamentalists and other deluded seers and scryers of all the monotheistic religions have even found in these texts predictions as precise as the Irish Potato Famine of 1845—49, the earthquakes in California of 1923 and 1925, and the AIDS pandemic. One fine example of these crystal–ball gazers was the Reverend John Cumming (1807—1881), about whom George Eliot felt moved to write a blistering attack.[14] He preached regularly to huge audiences in Covent Garden in London and published around one hundred and eighty books, 'proving' that the papacy was the anti–Christ and that prophecies in the Old Testament book of Daniel and the New Testament book of Revelation predicted the French Revolution, the invention of the telegraph and many other modern innovations. He even managed to pin–point the year of Christ's return using biblical sources: he settled on the year 1867. Similar groups in the USA have expected Christ's imminent return, but so far all is quite on the western front—and on all others, and is likely to remain so.

---

[14] See Christopher Hitchens, *The Portable Atheist* (Philadelphia: Da Capo Press, 2007), pp. 75—92. An Islamic preacher says AIDS is a punishment on homosexuals from Allah—see http://www.youtube.com/watch?v=IoFKNSCsG2Y On Monday 27 November 1989 there was a conference in the Vatican and it was reported that, 'The meeting strengthened Roman Catholic officialdom's stand against advocating condom use for homosexuals or distribution of sterile needles to drug addicts, particularly in a tough opening speech by New York's John Cardinal O'Connor. Father Rocco Buttiglione of Liechtenstein's International Academy of Philosophy went so far as to suggest that the AIDS scourge could be a "divine punishment," but quickly added that it was aimed not just at sexual misconduct but at all modern forms of sinfulness. The various flare-ups tended to obscure the repeated theme on which everyone at the conference agreed: AIDS is a horrendous health crisis that demands every bit of compassion and care the church can muster.' Reported in '*TIME Magazine*'.

Figure 49: Rev. John Cumming predicts "The End of the World", *Vanity Fair,* **13 April 1872.**

The lack of a single, complete canonical text raised difficult issues for the Christian Church in particular: we have mere fragments of texts from many versions scattered far and wide, all of which were copied many times, and as such they were subjected to the introduction of mistakes, etc. To compound this problem, there are questions of translation from one language into another and, in some cases, back again into other languages, and it is inconceivable that changes did not occur. There are also huge linguistic problems since meanings of words have been lost, symbols for vowels and other diacritical marks were absent in the early Hebrew of the Old Testament, and the Arabic of the Koran etc. Any linguist is well aware of all these issues and many more. As for the formation of the New Testament in the form we know it today, there was a huge debate over which of the many manuscripts, letters and memoirs extant at the time, should form a definitive and authoritative canon: the Book of Revelation almost escaped being selected for the Bible, to name but one text from the vast array of possible candidates, which belies the whole concept of the Bible being *the single* word of God. There are also many other narrative accounts of Jesus and his family which never been included in the New Testament: there is a Gospel of Peter and yet another of Judas, a First Letter of Clement, a Letter of Barnabas, yet another Apocalypse (Revelation) by Peter, Shepherd of Hermas, and many more. The New Testament canon was not settled in a form similar to that which we would recognize today until the fourth century AD, and the Protestant and Catholic branches of Christianity cannot agree on which books are canonical. There are also major problems of interpretation because many books are narrated in poetic, mystical language, so obscure as to make the real, definitive sense difficult to ascertain. D'Holbach draws attention to many of these thorny problems in his *Christianity Unveiled*.

The composition of the canon was one thing, but the need to find a definitive text with as few mistakes and alterations as possible was a problem openly admitted by many early church commentators—and alas not widely admitted today—and many efforts were made to compare as wide a range as possible of copied texts to try and find some way of getting back to the original wording, and therefore the sense, of the original New Testament scriptures. John Mill (*c.* 1645—1707) spent over thirty years amassing materials for comparison to come up with a definitive version of the original Greek New Testament and he used one hundred manuscripts for that purpose. Even so, when Mill published his edition of the Greek New Testament in 1707, based on an edition published as early as 1550, there were no fewer than thirty thousand points of variation. Under such circumstances, how can

Figure 50: *The Covenant of Judas, J. Franklin, Illustrated London News, 13 April 1850.*

Evangelical Fundamentalists claim to know the Word of God?[15] Textual problems with the Old Testament are even greater, given the greater antiquity of the manuscripts.

As far as the Koran is concerned, the establishing of a definitive version was a political act: Uthman, the governor of Medina, collected various copies of the Koran in the seventh century AD, keeping one version only—perhaps wisely (?!), having burned all the others in the vain hope of avoiding confrontation and schisms. Today we do not know what textual variations there might have been in those burnt copies.

Hence, all these holy books, claiming to be the exclusive expression of a single truth, are nothing more than a hotchpotch of texts which have been passed down orally at first, subject to considerable variation, subsequently edited and re–edited, and then often elaborated for political ends.

Another major claim made by each of the monotheistic religions for their sacred text is that their book is without fault, that it is perfect, as God is perfect, and that it contains no contradictions or mistakes. In *Christianity Unveiled*, D'Holbach points out some of the major contradictions within details of the gospels, and other writers have indicated many instances of implausible passages: there are thirty-four references to dragons in the Old and New Testaments (e.g., Deut. 32: 33–*King James Version*); the author of Psalm 19 clearly believes that the sun goes round the earth; there are two versions of the creation myth which do not correspond—in one of them plant life is created before the sun, meaning that the process of photosynthesis would have been impossible. Scholars have also analyzed a number of Old Testament books in particular and have seen clear evidence of multiple authorship, which also raises major problems.[16] However, it is indisputable that these ancient texts are fascinating works of early literature in their own right and present interesting archaeological, philosophical and linguistic challenges. They have also been the source and inspiration for a great deal of magnificent European literature, art and music: it is such a shame that they have been taken too literally and used as the most powerful, vicious weapon in the Church's armoury.

The early Church was riven with strife and schisms over doctrinal issues, which arose because different and often isolated groups emphasized one particular teaching or preacher, or holy text above all others. Constantine

---

[15] Bart Ehrman, *Misquoting Jesus: The Story Behind Who Changed the Bible and Why* (N.Y.: HarperOne/HarperCollins, 2005), pp. 83—88 and p.101.

[16] One of the best recent and scholarly books of this type is G. Greenberg, *101 Myths of the Bible: How Ancient Scribes Invented Biblical History* (Naperville, Illinois: Sourcebooks, Inc., 2000).

wanted to put a stop to this, as did many other sovereigns, in order to create a unified church. The Church comprised small, scattered cliques of believers, who increasingly withdrew from Roman society, cutting themselves off from public events, especially those involving sacrificial, pagan rites. The Christians' own celebrations and rites set them apart still further from the rest of society and Roman rulers had to decide how long they would tolerate such divisions: they regarded cliques as potential sources of sedition. By the time of Diocletian (AD 245—316), the Christian community was already large enough to cause him concern over this disjunction from the rest of society, in part marked by their refusal to show allegiance to the gods of the empire, and his attempts to bring them into line resulted in a fierce bout of persecution.

The early Church needed a canon of approved texts or scriptures to unite all believers and avoid individual groups going their own way, which they were doing in any case. St Paul, having been brought up in the Jewish tradition with its definitive canonical texts, was concerned to unite all disparate groups with standard texts and rites, and to maintain purity within Christian teaching and practices. When individual Christian groups fell into what was perceived as error, epistles were written to them to correct their departure from accepted truth and urge them to fall back in line. These letters eventually became part of the New Testament scriptures and were deemed to be divinely inspired. As time wore on, eyewitnesses to Christ's ministry, who had learned of his teaching first hand, were beginning to die out and reliance on an oral tradition was perilous for preserving truth and doctrinal purity. Some church groups were isolated, being great distances apart and, in days when travel was not easy, they were bound to drift doctrinally and follow their own particular teaching. Furthermore, some early Christians believed that revelation was an on–going process and there were those who claimed that they had been the recipients of yet further revelations. Slowly a canon began to emerge and be accepted, but in the second century there were still major differences between the western and eastern churches, which went unresolved until the fourth century. St Paul himself was the only early theologian who had never read any of the gospels.

As far as Paul's faith is concerned, it was based on an emotional response and a rejection of empirical knowledge. It is likely that Paul was ignorant of Greek philosophy and his approach to his faith was irrational: in Acts 17 he admits to having been ridiculed by Stoics and Epicureans in Athens, and he makes several statements which denigrate intellectual rigour, claiming that the seemingly irrational nature of his faith is God's wisdom revealed to him personally, which defies all logic. He knows that his faith does not stand up to intellectual scrutiny and he glories in irrationality and mysticism, having recourse instead to divine revelation and inspiration: this is blatantly obvious in Romans 1 and 2 Corinthians 11. Hence Paul flies in the face of classical, rational argument and it is small wonder that philosophers of the day held him in contempt. In fact, after a number of people had been converted in Ephesus under Paul's influence, a bonfire was held of scrolls and books, and doubtless this anti–intellectual, barbarous act went on with Paul's assent: having been unable to win the argument on an intellectual, rational basis, he simply burnt the wisdom of the ancients. This practice still takes place in the modern era by religious fanatics and it was even approved of fairly recently by the Catholic Church, as expressed in the *Catholic Encyclopedia* of 1917: 'Everywhere the books declared dangerous were cast into the fire—the simplest and most natural execution of censorship.' Hence, in St Paul the Church has a prime example of one who will not listen to intellectual argument, who wallows in his own ignorance and even prides himself in it, and to this he adds the barbarism of burning books. The Christian Church developed a tradition of banning and burning books to stifle debate and dissent from its earliest history, and the cases of Copernicus and Galileo have become *causes célèbres*. Greek and Latin classical literature on philosophy, logic, science and the arts, largely destroyed under Christian rule, were translated back from Arabic translations into Latin in an era when Islam was flourishing intellectually and much more tolerant than it is today. Papal prohibitions in 1210 and 1215 restricted the teaching of Aristotle's works, and by 1272 all discussion of any purely theological matter was forbidden. As Helen Ellerbe points out, 'St Bernard of Clairvaux gave voice to Church sentiment when he said "...everything is treated contrary to custom and tradition." He went on to write: "The faith of simplicity is mocked, the secrets of Christ profaned; questions on the highest things are impertinently asked, the Fathers scorned because they were disposed to conciliate rather than solve such problems. Human reason is snatching everything to itself, leaving nothing for faith."' Ellerbe continues:

> Orthodox Christians expressed disdain for the flourishing creativity and declared support of the arts to be heathen and pagan. The outspoken fifteenth century Dominican prophet Girolano Savonarola believed that classical poets should be banished and that science, culture and education should return entirely to the hands of monks. He wrote: 'The only good thing that we owe to Plato and Aristotle is that they brought forward many arguments which we can use against the heretics. Yet they and other philosophers are now in hell... It would be good for religion if many books that seem useful were destroyed. When there were not so many books and not so many arguments and disputes, religion grew more quickly than it has since.'[17]

---

[17] Helen Ellerbe, *The Dark Side of Christian History* (Windermere, Florida: Morningstar and Lark, 2004), pp. 54—57.

Figure 51: *St Dominic and the Albigenses*, Pedro Berruguete (*c*. 1495).
Albigenses is another name for the Cathars.
St Dominic, shown with a halo, looks on as his writings miraculously refuse to burn.

Ellerbe states also that, 'The losses in science were monumental. In some cases the Christian Church's burning of books and repression of intellectual pursuit set humanity back as much [sic] as two millennia in its scientific understanding. Already in the sixth century BC **Pythagoras** had come up with the idea that the earth revolved around the sun.'[18]

One of the chief Christian doctrines to divide and split the early Church was Manichaeism, which occurred in the third century AD. The movement was founded in Persia by Mani (or Manes, or Manichaeus), an Iranian who was known as the 'Apostle of Light' and supreme 'Illuminator'. He preached throughout the Persian Empire and India, which disrupted the peace to such an extent that he was attacked by Zoroastrian priests and was condemned and imprisoned; he died around AD 274—277. Mani saw himself as one prophet of a long line, from Adam to Zoroaster through to Jesus (including Buddha), teaching his own form of divine revelation which moved significantly away from Christianity. His belief in a single, omnipotent God and creator grapples with the problem of pain and evil in the world and why God either creates or allows it. He imagined an evil force working against God, and thus a dualistic theology emerged. By shifting the blame for evil from God onto another, opposing force, God was to some extent being absolved of its consequences. Salvation from such evil was offered through a special revelation of the nature of evil itself—or gnosis, and this inner illumination shed light on the evil self, previously obscured by ignorance, allowing the enlightened soul to seek and take the path to salvation. The Manicheans adhered to a strict ascetic life of sacramental rites through prayer, almsgiving, fasting and general extreme austerity. Women were seen as temptresses and morally weak, an image supported by the Serpent and Eve myth in Genesis, and sex was regarded as an integral part of the forces of evil. The movement had wide appeal and its message spread far, partly because translations of its texts were made into many languages, and partly because frenetic missionary zeal was expected of its adherents. Although the Christian Church condemned Manichaeism as a heresy, it borrowed a great deal from its asceticism and phobia about sex and women, support for which the Church managed to find in the misogyny of SS Paul and Timothy.[19]

---

[18]   Ibid., p. 44.

[19]   'But if they cannot contain [themselves], let them marry: for it is better to marry than to burn', (I Cor. 7: 9).

'Traitors, heady, highminded, lovers of pleasures more than lovers of God; Having a form of godliness, but denying the power thereof: from such turn away. For of this sort are they which creep into houses, and lead captive silly women laden with sins, led away with divers lusts, ever learning, and never able to come to the knowledge of the truth.' (2 Tim. 3: 4–7).

Arianism was another sect of the early Christian Church, which was also deemed to be a heresy. It was first promoted by Arius (*c*. AD 250—336) who was a priest in Alexandria, Egypt. He proposed that Christ was not truly divine since he was the son of God, i.e., he was the created progeny of God, and as such, he was not equal with God. Arius found many New Testament references to support his view, since the gospels said that Christ was 'begotten of the father'.[20] Hence, Arius believed Christ was not consubstantial or coeternal with God the Father, there being once a time before he was 'begotten' and therefore he had not always existed. Arius attracted a considerable following and all such believers were excommunicated by the Church. This was one of a number of times that the divinity of Christ was challenged in the history of the Church.

There was a break–away group in the third century AD who rallied around a bishop called Donatus, whose base was the Church in northern Africa, where Christianity had grown rapidly. These so–called Donatists, named after their leader, refused to accept sacraments from priests and bishops who had either renounced or compromised their faith under the persecution engineered by Diocletian. They declared that, having compromised themselves in this way, those priests were unfit to serve as ministers and that they had forfeited their spiritual authority to administer the sacraments. Consequently, they appointed their own rival bishop in the person of Donatus, claiming that they were the true Church of martyrs. The schism rumbled on for the best part of a century.

Another sect mentioned by d'Holbach in his treatise was the Ebionites, who were members of an early group of former Jews, living in and around Palestine during the first century AD. The sect took its name from the Hebrew word for 'poor', i.e., *ebyonim* or *ebionim*. The sect seems to have arisen sometime in the late first century and lasted until around the fourth. Its adherents were monotheists and believed that Jesus was the Messiah, but they rejected his miraculous birth, supposing instead that he was the natural son of Joseph and Mary. Basically, they followed the Jewish law and they also adopted vegetarianism and a life of poverty. Their insistence on vegetarianism was based on the fact that any meat butchered and procured as an offering to pagan idols would thus be avoided and they would not be tainted by it: they understood from the Old Testament that Jehovah hated all forms of idolatry with a passion and they wanted no part of it—even inadvertently.

There was also a group called the Cerinthians, so named after their founder Cerinthus, who flourished around AD 100. Cerinthians accepted only the

---

[20]   See John 1:18; 3:16 & 18; Acts 13:33, amongst many other references.

Gospel of Matthew as divinely inspired. They rejected God as creator of the world and the divinity of Jesus, preferring instead to imagine that Jesus was the embodiment of a spiritual form of the Christ, received at the point of baptism and who departed as a spirit from his body at the time of the crucifixion. They could not countenance the idea of God being physically born and killed. Like many of the early Christian sects, there was a strong millenarian, apocalyptic element to their beliefs: most early believers thought they would witness the actual triumphant return of Christ in their own lifetime.[21]

There was a Jewish sect which flourished from the second century BC to the first century AD known as the Essenes, about whom there is a good deal of controversy. Some scholars believe they lived in secluded desert colonies set apart from the rest of society, whereas others believe they could also be found living in towns. They were vegetarians and lived a celibate life in communities with strict rules similar to the monastic groups which were to form later in the history of the Christian Church. Like a number of early Jewish sects, they had an eschatological outlook, believing that they, along

---

[21]   They took their inspiration and beliefs from a prophecy made by Christ himself, reported in Matthew's Gospel (but not exclusively so): 'For there shall arise false Christs, and false prophets, and shall shew great signs and wonders; insomuch that, if it were possible, they shall deceive the very elect. Behold, I have told you before. Wherefore if they shall say unto you, Behold, he is in the desert; go not forth: behold, he is in the secret chambers; believe it not. For as the lightning cometh out of the east, and shineth even unto the west; so shall also the coming of the Son of man be. For wheresoever the carcase is, there will the eagles be gathered together. Immediately after the tribulation of those days shall the sun be darkened, and the moon shall not give her light, and the stars shall fall from heaven, and the powers of the heavens shall be shaken: And then shall appear the sign of the Son of man in heaven: and then shall all the tribes of the earth mourn, and they shall see the Son of man coming in the clouds of heaven with power and great glory. And he shall send his angels with a great sound of a trumpet, and they shall gather together his elect from the four winds, from one end of heaven to the other. Now learn a parable of the fig tree; When his branch is yet tender, and putteth forth leaves, ye know that summer is nigh: So likewise ye, when ye shall see all these things, know that it is near, even at the doors. Verily I say unto you, **This generation shall not pass, till all these things be fulfilled.** Heaven and earth shall pass away, but my words shall not pass away', (Matt. 24: 24–35). Mark 13 and Luke 21 contain similar predictions of cosmic events, and the bold text is specifically repeated verbatim—see Mark 13: 30 and Luke 21: 32. D'Holbach complains—quite rightly—that prophesies are often couched in vague language, but this one could not be more time-specific, and yet nothing has happened as predicted. Perhaps George Bush got his inspiration from such biblical passages when he stated, 'And now, we can see a new world coming into view. A world in which there is the very real prospect of a new world order.' (Speech reported in the *New York Times* of 7 March 1991.)

with very few others, would be saved at the end of time, which was not far off. It is thought that John the Baptist might have been an Essene and this sect has been associated with scroll fragments found in Qumran. Scholars have identified a number of Essene doctrines in the teaching of Christ himself, particularly his refutation of earthly possessions and the marital state.

Apart from the above sects, and one or two other minor groups mentioned in the footnotes in d'Holbach's text, there were doctrinal issues on which the early Church argued long and hard, and often with great personal bitterness. Sometimes these controversies were sufficiently divisive to create yet more whole new sects, whereas others continued to consider themselves as part of the Church. Needless to say, they all believed they possessed the one and only truth.

One of the most contentious doctrinal issues to whip the early Church into a real frenzy was the argument over the Trinity, the concept that although God was only one being, he was yet three persons, revealed as the Father, the Son and the Holy Spirit. The controversy over this issue went on for several centuries, since many believed that the Son of God was made or created, and as such, he was subservient to God, as already mentioned above. Believers struggled with the concept of the three persons of the godhead as one being, particularly since each person seemed to possess his own individual identity and role when interacting with the created universe. It was not until the fourth century in the Council of Nicaea in 325 that the matter was officially more or less settled, stating that the Son was 'of the same substance as the Father', but even then the controversy rumbled on for the next half–century. D'Holbach makes the concept of the Trinity a particular target for his criticism in *Christianity Unveiled*.

Another major disagreement amongst the Church Fathers was the doctrine of transubstantiation, the notion that the bread and wine symbols of Christ's body become the actual physical body and blood at the hands of the priest. It was a late controversy within the Church and the term 'transubstantiation' was first coined in the twelfth century. The claims for this transformation lie in a literal interpretation of Christ's words reported in the Gospel, i.e., 'This is my body' and 'this is my blood', (Matt. 26). Again this is a doctrine targeted for severe criticism by d'Holbach in several of his works. The import of this teaching is rather gruesome, as the Russian writer Tolstoy pointed out: if the host and the wine literally transform into the body and blood of Christ, then eating and drinking them is tantamount to cannibalism.

The diversity of religious views and the variation in beliefs over the nature of and events in the life of Christ, and the Church's desire to promote the concept that the New Testament was a fulfilment of Old Testament prophesies, all combined to make the need for a definitive canonical text even more urgent. The linking of the Old and New Testaments, making out that they were *one inspired work*, gave rise to all manner of glaring discrepancies, as d'Holbach points out. The vague language in which the Old Testament prophecies were couched meant that they were all things to all men, both to the Jews who rejected Christ, and to the Christians who obviously accepted him. Recognizing the fraught nature of biblical interpretation and obviating the many glaring contradictions in the Scriptures was a mine–field, so the Church declared itself to be the sole arbiter of truth: truth was what the Church Fathers said it was, and not necessarily what it appeared to be, and it was the duty of the faithful simply to accept it without question. Despite the fact that the masses were generally illiterate, the idea that the common herd might actually get their hands on the sacred text and challenge accepted interpretation filled the Church with horror. With time, the *Vulgate* version of the scriptures was produced through the efforts of St Jerome and the Latin language of the scriptures and the mass were a means of setting the clergy in awe of the masses. Initially, many books of the Bible were available in Latin by the year 405, but they were only all accessible in a form we now would recognize as the Bible as late as the sixth century. Gradually the Church pronounced on many matters of faith generally beyond the scope of the Bible, on issues such as freewill, sexual conduct, heaven and hell, the forgiveness of sins, the cult of the Virgin Mary, and many other issues. All aspects of faith were prescribed and set down effectively in tablets of stone and dissenters were dealt with harshly. When in the 1520s, William Tyndale (1490—1536) became convinced that every Christian ought to have the Bible accessible in his or her own vernacular, he was pronounced a heretic. The Catholic authorities prevented him from undertaking the work of producing a new translation of the Bible in English, forcing him to emigrate to Germany to realize his project. His completed New Testament had to be printed abroad and the church authorities in England did all they could to suppress its distribution and dissemination.

Europe entered a period of what used to be called the Dark Ages, from about 500—1000, but historians shy away from the term nowadays because of the value judgment the term infers. From the point of view of the progress of knowledge and science, it was literally a period of darkness, as the Christian Church assumed leadership and control of virtually all aspects of learning, teaching, education, science and the creative arts.

The Western Roman Empire collapsed in the fifth century under constant attack from Germanic tribes. Rome was sacked in AD 410 and with it the political structure and social climate of the Western world changed. The Roman Empire had served as a cohesive force for most of Europe until that time and many improvements had been made to ameliorate life: roads had been built and there had been a general investment in the infrastructure—water supplies and sewerage systems had been provided in urban settlements, and in the countryside agriculture had been organized in a generally efficient way. Europe was gripped by wars and skirmishes in a bid to seize power under local strongmen and powerful families, such as the Lombards in Italy. All this had a devastating effect on trade, not to mention the plagues and epidemics which ravaged the population. Worst of all for the general progress of mankind was the decline in scholarly and artistic endeavour, then entirely in the grip of the Church. Both the clergy and the laity at this time viewed mankind's existence as beset by the struggle between the forces of God and the Devil: demons and devils roamed large, responsible for all ills that befell people or were sent as a punishment from a censorious god. Pagan and animistic ideas were also common amongst most simple folk, who were predominantly rural dwellers. Anything that people did not understand, such as disease, was put down to the work of the devil and his 'angels'. The Church and its sacraments provided the only refuge in the face of this unseen enemy and secular learning of every description was viewed with the utmost suspicion. The Church of Rome in the West and the Orthodox Church in the East were mired in superstition and ignorance, and regular campaigns were waged against all views not conforming to Christian dogma, particularly pagan beliefs. Education was offered exclusively to the clergy, but even then a Pauline pride in ignorance reigned, as already pointed out. The reading of any literature outside devotional works was condemned and the laity was forbidden to read the Scriptures, although few were able to do so, even if they had the desire. Even a relatively well–educated pope such as Gregory I (the Great) was to write of the Latin language, the lingua franca of the European Church: 'I despise the proper construction and cases, because I think it very unfitting that the words of the celestial oracle should be restricted by the rules of Donatus.' After sporadic orgies of book burning and destroying libraries, comprising mostly the works of Græco–Roman philosophers, the prominent Greek Father of the Church, biblical interpreter and archbishop of Constantinople, St John Chrysostom was to declare with pride that, 'Every trace of the old philosophy and literature of the ancient world has vanished from the face of the earth.'[22] He also issued a command to Orthodox believers, saying, 'Empty your minds of secular knowledge'. So much for one whose sobriquet was the 'Golden Mouthed'! St John, whom d'Holbach mentions in his *Christianity Unveiled*, enjoyed great popularity amongst the common people and he managed to attract great crowds when he preached. The whole attitude of the Church towards ancient culture was to jettison it and even expunge it. Early Christian zealots vandalized and defaced all

---

[22]   Quoted in Helen Ellerbe, p. 48.

manner of Græco–Roman artefacts, condemning them as the product of pagan worship, including the famous Elgin Marbles. History was later to repeat itself whenever other systems of belief claimed to have a monopoly on truth: the Bolsheviks in Russia in the early twentieth century destroyed religious icons and Orthodox churches and the Taliban committed similar acts of vandalism in March 2001, when they dynamited the huge Buddhas of Bamyan. All regimes claiming a unique insight and possession of one truth have always been ruthless in the way they treated other cultures that had preceded them.

In Europe of the middle ages a vast industry grew up around the collecting, buying and selling—and even forging—of religious relics, from the blood, bones and artefacts of saints and martyrs, to finding pieces of the 'true cross'. The Turin Shroud proved to be a prime example of medieval religious forgery, yet the Catholic Church continues to regard such objects as sacred and worthy of veneration, imbued with magical powers. All these elements were small but significant ways the Church and its bishops, in particular, accrued kudos and an air of authenticity, mystery, power, and influence over an ill–educated, gullible people. As a further hold over the people, the Church also gradually assumed the responsibility for giving alms to the poor and providing rudimentary medical services. This is not to imply that all people in monastic orders acted solely for ulterior motives, but it is a fact that anyone seeking help from the Church was made to feel a moral obligation and a debt to it, and offering such social succour was used as yet another lever of control, power and domination.

St Januarius (San Gennaro, Bishop of Naples) although consigned to a furnace to be roasted alive, emerged unscathed. Subsequently, he was thrown into the amphitheatre at Pozzuoli to be eaten alive by starved wild bears. Even so, the animals refused to eat him. He was eventually beheaded.

Characteristically, there is very limited information about his life and works. He is famous for the miraculous liquefaction of his blood, first reported in 1389. Dried blood, reputed to be his, is stored in vials in a reliquary, which, when paraded in public three times a year and brought near to his body, supposedly liquefies.

Figure 52: St Januarius (*c.* 275—305)

Figure 53: *The Hero and the Saint.* A print from *Punch, or the London Charivari*, 22 September 1860.
The priest is being directed over the edge of a cliff, clutching a miraculous *Winking Picture*, satirically depicted with a hidden mechanical device, and a bottle of the 'Blood of St Januarius'..

Whilst amassing vast fortunes, yet stigmatizing the lending of money at interest—a practice which Muslims still follow because it is condemned by the Koran—the Christian Church owned vast tracts of land and property.[23] Bishops operated territories under a feudal system, but they gradually became closely associated with cities; they sought freedom from paying taxes for themselves and sold indulgencies for the remission of sins and ecclesiastical offices. These practices were referred to as 'simony', after Simon Magus mentioned in Acts chapter 18, who tried to buy from the Apostles the power to confer gifts of the Holy Spirit upon people. A great deal of land and property was also in the hands of monastic orders. All in all, the Church in this early medieval period was more to do with money and power than with spiritual matters and it made sure that it was at the very centre of imperial force and military might. Rulers also knew that it was essential to keep the church hierarchy on their side because of the obvious power and influence they had over the common people. As d'Holbach points out, sovereigns were also cognisant of the cohesive role religion played in society. During this period, the Church was shrewd enough to allow the common people to continue with their pagan festivities and social practices, but they shifted the focus slightly by providing a veneer of Christianity, as per Pope Gregory I's recommendations to his emissary in Britain, St Augustine of Canterbury:

> ... the people will have no need to change their place of concourse; where of old they were wont to sacrifice cattle to demons, thither let them continue to resort on the day of the Saint to whom the Church is dedicated, and slay their beasts, no longer as a sacrifice to demons, but for a social meal in honour of Him whom they now worship.[24]

Thus the celebration of the Winter Solstice, rooted in paganism, was hijacked by the Church and was eventually to become a celebration of Christ's birth. In the twentieth century, the Bolsheviks in Russia took a similar approach, as they vainly tried to eradicate religion partly by stripping off the label 'Christian' and rebranding religious popular customs in line with

---

[23] The Koran 2: 275—76 forbids 'usury' but Muslims have gone to great lengths, aided by governments, to make sure that Muslims can still obtain mortgages to buy property without violating the letter of the law. This kind of wriggling out of what is obviously the spirit of the law by devious means is practised by vast numbers of believers of the three monotheistic religions, whenever their medieval beliefs clash markedly with modern social practices and when they want to avoid breaking the rules without actually transgressing the letter of the law. Similarly, when Jews wish to get round the ridiculous inconveniences of strict Sabbath observance, they establish an 'eruv', an 'enclosure', in which it is permitted to go about one's daily life relatively normally without breaking any rules: they enclose an area with a simple piece of wire, thus obviating the original, ludicrous command.

[24] Ellerbe, p. 52.

their own vision. The Christian Church transformed paganism in line with its own traditions by hijacking popular festivities and when this had been successfully completed, the event was made to look as though it had its origins in Christianity. This is certainly true of the ancient pagan tradition of 'well dressing' in Derbyshire.

Figure 54: Well Dressing in Derbyshire.

A typical design, predominately rendered in flower petals on a clay-coated board.

The common people could still not read any of the religious texts on which their faith was based—in fact, they were under pain of death not to do so, and therefore they learned of Christian myths and legends through priests and religious art: the frescoes in churches such as the Cappella Scrovegni, Padua assumed a sort of comic strip illustration of the bare essentials of Christ's life, miracles and passion. The Church also immortalized and mythologized the saints, elevating them to the status of demi–gods, notably in frescoes which we still admire today for their outstanding beauty and artistry: the Church of Santa Maria del Carmine in Florence is famous for its depiction in frescoes of the life of St Peter in the Brancacci Chapel, which shows St Peter unrealistically depicted against a background of Florentine buildings, and the painter Masaccio also injected a good measure of pathos in his depiction of the expulsion of Adam and Even from the Garden of Eden.

The Church largely had a monopoly on education and all forms of artistic creativity; it was to be some time before secular schools were established to provide an elementary education. Universities were originally bastions of religious orthodoxy with a tight grip on what could be taught in them, but gradually this grip was loosened and the universities founded in Paris, Oxford, Toulouse, Montellier, Cambridge, Salerno, Bologna and Salamanca gave rise to many brilliant men of science and literature, who were independent thinkers and challenged the Church and its dogmas.

With time, the three great monotheistic religions took on their own distinctive features and great enmity grew up between them, however many of the contentious issues were not so much doctrinal, as issues over power, influence and trade. Muslim expansion in the Middle East, and in particular the empire's control over 'sacred' sites such as Jerusalem, caused particular friction between the forces of Christianity and Islam. Holy wars or Crusades raged from the late eleventh century, promoted by Western Christians to check centuries of Muslim expansion. The combatants were successfully persuaded to take part in order to expiate their sins. Some prominent leaders of the Christian Church were virulently anti–Jewish, most notably SS John Chrysostom and Jerome, who promulgated the image of the Jews as a nation of deicidal apostates to be held eternally responsible for the death of Christ. Such views fanned the flames of hate and prejudice which persist even today: Mel Gibson's film *The Passion of Christ* (2004) became mired in controversy over who was responsible for the death of Christ. This accusation was levelled at the Jews by the Catholic Church for centuries, until the Second Vatican Council in 1965.

However, the Christian Church did not need to go as far as the so–called 'Holy Land' to find victims to persecute: they had the Cathars on their own doorstep in France and Italy.

Figure 55: Burning Cathars. Ilustration from *The History of Protestantism* by J.A. Wylie (1878).

The Cathars were a Christian religious sect who believed that man's existence in all its manifestations was riddled with a duality of good and evil, with an emphasis on the evil because of Adam's fall from God's grace. They believed the material world was evil. Though this sect had existed in the eleventh century and even earlier, it regained a considerable amount of popularity in the twelfth and it even became quite powerful in small enclaves—mainly in France and Italy. They appointed their own bishops and hierarchy, and set out their own very strict rules of religious observance. The Cathars rejected much of the Old Testament and the Incarnation of Christ, whom they regarded as a mere angel of God, but they levelled their severest criticism at the Catholic Church, much to its annoyance: they viewed its hierarchy and practices as corrupt, based wholly on avarice and worldly power. They thought that the Roman Church had strayed far from the simplicity of the original apostolic message, which of course was perfectly true. Pope Innocent III (1198—1216) unsuccessfully tried to diminish Cathar influence by preaching against them, but when this proved ineffectual, a crusade was initiated and it lasted over thirty years. Barons from northern France were mobilized against forces in the south and appalling numbers of people perished, decimating the people, culture and economy of the Languedoc and Provence. It is said that 20,000 people were killed in the town of Bésiers alone, and the papal legate Arnaud–Amaury was to report back to Pope Innocent III: 'Today, your Holiness, twenty thousand heretics were put to the sword, regardless of rank, age, or sex.' He had famously given the order, 'Kill them all. God will know his own.'[25] This carnage included women and children. There were other sites where such slaughter of their own Christian kindred took place in the area and it is estimated that around one million people were killed during this home–grown, European crusade. D'Holbach mentions such Christian assaults upon fellow Christians and these details are given to illustrate but one example of the point he makes in his polemic.

The Christian Church finally split along the broader lines of the Eastern and Western Church, fault–lines which had been developing for centuries. The Eastern Church, based in Constantinople, had retained its respect for art, literature and education, much more so than its western counterpart, and it had maintained a certain kudos derived from its linguistic heritage: it commonly used the Septuagint, the earliest Greek translation of the original Hebrew Old Testament, a version imbued with gravitas and moral superiority over any other. Many scholars of the Western Church did not know Greek— they knew Latin only. Much of the language used in the early Church had

---

[25] *Patrologia Latinae cursus completus*, series Latina, 221 vols, ed. J-P Migne (Paris, Vol 216: col 139). See also Ellerbe, pp. 74–75.

been Greek, which had been retained as the official language of law, government and, of course, classical Greek literature. Generally in the West medieval scribes could not read Greek, and the language, along with its cultural heritage, became synonymous with gibberish or a lack of understanding. (This is possibly the origin of the phrase, 'It's all Greek to me'.) Also between the Eastern and Western Churches major differences in ritual and emphases on doctrinal issues had developed. Hence in 1054, the two prodigious church traditions represented by Rome and Constantinople formalized their separation in an atmosphere of increasing rivalry and enmity, claims and counterclaims of being the true Church. Jews were caught in the cross–fire and seemed to become the enemy of all, including Islam.

The Revival of Philosophy in Western Europe

After a period of stagnation in the development of logic and dialectic, the works of Aristotle became known again in the late twelfth century through the arrival from Spain and Sicily of translations of a large proportion of the corpus of his works, translated back from Arabic translations, along with scholarly commentaries. These works were largely the fruit of the labours of a Muslim philosopher called Averroës (1126—1198) between 1169 and 1195, who commented on many of Aristotle's works and he was hugely influential not only in the Islamic world, but also in Europe. Through Aristotle's works on metaphysics, and ethics in particular, the Dominican thinkers St Albertus Magnus and St Thomas Aquinas applied Aristotle's systematic approach to Christianity. Aquinas dedicated some twenty–five years to rethinking Aristotle and thus he elevated theology from accepting dogmas as mere articles of faith (though some faith was obviously still required), to setting it firmly upon a philosophical foundation. Though the opening of the western mind to philosophical discourse did not happen overnight, and there would still be many mountains to climb, there was a gradual renewed acceptance of Greek rationality and empiricism. Greek philosophy, as exemplified by Aquinas' work on Aristotle, was used to confront issues such as the proofs of the existence of God, free will, etc., which became known as Scholasticism: it was not so much a school of thought or a movement, but more a methodology. Scholastic thinking generally embraced logic, metaphysics and semantics, and it developed as a single discipline, being applied to biblical, as well as to secular, texts recently rediscovered from classical antiquity. Some conservative theologians within the Church were suspicious of studying any form of secular knowledge and were worried that non–devotional material would allow the reader to stray from the path of faith. Arguments and disputes in the twelfth century tended to centre on issues such as these.

As Islam spread from the seventh century AD onwards through the Middle East to Africa, Europe and beyond, the Arabs tolerated and even revered the Greek intellectual tradition. In the ninth and tenth centuries, most of the great Greek thinkers such as Aristotle, Plato, Hippocrates, Galen, Euclid and Ptolemy were accurately translated into Arabic by teams of scholars in order that their ideas might be studied by Arab intellectuals. Christianity had shunned intellectual enquiry and had placed greater emphasis upon blind faith, largely feeding off the irrational, such as miraculous phenomena, but despite their religious faith, the Arabs were beginning to take up where the Greeks had left off. The Muslim philosopher Averroës was typical of a much less dogmatic mind–set during this period of Islam, believing that 'religion and philosophy reached the same truths but by different routes and thus could exist alongside each other'.[26]

Towards the end of the twelfth century the first universities in Paris and Oxford were founded, where secular thought was taught. Albertus Magnus (Albert the Great) (1200—1280) was the first to introduce Aristotle to Europe, claiming that discoveries of God's creation could never contradict articles of faith and that there was harmony to be gained through a knowledge of the natural world, combined with the Scriptures. His student, Thomas Aquinas (1224/5—1274) adapted Aristotelian thought to Christianity and he became one of the great philosophers of the Roman Catholic Church: his voluminous writing and philosophy stood alone in its own right, and it became known as Thomism. Aquinas had studied at the university in Naples where he had been exposed to the works of both Jewish and Arab philosophers. He went on to study in Cologne, where he met Albertus, and then moved on to teach theology all over Italy. He produced two monumental works, *Summa contra gentiles* {*Summary Against the Gentiles*, but often left untranslated} between 1258 and 1264, which was a defence of Christianity against unbelievers, and his *Summa theologiae* {*Summary of Theology*}, written as a systematized summation of theological belief at the height of his career in Paris and Rome between 1265 and 1274. Whereas St Augustine had placed faith *above* reason, Aquinas restored reason to its rightful place and he did much to try to dispel the myth that it had been corrupted by original sin, rendering it untrustworthy, as Augustine had argued. Aquinas saw the human ability to reason as one of God's greatest gifts and believed that a better understanding of the natural world could only be to the greater glory of God and an increased understanding of him.

---

[26] Charles Freeman, *The Closing of the Western Mind: The Rise of Faith and the Fall of Reason* (London: Pimlico, 2003), p. 331.

Of course, as rationality and intellectual enquiry discovered more about the universe and empirical knowledge proved the Church to be wrong time and again about so many things taught as articles of faith, more clashes were inevitable, as the disputes with Copernicus and Galileo illustrate perfectly.

In the wake of the Cathar furore and the ubiquitous existence of alchemy, witchcraft and sorcery—hang–overs of European medieval paganism—Pope Gregory IX decided it was high time for a purge of heretical belief: to this end, he inaugurated a papal Inquisition to seek out and suppress heretics of all hues. Heretics, dissenters and doubters for any absolute regime, be it religious, such as the Roman Catholic Church, or secular, such as the Soviet Union in the twentieth century, saw such people as a pernicious influence and a major threat to unity and official dogma. The phenomenon referred to as the Inquisition was complex because it took various forms over a protracted period, depending on who was in charge and where it was taking place: torture was not used from the outset and the person deemed to be a heretic was given the chance to recant and return to the fold. The penalties were also not always death, depending on the degree of severity of the transgression, and often the 'sinner' got away with some form of religious penance. In northern Europe the Inquisition took a relatively mild form and was mostly applied in northern Italy and southern France, but the excesses of the Inquisition, now the stuff of legend, were all committed in Spain under Tomás Torquemada (1420—1498), the first grand inquisitor in Spain, whose name has become synonymous with the worst of Christian bigotry and cruel fanaticism. He was closely associated with the religious policy of King Ferdinand II and Queen Isabella I, to whom he was both confessor and adviser (to Isabella, from her childhood). He was convinced that the existence of the Marranos (Jewish 'converts'), Moriscos (Islamic converts), Jews and Moors was a threat to the religious and social life of Spain, and his influence with Catholic monarchs enabled him to affect their policies. In August 1483 he was appointed Grand Inquisitor for Castile and León, and on October 17 of that year his powers were extended to Aragon, Catalonia, Valencia, and Majorca. In his capacity as grand inquisitor, Torquemada reorganized the Spanish Inquisition, already established in Castile in 1478, establishing tribunals at Sevilla (Seville), Jaén, Córdoba, Ciudad Real, and, later, Zaragoza. In 1484 he promulgated twenty–eight articles for the guidance of inquisitors, whose competence was extended to include not only crimes of heresy and apostasy, but also sorcery, sodomy, polygamy, blasphemy, usury and other offences. Torture was authorized and widely used in order to obtain 'evidence'. These articles were supplemented by others promulgated between 1484 and 1498. The number of burnings at the stake during Torquemada's tenure has been estimated at about 2,000.[27]

This period of European history overturned so many of the basic tenets of justice and the judicial process: the accused was presumed guilty, not innocent and denied the right to counsel; the circumstances of the accusation were not fully explained or any accusers' names disclosed; friends and acquaintances were guilty by association.[28] Also church inquisitors often profited handsomely from the whole process, accepting money like a form of 'protection racket' to ensure a person did not fall foul of them, but part of the sentence in some of the most serious cases involved the confiscation of goods, property and money, which they kept. The seeking out 'heresy' obviously paid. When the ultimate penalty was meted out, those found guilty were burned at the stake and the Church managed to find scriptural sanction for this in the Gospel of John, '*If a man abide not in me, he is cast forth as a branch, and is withered; and men gather them, and cast them into the fire, and they are burned.*'[29]

Not content with the destruction of human life in Europe, in 1570 Christians 'established an independent tribunal in Peru and the city of Mexico for the purpose of "freeing the land, which has become contaminated by Jews and heretics".' This resulted in any native who did not convert to Christianity being burned at the stake.[30] This kind of behaviour was repeated in other 'pagan' lands also.

After the major doctrinal issues that divided the Church between Rome and Constantinople in the fifth to the sixth centuries, and the subsequent major split between the Churches of the West and East in the ninth, there ensued another century of in–fighting—this time exclusively within the Western Church during the fourteenth over the location of the papal seat. The issue was whether the seat ought to be in Avignon or Rome: again this had little to do with religious dogma and everything to do with politics and power.

Hardly had the Church's appalling behaviour during the Inquisition faded to but a dim memory, than the next major calamity to befall Western Christendom arose: it was the Reformation, and this time it would cause a major split within the Western Church, which divided it permanently

---

[27] 'Torquemada, Tomás de.' *Encyclopaedia Britannica 2008 Ultimate Reference Suite* (Chicago: Encyclopædia Britannica, 2008).

[28] Ellerbe, op. cit., p. 78. There are echoes here of Guantanamo Bay!

[29] These sentiments are echoed in many verses of the Gospels, e.g., Matt. 7: 19; Luke 3: 9, etc.

[30] Ellerbe, p. 88.

Figure 56: *Burning Maria and Ursula van Backum.* Illustration by Jan Luiken (1649—1712), from *The Martyrs' Mirror*, Thieleman J. van Braght (Amsterdam, 1685).

into Roman Catholic and Protestant factions. No wonder d'Holbach repeatedly refers to the Church's constant in–fighting and skirmishes, and as he also points out, many of these directly involved rulers of all kinds, too numerous to mention here.

The fundamental split between the Roman Catholic and Protestant Churches occurred over a protracted period and the events leading up to it were complex: the schism, known as the Reformation, took place in the sixteenth century. The chief protagonists were John Calvin (1509—1564) and Martin Luther (1483—1546), but there was a host of minor and not–so–minor characters who collectively played an important role. The Reformation did not come out of the blue: the Church of Rome had long suffered and tried to silence its trenchant critics over its overt lust for riches and power, and by the Middle Ages the institution seemed to have strayed far from Christ's and the early apostles' message of a simple life of self–sacrifice and preaching the gospel. Men such as Jan Hus (1370—1415), the Czech religious reformer, were critical of the Church's obsession with land, wealth and power, but there were also wrangles over doctrinal issues. The Church's accumulation of wealth through the selling of indulgencies, which was a rich man's charter for paying their way out of sin, revolted Hus and a good number of poor priests, who could see it growing fat on the proceeds of selling forgiveness for sins committed which had no basis in Holy Writ. For his dissention, the Church burned Hus at the stake. John Wycliffe (1330—1384), a Yorkshireman, voiced similar objections in England, and these men were forerunners of the Reformation. However, the Reformation was not solely about ecclesiastical reform and dissention: it had major social, economic and political ramifications, the effects of which are still felt to this day.

Whilst for the masses it was business as usual, within the Church of the sixteenth century a number of scholars attacked it in the form of an in–house *coup*, chief amongst them being Erasmus of Rotterdam (1469—1536) and Martin Luther (1483—1546), whose salvo shook the hierarchy for its involvement in politics and power–grabbing, and being more concerned over temporal, than spiritual, power. Luther is said to have pinned a list of 'Ninety–Five Theses', or points for reform, on a church door in Wittenberg on 31 October 1517—the traditional date cited for the beginning of the Reformation, although some scholars have questioned the veracity of this event. Luther found the papal sale of 'indulgencies', or 'pardons for sin', particularly offensive and seedy, believing it to be contrary to biblical teaching. This issue had a knock–on effect, giving rise to a debate on a very basic issue: how might a person be granted divine grace and forgiveness, and who had the power or right to dispense pardons? This need to re–assess such a fundamental and essential tenet of Christian teaching is indicative of just how far the whole church edifice had strayed from the original gospel message.

Whilst church corruption featured in Luther's list of complaints, he also raised a number of doctrinal and theological issues which were the real cause of such a seismic schism in the Catholic Church, leading to the formation of the Protestant faction.

The doctrine of predestination was pivotal as events unfolded. The principal proponents of predestination were Martin Luther and John Calvin. The doctrinal issues revolved around whether the Church had the power to mediate between God and man by providing a route to salvation through good works, faithful service, intercession by saints, etc., and God's mother, just for luck, or whether, as St Paul maintained in his Epistles, based on Christ's teaching, salvation was a matter of God's personal choice in nominating a person to be saved from eternal damnation. Calvin preached that a person was specially *'chosen before the foundation of the world'* to become one of God's *'elect'*, and without this overt favourism on God's part, a person was doomed, despite all best efforts. Calvin's chief text for these ideas is to be found in the Book of Ephesians, where St Paul writes, *'Blessed be the God and Father of our Lord Jesus Christ, who hath blessed us with all spiritual blessings in heavenly places in Christ: According as **he hath chosen us in him before the foundation of the world**, that we should be holy and without blame before him in love: **Having predestinated us unto the adoption of children by Jesus Christ to himself, according to the good pleasure of his will**...'*, (Eph. 1: 3—5; the same ideas are expressed in 1 Peter 1: 20.) Hence, the inference to be drawn is that man does not choose God, but God chooses man. Also, Luther and Calvin maintained that the only source of authority was Scripture, not the pope, and that man, having inherited Adam's corrupt and sinful nature, could only be justified by faith through Christ and by no other means—no number of 'good works' would do the trick of keeping a person out of hell fire. Thus the gift of salvation was arrested from the money-grubbing grasp of the Catholic Church and transferred to a personal relationship with Christ—free at the point of delivery, provided that one had been selected first. This was indeed a seismic shift in thinking.

For his temerity Luther was excommunicated in 1521, and the reforms which ensued split the Church into Roman Catholic and Protestant factions. Within these two broad camps other cliques rallied, based on tenuous, hair-splitting theological emphases: there were those who insisted that baptism should be a conscious decision made by an adult who had accepted Christ as a personal saviour (the Anabaptists), and yet others rejected the idea of transubstantiation—an 'old chestnut' for renewed debate, as critics went back

345

to first principles laid down in the Scriptures. There were other issues which caused the Church to fracture into sects, many of which still exist today.

Figure 57: Portrait of Sir Thomas More, Hans Holbein the Younger (1527). (Source: Wikipedia.)

In England, the process and results of the Reformation were as political as they were religious. Angered by Pope Clement VII's refusal to grant a dissolution of his marriage to Catherine of Aragon, Henry VIII repudiated papal authority and the Catholic Church with it: in 1534 he established the Anglican Church, nominating himself as its supreme head—a title which exists even today. The clergy were forced by Henry to accede to these new offices and when the recalcitrant Sir Thomas More (1477—1535) refused, he was executed. (Predictably the Catholic Church canonized him in 1935, though why they had waited so long to do so is not clear.)

There were further disputes over whether common men and women had the right to read the Bible for themselves—an act deemed dangerous by many clerics, and Bergier expresses this sentiment in his refutation. For their temerity in doing so—were they able—the Church's punishment was death at this time. This issue provided the impetus for making new translations of the Bible and the preparation of the Book of Common Prayer. In Scotland, John Knox (1514—1572), heavily influenced by Calvin in Geneva, led the establishment of the Presbyterian Church. Most Englishmen had had to wait until the late thirteenth and early fourteenth century before work had been undertaken to translate the Bible from a Latin translation of the original Hebrew and Greek into English (known as the Wycliffe Bible). However, there was tremendous opposition to this translation by the Church and copies of it were burned when they were found. The brief efflorescence of the Protestant movement during the short reign of Edward VI (1547—53) saw the reissue of the biblical texts in English, but no fresh attempts at a revision. The repressive rule of Edward's successor Mary, a Roman Catholic, put an end to the printing of Bibles in England for several years. The persecution of Protestants caused the focus of English biblical scholarship to be shifted abroad where it flourished in greater freedom. A colony of Protestant exiles led by Coverdale and John Knox (the Scottish Reformer), and under the influence of John Calvin, published the New Testament in 1557. The Geneva Bible, originally published in 1560, was not printed in England until 1576, but it was allowed to be imported without hindrance. The accession of Elizabeth I in 1558 put an end to the persecution. The Geneva Bible then gained instantaneous and lasting popularity over all other versions. Its technical innovations contributed not a little to its becoming for a long time the family Bible of England, which, next to Tyndale, exercised the greatest influence upon the *King James Version*. The first full translation of the New Testament to appear in France was in 1523, which was a translation from the Latin *Vulgate* and not from the original Greek. The full Bible translated from the original Hebrew and Greek did not appear in France until 1535.

As doctrinal and theological disputes raged and the Protestant Church formed, this upheaval served as an impetus for the Roman Catholic Church to examine its own stance on a number of issues and re–assert its authority and teaching. It rejected the concept that Scripture had the final word on all matters doctrinal, recognizing that various personal emphases may be read into Scripture. The Catholic Church reaffirmed its position that reading and interpreting the Bible had to go hand in hand with what the Church taught, as expressed by the vast body of writings produced by its own Church Fathers and saints. Personal reading and understanding of Scripture amongst the masses was and never has been promoted by the Catholic Church, which preferred to tell its adherents what to believe, rather than encourage personal interpretation, as became the practice in the Protestant tradition. The *imposition* of a body of belief was a strong, unifying force throughout the Catholic confession, much more so than amongst Christians of other persuasions.

The Reformation led the Catholic Church to restate its position on many issues and this process became known as the Counter Reformation, a distinct historical movement in sixteenth–century Europe. The expression of the Roman Catholic Church's reforms during this period was voiced through the Council of Trent, which met intermittently between 1545 and 1563, and the outcome of the Council was seen as the last word in Catholic doctrine at that time. The Church affirmed that salvation was to be had through the auspices of the teaching of the Catholic Church, along with good works and faith, and it also reaffirmed the primacy of the Latin *Vulgate* version of the Bible—a closed book to virtually all its faithful at the time.

The Catholic Church also formalized its provisions for the education of priests in seminaries under strict church control, and many of the corrupt practices regarding the regulation and accumulation of wealth were reformed. The celebration of mass was also prescribed and made more or less universal. All in all, the Roman Catholic Church was reformed in a way one would recognize today.

The emphasis on teaching and preparing men for the priesthood brought the Jesuits, or the religious order known as the Society of Jesus, founded in 1534, into particular prominence: they became the vanguard in the reconstruction of church life and teaching in the aftermath of the Reformation. Above all, they were active in educating members of the nobility and by this they insinuated themselves yet again into a position close to political power and influence. They were also entrusted with much of the Church's missionary work abroad, though it did not fall exclusively within their remit.

A further controversy in France was caused by the posthumous publication of a work entitled *Augustinus* (1640) by a Dutch theologian named Cornelius Jansen, who defended the doctrines of Augustine against the then dominant theological trends within Roman Catholicism. The book's special target was the teachings and practices of the Jesuits, who, Jansen claimed, had erred in the opposite direction while opposing Luther and Calvin in their definition of the doctrine of grace: by emphasizing human responsibility at the expense of divine initiative, Jansen believed that the Jesuits had relapsed into the Pelagian heresy, which Augustine had fought against in the early fifth century. Jansen asserted the Augustinian doctrine of original sin, including the teaching that man cannot keep the commandments of God without a special gift of grace and that the converting grace of God is irresistible. In essence his ideas were tantamount to Calvinism and his book caused a long, bitter controversy. The debate developed into a more general campaign against Jesuit theology and Pope Innocent X (reigned 1644—55) issued his bull *Cum occasione* {*With Occasion*} against Jansenism in 1653, but Jansenism was espoused by the French philosopher Blaise Pascal in his *Lettres provinciales* {*Provincial Letters*} (1656—57), adding more fuel to the fire. The next pope, Clement XI (reigned 1700—21), promulgated his constitution *Unigenitus* {*Only–Begotten*} and Pascal's book *Provincial Letters* ended up on the *Index of Prohibited Books* in 1657.

The *Index Librorum Prohibitorum* {*Index of Prohibited* [or *Forbidden*] *Books*} was instituted in the wake of the Counter Reformation, upon which d'Holbach's works were placed, once their authorship could be attributed to him. It remained in place until 1966 and grew in length, as one might expect, as all works which criticized the Church and voiced atheist ideas were added to it, along with works of authors who later expressed left–wing and communist ideas. As already stated, not a single work of Hitler's was ever placed on it.

During the Reformation, the Catholic Church lost influence in some geographical areas where it had previously been powerful: these were most of the 'German *lands*' (semi–autonomous areas in Germany and Austria, governed locally), where Luther's influence was felt the keenest. However, by the end of the sixteenth century Bavaria and Austria became predominantly Catholic again. Tragically, it was through yet more violent means that further geographical areas were regained for Catholicism. 'The Wars of Religion' (1562 to 1598), resulted in France becoming Catholic again, but Protestants were given a limited guarantee though the Edict of Nantes (1598) that they would be tolerated, rather than persecuted. This was effective for a time, until the edict was revoked in 1685, when the Huguenots (as French Protestants were known) were ejected from France (see below). Catholicism was restored in Poland and Bohemia also.

Europe suffered enormous damage and loss of human life in a series of wars known as 'The Thirty Years' Wars' (1618 to1648), and whilst these struggles were over commercial, dynastic and territorial issues, they were also fuelled by religious prejudice. D'Holbach makes reference to some of these events and the general reader can set aside the historical minutiae involved, whilst acknowledging that sovereigns got embroiled in disputes and military action in which the clergy and church hierarchy played a distinctive role, as they all jostled for power and influence with their neighbours.

The Huguenots were a significant group in the sixteenth and seventeenth centuries. (The origin of their name is not clear.) The first Huguenot community to be founded on French territory was in Meaux in 1546 and the Huguenot Church in Paris was founded in about 1555, against a good deal of religious persecution and opposition from the Catholics. The violence and confusion engendered during the 'Wars of Religion' produced in France a famous incident called the Massacre of St Bartholomew's Day, when almost all the leading Huguenots in Paris were slain. The Paris massacre was repeated throughout France, as Protestants were killed in their thousands. The Huguenots at first hoped that the crown of France would pass to a Huguenot, but when it became obvious that this would not happen, they fought for full religious and civil liberties within the state. After forty years of strife, Henry IV promulgated the Edict of Nantes in April 1598, granting the Huguenots their religious and political freedom. However, civil wars occurred again in the 1620s under King Louis XIII and eventually the Huguenots were defeated. The Peace of Alès was signed in 1629, whereby the Huguenots were allowed to retain their freedom of conscience but lost all their military advantages. This was enough to neutralize them as a political force and they became loyal subjects of the king. Their remaining rights under the Edict of Nantes were confirmed by a royal declaration in 1643 on behalf of the infant king, Louis XIV. However, the Roman Catholic clergy could never accept the Huguenots and they worked to deprive them of their rights. General harassment and the forcible conversion of thousands of Protestants were wide–spread for many years. Finally in 1685 Louis XIV revoked the Edict of Nantes and, fearing yet more persecution, the Huguenots emigrated *en masse*, resulting in France losing more than 400,000 of its Protestant inhabitants over the next several years. Many emigrated to England, Prussia, the Netherlands and America, and continued to be the useful, productive citizens in their adopted countries as they had been in France. Many Huguenots had been urban people, working in commerce and industry, and their absence caused considerable financial damage to France and a serious loss of skilled workers for the coming Industrial Revolution.

The Rise and Influence of Deism

One of the chief religious influences amongst intellectuals in d'Holbach's time and evident in his coterie was Deism, an unorthodox religious belief which was mainly confined to England, France and Germany, and which subsequently spread to America. As a belief system, it started around the first half of the seventeenth century with Edward Herbert and it ended with Viscount Bolingbroke (Henry St John) around the middle of the eighteenth century. The main centres of deist belief—England and France—had a symbiotic relationship, a cross–fertilization of the writings of French and English philosophers. D'Holbach translated a number of English deist texts into French, though there were fewer translations the other way. The high point of Deism occurred in England from around 1689 to 1742, where people were freer than in France to express dissenting and unorthodox views on religious issues.

Deism is called a 'natural religion' because it relies for its ideas not on revealed dogma and sacred texts, but upon personal experience and a sense of innate religiosity. Both Protestant and Catholic churches were hostile to these ideas, and the reverse was also true. Deists believed in a rather nebulous, creator god whose handiwork was complete at the point of creation and who intervened little, if at all, in human affairs, like Plato's Demiurge. They used the analogy of a watch as evidence of the divine being, i.e., the Watchmaker argument (see pp. liv & 285). They also rejected most forms of divine, written revelation and they certainly refused to believe it was inspired by the Holy Spirit and inerrant.

When this controversy was at its peak (1754—56), John Leland put together a compendium of Deist thought under the characteristically long title of *A View of the Principal Deistical Writers that Have Appeared in England in the Last and Present Century: with Observations upon Them, and Some Account of the Answers that Have Been Published Against Them.*[31] Those

---

[31] Originaly published in 1754 and reprinted with an Appendix and Introduction by W.L. Brown, D.D. and Cyrus R. Edmonds (resp.) in 1837 in London. The latter edition can be read as a Google DigitalBook at http://books.google.co.uk/books?hl=en&id=Rt9J

who contributed to the work represent a fairly comprehensive list of English Deists: Lord Herbert of Cherbury, Thomas Hobbes, Charles Blount, the Earl of Shaftesbury, Anthony Collins, Thomas Woolston, Matthew Tindal, Thomas Morgan, Thomas Chubb and the Viscount Bolingbroke. To this list, John Toland can be added, particularly since d'Holbach translated his *Letters to Serena* (1704), which appeared in his volume *Lettres Philosophiques {Philosophical Letters}* (1768), and his influence is to be detected in several of d'Holbach's works, notably *Christianity Unveiled*, in which he mentions the Ebionite sect (q.v.), about whom Toland wrote in his *Nazarenus* (1718). Also the work of **Peter Annet** (1693—1769) must be mentioned, since there is a work, often attributed to him, entitled *A History of the Man after God's own Heart* (1761), which d'Holbach also translated as *David, ou l'Histoire de l'Homme selon le Cœur de Dieu {David, or the History [or Story] of the Man After God's Own Heart}* (1768). These men all represented quite a broad church (in a figurative sense) in terms of belief—some writing in more militant, radical terms than others, and each one putting his own individual emphasis on a particular aspect. Toland stressed the rational element in natural religion, set out in his treatise *Christianity Not Mysterious: or a Treatise Shewing That There is Nothing in the Gospel Contrary to Reason, Nor above It* (1696), saying:

> On the contrary, we hold that Reason is the only foundation of all certitude, and that nothing revealed, whether as to its manner or existence, is more exempted from its disquisitions than the ordinary phenomena of nature. Wherefore, we likewise maintain, according to the title of this discourse, that *there is nothing in the Gospel contrary to reason, nor above it; and that no* Christian doctrine can be properly called a mystery...[32]

Other thinkers, like Shaftesbury, who would not have owned the label 'Deist', but whose views were almost identical to theirs, emphasized the emotive quality of a personal religious experience. All agreed in denouncing religious intolerance, especially as exemplified by the many wars, inquisitions and bitters schisms, which religious belief had fomented within orthodox Christianity of all hues. Many Deists also played down Christianity's claims to uniqueness and they took an interest in the teaching of Buddha and Muhammad: a number of them also analysed ancient religions and drew general inferences from them.

AAAAMAAJ&dq=leland+%22A+View+of+the+Principal+Deistical+Writers%22&sa=X&oi=book_result&resnum=1

[32] John Toland, *Christianity Not Mysterious* (London: Sam Buckley, 1696), p. 6.

Figure 58: John Toland (1670—1722).

This is the only known portrait of John Toland which appeared in the third volume
of *Versuch einer Vollständige Engländische Freydenker-Bibliothek* [*An Attempt of a
Complete Library of English Free-Thinkers*], U. G. Thorschmid (1766).

**Figure 59: Matthew Tindal (1657—1733), John Faber Jr.,
after Matthew Dandridge (1733).**

Most Deists accepted the moral teaching of the Bible but rejected much of its historicity and prophetic claims. Toland was virulent in his denial of all aspects of mystery and chimeras, and all were united against all forms of religious fanaticism.

In France, Deistic ideas were embraced chiefly by Pierre Bayle, Voltaire, D'Alembert, Montaigne, Montesquieu, and to a large extent Rousseau. Deism became known in Germany largely through translations of Shaftesbury's works, partly through the philosopher and mathematician Leibniz, who adopted a position similar to that of Voltaire's. It is also claimed that English Deists influenced the whole officer corps of Frederick the Great, whose favourite reading was Collins and Tindal.

The ideas and theories of Boulanger (1722—1759) on floods and natural disasters as man's impetus to look for a deity (see p. liii) are reflected in David Hume's ideas, as expressed in his *The Natural History of Religion* (1757):

> The primary religion of mankind arises chiefly from an anxious fear of future events; and what ideas will naturally be entertained of invisible, unknown powers, while men lie under dismal apprehensions of any kind, may easily be conceived. Every image of vengeance, severity, cruelty, and malice must occur, and must augment the ghastliness and horror which oppresses the amazed religionist. [...] And no idea of perverse wickedness can be framed, which those terrified devotees do not readily, without scruple, apply to their deity.[33]

In many ways this was exemplary of the kind of cross–fertilization of ideas being bandied across the English Channel. Nor were these cross–currents restricted to philosophical circles: it is known that the poet Percy Bysshe Shelley (1792—1822) had been a diligent reader from an early age of Helvétius, d'Holbach, Condorcet and Volney, and there are clear signs of their influence in his poetry, and especially in his *Queen Mab* (1813), where the poet quotes d'Holbach's *System of Nature* extensively in his notes to that poem.[34]

By the end of the eighteenth century, Deism had also spread to America through Thomas Paine's *The Age of Reason* (1794) and Benjamin Franklin, who had visited Paris and knew a number of intellectuals there, including

---

[33] David Hume, *The Natural History of Religion*, Section XIII.

[34] For an analysis of the influence of d'Holbach's *System of Nature* upon Shelley's *Queen Mab*, see J.W. Beach, *The concept of Nature in Nineteenth-Century English Poetry* (New York: Macmillan, 1936), pp. 215—228. The compendium of Christopher Hitchens, *The Portable Atheist* (see Bibliography) also contains an extract of Shelley's writing on religion.

d'Holbach. Deist ideas spread to such an extent that the first three presidents of the United States of America held deistic convictions. Sadly that relatively liberal tradition has become mired in bible–bashing Christianity and the delusion that God harbours a special place in his heart for America. This is a conviction that would have horrified Paine and the Founding Fathers, as Michael Moore has pointed out:

> The Founding Fathers would never have uttered the presumptuous words, 'God Bless America.' That, to them, sounded like a command instead of a request, and one doesn't command God, even if they are America [sic]. In fact, they were worried God would punish America. During the Revolutionary War, George Washington feared that God would react unfavorably against his soldiers for the way they were behaving. John Adams wondered if God might punish America and cause it to lose the war, just to prove His point that America was not worthy. They and the others believed it would be arrogant on their part to assume that God would single out America for a blessing. What a long road we have travelled since then.[35]

By the end of the 1800s, Deism was more or less a spent force and it evolved into other belief systems and philosophies: the writings of Hume, Kant and Darwin were contributory factors to its decline and to religious belief in general, which had been seriously challenged by the Age of the Enlightenment.

---

[35] Monday, March 24th, 2008
So? ... A Note from Michael Moore
This article can be read at
http://www.michaelmoore.com/words/message/index.php?messageDate=2008-03-24

Figure 60: *Venus and Adonis,* Titian (c. 1555)

Glossary

I have relied heavily on information given in the *Encyclopædia Britannica* as on the DVD of the *Encyclopaedia Britannica 2008 Ultimate Reference Suite*, (Chicago: Encyclopædia Britannica) for much of the information provided in this Glossary: the original entries in the encyclopaedia are much more detailed and well worth reading Where other sources have been used substantially, they are acknowledged.   One such is the *Catholic Encyclopedia*, accessible on–line at http://www.catholic.org/encyclopedia/; however one has to bear in mind that the information contained there is not always impartial.

Achilles was a mythical character who was the bravest, most handsome and the greatest warrior of the army of Agamemnon in the Trojan War. One of the non–Homeric tales of his childhood relates that Thetis dipped Achilles in the waters of the River Styx, by which he became invulnerable, except for the part of his heel by which she held him; whence the proverbial 'Achilles' heel'.

Acosta, Father Joseph de (*c.* 1540—1600) was a Jesuit priest and ethnographer who wrote a multi–volume work entitled *Historia natural y moral de la Indias* {*A Natural and Moral History of the Indias*, i.e., South America}, which was published in Barcelona in 1591, and appeared subsequently in many editions.

Adonis was a youth in Greek mythology of remarkable beauty, the favourite of the goddess Aphrodite. He was the product of an incestuous love affair between Smyrna (Myrrha) and her father, the Syrian king Theias. Charmed by his beauty, Aphrodite put the newborn infant Adonis in a box and entrusted his care to Persephone, the queen of the Underworld, who subsequently refused to give him up. On appeal to Zeus, King of the Gods, it was decided that Adonis should spend each year equally between Persephone and Aphrodite, and the remaining four months were at his own disposal. Adonis became an enthusiastic hunter, but he met his end on one trip by a wild boar. Aphrodite again pleaded for him with Zeus, this time for his life, and he allowed him to spend half of each year with her and half in the Underworld. The central idea of the myth is the cyclical death in winter and revival or rebirth in spring.

Akenside, Mark (1721—1770) was a poet and physician, best known for his poem *The Pleasures of Imagination*, an eclectic philosophical essay that takes as its starting point papers on the same subject written by Joseph Addison for *The Spectator*. The poem was written in blank verse, after Milton, Virgil's *Georgics*, and Horace's *Epistles*. Samuel Johnson said his politics were characterized by an 'impetuous eagerness to subvert and confound, with very little care what shall be established', and he is caricatured in the republican doctor of Tobias Smollett's *The Adventures of Peregrine Pickle*. Akenside published further volumes of poetry with the ode as his favourite form. Initially Akenside studied for the ministry, but later changed to medicine. In 1744, he turned to satire with his *An Epistle to Curio*, occasioned by the political volte–face made by William Pulteney who, despite his long–standing Whig sympathies, accepted the earldom of Bath from a Tory ministry. He was an accomplished physician who attended the queen, Charlotte Sophia of Mecklenburg–Strelitz, wife of George III.

Aharimane q.v. Zoroaster/Zoroastrianism

Amenophis, King is more commonly known as King Akhenaton in the modern era, but he is also known as Akhnaton, or Ikhnaton, and as king of Egypt (1353—36 BC) he is known as Amenhotep IV; he established a new monotheistic cult of Aton. (It is thought that his name Akhenaton means *'One Useful to Aton'*.) The religion of ancient Egypt was static and traditional, and on the assumption that the gods had established order the people were urged to hold fast to the *status quo*. When changes did occur, religion tried to incorporate them into the system as though they came from the creation. By the time Akhenaton took the throne as the fourth pharaoh named Amenhotep, the eighteenth dynasty (1539—1292 BC) had run for nearly two hundred years and there had been a century of imperial conquest and control of foreign lands. Egypt dominated Palestine, Phoenicia and Nubia. The nation was powerful and rich, and courted by lesser princes. To maintain these gains, a military and political group controlled all culture: the Egyptian state had always been theocratic, i.e., ruled by a god or gods, and this group acted in tandem with the priesthood. The richest and most powerful of the gods, such as Amon of Thebes, or Re of Heliopolis, was said to dictate the purpose of the state. The king had to apply to the gods for oracles directing his major activities. In return for wealth, elegance and the role of the leading actor in a drama of imperial success, the pharaoh had relinquished his religious (and military) authority to others. Within his first few years as pharaoh, Akhenaton made changes: he abandoned the temple to Re–Harakhte and began to build a place to worship a new form of sun–god—the disk of the sun, called the Aton. It had been a little–known deity for two generations before him. The Aton was never shown in human or animal form, but as the extended rays of the sun disk conferring blessings upon men. This was the life–giving and life–sustaining power of the sun. He had no image in the hidden sanctuary of a temple, but was to be worshiped out in sun–warmed openness. The Aton religion was an adoration of nature without an ethical code. Men were asked only to be grateful to the sun for life and warmth. It was unlike the awesome austerity of the great gods of former Egypt, who might punish man for disobedience. It was quite unlike the heavy demands that the Hebrew god would lay upon his people. In the Aton religion there was no 'Thou shalt...' and 'Thou shalt not...'

Figure 61: The Sun–God, Aton or Aten.

Note that this representation of the Sun-God broke with convention and was diagramatic in appearance rather than with human or animal form.

Figure 62: The conventional Sun–God, Re.

Ammonius (fl. *c.* 550) held the chair of philosophy at Alexandria and is known chiefly for his commentaries on Aristotle, though he was also a distinguished astronomer and geometrician. He taught all the important Platonists who followed him in the late–fifth and early–sixth centuries, such as Asclepius, Philoponus and Simplicius, amongst others. During his tenure in Alexandria the school was an important centre of Christian culture, which at times was subjected to hostile attacks, of which Hypatia (q.v.) was the most famous example.

Ammonius Saccas (fl. 3rd century AD) was a Greek philosopher from Alexandria who is often credited with being one of the founders of Neo-Platonism. Some Christian writers have suggested that Ammonius Saccas was a Christian, but it is now assumed that there was a different Ammonius of Alexandria who wrote Biblical texts. Not much is known about the life of Ammonius Saccas. He had a humble background and appears to have earned his living as a porter in the docks of Alexandria, hence his nickname of 'Sack–bearer' (*Sakkas* for *sakkophoros*). Most details of his life come from the fragments left from Porphyry's writings. The most famous pupil of Ammonius Saccas was Plotinus, who studied under Ammonius for eleven years. According to Porphyry, in 232, at the age of 28, Plotinus went to Alexandria to study philosophy:

> In his twenty–eighth year he [Plotinus] felt the impulse to study philosophy and was recommended to the teachers in Alexandria who then had the highest reputation; but he came away from their lectures so depressed and full of sadness that he told his trouble to one of his friends. The friend, understanding the desire of his heart, sent him to Ammonius, whom he had not so far tried. He went and heard him, and said to his friend, 'This is the man I was looking for.' From that day he stayed continually with Ammonius and acquired so complete a training in philosophy that he became eager to make acquaintance with the Persian philosophical discipline and that prevailing among the Indians. (Porphyry, *Life of Plotinus*, cited in Reale, G., *A History of Ancient Philosophy IV: The Schools of the Imperial Age* [N.Y.: SUNY Press, 1990], p. 298.)

Porphyry makes the allegation that the parents of Ammonius were Christians, but upon learning Greek philosophy, Ammonius rejected his parents' religion for paganism. This conversion is contested by the Christian writers Jerome and Eusebius—the latter stated:

> Such are the allegations made by Porphyry in the third book of his treatise against the Christians. He tells the truth about Origen's teaching and wide learning, but plainly lies—for opponents of Christianity are quite unscrupulous—when he says that he came over from the Greek camp, and that Ammonius lapsed from the service of God into paganism. For Origen clung firmly to the Christian principles his parents had taught him, as this record has already shown; and Ammonius' inspired philosophy remained pure and intact to the very end of his life. To this, surely, his literary labours bear witness, for the works that he bequeathed to posterity have won him a very wide reputation—for instance the book entitled *The Harmony of Moses and Jesus*, and the many other works treasured by discriminating readers. (Eusebius, *The History of the Church*, [Penguin, revised edition, 1989], p. 196.)

However we are told by Longinus that Ammonius wrote nothing (Longinus, quoted by Porphyry, *Life of Plotinus*, xx.), and if Ammonius was the principle influence on Plotinus, then it is unlikely that Ammonius would have been a Christian. One way to explain much of the confusion concerning Ammonius is to assume that there were two people called Ammonius: Ammonius Saccas who taught Plotinus, and an Ammonius the Christian who wrote biblical texts. To add to the confusion, it seems that Ammonius had two pupils called Origen: Origen the Christian, and Origen the Pagan. It is quite possible that Ammonius Saccas taught both Origens. Among Ammonius' other pupils there were Herennius and Cassius Longinus. It seems to do little to support Bergier's refutation to quote such doubtful sources; see footnote on p. 237 of this volume. (Based on information in *Wikipedia*.)

Anastasius Sinaita, Saint (fl. 7th century) was a theologian and abbot of the Monastery of St Catherine, on Mt Sinai—hence his name Sinaita—whose writings, public disputes with various heretical movements in Egypt and Syria, and polemics against the Jews made him a foremost advocate of orthodox Christian doctrine in his day, specifically on the person and work of Christ, and he provided key documents for the history of early Christian thought.

Annet, Peter (1693—1769) was an English Deist who is thought to have written *A History of the Man after God's own Heart* (1761), an examination of the life of the biblical King David, which d'Holbach translated from English into French and published as *David, ou l'Histoire de l'Homme selon le Cœur de Dieu* {*David or the History of the Man After God's Own Heart*} (1768). A schoolmaster by profession, he became notorious for his attacks on orthodox theologians, the clergy and the literal acceptance of biblical texts. He was sentenced to the pillory and a year's hard labour on the grounds of blasphemous libel at the advanced age of 68. In his *Supernaturals Examined* (1747), Annet rejects all superstitious belief in miracles.

Anthony, Mark (82/81—30 BC) (also spelled Marc Anthony, Latin *Marcus Antonius*) was a Roman general under Julius Caesar and later triumvir (43—30 BC), who, with Cleopatra, queen of Egypt, was defeated by Octavian (the future emperor Augustus) in the last of the civil wars that destroyed the Roman Republic. Religious propaganda declared Cleopatra the New Isis, or Aphrodite, to his New Dionysus, and it is possible (but unlikely) that they contracted an Egyptian marriage, which would not have been recognized in Roman law, since Romans could not marry foreigners.

Anthony, Saint (251—356 AD) (known also as *Antonios*) was a religious hermit and one of the earliest monks, considered the founder and father of organized Christian monasticism. His rule represented one of the first attempts to codify guidelines for monastic living. A disciple of Paul of Thebes, Anthony began to practise an ascetic life at the age of twenty and after fifteen years he withdrew to live in absolute solitude on a mountain by the Nile called Pispir (now Dayr al–Maymūn), where he lived from about 286 to 305. During the course of this retreat, he began his legendary combat against the devil, withstanding a series of temptations famous in Christian theology and iconography. He emerged from his retreat in about 305 to instruct and organize the monastic life of hermits, who imitated him and who had established themselves nearby. When Christian persecution ended after the Edict of Milan (313), he moved to a mountain in the Eastern Desert, between the Nile and the Red Sea, where the monastery Dayr Mārī Antonios still stands. Here he remained, receiving visitors and, on occasions, crossing the desert to Pispir. He ventured twice to Alexandria, the last time (*c.* 350) to preach against Arianism (q.v.). The early monks who followed Anthony into the desert considered themselves the vanguard of God's army and they attempted to attain the same state of spiritual purity and freedom from temptation they saw in Anthony by fasting and performing other ascetic practices. Anthony's spiritual combats with what he envisioned as the forces of evil made his life one long struggle against the Devil. According to St Athanasius (q.v.), the bishop of Alexandria, the devil's assaults on Anthony took either seductive or horrible forms of visions: at times the devil appeared in the guise of a monk bringing bread during his fasts or in the form of wild beasts, women or soldiers, sometimes beating the saint and leaving him in a deathly state. Anthony endured many such attacks and those who witnessed them were convinced they were real. His temptations became legendary and they have often been used in literature and art, notably in the paintings of Hieronymus Bosch, Matthias Grünewald and Max Ernst.

Antonine is either of the Roman emperors Antoninus Pius (reigned AD 138—161) and his adopted heir Marcus Aurelius (161—180). The term 'Antonines' also usually includes Lucius Verus (161—169), another adopted heir of Antoninus Pius and co–emperor with Marcus Aurelius, as well as Commodus (176—192), son of Marcus Aurelius and co–emperor and then sole emperor. The Antonine period 138—180 was one of great internal peace and prosperity, when the sense of unity, the reconciliation of peoples, was greatest throughout the Roman Empire.

Apollonius of Tyana (fl. 1st century AD) was a Neo–Pythagorean who became a mythical hero during the time of the Roman Empire. Empress Julia Domna instructed the writer Philostratus to write a biography of Apollonius, and it is speculated that her motive for doing so stemmed from her desire to counteract the influence of Christianity on Roman civilization. The biography portrays a figure much like Christ in temperament and power, and claims that Apollonius performed certain miracles. The biography is widely believed to be based more on fiction than on fact. Many of the pagans in the Roman Empire believed what was said in this work and it kindled religious feeling in many of them. Shrines and other memorials were erected to honour and worship Apollonius.

Aquinas, St Thomas (AD 1224/5—1274) (also called Aquinas, and in Italian *San Tommaso d'Aquino*, by–name *Doctor Angelicus* {Angelic Doctor}), was an Italian Dominican theologian and the foremost medieval Scholasticist. He developed his own conclusions from Aristotelian premises, notably in the metaphysics of personality, creation and Providence. As a theologian he was responsible in his two masterpieces, the *Summa theologiae* {*Summary of Theology*} and the *Summa contra gentiles* {*Summary Against the Gentiles*, although often left untranslated}, for the classical systematization of Latin theology; and as a poet he wrote

Figure 63: *St Anthony Tormented by Demons*, Martin Schongauer (*c.* 1470).

some of the most gravely beautiful eucharistic hymns in the Church's liturgy. His doctrinal system and the explanations and developments made by his followers are known as Thomism. Although many modern Roman Catholic theologians do not find St Thomas altogether congenial, he is nevertheless recognized by the Roman Catholic Church as its foremost Western philosopher and theologian.

Armenia. Modern Armenia comprises only a small portion of ancient Armenia, one of the world's oldest centres of civilization. At its height, Armenia extended from the south–central Black Sea coast to the Caspian Sea and from the Mediterranean Sea to Lake Urmia in present–day Iran. Ancient Armenia was subjected to constant foreign incursions and it finally lost its autonomy in the fourteenth century AD. The centuries–long rule of Ottoman and Persian conquerors imperilled the very existence of the Armenian people. Eastern Armenia was annexed by Russia during the nineteenth century; western Armenia remained under Turkish rule, and in 1894—96 and 1915 Turkey perpetrated systematic massacres and forced deportations of Armenians. In the fourth century AD the ruler of Armenia converted to Christianity and thus created a permanent gulf between Christian Armenia and Muslim Persia, now modern Iran.

Aristotle (384—322 BC) (Greek name—*Aristoteles*) was an ancient Greek philosopher and scientist, one of the two greatest intellectual figures produced by the Greeks (the other being Plato). He surveyed the whole of human knowledge as it was known in the Mediterranean world of his day. More than any other thinker, Aristotle determined the orientation and content of Western intellectual history. He was the author of a philosophical and scientific system that through the centuries became the support and vehicle for both medieval Christian and Islamic scholastic thought: Western culture was Aristotelian until the end of the seventeenth century. Even after the intellectual revolutions of centuries to follow, Aristotelian concepts and ideas remained embedded in Western thinking. Aristotle's intellectual range was vast, covering most of the sciences and many of the arts. He worked in physics, chemistry, biology, zoology, botany, psychology, political theory, ethics, logic, metaphysics, history, literary theory and rhetoric. His greatest achievements were in two unrelated areas: he invented the study of formal logic, devising for it a finished system, known as Aristotelian syllogistic, that for centuries was regarded as the sum of logic; and he pioneered the study of zoology, both observational and theoretical, in which his work was not surpassed until the nineteenth century.

Arnauld, Antoine (1612—1694) was also known as 'The Great Arnauld'. He was a leading seventeenth–century theologian of Jansenism—a Roman Catholic movement that maintained doctrines which the Catholic Church regarded as heretical on issues over free will and predestination, a doctrine close to Calvinism. Arnauld studied theology at the Sorbonne and he was ordained into the Roman Catholic priesthood in 1641. He published his treatise *De la fréquente communion* {*On Frequent Communion*} (1643), defending controversial Jansenist views on the Eucharist and on penance. With his *Théologie morale des Jésuites* {*Moral Theology of the Jesuits*} (1643), Arnauld launched his long polemical campaign against the Jesuits. During the period of the great persecution of the Jansenists (1661—69), Arnauld emerged as their foremost apologist.

Athanasius (AD 293—373) was a theologian, ecclesiastical statesman and Egyptian national leader. He was the chief defender of Christian orthodoxy in the fourth–century fight against Arianism, the claim (regarded as a heresy) that the Son of God was not consubstantial (of the same substance) as God the Father, because the gospel refers to him as 'begotten of the Father'—the implication being that he was created by him. His important works include *The Life of St. Antony* and *Four Orations against the Arians*. While in Egypt, he established important contacts with the Coptic monks of Upper Egypt and their leader Pachomius. He was exiled and banished several times for his meddling in Egyptian affairs of state: when rulers moved to operate pro–Arian policies, he did all he could to hinder them.

Astarte (also spelled Athtart or Ashtart) was a great goddess of the ancient Middle East and chief deity of Tyre, Sidon and Elat, which were all important Mediterranean seaports. Hebrew scholars now feel that the goddess Ashtoreth mentioned so often in the Bible is a deliberate conflation of the Greek name 'Astarte' and the Hebrew word *boshet*, 'shame', indicating the Hebrews' contempt for her cult. Ashtaroth, the plural form of the goddess's name in Hebrew, became a general term denoting goddesses and paganism. King Solomon, married to foreign wives, 'followed Astarte the goddess of the Sidonians' (1 Kgs. 11: 5). Later the cult places to Ashtoreth were destroyed by Josiah. Astarte/Ashtoreth is the Queen of Heaven to whom the Canaanites burned offerings and poured libations (Jeremiah 44). Astarte, goddess of war and sexual love, shared so many qualities with her sister, Anath, that they may originally have been a single deity. Their names together are the basis for the Aramaic goddess Atargatis. Astarte was worshiped in Egypt and Ugarit, and among the Hittites, as well as in Canaan. Her Akkadian counterpart was Ishtar. Later she became assimilated with the Egyptian deities Isis and Hathor (a goddess of the sky and of women), and in the Græco–Roman world with Aphrodite, Artemis and Juno.

Figure 64: Second-century marble bust of Attis.

Attis (also spelled Atys) was the mythical consort of the Great Mother of the Gods. He was worshipped in Phrygia, Asia Minor, and later throughout the Roman Empire, where he assumed the persona of a solar deity in the second century AD. The worship of Attis and the Great Mother included the annual celebration of mysteries on the return of the spring season—q.v. **Adonis**. Attis, like the Great Mother, was probably indigenous to Asia Minor, adopted by the invading Phrygians and blended by them with a mythical character of their own. According to the Phrygian tale, Attis was a beautiful youth born of Nana, the daughter of the river Sangarius, and the hermaphroditic Agdistis. Having become enamoured of Attis, Agdistis made a frenzied attack on him as he was about to be married, resulting in Attis castrating himself and dying. Agdistis prevailed upon Zeus in an act of repentance to grant that the body of the youth should never decay or waste—apparently like many Catholic saints. Other versions also exist, but they all retain the essential etiological feature, the self–castration. Attis was fundamentally a vegetation god, and in his self–mutilation, death and resurrection, he represents the fruits of the earth which die in winter only to rise again in the spring. In art, Attis was frequently represented as a youth, with the distinctive Phrygian cap and trousers.

Augustine, Saint (AD 354—430) (also called Saint Augustine of Hippo, whose original Latin name was *Aurelius Augustinus*) was the bishop of Hippo from 396 to 430, one of the Latin Fathers of the Church, one of the Doctors of the Church, and perhaps the most significant Christian thinker after St Paul. Augustine's adaptation of classical thought to Christian teaching created a theological system of great power and lasting influence. His numerous written works, the most important of which are *Confessions* (397) and *City of God* (413—426/427) shaped biblical exegesis and helped lay the foundation for much of medieval and modern Christian thought. Intellectually, Augustine represents the most influential adaptation of the Platonic tradition with Christian ideas that ever occurred in the Latin Christian world. Augustine received the Platonic past in a far more limited and diluted way than did many of his Greek–speaking contemporaries, but his writings were so widely read and imitated throughout Latin Christendom that his particular synthesis of Christian, Roman and Platonic traditions laid down a tradition that lasted for centuries. Both modern Roman Catholic and Protestant Christianity owe much to Augustine, though in some ways each community has at times been embarrassed to own up to that allegiance in the face of irreconcilable elements in his thought. Augustine's volume *Confessions* recounts his early life with immense persuasiveness, but his goal was clearly self–justificatory, and as such his choice of details and incidents is highly selective. He also wrote at length on church issues and heresies, as exemplified in his work *On Genesis: Against Manicheans*, q.v. Mani.

Averroës (1126—1198) (called in medieval Latin *Averrhoës*; and in Arabic in full *Abū al–Walīd Muhammad ibn Ahmad ibn Muhammad ibn Rushd*, or *Ibn Rushd* for short) was an influential Islamic religious philosopher who integrated Islamic traditions with ancient Greek thought. He produced a series of summaries and commentaries on most of Aristotle's works (1169—95) and on Plato's *Republic*, which exerted a considerable influence in both the Islamic world and Europe for centuries. He wrote the *Decisive Treatise on the Agreement between Religious Law and Philosophy, Examination of the Methods of Proof Concerning the Doctrines of Religion*, and *The Incoherence of the Incoherence*—all in defence of the philosophical study of religion against theologians.

Babylon was one of the most famous cities of antiquity. It was the capital of southern Mesopotamia (Babylonia) from the early second millennium to the early first millennium BC, and capital of the Neo–Babylonian (Chaldean) empire in the seventh and sixth centuries BC, when it was at the height of its splendour. Its extensive ruins on the Euphrates River, about fifty–five miles (eighty–eight km) south of Baghdad, lie near the modern town of Al–Ḥillah, in Iraq. From the ninth to the late seventh century, Babylon was almost continuously under Assyrian suzerainty, usually wielded through native kings, though sometimes Assyrian kings ruled in person. Close Assyrian involvement in Babylon began with Tiglath–pileser III (744—727 BC) as a result of Chaldean tribesmen pressing into city territories, several times usurping the kingship. Disorders accompanying increasing tribal occupation finally persuaded the Assyrian monarch Sennacherib (704—681 BC) that peaceful control of Babylon was impossible and in 689 he ordered the city to be destroyed. His son Esarhaddon (680—669 BC) rescinded that policy and, after expelling the tribesmen and returning the property of the Babylonians to them, he undertook to rebuild the city. In the mid–seventh century, civil war broke out between the Assyrian king Ashurbanipal and his brother. Ashurbanipal laid siege to the city, which fell to him in 648 after famine had driven the defenders to cannibalism. After Ashurbanipal's death, a Chaldean leader, Nabopolassar, in 626 made Babylon the capital of a kingdom that under his son Nebuchadrezzar II (605—561 BC) became a major imperial power. Nebuchadrezzar undertook a vast program of rebuilding and fortification in Babylon, and labour gangs from many lands increased the multi–racial composition of the population. Nebuchadrezzar's most important successor, Nabonidus (556—539 BC), campaigned in Arabia for a decade, leaving his son Belshazzar as regent in Babylon. Nabonidus failed to protect the property rights or religious traditions of the capital and attempted building operations elsewhere to rival Marduk's great temple of Esagila. When the Persian Achaemenian dynasty under Cyrus II attacked in 539 BC, the capital fell almost without resistance; a legend (accepted by some as historical) that Cyrus achieved entry by diverting the Euphrates is unconfirmed in contemporary sources. Under the Persians, Babylon retained most of its institutions, became capital of the richest satrapy in the empire, and was, according to the fifth–century (BC) Greek historian Herodotus, the world's most splendid city. A revolt against Xerxes I (482) led to the destruction of its fortifications and temples and to the melting down of the golden image of Marduk. In 331 BC Babylon surrendered to the Macedonian king Alexander the Great, who confirmed its privileges and ordered the restoration of the temples. Alexander, recognizing the commercial importance of the city, allowed its satrap to coin money and began constructing a harbour to foster trade. In 323, Alexander died in the palace of Nebuchadrezzar; he had planned to make Babylon his imperial capital. Alexander's conquest brought Babylon into the orbit of Greek culture and Hellenistic science was greatly enriched by the contributions of Babylonian astronomy. After a power struggle among Alexander's generals, Babylon passed to the Seleucid dynasty in 312 BC. The city's importance was much reduced by the building of a new capital, Seleucia on the Tigris, where part of Babylon's population was transferred in 275. The present site, an extensive field of ruins, contains several prominent mounds and excavations continue to the present time.

Barbier, Antoine–Alexandre (1765—1825) was a French librarian and bibliographer who compiled a standard reference directory of anonymous writings and helped preserve scholarly books and manuscripts during and after the French Revolution. In 1794 Barbier became a member of the temporary commission of the arts and was charged with distributing books confiscated during the Revolution among the various libraries. A few years later, under the Directory, he became a member of the council for the preservation of works in the arts and sciences. During his work he discovered and saved the letters and manuscripts of many important people whose work would otherwise have been lost. Although Barbier had been ordained a priest, his main passion was for books, and in 1801 he was released from his orders. He became librarian successively to the Directory, to the Conseil d'État, and, in 1807, to Napoleon, for whom he also researched scholarly answers to political and religious problems. His *Dictionnaire des ouvrages anonymes et pseudonymes* (*Dictionary of Anonymous and Pseudonymous Works*) (1806—1809) is still a standard library work of reference. He helped found the libraries of the Louvre museum, and, under Louis XVIII, he was administrator of the king's private libraries until he was abruptly dismissed in 1822.

Figure 65: Pierre Bayle (1647—1706). Plate from the fifth edition of
Dictionaire Historique et Critique **(1734).**

Bayle, Pierre (1647—1706) was a philosopher whose *Dictionaire* [sic] *historique et critique* {*Historical and Critical Dictionary*} (1697) was roundly condemned by the French Reformed Church of Rotterdam and by the French Roman Catholic Church because of its numerous annotations deliberately designed to destroy orthodox Christian beliefs. He was an important figure of the Enlightenment as a forerunner of the *Encyclopédistes*. The son of a Calvinist minister who briefly embraced Roman Catholicism in 1669, he worked as a tutor and progressed to teach philosophy at the Protestant Academy of Sedan from 1675 to 1681. He published his anonymous reflections on the comet of 1680 under the title *Pensées sur la Comète* {*Thoughts on the Comet*}, deriding the commonly held superstition that comets presage catastrophe. He also questioned many Christian traditions, thus arousing the ire of a Calvinist colleague, Pierre Jurieu. Bayle's plea for religious toleration (even for atheists) eventually convinced Jurieu that Bayle was an atheist in disguise. The rift between the two was complete when Bayle advocated a conciliatory attitude toward the anti–Calvinist government of Louis XIV: in 1693, Bayle was deprived of his Rotterdam professorship. Thereafter, Bayle devoted himself to his famous *Dictionaire*. The first edition of the *Dictionaire historique et critique* (in 16 volumes) was published in Geneva in 1697 and reprinted in Paris in 1820—1824. The bulk of the *Dictionaire* consists of quotations, anecdotes, commentaries and erudite annotations that cleverly unpick whatever orthodoxy the articles contain. Vehement objections were voiced, particularly to the article 'David', to the bias in favour of Pyrrhonistic (radical) scepticism, atheism and Epicureanism, and to the use of Scripture to introduce indecencies. This oblique method of subversive criticism was adopted by the eighteenth–century *Encyclopédistes*. Bayle's last major work was entitled *Réponse aux questions d'un provincial* {*Reply to the Questions of a Provincial Man*} and was published between 1704 and 1707 (in 4, 5 or 6 volumes, depending on the edition), originally in Rotterdam. It is an amalgam of articles on diverse subjects, on philosophical and theological questions, but also on literary subjects. (Bayle's *Dictionary* can be consulted on the internet as part of is a co–operative enterprise of *Analyse et Traitement Informatique de la Langue Française* [ATILF] {*The Project for American and French Research on the Treasury of the French Language*} [ARTFL] of the Centre National de la Recherche Scientifique [CNRS], the Division of the Humanities, the Division of the Social Sciences, and Electronic Text Services [ETS] of the University of Chicago.)

DICTIONAIRE HISTORIQUE ET CRITIQUE,

PAR

Mʳ. PIERRE BAYLE.

CINQUIEME EDITION,

REVUE, CORRIGÉE, ET AUGMENTÉE.

AVEC LA VIE DE L'AUTEUR,

PAR Mʀ. DES MAIZEAUX.

TOME PREMIER.

A———B.

A AMSTERDAM.	Chez P. BRUNEL, P. HUMBERT, J. WETSTEIN & G. SMITH, F. L'HONORE' & Fils, Z. CHATELAIN, COVENS & MORTIER, PIERRE MORTIER, F. CHANGUION, J. CATUFFE, & H. UYTWERF.	
A LEIDE,	Chez SAMUEL LUCHTMANS.	*LIBRAIRES.*
A LA HAYE,	Chez P GOSSE, J. NEAULME, A. MOETJENS, G. BLOCK, & A. VAN DOLE.	
A UTRECHT,	Chez ETIENNE NEAULME.	

M D C C X L.

AVEC PRIVILEGE.

**Figure 66: Frontispiece of a reprint of the fifth edition of the
Dictionaire Historique et Critique (1740).**

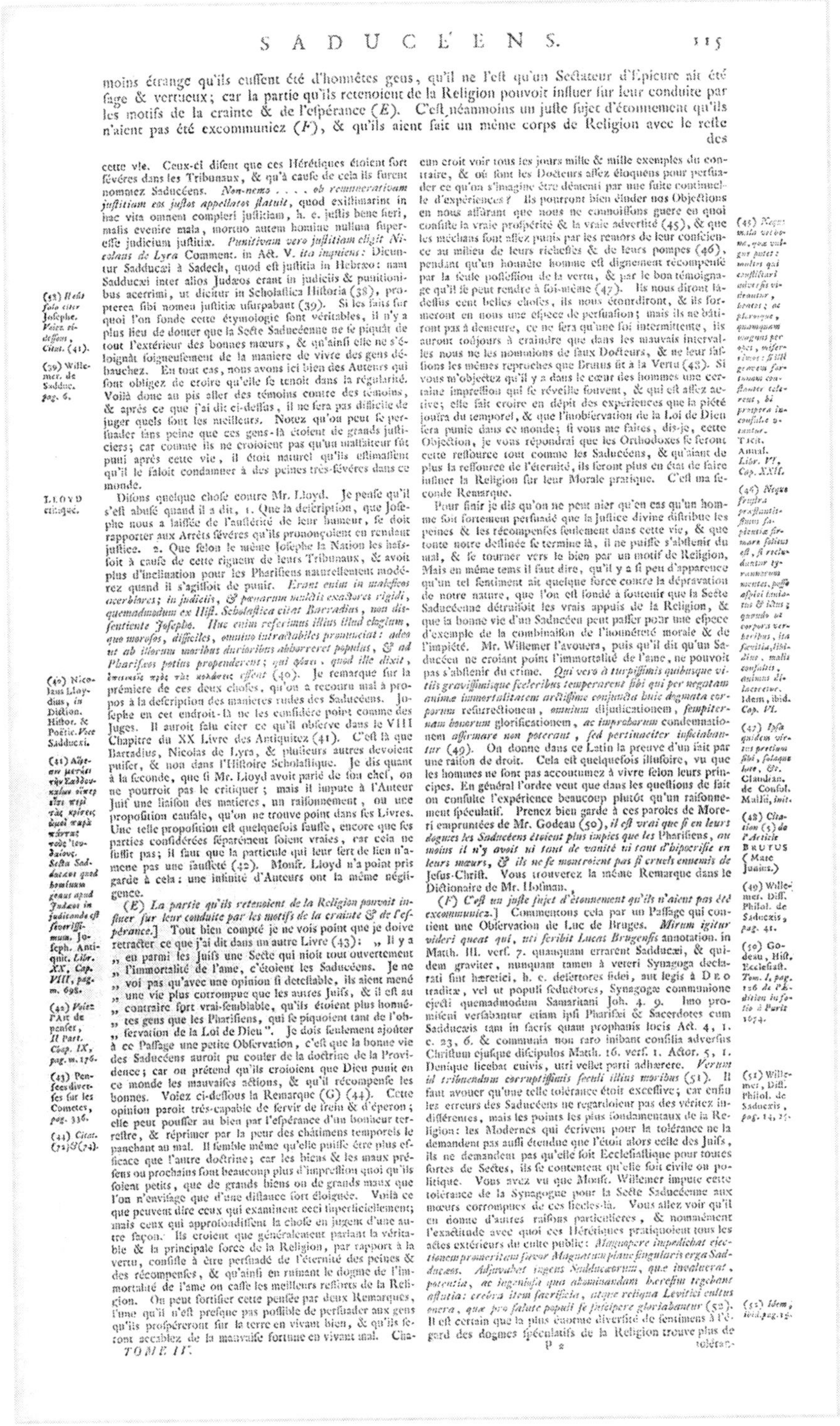

SADUCÉENS. 115

moins étrange qu'ils eussent été d'honnêtes gens, qu'il ne l'est qu'un Sectateur d'Epicure ait été sage & vertueux; car la partie qu'ils retenoient de la Religion pouvoit influer sur leur conduite par les motifs de la crainte & de l'espérance (*E*). C'est néanmoins un juste sujet d'étonnement qu'ils n'aient pas été excommuniez (*F*), & qu'ils aient fait un même corps de Religion avec le reste des

cette vie. Ceux-ci disent que ces Hérétiques étoient fort sévéres dans les Tribunaux, & qu'à cause de cela ils furent nommez Saducéens. *Non-nemo . . . . ob remunerativam justitiam eos justos appellatos statuit*, quod existimarint in hac vita omnem compleri justitiam, h. e. justis bene fieri, malis evenire mala, mortuo autem homine nullum superesse judicium justitiæ. *Punitivam vero justitiam eligit Nicolaus de Lyra* Comment. in Act. V. *ita inquiens:* Dicuntur Sadducæi à Sadech, quod est justitia in Hebræo: nam Sadducæi inter alios Judæos erant in judiciis & punitionibus acerrimi, ut dicitur in Scholastica Historia (38), propterea sibi nomen justitiæ usurpabant (39). Si les faits sur quoi l'on fonde cette étymologie sont véritables, il n'y a plus lieu de douter que la Secte Saducéenne ne se piquât de tout l'extérieur des bonnes mœurs, & qu'ainsi elle ne s'éloignât soigneusement de la maniere de vivre des gens débauchez. En tout cas, nous avons ici bien des Auteurs qui sont obligez de croire qu'elle se tenoit dans la régularité. Voilà donc au pis aller des témoins contre des témoins, & aprés ce que j'ai dit ci-dessus, il ne sera pas difficile de juger quels sont les meilleurs. Notez qu'on peut se persuader sans peine que ces gens-là étoient de grands justiciers; car comme ils ne croioient pas qu'un malfaiteur fût puni après cette vie, il étoit naturel qu'ils estimassent qu'il le faloit condamner à des peines très-sévéres dans ce monde.

Disons quelque chose contre Mr. Lloyd. Je pense qu'il s'est abusé quand il a dit, 1. Que la description, que Josephe nous a laissée de l'austérité de leur humeur, se doit rapporter aux Arrêts sévéres qu'ils prononçoient en rendant justice. 2. Que selon le même Josephe la Nation les haïssoit à cause de cette rigueur de leurs Tribunaux, & avoit plus d'inclination pour les Pharisiens naturellement modérez quand il s'agissoit de punir. *Erant enim in maleficos acerbiores; in judiciis, & pœnarum mulctis exactores rigidi, quemadmodum ex Hist. Scholastica citat Barradius, non dissentiente Josepho. Hunc enim referimus illius illud elogium, quo morosos, difficiles, omnino intractabiles pronunciat: adeo ut ab illorum moribus durioribus abhorreret populus, & ad Pharisæos potius propenderent; qui φύσει, quod ille dixit, ἐπιεικῶς πρὸς τὰς κολάσεις essent* (40). Je remarque sur la prémiere de ces deux choses, qu'on a recouru mal à propos à la description des manieres rudes des Saducéens. Josephe en cet endroit-là ne les considére point comme des Juges. Il auroit falu citer ce qu'il observe dans le VIII Chapitre du XX Livre des Antiquitez (41). C'est là que Barradius, Nicolas de Lyra, & plusieurs autres devoient puiser, & non dans l'Histoire Scholastique. Je dis quant à la seconde, que si Mr. Lloyd avoit parlé de son chef, on ne pourroit pas le critiquer; mais il impute à l'Auteur Juif une liaison des matieres, un raisonnement, ou une proposition causale, qu'on ne trouve point dans ses Livres. Une telle proposition est quelquefois fausse, encore que ses parties considérées séparément soient vraies, car cela ne suffit pas; il faut que la particule qui leur sert de lien n'amene pas une fausseté (42). Monsr. Lloyd n'a point pris garde à cela: une infinité d'Auteurs ont la même négligence.

(*E*) *La partie qu'ils retenoient de la Religion pouvoit influer sur leur conduite par les motifs de la crainte & de l'espérance.*] Tout bien compté je ne vois point que je doive retracter ce que j'ai dit dans un autre Livre (43): „ Il y a „ eu parmi les Juifs une Secte qui nioit tout ouvertement „ l'immortalité de l'ame, c'étoient les Saducéens. Je ne „ voi pas qu'avec une opinion si detestable, ils aient mené „ une vie plus corrompue que les autres Juifs, & il est au „ contraire fort vrai-semblable, qu'ils étoient plus honnêtes gens que les Pharisiens, qui se piquoient tant de l'ob„ servation de la Loi de Dieu". Je dois seulement ajoûter à ce Passage une petite Observation, c'est que la bonne vie des Saducéens auroit pu couler de la doctrine de la Providence; car on prétend qu'ils croioient que Dieu punit en ce monde les mauvaises actions, & qu'il récompense les bonnes. Voiez ci-dessous la Remarque (G) (44). Cette opinion paroit très-capable de servir de frein & d'éperon; elle peut pousser au bien par l'espérance d'un bonheur terrestre, & réprimer par la peur des châtimens temporels le panchant au mal. Il semble même qu'elle puisse être plus efficace que l'autre doctrine; car les biens & les maux présens ou prochains font beaucoup plus d'impression quoi qu'ils soient petits, que de grands biens ou de grands maux que l'on n'envisage que d'une distance fort éloignée. Voilà ce que peuvent dire ceux qui examinent ceci superficiellement; mais ceux qui approfondissent la chose en jugent d'une autre façon. Ils croient que généralement parlant la véritable & la principale force de la Religion, par rapport à la vertu, consiste à être persuadé de l'éternité des peines & des récompenses, & qu'ainsi en ruinant le dogme de l'immortalité de l'ame on casse les meilleurs ressorts de la Religion. On peut fortifier cette pensée par deux Remarques, l'une qu'il n'est presque pas possible de persuader aux gens qu'ils prospéreront sur la terre en vivant bien, & qu'ils seront accablez de la mauvaise fortune en vivant mal. Chacun croit voir tous les jours mille & mille exemples du contraire, & où sont les Docteurs assez éloquens pour persuader ce qu'on s'imagine être démenti par une suite continuelle d'expériences? Ils pourront bien éluder nos Objections en nous assûrant que nous ne connoissons guere en quoi consiste la vraie prospérité & la vraie adversité (45), & que les méchans sont assez punis par les remors de leur conscience au milieu de leurs richesses & de leurs pompes (46), pendant qu'un honnête homme est dignement récompensé par la seule possession de la vertu, & par le bon témoignage qu'il se peut rendre à soi-même (47). Ils nous diront là-dessus cent belles choses, ils nous étourdiront, & ils formeront en nous une espece de persuasion; mais ils ne bâtiront pas à demeure, ce ne sera qu'une foi intermittente, ils auront toûjours à craindre que dans les mauvais intervalles nous ne les nommions de faux Docteurs, & ne leur fassions les mêmes reproches que Brutus fit à la Vertu (48). Si vous m'objectez qu'il y a dans le cœur des hommes une certaine impression qui se réveille souvent, & qui est assez active; elle fait croire en dépit des expériences que la piété jouïra du temporel, & que l'inobservation de la Loi de Dieu sera punie dans ce monde; si vous me faites, dis-je, cette Objection, je vous répondrai que les Orthodoxes se feront cette ressource tout comme les Saducéens, & qu'aiant de plus la ressource de l'éternité, ils seront plus en état de faire influer la Religion sur leur Morale pratique. C'est ma seconde Remarque.

Pour finir je dis qu'on ne peut nier qu'en cas qu'un homme soit fortement persuadé que la Justice divine distribue les peines & les récompenses seulement dans cette vie, & que toute notre destinée se termine là, il ne puisse s'abstenir du mal, & se tourner vers le bien par un motif de Religion, Mais en même tems il faut dire, qu'il y a si peu d'apparence qu'un tel sentiment ait quelque force contre la dépravation de notre nature, que l'on est fondé à soutenir que la Secte Saducéenne détruisoit les vrais appuis de la Religion, & que la bonne vie d'un Saducéen peut passer pour une espece d'exemple de la combinaison de l'honnêteté morale & de l'impiété. Mr. Willemer l'avouera, puis qu'il dit qu'un Saducéen ne croiant point l'immortalité de l'ame, ne pouvoit pas s'abstenir du crime. *Qui vero à turpissimis quibusque vitiis gravissimisque sceleribus temperarent sibi qui per negatam animæ immortalitatem arctissime conjuncta huic dogmata corporum* resurrectionem, *omnium* dijudicationem, *sempiternam bonorum* glorificationem, *ac improborum* condemnationem *affirmare non poterant, sed pertinaciter inficiabantur* (49). On donne dans ce Latin la preuve d'un fait par une raison de droit. Cela est quelquefois illusoire, vu que les hommes ne sont pas accoutumez à vivre selon leurs principes. En général l'ordre veut que dans les questions de fait on consulte l'expérience beaucoup plutôt qu'un raisonnement spéculatif. Prenez bien garde à ces paroles de Moreri empruntées de Mr. Godeau (50), *il est vrai que si en leurs dogmes les Saducéens étoient plus impies que les Pharisiens, au moins il n'y avoit ni tant de vanité ni tant d'hipocrisie en leurs mœurs, & ils ne se montroient pas si cruels ennemis de* Jesus-Christ. Vous trouverez la même Remarque dans le Dictionaire de Mr. Hofman.

(*F*) *C'est un juste sujet d'étonnement qu'ils n'aient pas été excommuniez.*] Commentons cela par un Passage qui contient une Observation de Luc de Bruges. *Mirum igitur videri queat qui, uti scribit Lucas Brugensis* annotation. in Matth. III. vers. 7. quanquam errarent Sadducæi, & quidem graviter, nunquam tamen à veteri Synagoga declarati sint hæretici, h. e. desertores fidei, aut legis à DEO traditæ, vel ut populi seductores, Synagogæ communione ejecti quemadmodum Samaritani Joh. 4. 9. Imo promiscui versabantur etiam ipsi Pharisæi & Sacerdotes cum Sadducæis tam in sacris quam prophanis locis Act. 4, 1. c. 23, 6. & communia non raro inibant consilia adversus Christum ejusque discipulos Matth. 16. vers. 1. Actor. 5, 1. Denique licebat cuivis, utri vellet parti adhærere. *Verum id tribuendum corruptissimis seculi illius moribus* (51). Il faut avouer qu'une telle tolérance étoit excessive; car enfin les erreurs des Saducéens ne regardoient pas des véritez indifférentes, mais les points les plus fondamentaux de la Religion: les Modernes qui écrivent pour la tolérance ne la demandent pas aussi étendue que l'étoit alors celle des Juifs, ils ne demandent pas qu'elle soit Ecclesiastique pour toutes sortes de Sectes, ils se contentent qu'elle soit civile ou politique. Vous avez vu que Monsr. Willemer impute cette tolérance de la Synagogue pour la Secte Saducéenne aux mœurs corrompues de ces siecles-là. Vous allez voir qu'il en donne d'autres raisons particulieres, & nommément l'exactitude avec quoi ces Hérétiques pratiquoient tous les actes extérieurs du culte public: *Magnopere impediebat ejectionem promeritam favor Magnatum plane singularis erga Sadducæos. Adjuvabat ingens Sadducæorum, quæ invaluerat, potentia, ac ingeniosa qua abominandam hæresin tegebant astutia: crebra item sacrificia, atque reliqua Levitici cultus onera, quæ pro salute populi se suscipere gloriabantur* (52). Il est certain que la plus énorme diversité de sentimens à l'égard des dogmes spéculatifs de la Religion trouve plus de tolérance

TOME IV. P 2

Figure 67: A page from Bayle's *Dictionaire*, showing its original, innovative layout.

Bazilidians were a Christian Muslim sect who existed in Arabia: they rejected the crucifixion of Christ. Apart from this fact, information on them is hard to come by. (Source: *Questions sur l'Encyclopédie (1752—1770)* in *Collection complette* [sic] *des œuvres de M. de Voltaire* [Genève, {Cramer}, 1768—1777], vols. XXII—XXV.)

Bellarmine, Saint Robert (1542—1621) (in Italian in full *San Roberto Francesco Romolo Bellarmino*) was an Italian cardinal and theologian, an opponent of the Protestant doctrines of the Reformation. Bellarmine entered the Society of Jesus in 1560, i.e., he was a Jesuit. After studying in Italy in Rome, Mondovì and Padua, he was sent to Louvain in the Spanish Netherlands, where he was ordained in 1570 and began to teach theology. He was forced by the strength of Protestantism and the Augustinian doctrines of grace and free will prevailing in the Low Countries to define his theological principles. He returned to Rome where he lectured at the new Jesuit College. Made a cardinal by Pope Clement VIII in 1599, he was subsequently appointed archbishop of Capua (1602). As a consultor of the Holy Office, he took a prominent part in the first examination of Galileo's writings. Bellarmine, somewhat sympathetic to Galileo's views, granted him an audience in which he warned him not to defend the Copernican theory, but to regard it only as a hypothesis. Acting at the behest of the Holy Office and fearing scandal at a time when Roman Catholicism and Protestantism were at odds with each other, Bellarmine thought it best to have the Copernican theory declared 'false and erroneous'. Bellarmine's most influential writings were a series of lectures published under the title *Disputationes de controversiis Christianae fidei adversus huius temporis haereticos* {*Lectures Concerning the Controversies of the Christian Faith Against the Heretics of This Time*} (1586—93). They contained a lucid and uncompromising statement of Roman Catholic doctrine. He took part in the preparation of the Clementine edition (1591—92) of the *Vulgate*, and his catechism of 1597 greatly influenced later works. In 1610 he published *De Potestate Summi Pontificis in Rebus Temporalibus* {*Concerning the Power of the Supreme Pontiff in Temporal Matters*}, a reply to William Barclay's *De Potestate Papae* {*Concerning the Power of the Pope*} (1609), which denied all temporal power to the pope. Bellarmine's autobiography first appeared in 1675. A complete edition of his works was published in 12 volumes between 1870 and 1874.

Bernard, Saint (1090—1153) was a Cistercian monk and mystic, the founder and abbot of the abbey of Clairvaux and one of the most influential churchmen of his time. He was a close confidant to several popes and as such had considerable power and influence. Pope Eugenius III and King Louis VII of France induced Bernard to promote the cause of a Second

Crusade (1147—49) to quell the prospect of a great Muslim surge engulfing both Latin and Greek Orthodox Christians. The crusade ended in failure because of Bernard's inability to account for the quarrelsome nature of politics, peoples, dynasties and adventurers. He was an idealist imbued with ascetic ideals, who imputed his own integrity of motive to the hearts of the crusaders, most of whom were merely bloodthirsty fanatics. He got involved in a number of theological and doctrinal debates, arguing powerfully against those the Church perceived to be heretics. His greatest literary endeavour was *Sermons on the Canticle of Canticles*, i.e., on the Song of Solomon. It revealed the gentle nature of his teaching, often described as 'sweet as honey', as in his later title '*doctor mellifluous*'. D'Holbach alludes to St Bernard's honey epithet in his footnote on p. 150, by calling him 'mild'.

Bolingbroke, Henry Saint John, 1st Viscount, Baron Saint John Of Lydiard Tregoze (1678—1751) was a prominent Tory politician and a major political propagandist in opposition to the Whig Party led by Sir Robert Walpole. In 1701 he entered Parliament, where his able oratory and his support of partisan Tory measures, including attacks on the previous Whig ministry and on the Protestant Dissenters, the Whigs' staunchest allies, caused him to be noticed. He briefly occupied a government post, providing troops and equipment for the War of the Spanish Succession against France, but he failed to be re–elected to the Parliament of 1708 to 1710. He fell foul of the government during George I's reign and he felt it expedient to flee to France, where he mixed with prominent thinkers and men of letters, including Voltaire. Free from political concerns and duties, he turned his attention to biblical, historical and philosophical issues, and wrote several works, including *Reflections upon Exile* and *Reflections Concerning Innate Moral Principles*. As far as his philosophy is concerned, Bolingbroke is known for his Deist beliefs, asserting that God exists and can be known through reason, but his religious views were only really revealed through works published after his death. He evinces a belief that God is omnipotent and omniscient and always does what is best for man, even when reason would indicate to the contrary. He also believed that God's morality could not be fully grasped by the human mind. He further believed that man's moral code could be determined through reason, based on a sense of the divine.

Boulainvilliers, Henri de, Comte de Saint–Saire (1658—1722) was primarily a historian and political: by training he was a classicist and historian, but as a man typical of his time, he was also well–read in the sciences. He read widely and was familiar with the works of Descartes, Spinoza, Newton and Locke. His later writing came close to the ideas of Montesquieu. In addition to writing on history, Boulainvilliers also wrote on philosophy in *L'Idée d'un système général de la nature* {*The Idea of a General System of Nature*} (1683); on comparative religions in *Histoire de la religion et de la philosophie ancienne* {*History of Religion and Ancient Philosophy*} (*c.* 1700); and also on occultism and astrology.

Boulanger, Nicolas–Antoine (1722—1759) was an engineer, scientist and mathematician, who ultimately turned to the study of ancient and oriental languages and wrote a number of philosophical treatises. All his works were published after his untimely death by Helvétius, d'Holbach and Diderot, who were so convinced of the quality and originality of them that they would not see them consigned to oblivion. It was to Boulanger that *Christianity Unveiled* was first pseudonymously attributed. His *Recherches sur l'origine du despotisme oriental* {*Research into the Origins of Oriental Despotism*} (1761) and *Antiquité dévoilée par ses usages* {*Antiquity Unveiled through its Customs*} (1765), the title of which bears not a little resemblance to d'Holbach's work in this volume, developed the theory that the origin of religion and despotism were the responses of early civilizations to cataclysmic events, such as floods, etc.

Brahmā is one of the chief gods of Hinduism, along with Vishnu and Śhiva. He is represented in art as having four faces and arms, seated a lotus.

Figure 68: The Hindu god Brahmā.

Bullet, Jean–Baptiste (1699—1775) was a priest who wrote, amongst other works, *Histoire de l'établissement du christianisme, tirée des seuls auteurs juifs et païens, où l'on trouve une preuve solide de la vérité de cette religion* {*History of the Establishment of Christianity, taken solely from Jewish and Pagan Writers, wherein is to be found Solid Proof of the Veracity of this Religion*} (Lyon, 1764). Jean–Baptiste Bullet was professor of theology at the University of Besançon, Bergier's Alma Mater.

Cabbala (also spelt Kabala, Kabbalah, Cabala, or Cabbalah) is a form of esoteric Jewish mysticism that appeared in the twelfth and following centuries. Cabbala has always been essentially an oral tradition in that initiation into its doctrines and practices is conducted by a personal guide to avoid the dangers inherent in mystical experiences. Esoteric Cabbala is also a tradition inasmuch as it lays claim to secret knowledge of the unwritten Torah (divine revelation) which was supposedly communicated by God to Moses and Adam. Though observance of the Law of Moses remained the basic tenet of Judaism, Cabbala provided a means of approaching God directly. It thus gave Judaism a religious dimension, whose mystical approaches to God were viewed by some as dangerously pantheistic and heretical.

Calmet, Dom Augustin (1672—1757) was a celebrated exegete, one of the Catholic Church's 'big guns' in that discipline. He was educated at the Benedictine priory of Breuil and in 1688 he joined the same order in the Abbey of St–Mansuy at Toul. He was ordained in 1696 and taught philosophy and theology. He became professor of exegesis, spending most of his life working on his *Commentaire littéral sur tous les livres de l'Ancien et du Nouveau Testament* {*Literal Commentary on all the Books of the Old and New Testaments*}, volume one of which appeared in Paris in 1707 and ran to twenty–three quarto volumes, re–issued several times. So esteemed was the work that it was translated into Latin. But while it was received with high praise, even by Protestants, it had its critics: some difficult passages are often passed over lightly, and too frequently different explanations of a text are set down without a hint to the reader as to which is the right or preferable one. (Based on *Catholic Encyclopedia*, 1908.)

Calvinist is an adherent of Calvinism, a doctrinal position which is based heavily upon the teaching of St Paul in the New Testament, which states that in and of themselves people are so sinful that they are unable to perceive God's grace and are incapable of being saved, unless God has personally pre–ordained and selected them to accept his grace through Christ. St Paul stated in his Epistles to the Corinthians and the Ephesians, amongst other places, that God had personally predestined a small number of people, his 'elect', chosen by himself to be spared the torments of Hell: 'According as he hath chosen us in him before the foundation of the world, that we should be holy and without blame before him in love', (Eph. 1:4) and 'We are bound to give thanks alway to God for you, brethren beloved of the Lord, because God hath from the beginning chosen you to salvation through sanctification of the Spirit and belief of the truth', (2 Thess. 2:13). This emphasis on predestination and divine selection was advanced by John Calvin, a Protestant Reformer in the sixteenth century and it was bitterly opposed by the Catholic Church, as was Jansenism (q.v.), philosophically its near equivalent. Calvinism spread into England, Scotland, France, the Netherlands, the English–speaking colonies of North America, and parts of Germany and central Europe. This expansion began during Calvin's lifetime and was encouraged by him. Religious refugees poured into Geneva from many European countries, but especially from France during the 1550s as the French government became increasingly intolerant. Calvin welcomed these fugitives, trained many of them as ministers, sent them back to their countries of origin to spread the gospel and supported them with letters of encouragement and advice. Geneva thus became the centre of an international movement and a model for churches elsewhere. John Knox, the Calvinist leader of Scotland, described Geneva as 'the most perfect school of Christ that ever was on the earth since the days of the Apostles'. Calvinism was one of the main ideological aspects of the theological disputes which caused such a rift in the Western Christian Church during the period of the Reformation. As a philosophy, it raises serious moral issues: if mankind is incapable of perceiving and accepting God's grace through Christ, how can people be punished and condemned to an eternity of torment in Hell, having never been chosen by God to believe in him in the first place? Surely it would be unjust of God to condemn a person to eternal damnation, having consciously and expressly withheld the means to escape his wrath. When even St Paul saw the injustice and illogicality of this situation and knew that he had doctrinally painted himself into a corner—a total philosophical impasse—the best he could do was reply, 'Nay but, O man, who art thou that repliest against God? Shall the thing formed say to him that formed it, "Why hast thou made me thus?",' (Rom. 9: 20). Many fundamentalist Christians still espouse these ideas today.

Carthage (Phoenician—*Kart–hadasht* , or in Latin—*Carthago*) was a great city of antiquity, traditionally founded on the north coast of Africa by the Phoenicians of Tyre in 814 BC. It is now a residential suburb of the city of Tunis. Its Phoenician name means 'New Town'. From the middle of the third to the middle of the second century BC, Carthage was engaged in a series of wars with Rome. These wars, known as the Punic Wars, ended in the complete defeat of Carthage by Rome. When Carthage finally fell in

146 BC, the site was plundered and burned, and all human habitation there was forbidden.

Casuist was a theologian (or other person) who studies and resolves cases of conscience or doubtful questions regarding duty and conduct, often with a sinister application. [Source: *Oxford English Dictionary*.]

Cato, Marcu Porcius (234—149 BC) (known also as 'Cato the Censor', or 'Cato the Elder') was a Roman statesman, orator and the first Latin prose writer of importance. Cato was born of plebeian stock and fought as a military tribune in the Second Punic War. His oratorical and legal skills and his rigid morality attracted the attention of the patrician Lucius Valerius Flaccus, who helped him begin a political career in Rome. This success was followed by his election to the censorship in 184 BC, again with Flaccus as his colleague. (The censors were twin magistrates who acted as census takers, assessors and inspectors of morals and conduct.) As censor, Cato aimed at preserving the *mos majorum* {ancestral custom} and combating all Greek influences, which he believed were undermining traditional Roman standards of morality. He passed measures taxing luxury and strictly revised the list of persons eligible for the Senate. He checked abuses by tax gatherers and he initiated a programme of public building, including the Basilica Porta (the first market hall) in Rome.

Celsus, (fl. 2nd century AD) (Greek name *Kelsōs* [Κέλσος]) was a Greek philosopher and opponent of Christianity. He is known to us mainly through the reputation of his literary work, *The True Word* (also translated as *The True Account*, or *Doctrine*, or *Discourse*) (Λόγος Ἀληθής), which is almost entirely reproduced in excerpts by Origen in his counter–polemic *Contra Celsum* {Against Celsus} (248), written seventy or eighty years after Celsus' original work. Very little is known about his personal history except that he lived during the reign of Marcus Aurelius, that his literary activity falls between the years 175 and 180 AD, and that he wrote *The True Word* against the Christian religion. He is one of several writers named Celsus who appeared as opponents of Christianity in the second century; he is probably the Celsus who was known as a friend of Lucian. Some doubt this identification, however, because Origen writes that Lucian's friend was a follower of Epicurus, and the author of *The True Word* shows himself to follow Plato, and perhaps Philo. It is generally supposed that Celsus was a Greek or Roman. His professed acquaintance with Judaism and knowledge of Egyptian ideas and customs incline some historians to think he belonged to the Eastern portion of the empire. Those who believe him to have been a Roman explain his knowledge of Jewish and Egyptian matters by assuming that he acquired that knowledge either by travelling or mingling with the foreign population of Rome. *The True Word* is divided into two sections; one in which objections are put into the mouth of a Jewish interlocutor, and the other in which Celsus speaks for himself, as a pagan philosopher. Celsus ridiculed Christians for what he perceived to be an advocacy of blind faith instead of reason, the same criticism to which St Paul was subjected (q.v.). Abbé Bergier draws attention to the fact that Celsus said that Jesus was born of an illicit relationship between Joseph and a 'virgin' (see p. 209). Another commentator has also noted:

> Celsus, assuming the person of a Jew, represents him as speaking to Jesus, and reprehending him for many things. And in the first place he reproaches him with feigning that he was born of a virgin; and says, that to his disgrace he was born in a Judaic village from a poor Jewess, who obtained the means of subsistence by manual labour. He adds, that she was abandoned by her husband, who was a carpenter, because she had been found by him to have committed adultery. Hence, in consequence of being expelled by her husband, becoming an ignominious vagabond, she was secretly delivered of Jesus, who, through poverty being obliged to serve as a hireling in Egypt, learnt there certain arts for which the Egyptians are famous. Afterwards, returning from thence, he thought so highly of himself, on account of the possession of these [magical] arts, as to proclaim himself to be a God. Celsus also adds, that the mother of Jesus became pregnant with him through a soldier, whose name was Panthera.

He also adds a footnote: 'The same thing is said of Jesus in a work called *The Gospel according to the Jews, or Toldoth Jesu*. See Chap. I and II of that work.' (*Arguments of Celsus, Porphyry, and the Emperor Julian, Against the Christians*, translated by Nathaniel Lardner, [London: MDCCCXXX], pp. 4—5.) (For an extract of *Against Celsus*—see Origen.)

Cerinthian was a member of an ancient heretical group who denied the divinity of Jesus Christ and whose name is derived from their leader, the famous first–century heresiarch and contemporary of the apostle St John. Cerinthius was a great devotee of circumcision and other legal observances of theological law, and St Epiphanius asserts that he was the leader of a group which formed in Jerusalem against St Peter, because he had taken his ministry to the Gentiles. His particular form of heresy was very close to that of the Ebionites (q.v.). Cerinthius also declared that it was not God who had created the universe, that the god of the Hebrews was not the Lord God, but an angel, and that Jesus was born of Joseph and Mary in the same way as any other man, but that he surpassed others in his virtue and wisdom, implying that he was really an embodied 'spirit' or 'virtue', sent by God the Father, through whom he performed miracles. His sect denied the crucifixion and resurrection of Christ, and his disciples were said to have had all manner of visions. They also rejected the whole of the New Testament, except the Gospel of St Matthew, in which they found the circumcision of Christ and therefore they insisted on the necessity of this religious law being upheld. Some ancients attributed the authorship of the book of Revelation of St John, i.e., the Apocalypse, to Cerinthius. (Source—abridged from: *Encyclopédie, ou Dictionnaire Raisonné des Sciences, des Arts et des Métiers*.)

Figure 69: *The Four Riders of the Apocalypse*, **Albrecht Dürer (1497—98).**

381

Chalcidius (*c*. AD 300) (also known as Calcidius) was a scholar who wrote a commentary on Plato's *Timaeus* in the fourth century (not the third, as Bergier suggests on p. 239), which exerted an important influence on the medieval interpretation of the work. It is also not known whether Chalcidius was a pagan or a Christian—scholarship is divided on this issue. He is often called a Christian exegete. One scholar has called him 'more Platonist than Christian', and he points out that Chalcidius stated that 'he calls the Jews a more holy sect', which throws doubt on his own Christianity. (See Dr Ralph Cudworth, *The True Intellectual System of the Universe wherein all the Reason and Philosophy of Atheism is Confuted and its Impossibility Demonstrated, with a Treatise concerning Eternal and Immutable Morality*, with notes and a dissertation by Dr J.L. Mosheim, translated by John Harrison [London: 1845], p. 463, footnote № 5.) A Christian Platonic theism of the type of which Boethius is the finest example arose, based on a reading of the *Timaeus* from a Christian point of view. Chalcidius commented on the adoration of the Magi, noting that:

> There is another more sacred and venerable history which says that the rising of a certain star foretold, not diseases and death, but the descent of the glorious God for the sake of human salvation and mortal affairs. Which star having been beheld by the wise men of the Chaldeans, versed in the contemplation of celestial things, they are said to have sought for the recent birth of God: and having found the august child, to have worshipped him, and presented unto him gifts suitable to so great a God; which things are much better known to thee than to others.

The Christian church has always taken this passage as evidence in support of the biblical story, but Chalcidius' work was written for a Christian audience and it merely reports what was believed at the time: we know nothing of Chalcidius' own opinion and his statement above is hardly an endorsement of the biblical myth as historical fact.

Chaldea was an ancient land, frequently mentioned in the Old Testament. It was part of southern Babylonia, now the modern southern Iraq. Chaldean priests and scholars were noted for their knowledge of astrology and astronomy, and the associated 'art' of foretelling the future. The Old Testament claims that Abraham came from Ur of the Chaldees, i.e., the people of Chaldea: 'And Terah took Abram his son, and Lot the son of Haran his son's son, and Sarai his daughter in law, his son Abram's wife; and they went forth with them from Ur of the Chaldees, to go into the land of Canaan; and they came unto Haran, and dwelt there', (Gen. 11: 31). However, this is yet another example of a late bit of editing the scriptural text, which is not supported by historical evidence. 'Ur of the Chaldees did not exist until about the eighth century BC, about one thousand years after the time of Abraham. The Mesopotamian city of Ur has a history dating back to at least the third millennium BC. The name Chaldees refers to the "land of the people of Chaldea," located just south of Babylon in southern Mesopotamia. Little is known of Chaldea prior to the eighth century BC. At this time, it temporarily captured the throne of Babylon and ruled the entire region, including Ur. From that time on, although it didn't rule continuously in Babylon, its name came to be associated with southern Mesopotamia. In 587 BC, the Chaldeans conquered the kingdom of Judah and transferred the Hebrew elite to Babylon. [...] The anachronistic Mesopotamian genealogy of Abraham and his relatives shows that it was a late invention intended to place Hebrew origins in the cultural centre of the powerful Mesopotamian empires that followed after the defeat of the Chaldeans by the Persians, and intended to enhance Hebrew prestige within the Babylonian community.' (Greenberg, op. cit., pp. 115—116.)

Charles I (1600—1649), King of England, was charged with high treason and other high crimes against the realm of England. He clashed many times with Parliament and Cromwell, provoking a civil war which led to his execution. He maintained that he stood for 'the liberty of the people of England'. The sentence of death was read on 27 January 1649 and his execution was ordered as a tyrant, traitor, murderer and public enemy. The sentence was carried out on a scaffold erected outside the banqueting hall of Whitehall on the morning of 30 January 1649. The King went bravely to his death, still claiming that he was 'a martyr for the people'. He was sincerely and keenly religious and he clashed with the Puritan majority in Parliament over both religious and secular issues. His decision in 1637 to impose upon Scotland a new liturgy, based on the English *Book of Common Prayer*, although approved by the Scottish bishops, met with concerted resistance. When many Scots signed a national covenant to defend their Presbyterian religion, the King decided to enforce his ecclesiastical policy with the sword. He was outmanoeuvred by a well–organized Scottish covenanting army, and by the time he reached York in March 1639, the first of the so–called Bishops' Wars was already lost.

Cheremon was a historian and scribe who worked closely with Maneto (q.v.). Little is known about him, apart from the fact that he collaborated with Maneto in writing what some commentators have described as 'scurrilous anti–Jewish writings of the past'. (Frank N. Magill, *Dictionary of World Biography: The Ancient World Vol 1* [Fitzroy Dearborn, 1998], p. 485.)

Chrysostom, St John (AD 347—407) was an early Church Father, biblical interpreter and archbishop of Constantinople; the zeal and clarity of his preaching, which appealed especially to the common people, earned him the Greek sobriquet meaning 'golden–mouthed', or *chrysostomos* in Greek —hence his name. His tenure as archbishop was stormy and he died in exile. His relics were brought back to Constantinople in about 438, and he was later declared Doctor (teacher) of the Church. Chrysostom preached many sermons about spurning riches and wealth, embracing poverty, and warning against amassing terrestrial goods instead of heavenly wealth. One such sermon, typical of this attitude, is entitled 'The Rich Man and Lazarus'. A less charitable and rather ugly side of his Christian views was his virulent anti–Semitism, expressed in works such as *Adversus Judaeos* [*Against the Jews*], homilies accusing the Jews of being Christ–killers, amongst other things, which have been described as 'the most horrible and violent denunciations of Judaism to be found in the writings of a Christian theologian', (James Parkes, *Prelude to Dialogue* [London: 1969], p. 153). These works were widely used by the Nazi Party in Germany and Austria during World War II, and they are still quoted by some right–wing groups.

Cicero, Marcus Tullius (106—43 BC) (English byname 'Tully') was a Roman statesman, lawyer, scholar and writer, who vainly tried to uphold republican principles in the final civil wars that destroyed the Republic of Rome. His writings include books of rhetoric, orations, philosophical and political treatises, and letters. He is remembered in modern times as the greatest Roman orator and innovator of what became known as Ciceronian rhetoric. He wrote one work of particular interest for this volume, viz., his treatise entitled *On Divination*, written in 45 BC. It provides great insight into the Roman religion and deals with all manner of divination, including dreams, oracles, augurs, etc.

Clarke, Samuel (1675—1729) was a theologian, philosopher and exponent of Newtonian physics, remembered for his influence on eighteenth–century English theology and philosophy. In 1698 Clarke became a chaplain to the bishop of Norwich and in 1706 to Queen Anne. In 1704 to 1705 he gave two sets of lectures, subsequently published as *A Demonstration of the Being and Attributes of God* (1705) and *A Discourse Concerning the Unchangeable Obligations of Natural Religion* (1706). In the first set he attempted to prove the existence of God by a method 'as near to Mathematical [sic], as the nature of such a Discourse [sic] would allow'. In the second, he argued that the principles of morality are as certain as the propositions of mathematics and thus can be known by reason, unassisted by faith—an approach sometimes called 'ethical rationalism'. David Hume's criticism of religion arose in part from his dissatisfaction with Clarke's effort to prove the existence of God. Clarke also spurred a vehement and prolonged controversy with his *Scripture Doctrine of the Trinity* (1712), which led many of his opponents to accuse him of Arianism (the belief that Christ is neither fully man nor fully God). A friend and disciple of Isaac Newton at the University of Cambridge, Clarke helped to spread Newton's scientific and philosophical views.

Clément, Jacques (1567—1589) was a fanatical Dominican monk who assassinated King Henry III of France on 1 August 1589. He was born in Serbonnes and was part of the Catholic League, whose mission it was to *'tuer tous les hérétiques'* {*'kill all the heretics'*}. On the pretext of handing over a secret note to the king, he stabbed him when they were alone and he was killed in the act by the king's guards.

Codex Theodosianus was the product of a codification or setting out of all the laws since Constantine I (*c.* AD 272—337) in clear terms. It was carried out at the instigation of Theodosius II (401—450)—hence it's name. Theodosius was an Eastern Roman emperor from 408 to 450. He was a gentle, scholarly, easily dominated man who allowed his government to be run by a succession of relatives and ministers. Theodosius' name is associated with three important projects. The first was the erection of an impregnable wall around Constantinople (413), which was actually the work of Anthemius. The second was founding the University of Constantinople in 425, and the third in supervising the compilation of the Theodosian Code (published 438). Theodosius died from injuries suffered during a hunting accident.

Collins, Anthony (1676—1729) was a prolific and provocative English Deist and freethinker, friend of the philosopher John Locke. He wrote an essay entitled *'Essay concerning the use of Reason in propositions the evidence whereof depends on Human Testimony'* (1707) in which he demanded that revelation should conform to man's ideas of God drawn from nature—a stance typical of the Deists. He also wrote *'Ignorance is the foundation of Atheism and Free–Thinking the Cure of it'* (1713), again a work typical of Deists, who were doubters, but not atheists. All his works were published

Figure 70: Anthony Collins (1676—1729).

anonymously and his *Essay* immediately caused a sensation, eliciting numerous counter–arguments in writing. The Deists were engaged in a constant battle with other Deists and members of the Church, producing essays and refuting those of others.

Cœnobite (or cenobite) is a person living in a religious community, as opposed to an *anchoret*, who lives in solitude.

Constantine (? to AD 411) (name in Latin in full Flavius Claudius Constantinus) was a usurping Roman emperor who was recognized as co–ruler by the Western emperor Honorius in 409. Proclaimed emperor by his own army in Britain in 407, Constantine crossed to the European continent with a force of British troops; by the end of the year he controlled eastern Gaul. Constantine established himself at Arelate (now Arles, in France) and was joined by Roman legions from Spain. He appointed his son Constans as caesar (junior emperor) and sent him to suppress a revolt led by relatives of Honorius. After the fall of Honorius' general Stilicho, the effective ruler of the Western empire, Constantine threatened to invade Italy. Honorius was forced to recognize him as joint emperor in 409. In 411 Constantine entered Italy, but he was driven back to Arelate and besieged by Honorius' generals. He surrendered and was executed.

Corinth (in Greek–*Kórinthos*) is an ancient and modern city of the Peloponnesus in south–central Greece. The remains of the ancient city lie about 50 miles (80 km) west of Athens. Corinth had great strategic and commercial importance in ancient times. In 146 BC Corinth was destroyed by the Roman general Lucius Mummius.

Council of Basle (or Basel) was a general council of the Roman Catholic Church held in Basle, Switzerland. It was called by Pope Martin V a few weeks before his death in 1431 and then confirmed by Pope Eugenius IV. Meeting at a time when the prestige of the papacy had been weakened by the Great Schism (1378—1417), it was concerned with two major problems: the question of papal supremacy and the Hussite heresy. (The Hussites were followers of the Bohemian religious reformer Jan Hus, [q.v.]: see also p. 344.) The Council was inaugurated in 1431, but made little progress: eventually it declared that a general council draws its powers immediately from God and that even the pope is subject to a council's direction. It also resolved that the dissenting Hussites were received back into the Catholic Communion, but further squabbling between the pope and the Council gradually led to its loss of prestige. The Council proposed several antipapal measures and in 1437 Pope Eugenius transferred it to Ferrara, Italy, in order to consider reunion with the Greeks. Many of the bishops at Basel accepted the move to Ferrara, but several remained at Basle as a rump council, i.e., a break–away body which declared Eugenius deposed, and in 1439 it elected as his successor a layman, the Duke of Savoy, Amadeus VIII, who took the name Pope Felix V. The next ten years of this rump council were important only because the princes used it to strengthen their control over the churches in their own territories. On the death of Eugenius in 1447, his successor, Nicholas V, brought about the abdication of Felix V and ended the rump council in April 1449. It is a prime example of the schismatic nature of the Church and the interplay of spiritual and temporal rulers, vying for power and influence to protect and further their own interests.

Cyrenius (*c.* 51 BC—AD 21) (Latin name Publius Sulpicius Quirinius, or Greek Κυρήνιος—Kyrenios or Cyrenius,) was a Roman aristocrat, whose governorship of Syria is one of the chronological anchors for the birth of Jesus. He was born near Rome of an aristocratic family and, as was common, he served in the Roman army, possibly participating in Octavian's campaign that culminated in the Battle of Actium in 31 BC. He served in Spain with distinction and eventually became governor of Crete and Cyrene in 14 BC; six years later he was dispatched to govern Pamphylia–Galatia (in modern Turkey). By AD 1, Quirinius had become chief advisor to Augustus' grandson Gaius Caesar, until the latter died from wounds suffered during a campaign. When Augustus' support shifted to his stepson Tiberius, Quirinius entered the latter's camp of followers. After the banishment of Herod Archelaus in AD 6, Judaea came under direct Roman administration. Judea was the southernmost of the three traditional divisions of ancient Palestine; the other two were Galilee in the north and Samaria in the centre. No clearly marked boundary divided Judaea from Samaria, but the town of Beersheba was traditionally the southernmost limit. The region presents a variety of geographic features, but the real core of Judaea was the upper hill country, known as Har Yehuda (*'Hills of Judaea'*), extending south from the region of Bethel (at present–day Rām Allāh) to Beersheba and including the area of Jerusalem, Bethlehem and Hebron. Quirinius was entrusted with the task of carrying out a census to assess the new province for tax purposes. Quirinius served as governor of Syria with nominal authority over Judaea until AD 12, when he returned to Rome as a close associate of Tiberius. Despite New Testament references to actual people like Cyrenius, it is impossible to piece together a full biography and accurate chronology of Jesus' life and ministry, not least because of conflicting accounts of the gospel writers, who showed little concern for such difficulties. The indifference of early secular historians, the confusions and approximations attributable to the simultaneous use of Roman and Jewish calendars, all make establishing a chronology of Jesus' life very difficult. Hence only an approximate chronology may be reconstructed from a few, somewhat conflicting facts. The points of reference are best taken from knowledge of the history of the times reflected in the passages. According to Matthew, Jesus was born near the end of the reign of Herod the Great, thus before 4 BC. In Luke 2: 1—2, Jesus is said to have been born at the time of a census when Quirinius was governor of Syria. Such a census did occur, but in AD 6—7.

Because this was after Herod's death and not in agreement with a possible date of Jesus' baptism, this late date is unlikely. There may have been an earlier census under another governor; an inscription in the Lateran Museum records an unnamed governor who twice ruled Syria, and the suggestion has been made that this was, indeed, Quirinius and that in an earlier time a reported census according to Roman calculation might have been carried out *c.* 8 BC, one of a series of such. With such speculation and the combined evidence of Matthew and Luke, an approximate year of Jesus' birth might be 7—6 BC.

Cyril, Saint was one of two saints, usually referred to in partnership with Methodius: they lived from AD 827—869 and AD 825—884 respectively. They were brothers who became famous for taking Christianity to the Danubian Slavs and for influencing the religious and cultural development of all Slavic peoples, receiving the title 'Apostles of the Slavs'. Both were outstanding scholars, theologians and linguists, and they are highly regarded by the Russian Orthodox Church. In 860, Cyril (originally named Constantine), who had gone on a mission to the Arabs and been professor of philosophy at the patriarchal school in Constantinople, worked with Methodius, the abbot of a Greek monastery, for the conversion of the Khazars northeast of the Black Sea. In 862, when Prince Rostislav of Great Moravia asked Constantinople for missionaries, the emperor Michael III and the patriarch Photius named Cyril and Methodius. In 863 they started their work among the Slavs, using Slavonic in the liturgy. They translated the Holy Scriptures into the language later known as Old Church Slavonic (or Old Bulgarian) and invented a Slavic alphabet based on Greek characters, which in its final (Cyrillic) form is still in use as the alphabet for modern Russian and a number of other Slavic languages. They were both canonized by the Eastern Church.

Daniel was a prophet who gave his name to a book in the Old Testament— The Book of Daniel, also called the *Prophecy of Daniel,* a book found in the *Ketuvim (Writings),* the third section of the Jewish canon, but placed among the Prophets in the Christian canon. The first half of the book (chapters 1—6) contains stories in the third person about the experiences of Daniel and his friends under Kings Nebuchadrezzar II, Belshazzar, Darius I and Cyrus II; the second half, written mostly in the first person, contains reports of Daniel's three visions and one dream. The second half of the book names as author a certain Daniel who, according to chapter 1, was exiled to Babylon. The language of the book—part of which is Aramaic (2:4—7:28)—probably indicates a date of composition later than the Babylonian Exile (sixth century BC). Numerous inaccuracies connected with the period of exile (no deportation occurred in 605 BC; Darius was a *successor* of Cyrus, not a *predecessor*; etc.) tend to confirm this judgment.

Because its religious ideas do not belong to the sixth century BC, numerous scholars date Daniel in the first half of the second century BC and relate the visions to the persecution of the Jews under Antiochus IV Epiphanes (175—164/163 BC). Daniel, extolled for his upright character, is presented as a model for the persecuted community. The unknown author may have drawn inspiration from Ugaritic and Phoenician sources that speak of a legendary figure, noted for his righteousness and wisdom. The book takes an apocalyptic view of history: the end time is vividly anticipated, when the reign of God will be established and the faithful, through a resurrection of the just, will be relieved of their suffering. The book exhorts its hearers and readers to endure, even to the point of martyrdom. In the Roman Catholic Old Testament, the book includes also 'The Prayer of Azariah', 'Song of the Three Young Men', 'Susanna' and 'Bel and the Dragon'— writings considered apocryphal by Jews and Protestants.

David, King (? to *c.* 962 BC) was the second of the Israelite kings (after Saul), reigning *c.* 1000 to *c.* 962 BC, who established a united kingdom over all Israel, with Jerusalem as its capital. In the Jewish tradition, he became a model king and the founder of an enduring dynasty, around whom messianic expectations of the people of Israel proliferated. In the New Testament Jesus is represented as descending from the lineage of David and the fulfilment of the messianic prophecies. David is also held in high esteem in the Islamic tradition. In the New Testament he is described as a 'man after God's own heart': 'And afterward they desired a king: and God gave unto them Saul the son of Cis, a man of the tribe of Benjamin, by the space of forty years. And when he had removed him, he raised up unto them David to be their king; to whom also he gave their testimony, and said, "I have found David the son of Jesse, a man after mine own heart, which shall fulfil all my will",' (Acts 13: 21—22). D'Holbach, less admiring of him, mentions him in his *Portable Theology*:

> He is one of the greatest saints in Paradise, a true model for kings. He was rebellious, lewd, adulterous and a murderer, etc. He slept with women and then had their husbands killed off. However, he was truly pious and nicely under the priests' thumb, through which he earned the sobriquet of 'a man after God's own heart'. God, even up to this present era, is never in a better mood than when He is being entertained by the farces this holy man got up to.

Figure 71: *David and Goliath*, Gustave Doré (1832—1883).
Illustration from an edition of *The Bible* (1865).

The reference to David's adulterous behaviour is based on the story, narrated in the Old Testament, when David fell in love with Bathsheba, wife of the Hittite Uriah, who became pregnant by him. David had her husband killed and then married her. Their first child died—God specifically made the child fall ill to punish the couple (2 Sam. 12: 15), but she had another child who grew up to become King Solomon. Bathsheba played a key part in the politics of King David's court. The story of his seduction of Bathsheba is told in both 2 Sam. 11 & 12 and 1 Kgs. 1 & 2. David was also fêted for killing masses of other tribes and people who displeased God: 'And the women answered one another as they played, and said, "Saul hath slain his thousands, and David his ten thousands",'—see 1 Sam. 18: 7. There is another passage (to which d'Holbach refers in his text), which shows David's behaviour as truly shocking and it is quoted here from the *Vulgate*:

> Then David gathered all the people together, and went out against Rabbath: and after fighting, he took it. And he took the crown of their king from his head, the weight of which was a talent of gold, set with most precious stones, and it was put upon David's head, and the spoils of the city which were very great he carried away. And bringing forth the people thereof he sawed them, and drove over them chariots armed with iron: and divided them with knives, and made them pass through brick kilns: so did he to all the cities of the children of Ammon: and David returned, with all the army to Jerusalem.' (*Vul.* 2 Kgs. 12: 29—31 or *King James Version* 2 Sam. 12: 29—31.)

Such is the ideal king and a 'man after God's own heart'. As an ideal king, David clearly holds a special place in God's affections, as 1 Sam. 18: 14 states: 'And David behaved himself wisely **in all his ways**; and the Lord was with him.' In the New Testament, David is equally revered and Jesus' putative direct ancestry from him, as claimed in his recorded genealogy, is more than suspect. Given the amount of carnage God commanded in the Old Testament, perhaps David is truly a 'man after God's own heart'.

De Burigny, Jean Levesque (1692—1785) was a historian who, in 1713, with his brothers, Champeaux and Lévesque de Pouilly, began to compile a dictionary of universal knowledge, similar to an encyclopaedia, which comprised twelve large manuscript folios and afforded Burigny ample material for his subsequent works. He was well–connected with writers and philosophers of his day and he made a considerable contribution to Saint–Hyacinthe's work *L'Europe savante*, in twelve volumes. His publications on historical topics earned him the reputation of a serious scholar.

Deism was an unorthodox religious attitude that found expression among a group of English writers beginning with Edward Herbert (later 1st Baron

Herbert of Cherbury) in the first half of the seventeenth century and ending with Henry St. John, 1st Viscount Bolingbroke (q.v.), in the middle of the eighteenth century. In general, it refers to what can be called a 'natural religion', the acceptance of a certain body of religious knowledge that is innate in everyone, or that can be acquired by the use of reason, as opposed to knowledge acquired either through revelation or the teaching of any church. Though an initial use of the term occurred in sixteenth–century France, the later appearance of the doctrine on the Continent was stimulated by the translation and adaptation of the English models. The high point of Deist thought occurred in England from about 1689 to 1742, during a period when, despite widespread counterattacks from the established Church of England, there was relative freedom of religious expression following the Glorious Revolution that ended the rule of James II and brought William and Mary to the throne. Deism took deep root in eighteenth–century Germany after it had ceased to be a vital subject of controversy in England. At times in the nineteenth and early twentieth centuries, the word Deism was used theologically in contradistinction to 'theism', the belief in an imminent God who actively intervened in the affairs of man. In this sense Deism was represented as the view of those who reduced the role of God to a mere act of creation in accordance with rational laws discoverable by man and held that, after the original act, God virtually withdrew, refraining from further interference in the processes of nature and human affairs.

Descartes, René (1596—1650) was a French mathematician, scientist and philosopher. He has been called the father of modern philosophy because he was one of the first to abandon scholastic Aristotelianism and he formulated the first modern version of mind–body dualism. He promoted the development of a new scientific method grounded in observation and experiment. He dismissed apparent knowledge derived from authority, the senses and reason by systematically applying an original system of methodical doubt, ultimately to express the now famous conclusion that the only thing he knew for sure is that he knows he exists, declared through the dictum often cited in Latin, though originally written in French—'*Cogito, ergo sum*' {'*I think, therefore I am*'}, or '*Je pense, donc je suis.*' His *Discourse* was one of the first important works to be written in French, as opposed to the customary Latin, so that it would reach a wider audience. In the *Discourse* he also provided a provisional moral code for use while seeking truth, comprising the following tenets: (i) obey local customs and laws; (ii) make decisions on the best evidence and then stick to them firmly, as though they were certain; (iii) change desires rather than the world; and (iv) always seek truth. Descartes' metaphysics are rationalist, based on the postulation of innate ideas of mind, matter and God, but his physics and physiology, based on sensory experience, are mechanistic and empiricist.

Diderot, Denis (1713—1784) was one of the greatest minds in France of his time. He was a man of letters and a philosopher who, from 1745 to 1772, served as chief editor of the *Encyclopédie*, one of the principal works of the Age of Enlightenment. He was educated by the Jesuits and he obtained his degree of Master of Arts at the University of Paris in 1732. He almost entered the church as a career, but he eventually turned atheist and expressed his ideas in a work entitled *Pensées philosophiques* {*Philosophical Thoughts*} (1746), which caused a sensation. Many of the ideas he expressed in them came from a work by the third Earl of Shaftesbury (one of the principal English Deists [q.v.]; see also p. 350) entitled *Inquiry Concerning Virtue* (1699), which Diderot had translated into French in 1745. In 1755 he met Sophie Volland, with whom he formed an attachment that was to last more than twenty years. Their liaison was founded on a common love of literature, philosophy and many other things, and it generated a prolific amount of correspondence which forms a fascinating insight not only into Diderot's own personality and character, but also into the ideas and intellectual ethos of the time. His closest friend Grimm (q.v.) wrote comments on d'Holbach's *Christianity Unveiled*, which are translated and included in this volume.

Diodorus Siculus (fl. 1st century BC) (also known as Diodorus of Sicily) was a Greek historian, the author of a universal history, known as *Bibliotheca historica* {*Historical Library*}. Diodorus lived at the time of Julius Caesar and Augustus, and his own statements make it clear that he travelled in Egypt in 60—57 BC, spending several years in Rome. His history consisted of forty books and was divided into three parts. The first treats of the mythic history of the non–Hellenic and Hellenic tribes to the destruction of Troy; the second ends with Alexander's death; and the third continues the history as far as the beginning of Caesar's Gallic War. The *Bibliotheca* is invaluable where no other continuous historical source has survived and, to some extent, it makes up for works lost by earlier authors, from which it was compiled. Diodorus does not always quote his authorities, but in the books that have survived his most important sources for Greek history were certainly Ephorus (for the period 480—340 BC) and Hieronymus of Cardia (for 323—302 BC).

Ditton, Humphry (1675—1715) was an English mathematician who started his academic career by studying theology, but he later devoted himself to mathematics and published widely in that field. However, he wrote a work entitled *Discourse on the Resurrection of Jesus Christ*, published in 1714.

Dodwell, Henry (1641—1711) was an academic who wrote numerous treatises in defence of the Anglican Church. He was educated at Trinity College, Dublin, where he taught for ten years before taking up posts at various other academic institutions, including Oxford. He refused to swear the Oath of Allegiance to William III in 1689 and thereby he lost his post. His work *De jure sacerdotale {On the Law of the Clergy}* was published in London in 1689.

Dominic, Saint (1170—1221) (in Spanish *Santo Domingo De Guzmán*) was the founder of the Order of Friars Preachers (Dominicans), a religious order of mendicant friars with a universal mission of preaching. It had a centralized organization and government, and placed great emphasis on scholarship. St Dominic met Francis of Assisi (q.v.) and the friendship of the two saints is a strong tradition in both the Franciscan and the Dominican orders. In the summer of 1216, Dominic met with sixteen companions in Toulouse and this meeting has been called the *capitulum fundationis {chapter* (or *meeting) of foundation}*, which was the basis for the foundation of the Dominican Order. The rule of St Augustine was adopted, as well as a set of *consuetudines {customs}*, partly based on those of the canons regular, concerning the divine office, monastic life and religious poverty, which are all still the core of Dominican legislation. After the death of Innocent III, Dominic, once more in Rome, received formal sanction for his order in 1216 from his successor Honorius III. This original community spawned many others, first in Paris and Bologna, adjacent to the universities there, which further enhanced the Dominican emphasis on scholarship, and thereafter the order spread all over Europe.

Dowdeswell, William (1721—1775) was an English politician. He was educated at Westminster School, Christ Church College (Oxford), then at the University of Leiden, where he met d'Holbach. He became a Member of Parliament for the family borough of Tewkesbury. He was a prominent Whig and was appointed Chancellor of the Exchequer in 1765.

Dumarsais, César Chesneau, sieur Dumarsais or **Du Marsais** (1676—1756) was a French philosopher and grammarian. He studied law in Paris, but he had to abandon furthering his career for lack of funds. D'Alembert called him the 'La Fontaine of philosophers', such was his wisdom and rare insight into human nature and many other fields of knowledge. He died in penury and D'Alembert wrote of him in the *Encyclopédie* (Volume V), 'He lived in poverty, neglected by the fatherland, which he enlightened.' He is chiefly remembered for a Latin primer, treatises on grammar, rhetoric and comparative lexicography, a work entitled *Nouvelles Libertés de penser {New Ways of Free-Thinking}* (1743), and *Examen de la religion chrétienne {Examination of the Christian Religion}* (1745).

Ebionite was a member of an early ascetic sect of Jews who followed Jesus of Nazareth. The Ebionites were one of several such sects that originated in and around Palestine in the first century AD and included the Nazarenes and Elkasites. The name of the sect is thought to originate from the Hebrew *ebyonim,* or *ebionim,* meaning 'poor', and not from the name of any leader, as has frequently been claimed. Little information exists on the Ebionites and the surviving accounts are subject to considerable debate. The first mention of the sect is in the works of the Christian theologian St Irenaeus, notably in his *Adversus haereses {Against Heresies}* (c. 180); other sources include the writings of Origen and St Epiphanius of Constantia. Several of these early church commentators accused them of altering sacred writings to fit in with their own views—a practice which was widespread in the early church: for example, they were accused of doctoring the Gospel of Matthew by cutting out the details of the so–called 'Virgin Birth' of Christ, because it did not fit in with their views. The Ebionite movement may have arisen about the time of the destruction of the Jewish Temple in Jerusalem (AD 70). Its members evidently left Palestine to avoid persecution and settled in Transjordan (notably at Pella) and Syria, and were later known to be in Asia Minor and Egypt. The sect seems to have existed into the fourth century. Most of the features of Ebionite doctrine were anticipated in the teachings of the earlier Qumrān sect, as revealed in the Dead Sea Scrolls. They believed in one God and taught that Jesus was the Messiah and the true 'prophet' mentioned in Deut. 18: 15. As already noted, they rejected the Virgin Birth of Jesus, holding instead that he was the natural son of Joseph and Mary. The Ebionites believed Jesus became the Messiah because he obeyed the Jewish Law. They themselves faithfully followed Jewish law, although they removed what they regarded as interpolations in order to uphold their teachings, which included vegetarianism, holy poverty, ritual ablutions and the rejection of animal sacrifices. The Ebionites also held Jerusalem in great veneration. The early Ebionite literature is said to have resembled the Gospel of Matthew, without the birth narrative and some other features. They later found this unsatisfactory and developed their own literature, some of which has survived only in fragments, i.e., from quotations from their opponents, such as the fourth–century heresy–hunter, Epiphanius of Salamis. These fragments can be read in Bart Ehrman, *Lost Scriptures: Books that Did Not Make It into the New Testament* (Oxford: OUP, 2003/5), pp. 11—14.

Edict of Nantes was a law promulgated at Nantes in Brittany on 13 April 1598, by Henry IV of France. It granted a large measure of religious liberty to his Protestant subjects, known as Huguenots (see pp. 349 *et seqq.*). The edict upheld Protestants' freedom of conscience and permitted them to hold public worship in many parts of the kingdom, though not in Paris. It granted them full civil rights and established a special court, the *Chambre de l'Édit*, composed of both Protestants and Catholics, to deal with disputes arising from the Edict. Protestant pastors were to be paid by the state and released from certain obligations; finally, the Protestants could keep the places they were still holding in August 1597 as strongholds, or *places de sûreté*, for eight years, the expenses of garrisoning them being met by the king. The edict also restored Catholicism in all areas where Catholic practice had been interrupted; and it made any extension of Protestant worship in France legally impossible. Nevertheless, it was much resented by Pope Clement VIII, by the Roman Catholic clergy in France and the *Parlements*—supreme courts, heavily infiltrated by the Catholic Church. Catholics tended to interpret the Edict in its most restrictive sense. The Cardinal de Richelieu, who regarded its political clauses as a danger to the state, annulled them by the Peace of Alès (1629). On 18 October 1685, Louis XIV revoked the Edict of Nantes and deprived the French Protestants of all religious and civil liberties. Within a few years, more than 400,000 Huguenots emigrated—to England, Prussia, Holland and America—depriving France of its most industrious commercial class.

Edward, Saint (1003—1066) (also known as 'the Confessor') was king of England from 1042 to 1066. Although he was a listless, ineffectual monarch, overshadowed by powerful nobles, his reputation for piety evidently preserved much of the dignity of the crown. His close ties to Normandy prepared the way for the conquest of England by Normans under William, Duke of Normandy (later King William I, The Conqueror), in 1066.

Ehud (sometimes spelled Aod in OT. See Judg. 3: 12—4: 1) was the son of Gera, the Benjaminite, an Israelite hero who delivered Israel from eighteen years of oppression by the Moabites. A left–handed man, Ehud tricked Eglon, king of Moab, and killed him. He then led the tribe of Ephraim to seize the fords of the Jordan, where they killed about 10,000 Moabite soldiers. As a result, Israel enjoyed peace for about eighty years.

Elijah (fl. in 9th century BC) (also spelled Elias, or Elia, Hebrew *Eliyyahu*) was a Hebrew prophet who ranks with Moses in saving the religion of Yahweh from being corrupted by the nature worship of Baal. Elijah's name means *Yahweh is my God* and is spelled Elias in some versions of the Bible. The story of his prophetic career in the northern kingdom of Israel during the reigns of Kings Ahab and Ahaziah is told in 1 Kgs. 17—19 and 2 Kgs. 1—2 in the Old Testament. Elijah claimed that there was no reality except the God of Israel, stressing monotheism to the people with possibly unprecedented emphasis. He is commemorated by Christians on 20 July

Figure 72: *Elijah Taken into Heaven*, Julius Schnoor von Carolsfeld (*c.* 1851).

and is recognized as a prophet by Islam. Elijah's deepest prophetic experience takes place on his pilgrimage to Horeb, where he learns that God is not in the storm, the earthquake, or the lightning. Nature, so far from being God's embodiment, is not even an adequate symbol. God as invisible spirit is best known in the intellectual word of revelation, as 'the still, small voice'. The transcendence of God receives here one of its earliest expressions. Elijah's story also expresses, for the first time, a thought that was to dominate Hebrew prophecy: in contrast to the bland hopes of the people, salvation is bestowed only on a 'remnant', i.e., those purified by God's judgment. The theme of the later prophets, viz., that morality must be at the heart of ritual worship, is also taught by Elijah, who upholds the unity of law and religion against the despotic cruelty of a king influenced by a pagan wife. Elijah's work may also be regarded as a protest against every effort to find religious experience in self–induced ecstasy and sensual frenzy, rather than in a faith allied to morality and the law of God.

Elysium q.v. **Tartarus.**

Epictetus (AD 55—135) was a Greek philosopher associated with the Stoics, remembered for the religious tone of his teachings, which commended him to numerous early Christian thinkers. As far as is known, Epictetus wrote nothing. His teachings were transmitted by Arrian, his pupil, in two works: *Discourses*, of which four books are extant; and the *Encheiridion* (or *Manual*), a condensed aphoristic version of the main doctrines. In his teachings, Epictetus followed the early Stoics, rather than the later group, reverting to Socrates and Diogenes, the philosopher of Cynicism, as historical models of the sage. Primarily interested in ethics, Epictetus described philosophy as learning 'how it is possible to employ desire and aversion without hindrance'. He believed *true education* consisted in recognizing that there is only one thing that belongs to an individual fully—his will or purpose. God, acting as a good king and father, has given each being a will that cannot be compelled or thwarted by anything external. Men are not responsible for the ideas that present themselves to their consciousness, though they are wholly responsible for the way in which they react to them. Epictetus stated, 'Two maxims we must ever bear in mind—that apart from the will there is nothing good or bad, and that we must not try to anticipate or to direct events, but merely to accept them with intelligence.' Man must believe there is a God whose thought directs the universe.

D'Epinay, Madame (1726—1783) (name in full Louise–Florence–Pétronille Tardieu d'Esclavelles, dame de La Live d'Épinay) was a distinguished figure in higher literary circles in eighteenth–century France. Though she wrote a good deal herself, she is principally remembered for her friendships with three of the most outstanding French writers and thinkers of her day—Denis Diderot, Baron Friedrich de Grimm, and Jean–Jacques Rousseau, with whom she exchanged copious correspondence. Her memoirs, entitled *Mémoires et Correspondance de Madame D'Epinay* {*Memoirs and Letters of Mme D'Epinay*} were published in Paris in 1818 in three volumes and they are an invaluable insight into the life and times of these literary figures.

Epiphanius, Saint (AD 310—403) was Archbishop of Salamis and his life is described by Tillemont (q.v.), and others. He was an opponent of Origen (q.v.) and he played an important role in ecclesiastical affairs, particularly in debates on issues surrounding numerous so–called heresies. In about 394, carried away by an apparently excessive zeal, he went to Jerusalem to oppose the supposed Origenism of Bishop John and in 402 he went to Constantinople to combat the same pretended heresy of St John Chrysostom.

Epirus is the coastal region of north–western Greece and southern Albania. In the fifth century, Epirus was still on the periphery of the Greek world: to the fifth–century historian Thucydides, the Epirotes were 'barbarians'.

Essene was a member of a sect or brotherhood which flourished in Palestine from about the second century BC to the end of the first century AD. The New Testament does not mention them and accounts given by Josephus (q.v.), Philo of Alexandria (q.v.), and Pliny the Elder (q.v.) sometimes differ in significant details, perhaps indicating a diversity that existed among their communities. The Essenes clustered in monastic groups which generally excluded women. Property was held in common and all details of daily life were regulated by officials. The Essenes were never numerous; Pliny fixed their number at some 4,000 in his day. Like the Pharisees, the Essenes meticulously observed the Law of Moses, the Sabbath and ritual purity. They also professed belief in immortality and divine punishment for sin. But, unlike the Pharisees, the Essenes denied the resurrection of the body and refused to involve themselves in public life. With few exceptions, they shunned Temple worship and were content to live ascetic lives of manual labour in seclusion. The Sabbath was reserved for day–long prayer and meditation on the Torah (the first five books of the Bible). Oaths were frowned upon, but once taken they could not be rescinded. Josephus devotes a paragraph to the Essenes in his *Jewish Antiquities*, stating:

> The doctrine of the Essenes is wont to leave everything in the hands of God. They regard the soul as immortal and believe that they ought to strive especially to draw near to righteousness. They send votive offerings to the temple, but perform their sacrifices employing a different ritual of purification. For this reason they are barred from those precincts of the temple that are frequented by all the people and perform their rites by themselves. Otherwise they are of the highest character, devoting themselves solely to agricultural labour. They deserve admiration in contrast to all others who claim their share of virtue because such qualities as theirs were never found before among any Greek or barbarian people, nay, not even briefly, but have been among them in constant practice and never interrupted since they adopted them from old. Moreover, they hold their possessions in common, and the wealthy man receives no more enjoyment from his property than the man who possesses nothing. The men who practise this way of life number more than four thousand. They neither bring wives into the community nor do they own slaves, since they believe that the latter practice contributes to injustice and that the former opens the way to a source of dissension. Instead they live by themselves and perform menial tasks for one another. They elect by show of hands good men to receive their revenues and the produce of the earth and priests to prepare bread and other food. Their manner of life does not differ at all from that of the so–called Ctistae among the Dacians, but is as close to it as could be. (Josephus, *Jewish Antiquities: Books XVIII–XIX*, translated by L.H. Feldman, [Cambridge, Mass.: Harvard University Press/Loeb Classical Library, 2000], pp. 15—21.)

Euclid (Greek *Eukleides*) is the most famous mathematician of Græco–
Roman antiquity, best known for his treatise on geometry called *The
Elements*. Almost nothing is known of his life, except that he flourished in
Alexandria, Egypt, around 300 BC.

Eusebius (fl. in 4th century AD) (also known as Eusebius Pamphili) was a
bishop, exegete, polemicist and historian, whose account of the first
centuries of Christianity, in his *Church* (or *Ecclesiastical*) *History* is a
landmark in Christian historiography. His *Church History* and *Chronicle*
are two of the greatest historical works that have survived. The *Chronicle*
has been lost in the original as a whole, but it has been reconstructed in
parts from excerpts from other sources. The second part has been
completely preserved in a Latin translation by Jerome, and both parts are
still extant in an Armenian translation. The loss of the Greek originals has
made the Armenian translation doubly valuable. The *Chronicle* was
written before *Church History*. Eusebius was baptized and ordained at
Caesarea, where he was taught by the learned presbyter Pamphilus, to
whom he was bound by ties of respect and affection, and from whom he
derived the name 'Eusebius Pamphili' (*son* or *servant of Pamphilus*).
Pamphilus was persecuted for his beliefs by the Romans and was martyred
in 310. Eusebius may himself have been imprisoned by the Roman
authorities at Caesarea, and he was taunted many years later with having
escaped by performing some act of submission. Eusebius wrote
voluminously, but his vast erudition is not matched by clarity of thought or
attractiveness of presentation. His fame rests chiefly on his *Church
History*, which he probably began to write during the Roman persecutions
and revised several times between 312 and 324. In this work Eusebius
produced what may be called, at best, a fully documented history of the
Christian Church, and, at worst, collections of passages from his sources.
As Eusebius constantly quoted or paraphrased his sources, he preserved
portions of earlier works that are no longer extant. His *Chronicle* was an
outline of world history and he carried this annalistic method over into his
Church History, constantly interrupting his narrative of church history to
insert the accession of Roman emperors and bishops of the four great sees
(Alexandria, Antioch, Jerusalem and Rome). He enlarged his work in
successive editions to cover events down to 324, the year before the
Council of Nicaea. Eusebius, however, was not a great historian. His
treatment of heresy, for example, is inadequate and he knew next to
nothing about the Western Church. His historical works are really
apologetic, showing by facts how the Church had vindicated itself against
heretics and heathens. After the Emperor Constantine's death in 337, he
wrote his *Life of Constantine*, a panegyric that possesses some historical
value, chiefly because of its use of primary sources.

Ezekiel (fl. in 6th century BC) (also spelt 'Ezechiel', in Hebrew *Yeḥezqel*) was a prophet/priest of ancient Israel and he has traditionally been regarded as the author of an Old Testament book that bears his name. Ezekiel's early oracles (from *c.* 592 BC) in Jerusalem were pronouncements of violence and destruction; his later statements addressed the hopes of the Israelites exiled in Babylon. The faith of Ezekiel in the ultimate establishment of a new covenant between God and the people of Israel has had profound influence on the post–exilic reconstruction and reorganization of Judaism. His ministry was conducted in Jerusalem and Babylon in the first three decades of the sixth century BC. For Ezekiel and his people, these years were bitter ones because the remnant of the Israelite domain, the little state of Judah, was eliminated by the rising Babylonian empire under Nebuchadrezzar (reigned 605—562 BC). Jerusalem surrendered in 597 BC. Israelite resistance was nevertheless renewed, and in 587—586 the city was destroyed after a lengthy siege. In both debacles, and indeed again in 582, large numbers from the best elements of the surviving population were forcibly deported to Babylonia. Before the first surrender of Jerusalem, Ezekiel was a functioning priest, probably attached to the Jerusalem Temple staff. He was among those deported in 597 to Babylonia, where he was located at Tel–abib on the Kebar canal (near Nippur). It is evident that he enjoyed a high status amongst his fellow exiles. Ezekiel's religious call came in July 592 when he had a vision of the 'throne–chariot' of God. He subsequently prophesied until 585, and then is not heard of again until 572. His latest datable utterance can be dated about 570 BC, twenty–two years after his first. His earlier oracles to the Jews in Palestine were pronouncements of God's judgment on a sinful nation for its apostasy. Ezekiel said that Judah was guiltier than Israel and that Jerusalem would fall to Nebuchadrezzar and its inhabitants would be killed or exiled. According to him, Judah trusted in foreign gods and foreign alliances, and Jerusalem was a city full of injustice. Pagan rites abounded in the courts of the Temple. After the fall of Jerusalem and his period of silence, Ezekiel then addressed himself more pointedly to the exiles and sought to direct their hopes for their restoration as a nation. His theme changed from the harsh judgment of God to promises of a more favoured future. Ezekiel prophesied that the exiles from both Judah and Israel would return to Palestine, leaving none in the Diaspora. In the imminent new age, a new covenant would be made with the restored house of Israel, to whom God would give a new spirit and a new heart. The restoration would be an act of divine grace, for the sake of God's name and personal reputation. Ezekiel's prophecies conclude with a vision of a restored Temple in Jerusalem. More than any of the classical biblical prophets, Ezekiel was given to symbolic actions, strange visions and even trances (although it is quite gratuitous to deduce from these, and from his words 'I fell upon my face' [1: 28], that he was a cataleptic). He ate a scroll on which words of prophecy are written, in order to symbolize his appropriation of the message (3: 1—3). He lay down for an extended time to symbolize Israel's punishment (4: 4 *et seqq.*). He was apparently struck dumb on one occasion for an unspecified length of time (3: 26). Like other prophets before him, he uses the analogous relationship of a husband to an unfaithful wife to describe the relationship of the Israelites with their god, and therefore he understands the collapse of the life of Judah as a judgment for essential infidelity. His book is valuable for understanding life in Babylonian exile.

Fairy, also spelled *faerie* or *faery*, is a mythical being of folklore and romance, usually having magic powers and dwelling on earth in close relationship with humans. It can appear variously; as a dwarf–like creature, typically having green clothes and living underground or in stone heaps, and characteristically exercising magic powers to benevolent ends; as a diminutive sprite, commonly in the shape of a delicate, beautiful, ageless, winged woman dressed in diaphanous white clothing; as an inhabitant of fairyland, but making usually well–intentioned intervention in personal human affairs; or as a tiny, mischievous, and protective creature, generally associated with a household hearth, like some sprites in Russian folklore, notably the *domovoi*. While the term *fairy* goes back only to the Middle Ages in Europe, analogues to these beings in varying forms appear in both written and oral literature, from the Sanskrit *gandharva* (semidivine celestial musicians) to the nymphs of Greek mythology and Homer, the *jinni* of Arabic mythology, and similar folk characters of the Samoans, of the Arctic peoples, and of other indigenous Americans. The common modern depiction of fairies in children's stories represents a bowdlerization of what was once a serious and even sinister folkloric tradition. The fairies of the past were feared as dangerous and powerful beings, sometimes friendly to humans, but they could also be cruel and mischievous at times. Fairies are usually conceived as being characteristically beautiful or handsome, having lives corresponding to those of human beings, though of longer duration: they have no souls and they simply perish at death. They often carry off children, leaving changeling substitutes, and they also whisk adults off to fairyland, which resembles pre–Christian abodes of the dead. People transported to fairyland cannot return if they eat or drink there. Fairy and human lovers may marry, though only with restrictions whose violation ends the marriage and, often, the life of the human. Some female fairies are deadly to human lovers. Fairies are said to be of human size or smaller, down to a height of three inches (7.5 cm) or less. Female fairies may tell fortunes, particularly prophesying at births and foretelling deaths. Several herbs, especially St John's wort and yarrow, are potent against fairies, and hawthorn trees, foxglove and groundsel are so dear to them that abuse of these plants may bring retribution. Fairy lore is particularly prevalent in Ireland, Cornwall, Wales and Scotland. Fairies are common in literature from the Middle Ages onwards and appear in the writings of the Italians Matteo Boiardo and Ludovico Ariosto, the English poet Edmund Spenser, the Frenchman Charles Perrault, and the Dane Hans Christian Andersen, among others.

Figure 73: *Prince Arthur and the Fairy Queen,* Johann Heinrich Füssli (1788).

Fontenelle, Bernard le Bovier, sieur de (1657—1757) was a French scientist and man of letters, described by Voltaire as the most universal mind produced by the era of Louis XIV. Many of the characteristic ideas of the Enlightenment are found in embryonic form in his works. Fontenelle was educated at the Jesuit College in Rouen. He did not settle in Paris until he had passed the age of thirty and had become famous as the writer of operatic librettos. His literary activity during the years 1683—88 won him a great reputation. The *Lettres galantes* {*Gallant Letters*}, originally published in 1683, then augmented in 1685, contributed to this, but the *Nouveaux Dialogues des morts* {*New Dialogues of the Dead*} (1683—1684) enjoyed a greater success and is more interesting to the modern reader. The *Dialogues* were conversations modelled on the dialogues of Lucian between such figures as Socrates and Montaigne, Seneca and Scarron, and served to disseminate new philosophical ideas. The popularization of philosophy was carried further by his *Histoire des oracles* {*History of Oracles*} (1687), based on a Latin treatise by the Dutch writer Anton van Dale (1683). Here Fontenelle subjected pagan religions to criticisms which the reader would inevitably see as applicable to Christianity as well. The same anti–religious bias is seen in his amusing satire *Relation de l'île de Bornéo* {*Account of the Island of Borneo*} (1686), in which a civil war in Borneo is used to symbolize the dissensions between Catholics based in Rome and Calvinists based in Geneva. Fontenelle's most famous work was the *Entretiens sur la pluralité des mondes* {*Conversations on the Plurality of Worlds*} (1686—1688). These charming and sophisticated dialogues were more influential than any other work in securing acceptance of the Copernican system, still far from commanding universal support in 1686. Fontenelle's basis of scientific documentation was meagre, and some of his figures were wildly erroneous even for his own day. He was unfortunate in the moment of his publication: the Cartesian theory of vortices, on which his work was based, was refuted the next year in Isaac Newton's *Principia*. The *Entretiens* were nevertheless exceedingly successful. Fontenelle was elected to the *Académie Française* {*French Academy*} in 1691 and was elected to the *Académie des Inscriptions* {*Academy of Inscriptions*} in 1701, of which Bergier was also a member—see p. 169 (footnote) of this volume. As permanent secretary of the Académie des Sciences from 1697, Fontenelle held a highly influential office. He published the memoirs presented to the academy and wrote its history. He kept abreast of new developments in science, corresponding with scientists in most European countries, and developed his talent for lucid popular exposition, notably in some of his obituary notices read to the academy (e.g., those of Newton and Gottfried Wilhelm Leibniz). Fontenelle was a close friend of Montesquieu and well–known to Voltaire, who mocked him in his *Micromégas* (1752), a dissertation on the smallness of man in relation to the cosmos, in which Fontenelle famously stated, 'Behold a universe so immense that I am lost in it. I no longer know where I am. I am just nothing at all. Our world is terrifying in its insignificance.' Fontenelle's most original contribution was in his approach to historiography, shown in his *De l'origine des fables* {*On the Origin of Fables*} (1724), in which he supports the theory that similar fables arise independently in several cultures and he also tentatively addresses himself to comparative religion.

Francis, Saint (1181/82—1226) (known also as 'St Francis of Assisi', or in Italian *San Francesco d'Assisi*, baptized Giovanni, renamed Francesco: his original name was Francesco di Pietro di Bernardone.) He was the founder of the Franciscan order of the *Friars Minor* (*Ordo Fratrum Minorum*), the woman's *Order of St Clare* (or *Poor Clares*), and the lay *Third Order*. He was also a leader of the movement of evangelical poverty in the early thirteenth century. His evangelical zeal, consecration to poverty, charity and personal charisma drew thousands of followers and his devotion to the human Jesus and his desire to follow Jesus' example reflected and reinforced important developments in medieval spirituality. The *Poverello* {Italian *Poor Little Man*} is one of the most venerated religious figures in Roman Catholic Catholicism, and he and Catherine of Siena are the patron saints of Italy. In 1979 Pope John Paul II recognized him as the patron saint of ecology. Francis was prone to having heavenly visions which contributed to his conversion to the apostolic life. He had a vision of Christ while he prayed in a grotto near Assisi and an experience of poverty during a pilgrimage to Rome, where, in rags, he mingled with the beggars before St Peter's Basilica and begged alms. In another incident he not only gave alms to a leper (for whom he had always felt a deep repugnance), but he also kissed his hand. Among such episodes, the most important, according to his disciple and first biographer, Thomas of Celano, occurred at the ruined chapel of San Damiano outside the gate of Assisi when Francis heard the crucifix above the altar command him: 'Go, Francis, and repair my house which, as you see, is well–nigh in ruins.' Francis renounced worldly goods and family ties to embrace a life of poverty. He repaired the Church of San Damiano, refurbished a chapel dedicated to St Peter the Apostle, and then restored the now–famous little chapel of *St Mary of the Angels* (*Santa Maria degli Angeli*), the *Porziuncola*, on the plain below Assisi, where he decided to lead a life of poverty. In 1209 he composed for his mendicant disciples, or friars, a simple rule or *Regula primitiva*, drawn from passages in the Bible. He then led the group of twelve disciples to Rome to seek the approval of Pope Innocent III, an important step that demonstrated Francis's recognition of papal authority. This event which, according to tradition occurred on 16 April 1210, marked the official founding of the Franciscan order. They preached and worked first in Umbria and then, as their numbers grew rapidly, in the rest of Italy. Certainly the love of poverty is part of his spirit, so much so that in his last writing, the *Testament*, composed shortly before his death in 1226, he declared unambiguously that absolute personal and corporate poverty was the essential life–style for the members of his order. However, it was not mere external poverty he sought, but the total denial of self (as in 2 Phil. 2: 7), which d'Holbach finds useless to society (see p. 120).

Figure 74: St Francis of Assisi, characteristically depitcted with birds.

Fréret, Nicholas (1688—1749) was one of the finest minds of his age, who studied classics, history and mythology of the Greeks, Celts, Germans, Chinese, and many more. He studied law and began to practise at the bar to please his father, but he soon followed his own path, despite his young years. At nineteen he was admitted to a society of learned men before whom he read memoirs on the religion of the Greeks, on the worship of Bacchus, Ceres, Cybele and Apollo. He was hardly twenty–six years of age when he was admitted as pupil to the *Académie des Inscriptions* {*Academy of Inscriptions*}—(q.v., Fontenelle). His chief fame today lies in his *Lettre de Thrasybule à Leucippe* {*Letter from Thrasybulus to Leucippus*} (1768). His *Letter* had not been intended for publication by him because it debunks Christianity as just one religion amongst many, and yet Fréret had to maintain the outward image of an establishment persona in his capacity as Associate of the Academy of Inscriptions. However, he did have to spend a period in the Bastille prison, having been accused of libelling the monarchy. His *Letter* was circulated in manuscript form amongst a small circle of people who enjoyed reading anti–religious works. There has long been a controversy over whether Fréret was actually the author of the *Letter*, but in 1986 scholars established him as the definitive author.

Galiani, Ferdinando (1728—1787) (known also as Abbé Galiani) was a priest, diplomat (secretary to the Neapolitan ambassador in Paris, 1759—1769), and an economist of considerable originality. He wrote with ease in French, as well as in his native Italian, and his collection of letters is a valuable source of information on European economic, social and political life. Galiani published two treatises, *Della moneta* {*On Money*} (1750) and *Dialogues sur le commerce des blés* {*Dialogues on the Grain Trade*} (1770). He was a close friend of Diderot and a member of d'Holbach's circle.

Garrick, David (1717—1779) was an actor, producer, dramatist, poet and co–manager of the Drury Lane Theatre, London. Initially enrolled as a student of law in London, and subsequently an apprentice vintner with his uncle in Lisbon, Garrick entered the theatre in 1741, standing in for an indisposed actor. He had a meteoric rise in the theatre and became a renowned interpreter of Shakespeare. In 1745 to 1746 he took part in negotiations to buy the theatre in Drury Lane in partnership with others. There, he went from strength to strength as an actor and manager, and he made Drury Lane Theatre the most successful in London, though his career and the theatre were not without their major setbacks, through which Garrick showed great determination and fortitude. In 1763 Garrick and his wife departed for a continental tour. They enjoyed sightseeing in Italy in aristocratic company, but Mrs. Garrick suffered agonies from what was, apparently, a slipped disk, and Garrick contracted typhoid in Venice and nearly died in Munich. They wintered in Paris, where Garrick enlarged his acquaintance with French literary and theatrical celebrities, Shakespearean enthusiasts and the *philosophes*. After returning (spring 1765), he appeared in no new parts and ten years later he sold his share in the theatre, subsequently to lead a happy retirement with his library, garden, dogs, and family. He frequently exchanged letters with d'Holbach and visited him whenever he could. He hosted d'Holbach in his house in Hampton in 1765 when d'Holbach made one of his rare trips abroad, to England, which was not to his liking: see footnote, p. xlix.

Gibbon, Edward (1737—1794) was an English rationalist historian and scholar best known as the author of *The History of the Decline and Fall of the Roman Empire* (1776—88), a continuous narrative from the second century AD to the fall of Constantinople in 1453. Having spent a considerable amount of time in Lausanne in his youth, where he learned French, he published his first work, written in French, *Essai sur l'étude de la littérature* (1761) {*An Essay on the Study of Literature*}, after which time he spent a period of study in England, only to leave again for Paris in 1763, where he made the acquaintance of several *philosophes*—Denis Diderot, d'Alembert and d'Holbach, amongst others. In 1764, Gibbon went to Rome, where he made an exhaustive study of the antiquities and was inspired to write of the decline and fall of the city, and some time was yet to pass before he decided on the history of the empire.

Gomarus, Franciscus (1563—1641) a Dutch Calvinist theologian and leader of the religious sect known as Contra–remonstrants, or Counter–remonstrants, who upheld the theological position known as supralapsarianism, which claimed that God is not the author of sin, yet they accepted the Fall of Man as an active decree of God. They also opposed toleration for Roman Catholics, Jews and for other Protestants. In opposing the Gomarists, Johan van Oldenbarnevelt, one of the great statesmen of the Netherlands, became embroiled in a religious controversy which had political implications, and he was eventually found guilty of treason and executed. At about the same time, the Gomarists took control of the Dutch Reformed Church. Their intransigence helped lead to a renewal of war with Spain in 1621. Hence, it was not Gomarus himself who 'set Holland on fire' (see p. 154), but the import of his ideas.

Grimm, Friedrich Melchior (1723—1807) was a diplomat and a literary and political correspondent for several European courts. He occasionally wrote for the *Mercure de France*—a prestigious literary gazette, founded in 1672—on topics of German culture.

Figure 75: Franciscus Gomarus (1563—1641).

His own periodical, the *Correspondance littéraire, philosophique et critique* {*Literary, Philosophical and Critical Correspondance*} is an invaluable memoir of the time. Grimm came to Paris around the end of 1748 and we know from Rousseau's *Confessions* that they met in 1749 and that he introduced Grimm to Parisian salon life, and to Diderot in particular, though Rousseau would end up falling out with them later. Grimm corresponded with many literary figures and also with people of high status, such as Catherine the Great of Russia, to whom he mentioned d'Holbach, whose book she treasured.

Guebres (or Ghebers) were adherents of the ancient Persian religion of Zoroastrianism, the ancient pre–Islamic religion of Iran. There are many more of its adherents in India, where they are called Parsees, where the religion is referred to as Parsiism. It was founded by the Iranian prophet and reformer Zoroaster in the sixth century BC, and it is a religion which contains both monotheistic and dualistic features. It influenced the other major Western religions—Judaism, Christianity and Islam.

Gymnosophists were ancient Indian Hindu philosophers of ascetic habits who wore no or little clothing, refrained from eating meat, and gave themselves up to mystical contemplation. They were known to the ancient Greeks through reports brought back by Alexander the Great (356—323 BC).

Habakkuk is the eighth of twelve Old Testament books which bear the names of the Minor Prophets. The book betrays the influence of liturgical forms, suggesting that either Habakkuk was a cult prophet or that those responsible for the final form of the book were cult personnel. It is difficult to fix the date of the book, but the mention of the Chaldeans as Yahweh's agent (1: 6) suggests the period of Chaldean power following their successful revolt against the Assyrians in 626 BC. A more precise date depends on the identity of 'the wicked' and 'the righteous', who are mentioned in the book. If 'the wicked' are the Assyrians, and 'the righteous' are the Judaeans, then the book must be dated before 612 BC, when the Assyrian Empire finally fell. According to this interpretation, Habakkuk announced the eventual collapse of the wicked oppressors (Assyrians) of the people of Judah. In the meantime, he consoled the people by saying, 'the righteous shall live by his faith', (2:4). Chapter 3, a psalm complete with musical directions, does not appear in the Habakkuk commentary from Qumrān, but there is as yet no convincing reason to deny its authenticity.

Hades *q.v.* **Tartarus.**

Hell *q.v.* **Tartarus.**

Helots q.v. **Lacedemonians.**

Helvétius, Claude–Adrien (1715—1771) was a philosopher, most noted for his philosophical work *De l'Esprit {On the Mind}* (1758), which was an attack on all religion–based concepts of morality. The book cause such offence that is was ordered to be burned in public and the author was ordered to recant. As part of the backlash against this kind of challenge to accepted concepts of morality and religious beliefs, other works were also condemned and burnt, i.e., some by Voltaire and others, and the publication of the *Encyclopédie*, which came out in stages, was temporarily suspended.

Figure 76: Claude-Adrien Helvétius (1715—1771), from an engraving by Augustin de Saint-Aubin, after a painting by Michel van Loo (1755). (Source: Wikipedia.)

Hercules was a Roman mythological god, equivalent to the Greek god Heracles, the most famous of the Græco–Roman legendary gods. His first task was to strangle two serpents while only a baby, and it was to him that the twelve 'labours', or exceedingly difficult tasks, were assigned, which included the slaying of the nine–headed Hydra, the shooting of the monstrous man–eating birds of the Stymphalian marshes, and the production from the lower world of the triple–headed dog Cerberus, guardian of its gates.

Hieronymus q.v. **Jerome, St.**

Hindustan (or Indostan) was the old name generally used to refer to part of the Indian continent, derived from 'Hindu' and 'stan', i.e., *Land of the Hindus*. Generally it referred to northern India. The term was in common use from the late sixteenth to the late nineteenth centuries.

Hobbes, Thomas (1588—1679) was an English philosopher and political theorist, best known for his publications on individual security and the social contract, which are important statements of both the nascent ideas of liberalism and the long–standing assumptions of political absolutism characteristic of the times. Hobbes's masterpiece was *Leviathan, or the Matter, Form, and Power of a Commonwealth, Ecclesiastical and Civil* (1651). In the first two parts, 'Of Man' and 'Of Commonwealth', he reworked the ground already covered in his earlier treatises; in the last two, *Of a Christian Commonwealth* and *Of the Kingdom of Darkness*, he embarked upon a discussion of Scripture and made a vigorous attack on the attempts of papists and Presbyterians to challenge the right of the sovereign. Hobbes's reputation as a thinker rests mainly on his contributions to the philosophy of man, in which he propounded an influential egoistic psychology. In moral theory, he is generally regarded as a pioneer of the Utilitarian school: he justified obedience to moral rules on a purely secular basis, as the means to 'peaceable, social, and comfortable living'. Yet he also said that the laws of nature were God's commands. The contentiousness of his work meant that Hobbes had to live in exile for a number of years, chiefly in Paris, where he associated with many intellectuals—both scientists and philosophers. However, he returned to England to face his critics and detractors. Over the years he has gradually been accorded recognition as one of the greatest English political thinkers.

Huguenot is a generic term for any of a whole range of Protestant believers in France in the sixteenth and seventeenth centuries, many of whom suffered severe persecution for their faith. The origin of the name is uncertain, but it appears to have come from the word *aignos*, derived from the German *Eidgenossen* (confederates bound together by oath), which used to describe, between 1520 and 1524, the patriots of Geneva hostile to the Duke of Savoy. The spelling *Huguenot* may have been influenced by

Figure 77: Frontispiece of *Leviathan*, Thomas Hobbes (1651).

the personal name Hugues, 'Hugh', after Besançon Hugues (d. 1532), leader of the Geneva movement. After the Protestant Reformation began in Germany (1517), the reform movement spread quickly in France, especially in places that had suffered economic depression and among those who had grievances against the established order of government. The French Protestants soon experienced persecution, however, and the first French martyr, Jean Vallière, was burned at the stake in Paris in August 1523. Despite persecution, the movement progressed, but measures against it were redoubled after the 'Affair of the Placards' (October 1534), when posters attacking the mass were found on walls throughout Paris and even on the door of King Francis I's bedroom at Amboise. Thereafter the number of Protestant refugees from persecution increased. Many went to Strasburg, then a free city of the Holy Roman Empire, where Martin Bucer had organized a Reformed church. The most famous of these exiles was John Calvin, (q.v. Calvinist/Calvinism), who left for Basle (or Basel) in the autumn of 1534. In Basle he is thought to have written his *Institutes of the Christian Religion*, which was prefaced by a letter to Francis I, pleading the cause of the Reformers in France. In 1538 Calvin visited Strasburg on Bucer's invitation and organized the French community there. The first Huguenot community on French territory was that of Meaux, founded in 1546. The Huguenot Church in Paris was founded about 1555 and, in spite of persecution, the Reformers increased in numbers. After civil wars and other struggles in which Huguenots hoped the French crown would pass to a Protestant king, rather than to a Catholic, the Huguenots gradually lost civil liberties and became a much persecuted group in France: the French Roman Catholic clergy found it impossible to accept the Huguenots and worked to deprive them of all their rights. General harassment and the forcible conversion of thousands of Protestants were part of official policy for many years, which forced more than 400,000 of France's Protestant inhabitants to emigrate to England, Prussia, the Netherlands and America, where they became very useful citizens in their adopted countries: their austere religious convictions made them law–abiding citizens with a strong work ethic and many were urban dwellers engaged in commerce and industry, and their absence would seriously hurt France in the forthcoming Industrial Revolution.

Hume, David (1711—1776) was a Scottish philosopher, historian, economist and essayist, known especially for his philosophical empiricism and scepticism. Hume conceived of philosophy as the inductive, experimental science of human nature. Taking the scientific method of the English physicist Sir Isaac Newton as his model and building on the epistemology of the English philosopher John Locke, Hume tried to describe how the mind works in acquiring what is called knowledge. He concluded that no theory of reality is possible; there can be no knowledge of anything beyond experience. Despite the enduring impact of his theory of knowledge, Hume seems to have considered himself chiefly as a moralist. He had a nervous breakdown while very young in 1729, from which it took him a few years to recover and he took himself off to France for three years. Most of this time he spent at La Flèche on the Loire, in the old Anjou, studying and writing *A Treatise of Human Nature*. The *Treatise* was Hume's attempt to formulate a complete philosophical system, aimed at explaining man's process of knowing, describing in order the origin of ideas, the ideas of space and time, etc. He also enquired into the senses, the 'passions' of man, and moral goodness in terms of experiencing a sense of approval or disapproval, and the consequences either to oneself or to others. His works were widely translated into French and they exerted considerable influence on the *Encyclopédists*. He was well–known in d'Holbach's circle and the latter translated some of Hume's essays into French (see p. l).

Hus, Jan (1370—1415) (also spelled Huss) was the most important fifteenth –century Czech religious Reformer, whose work was transitional between the medieval and the Reformation periods, and it anticipated the Lutheran Reformation by a full century. He was embroiled in the bitter controversy of the Western Schism for his entire career and was convicted of heresy at the Council of Constance, then burned at the stake. Hus studied Wycliffe's works and later his theological writings, which were brought into Prague in 1401. Hus was influenced by Wycliffe's underlying principles, though he never accepted their extreme implications, and he was particularly impressed by Wycliffe's proposals for reform of the Roman Catholic clergy. After years of bitter recriminations and threats, Hus's enemies succeeded in having him tried before the Council of Constance as a Wycliffite heretic. All that the earnest intervention by the Bohemian nobles could obtain for him was three public hearings at which he was allowed to defend himself; he succeeded in refuting some of the charges against him. The council urged Hus to recant in order to save his life, but the majority of its members regarded him as a dangerous heretic, fit only for death. When he refused to recant, he was solemnly sentenced on 6 July 1415, and subsequently burned at the stake. (See also p. 344.)

Hypatia (AD 370—415) was an Egyptian Neo-Platonist philosopher who was the first notable woman intellectual in mathematics. As the daughter of Theon, also a famous mathematician and philosopher, Hypatia became the recognized head of the Neo-Platonist school of philosophy at Alexandria in about AD 400, and her eloquence, modesty and beauty, combined with her remarkable intellectual gifts, attracted a large number of pupils. Among

Figure 78: Jan Hus being burned by the Church as a heretic, after Diebold Schilling the Older, from the *Spiezer Chronicle* (1485).

them was Synesius of Cyrene, afterward bishop of Ptolemais (*c.* 410), several of whose letters to her are still extant. Hypatia lectured on mathematics and on the philosophical teachings of two Neo–Platonists: Plotinus (*c.* AD 205—270), the founder of Neo-Platonism, and Iamblichus (*c.* AD 250—330), the founder of the Syrian branch of Neo-Platonism. She symbolized learning and science at a time in Western history when they were largely identified with paganism. This put Hypatia in a precarious situation: Theodosius I, Roman emperor in the East from 379 to 392 and then emperor in both the East and West until 395, initiated an official policy of intolerance towards paganism and Arianism in 380. In 391, in reply to Theophilus, the bishop of Alexandria, he gave permission to destroy Egyptian religious institutions. Christian mobs obliged by destroying the Library of Alexandria, the Temple of Sarapis, and other pagan monuments. Although legislation in 393 sought to curb violence, and in particular the looting and destruction of Jewish synagogues, a renewal of disturbances occurred after the accession of Cyril to the patriarchate of Alexandria in 412. Tension culminated in the forced, albeit illegal, expulsion of Alexandrian Jews in 414 and the murder of Hypatia, the most prominent Alexandrian pagan, by a fanatical mob of Christians in 415. The departure soon afterward of many scholars marked the beginning of the decline of Alexandria as a major centre of ancient learning.

Iamblichus (*c.* AD 250—*c.* 330) was a Syrian philosopher, a major figure in the philosophical school of Neo-Platonism and the founder of its Syrian branch. Though only his minor philosophical works have survived, the basic elements of Iamblichus' system can be understood from the references to his teachings in the writings of the fifth–century philosopher Proclus. He wrote (in Greek) the treatise known under the Latin name *De Mysteriis* {usually translated as *On the Egyptian Mysteries*}, and his other works include: *On the Pythagorean Life*; *The Exhortation to Philosophy*, or *Protrepticus*; *On the General Science of Mathematics, On the Arithmetic of Nicomachus*; and *Theological Principles of Arithmetic*. More than any other single philosopher, Iamblichus has generally been credited with the transformation of the Neo-Platonism advocated by Plotinus earlier in the third century into a pagan religious philosophy, best known from the works of Proclus. Iamblichus asserted that a higher 'One' exists outside the range of human knowledge and qualifications. To the three existing ethical virtues of Neo-Platonism—political, purifying and exemplary—he added the contemplative virtue and placed above all four the priestly, or unifying, virtues by which men obtain ecstatic union with the 'One'. Iamblichus was known for the next two centuries as 'the divine', or 'inspired', for his emphasis on theurgy and his elevation of the non–intellectual virtues.

Index of Prohibited Books (or *Index Librorum Prohibitorum*) was a list of books once forbidden by Roman Catholic Church as dangerous to the faith or morals of Roman Catholics. Books of almost any kind, from works of literature to works on theology, were placed on the Index to prevent the contamination of the faith or the corruption of morals through the reading of theologically erroneous or immoral books. The first catalogue of forbidden books in this guise was published in 1559 by the Sacred Congregation of the Roman Inquisition (a precursor to the Congregation for the Doctrine of the Faith). The last and twentieth edition of the Index appeared in 1948. The list was suppressed in June 1966. The works of many writers who dared criticize the Catholic Church, even in relatively mild terms, such as the modern French writer André Gide (1869—1951), were placed on the Index, as well as works of a more overt and left–wing persuasion, such as the works of Jean–Paul Sartre (1905—1980).

Isaiah (fl. in 8th century BC) (whose name in Hebrew is *Yesha'yahu {God Is Salvation}*) was a prophet, after whom the biblical Book of Isaiah (also spelled *Isaias*) is named. He was a significant contributor to the Jewish and Christian traditions. His call to prophecy in about 742 BC coincided with the beginnings of the westward expansion of the Assyrian empire, which threatened Israel and which Isaiah proclaimed to be a warning from God to a godless people. The Book of Isaiah, of which only some of the first thirty–nine chapters are attributed to him, is one of the major prophetical writings of the Old Testament. The superscription identifies Isaiah as the son of Amoz and his book as 'the vision of Isaiah [...] concerning Judah and Jerusalem in the days of Uzziah, Jotham, Ahaz, and Hezekiah, kings of Judah.' According to 6: 1, Isaiah received his call 'in the year that King Uzziah died' (742 BC), and his latest recorded activity is dated in 701 BC. However, only chapters 1—39 can be assigned to this period. Chapters 40—66 are much later in origin and therefore known as Deutero–Isaiah (Second Isaiah). Sometimes a further distinction is made between Deutero–Isaiah (chapters 40—55) and Trito–Isaiah (chapters 56—66). Chapters 1—39 consist of numerous sayings and reports of Isaiah, along with several narratives about the prophet, attributed to his disciples. The growth of the book (chapters 1—39) was a gradual process, its final form dates perhaps from as late as the fifth century BC, a date suggested by the arrangement of the materials and late additions. In spite of the lengthy and complicated literary history of the book, however, Isaiah's message is clearly discernible. He was much influenced by the cult in Jerusalem, and the exalted view of Yahweh in the Zionist traditions is reflected in his message. He was convinced that only an unshakable trust in Yahweh, rather than in political or military alliances, could protect Judah and Jerusalem from the advances of their enemies, i.e., the Assyrians, at this period. He called for the recognition of Yahweh's sovereignty and he passionately denounced anything which worked against or obscured Yahweh's purposes—from social injustices to meaningless cult observances. Although Isaiah pronounced Yahweh's judgment upon Judah and Jerusalem for their unfaithfulness, he also announced a new future for those who relied on him. Deutero–Isaiah (chapters 40—55), consisting of a collection of oracles, songs and discourses, dates from the Babylonian Exile (sixth century BC). The anonymous prophet is in exile and looks forward to the deliverance of his people. The destruction of Babylon is prophesied and the return of the exiles to their homeland is promised. The 'servant–of–Yahweh songs', in Deutero–Isaiah (42:1—4; 49:1—6; 50:4—9; 52:13—53:12), have generated animated discussions among scholars, but the ideas reflected in the songs suggest that they were written under the influence of the ideology of the king—the anointed one who, through his righteous rule, had the power to effect his people's deliverance. Trito–

Isaiah (chapters 56—66), coming from a still later period, reflects a Palestinian point of view, with the latter chapters in particular addressed to the cultic concerns of the restored community. The diversity of materials in these chapters suggests a multiple authorship. How the three 'Isaiahs' came together is not known.

Jael was an Old Testament character, the wife of Heber, a member of the tribe of Hobab, the father–in–law of Moses. After a battle with a rival tribe under the command of Sisera, all men were killed, apart from Sisera himself, who escaped and ended up taking refuge in Jael's tent. Exhausted and thirsty from battle, and after satisfying his thirst, Sisera fell asleep, whereupon Jael hammered a large nail through his temple, pinning him to the ground, as narrated in Judg. 4: 21—23:

> Then Jael Heber's wife took a nail of the tent, and took an hammer in her hand, and went softly unto him, and smote the nail into his temples, and fastened it into the ground: for he was fast asleep and weary. So he died. And, behold, as Barak pursued Sisera, Jael came out to meet him, and said unto him, 'Come, and I will shew thee the man whom thou seekest.' And when he came into her tent, behold, Sisera lay dead, and the nail was in his temples. So God subdued on that day Jabin the king of Canaan before the children of Israel.

In the next chapter of Judges, the Angel of the Lord praises Jael for her sterling work:

> 'Blessed above women shall Jael the wife of Heber the Kenite be, blessed shall she be above women in the tent. He asked water, and she gave him milk; she brought forth butter in a lordly dish. She put her hand to the nail, and her right hand to the workmen's hammer; and with the hammer she smote Sisera, she smote off his head, when she had pierced and stricken through his temples. At her feet he bowed, he fell, he lay down: at her feet he bowed, he fell: where he bowed, there he fell down dead.' (Judg. 5: 24—27.)

Clearly she was not a woman to trifle with! It is appalling that the Bible lauds and sets up these kinds of monsters as 'blessed' and pleasing in the eyes of God, and the fact that this kind of behaviour pleases God says as much about his outlook as it does about the deranged, pathological killers he favours. And what happened to the imprecation to show hospitality to a stranger, not to mention '*Thou shalt not kill*'? The utter inconsistency of God in the Old Testament can be seen in an incident when some hostile forces turn up and they are treated quite differently:

> And the king of Israel said unto Elisha, when he saw them [i.e., the Arameans], 'My father, shall I smite them? Shall I smite them?' And he answered, 'Thou shalt not smite them: wouldest thou smite those whom

thou hast taken captive with thy sword and with thy bow? Set bread and water before them, that they may eat and drink, and go to their master.' And he prepared great provision for them: and when they had eaten and drunk, he sent them away, and they went to their master. So the bands of Syria came no more into the land of Israel. (II Kgs. 6: 21—23.)

Jansenist was a member of a small sect of Christians, generally based in Holland, whom the main body of the Catholic Church regarded as heretical. A schism developed within the Roman Catholic Church in Holland in 1702, when Petrus Codde, archbishop of Utrecht, was accused of heresy for suspected sympathy with Jansenism, a doctrine emphasizing God's grace and predestination, akin to Calvinism (q.v.), which was condemned by Pope Alexander VII in 1656. Many of the Dutch clergy and laity remained loyal to Codde and left the Roman Catholic Church. Several French Jansenists subsequently settled in Holland and joined the small group of their Dutch counterparts. In 1723 the Church elected Cornelius Steenhoven as its own bishop and remained separate from main–stream Catholicism, particularly when the pope declared himself to be infallible in matters of religious doctrine.

Jeremiah (*c*. 650—*c*. 570 BC) (whose name in Hebrew is *Yirmeyahu*, and in the Latin *Vulgate* 'Jeremias') was a Hebrew prophet, reformer and author of an Old Testament book, bearing his name. He was closely involved in the political and religious events of a crucial era in the history of the ancient Near East; his spiritual leadership helped his fellow countrymen survive disasters that included the capture of Jerusalem by the Babylonians in 586 BC and the exile of many Judaeans to Babylonia. Jeremiah was born and grew up in the village of Anathoth, a few miles northeast of Jerusalem, in a priestly family. In his childhood, he must have learned some of the traditions of his people, particularly the prophecies of Hosea, whose influence can be seen in his early messages. The era in which Jeremiah lived was one of transition for the ancient Near East. The Assyrian Empire, which had been dominant for two centuries, declined and fell. Its capital, Nineveh, was captured in 612 by the Babylonians and Medes. Egypt had a brief period of resurgence (664—525), but did not prove strong enough to re–establish an empire. The new, world power was the Neo–Babylonian Empire, ruled by a Chaldean dynasty, whose best known king was Nebuchadrezzar. The small and comparatively insignificant state of Judah had been a vassal of Assyria and, when Assyria declined, asserted its independence for a short time. Subsequently, Judah vacillated in its allegiance between Babylonia and Egypt, ultimately becoming

Figure 79: *Jeremiah's Call*, **Julius Schnoor von Carolsfeld (*c.* 1851).**

a province of the Neo–Babylonian Empire. Jeremiah's early messages to the people were condemnations of them for their false worship and social injustice, with a summons to repentance. He proclaimed the coming of a foe from the north, symbolized by a boiling pot that would cause great destruction. This foe has often been identified with the Scythians, nomads from southern Russia, who supposedly descended into western Asia in the seventh century and attacked Palestine. Some scholars have identified the northern foe with the Medes, the Assyrians, or the Chaldeans (Babylonians); others have interpreted his message as vague, eschatological predictions, not concerning a specific people. Jeremiah had more to say about repentance than any other prophet. He called upon men to turn away from their wicked ways and dependence upon idols and false gods, and to return to their early, covenantal loyalty to Yahweh. Repentance thus had a strong ethical colouring, since it meant living in obedience to Yahweh's will for the individual and the nation. In the latter part of his career, Jeremiah had to struggle against the despair of his people and give them hope for the future. He expressed his own hope vividly by an action that he undertook when the Babylonians were besieging Jerusalem and he was in prison. From a cousin he bought a field in Anathoth, his native town. In the presence of witnesses he weighed out the money and made contracts, saying, 'For thus saith the Lord of hosts, the God of Israel; "Houses and fields and vineyards shall be possessed again in this land",' (Jer. 32: 15). In this and other ways, he expressed his hope for a bright future for Israel in its own land. D'Holbach refers to this incident in *Christianity Unveiled*—see footnote on p. 55.

Jerome of Prague (1365—1416) was a Czech philosopher and theologian, whose advocacy of sweeping religious reform in the Western Church made him one of the first Reformation leaders in central Europe. As a student at the Charles University of Prague, Jerome came under the influence of the Czech Reformer Jan Hus, with whom he collaborated in criticizing the Roman Catholic Church and in debating theological issues throughout

Figure 80: Jerome of Prague being burned at the stake, from John Foxe, *Actes and Monuments* (*Book of Martyrs*) (1563).

Bohemia, Poland and Germany. After obtaining a bachelor's degree in 1398, he continued his studies at Oxford and adopted the philosophical theology of the English Reformer John Wycliffe. He returned to Prague in 1401 to teach at the university, where he began spreading Wycliffe's teaching. The Christian Church, according to Jerome's views, is the community of those chosen by God for salvation and is not defined in legal terms, devised by a rigid, ministerial structure. Moreover, he advocated the need for poverty in the Church and called for the expropriation of church lands. In the order of worship, he insisted that the wine of Holy

Communion be extended to the laity, as practised by the early Church, and asked for more freedom in preaching. In April 1415, against the advice of his followers, Jerome went secretly to the Council of Constance in an unsuccessful attempt to defend the teaching of the imprisoned Jan Hus (q.v.). As he was leaving Constance, he was arrested and imprisoned. Confined for more than a year and ill, he disavowed the condemned doctrine of Wycliffe and Hus after repeated interrogation by the conciliar tribunal. Accused of ambiguity and insincerity at his final appearance before the Council (May 1416), he then withdrew all earlier retractions of reform views and declared that his confession of Roman Catholic orthodoxy had come out of fear and weakness. Accordingly, he was judged a relapsed heretic and sentenced to burn at the stake. The Bohemian Hussite Church considers Jerome (with Hus) the first martyr for the Protestant Reformation.

Jerome, St (*c*. AD 347—419/420) was a biblical translator and monastic leader, traditionally regarded as the most learned of the Latin Fathers. He is also known in Latin as Hieronymus, or in full Eusebius Hieronymus, and also by the pseudonym Sophronius. He lived for a time as a hermit, became a priest, then served as secretary to Pope Damasus, and in about 389 established a monastery at Bethlehem. His numerous biblical, ascetical, monastic and theological works profoundly influenced the early Middle Ages. He is known particularly for his Latin translation of the Bible, known as the *Vulgate*.

Joinville q.v. **Louis, St.**

Josephus, Flavius (AD 37/38—100), whose original name was *Joseph Ben Matthias*, was a Jewish priest, scholar and historian, who wrote valuable works on the Jewish revolt of AD 66—70 and on earlier Jewish history. His major books are *History of the Jewish War* (AD 75—79), *The Jewish Antiquities* (AD 93), and *Against Apion*. Flavius Josephus was born of an aristocratic priestly family in Jerusalem. According to his own account he was a precocious youth who, by the age of fourteen, was consulted by high priests in matters of Jewish law. At sixteen he undertook a three–year sojourn in the wilderness with the hermit Bannus, a member of one of the ascetic Jewish sects which flourished in Judaea around the time of Christ. Returning to Jerusalem, he joined the Pharisees—a fact of crucial importance in understanding his later collaboration with the Romans. The Pharisees, despite the unflattering portrayal of them in the New Testament, were for the most part intensely religious Jews and adhered to a strict, though non–literal, observance of the Torah. Politically, however, the Pharisees had no sympathy with the intense Jewish nationalism of such sects as the military patriotic Zealots and were willing to submit to Roman rule if only they were assured their religious independence. There is absolutely nothing about the existence of Christ in his *Jewish War*, but there is a reference in the *Jewish Antiquities*. This passage has been much lauded by church apologists, who have made more of it than it merits. Josephus states:

> About this time there lived Jesus, a wise man, if indeed one ought to call him a man. For he was one who wrought surprising feats and was a teacher of such people as accept the truth gladly. He won over many Jews and many of the Greeks. He was the Messiah. When Pilate, upon hearing him accused by men of the highest standing amongst us, had condemned him to be crucified, those who had in the first place come to love him did not give up their affection for him. On the third day he appeared to them restored to life, for the prophets of God had prophesied these and countless other marvellous things about him. And the tribe of the Christians, so called after him, has still to this day not disappeared. (Book XVIII, 63— 64, pp. 49—51. Josephus, *Jewish Antiquities*, translated by Louis H. Feldman, [Cambridge, Mass.: Harvard U.P./Loeb Classical Library, 2000].)

This passage has spawned an enormous amount of literature, for and against its authenticity. Scholars have stated that the language and style of the writing generally fit with the rest of the text. However, its detractors are of the opinion that Josephus, as a loyal Pharisaic Jew, could not possibly have written that Jesus was the Messiah. Furthermore, the passage sits ill within the narrative flow of the context around it. In a word, the passage is suspect, to say the least, and many authorities are of the opinion that it was inserted at a much later date by a sympathetic copyist. For further information and more arguments, see the footnote on p. 49 in the edition cited. It is significant that the last remaining works of Josephus are defences—the autobiography is a defence of his part in the Jewish revolt, and *Against Apion* is a defence of his Jewish heritage.

Judith is a character in a non–canonical book of the Old Testament, whose name it bears. The Book of Judith tells the story of a beautiful widow who single–handedly saved the town of Bethulia, which was being besieged by forces of the King of Assyria, Nebuchadnezzar. When it looked as though the Judeans were going to be forced to surrender, Judith used her feminine charms to ingratiate herself with the military commander, whom she decapitated and brandished the evidence—his severed head—in a bag. The Assyrians fled in fear and the Israelites helped themselves to the booty. This was seen as a great victory for Jehovah and Judith. At the end of the book, Judith is praised and the people celebrate in song:

> So all the people plundered the camp for thirty days. They gave Judith the tent of Holofernes and all his silver dishes and his beds and his bowls and all his furniture; and she took them and loaded her mule and hitched up her carts and piled the things on them. Then all the women of Israel gathered

to see her, and blessed her, and some of them performed a dance for her; and she took branches in her hands and gave them to the women who were with her; and they crowned themselves with olive wreaths, she and those who were with her; and she went before all the people in the dance, leading all the women, while all the men of Israel followed, bearing their arms and wearing garlands and with songs on their lips. (Judith 15: 11—13).

The story ends happily:

After this every one returned home to his own inheritance, and Judith went to Bethulia, and remained on her estate, and was honoured in her time throughout the whole country. Many desired to marry her, but she remained a widow all the days of her life after Manasseh her husband died and was gathered to his people. She became more and more famous, and grew old in her husband's house, until she was one hundred and five years old. She set her maid free. She died in Bethulia, and they buried her in the cave of her husband Manasseh, and the house of Israel mourned for her seven days. Before she died she distributed her property to all those who were next of kin to her husband Manasseh, and to her own nearest kindred. And no one ever again spread terror among the people of Israel in the days of Judith, or for a long time after her death. (Judith 16: 21—25).

The Book of Judith is thought to have been written originally in Hebrew around 100 BC, but the oldest existing text is thought to be a Hebrew translation of a Latin version of the original. It is not generally accepted as a Book of the Bible by many Christians, although it was included in the Septuagint, the Greek version of the Hebrew Bible, and it is accepted by the Roman Catholic Church.

Julian (AD 331/332—363), whose original name was Flavius Claudius Julianus, was a **Roman** Emperor and was known as 'Julian the Apostate' (in Latin *Julianus Apostata*). He was Roman emperor from AD 361 to 363 and a nephew of Constantine the Great. He was a noted scholar and military leader, proclaimed emperor by his troops. A persistent enemy of Christianity, he publicly announced his conversion to paganism in 361, thus acquiring the epithet 'the Apostate'. In 351 he converted to the pagan Neo-Platonism, recently 'reformed' by Iamblichus (q.v.), and was initiated into theurgy by Maximus of Ephesus. He studied in Pergamum, Ephesus, and later in Athens. He adopted the cult of the 'Unconquered Sun'. That his literary talent was considerable is demonstrated in his surviving works, most of which illustrate his deep love of Hellenic culture. Julian had been baptized and raised a Christian and although he outwardly conformed until he was supreme, Christianity in its official guise meant to him the religion of those who had murdered his father, his brother and many of his relations and as such, it was hardly likely to commend itself to him. He found far more solace in his philosophical speculations. While emperor, he issued proclamations in which he declared his intention to rule as a philosopher, on the model of Marcus Aurelius. All Christian bishops exiled by Constantius were allowed to return to their sees (although the purpose of this may have been to promote dissension among the Christians), and an edict of 361 proclaimed freedom of worship for all religions. However, this initial toleration of Christianity was coupled with a determination to revive paganism and raise it to the level of an official religion with an established hierarchy. Julian apparently saw himself as the head of a pagan church. He performed animal sacrifices and was a staunch defender of a sort of pagan orthodoxy, issuing doctrinal instructions to his clergy. Not surprisingly, this incipient fanaticism soon led from passive toleration to outright suppression and persecution of Christians. Pagans were openly preferred for high official appointments, Christians were expelled from the army and they prohibited from teaching classical literature and philosophy. Julian wrote an attack on Christianity, which he calls 'the trickery of the Galileans', in his *Against the Galileans*, that is known today only by fragmentary citation, stating, 'The trickery of the Galileans has nothing divine in it... It appeals to rustics only, and it is made up of fables and irrational falsehoods.' His project to rebuild the Jewish Temple in Jerusalem was designed rather to insult the Christians than to please the Jews who, long accustomed to the worship of the synagogue, would have found the revival of animal sacrifice acutely embarrassing. The plan was rather abruptly dropped, as Bergier notes in his refutation—see p. 251.

Justin, Saint (AD 100—165) was one of the most important of the Greek philosopher–apologists in the early Christian Church. His writings represent the first positive encounter of Christian revelation with Greek philosophy and laid the basis for a theology of history. A pagan reared in a Jewish environment, Justin studied Stoic, Platonic and other ancient philosophies, and then became a Christian in 132, possibly at Ephesus, near modern Selçuk, Turkey. Soon after 135 he began wandering from place to place proclaiming his newfound Christian philosophy in the hope of converting educated pagans to it. He spent a considerable time in Rome. Some years later, after debating with the cynic Crescens, Justin was denounced to the Roman prefect as subversive and condemned to death. Authentic records of his martyrdom survive. Justin's distinctive contribution to Christian theology is his conception of a divine plan in history, a process of salvation structured by God, wherein the various historical epochs have been integrated into an organic unity directed toward a supernatural end; the Old Testament and Greek philosophy met to form the single stream of Christianity. Justin's concrete description of the sacramental celebrations of Baptism and the Eucharist remain a principal source for the history of the primitive Church. Justin serves, moreover, as a crucial witness to the status of the second–century New Testament corpus, mentioning the first three gospels and quoting and paraphrasing the letters of Paul and I Peter; he was the first known writer to quote from the Acts of the Apostles. Most important of his works deemed genuine are two 'Apologies' and the *Dialogue with Trypho*. The first, or *Major Apology*, was addressed in about AD 150 to the Roman emperors Antoninus Pius and Marcus Aurelius. In the first part of the *First Apology*, Justin defends his fellow Christians against the charges of atheism and hostility to the Roman state.

Justus of Tiberias (fl. second half of 1st century AD) was a contemporary of Josephus, who mentions him. Like Josephus, he wrote a *History of the Jewish War*, but this work is lost. Although his work has not survived, we know from a comment made by Photius (born *c.* 820, died some time in tenth century), a saint and Patriarch of Constantinople (858—867 and 877—886), that he found not a single reference to the birth, life events, or the miracles of Jesus Christ in his writing, though he looked long and hard, and this was a source of his own great personal chagrin.

Kami were an object of worship in Shintō and other indigenous religions of Japan. The term *kami* is often translated as *god*, *lord* or *deity*; but it also includes other forces of nature, both good and evil, which, because of their superiority or divinity, become objects of reverence and respect. The sun goddess Amaterasu Ōmikami and other creator spirits, illustrious ancestors, and both animate and inanimate things, such as plants, rocks, birds, beasts and fish, may all be treated as *kami*. In early Shintō, the heavenly *kami* (*amatsukami*) were considered nobler than the earthly *kami* (*kunitsukami*), but in modern Shintō this distinction is no longer made. *Kami* are manifested in, or take residence in, a symbolic object such as a mirror, in which form they are usually worshiped in Shintō shrines. Shintō myths speak of the '800 myriads of *kami*' to express the infinite number of potential *kami*, and new ones continue to be recognized.

Lacedemonians were the inhabitants of Lacedaemon, the ancient capital of Laconia in the south–east Peloponnese, better known as Sparta. The Helots, whose ethnic origins are uncertain, were state–owned serfs of the Spartans, reduced to servility after their land had been conquered, around the eighth century BC.

Lactantius (AD 240—320) (in Latin in full *Lucius Caecilius Firmianus Lactantius*, Caecilius, is also spelled Caelius) was a Christian apologist and one of the most reprinted of the Latin Church Fathers, whose *Divinae institutiones* {*Divine Precepts*}, a classically styled philosophical refutation of early fourth–century, anti–Christian tracts, was the first systematic Latin account of the Christian attitude toward life. Lactantius was referred to as the 'Christian Cicero' by Renaissance humanists. Lactantius was

427

appointed a teacher of rhetoric at Nicomedia (later İzmit, Turkey) by the Roman emperor Diocletian. When the emperor began persecuting Christians, however, Lactantius resigned his post in about 305 and returned to the West. Later, in about 317, he came out of retirement to tutor Emperor Constantine's son Crispus, at Trier. Only Lactantius' writings dealing with Christianity have survived. His principal work, the *Divine Precepts,* depended more on the testimony of classical authors than on that of sacred Scripture. It repudiated what he termed the deluding superstitions of pagan cults, proposing in their place the Christian religion as a theism or rationalized belief in a single Supreme Being, who is the source creating all else. In a companion work, *On the Death of Persecutors,* Lactantius held that the Christian God—in contradistinction to the remote, unconcerned god of Stoic deism—could intervene to right human injustice. Moreover, he maintained that Roman justice could be better perfected by rooting it in the Christian doctrine of divine fatherhood, uniting the human race in a universal fraternity through the mediation of Christ, than by basing it on the Latin concept of *aequitas {equity}.* Limited by a shallow view of religion as popular morality, Lactantius was more adept in showing the incongruity of heathen polytheism than in establishing Christian teaching.

La Harpe (or Laharpe), Jean–François de (1739—1803) was a critic and unsuccessful playwright who wrote severe and provocative works of criticism and history of French literature. He was imprisoned at nineteen for allegedly writing a satire against his protectors at college and the experience seems to have turned him into a bitter, caustic man. Of the many uninspired plays he wrote, the best are perhaps his first tragedy, *Warwick* (1763), and *Mélanie* (1778), a pathetic drama never performed. He wrote criticism for, and was editor of, the *Mercure de France,* becoming respected, though often disliked, for his unsympathetic views. In 1786, after being coldly admitted to the French Academy, he began to lecture at the newly established *Lycée.* His lectures, published as the *Cours de littérature {Lessons in Literature},* in sixteen volumes (1799—1805), show La Harpe at his best; he brought a clear and intelligent understanding to his treatment of seventeenth–century literature, also exemplified in his *Commentaire sur Racine {Commentary on Racine}* (1807). Although an extreme revolutionary, he became suspect and was imprisoned in April 1794. Shocked by the horrors around him, he became an ardent Roman Catholic and reactionary, attacking his former friends when he returned to the *Lycée.* His *Œuvres* were published in 1821.

Lar (plural *Lares*) were any of numerous tutelary deities in Roman pagan religion. They were originally gods of the cultivated fields, worshipped by each household at the crossroads where its allotment joined those of others.

Later, the *lares* were worshipped in houses in association with the *penates*, the gods of the 'storeroom' (*penus*) and by analogy of the family's prosperity; the household *lar* (*familiaris*) was conceived as the centre of the family and of the family cult. Originally each household had only one *lar*. It was usually represented as a youthful figure, dressed in a short tunic, holding in one hand a drinking horn, in the other a cup. Under the empire, two of these images were commonly to be found, one on each side of the central figure of the *genius*, of Vesta, or of some other deity. The whole group came to be called indifferently *lares* or *penates*. A prayer was said to the *lar* every morning, and special offerings were made at family festivals. The public *lares* belonged to the state religion. Among these were included the *Lares compitales*, i.e., 'deities who presided over crossroads' (the *compita*), and by extension the whole neighbouring district. They had a special annual festival, called the *Compitalia*. The state itself had its own *lares*, called *praestites*, i.e., the 'protecting deity–guardians of the city'. They had a temple and altar on the Via Sacra (Holy Way or Street) and were represented as men wearing the *chlamys* (military cloak), carrying lances, seated, with a dog (the emblem of watchfulness) at their feet.

Lavater, Johann Kaspar (1741—1801) was a Swiss writer, Protestant pastor, and founder of physiognomics, an anti–rational, religious and literary movement. Lavater served as pastor of St Peter's Church in Zürich. He was deported to Basle for a time because of his protest against the violence of the French Directory. His studies in physiognomy and his interest in 'magnetic' trance conditions had their source in his religious beliefs, which drove him to search for demonstrable traces of the divine in human life. His belief in the interaction of mind and body led him to seek influences of the spirit upon the features. His multi–volume *Physiognomische Fragmente zur Beförderung der Menschenkenntnis und Menschenliebe {Essays on Physiognomy}* (1775—78) established his reputation throughout Europe. Goethe worked with Lavater on the book and the two enjoyed a warm friendship, which was later severed by Lavater's zeal for conversion: he tried to convert many prominent Europeans and men of letters. Lavater's most important books are *Aussichten in die Ewigkeit {Prospects of Eternity}*(1768—78), *Geheimes Tagebuch von einem Beobachter seiner selbst {Secret Journal of a Self Observer}* (1772—73), *Pontius Pilatus {Pontius Pilate}* (1782—85), and *Nathanael* (1786).

Le Tellier, Michel (1643—1719) was born into a simple peasant family, but he rose to great heights in the Catholic Church, including being appointed confessor to Louis XIV. Of him, Louis XIV is reputed to have remarked to the Duc d'Harcourt: 'His greatest happiness would be to shed his blood for the Church, and I do not believe there is a single soul in my entire kingdom who is more fearless and more saintly.' (Source: *Catholic Encyclopedia*, 1917.)

Livy (59—64 BC to AD 17) (Latin name in full *Titus Livius*) was one of the most influential of Roman historians who recorded and described historical events of his time, along with Sallust and Tacitus. Livy's most ambitious project was a detailed history of Rome from its earliest times, but narrated from his own personal perspective, which was quite different from that of other chroniclers of Roman history. Livy emphasized the moral character of historical figures to the detriment of pure historical fact.

Longinus (fl. in 1st century BC) (also known as *Dionysius Longinus*) was a scholar who wrote a treatise on literary style, the *Treatise on the Sublime* (in Greek *Peri Hypsous*), usually attributed to him. *On the Sublime* is an incomplete work, the oldest manuscript of which dates from the tenth century, and it is one of the great seminal works of ancient literary criticism, in which the author expresses his admiration for 'greatness' or 'the sublime' in writing analysed in illustrative passages from Homer, Sappho, Plato and the biblical book of Genesis. In his treatise, Longinus notes that writers and poets have attributed to the gods and men great, mighty characteristics and powers, stating, 'Homer has done his best to make the men in the *Iliad* gods and the gods men': in so doing, he portrayed them as great. With reference to Moses, (as mentioned by Bergier) he writes: 'So, too, the lawgiver of the Jews, no ordinary man, having formed a worthy conception of divine power and given expression to it, writes at the very beginning of his *Laws*, "God said"—what? "Let there be light," and there was light, "Let there be earth," and there was earth.' (Longinus, *On the Sublime*, translated by W.H. Fyfe, revised by Donald Russell, in Aristotle, *Poetics*, Longinus, *On the Sublime*, and Demetrius, *On Style*, {all three works in one vol.} [Cambridge, Mass.: Harvard University Press, Loeb Classical Library, 1999], pp. 189—191.)

Louis XIV (1638—1715) was a king of France who had several sobriquets 'Louis The Great', 'Louis The Grand Monarch', or 'The Sun King', {in French *Louis Le Grand, Louis Le Grand Monarque*, or *Le Roi Soleil*}, who ruled France from 1643 to 1715, principally from his magnificent palace at Versailles, during one of the French monarchy's most flamboyant periods: he is the symbol of absolute monarchy in the classical age. As far as his foreign policy was concerned, he pushed back France's borders in a series of wars between 1667 and 1697: he did so in the east at the expense of the Habsburgs and then, in the War of the Spanish Succession (1701—14) he engaged a hostile European coalition in order to secure the Spanish throne for his grandson. To France's traditional enemies, Louis added the entire Protestant world by a crass act born of his religious fervour. His mother had inculcated in him a narrow and simplistic religion, and he understood nothing of the Reformation. He viewed French Protestants as potential rebels and, having unsuccessfully tried to convert them by force, he revoked the Edict of Nantes (q.v.) in 1685, which had guaranteed their freedom of worship. The revocation was followed by a period of vicious persecution and it drove many artisans—the Huguenots (q.v.)—from France, much to her economic detriment.

Louis, St., more usually known as Louis IX (1214—1270), king of France from 1226 to 1270: he was also called Saint Louis because of his religious devotion. He led the Seventh Crusade to the Holy Land in 1248—50 and died on another crusade to Tunisia. He was attended by Joinville, known as *Jean, sire de Joinville* (1224—1317). As a member of the lesser nobility of Champagne, Joinville first attended the court of Louis IX at Saumur (1241), probably as a squire. The young Joinville took the crusader's cross at the same time as the King (1244) and set out with him (in August 1248) on his expedition to Egypt, from where the crusaders planned to attack Syria. The entire army with Louis and Joinville were captured and ransomed, whereupon they returned to France in 1254. While in Syria, Joinville wrote the first draft of a minor work, his *Credo,* a rather naive statement of belief that was probably revised later. He refused to accompany the King on his fatal crusade to Tunis (1270), having previously told him that it was folly. Joinville lived to testify for the canonization of the King in 1282. Joinville's major work was the *Histoire de Saint–Louis {History of St Louis},* possibly started as early as the 1270s, but the final form was commissioned by Jeanne of Champagne and Navarre, wife of King Philip IV the Fair; it was not completed at the time of her death (1305) and so was presented in 1309 to her son Louis X. The *Histoire* is a personal account, which, in the course of setting forth the exploits of his idol, King Louis IX, reveals Joinville himself as a man of deep emotions: simple, honest, straightforward and affectionate. He makes no attempt to conceal his occasional cowardice, his lack of piety, his tactlessness or his garrulousness. The main interest of the account lies in the details of the Crusade—the financial hardships, the dangers of sea voyages, the ravages of disease, etc. Also of interest in the book are descriptions of Muslim customs.

Lustral water refers to the Roman *lustrum* or 'purificatory sacrifice'. In Roman times a census was taken every five years, followed by a purification ceremony, during which water was used to purify the people.

Machabees, Books of the, is the title of four books, of which only Books I & II are regarded by the Catholic Church as canonical: Protestants regard all four books as apocryphal. The first two have been so named because they relate the history of the rebellion of the Machabees, the fourth because it speaks of the Machabee martyrs. The third, which has no connection whatever with the Machabee period, no doubt owes its name to the fact that, like the others, it deals with a period of persecution of the Jews. In contrast to what Bergier says of the written style of these works, the *Catholic Encyclopedia* notes, 'The narrative both in style and manner is modelled on the earlier historical books of the Old Testament. The style is usually simple, yet it at times becomes eloquent and even poetic.' The original language was Aramaic or Hebrew, which was subsequently translated into Greek, like the Septuagint version of the Bible. The *Catholic Encyclopedia* goes on to note that, 'Not only is the structure of the sentences decidedly Hebrew (or Aramaic); but many words and expressions occur which are literal renderings of Hebrew idioms.' It is almost futile for Bergier to make a point about the written style of a translation of a translation, because any work which has undergone this treatment inevitably loses its original qualities and the arguments simply become conjecture.

Macrobius, Ambrosius Theodosius (fl. AD 400) was a Latin grammarian and philosopher, whose most important work is *Saturnalia*. Little is known about his life: he may have been a praetorian prefect in Spain (399), proconsul in Africa (410), and grand chamberlain (422). *Saturnalia*, which is dedicated to Macrobius' son Eustachius, purports to give an account of discussions in private houses on the day before the Saturnalia (a winter festival celebrated on December 17—24 and a time of wild merrymaking and domestic celebrations) and on three days during that festival. Macrobius also wrote a commentary on Cicero's *Somnium Scipionis* {*The Dream of Scipio*} from *De Republica* {*On the Republic*}. There is a reference to King Herod killing the 'Innocents', i.e., the babies reported in the Gospel of Matthew (2: 16), but no new evidence or sources are quoted and the remark is typical of the tittle–tattle style of the *Saturnalia*. The whole work takes the form of an imaginary dialogue between about a dozen characters, who may well not have been actual historical characters themselves. There is a long discussion on the works and written style of Virgil, and also a good deal of information on the pagan gods, etc., plus some remarks on astrology and the zodiac, *inter alia*. There are no references at all to Christianity and only a fleeting reference—more of a humours quip—on Herod: cf., Bergier's refutation, p. 207.

Maneto (fl. *c.* 300 BC) (also spelled Manethos, or Manethon) was an Egyptian priest who wrote a history of Egypt in Greek, probably for Ptolemy I (305—282 BC). Maneto's history has not survived, except for some fragments of narrative in Josephus' treatise *Against Apion* and tables of dynasties, kings and lengths of reigns in the works of Julius Africanus, Eusebius and George Syncellus. The fragments thus preserved showed that

Maneto's work was based on good native sources. These fragments have been of much service to scholars in confirming the succession of kings where the archaeological evidence was inconclusive, and Maneto's division of the rulers of Egypt into thirty dynasties is still accepted.

Mani (AD 216—*c.* 274) (also called Manes, or Manichaeus) was an Iranian and the founder of the Manichaean religion, a church advocating a dualistic doctrine that viewed the world as a fusion of spirit and matter, the original contrary principles of good and evil, respectively.

Marca, Pierre de (1594—1662) was a French bishop and scholar of a family distinguished in the magistracy. After studying law in the University of Toulouse, he became councillor (1615), and then president (1621), of the Parliament of Pau, and finally intendant of Béarn (1631), where his influence greatly helped to restore the Catholic religion almost extinguished by the queen, Jeanne d'Albret. Amongst other works, he wrote *Histoire de Béarn* {*History of Béarn*} and a treatise at Cardinal Richelieu's instigation *Concordia sacerdotii et imperii* {*Harmony between the Priesthood and the State*} (1641).

Marcellinus, Ammianus (*c.* AD 330—395) was the last major Roman historian, whose work continued the history of the later Roman Empire to 378. Born of a noble Greek family, Ammianus served in the army of Constantius II in Gaul and Persia. He fought against the Persians under Julian the Apostate (q.v.) and took part in the retreat of his successor, Jovian. Leaving the army at Antioch, he travelled to Egypt and Greece, eventually settling in Rome. There he wrote his Latin history of the Roman Empire from the accession of Nerva to the death of Valens, thus continuing the work of Tacitus. This history, *Rerum gestarum libri* {*The Chronicles of Events*}, better known as *History* in English, consisted of thirty–one books, of which only the last eighteen, covering the years AD 353—378, survive. It is a clear, comprehensive account of events by a writer of soldierly qualities, independent judgment and wide reading. Drawing upon his own experience, Ammianus portrayed vivid pictures of the empire's economic and social problems. A pagan who was tolerant to other religions, he took a detached view of the intellectual trends of the day. His judgment in political affairs was limited only by his own straightforward attitude. He used the regular techniques of later Roman historiography—rhetoric in speeches, ethnographical digressions in descriptions, etc. He wrote with vivid and striking dramatic power in a conscious imitation of Tacitus.

Maréchal, Pierre–Sylvain (1750—1803) was a French poet, playwright and publicist, whose plan for a secular calendar, presented in his *Almanach des honnêtes gens* {*Almanac of Notable People*} (1788) was subsequently the basis for the French republican calendar adopted in 1793. By profession a lawyer and librarian, Maréchal was a materialist and an atheist in his philosophy. After writing some erotic poetry, he turned his talents to anti–religious propaganda. He parodied the Bible in *Livre échappé au Déluge {Book Salvaged from the Flood}* (1784) and compiled his own *Dictionnaire des athées anciens et modernes {Dictionary of Ancient and Modern Atheists}* (1800).

Marie Alacoque, Saint (1647—1690) was a French Catholic nun who had visions of Christ, during which she claimed he showed his 'sacred heart' to her and through her efforts the Roman Catholic Church made the physical heart of Jesus an object of devotion. The use of Jesus' heart to symbolize his love for mankind is not found in the Bible, but in the writings of some medieval mystics. Marie Alacoque was born in L'Hautecour, Burgundy, in France and it is said that as a child she preferred silence and prayer to play, and her fanatical devotion led her to self–harming, from which she became temporarily paralyzed. She continued to inflict pain and suffering upon herself by excessive fasting and self–laceration, believing that she was undergoing the very passion of Christ. Assisted by Claude de la Colombière, a Jesuit priest who believed the stories of her visions, Marie Alacoque called for the establishment of a feast in honour of the Sacred Heart and for prayers of reparation for sins, especially for those directed against the Eucharist. In 1856 Pope Pius IX introduced the feast into the general calendar of the Roman Catholic Church. In addition to the feast, now celebrated on the Friday of the third week after Pentecost, devotion includes acts of consecration and honour given to the image of the Sacred Heart. Such images are often depicted with a wounded heart, encircled by a crown of thorns and radiating light.

It is claimed that when her tomb was opened in the chapel at Paray, her body had not decomposed and two miracles then happened instantaneously. Miracle cures are still claimed. Marie Alacoque was canonized in 1920. She also left a number of devotional texts.

Figure 81: Devotional picture of 'The Sacred Heart of Jesus'.

Marie–Madeleine de Pazzi, Saint (1566—1607) (her original Italian name was *Santa Maria Maddalena de' Pazzi*) was a Carmelite nun who was born in Florence. From an early age she went in for acts of extreme self–harm, wearing a crown of thorns on her head in imitation of Christ's passion. She avowed never to marry, espousing Christ as her only 'husband', and she wrote, '*Je livrerais plutôt ma tête au bourreau que ma chasteté à un homme*', {'*I would rather surrender my head to the executioner than offer my chastity to a man*'}. (Abbé L. Jaud, *Vie des Saints pour tous les jours de l'année* [Tours, Marne, 1950].)

Marmontel, Jean–François (1723—1799) was a poet, dramatist, novelist, and critic, who is remembered for his autobiographical work *Mémoires d'un père* {*Memoirs of a Father*} (1804), written in retirement away from Paris during the Revolution. Some of his works appeared in the prestigious literary journal *Mercure de France* and he contributed to the *Encyclopédie* on literary terms and word forms. His works *Bélisaire* (1767) and *Les Incas* (1777) make a plea for religious tolerance and denounce fanaticism, for which Marmontel was roundly attacked from many quarters. He also wrote opera libretti.

Mary, reputed to be a virgin at the time she gave birth to Jesus Christ. In his *Portable Theology*, d'Holbach notes that: 'Saint Mary the Virgin is the mother of the Son of God and the mother–in–law of the Church: she was spiritually "overshadowed" by God the Father who, being only pure spirit, never consummated the marriage because one clearly needs to have a body to enact this ceremony.' According to some sources, Mary was said to have been either a 'hairdresser' or a 'milliner': there is confusion because the French term used (*coiffeuse*) can mean both. It seems likely that the translation 'hairdresser' would be more appropriate, based on information from the original Talmud story, which claims that there was a man named Ben Stada, reputed to be black magician. His mother was named Miriam and also called Stada. His father was named Pappos Ben Yehudah. Miriam (Stada) had an affair with Pandira from which Ben Stada was born and some historians claim that Ben Stada, also known as Ben Pandira, was Jesus. His mother's name was Miriam, which bears close resemblance to the name Mary. Additionally, Miriam was called a women's hairdresser, or '*megadla nashaia*', in Hebrew. The phrase '*Miriam megadla nashaia*' sounds similar to Mary Magdalene, a well–known New Testament figure. It amused d'Holbach and some of the other *Encyclopédistes* to repeat this rather far–fetched allegation, which outraged the Church. The story, however, is not without some serious scholarship, as the following passage indicates: 'Now one of the most important details of the confused legend in the Talmud concerning the pre–Christian Jesus Ben Pandira, who is conjoined with Ben Stada, is that the mother is in one place named Miriam

Magdala, Mary the nurse, or the hairdresser (Jastrow, *Dict. of the Targ. and the Midr. Lit.*, part 2, p. 213, 1888). As Isis, too, plays the part of a hair–dresser (Plut., *De Is. et Osir.*, 15), it seems clear that we are dealing here also with myth, not with biography. In the Gospels we have Mary the Magdalene, that is, of the supposed place Magdala, which Jesus in one text (Matt. 15:39) visits. But Magdala at most simply means "a tower", or "high place" (the same root yielding the various senses of nursing, rearing, and hair–dressing)...' (Quoted from J.M. Robertson, *Christianity and Mythology* [1900], in T.J. Thorburn, *The Mythical Interpretation of the Gospels: Critical Studies in the Historic Narratives* [N.Y.: Charles Scribner's Sons, 1916], p. 5.)

Meister, Jacques–Henri (1744—1826) was a Swiss writer of an exiled Protestant family, whose book *De l'origine des principes religieux {On the Origin of Religious Principles}* (1768) caused him to be stripped of his ministerial post in Zurich and his political and civil rights, which were only restored to him in 1772. As Grimm's (q.v.) secretary from 1773 onwards, he edited much of his *Correspondance littéraire, philosophique et critique*, which was a literary and philosophical journal published serially between 1747 and 1793 to an undisclosed group of subscribers, thereby obviating the watchful eye of the censor. The journal was sent to some extremely well–placed individuals, such as Catherine the Great of Russia, Frederick the Great of Prussia, and the future Gustav III of Sweden. This ensemble of journals forms an invaluable insight into eighteenth–century French aristocratic society. Meister was a friend and collaborator of Diderot (q.v.) and many of the finest minds in France.

Menander (342—292 BC) was an Athenian dramatist, whom ancient critics considered the supreme poet of Greek New Comedy, i.e., the last flowering of Athenian stage comedy. During his life, his success was limited; although he wrote more than a hundred plays, he won only eight victories at Athenian dramatic festivals.

Mennonite was a member of the Protestant Church that arose out of the Anabaptists, a radical reform movement of the sixteenth–century Reformation. It was named after Menno Simons, a Dutch priest who consolidated and institutionalized the work initiated by moderate Anabaptist leaders. Mennonites are found in many countries of the world but are concentrated most heavily in the United States and Canada. Anabaptist–Mennonite thought has been characterized by its insistence on a separation between religion and the world. The persecutions of the sixteenth century forced Anabaptists to withdraw from society in order to survive, a strategy that became central in Mennonite theology. Consequently, most Mennonites have remained tightly bound to their

CORRESPONDANCE

LITTÉRAIRE, PHILOSOPHIQUE ET CRITIQUE

PAR

GRIMM, DIDEROT

RAYNAL, MEISTER, ETC.

REVUE SUR LES TEXTES ORIGINAUX

COMPRENANT

outre ce qui a été publié à diverses époques

LES FRAGMENTS SUPPRIMÉS EN 1813 PAR LA CENSURE

LES PARTIES INÉDITES

CONSERVÉES A LA BIBLIOTHÈQUE DUCALE DE GOTHA ET A L'ARSENAL A PARIS

NOTICES, NOTES, TABLE GÉNÉRALE

PAR

MAURICE TOURNEUX

TOME CINQUIÈME

PARIS

GARNIER FRÈRES, LIBRAIRES-ÉDITEURS

6, RUE DES SAINTS-PÈRES, 6

1878

Figure 82: Facsimile of *Correspondance littéraire, philosophique et critique* (1878).

communities, subjected themselves to rigorous group discipline and wear distinctive clothing (e.g., the 'plain coat'—a jacket without lapels—for men and the 'covering'—a small hat made of lace—for women). Their isolation encouraged the sectarian virtues of frugality, hard work, piety and mutual helpfulness, but also frequently led to schism. However, by the mid–twentieth century Mennonites were deeply involved in the social, educational and economic world around them, a situation that led to revolutionary changes in their life and thought. It also prompted a new search for identity as a distinct group in the modern world, through study of their denominational history, sociological analysis and theological interaction with other groups.

Meslier, Jean (1664—1729) was a rural parish priest who worked virtually all his life, for forty years, in Étrépigny, in Champagne. When he died, it was found he had left three copies of a lengthy manuscript in his house, intended as a summation of his ideas to be read by his parishioners. The full title of the work gives a good indication of the content of these manuscripts: '*Memoir of the Thoughts and Feelings of Jean Meslier, Priest of Estrépigny and Galaives on a Part of the Errors and Abuse of the Conduct of the Government and Men, in which One can See Clear and Obvious Demonstrations of the Vanity and Falsity of all Gods and Religions of the World, Addressed to his Parishioners after his Death, to Serve them as a Testimony for them and all Such Similar People*'. After a title such as that, it comes as no surprise that their village curate denounced religion as a lie. These manuscripts were further copied clandestinely and it is known that there were about a hundred in circulation. When one had come to Voltaire's attention in 1735, he published extracts of the work in 1762, but in editing it, he put a Deist (q.v.) slant on the work, absent in the original manuscript. It is stated that Meslier's dying wish (unrecorded) was that: '*Je voudrais, et ce sera le dernier et le plus ardent de mes souhaits, je voudrais que le dernier des rois fût étranglé avec les boyaux du dernier prêtre*' {'*I would like—and this would be my last and most ardent wish—that the last king be strangled with the guts of the last priest.*'}. It is only recently that Meslier's text has become readily available in a scholarly version, encouraged by the indefatigable efforts of the writer and philosopher Michel Onfray (see Bibliography).

Mirabaud, Jean–Baptiste de (1675—1760) was an officer and subsequently a private tutor to the children of the Duchess of Orléans. He was a friend of the fabulist La Fontaine and he became a member of the French Academy of Science in 1726, eventually rising to the position of permanent secretary of the Academy. He wrote *Le Monde, son origine et son antiquité* {*The World—Its Origin and Antiquity*} (1751) and *Opinions des Anciens sur les Juifs et Réflextions sur l'Evangile* {*Opinions of the*

Ancients on the Jews and Reflections on the Gospel}, published posthumously in 1769. It was to Mirabaud that d'Holbach's *System of Nature* was attributed.

Mithras (also spelled 'Mithra', in Sanskrit *Mitra*) was the god of light, in ancient Indo–Iranian mythology, whose cult spread from India in the east to as far west as Spain, Great Britain and Germany. The first written mention of the Vedic Mitra dates to 1400 BC. His worship spread to Persia and, after the defeat of the Persians by Alexander the Great, throughout the Hellenic world. In the third and fourth centuries AD, the cult of Mithra, carried and supported by the soldiers of the Roman Empire, was the chief rival to the newly developing religion of Christianity. The Roman emperors Commodus and Julian were initiates of Mithraism, and in 307 Diocletian consecrated a temple on the Danube River to Mithras, 'Protector of the Empire'. According to myth, Mithras was born bearing a torch and armed with a knife, beside a sacred stream and under a sacred tree, a child of the earth itself. He soon rode, and later killed, the life–giving cosmic bull, whose blood fertilizes all vegetation. Mithras's slaying of the bull was a popular subject of Hellenic art and became the prototype for a bull–slaying ritual of fertility in the Mithraic cult. As god of light, Mithras was associated with the Greek sun god, Helios, and the Roman *Sol Invictus* (the *Unconquered Sun*). He is often paired with Anahita, goddess of the fertilizing waters.

Monks *q.v.* either under **Trappist** or **Septfonds**.

Montesquieu, Charles–Louis de Secondat, baron de La Brède et de (1689—1755) was a French political philosopher whose *magnum opus*, *L'Esprit des Lois* {*The Spirit of Laws*} (1750), was a major contribution to political theory. Montesquieu was born into a modest military family, ennobled in the sixteenth century for services to the crown. In 1721 he surprised all but a few close friends by publishing his *Lettres persanes* {*Persian Letters*} (1722), in which he gave a brilliant, satirical portrait of French, and particularly Parisian, civilization, supposedly seen through the eyes of two Persian travellers. This exceedingly successful work mocks the reign of Louis XIV, which had only recently ended; it pokes fun at all social classes, discusses, in its allegorical story of the Troglodytes, the theories of Thomas Hobbes relating to the state of nature. It also makes an original, if naive, contribution to the new science of demography, continually compares Islam and Christianity, and it reflects the controversy over the papal bull *Unigenitus* (q.v.), which was directed against the dissident Catholic group known as the Jansenists. Satire on Roman Catholic doctrine abounds, infused throughout with a new spirit of vigorous, disrespectful and iconoclastic criticism. The work's anonymity was soon penetrated and Montesquieu's identity was uncovered, making him instantly famous. The new ideas fermenting in Paris had received their most scintillating expression. About this time he made the acquaintance of the English politician Viscount Bolingbroke (q.v.), whose political views were later to be reflected in Montesquieu's analysis of the English constitution. Bolingbroke was just one of a wide circle of friends Montesquieu made in England. He produced other works, but it is for his *Spirit of Laws* that he is best remembered. It consisted of two quarto volumes, comprising thirty–one books in 1,086 pages and it is one of the great works in the history of political theory and in the history of jurisprudence. Its author acquainted himself with all previous schools of thought, but identified personally with none.

Moor is a term for a Moroccan or, formerly, a member of the Muslim population of Spain of mixed Arab, Spanish and Berber origins, who created the Arab Andalusian civilization and subsequently settled as refugees in North Africa between the eleventh and seventeenth centuries. By extension (corresponding to the Spanish *moro*), the term occasionally denotes any Muslim in general, as in the case of the Moors of Sri Lanka (Ceylon), or of the Philippines. The word derives from the Latin *Mauri*, first used by the Romans to denote the inhabitants of the Roman province of Mauretania, comprising the western portion of modern Algeria and the north–eastern portion of modern Morocco. Modern Mauritanians are also sometimes referred to as Moors (as in the French *maure*); the Islamic Republic of Mauritania, however, lies in the large Saharan area between Morocco and the republics of Senegal and Mali.

Morellet, André, Abbé (1727—1819) was a theologian, as his name suggest, but he was also a Master of Theology. He was a pamphleteer and an economist, as well as a fine memoirist, who left a valuable, elegantly written memoir of the period, *Mémoires sur le XVIIIe siècle et la Révolution {Memoirs of the Eighteenth Century and the Revolution}*, published after his death in 1821. Though he was educated by the Jesuits and took holy orders, he was a man of immensely liberal, balanced views. As well as being a regular guest *chez* d'Holbach, he also frequented one of the other major Parisian salons, that of Mme Geoffrin, which meant he had a very wide circle of acquaintances and friends, and he was very much 'in the know' within Parisian intellectual circles. He was known for his quick, biting wit, which prompted Voltaire's own wit to dub him 'L'Abbé Mord–les' {'Abbé Bite–Them'}.

Moses (fl. in 14th to 13th centuries BC) (in Hebrew *Moshe*) was a Hebrew prophet, teacher and leader who, in the thirteenth century BC, reputedly delivered the Israelites from Egyptian slavery. In the Covenant ceremony at Mt Sinai, where the Ten Commandments were delivered, he founded the religious community known as Israel. As the interpreter of these Covenant stipulations, he was the organizer of the community's religious and civil traditions. In the Judaic tradition, he is revered as the greatest prophet and teacher, and Judaism has sometimes loosely been called Mosaism, or the Mosaic faith, in Western Christendom. His influence continues to be felt in the religious life, moral concerns and social ethics of Western civilization. Most scholars of biblical exegesis dismiss the time–honoured claim that Moses was the author of the first five books of the Bible, viz., Genesis, Exodus, Leviticus, Numbers and Deuteronomy, collectively referred to as the Pentateuch, which are a corner–stone of both the Jewish and Christian religions. They tell how the relationship between God and the people of Israel, God's chosen people, developed and about the establishment of a covenant between God and the early patriarchs, Abraham, Isaac and Jacob, through to the flight from Egypt, where the Israelites were slaves, and up to the point when they entered the Promised Land. Although there is no direct claim that these books were written by Moses himself, the Bible itself tells us that Moses kept written records, and Greenberg states, 'Over the course of several centuries, despite aggressive opposition by the churches, a handful of scholars pointed out a number of logical inconsistencies in the idea of Mosaic authorship for these works', not least since one passage in Deuteronomy describes the burial of Moses, indicating that the passage was written well after the death of Moses and therefore it could not have been written by him.' (See Gary Greenberg, *101 Myths of the Bible: How Ancient Scribes Invented Biblical History* [Illinois: Sourcebooks, Inc., 2002]). Greenberg also goes on to state that, 'The Bible has several contradictory accounts of what laws the Israelites were given, how many they received, and where and when they got them. The traditional version of the Ten Commandments as given [Exod. 20: 1— 17] was a late invention, created no earlier than the seventh century BC.' (Greenberg, pp. 215—225.) The *Encyclopædia Britannica* also points out many historical inaccuracies of the biblical account of the people of Israel, much of which is not supported by archaeological evidence. (See *Britannica* under 'Moses'.) Although time undoubtedly enhanced the portrait of Moses, a basic picture emerges from the sources. Five times the narratives claim that Moses kept written records (Ex. 17: 14; 24: 4; 34: 27—28; Num. 33: 2; and Deut. 31: 9 & 24—26). Even with a generous interpretation of the extent of these writings, they do not amount to more than a fifth of the total Pentateuch; therefore, the traditional claim of Mosaic authorship of the whole Pentateuch is untenable. In a general sense, the first five books of the Hebrew Bible can be described as Mosaic in spirit, but not written by him, and without him there would have been no Israel and no collection known as the Torah. Moses was a gifted, well– trained person, but his true greatness was probably due to what he believed to be his personal experience of and relationship with Yahweh. This

441

former stammering murderer understood his preservation and destiny as coming from the grace of a merciful Lord who had given him another chance. Because of the uniqueness of his situation, Moses had to function in a number of roles. As Yahweh's agent in the deliverance of the Hebrews, he was their prophet and leader. As mediator of the Covenant, he was the founder of the community. As interpreter of the Covenant, he was an organizer and legislator. As intercessor for the people, he was their priest. Therefore, Moses had a special combination of gifts that made him impossible to replace. Although his successor, Joshua, and the priest Eleazar, the son of Aaron, tried to do so, together they did not measure up to him. Later prophets were great men who spoke out of the spirit that Moses had, but they were not called to function in so many roles. D'Holbach makes a number of deprecatory comments about Moses' behaviour and career (see p. 21), based on details found in biblical passages. After having been found in the bulrushes in a basket by pharaoh's daughter, Moses was raised and educated in the royal court in Egypt and he worked for the pharaoh. Moses had been witness to the abuse of one of the Hebrew slaves by the king's overseers and he killed the Egyptian, afterwards hiding the body in the hope that no one would find it:

> And it came to pass in those days, when Moses was grown, that he went out unto his brethren, and looked on their burdens: and he spied an Egyptian smiting an Hebrew, one of his brethren. And he looked this way and that way, and when he saw that there was no man, he slew the Egyptian, and hid him in the sand. And when he went out the second day, behold, two men of the Hebrews strove together: and he said to him that did the wrong, 'Wherefore smitest thou thy fellow?' And he said, 'Who made thee a prince and a judge over us? Intendest thou to kill me, as thou killedst the Egyptian?' And Moses feared, and said, 'Surely this thing is known.' Now when Pharaoh heard this thing, he sought to slay Moses. (Exod. 2: 11—15).

The murder became common knowledge and Moses had to flee from Pharaoh, as the biblical account continues. He settled into a priest's family and took his daughter as his wife, as d'Holbach points out in his text:

> [Moses] dwelt in the land of Midian: and he sat down by a well. Now the priest of Midian had seven daughters: and they came and drew water, and filled the troughs to water their father's flock. And the shepherds came and drove them away: but Moses stood up and helped them, and watered their flock. And when they came to Reuel their father, he said, 'How is it that ye are come so soon to day?' And they said, 'An Egyptian delivered us out of the hand of the shepherds, and also drew water enough for us, and watered the flock.' And he said unto his daughters, 'And where is he? Why is it that ye have left the man? Call him, that he may eat bread.' And Moses was content to dwell with the man: and he gave Moses Zipporah his

daughter. And she bare him a son, and he called his name Gershom: for he said, "I have been a stranger in a strange land.' (Exod. 2: 15—22).

Hence, Moses was a murderer and he married into an idolatrous family. God's constant complaint about the Israelites was that they continuously chased after idols: given all these facts, Moses seems to have been a rather dubious choice for a leader of God's chosen people. D'Holbach also makes mention of the Children of Israel stealing the Egyptians' possession and Moses performing magic tricks (see p. 21):

> And the children of Israel did according to the word of Moses; and they borrowed of the Egyptians jewels of silver, and jewels of gold, and raiment: And the Lord gave the people favour in the sight of the Egyptians, so that they lent unto them such things as they required. And they spoiled the Egyptians. (Exod. 12: 35—6).

'Borrowed' here is a euphemism for 'took'! The supernatural acts which Moses did was to turn a staff into a serpent and back into a staff again, and similarly, he put his hand in his tunic and it emerged leprous, and when he inserted it again, it came out cured. These events are recorded in the book of Exodus, ch. 4.

Naigeon, Jacques–André (1738—1810) was a close friend of d'Holbach and Diderot, and he collaborated extensively with d'Holbach on editing and preparing material for publication. He contributed articles to the *Encyclopédie* on philosophical matters relating to religious belief, he did a good deal of translating and he compiled a *Dictionnaire de philosophie ancienne et modern* {*Dictionary of Ancient and Modern Philosophy*} and he wrote most of *Le Militaire philosophe, ou Difficulties sur la religion* {*The Militant Philosopher or Difficulties of Religion*} (1768), with d'Holbach contributing the final chapter. He was known for being quite a garrulous, militant atheist, whereas d'Holbach, at least personally and in polite society, took a more moderate tone. He wrote d'Holbach's obituary which is translated and included in this volume.

Nebuchadnezzar II (*c*. 630—561 BC) was the greatest king of the Chaldean dynasty of Babylonia, known for his military might and he played an important role in the history of the Jewish nation. Nebuchadnezzar made a first attack on the Temple at Jerusalem in 604 BC from where he removed treasures. On one of his subsequent campaigns he attacked the Arab tribes of north–western Arabia and Judah in 597 BC and he captured Jerusalem. According to biblical sources, this second attack on Jerusalem resulted in its capture in 587/586 and in the deportation of prominent citizens, with a further deportation in 582. He totally destroyed the Temple in 587/586. This destruction and the deportations of Jews to Babylonia in 586 and 582 were seen as fulfilling prophecies and, therefore, strengthened Judaic religious beliefs, awakening the hope of a re–establishment of an independent Jewish state. Nebuchadnezzar's expansionist policies greatly extended the boundaries of the Babylonian empire.

Nicole, Pierre (1625—1695) was a French theologian, author, moralist and controversialist, whose (chiefly polemical) writings supported the Roman Catholic reform movement known as Jansenism. Educated in Paris, Nicole taught literature and philosophy at Port–Royal des Champs, a Cistercian abbey and a stronghold of Jansenism. He wrote several textbooks with the Jansenist leader Antoine Arnauld and others, among them *La Logique, ou L'art de Penser* {*Logic, or The Art of Thinking*} (1662). Nicole was an influential spokesman from 1655 to 1668 through his writing or editing of most of the Jansenist pamphlets. From 1669, Nicole used his talents to defend Catholic dogma against Protestant criticism. A friend of the French philosopher Blaise Pascal (q.v.), he used one of his numerous pseudonyms to translate into Latin Pascal's *Provinciales* {*Provincial Letters*}.

Numantia was a Celtiberian town located near modern Soria in Spain on the upper Douro (Duero) River. Founded on the site of earlier settlements by Iberians who penetrated the Celtic highlands about 300 BC, it later formed the centre of Celtiberian resistance to Rome, withstanding repeated attacks. Finally, Scipio Aemilianus (Numantinus) blockaded it (133 BC) by establishing six miles of continuous ramparts around it. After an eight–month siege, Numantia was reduced to extreme hunger and the survivors capitulated: its destruction ended all serious resistance to Roman power in Celtiberia. Numantia was later rebuilt by the emperor Augustus, but it was of little importance.

Odin (alternatively known as 'Wodan', 'Woden', or 'Wotan') is one of the chief gods of Norse mythology, from which the English day Wednesday is derived: the Old English *Wodnes dæꝫ* 'the day of [the god] Woden' is a translation from the Roman historian Tacitus, who stated that the Teutons worshipped Mercury, or *dies Mercurii* in Latin. Odin was a god of war and he was reputed to be the protector of those who had fallen in battle.

Origen (AD 185—254) (also known in Latin as *Origenes Adamantius*) was a leading biblical scholar of the early Greek Church, into whose hands came an anti–Christian treatise written by Celsus (q.v.)—one of several writers who wrote works of a polemical nature against the early Christian Church around the second century AD. Celsus' work was entitled *The True Word* (or it could also be translated as *The True Discourse*), in which he attacked Christianity first from a Jewish perspective, then from a philosophical, Platonist perspective. It denied the Messianic mission of Christ, the Virgin Birth and accounts of the miracles, which he explained by referring to the renowned 'magical' tricks of the Egyptians, an accusation d'Holbach uses in his treatise. Origen wrote a refutation of Celsus' work, called *Contra Celsum* {*Against Celsus*}, originally written in Greek, but translated into Latin.

Origen's *Against Celsus* states:

> 'But,' continues Celsus, 'what great deeds did Jesus perform as being a God? Did he put his enemies to shame, or bring to a ridiculous conclusion what was designed against him?' Now to this question, although we are able to show the striking and miraculous character of the events which befell Him, yet from what other source can we furnish an answer than from the Gospel narratives, which state that 'there was an earthquake, and that the rocks were split asunder, and the tombs opened, and the veil of the temple rent in twain from top to bottom, and that darkness prevailed in the day–time, the sun failing to give light?' But if Celsus believe the Gospel accounts when he thinks that he can find in them matter of charge against the Christians, and refuse to believe them when they establish the divinity of Jesus, our answer to him is: 'Sir, either disbelieve all the Gospel narratives, and then no longer imagine that you can found charges upon them; or, in yielding your belief to their statements, look in admiration on the Logos of God, who became incarnate, and who desired to confer benefits upon the whole human race.' And this feature evinces the nobility of the work of Jesus, that, down to the present time, those whom God wills are healed by His name. And with regard to the eclipse in the time of Tiberius Caesar, in whose reign Jesus appears to have been crucified, and the great earthquakes which then took place, Phlegon too, I think, has written in the thirteenth or fourteenth book of his Chronicles. (*Against Celsus*, Book II, Chapter XXXIII.)

Ormazd q.v. **Zoroaster/Zoroastrianism**.

Osiris (also called *Usiri*) is one of the most important gods of ancient Egypt. The origin of Osiris is obscure; he was a local god of Busiris, in Lower Egypt, and may have been a personification of underworld fertility, or possibly a deified hero. By about 2400 BC, however, Osiris clearly played a double role: he was both a god of fertility and the embodiment of the dead and resurrected king. This dual role was in turn combined with the Egyptian concept of divine kingship, because the king, upon death, became Osiris, god of the underworld, and the dead king's son, i.e., the living king, was identified with Horus, a god of the sky. Osiris and Horus were thus father and son. The goddess Isis was the mother of the king and was thus the mother of Horus and consort of Osiris. The god Seth was considered the murderer of Osiris and adversary of Horus.

Pantheism is the doctrine that the universe conceived of as a whole is God and, conversely, that there is no God but the combined substance, forces and laws that are manifested in the existing universe. The cognate doctrine of panentheism asserts that God includes the universe as a part, though not the whole, of his being. Both 'pantheism' and 'panentheism' are terms of recent origin, coined to describe certain views of the relationship between God and the world that are different from that of traditional Theism. As reflected in the prefix 'pan–' (Greek παν, 'all'), both of the terms stress the all–embracing inclusiveness of God, as compared with his separateness as emphasized in many versions of Theism. On the other hand, pantheism and panentheism, since they stress the theme of immanence, i.e., of the indwelling presence of God, are themselves versions of Theism conceived in its broadest meaning. Pantheism stresses the identity between God and the world, panentheism (Greek ἐν, plus θεός 'in' and 'God') that the world is included in God, but that God is more than the world. The adjective 'pantheist' was introduced by the Irish Deist (q.v. Deism) John Toland in the book *Socinianism Truly Stated* (1705). The noun 'pantheism' was first used in 1709 by one of Toland's opponents. The term 'panentheism' appeared much later, in 1828. Although the terms are recent, they have been applied retrospectively to alternative views of the divine being as found in the entire philosophical traditions of both the East and West.

Paradise q.v. **Tartarus.**

Paralipomenon, (The) is the older name for the Books of Chronicles (I & II) in the Old Testament, which largely parallel the Davidic books of Samuel and Kings. For this reason, they were known as 'Supplements' in the Septuagint version of the Bible. Generally the books can be divided into four parts based on their content: (i) The beginning of I Chronicles (chapters 1—10) mostly contains genealogical lists, concluding with the House of Saul (q.v.) and Saul's rejection by God, which sets the stage for the rise of David (q.v.); (ii) chapters 11—29 form a history of David's reign (iii) II Chron. (chapters 1—9) begins with a history of King Solomon's reign (David's son); (iv) the rest of II Chron. (chapters 10—36) is a chronicle of the kings of Judah to the time of the Babylonian exile and concludes with the call by Cyrus the Great for the exiles to return to their land.

Pascal, Blaise (1623—1662) was a French mathematician, physicist, religious philosopher and master of prose. He laid the foundation for the modern theory of probabilities, formulated what has come to be known as 'Pascal's law of pressure', and propagated a religious doctrine emphasising an experience of God through the heart, rather than through reason. Pascal's most celebrated work in the field of theology was to be a weighty tome under the title of *Apologie de la religion chrétienne {Apology of the Christian Religion}*, a consequence of his meditations on miracles and other proofs of Christianity. The work remained unfinished at his death. Between the summers of 1657 and 1658, he put together most of the notes and fragments which editors have published under the title *Pensées {Thoughts}*. In it, Pascal shows man without grace to be an incomprehensible mixture of greatness and abjectness, incapable of truth or of reaching the supreme good to which his nature aspires. The work is famous for his idea of the 'wager' as a means of overcoming man's scepticism, i.e., if God does not exist, the sceptic loses nothing by believing in him, and if he does exist, the sceptic gains eternal life by believing in him. Pascal insists that men must be brought to God through Jesus Christ alone, because a creature could never know the infinite, had Jesus not descended to assume the proportions of man's fallen state.

Paul, Saint (AD 10?—67?) (original name 'Saul of Tarsus') was a first–century Jew who, after first being a bitter enemy of Christianity, later became an important figure in church history. He converted only a few years after the death of Jesus and became the leading apostle or missionary of what was then the new movement of Christianity, and he played a decisive role in spreading Christianity beyond the limits of Judaism to become a worldwide religion. His surviving letters are the earliest extant Christian writings. They reveal both theological skill and pastoral understanding and have had lasting importance for Christian life and thought. Before his conversion to Christianity, Saul (aka Paul) was a member of the Pharisees (q.v.), a Jewish sect which held fast to the teachings of Moses and thereby rejected the claims of Christ, so as such, he was a sworn enemy of Christianity. He was a fearsome persecutor of the early Christian Church, as narrated in the book of Acts chapter 8. It took a 'miracle' to convert him, which occurred in the guise of a direct confrontation with God on the road to Damascus (narrated in Acts 9), to turn him into an ardent Christian. D'Holbach makes the point that if the arguments and eye–witness accounts of the miracles of Christ were so compelling at the time, why had Saul not been convinced and converted by them, especially since temporally he was so close to the events, which would have still been fresh in living memory? (This edition, p. 48.)

Peloponnesian War was fought in 431—404 BC between the two leading city–states in ancient Greece—Athens and Sparta. Each stood at the head of alliances which, between them, included nearly every Greek city–state. The fighting engulfed virtually the entire Greek world and it was properly regarded by Thucydides, whose contemporary account of it is considered to be among the world's finest works of history, as the most momentous war up to that time.

Penates (or normally *Di Penates*) were household gods of the Romans and other Latin peoples. In the narrow sense, they were gods of the *penus* ('household provision'), but by extension their protection encompassed the entire household. They are associated with other deities of the house, such as *Vesta*, and the name was sometimes used interchangeably with that of the *lares* (q.v.), any of various tutelary deities. The *penates* are all or some

447

specific group of deities with household connections, but their number and precise identity were a puzzle even to the ancients. The *penates* were worshiped privately as protectors of the individual household and also publicly as protectors of the Roman state. Each house had a shrine with images of them and worshiped at the family meal and on special occasions. Offerings were of portions of the usual meal or of special cakes, wine, honey, incense and, more rarely, of a blood sacrifice. The state as a whole worshiped the *penates publici* or 'public penates'. This state cult occupied a significant role as a focal point of Roman patriotism and nationalism.

Pharisees and **Sadducees** were distinct factions of the Jewish religion. The Pharisees were members of a Jewish religious party that flourished in Palestine during the latter part of the Second Temple period (515 BC to AD 70). Their insistence on the binding force of oral tradition ('the unwritten Torah') still remains a basic tenet of Jewish theological thought. When the *Mishna* (the first constituent part of the Talmud) was compiled about AD 200, it incorporated the teachings of the Pharisees on Jewish law. The Pharisees (in Hebrew *Perushim*) emerged as a distinct group shortly after the Maccabaean revolt, around 165—160 BC; it is generally believed they were spiritual descendants of the Hasideans. The Pharisees emerged as a party of laymen and scribes in contradistinction to the Sadducees, i.e., the party of the high priesthood who had traditionally provided the sole leadership of the Jewish people. The basic difference that led to the split between the Pharisees and the Sadducees lay in their respective attitudes toward the Torah (the first five books of the Old Testament) and the problem of finding in it answers to questions and bases for decisions about contemporary legal and religious matters, arising under circumstances far different from those of the time of Moses. In their response to this problem, the Sadducees refused on the one hand to accept any precept as binding, unless it was based directly on the Torah, i.e., the Written Law. On the other hand, the Pharisees believed that the Law that God had given to Moses was twofold, consisting of the Written Law and the Oral Law, i.e., the teachings of the prophets and the oral traditions of the Jewish people. Whereas the priestly Sadducees taught that the written Torah was the only source of revelation, the Pharisees accepted the principle that the Law could evolve, i.e., that men must use their reason in interpreting the Torah and applying it to contemporary problems and changing circumstances. Rather than blindly follow the letter of the Law, even if it conflicted with reason or conscience, the Pharisees harmonized the teachings of the Torah with their own ideas, or found their own ideas suggested or implied in it. They interpreted the Law according to its spirit; when in the course of time a law had been outgrown or superseded by changing conditions, they gave it a new, more acceptable meaning, seeking scriptural support for their actions through a ramified system of hermeneutics (the art or science of interpretation). It was due to this progressive tendency of the Pharisees that their interpretation of the Torah continued to develop and has remained a living force in Judaism.

Philip II (1165—1223) was a king of France, whose sobriquet was Philip Augustus (in French *Philippe Auguste*), the first of the great Capetian kings of medieval France. He reigned from 1179 to 1223, gradually reconquering the French territories held by the kings of England and also furthered the royal domains northward into Flanders and southward into Languedoc. He was a major figure in the Third Crusade to the Holy Land in 1191. Throughout his reign, Philip kept a close watch over the French nobility, which he brought effectively to heel. He maintained excellent relations with the French clergy, leaving the canons of the cathedral chapters free to elect their bishops and he favoured the monastic orders.

Philo of Alexandria or **Philo Judeus** (15/10 BC—AD 45/50) was a Greek–speaking Jewish philosopher, the most important representative of Hellenistic Judaism. His writings provide the clearest view of this development of Judaism in the Diaspora. As the first to attempt to synthesize revealed faith and philosophical reasoning, he occupies a unique position in the history of philosophy and he has been eagerly embraced by Christians as a forerunner of Christian theology, primarily for his attempts to reconcile the Greek philosophical tradition with the Hebrew tradition, as revealed through the Hebrew Scriptures. Hence, he takes Plato's concept of the creation *ex nihilo*, as expressed in his *Timaeus* (q.v. Plato) and combines it with the Genesis account of creation. Also of note is his thinking on *Logos*, the term widely used in the Græco–Roman tradition and in Judaism to designate a rational, intelligent and creational principle of the universe, with which God is associated in the Old Testament and with which Christ as 'the Word' is associated in the New, i.e., in Matthew's Gospel. He mentions the Essenes (q.v.) and their waiting for a Messiah, but he makes not a single mention of Jesus Christ or Christians, which, given his proximity to New Testament events in both time and location, is very strange.

Philostratus (AD 170—*c.* 245) is an ancient Greek writer who studied at Athens and subsequently, after the year 202, entered the circle of the philosophical Syrian empress of Rome, Julia Domna. On her death, Philostratus settled in Tyre. He wrote the *Gymnasticus* (a treatise dealing with athletic contests); a life of the Pythagorean philosopher Apollonius of Tyana; *Bioi sophiston* {*Lives of the Sophists*}, treating both the classical Sophists of the fifth century BC and later philosophers and rhetoricians; a discourse on nature and law; and the *Epistles* (known in English as *Love*

Letters), of which one forms the basis of the English poet Ben Jonson's '*Drink to Me Only with Thine Eyes.*'

Phineas (or Phinehas, as it is spelled in the *King James Version* of the Bible) is a character from the Old Testament, who was involved in a particularly violent story told in Numbers 25. God, angry that the Israelites had interbred with other tribes, proceeded to smite them:

> And Israel abode in Shittim, and the people began to commit whoredom with the daughters of Moab. And they called the people unto the sacrifices of their gods: and the people did eat, and bowed down to their gods. And Israel joined himself unto Baalpeor: and the anger of the Lord was kindled against Israel. And the Lord said unto Moses, 'Take all the heads of the people, and hang them up before the Lord against the sun, that the fierce anger of the Lord may be turned away from Israel.' And Moses said unto the judges of Israel, 'Slay ye every one his men that were joined unto Baalpeor.' And, behold, one of the children of Israel came and brought unto his brethren a Midianitish woman in the sight of Moses, and in the sight of all the congregation of the children of Israel, who were weeping before the door of the tabernacle of the congregation. And when Phinehas, the son of Eleazar, the son of Aaron the priest, saw it, he rose up from among the congregation, and took a javelin in his hand; and he went after the man of Israel into the tent, and thrust both of them through, the man of Israel, and the woman through her belly. So the plague was stayed from the children of Israel. And those that died in the plague were twenty and four thousand. And the Lord spake unto Moses, saying, 'Phinehas, the son of Eleazar, the son of Aaron the priest, hath turned my wrath away from the children of Israel, while he was zealous for my sake among them, that I consumed not the children of Israel in my jealousy.' (Num. 25: 1—11).

Phlegon of Tralles (fl. in 2nd century AD), was a Greek writer in Asia Minor and freedman of the emperor Hadrian. His chief work was the *Olympiads*, a historical compendium in sixteen books, from the first down to the two–hundred–and–twenty–ninth Olympiad (776 BC to AD 137), of which several chapters are preserved in Eusebius' *Chronicle*, and in the writing of St Photius and in George the Syncellus, a Byzantine historian. Two small works by Phlegon are extant: *On Marvels*, containing some stories about ghosts, prophecies by heads, monstrous births (Siamese twins), hermaphrodites and giant skeletons, and *On Long–lived Persons*, a list of Italians who had passed the age of one hundred, taken from the Roman censuses.

Phoenicia was an ancient kingdom which roughly corresponds to modern Lebanon. The Phoenicians were noted for being tradesmen, craftsmen and merchants, and their religion—what little is known about it—was based on gods and goddesses who personified natural phenomena.

Phrygia was an ancient district in west–central Anatolia, named after a people whom the Greeks called Phryges and who dominated Asia Minor between the Hittite collapse (twelfth century BC) and the Lydian ascendancy (seventh century BC).

Plato (428/427—348/347 BC) was an ancient Greek philosopher, the second of the great trio of ancient Greeks—Socrates, Plato and Aristotle—who between them laid the philosophical foundations of Western culture. Building on the life and thought of Socrates, Plato developed a profound and wide–ranging system of philosophy. His thought has logical, epistemological and metaphysical aspects; but its underlying motivation is ethical. It sometimes relies upon conjectures and myth, and it is occasionally mystical in tone; but fundamentally Plato was a rationalist, devoted to the proposition that reason must be followed wherever it leads. Thus the core of Plato's philosophy is a system of rational ethics. One aspect of his philosophy, which is particularly relevant to the subject matter in hand, is his theory of the creation of the world and the universe, as discussed primarily in his treatise *Timaeus*, probably written around 361—347 BC. Plato's Creator of the Universe was the Demiurge, an impersonal god—and certainly one not to be worshipped as Yahweh or Jehovah—who fashioned the world *ex nihilo* from a concept in his mind, rather as a carpenter might make a table according to a design he had thought up. Once having made the world, the intervention of this god in the affairs of men was negligible. Plato's idea of a creator god was one of very few theories of creation amongst the ancients. Plato also deals elsewhere (in his treatise *Theaetetus*) with the concept of knowledge and *logos*, the Greek notion of a universal principle of rationality and self–expression. The term *logos* was adopted by John at the beginning of his gospel (translated as 'the Word'), drawn both from the Hebraic notions of the Wisdom (later transformed into the Greek, feminine concept of 'Sophia) and the Word of God, and associated it as a concept with Jesus, the son of God become Christ, as the second Person of the Trinity. The whole concept of the Trinity posed a particularly thorny problem for biblical apologists and the concept caused a great deal of division in the early Church, taking centuries to settle, or rather, to concoct and elaborate, since it has little basis in revealed Scripture: see the essay on church history in the Appendix. D'Holbach makes reference to the concept of *logos* in several places in his treatise: see pp. 62 & 449.

Pliny (The Elder) (AD 23—79) (Latin name in full *Gaius Plinius Secundus*) was a Roman savant and author of the celebrated *Natural History*, an encyclopaedic work of uneven accuracy that was an authority on scientific matters up to the Middle Ages. Pliny's last assignment was that of commander of the fleet in the Bay of Naples, where he was charged with

451

the suppression of piracy. Learning of an unusual cloud formation—later found to have resulted from an eruption of Mt Vesuvius—Pliny went ashore to ascertain the cause and to reassure the terrified citizens, where he was overcome by the fumes resulting from the volcanic activity, and died on 24 August 79, according to his nephew's report. As a writer, Pliny had a penchant for giving credence to unsupported claims, fables and exaggerations. He also had a belief in magic and superstition, which helped shape scientific and medical theory in subsequent centuries. Perhaps the most important of the pseudoscientific methods advocated by him was the doctrine of signatures: a resemblance between the external appearance of a plant, animal, or mineral and the outward symptoms of a disease was thought to indicate the therapeutic usefulness of the plant: hence the plant *Pulmonaria*, common name 'lungwort', which resembled a lung, was believed to be beneficial to lung conditions. Pliny had also been in Palestine for a period of five years, from AD 65 to 70, and yet given his taste for folklore and his proximity to the events of the crucifixion of Christ in terms of both time and location, it seems rather curious that he never mentioned anything to do with Christ—either his passion, or his miracles.

Pliny (The Younger) (AD 61/62—*c.* 113) (Latin name in full *Gaius Plinius Caecilius Secundus*) was a Roman author and administrator who left a collection of private letters of great literary charm, intimately illustrating public and private life in the heyday of the Roman Empire. He was born into a wealthy family and adopted by his uncle, Pliny the Elder, and he began to practise law at the age of eighteen. His reputation in the civil–law courts placed him in demand in the political court which tried provincial officials for extortion. His most notable success was securing condemnation of a governor in Africa and a group of officials from Spain. Meanwhile, he had attained the highest administrative posts, becoming praetor (in AD 93) and consul (AD 100). Pliny had financial ability and successively headed the military treasury and the senatorial treasury (94—100). After administering the drainage board of the city of Rome (104—106), he was sent (*c.* 110) by Emperor Trajan to investigate corruption in the municipal administration of Bithynia, where apparently he died two years later. Like his contemporary, the historian Tacitus (q.v.), Pliny was conventional, accepting the Roman Empire, serving under 'good' and 'bad' emperors, and making the conventional complaints against the latter in his writings. Between 100 and 109 he published nine books of selected private letters, beginning with those covering events from the death of Emperor Domitian (October 97) to the early part of 100. The tenth book contains addresses to Emperor Trajan on sundry official problems and the emperor's replies. One such letter is worth quoting because Christian apologists usually use this letter to 'prove' the piety and determination of early

Christian communities, however there is strong evidence to suggest from the description of their habits, that he is writing about Essenes, and not early Christians.

To the Emperor Trajan

It is my invariable rule, Sir, to refer to you in all matters where I feel doubtful; for who is more capable of removing my scruples, or informing my ignorance? Having never been present at any trials concerning those who profess Christianity, I am unacquainted not only with the nature of their crimes, or the measure of their punishment, but how far it is proper to enter into an examination concerning them. Whether, therefore, any difference is usually made with respect to ages, or no distinction is to be observed between the young and the adult; whether repentance entitles them to a pardon; or if a man has been once a Christian, it avails nothing to desist from his error; whether the very profession of Christianity, unattended with any criminal act, or only the crimes themselves inherent in the profession are punishable; on all these points I am in great doubt. In the meanwhile, the method I have observed towards those who have been brought before me as Christians is this: I asked them whether they were Christians; if they admitted it, I repeated the question twice, and threatened them with punishment; if they persisted, I ordered them to be at once punished: for I was persuaded, whatever the nature of their opinions might be, a contumacious and inflexible obstinacy certainly deserved correction. There were others also brought before me possessed with the same infatuation, but being Roman citizens, I directed them to be sent to Rome. But this crime spreading (as is usually the case) while it was actually under prosecution, several instances of the same nature occurred. Anonymous information was laid before me containing a charge against several persons, who upon examination denied they were Christians, or had ever been so. They repeated after me an invocation to the gods, and offered religious rites with wine and incense before your statue (which for that purpose I had ordered to be brought, together with those of the gods), and even reviled the name of Christ: whereas there is no forcing, it is said, those who are really Christians into any of these compliances: I thought it proper, therefore, to discharge them. Some among those who were accused by a witness in person at first confessed themselves Christians, but immediately after denied it; the rest owned indeed that they had been of that number formerly, but had now (some above three, others more, and a few above twenty years ago) renounced that error. They all worshipped your statue and the images of the gods, uttering imprecations at the same time against the name of Christ. They affirmed the whole of their guilt, or their error, was, that they met on a stated day before it was light, and addressed a form of prayer to Christ, as to a divinity, binding themselves by a solemn oath, not for the purposes of any wicked design, but never to commit any fraud, theft, or adultery, never to falsify their word, nor deny a trust when they should be called upon to deliver it up; after which it was their custom to separate, and then reassemble, to eat in common a harmless meal. From this custom, however, they desisted after the publication of my edict, by which, according to your commands, I forbade the meeting of any assemblies. After receiving this account, I judged it so much the more necessary to endeavour to extort the real truth, by putting two female slaves to the torture, who were said to officiate in their religious rites: but all I could discover was evidence of an absurd and extravagant superstition. I deemed it expedient, therefore, to adjourn all further proceedings, in order to consult you. For it appears to be a matter highly deserving your consideration, more especially as great numbers must be involved in the danger of these prosecutions, which have already extended, and are still likely to extend, to persons of all ranks and ages, and even of both sexes. In fact, this contagious superstition is not confined to the cities only, but has spread its infection among the neighbouring villages and country. Nevertheless, it still seems possible to restrain its progress. The temples, at least, which were once almost deserted, begin now to be frequented; and the sacred rites, after a long intermission, are again revived; while there is a general demand for the victims, which till lately found very few purchasers. From all this it is easy to conjecture what numbers might be reclaimed if a general pardon were granted to those who shall repent of their error. (Pliny, *Letters*, № XCVII.)

Plutarch (AD 46—*c.* 119) (name in Greek *Plutarchos*, and in Latin *Plutarchus*) was a biographer and author, whose works strongly influenced the evolution of the essay, the biography and historical writing in Europe from the sixteenth to the nineteenth century. Among his approximately 227 works, the most important are the *Bioi parallēloi {Parallel Lives}*, in which he recounts the noble deeds and characters of Greek and Roman soldiers, legislators, orators and statesmen, and the *Moralia* or *Ethica*, a series of more than sixty essays on ethical, religious, physical, political and literary topics. By his own admission, Plutarch was less concerned about factual events, favouring the character of those whose lives he described:

> It is not histories I am writing, but lives; and in the most glorious deeds there is not always an indication of virtue of vice, indeed a small thing like a phrase or a jest often makes a greater revelation of a character than battles where thousands die. (Plutarch, *Life of Alexander/Life of Julius Caesar, Parallel Lives.*)

However, he makes not a single mention of Jesus, though it must be stated clearly that it is estimated that possibly up to a half of the corpus of Plutarch's work has not survived.

Pomponazzi, Pietro (1462—1525) (name in Latin *Petrus Pomponatius*) was an Italian philosopher and an alchemist. He was a leading representative of Renaissance Aristotelianism who interpreted Aristotle in the light of the Humanism of his own time. He wrote a treatise on the immortality of the soul, *Tractatus de immortalitate animae* (1516), which was publicly burned in Venice during the Italian Inquisition because it maintained that the soul was not immortal: it followed the ideas of Aristotle, rather than those of the Church. He managed to escape personal persecution because he enjoyed the protection of a cardinal. His other main works were published after his death, i.e., *De incantationibus* {*On Incantations*} (1556), which proposed a natural explanation for several reputedly miraculous phenomena, and *De fato* {*On Fate*} (1567), which discusses predestination and free will.

Porphyry (*c.* AD 234—*c.* 305) (original name Malchus) was a Neo-Platonist Greek philosopher, important both as an editor and as a biographer of the philosopher Plotinus and for his commentary on Aristotle's Categories, which set the stage for medieval developments of logic and the problem of universals. Porphyry's original Syrian name (meaning *king*) was Hellenize at Athens by Cassius Longinus, his teacher of rhetoric (the new name signifying 'imperial purple', an allusion to the status of a king). Porphyry studied philosophy in Rome (263—268?) under Plotinus, who gently rescued him from a suicidal depression. In 301 he produced his most important work, *Enneads*, a systematized and edited collection of the works of Plotinus to which was prefixed a biography, unique for its reliability and informativeness. Porphyry's voluminous writings extended to philosophy, religion, philology and science, and show scholarly care in citing authorities. Surviving fragments of his *Against the Christians*, a work in fifteen books, which was condemned in 448 to be burned, marked him as a fierce critic of the 'new religion'. He wrote other anti–Christian works, notably his *Preparation of the Gospel* and *Demonstration of the Gospel*, against which Eusebius wrote a refutation, which has not survived. He also lectured on Plotinus and was tutor to the Syrian philosopher Iamblichus. He wrote a life of the mathematician Pythagoras and preserved precious fragments of earlier philosophy in his *On Abstinence*, a plea for vegetarianism.

Prétextat (date of birth unknown) was Bishop of Rouen, who was assassinated in 586 on the orders of Fredegund, queen consort of Chilperic I, the Merovingian Frankish king of Soissons. He incurred Fredegund's ire by criticizing her and denouncing her behaviour. He became a saint and his feast day is celebrated on 24 February.

Priestley, Joseph (1733—1804) was an English clergyman, political theorist and physical scientist whose work contributed to advances in liberal political and religious thought, and in experimental chemistry. He is best remembered for his contribution to the chemistry of gases.

Purgatory & Limbo in the Roman Catholic faith (the only sect to embrace this idea) are the place or condition of punishment for those who have died in God's grace but have not been purged of venial sins, or have not sought full atonement for their sins: these souls had thus to be purified before entering heaven. The origins of the idea of purgatory can be traced to religions of the ancient Middle East, and especially to the Jewish and Christian Scriptures, though there is nothing precise in canonical Christian scripture to suggest the existence of such a place. The notion of purgatory inherited general characteristics from the Jewish view of the underworld and, according to Christian theologians, was prefigured in II Maccabees 12: 42—45:

> Besides, that noble Judas exhorted the people to keep themselves from sin, forsomuch as they saw before their eyes the things that came to pass for the sins of those that were slain. And when he had made a gathering throughout the company to the sum of two thousand drachms of silver, he sent it to Jerusalem to offer a sin offering, doing therein very well and honestly, in that he was mindful of the resurrection: For if he had not hoped that they that were slain should have risen again, it had been superfluous and vain to pray for the dead. And also in that he perceived that there was great favour laid up for those that died godly, it was an holy and good thought. Whereupon he made a reconciliation for the dead, that they might be delivered from sin.

It has to be said that this is a pretty thin pretext on which to establish the whole concept of Purgatory, as invented by the Catholic Church. Christian Scriptures and the Apocrypha also contain indirect references to the idea. The most important allusions to it may be found in Paul's Epistle to the Romans and in the story of Lazarus in Luke's Gospel, which mentions souls resting in the 'bosom of Abraham': 'And it came to pass, that the beggar died, and was carried by the angels into Abraham's bosom: the rich man also died, and was buried; And in hell he lift up his eyes, being in torments, and seeth Abraham afar off, and Lazarus in his bosom', (Luke 16: 22—23).

Beda venerabilis

Figure 83: The Venerable Bede, from the *Nuremberg Chronicle* (1493).

During late antiquity and the early Middle Ages, the idea of purgatory developed as a place of temporal punishment or brief sojourn before admittance into heaven. Theologians, beginning with St Augustine, cultivated the idea and references to it appear in a variety of sources, including Bede's history: in his *Historia Ecclesiastica gentis Anglorum* {*The Ecclesiastical History of the English People*} (completed around 732), he tells the story of '*How Queen Etheldrida always preserved her virginity, and her body suffered no corruption in the grave*', (Book IV, ch. 19), despite the fact that she had been married for twelve years and buried for sixteen, after which her exhumed body was found to be 'uncorrupted'. The woman is instantly dubbed a 'bride of Christ' and a poem follows in the following chapter (20), lauding virginity and affirming that the faithful shall pass into 'greater glories' which 'await them above the spheres'.

Figure 84: Gustave Doré's dipiction of Purgatory for Dante's *Purgatorio*, Canto XXIV.

As part of a broader wave of systematization during the twelfth and thirteenth centuries, the teachings concerning purgatory were refined by scholastic theologians such as Peter Lombard and Thomas Aquinas. The idea received its most famous treatment, however, in the second book of Dante's *Divine Comedy*. Finally, the councils of Lyon (1274), Florence (1438—45), and Trent (1545—63) provided official sanction and

457

authoritative definition to the teaching of the theologians. The other place for interim suffering is Limbo, which, in Roman Catholic theology, is the border place between heaven and hell where souls, not condemned to be punished, are deprived of entry to heaven. The word is of Teutonic origin, meaning *border*, or *anything adjoining*. The concept of Limbo probably developed in the European Middle Ages. The question of the destiny of infants dying unbaptized presented itself to Christian theologians at a relatively early period. Many theologians were squeamish about the idea of consigning innocent children directly to Hell, despite the fact that their inherited sin from Adam demanded that they be so confined, so the invention of Limbo seemed to be a good compromise, without appearing too vicious. The concept of Limbo remained rather vague and ill–defined in modern Roman Catholic doctrine. After peddling for centuries this bizarre compromise of salvation, the Vatican recently reformed its ideas, acting on the advice of a papal committee, which had been discussing the concept of Limbo for years—what an interesting symposium that must have made! The Vatican's International Theological Commission recommended, in a forty–one–page report (no less!) that, 'Our conclusion is that there are serious theological and liturgical grounds for hope that unbaptized infants who die will be saved and brought into eternal happiness.' The panel added that while this is not 'sure knowledge', it comes in the context of a loving and just God who 'wants all human beings to be saved'. (*Los Angeles Times*, 21 April 2007—one of many newspapers to report the findings and recommendations of the commission.)

Pyrrhon/Pyrrhonisn/Pyrrhonist. Pyrrhon of Elis (*c.* 360—272 BC) (also spelt *Pyrrho*) was a Greek philosopher from whom Pyrrhonism takes its name; he is generally accepted as the father of Scepticism. A former pupil of Anaxarchus of Abdera, he established himself as a teacher at Elis in 330 BC. Believing that equal arguments can be offered on both sides of any proposition, he dismissed the search for truth as a vain endeavour. While travelling with an expedition under Alexander the Great, Pyrrhon saw in the fakirs of India an example of happiness flowing from their indifference to circumstances. He concluded that man must suspend judgment (or practise *epochē*) on the reliability of sense perceptions and simply live according to reality as it appeared. Pyrrhonism permeated the Middle and New Academy of Athens and strongly influenced philosophical thought in seventeenth–century Europe with the republication of the Sceptical works of Sextus Empiricus, who had codified Greek Scepticism in the third century AD. Pyrrhon's teaching was preserved in the poems of Timon of Phlius, who studied with him.

Pythagoras (*c.* 580—*c.* 500 BC) was a Greek philosopher, mathematician, and founder of the Pythagorean brotherhood. He settled in Croton in southern Italy in about 525 BC and established the Pythagoreans who, although religious in nature, formulated principles that influenced the thought of Plato and Aristotle, and contributed to the development of mathematics and Western rational philosophy. Their fame rests on some very influential ideas, which include those of; (i) the metaphysics of number and the conception that reality, including music and astronomy, is at its deepest level mathematical in nature; (ii) the use of philosophy as a means of spiritual purification; (iii) the heavenly destiny of the soul and the possibility of its rising to a union with the divine; (iv) the appeal to certain mystical symbols; (v) the Pythagorean theorem; and (vi) the demand that members of the order shall observe a strict loyalty and secrecy. By laying stress on certain inner experiences and intuitive truths revealed only to the initiated, Pythagoreanism seems to have represented a soul–directed subjectivism alien to the mainstream of pre–Socratic Greek thought, centring on the Ionian coast of Asia Minor (Thales, Anaximander, Anaxagoras and others), which was preoccupied with determining what the basic cosmic substance is. In contrast with such Ionian naturalism, Pythagoreanism was akin to trends seen in mystery religions and emotional movements, such as Orphism, which often claimed to achieve a spiritual insight into the divine origin and nature of the soul through intoxication. Yet there are also aspects of it that appear to have owed much to the more sober, 'Homeric' philosophy of the Ionians. The Pythagoreans, for example, displayed an interest in metaphysics (the nature of Being), as did their naturalistic predecessors, though they claimed to find its key in mathematical form, rather than in any substance. They accepted the essentially Ionian doctrines that the world is composed of opposites (wet–dry, hot–cold, etc.) and generated from something unlimited; but they added the idea of the imposition of limit upon the unlimited and the sense of a musical harmony in the universe. Again, like the Ionians, they devoted themselves to astronomical and geometrical speculation. Combining, as it does, a rationalistic theory of number with a mystic numerology and a speculative cosmology with a theory of the deeper, more enigmatic reaches of the soul, Pythagoreanism interweaves rationalism and irrationalism more inseparably than does any other movement in ancient Greek thought.

Quaker was the name given to a member of a religious sect known also as 'Friends' Church', or 'The Religious Society of Friends', a Christian group that arose in mid–seventeenth–century England, dedicated to living in accordance with the 'Inward Light', or direct inward apprehension of God, without creeds, clergy or other ecclesiastical forms. As most powerfully expressed by George Fox (1624—91), Friends felt that their 'experimental' discovery of God would lead to the purification of all of Christendom. Friends founded one American colony and were dominant for a time in several others, and though their numbers are now comparatively small, they continue to make disproportionate contributions to science, industry, and especially to the Christian effort for social reform.

Quintilian (AD 35—96) (name in Latin in full *Marcus Fabius Quintilianus*) was a Latin teacher and writer, whose work on rhetoric, *Institutio oratoria* {*Institutes of Oratory*}, is a major contribution to educational theory and literary criticism. Quintilian was born in northern Spain, but he was probably educated in Rome, where afterward he received some practical training from the leading orator of the day, Domitius Afer. He then practised for a time as an advocate in the law courts. He left for his native Spain sometime after AD 57, but returned to Rome in 68 and began to teach rhetoric, combining this with advocacy in the law courts. Under the emperor Vespasian (ruled 69—79), he became the first teacher to receive a state salary for teaching Latin rhetoric, and he also held his position as Rome's leading teacher under the emperors Titus and Domitian, retiring probably in 88. Toward the end of Domitian's reign (81—96), he was entrusted with the education of the Emperor's two heirs (his grandnephews), and through the good agency of the boys' father, Flavius Clemens, he was given the honorary title of consul (*ornamenta consularia*). His own death, which probably took place soon after Domitian's assassination, was preceded by that of his young wife and two sons. Quintilian's great work, the *Institutio oratoria,* in twelve books, was published shortly before the end of his life. He believed that the entire educational process, from infancy onward, was relevant to his major theme of training an orator. During his general discussion of invention, he also considers the successive, formal parts of a speech, including a lively chapter on the art of arousing laughter.

Ramsay, Allan (1686—1758) was a Scottish poet and literary antiquary, who maintained national poetic traditions by writing Scots poetry and by preserving the work of earlier Scottish poets at a time when most Scottish writers had been Anglicized. He was admired by Robert Burns as a pioneer in the use of Scots in contemporary poetry. His *Fables and Tales* (1722—30) includes versions of the fables of Jean de La Fontaine and Antoine Houdar de La Motte in Scots.

Ravaillac, François (1578—1610) was a fanatical Roman Catholic who assassinated King Henry IV of France in Paris on 14 May 1610. When Henry III was murdered (1589), Épernon, one of the most powerful new magnates in French politics at the turn of the seventeenth century, at first refused to serve Henry IV, who was then still a Protestant, and he even made a secret treaty with Spain. However, when Henry was established as king, Épernon appeared at court posing as a loyal subject. He joined in every conspiracy of the reign without ever being caught and there are grounds for believing that he helped to arrange the murder of the king by François Ravaillac, who is known to have received money from Épernon's mistress, Catherine du Tillet, and who was kept in protective custody by Épernon for a whole day after the murder.

Raynal, Guillaume–Thomas, abbé de (1713—1796) was a writer on history and a propagandist. He was educated by the Jesuits and joined their order, which he abandoned for a career in writing. He edited the literary journal *Mercure de France* from 1750 to 1754. His chief work was a huge six–volume history of the East and West Indies entitled *Histoire des deux Indes* {*History of the Two Indias*}, initially published in 1770, and subsequently expanded. In the work, he denounced European cruelty carried out in the colonies, which was largely fuelled by religious intolerance. Needless to say, the work was placed on the Vatican's *Index of Prohibited Books* (q.v.) and condemned to be burned, as a consequence of which he was forced into exile in Switzerland.

Romilly, Samuel (Sir) (1757—1818) was an English legal reformer whose chief efforts were devoted to lessening the severity of English criminal law. His attacks on the laws authorizing capital punishment for a host of minor felonies and misdemeanours, such as begging by soldiers and sailors without a permit, were partly successful during his lifetime and contributed to reforms carried out after his death. Called to the bar in 1783, Romilly became known as the outstanding chancery lawyer in England and served as chancellor of Durham from 1805 to 1815. In 1806 he was appointed Solicitor General and entered the House of Commons, and he was knighted. Influenced by the libertarianism of Jean–Jacques Rousseau (q.v.), he supported the French Revolution in its early stages, though conservative reaction in England to the revolution's excesses subsequently hindered his work. His vision for the mitigation of punishment in criminal law was based in part on the criminology of Cesare Beccaria and the utilitarian philosophy of Jeremy Bentham. Distressed by the death of his wife, Romilly committed suicide in 1818. His *Memoirs* appeared in 1840.

Rousseau, Jean–Jacques (1712—1778) was a French philosopher, writer and political theorist of considerable importance in the tradition of French thought. He was of a very modest class by birth, but he was taken under the wing of a Savoy benefactress named the Baronne de Warens, who provided him with a refuge in her home, employing him as her steward. She also furthered his education to such a degree that the boy who had arrived on her doorstep as a stammering apprentice, never having attended school, developed into a philosopher, a man of letters and a musician.

When Rousseau arrived in Paris at the age of thirty, he met another young man from the provinces seeking literary fame in the capital—Denis Diderot (q.v.), through whom he gained access to all the most brilliant minds of France at the time on account of their efforts on the *Encyclopédie*. He wrote music as well as prose, and one of his operas, *Le Devin du village* {*The Village Soothsayer*} (1752), attracted universal admiration—not least from the king and his court. When an Italian opera company arrived in Paris in 1752 to perform works of *opera buffa* (generally short, comic operas) by Pergolesi, Scarlatti and others, such works suddenly divided the French music–loving public into two excited camps—those who supported the new Italian opera, and those who adhered to the traditional French opera. The *philosophes* of the *Encyclopédie*—d'Alembert, Diderot and d'Holbach among them—entered the fray as champions of Italian music, and Rousseau, who was a very knowledgeable musician, led the campaign for the reform of French music, arguing for much greater freedom of expression and form, breaking with the strictures of French Classicism. One of Rousseau's first major works of philosophy was his *Discours sur l'origine de l'inegalité* {*Discourse on the Origin of Inequality*} (1755), which distinguishes between two kinds of inequality—natural and artificial; the first arising from differences in strength, intelligence, etc., the second from societal conventions. It is the inequalities of the latter sort that he sets out to explain. He totally rejected the concept of man fallen from God's grace through Adam, etc., i.e., the concept of original sin, as expounded in Genesis and as taught by the Catholic Church, amongst other religions. Rousseau shows how men are different from animals in that they have the ability not to follow their instinct and so they are at liberty to make rational choices. He also expressed his belief in man's ability to improve and perfect his own surroundings or the society in which he lives. All these ideas conjoin to reject the rather dismal, hopeless position of man, wallowing in a state of original sin, which required God's grace to haul mankind out of the mire engendered by the Fall. In his second major work, *Du Contrat social* {*The Social Contract*} (1762), Rousseau begins with the sensational opening sentence: 'Man was born free, but everywhere he is in chains', and proceeds to argue that men need not remain so. If a civil society or state could be based on a genuine social contract, as opposed to the fraudulent social contract depicted in the *Discourse on the Origin of Inequality*, men would receive, in exchange for their independence, a better kind of freedom, namely true political, or republican, liberty. Such liberty is to be found in obedience to a self–imposed law. In 1762, upon the publication of his treatise on education *Émile*, the pious Jansenists of the French *Parlements* were scandalized and an order was issued to burn the book: Rousseau spent the rest of his life as a fugitive moving from one refuge to another. Although its subtitle is *On*

Education, it is basically a treatise on the nature of man and Rousseau states his view that mankind is basically good, which flies in the face of the Christian view of man as 'fallen' and in a desperate need of God's grace and salvation. He wrote his memoirs, which he called in French *Confessions* {*Confessions*} (1781—1788), which contain a frank account of his intellectual and sexual development, though seen very much from his own point of view: he was paranoid and apt to see conspiracies and ill–will directed at him everywhere, even when there were probably none.

Roux, Auguste (1726—1776) was a French doctor and an editor of the prestigious *Journal de Médicine* {*Journal of Medicine*}. He was appointed professor of the Faculty of Medicine in Paris in 1771 and he was the author of several works on medicine and natural history. (Source: *Brokhaus and Efron Encyclopaedia*, {in Russian}, St Petersburg, 1890—1916.)

Sadducees q.v. **Pharisees**.

Saint–Lambert, Jean–François de (1716—1803) served in the French army, after which he dedicated himself to literature, principally poetry, and then to philosophy. He wrote many articles for the *Encyclopédie*. As a close friend of d'Holbach, it was he who took the manuscript of *Christianity Unveiled* to be printed and published in the strictest secrecy.

Samuel (fl. in 11th century BC) (Hebrew name is *Shmu'el*) was a religious hero in the history of Israel, represented in the Old Testament in every role of leadership open to a Jewish man of his day—seer, priest, judge, prophet and military leader. His greatest distinction was his role in the establishment of the monarchy in Israel. Information about Samuel is contained in The First Book of Samuel (called in the Roman Catholic canon or *Vulgate* 'The First Book of Kings'). The ancient designation of the two books of Samuel does not indicate that he is the author—in fact, his death is related in I Sam. 25. Therefore, it is difficult to deduce what the title was intended to mean. On the orders of Yahweh, Samuel anointed Saul as king over the Israelites (chapters 9—10). Saul was vindicated as king by his leadership of Israel in a campaign against the Ammonites (chapter 11); after this, Samuel retired from the leadership of Israel (chapter 12). He reappeared, however, to announce the oracle of Yahweh, rejecting Saul as king, once for arrogating to himself the right of sacrifice (chapter 13), and a second time for failing to carry out Yahweh's instructions over the spoils of war after defeating the Amalekites (chapter 15). By the oracle of Yahweh, Samuel secretly anointed David as king (chapter 16). He then faded into the background, appearing at the sanctuary of Naioth (chapter 19). He died and his ghost was evoked by a necromancer or sorceress, at the request of Saul, a practice which is condemned as sinful in the text. He then announced a third time the rejection of Saul (chapter 28). D'Holbach makes reference to Samuel and Saul's behaviour in I Kgs. 15 (*King James Version*)—see p. 55 & also p. 446. When Saul did not carry out God's orders and kept back some of the possessions of the people of Amalec (or Amalek), Samuel becomes enraged and takes his temper out on one of the opposing kings, i.e., King Agag, who is summarily executed by him, as narrated in I Kgs. 15 (*Vulgate*), or I Sam. 15 (*King James Version*). The execution of Agag is particularly gruesome, especially as narrated in the *Vulgate*:

> And Samuel said: 'Bring hither to me Agag, the king of Amalec.' And Agag was presented to him very fat, and trembling. And Agag said: 'Doth bitter death separate in this manner?' And Samuel said: 'As thy sword hath made women childless, so shall thy mother be childless among women.' And Samuel hewed him in pieces before the Lord in Galgal. (1 Kgs. 15, *Vulg.*)

D'Holbach's opinion of Samuel is revealed in his *Portable Theology*, where he notes that Samuel was a 'cantankerous, Jewish prophet who had never studied human rights in Grotius or Pufendorf: he hacked to pieces kings of other countries and appointed and sacked kings from amongst his own people. Otherwise, he was a good man, so long as one shared his opinions.' Grotius (1583—1645) was a Dutch jurist and scholar whose masterpiece *De Jure Belli ac Pacis* {*On the Law of War and Peace*} (1625) is considered one of the greatest contributions to the development of international law, and Pufendorf (1632—1694) was a German jurist and historian, best known for his defence of the idea of natural law.

Samson (in Hebrew *Shimshon*) was an Israelite hero portrayed in an epic narrative in the Old Testament (Judg. 13—16). He was a Nazirite (one set aside for God by a vow to abstain from strong drink, shaving, hair–cutting and from contact with corpses), and a legendary warrior, whose incredible exploits hint at the weight of Philistine pressure on Israel during much of the early, tribal period of Israel in Canaan (1200—1000). The Book of Judges ranks him with other divinely inspired warriors who delivered the community to establish themselves as its judges. Samson is reputed to possess extraordinary physical strength and the moral of his saga relates the disastrous loss of his power to the violation of his Nazirite vow. Credited with remarkable exploits, such as the slaying of a lion and moving the gates of Gaza, he first broke his religious promises by feasting with a woman who was also a Philistine, one of Israel's mortal enemies. Other remarkable deeds followed, such as his decimating the Philistines in a private war. On another occasion he repulsed their assault on him at Gaza, where he had gone to visit a prostitute. He finally fell victim to his foes through the love of Delilah, who tricked him into revealing the secret of his strength, i.e., his long, uncut hair, which she proceeded to cut, thus betraying him whilst he slept. He was captured, blinded and enslaved by the Philistines, but in the end he was granted his revenge: through the return of his old strength, he demolished the great Philistine temple of the god Dagon at Gaza, destroying his captors and himself (Judg. 16: 4—30).

Figure 85: *Death of Samson*. Plate from *The Doré Gallery of Bible Illustrations* (1870).

Saul—see under **Samuel**.

Saurin (1659—1737) was a French mathematician. He was the son of a Protestant minister and brother of a Protestant theologian; he became a minister of religion himself in 1684. His preaching and views soon attracted enemies from the Church and he emigrated to Switzerland for a while, but he had to leave, having also become embroiled in religious disputes there. He converted to Catholicism in 1690 and returned to live in France. He published widely on mathematics and edited the *Journal des savants {Scientists' Journal}*, a platform for intellectual and scientific debate and the earliest scientific journal to be published in Europe. He also became a member of the French Academy of Science. He spent a number of months in prison for allegedly publishing some blasphemous poems in 1710, after which time he spent the rest of his life working on differential calculus.

Seneca (4 BC—AD 65) (known as *Seneca the Younger*) was a Roman philosopher, statesman, orator and tragedian. He was Rome's leading intellectual figure in the mid–first century AD and was virtual ruler with his friends of the Roman world between 54 and 62 during the first phase of the Emperor Nero's reign and he had been Nero's tutor. Although a contemporary of the disciples and of Christ himself, Seneca makes not a single mention of any New Testament story, or even of the existence of Christ. It is also strange that St Paul, who was such an important figure in the early Christian Church, was never mentioned in the writing of such influential men as Seneca: there is not a single mention of Paul among any Jewish or Roman contemporaries. Conscious of this fact, a series of letters was forged in the fourth century, claiming to be correspondence between St Paul and Seneca, with the express aim of raising Paul's profile and status: the false letters have Seneca praising Paul for his intellectual brilliance and they affirm that his letters have been read out to none other than Nero himself, as a mark of their brilliance. These letters can be read in Bart Ehrman's *Lost Scriptures: Books that Did Not Make It into the New Testament* (Oxford: OUP, 2003), pp. 160—164.

Septfonds Monks were those who established a monastery in the region of Tarne–et–Garonne in the early part of the twelfth century, which grew to comprise the whole town. The abbey was called *Sancta Maria de Septem Fontibus* or *Holy Mary of the Seven Fountains*. Hostility from Henry II, the King of England, forced the monks to depart from the town which fell into disrepair. Its fortunes were revived in the mid–thirteenth century, but religious disputes and wars in the sixteenth century caused its downfall again.

Figure 86: *Nadie nos ha visto* [Nobody has seen us], from *Los Caprichos*, Goya (1799).

Servetus, Michael (1511?–1553) (in Spanish *Miguel Servet*) was a Spanish physician and theologian whose unorthodox teachings led to his condemnation as a heretic by both Protestants and Roman Catholics, and to his execution by Calvinists from Geneva. While living in Toulouse, Servetus studied law and delved into the problem of the Trinity. In

February 1530, he accompanied his patron, the Franciscan Juan de Quintana, to the coronation of Emperor Charles V at Bologna. Distressed by papal ostentation and by the emperor's deference to the worldly pope, he left his patron and visited Lyon, Geneva and Basle. In Basle and Strasbourg he met with various Reformation leaders. Servetus published his new ideas on the Trinity in *De Trinitatis erroribus libri vii {On Errors of the Trinity}* (1531), attacking orthodox teaching and attempting to form a view of his own, which was mystical and beyond canonical scriptural teaching. Although both Catholics and Protestants may have had difficulty following Servetus' involved speculations, what he proposed was clearly odious to them. He therefore published a revised formulation, *Dialogorum de Trinitate libri ii {Two Dialogues on the Trinity}* (1532). Later he published a work on astrology, maintaining that the stars influenced health; despite attacks by the medical faculty, he matriculated in medicine at Paris in 1538 and subsequently became physician to the archbishop at Vienne, France. Servetus remained outwardly a conforming Catholic while pursuing his private theological studies. Soon he published his most important work at Lyon, his *Biblia sacra ex Santis Pagnini tra[ns]latione {Translation of the Holy Bible from the St Pagnini Version}* (1542), notable for its theory of prophecy. Servetus forwarded the manuscript of an enlarged revision of his ideas, the *Christianismi Restitutio {The Restoration of Christianity}*, to Calvin in 1546 and expressed a desire to meet him. After their first few letters, Calvin would have nothing more to do with him and kept the manuscript. He declared to his eloquent French preacher colleague Guillaume Farel that if Servetus ever came to Geneva, he would not allow him to leave alive. When some of Servetus' letters to Calvin fell into the hands of Guillaume de Trie, a former citizen of Lyon, he exposed Servetus to the inquisitor general at Lyon. Servetus and his printers were seized. During the trial, however, Servetus escaped and the Catholic authorities had to be content with burning an effigy of him. He quixotically appeared in Geneva and was recognized, arrested and tried for heresy in 1553. Calvin played a prominent part in the trial and pressed for execution, although by beheading rather than by fire. Despite his intense bible–based belief and his wholly Christ–centred view of the universe, Servetus was found guilty of heresy, mainly on his views of the Trinity and Baptism. He was burned alive at Champel. The eminent theologian Calvin, the darling of Christian Fundamentalists and Reformed Church believers, seemed to have forgotten to love his neighbour and the Sixth Commandment, 'Thou shalt not kill (or murder)'. What men of god will do when they know they are right!

Figure 87: Michael Servetus—note him being burned at the stake.

Figure 88: John Calvin (1509—1564).

Shaftesbury (1671—1713) was an English politician and philosopher, grandson of the famous 1st earl and one of the principal English Deists. His early education was directed by John Locke, and he attended Winchester College. He entered Parliament in 1695 and, succeeding as 3rd Earl of Shaftesbury in 1699, attended Parliament regularly in the House of Lords for the remainder of William III's reign. He pursued an independent policy in the House of Lords as well as in the House of Commons. In July 1702 he retired from public life. Shaftesbury's philosophy owed something to the Cambridge Platonists, who had stressed the existence in man of a natural moral sense. Shaftesbury advanced this concept against both the orthodox Christian doctrine of the Fall and against the premise that the state of nature was a state of unavoidable warfare. Shaftesbury's Neo-Platonism, his contention that what man sees of beauty or truth is only a shadow of absolute beauty or truth, dominated his attitude to religion and to the arts. During his lifetime his fame as a writer was comparatively slight, for he published little before 1711; in that year appeared his *Characteristicks of Men, Manners, Opinions, Times*, in which his chief works were assembled. The effect of this book was immediate and was felt in Europe, as well as in England; in fact, English Deism was transmitted to Germany almost entirely through translations of his writings. Alexander Pope, Joseph Butler, Francis Hutcheson, Mark Akenside, Samuel Taylor

Coleridge and Immanuel Kant were among those who were, to some degree, affected by Shaftesbury.

Shaker was the name given to a member of the United Society of Believers in Christ's Second Appearing, a celibate millenarian group which established communal settlements in the United States in the eighteenth century. Based on the revelations of Ann Lee and her vision of the heavenly kingdom to come, Shaker teaching emphasized simplicity, celibacy and work. Shaker communities flourished in the mid–nineteenth century and contributed a distinctive style of architecture, furniture and handicraft to American culture. The communities declined in the late nineteenth and early twentieth centuries. The Shakers derived originally from a small branch of English Quakers founded by Jane and James Wardley in 1747. They may have adopted the French Camisard's ritual practices of shaking, shouting, dancing, whirling and singing in tongues while in a state of religious ecstasy. The Shaker doctrine, as it came to be known in the United States, was formulated by Ann Lee, a textile worker in Manchester. 'Mother Ann', as she was known to her followers, had a troubled marriage and had suffered difficulties while pregnant (she had four children, all of whom died young), and in 1758 she converted to the 'Shaking Quakers'. After enduring persecution and imprisonment for participation in noisy worship services, she had a series of revelations: from then on she regarded herself and was considered by her followers as the female aspect of God's dual nature (e.g., male and female), and the second Incarnation of Christ. She developed an elaborate theology and established celibacy as the cardinal principle of the community. In 1774 Mother Ann came to America with eight disciples, having been charged by a new revelation to establish the millennial church in the New World. Settling in 1776 at Niskeyuna (now Watervliet), New York, the small group benefited from an independent revival movement that was sweeping the district, and within five years it grew to several thousand members. After Mother Ann's death (1784), the Shaker Church came under the leadership of Elder Joseph Meacham and Eldress Lucy Wright. Together they worked out the distinctive pattern of Shaker social organization, which consisted of celibate communities of men and women living together in dormitory–style houses and holding all things in common. The first Shaker community, established at New Lebanon, New York, in 1787, retained leadership of the movement as it spread through New England and westward into Kentucky, Ohio and Indiana. By 1826, eighteen Shaker villages had been set up in eight states. Although often persecuted for pacifism or for bizarre beliefs falsely attributed to them, the Shakers won admiration for their model farms, orderly and prosperous communities, and fair dealing with outsiders. Their industry and ingenuity produced numerous (usually unpatented) inventions, including, among other things, the screw propeller, babbitt metal, a rotary harrow, an automatic spring, a turbine waterwheel, a threshing machine, the circular saw and the common clothespin. They were the first to package and market seeds and were once the largest producers of medicinal herbs in the United States. At the turn of the twenty–first century, there was one working Shaker village left— Sabbathday Lake, near New Gloucester, Maine; it had fewer than ten members. As d'Holbach points out in his *Christianity Unveiled*, any community founded on celibacy is bound to die out.

Sibyl (also called *Sibylla*) was a prophetess in Greek legend and literature. Tradition represented her as a woman of prodigious old age uttering predictions in ecstatic frenzy, but she was always a figure of the mythical past and her prophecies, delivered in Greek hexameters, were handed down in writing. In the fifth and early fourth centuries BC, she was always referred to in the singular; *Sibylla* was regarded as her proper name and she was reputed to be located in Asia Minor. From the late fourth century the number of sibyls was multiplied; they were localized traditionally at all the famous oracle centres and elsewhere, particularly in association with Apollo, and were distinguished by individual names, 'sibyl' being treated as a title. A famous collection of sibylline prophecies, the *Sibylline Books*, was traditionally offered for sale to Tarquinius Superbus, the last of the seven kings of Rome, by the Cumaean sibyl. He refused to pay her price, so the sibyl burned six of the books before finally selling him the remaining three at the price she had originally asked for all nine. The books were thereafter kept in the temple of Jupiter on the Capitoline Hill, to be consulted only in emergencies. A Judaean or Babylonian sibyl was credited with writing the Judeo–Christian *Sibylline Oracles*. Thus the sibyl came to be regarded by some Christians as a prophetic authority, comparable to the Old Testament. The concept of a pagan religion based on written texts is unusual, as opposed to the Judaic and Christian traditions, which based all their beliefs on sacred texts: in this sense, the Jews, Christians, and later the adherents of Islam, were all in a very real sense, 'people of the book', i.e., they all had written texts on which their faith was founded. The Koran refers to 'people of the book' chiefly to refer to those non–Muslims who revere the Jewish and Christian scriptures because they recognize that God has revealed himself through prophets, such as Abraham and Christ.

Siculus, Diodorus (fl. in 1st century BC in Sicily) was a Greek historian, the author of a universal history, *Bibliotheca historica* {*Library of History*}. He lived at the time of Julius Caesar and Augustus and it is clear from his own statements that he travelled in Egypt around 60—57 BC. Diodorus' *World history* was, in his own words, 'an immense work' that consisted of forty books, of which 1—5 and 11—20 have survived completely. (The last complete copy vanished when the Turks sacked Constantinople in 1453.) Bergier mentions Diodorus Siculus in his refutation in his defence of Moses, whom d'Holbach criticized (see p. 202), but what Diodorus says about Moses is hardly anything like an endorsement, let alone praising him as a man of honour and wisdom. The following passage from a fragment of Book VII (the only reference to Moses) shows Diodorus' views and attitude to life, which is one of using the law and the belief in gods of any description to keep law and order:

> For amongst the Egyptians, it is a sacred constitution, that they should at their greatest costs honour their parents and ancestors, who are translated to an eternal habitation. It is a custom likewise among them, to give the bodies of their parents in pawn to their creditors, and they that do not presently redeem them, fall under the greatest disgrace imaginable, and are denied burial after their deaths. One may justly wonder at the authors of this excellent constitution, who both by what we see practised among the living, and by the decent burial of the dead, did, (as much as possibly lay within the power of men), endeavour to promote honesty and faithful dealing one with another. For the Greeks, (as to what concerned the rewards of the just, and the punishment of the impious), had nothing amongst them but invented fables, and poetical fictions, which never wrought upon men for the amendment of their lives; but on the contrary, were despised and laughed at by the lewder sort. But among the Egyptians, the punishment of the bad, and the rewards of the good, being not told as idle tales, but every day seen with their own eyes, all sorts were warned of their duties, and by this means was wrought and continued a most exact reformation of manners and orderly conversation among them. For those certainly are the best laws that advance virtue and honesty, and instruct men in a prudent converse in the world, rather than those that tend only to the heaping up of wealth, and teach men to be rich. And now it is necessary for us to speak of the legislators of Egypt, who established such laws as are both unusual elsewhere, and admirable in themselves.

At this stage in the text, Diodorus praises the popular belief in the awesomeness of Jupiter and Apollo, and he states:

> This contrivance, it is said, has been made use of amongst divers other nations, who have reaped much advantage by observing such laws. For it is reported, that among the Aramaspi, Zathraustes pretended he received his laws from a good genius; and that Zamolxis, amongst the people called the Getes, patronised his by Vesta; and among the Jews, that Moses alleged the god called Jao, to be the author of his. And this they did either because they judged such an invention (which brought about so much good to mankind) was wonderfully commendable, and of a divine stamp; or that they concluded the people would be more observant, out of a reverend regard to the majesty and authority of those who were said to be the law—

makers. (Diodorus Siculus, *The Historical Library in Fifteen Books*, translated by G. Booth, in two vols [London: 1814], Vol I, pp. 92—93.)

It seems extraordinary that Bergier should regard his kind of passage as praise of Moses' wisdom and him as a law–giver.

Socrates (*c.* 470—399 BC) was a Greek philosopher whose philosophical thought was tremendously influential on ancient and modern philosophical thinking. Much of his thought is conveyed through the writing of Plato and Xenophon, because Socrates wrote nothing in his own hand that has survived. At the age of seventy, Socrates was accused of impiety and sentenced to death; Plato's *Apology*, written in several sections, purports to be the speech Socrates made at his trial.

Solon (*c.* 630—*c.* 560 BC) was an Athenian statesman, known as one of the Seven Wise Men of Greece. He ended exclusive aristocratic control of the government, substituted a system of control by the wealthy and introduced a new and more humane law code. He was also a noted poet.

Sophronius q.v. **Jerome, St.**

Spinoza (1632—1677) (Hebrew forename *Baruch*, Latin forename *Bendictus*, and in Portuguese known as *Bento De Espinosa*) was a Dutch–Jewish philosopher, the foremost exponent of seventeenth–century Rationalism. He was from a prosperous merchant family who were respected members of the Jewish community and it may be assumed that Spinoza attended the school for Jewish boys founded in Amsterdam in about 1638. Outside school hours, the boys had private lessons in secular subjects. Spinoza was taught Latin by a German scholar who may also have taught him German, and he knew to some extent all other significant Western European languages. Though his early studies were mainly Jewish, he was an independent thinker and had found more than enough in his religious studies to wean him from orthodox doctrines and interpretations of Scripture; moreover, the tendency to revolt against tradition and authority was much in the air in the seventeenth century. Jewish religious leaders in Amsterdam were fearful that heresies (which were no less anti–Christian than anti–Jewish) might give offence in a country that did not yet regard the Jews as citizens. Spinoza soon incurred the disapproval of the synagogue authorities. In conversations with other students, he had held that there was nothing in the Bible to support the views that God had no body, that angels really existed, or that the soul is immortal. He had also expressed his belief that the author of the Pentateuch (the first five books of the Bible) was no wiser in physics, or even in theology, than they were as mere students. The Jewish authorities, after trying vainly to silence Spinoza with bribes and threats, excommunicated him in July 1656, and he was banished from Amsterdam for a short period by the civil authorities. In his early work, he took issue with the philosophy of Descartes: the three points which he found unacceptable were (i) the transcendence of God, (ii) the substantial dualism of mind and body, (iii) and the ascription of free will both to God and to human beings. In Spinoza's eyes, those doctrines made the world unintelligible. It was impossible to explain the relation between God and the world, or between mind and body, or to account for events occasioned by free will. He completed a huge work on ethics also. From about 1665 onwards, Spinoza worked on his *Tractatus Theologico–Politicus* {*A Theologico–Political Treatise*}, which was published anonymously at Amsterdam in 1670. This work aroused great interest and was to go through five editions in as many years. It was intended 'to show that not only is liberty to philosophize compatible with devout piety and with the peace of the state, but that to take away such liberty is to destroy the public peace and even piety itself.' As this work shows, Spinoza was far ahead of his time in advocating the application of the historical method to the interpretation of the biblical sources. He argued that the inspiration of the prophets of the Old Testament extended only to their moral and practical doctrines, and that their factual beliefs were merely those appropriate to their time, having no philosophical significance. Complete freedom of scientific and metaphysical speculation is therefore consistent with all that is important in the Bible. Miracles are explained as natural events misinterpreted and stressed for their moral effect. Throughout the eighteenth century he was almost universally decried as an atheist—or sometimes used as a cover for the detailing of atheist ideas. The tone had been set by Pierre Bayle (q.v.), in whose *Dictionaire historique et critique* {*Historical and Critical Dictionary*} (1697) Spinozism was described as 'the most monstrous hypothesis imaginable, the most absurd', and even David Hume (q.v.) felt obliged to speak of the 'hideous hypothesis' of Spinoza. Late twentieth–century Europe demonstrated a greater philosophical interest in Spinoza, often from a left–wing or Marxist perspective. Unlike most philosophers, Spinoza and his work were highly regarded by Nietzsche.

Strabo (64/63 BC to AD 23?) was a Greek geographer and historian, whose *Geography* is his only complete, extant work, covering a remarkable range of peoples and countries known to classical antiquity. Bergier mentions Strabo in defence of Moses' good reputation against d'Holbach criticism of him (see p. 202), however the only reference to Moses in Strabo is a mere footnote, and it does nothing to enhance Moses' standing and status as a law–giver. The passage reads:

> Canobus is a city situated at a distance of one hundred and twenty stadia
> from Alexandria, if one goes on foot, and was named after Canobus, the

pilot of Menelaüs, who died there. It contains the temple of Sarapis, which is honoured with great reverence and effects such cures that even the most reputable men believe in it and sleep in it themselves on their own behalf, or others for them.

At this point in the text, a footnote is provided which states, '*Even Moses advocated this practice.*' The text continues:

> Some writers go on to record the cures, and others the virtues of the oracles there. But to balance all this is the crowd of revellers who go down from Alexandria by the canal to the public festivals; for every day and every night is crowded with people on the boats who play the flute and dance without restraint and with extreme licentiousness, both men and women, and also with the people of Canobus itself, who have resorts situated close to the canal and adapted to relaxation and merry–making of this kind. (Strabo, *Geography*, Book XVII, translated by Horace Leonard Jones, in 8 vols [Cambridge, Mass.: Harvard University Press/Loeb Classical Library, 1932], Vol VIII, pp. 63—65.)

Suard, Jean–Baptiste–Antoine (1733—1817) was a journalist and literary correspondent, who contributed to a number of literary journals. He was a close friend of d'Holbach, Helvétius and a number of minor intellectuals of the period. He corresponded regularly with Hume, Garrick and Wilkes, as did d'Holbach.

Suetonius (AD 69—c. 122) (Latin name in full *Gaius Suetonius Tranquillus*) was a Roman biographer and antiquarian whose writings include *De viris illustribus* {*Concerning Illustrious Men*}, a collection of short biographies of celebrated Roman literary figures, and *De vita Caesarum* {*Lives of the Caesars*}. The latter book, seasoned with snippets of gossip and scandal relating to the lives of the first twelve cæsars, secured him lasting fame. He was secretary to the emperor Domitian during the years AD 90 to 95, i.e., during the period of alleged intense persecution of Christians, and yet he mentions not a word about them or Christ. In the chapter on the life of Claudius (Book V), there is an ambiguous reference to a possible Christ: 'Since the Jews constantly made disturbances at the instigation of Chrestus, he [i.e., Claudius] expelled them from Rome.' (Suetonius, *The Lives of the Cæsars* [Cambridge, Mass.: Harvard U.P./Loeb Classical Library, 1914], p. 53.) It has been presumed by some scholars that 'Chrestus' was a typographical mistake and that it should really read 'Christus', i.e., 'Christ', a term which is used in the writing of Tacitus (q.v.). However, if Christ died around AD 29—33 (a commonly accepted 'window' for his death), he would not have been around during the reign of Claudius, who ruled from AD 41 to 54, and so 'Christus' (or 'Christ') could not possibly have been alive and fomenting sedition. Just because there is a similarity between the names 'Chrestus' and 'Christus', there is no textual or historical reason for assuming any typographical error, especially given the paucity of corroborating historical evidence from other authorities.

Tachard, Father was a Jesuit priest who was sent to Siam with a group of other observers to find out all they could about life and politics in Siam for the purposes of developing further trading: in 1680, Louis XIV had obtained exclusive rights to trade with Siam in spices and Father Tachard was amongst the group dispatched there. He wrote his findings and impressions in two books published in Paris in 1686.

Tacitus (AD 56—*c*. 120) (Latin name in full *Publius Cornelius Tacitus* or *Gaius Cornelius Tacitus*) was a Roman orator and public official, probably the greatest historian and one of the greatest prose stylists who wrote in Latin: his written style was highly refined and concise, typical of writing of what has become known as the 'Silver Age'. Among his works are (i) the *Germania* (describing the Germanic tribes), (ii) the *Historiae* {*Histories*}, concerning the Roman Empire from AD 69 to 96, and later (iii) the *Annals*, dealing with the empire in the period from AD 14 to 68. In the *Annals*, Tacitus mentioned the Christians as a group, whom Nero blamed for setting fire to Rome, so he duly punished them. Again, Christian apologists make much of this passage because it is one of the few independent sources outside the gospels, which mentions Christians:

> Such indeed were the precautions of human wisdom. The next thing was to seek means of propitiating the gods, and recourse was had to the Sibylline books [q.v.], by the direction of which prayers were offered to Vulcanus, Ceres, and Proserpina. Juno, too, was entreated by the matrons, first, in the Capitol, then on the nearest part of the coast, whence water was procured to sprinkle the fane and image of the goddess. And there were sacred banquets and nightly vigils celebrated by married women. But all human efforts, all the lavish gifts of the emperor, and the propitiations of the gods, did not banish the sinister belief that the conflagration was the result of an order. Consequently, to get rid of the report, Nero fastened the guilt and inflicted the most exquisite tortures on a class hated for their abominations, called Christians by the populace. Christus, from whom the name had its origin, suffered the extreme penalty during the reign of Tiberius at the hands of one of our procurators, Pontius Pilatus, and a most mischievous superstition, thus checked for the moment, again broke out not only in Judæa, the first source of the evil, but even in Rome, where all things hideous and shameful from every part of the world find their centre and become popular. Accordingly, an arrest was first made of all who pleaded guilty; then, upon their information, an immense multitude was convicted, not so much of the crime of firing the city, as of hatred against mankind. Mockery of every sort was added to their deaths. Covered with the skins of beasts, they were torn by dogs and perished, or were nailed to crosses, or were doomed to the flames and burnt, to serve as a nightly illumination, when daylight had expired. Nero offered his gardens for the spectacle, and was exhibiting a show in the circus, while he mingled with

the people in the dress of a charioteer or stood aloft on a car. Hence, even for criminals who deserved extreme and exemplary punishment, there arose a feeling of compassion; for it was not, as it seemed, for the public good, but to glut one man's cruelty, that they were being destroyed. (Tacitus, *Annals*, Book XV, Section XLIV.)

But for all his objectivity as a historian, Tacitus reports the general populous as being extremely superstitious and it is difficult to discern how objective Tacitus himself is from these beliefs:

At the close of the year people talked much about prodigies, presaging impending evils. Never were lightning flashes more frequent, and a comet too appeared, for which Nero always made propitiation with noble blood. Human and other births with two heads were exposed to public view, or were discovered in those sacrifices in which it is usual to immolate victims in a pregnant condition. And in the district of Placentia, close to the road, a calf was born with its head attached to its leg. Then followed an explanation of the diviners, that another head was preparing for the world, which however would be neither mighty nor hidden, as its growth had been checked in the womb, and it had been born by the wayside. (Ibid.)

Whenever a people's world is turned upside down and they are caught up in cataclysmic events, the general populous often has recourse to all manner of unusual signs and portents, as did the Russian peasantry at the onset of collectivization (1929—30) in Russia; it was generally rumoured that the policy of collectivization, imposed by Stalin from above, was the work of the Anti–Christ. It is difficult to judge to what extent Tacitus gives credence to these supernatural beliefs, or whether he is merely reporting a general consensus of opinion. Also, the text is full of difficulties and there are not a few textual variations in the various manuscripts—e.g., *Christianos* or *Chrestianos* and even *Christianus*, i.e., the singular, along with *Christus* and *Chrestos*; all these variations suggest strongly that this text has been altered by scribes and copyists, as many were, and it is not known whether these amendments were made intentionally or whether they were simply 'slips of the pen'. It is not even clear what Tacitus means to say, i.e., whether he implies that the charge of setting the fires brought against Christians was false; whether some Christians were arrested because they set fires and others because of their general 'hatred against humankind'; what those persons arrested 'confessed' to—arson or Christianity?—or whether they were executed by crucifixion or immolation, or in some other manner. But the real question concerns the historical reliability of this information and whether we are dealing with a later insertion by a Christian scribe, as is frequently alleged, or not. With regard to this particular source, the earliest extant manuscript for the *Annals* dates from the eleventh century, and therefore it must have been copied and recopied many times, most usually by generations of Christian scribes and apologists. The scope and opportunity to effect

477

alterations are obvious, and exactly the same problem exists with all the New Testament texts—a fact that Christian Fundamentalists and those who believe that the Bible is the literal, inspired word of God, pay scant attention to—if they even think about it at all. As Bart Ehrman has pointed out regarding New Testament texts, which goes for all ancient texts—both sacred and secular: 'Not only do we not have the originals, we don't have the first copies of the originals. We don't even have copies of the copies of the originals, or copies of the copies of the copies of the originals. What we have is copies made later—much later. In most instances, they are copies made many *centuries* [sic] later. And these copies all differ from one another, in many thousands of places.' (Bart D. Ehrman, *Misquoting Jesus: The Story Behind Who Changed the Bible and Why* [N.Y.: HarperOne, 2005], p. 10.)

The fact that Tacitus' claims are unsupported by any other contemporary source until Sulpicius Serverus in the late fourth century, through the writing of Eusebius, renders the testimony Tacitus offers as doubly suspicious. The dramatic, imaginative description of the tortures suffered by the scapegoats resembles the executions portrayed in later legendary Acts of Christian Martyrs. Even if this passage is granted credence, the fact that Tacitus was aware of a character called *Christus* and that he had followers named after him, does not, in and of itself, provide any independent evidence that Jesus even existed.

Tartarus was the infernal regions of ancient Greek mythology. The name was originally used for the deepest region of the world, the lower of the two parts of the underworld, where the gods locked up their enemies. It gradually came to mean the entire underworld. As such it was the opposite of Elysium (q.v.), where happy souls lived after death. Hades was another, similar concept, derived from the Greek Aïdes (*the Unseen*), also called Pluto, or Pluton (*the Rich*). In Greek mythology, these were the son of the Titans Cronus and Rhea, and the brother of the deities Zeus and Poseidon. After Cronus was killed, the kingdom of the underworld fell by lot to Hades. There he ruled with his queen, Persephone, over the infernal powers and over the dead, in what was often called 'the House of Hades', or simply 'Hades'. Though he supervised the trial and punishment of the wicked after death, he was not normally one of the judges in the underworld; nor did he personally torture the guilty, a task assigned to the Furies (or *Erinyes*). Hades was depicted as stern and pitiless, unmoved (like death itself) by prayer or sacrifice. Forbidding and aloof, he never quite emerges as a distinct personality from the shadowy darkness of his realm. The transformation of these ideas into the Christian concepts of Hell and eternal punishment are admirably portrayed in many works of fiction with great embellishment and imagination, having little to do with biblical sources; they most notably appear in Dante's *Divine Comedy* (*c.* 1310—14) and Milton's *Paradise Lost* (*c.* 1655—1667).

Tertullian (AD 155/160—*c.* 220) (name in Latin in full *Quintus Septimus Florens Tertullianus*) was an important early Christian theologian, polemicist and moralist who, as the initiator of ecclesiastical Latin, was instrumental in shaping the vocabulary and thought of Western Christianity. While receiving his education in Rome, he became interested in the Christian movement, but not until he returned to Carthage toward the end of the second century was he converted to the Christian faith (*c.* 192). He left no account of his conversion experience, but in his early works, *Ad martyras {To the Martyrs}*, *Ad nationes {To the Nations}*, *and Apologeticum {Defense}*, he indicated that he was impressed by certain Christian attitudes and beliefs, viz., the courage and determination of martyrs, their moral rigor and an uncompromising belief in one god. It is thought that he wrote his *Apologeticum* around 197. He wrote many books and treatises on various topics—from moral issues to what Christians should wear. Tertullian is usually considered the outstanding exponent of the outlook that Christianity must stand uncompromisingly against its surrounding culture. Bergier singles out chapter 21 of Tertullian's *Apologeticum* as bearing witness to the miracles of Christ, etc., but in essence, there is nothing in this chapter which cites independent evidence of Christ's existence and his miracles. In chapter 21, Tertullian is at pains to point out that the Jews are now fully out of favour with God because of the way in which they treated Jesus Christ:

> The Jews once were a people in such favour with God, upon the account of their forefathers' faith and piety, which was the root of all their greatness, both with respect to the increase of their families, and the advance of a kingdom, and their happiness was so unparalleled, that God Himself did them the honour even with His own mouth to prescribe them laws, whereby they might secure His omnipotence on their side, and never turn it against them. But how the degenerate children upon the stock of Abraham's faith, and in confidence of their forefathers' virtue, how egregiously they provoked God by deviating from His own positive institutions into profaneness and idolatry; although the Jews themselves will not confess this, yet the present calamities of that people are a sad and standing testimony against them. For they are now a dispersed vagabond people, banished country and climate, strolling about the world without any show of government, either divine or human, and so completely miserable that they have not the poor privilege to visit the Holy Land like strangers, or set a foot upon their native soil; and while the sacred writings did forethreaten these calamities, they did likewise continually inculcate that the time would come about the last days when out of every nation and country God would choose Himself a people that should serve Him more faithfully, upon whom He would shed a greater measure of grace in proportion to the merits of the founder of this new worship.

In his writing, he is clearly pro–Christian and anti–Jewish, which is no basis on which to offer historical evidence, but that said, he offers no additional evidence or sources to support the supernatural events at the time of the crucifixion of Christ, and he merely summarizes the events presented in the gospels. Tertullian offers the Jews another chance to accept Christ, telling them that they may yet repent and thereby receive God's grace:

> If you please now you may receive this great truth in the nature of a fable like one of yours, till I have given you my proofs; though it is a truth that could not be unknown to those among you who maliciously dressed up their own inventions on purpose to destroy it. The Jews likewise full well knew from their prophets that Christ was to come, and they are now in expectation of Him; and the great clashing between us and them is chiefly upon this very account, that they do not believe Him already come. For there being two advents of Christ described in the prophets, the first which is discharged and over, namely His state of humiliation and suffering in human flesh. The second, which is at hand, too, in the conclusion of the world, in which He will exert His majesty, and come in a full explication of divine glory. By not understanding the first, they fixed only upon the second advent, which is described in the most pompous and glaring metaphors, and which struck the carnal fancy with the most agreeable impressions. And it was the just judgment of God upon them for their sins that withheld their understandings from seeing this first coming, which had they understood, they had believed, and by believing had obtained salvation.

With regard to the point Bergier makes about 'Roman senators [being] witness to the effect that these miracles were recorded in their annals' (see p. 239.), Tertullian says:

> At length being fastened to the cross, and having cried out and commended His spirit into the hands of His Father, He gave up the ghost of His own accord, and so prevented the executioner's breaking His bones, by dying in His own time, and fulfilled a prophecy by so doing. Moreover, in the same moment He dismissed life, the light departed from the sun, and the world was benighted at noonday, and those men who acknowledged this eclipse, but were unacquainted with the prophecies that foretold it upon Christ's death, and finding it impossible to be solved by the laws of nature, at last roundly denied the fact; and yet this wonder of the world you have related, and the relation preserved in your archives to this day.' (*The Apology of Tertullian,* translated and annotated by W. Reeve, sometime Vicar of Cranford, Middlesex, in 2 vols [London: 1709], pp. 61 *et seqq.*)

He does not cite these sources or 'archives', or even quote them.

Thallus was possibly a pagan chronicler of unknown date, who is occasionally mentioned in the works of Christian apologists, modern and ancient, as a first–century pagan witness to the gospel claim of a darkening of the sky at the time of Christ's death, which is sometimes called an eclipse: see Mark 15: 33; Luke 23: 44; and Matt. 27: 51—53, whose account includes an earthquake, split rocks and zombies; John makes no mention of any such events, nor does Paul, or any other New Testament writer. Such events would not fail to be recorded in the works of Seneca (q.v.), Pliny (q.v.), Josephus (q.v.), or other relatively reliable historians, yet there is no mention of them. We know only of the possible existence of a Thallus from third–hand references to his writing, but only one historian—Eusebius, quoting another source—Julius Africanus, who mentions that Thallus wrote a historical account, but this has not been found. Josephus has traditionally been credited with making reference to a 'Thallus', but the text is corrupt. The sentence is now generally taken to read, 'Now there was, **in addition**, a certain man of Samaritan origin who was a freedman of the emperor'. However, the translation of the word 'in addition', which appears as ἄλλος in the original Greek, was presumed by scholars to have been mistakenly written for Θάλλος, i.e., 'Thallus the Samaritan'. This is now seriously disputed, which makes the very existence of a 'Thallus' even more doubtful, let alone anything supernatural he might have witnessed at the death of Christ. (See Josephus, *Jewish Antiquities*: Book XVIII, op. cit., footnote *f*, p. 107.) Christian apologists cite this very doubtful evidence because there is so little other historical evidence: that of Thallus is the most suspect. Further information can be found on the internet: http://www.infidels.org/library/modern/richard_carrier/thallus.html

Theophylactus (fl. *c.* 1050—1109) was archbishop of Bulgaria and he is celebrated mainly for his commentaries on the Bible and a few other works. There are scarcely any particulars of his life worth recording. He appears to have been a native of Constantinople, a deacon in the principal church there, and to have been appointed to the archbishopric of Bulgaria, the chief city of which was Acris, between 1070 and 1077. He wrote commentaries upon the gospels, the Acts, the Epistles of Paul and the Minor Prophets, which were founded on the commentaries of Chrysostom (q.v.).

Thérèse of Lisieux, Saint (1873—1897) (also called *Saint Teresa of the Child Jesus*, or the *Little Flower*; her original name was *Marie–Françoise–Thérèse Martin*) was a Carmelite nun whose service to her Roman Catholic order, although outwardly unremarkable, was later recognized for its exemplary spiritual accomplishments. She was named a Doctor of the Church by Pope John Paul II in 1997. Thérèse moved with her family to Lisieux in 1877 and was raised by an older sisters and an aunt. In the deeply religious atmosphere of her home, her piety developed early and intensively. At the age of only fifteen she entered the Carmelite convent at

Lisieux, having been refused admission a year earlier. Although she suffered from depression, a groundless feeling of guilt and, at the end of her life, religious doubts, she kept her vows to perfection and maintained a smiling, pleasant and unselfish manner. Before her death from tuberculosis, she acknowledged that because of her difficult nature not one day had ever passed without a spiritual struggle. Her burial site at Lisieux became a place of pilgrimage and a basilica bearing her name was built there (1929—54).

Figure 89: St Thérèse of Lisieux, Lyon Cathedral. (Source: Wikipedia).

Theseus was the mythical son of Aegeus and a great hero of Attic legend. Amongst other feats, he successfully attacked the fire–breathing bull of Marathon. His subsequent adventure was to tackle the Cretan Minotaur— half man, half bull—shut up in the legendary labyrinth on Crete. He united the various Attic communities into a single state and extended the territory of Attica to the Isthmus of Corinth.

Tibullus (55—19 BC) was a Roman poet, the second in the classical sequence of great Latin writers of elegiacs that begins with Cornelius Gallus and continues through Tibullus and Sextus Propertius to Ovid. Quintilian considered Tibullus to be the finest poet of them all.

Tillemont (1637—1698) (in full *Louis–Sébastien Le Nain de Tillemont*) was a French ecclesiastical historian, one of the earliest scholars to provide a rigorous appraisal of preceding historical writing. His works were objective and among the first of modern historical works to include a critical discussion of the principal sources for each period. As the son of a wealthy lawyer, Tillemont attended Port–Royal, the famous Jansenist school, where an austere form of Roman Catholicism was taught. He began his researches early (1655), scrupulously collecting literary and historical information concerning early Christianity. After entering the seminary at Beauvais (1661), Tillemont collaborated in publishing an edition of the writings of the Church Fathers (1669). In 1667 he took up residence at Port–Royal, becoming chaplain (1675), and later priest (1676). The Jansenist persecutions of 1679 forced him to settle on the family estate of Tillemont, where he remained to continue his studies in church history until his death. Tillemont's writings began to appear during his lifetime; the *Mémoires pour servir à l'histoire ecclésiastique des six premiers siècles,* in sixteen volumes {*Memoirs Useful for the Ecclesiastical History of the First Six Centuries*} (1693—1712), and *Histoire des empereurs,* in six volumes {*History of the Emperors*} (1690—1738), which were originally conceived as one work, but were published separately. These books deal with the history of the Christian Church and the Roman Empire to about AD 515, giving highly objective accounts as well as citing original sources. They were among the chief sources used by the English historian Edward Gibbon in his *Decline and Fall of the Roman Empire.*

Tindal, Matthew (1657—1733) was an English philosopher of a Deist persuasion, who has been described as the 'most learned of the English Deists'. He argued that the essential part of Christianity is its ethics, which, being clearly apparent to natural reason, renders revelation superfluous.

Titus (AD 39—81) (full title *Titus Vespasianus Augustus*, original name—*Titus Flavius Vespasianus*) was Roman emperor between AD 79 to 81. He led a campaign against the Jews and conquered Jerusalem in AD 70.

Toland, John (1760—1722) was an Irish–born British free–thinker, who studied at the universities of Glasgow, Edinburgh, Leiden (where d'Holbach also studied) and Oxford. He published his *Christianity Not Mysterious* (1696), in which he makes the fundamental assumption that all that is essential in Christianity must be understandable. It is therefore impossible for reasonable men to receive mysteries on the proclaimed authority of the Early Fathers, the Doctors of the Church, or an infallible pope. He declares that, 'The element of mystery must be eliminated from Christianity', and that we should not adore what we cannot comprehend. Needless to say, this caused an outrage and he was obliged to flee to Dublin, where he learned that the Irish Parliament had condemned his book and ordered his arrest, so he took refuge in England. He continued to write pamphlets and works challenging orthodox views of Christianity, one of which was his *Letters to Serena* (1704), which d'Holbach translated into French. In it, Toland set out a historical account of the rise of superstitious belief from which the human mind can never fully liberate itself. He believed that the Church's ceremonies and practices were a source and cause of mystery, which ought to be jettisoned in order to give free expression to the exercise of one's native ability to come to an understanding of God through reason.

Trappist monks were members of the Order of the Reformed Cistercians of the Strict Observance (O.C.S.O.), a branch of the Roman Catholic Cistercians, founded by the converted courtier Armand de Rancé (1626—1700), who had governed the Cistercian abbey of La Trappe in France, which he transformed (in 1662) into a community practising extreme austerity of diet, penitential exercises and absolute silence. He became its permanent abbot in 1664 and, for more than thirty years, kept the abbey under his forceful sway. In 1792 the monks were ejected from La Trappe and a number of them, led by Dom Augustine de Lestrange, settled at Val–Sainte in Fribourg (Switzerland), where they adopted an even more rigid lifestyle and made several foundations before their expulsion in 1798. Long years of wandering in Russia and Germany were followed in 1814 by a return to La Trappe; they were the first religious order to revive after the French Revolution and, at the death of Lestrange in 1827, they numbered seven hundred. Their increase has never ceased and, by the late twentieth century, there were abbeys worldwide, including several in England, Scotland, Canada, the United States, Australia and South Africa. The three existing congregations of Trappists were united by Pope Leo XIII as the independent Reformed Cistercians of the Strict Observance; they follow the primitive custom of Cîteaux with an emphasis on silence and austerity, but without the rigid regulations of the early Trappists. After World War II their growth was particularly notable in France and the United States.

Trenchard, John (1662—1723) was an English writer and politician, related to the same Dorset family as the Secretary of State Sir John Trenchard. Educated at Trinity College, Dublin, he inherited considerable wealth which permitted him to pursue a life of writing on politics as a Whig and an opponent of the High Church party. Amongst other works, he also wrote *The Natural History of Superstition* (1709). He published the weekly periodical *The Independent Whig* (with Thomas Gordon), and a series of essays from 1720 to 1723, again with Gordon, published first in the *London Journal* and then in the *British Journal* as *Essays on Liberty, Civil and Religious*. Trenchard was also a Member of Parliament for Taunton.

Tronchin, Théodore (1709—1781) was a doctor of Swiss origin, born in Geneva, but he lived many years in Paris. He was well known in European intellectual circles, active in learned bodies and academies, and he counted Voltaire amongst his patients. He was also the personal physician of the Duke of Orléans. He promoted the idea of vaccination, which he introduced into France, and he provided an article on vaccination for Diderot's *Encyclopédie*, through whom he knew many intellectuals; he was also acquainted with members of French salon society.

Typhon, (also spelt *Typhaon*, or *Typhoeus*) was the youngest son of Gaea (Earth) and Tartarus (of the nether world) in Greek mythology. He was described as a grisly monster with a hundred dragons' heads, who was conquered and cast into the underworld by Zeus. In other accounts, he was confined in the land of the Arimi in Cilicia or under Mount Etna, or in other volcanic regions, where he was the cause of eruptions. Typhon was thus the personification of volcanic forces. Among his children by his wife Echidna were Cerberus (q.v. Hercules), the three–headed hound of hell, the multiheaded Lernean Hydra and the Chimera. He was also the father of dangerous winds (typhoons), and he was identified with the Egyptian god Seth by later writers.

Ulysses is the English name for the mythological god Odysseus, hero of Homer's epic poem the *Odyssey* and one of the most frequently portrayed figures in Western literature. According to Homer, Odysseus was king of Ithaca. Homer portrayed Odysseus as a man of outstanding wisdom and shrewdness, eloquence, resourcefulness, courage and endurance. In the *Iliad*, Odysseus appears as the man best suited to cope with crises in personal relations among the Greeks and he plays a leading part in achieving the reconciliation between Agamemnon and Achilles. His bravery and skill in fighting are demonstrated repeatedly, and his willingness is shown most notably in the night expedition he undertakes with Diomedes against the Trojans. Odysseus' wanderings and the recovery of his house and kingdom are the central theme of the *Odyssey*, an epic in twenty–four books which also relates how he accomplished the capture of Troy by means of the wooden horse.

Unigenitus (in full *Unigenitus Dei Filius*) was a bull issued by Pope Clement XI on 8 September 1713, condemning the doctrines of Jansenism (see p. 348 and also under Arnauld and Calvinist), a dissident religious movement in France. The publication of the bull began a doctrinal controversy in France, lasting throughout much of the eighteenth century and it merged with the French Church's fight for autonomy, called Gallicanism, and with the opposition of the *Parlements* (supreme courts) to the crown. *Unigenitus,* which condemned 101 theological propositions of the Jansenist writer Pasquier Quesnel contained in the book *Réflexions morales {Moral Reflections}*, was issued at the request of the French king, Louis XIV, who wished to suppress the Jansenist faction. Louis was able to secure initial acceptance of the bull, but some French bishops (led by Louis–Antoine de Noailles, cardinal–archbishop of Paris) rejected it, and the *Parlement* of Paris accepted it only with reservations. The Jansenists were supported by the magistrates of the *Parlements,* who regarded the bull as an unwarranted papal interference in the affairs of the French Church. The crown, in supporting the pope and those French bishops who accepted the bull, found itself increasingly at odds with the *parlementaires.* The controversy over *Unigenitus* broke out in earnest after the death of Louis XIV in 1715. In 1717 four bishops appealed against the bull to a future ecumenical council (which they held to have authority over the pope). But the bishops' effective opposition ended with the death of Cardinal de Noailles in 1729. As a further blow to the Jansenist cause, a royal declaration of 1730 made the bull a law of the state and threatened ecclesiastics who rejected it with loss of lands. The final episode in the controversy occurred from 1749 to 1754 over the issue of *billets de confession.* The *billets* were papers affirming submission to the bull that suspected Jansenists were ordered to sign by the archbishop of Paris, Christophe de Beaumont. If they refused, the last sacraments and burial in consecrated ground would be denied them. The *Parlement* of Paris, claiming jurisdiction over matters of ecclesiastical discipline and supported by public opinion, opposed the *billets.* It ordered priests to administer the sacraments to every one of the faithful under pain of banishment and confiscation of goods. In 1754 King Louis XV forbade continuation of the dispute.

Vallée, Geoffroy (or *Geffroi de la Vallée*) (*c.* 1550—1574) is best remembered for a work entitled *La Béatitude des chrestiens, ou le Fléo de* *la foy* (*The Beatitude of the Christians, or the Scourge/Flail of Faith* (1573), who was reputed to have been hanged and burned in Paris in 1574, but this date is disputed. The work was so well repressed that only one copy could be located in 1714. There is almost no information on Geoffroy Vallée, apart from his being burned and hanged for heresy, but there is a short article on him in Bayle's *Dictionary* (1740 edition.). Bayle notes that: 'Some say he was burned for his atheism in Paris in the year 1571 and that he had composed a work entitled *L'Art de ne rien croire* {*The Art of Believing Nothing*}.' (Bayle, *Dictionaire Historique et Critique*, [Amsterdam, 1740], p. 423.) According to a scholarly edition of *The Art of Believing Nothing* (or *De arte nihil credenda*, as it was popularly known at the time), which was recently published with a short biography of de la Vallée, he wrote 'All religions have been mindful to deprive man of the joy of the body in God, in order to make them ever more miserable, while keeping the best things for those who invented them...' ('*L'Art de ne croire en rien suivi de Livre des trios imposteurs*', text edited with a preface by Raoul Vaneigem [Paris: Éditions Payot et Rivages, 2002], p. 23.) *The Art of Believing Nothing* is no more than a work of pamphlet length, but it scandalized the Church on account of its libertine stance. However, it is not an atheist work—it could better be described as deist.

Vanini, Lucilio (1585—1619) was an Italian priest and philosopher who proposed natural explanations for Christ's miracles. He led a somewhat itinerant life, wandering around France, Switzerland and the Low Countries, teaching and disseminating his anti–religious views. He had to flee from France on two occasions, having fallen foul of the Church and the French state on account of his views. He was arrested in November 1618 on the grounds of atheism and condemned to having his tongue cut out, to strangulation at the stake, and then his body was burned to ashes— just for good measure. The sentence was carried out on 9 February 1619.

Veil, (the) is a powerful symbol in religious thought and tradition and it carries many different meanings. It is a symbol of things hidden for modesty's sake: hence, Muslim women are encouraged to hide various parts of their bodies so as not to tempt men and arouse their passions, as the Koran states: '*And tell believing women that they should lower their gaze, guard their private parts, and not flaunt their charms beyond what it is acceptable to reveal; they should let their headscarves fall to cover their necklines and not reveal their charms except to their husbands, their fathers, their husbands' fathers, their sons, their husbands' sons, etc...*' Koran 24: 31. Injunctions to wearing clothing which show only the face and hands to a stranger are contained in the *Hadith* or 'prophetic tradition'. In similar vein, St Paul urges women to cover their heads as a sign of their respect and humility, and not flaunting their hair, with which the Muslim and Jewish traditions are also obsessed. As is noted in the Bible:

> But every woman that prayeth or prophesieth with her head uncovered dishonoureth her head: for that is even all one as if she were shaven. For if the woman be not covered, let her also be shorn: but if it be a shame for a woman to be shorn or shaven, let her be covered. For a man indeed ought not to cover his head, forasmuch as he is the image and glory of God: but the woman is the glory of the man. For the man is not of the woman: but the woman of the man. Neither was the man created for the woman; but the woman for the man. For this cause ought the woman to have power on her head because of the angels. Nevertheless neither is the man without the woman, neither the woman without the man, in the Lord. For as the woman is of the man, even so is the man also by the woman; but all things of God. Judge in yourselves: is it comely that a woman pray unto God uncovered? Doth not even nature itself teach you, that, if a man have long hair, it is a shame unto him? But if a woman have long hair, it is a glory to her: for her hair is given her for a covering. But if any man seem to be contentious, we have no such custom, neither the churches of God. (1 Cor. 11: 5—16).

The veil was also used to cover men's eyes from objects which were deemed too holy to be looked upon by ordinary people: hence, the Tabernacle or Altar of the Lord was screened by a veil, which, when Christ was crucified, was said to rip from top to bottom, symbolising that the way was now open to men to approach God directly through Christ. The symbolic tearing of the veil in the Temple at Jerusalem is mentioned in the Gospels of Matthew, Mark and Luke: Mark's account is typical of the other citations, 'And the veil of the temple was rent in twain from the top to the bottom.' (Mark 15: 38). When Moses had spoken directly to God on Mt Sinai, he had to cover his face with a veil because his face shone after speaking face to face with God: 'And till Moses had done speaking with them [i.e., the Israelites], he put a veil on his face.' (Exod. 34: 33). Yet having spoken to God face to face on this occasion, Moses' request to see God's glory is denied to him, because it would be more than he could cope with:

> Then Moses said, 'Now show me your glory.' And the Lord said, 'I will cause all my goodness to pass in front of you, and I will proclaim my name, the Lord, in your presence. I will have mercy on whom I will have mercy, and I will have compassion on whom I will have compassion. But,' he said, 'you cannot see my face, for no one may see me and live.' Then the Lord said, 'There is a place near me where you may stand on a rock. When my glory passes by, I will put you in a cleft in the rock and cover you with my hand until I have passed by. Then I will remove my hand and you will see my back; but my face must not be seen', (Exod. 33: 18—23).

The veil is also used as a symbol of protection: in the Russian Orthodox Church, the Festival of the Holy Veil is celebrated on 14 October every year. This festival is based on the myth that the Virgin Mary made an appearance in Constantinople in the tenth century and it became an official festive day in the Russian Church in about 1164. The appearance was supposed to have taken place in a church where the vestments of the Virgin herself were kept. She is said to have appeared with an angelic throng to a group of besieged people praying for deliverance, and she spread out her veil above the assembled faithful by way of a blessing, which saved them. Of course, in more prosaic contexts, a veil can be used as a means of covering up or hiding a secret or something shameful. Some of these symbolic meanings may be born in mind when considering d'Holbach's title.

Volland, Sophie (1716—1784) (full name *Louise Henriette Volland*), was the friend and mistress of Diderot from 1755 to1769, during which time they exchanged many letters on a great variety of subjects. Unfortunately no letters have survived of hers to him. Grimm, as one of Diderot's closest friends, wrote a letter to her, advising her on reading philosophical works of the day and it is translated and included in this volume. Diderot met Sophie Volland in 1755 and formed a relationship with her that was to last more than twenty years. His correspondence with Sophie, together with his letters written from and to others at the time, form one of the most fascinating documents on Diderot's personality, enthusiasms and ideas, and on the intellectual society of Paris: amongst these letters are those from Mme Louise d'Épinay, F.M. Grimm, the Baron d'Holbach, Ferdinando Galiani and other deistic writers and thinkers (*philosophes*), with whom he felt most at home.

Voltaire (1694—1778) (pseudonym of *François–Marie Arouet*) was one of the greatest of all French writers. Although only a few of his works are still read, he continues to be held in worldwide repute as a courageous crusader against tyranny, bigotry and cruelty. His writing embodies the characteristic qualities of the French mind—a critical capacity, wit and satire. His whole work vigorously propagates an ideal of progress to which men of all nations have remained responsive. His long life spanned the last years of classicism and the eve of the revolutionary era, and during this age of transition his works and activities influenced the direction taken by European civilization. Voltaire's background was middle class, though he was of doubtful paternity, and his mother died when he was very young. He attended the Jesuit college of Louis–le–Grand in Paris, where he learned to love literature, the theatre and social life. While he appreciated the classical taste the college instilled in him, the religious instruction of the fathers served only to arouse his scepticism and mockery. United with other thinkers of his day—men of letters and scientists—in the belief in the efficacy of reason, Voltaire was a *philosophe*, as the eighteenth century termed it. In the salons he professed an aggressive Deism, which scandalized the devout. He became interested in England, the country that tolerated more freedom of thought than France at that time; he visited the Tory leader Viscount Bolingbroke (q.v.), exiled in France, whom Voltaire admired to the point of comparing him to Cicero. On Bolingbroke's advice he learned English in order to read the philosophical works of John Locke. His intellectual development was furthered by an accident: as the result of a quarrel with a member of one of the leading French families, the Chevalier de Rohan, who had made fun of his adopted name, he was beaten up, taken to the Bastille, and then conducted to Calais on 5 May 1726, from where he set out for London. His destiny from that time on was exile and opposition. He returned to France at the end of 1728 or the beginning of 1729, and he frequently published literary works which caused a scandal: he also wrote less contentious works on history. He spent some time in Geneva, but even there he was viewed as a loose cannon on account of his ideas and, like the young disciple of philosophy in his philosophical fantasy *Candide* (1758), he retired to the secret happiness of metaphorically 'cultivating his own garden', in Ferney, a property he bought at the end of 1758 on the French–Swiss border: with easy access to the frontier he could thus safeguard himself against police incursion from either country. At Ferney, Voltaire entered on one of the most active periods of his life. Voltaire's writing is voluminous, comprising some fifty volumes, which cannot all be mentioned here. His works relevant to this volume are his *Dictionnaire philosophique portatif* {*Portable Philosophical Dictionary*} (1764). Typically, when it appeared it caused a sensation: Voltaire used an alphabetical, dictionary format to express his views on theology and modern religious beliefs regarded as heretical by the Catholic Church, and on many other subjects in a series of short essays comprising articles contributed by him to Diderot's *Encyclopédie*. The *Dictionary* also aimed criticism against French institutions which were the targets of Voltaire's personal hate, such as certain political institutions, the Bible and the Catholic Church. It was published anonymously in Geneva and when it appeared, the Chief Attorney of the Paris *Parlement*, a certain Omer Joly de Fleury, declared, 'I shall not die happy without having seen the philosopher [of this work] hang', and no less than the king, Louis XV, asked, 'Is there no way that man can be silenced?' Many people found the entry on St Peter, founder of the Catholic Church, particularly offensive. His *Traité sur la Tolérance* {*Treatise on Tolerance*} was published in 1763. His connection with Bolingbroke is attested by the fact that he wrote a work entitled *Examen Important de Milord Bolingbroke* {*Important Examination of Lord Bolingbroke*}, which bears the subtitle '*Written at the end of 1736*', but which was actually published in 1767 and ran to several editions, many of them subtly different. The work comprises several of Bolingbroke's own works, which had appeared in London in a collected edition of 1754 (in five volumes), and Voltaire took what he considered to be the most interesting pieces and reworked them in his own style. It is an examination of religious belief, written with Voltaire's usual scepticism, but from a deist point of view. In the section entitled 'The Person of Jesus', (chapter XI), Voltaire reiterates the dubious background of Christ and his paternity (see this volume, p. 208). Another work referenced in this edition is *Le Dîner du Comte Boulainvilliers* {*The Dinner of Count Boulainvilliers*} (1767): this work takes the form of a series of questions on religious issues put by the dinner guests to the host. It is an extremely witty, amusing piece and it targets Voltaire's usual *bêtes noires*, i.e., implicit trust in divine revelation, blind faith, clerics of the Catholic Church, etc. Although often called an atheist, Voltaire was really a Deist, but as he advanced in years, it has been speculated that he ended up virtually an atheist.

Warburton, William (1698—1779) was an Anglican bishop of Gloucester, a literary critic and an essayist, who frequently wrote in defence of Christianity, and in particular of the Christian revelation against Deists. He was not one to mince words, once describing some opponents against whom he was writing on one particular occasion as a 'pestilent herd of libertine scribblers with which the island is overrun', and his lively style often brought him into great controversies with intellectuals from home and abroad. He is known to have contributed articles to the *Encyclopédie* and written many collections of essays.

Wilkes, John (1725—1797) was an outspoken eighteenth–century journalist and popular London politician who came to be regarded as a victim of persecution and a champion of liberty, because he was repeatedly expelled from Parliament. His widespread popular support may have been the beginning of English Radicalism. Though from a modest background, he married well and was profligate with money, frequently landing himself in debt. He became Member of Parliament for Aylesbury and hoped to make up for his reckless overspending by political advancement. In 1762, as author of a political newspaper, the *North Briton*, he evoked popular English hatred for the Scots and wrote libellous innuendos about George III's mother and for that, and many more outspoken articles, he was thrown into the Tower of London, but a week later, to public delight, his release was ordered on the grounds that his arrest had been a breach of parliamentary privilege. Already a marked man, the government secured from Wilkes's private press the proof sheets of *Essay on Woman*, an obscene parody on Alexander Pope's *Essay on Man*, which had been written by Wilkes and Thomas Potter years before. Wilkes had commenced, but not completed, printing a dozen copies. At the start of the parliamentary session in November 1763, the essay was read by Lord Sandwich to the House of Lords, who voted it a libel and a breach of privilege. At the same time the Commons, on a government motion, declared him guilty of a seditious libel on a former misdemeanour. During the Christmas recess Wilkes, recovering from a wound sustained in a duel provoked by exchanges in the House, stole off to Paris to visit his daughter and decided not to return to face prosecution. On 20 January 1764, the ministers carried the motion for his expulsion from the Commons. He was tried in absentia and found guilty of publishing a seditious libel and an obscene and impious libel. Sentence was deferred pending his return and in due course he was pronounced an outlaw for impeding royal justice. He spent several years abroad, chiefly in Paris, where he attended d'Holbach's 'dinners', meeting other members of the group. When back in Parliament, he gained a reputation for being something of an opportunist, changing his views even to the extent of embracing an opposite stance in order to keep his parliamentary seat, which seriously damaged his popularity. Wilkes's wit was legendary: when Lord Sandwich quipped that Wilkes would die either of the pox or on the gallows, Wilkes retorted with a lightning response, 'That depends, my lord, whether I embrace your mistress or your principles.'

Woolaston, William (1659—1724) was a British Rationalist philosopher and moralist whose ethical doctrines influenced subsequent philosophy, as well as that of his own time. After studies at the University of Cambridge, Woolaston became a schoolteacher in Birmingham (1682) and soon afterward was ordained a priest. In 1688 he inherited the major part of his family's fortune from a cousin and was able to move to London to devote his life to scholarship and philosophy. There he and his wife lived a secluded life among a few friends; he wrote prolifically, but his exaggerated standards of taste caused him to destroy many of his manuscripts. His penchant for literary elegance is evident from his major work, *The Religion of Nature Delineated* (1724). Though some critics have seen the seeds of some twentieth–century ethical theories in his views, his theism was subject to severe attacks by the end of the eighteenth century, notably by David Hume in his *Dialogues Concerning Natural Religion* (1779).

Woolston, Thomas (1670—1733) was an English religious writer and Deist. Woolston became a fellow at the University of Cambridge in 1691. After studying the work of Origen (q.v.), Woolston began to interpret Scripture allegorically rather than literally. He soon came into conflict with the government and, when it was reported that his mind had become 'defective', he was deprived of his fellowship, and in 1721 went to live in London. He formally entered into the deist controversy with his book *The Moderator Between an Infidel and an Apostate* (1725). In addition to questioning prophecies and the Resurrection of Christ, Woolston insisted on an allegorical interpretation of biblical miracles. He applied his principles in particular in *A Discourse on Our Saviour's Miraculous Power of Healing* (1730), which reportedly sold 30,000 copies. Woolston thus played a pivotal role in the denial of the miracles in the gospel. In 1729, Woolston was arrested and tried for publishing the series, sentenced to a year's imprisonment and ordered to pay a fine with imprisonment, i.e., until the fine was paid. Unable to raise funds to pay the penalty, he died in confinement.

Zoroaster (*c.* 628—*c.* 551 BC) (in Old Iranian *Zarathushtra* or *Zarathustra*) was an Iranian religious reformer and founder of Zoroastrianism, or Parsiism, as it is known in India. His teaching centred on Ahura Mazdā, the highest god, who alone is worthy of worship. He is the creator of heaven and earth, i.e., of the material and the spiritual world. As the source of everything and the very centre of nature, he is the sovereign lawgiver, the originator of the moral order and judge of the entire world. In Zoroastrianism, The Wise Lord (*Ahuro Mazdao*—later *Ormazd*) is the primeval spiritual being, the All–father, who was existent before ever the world arose. It is from him that the world emanated, i.e., he is like the Christian Creator God, and its course is governed by his foreseeing eye. His guiding spirit is the Holy Spirit, which wills good: yet it is not free, but restricted, in this temporal epoch, by its antagonist and own twin–brother, the Evil Spirit (*angro mainyush,* or *Ahriman*), who, in the beginning, was banished by the Good Spirit, and since then drags out his existence in the darkness of Hell, as the principle of evil and the arch–devil. In the *Gathas*, the writings or 'hymns' of Zoroaster, the Good Spirit of Mazda and the Evil Spirit are the two great opposing forces in the world, and Ormazd himself is to a certain extent placed above them both. Later the Holy Spirit is made directly equivalent to Ormazd. There is a whole host of devils or minor malevolent spirits, called *daevas*, who are the inferior instruments of the Evil Spirit: they are the corrupted children of Ahriman, from whom all that is evil in the world emanate. The *daevas,* unmasked and attacked by Zoroaster as the true enemies of mankind, are still, in the *Gathas*, without doubt the perfectly definite gods of old popular belief—the idols of the people. For Zoroaster they sink to the rank of spurious deities and in his eyes their priests and votaries are idolaters and heretics. In a later developed system, the *daevas* are evil spirits in general and their number has increased to millions.

Figure 90: *Le Reliquaire*, W. Goodall. *The Illustrated London News*, 6 June 1863.

Bibliography

A Brief Survey of Available Literature on D'Holbach

D'Holbach still awaits a biographer in any language, let alone in French, the language of his adopted country. His life has not been subjected to the same kind of scholarly scrutiny with which that of his friends and contemporary philosophers of similar intellectual standing has been treated, at least by French scholars and other writers on the Enlightenment, although his ideas, as expounded in his *System of Nature*, have been more fully explored in a number of languages, as outlined below. His anti–Christian works, such as *Christianity Unveiled*, have received scant critical attention, and a number of his other works in the same vein have been subjected to even less analysis or none at all, viz., *La Théologie portative (Portable Theology)* (1767), *La Contagion sacrée (Sacred Contagion)* (1768), *Histoire Critique de Jésus Christ (Critical History of Jesus Christ)* (1770), etc., and many others. Many have not been translated into English as yet—see Bibliography for details. As will also be seen, many of the dates of publication, not to mention their authorship, are difficult to establish since false dates were frequently assigned, being pre– or post–dated from the date of composition as given on the title page, as well as pseudonyms or no name at all being assigned by way of authorship in order to avoid French censorship. Indeed, it is only as recent as 2006 that inexpensive editions in French of some of his texts have become available, before which time the reader had to rely on expensive antiquarian editions or on library holdings.

Books in English

There are many passing references to d'Holbach and his works in books to do with the Enlightenment, both in French and in English, which are too numerous to mention, but most refer to his *System of Nature*. D'Holbach's works were widely read in England by thinkers such as Deists and, as explained in the Introduction, he carried on a lively correspondence with, visited, and received as guests a number of prominent Englishmen. D'Holbach also relied on such people to bring him the latest publications written in English when visitors came to see and stay with him and some of these works he translated into French. Books having substantive sections on, or references to, d'Holbach's works are noted in the Bibliography here.

Books written in English primarily about d'Holbach and his works are few and they are all out of print: hence they are difficult to get hold of, except as library items—and even then, some of them are rare. One of the first publications of this type is by Julian Hibbert, *A Brief Sketch of the Life and Writings of Baron D'Holbach*, published by J. Watson, London, in 1834. The book is a mere pamphlet and it would have been a much more substantial work had the author not died before he had time to finish it: the editor and publisher, J. Watson, remarks that the 'lamented complier's' work was 'much too good to be wholly suppressed', so he published it as it was—unfinished.[1] It contains a brief biographical sketch of d'Holbach, the details of which are well–documented elsewhere, but it does contain a list of d'Holbach's publications which, though now superseded, was useful at the time of publication. Much more extensive and detailed research has been carried out subsequently on the issues of authorship and dates of publication to make Hibbert's list appear hopelessly dated and in some instances, quite misleading.

A useful study of d'Holbach and a good number of his writings, not just on religious superstition, but also his later works on morality, social organization, civil and religious liberty, and international law, etc., is W.H. Wickwar's, *Baron D'Holbach: A Prelude to the French Revolution*, first published in 1935. Wickwar goes into some considerable biographical detail of the baron's life, the intellectuals with whom he met regularly, those who influenced his thinking and the ideas he expressed—all examined in their historical setting. Generally the work is very informative, but many of his anti–Christian works are given short shrift, or the remarks he makes about some works are superficial. Also there are a number of typographical errors in the text and, whilst the book is generously furnished with references to his sources, a good number of footnotes are missing and they are organized and referenced in a chaotic fashion.

One text that is readily available, despite its age, is Cushing, *Baron D'Holbach: A Study of Eighteenth–Century Radicalism in France*, published in 1914. It was written as part of a doctoral degree, but despite this, it is a slim volume of scant detail, available as a print–on–demand edition of books no longer in stock. This work will be of very limited use to many readers since letters and documents to and from d'Holbach are reproduced untranslated in French and in German, but the volume does contain some of d'Holbach's own letters to Wilkes in English, which would be difficult to obtain elsewhere, since they are now archival material. The book contains a reasonable bibliography of d'Holbach's own writings which, like Hibbert's, has been generally superseded, but it has a general bibliography, albeit of limited use for readers who do not know French. Irritatingly, it has been reproduced without a single French accent throughout the entire book, whether simply part of a proper noun, such as in Helvétius, or even in the long passages of French reproduced from letters in the original language. To

---

[1] J. Hibbert, *A Brief Sketch of the Life and Writings of Baron D'Holbach* (London: Watson, 1834), p. 12.

say the least, this is sloppy and it can also make a semantic difference to the sense of the original.

An extremely detailed and readable book, which has the advantage of having being written relatively recently, is Kors *D'Holbach's Coterie: An Enlightenment in Paris*, published in 1976. Though it is not without its detractors and critics, Kors lists people who visited d'Holbach at his famous Thursday evening dinners, from *habitués* to those just passing through, and he gives a rather useful thumb–nail sketch of each person. The author tackles such questions as, whether these regular dinners were a hotbed of militant atheism, as has often been alleged, or were simply a forum for discussion of a more wide–ranging nature. The volume also contains a very useful bibliography, which has been compiled using the very latest scholarship, i.e.,Vercruysse's descriptive bibliography.

Finally, there is a work of considerable interest, containing a single, lengthy chapter on d'Holbach which is well–written and researched, but it is to be found in a doctoral thesis, not readily accessible to the general reader. It is Wattles, *Atheism in the Philosophe Movement from 1750 to 1775, with particular reference to Buffon, D'Alembert, Helvétius, D'Holbach and Diderot*. Wattles covers in some detail thinkers who had a considerable influence upon d'Holbach's thinking and he sets his numerous anti–religious publications published between 1767—1770 in context, giving possible sources for many of his ideas from works published by friends known to him or released anonymously for fear of falling foul of French censorship and ending up in the Bastille. Wattles makes the very valuable point that d'Holbach's irreligious and atheistic writings have been seen as a climax of philosophical thought of this kind, not merely because of the unprecedented boldness of their publication, but also because his writing represent a synthesis of a number of ideas which had already appeared in the seventeenth and eighteenth centuries.[2]

Books in French

As with general books written about the Enlightenment in any language, there are many passing references to d'Holbach in those written by French scholars, and there are a number of memoirs and letters written by fellow *philosophes* and members of the baron's own circle or from wider circles of French intellectual society, who have made comments about him. His name crops up in letters *en passant* in the correspondence of several people like Voltaire and Diderot, and by people in the thick of Parisian salon life, such as

---

[2]   See Bibliography for details. Chapter VI of the thesis discusses d'Holbach's life and works.

497

Mme D'Epinay, who corresponded at length with Grimm, Rousseau and others. Most references to d'Holbach in letters written to and by his fellow *philosophes* are useful and are commented upon in the appropriate sections of this book. References to d'Holbach in the correspondence of people like Mme D'Epinay are really only tittle–tattle and useful merely to shed light on his character and to help in an understanding of the milieu in which he lived and wrote. This is not to denigrate such memoirists and correspondents in any way, but so few people were apprised of the fact that d'Holbach was the real author of many of the works which caused such a stir in French intellectual circles. A remark made by the Contesse de Genlis on d'Holbach's *Système de la nature*, though disapproving of the work, is typical and indicative of the conscious efforts d'Holbach made to keep his authorship of contentious, anti–religious works a closely guarded secret: 'Sans nom d'auteur, mais ce méprisable ouvrage étoit du baron d'Holbach. *Ce qui n'a été su, avec certitude, qu'après sa mort*' (my italics)— '[Published] without the author's name, this despicable work was by the baron d'Holbach. *This fact was only known for sure after his death.*'[3] One thing is clear and emerges repeatedly in all sources of this kind—that d'Holbach and his wife were genial hosts, and all who met d'Holbach were impressed by his learning, which he wore lightly, and that he was an exceptionally generous man who kept his acts of generosity to himself. None of his contemporaries had a bad word to say about him, apart from the constantly whining, paranoid Rousseau, and even then the incident which so offended Rousseau was based on a misunderstanding. (Details of this and d'Holbach's relations with Rousseau are dealt with in the Introduction.)

Whole studies dedicated to d'Holbach and his writing in French are as thin on the ground as those written in English, and they have not been translated. Chief among them, if only because it is the only work of its kind *wholly* dedicated to a study of d'Holbach and his writing, is Hubert, *D'Holbach et ses Amis*, published in Paris in 1928. The book is divided into two sections: the first part sets d'Holbach and his coterie in the context of the era, principally around the ideas and compilation of Diderot's *Encyclopédie*, and the second part reproduces extracts from works mostly by d'Holbach, but also by Boulanger, Grimm, Damilaville and Diderot himself. The work is useful for its chronological treatment of when, where and how d'Holbach met luminaries of the Enlightenment, such as Diderot, Grimm, Buffon, Morellet, Naigeon, Boulanger, and many others. It is also useful in that the author

---

[3] Contesse de Genlis, *Les Diners du Baron D'Holbach* (Paris, 1822), p. 205, footnote. This work has generally been discredited by scholars as being more fabrication than fact and many of her remarks about what went on at d'Holbach's soirées were based on hearsay. However, on this point, I think she can be taken at her word.

tackles the question of why certain 'A–List' *philosophes* of the Enlightenment, such as d'Alembert, were not regular visitors or ever frequented a single one of his regular 'dinners'.

One of the most useful works on d'Holbach published in French is the unsurpassed—but rare and expensive—descriptive bibliography of d'Holbach's works by Vercruysse—*Bibliographie descriptive des écrits du baron d'Holbach*, published in 1971. Standing as a great testament to painstaking scholarship, Vercruysse's book adopts a chronological approach to all d'Holbach works, or those attributed to him, including those published under pseudonyms and attributed to other authors, and he prefaces each work with fully referenced remarks made by contemporaries and provides a detailed analysis of publication history and editions, including translations of works into foreign languages, where appropriate. It is the last word (dare one say 'Bible'?!) on matters bibliographical and it surpasses any bibliography to date, and probably for the foreseeable future, unless some astonishing new archive comes to light.

Of the many memoirists of the era, Morellet and Marmontel are the most forthcoming on d'Holbach's character and gatherings. Needless to say, Diderot mentions d'Holbach in many of his letters, which are very revealing.

Recent Editions of d'Holbach's Works

Œuvres Philosophiques, 5 vols (Paris: Editions Alive, 1998—2001)

La Théologie Portative, ou Dictionnaire abrégé de la religion chrétienne, text prepared and edited by Jean–Pierre Jackson (Paris: Editions Coda Poche, 2006)

Le Christianisme Dévoilé, text prepared and edited by Jean–Pierre Jackson (Paris: Editions Coda Poche, 2006)

Histoire critique de Jésus Christ, ou Analyse raisonnée des Evangiles, text prepared and edited by Jean–Pierre Jackson (Paris: Editions Coda Poche, 2007)

La Contagion sacrée, ou Histoire naturelle de la superstition, text prepared and edited by Jean–Pierre Jackson (Paris: Editions Coda Poche, 2006)

Translations into English of d'Holbach's Works

Baron d'Holbach, *Christianity Unveiled; being an Examination of the Principles and Effects of the Christian Religion*, translated by W.M. Johnson (N.Y.: Gordon Press, 1974)

Paul Henri Thiry, Baron d'Holbach, *Good Sense*, translated by Anna Knoop (N.Y.: Prometheus Books, 2004)

Paul Henri Thiry, Baron d'Holbach, *Ecce Homo! Or A Critical Inquiry into the History of Jesus of Nazareth: Being a Rational Analysis of The Gospels*, no translator given, reprint of the first American edition, revised and corrected, of 1827, (N.Y.: Gordon Press, 1977)

Paul Henri Thiry, Baron d'Holbach, *A letter to Eusebia, occasioned by Mr. Toland's "Letters to Serena"*, translated by W. Wotton (London: 1704)

Paul Henri Thiry, Baron d'Holbach, *The system of nature*, translated with an introduction by Robert D. Richardson, Jr., (N.Y.: Garland, 1984)

Baron d'Holbach, *The System of Nature*, adapted from the original translation of H.D. Robinson, 1868, introduced by Michael Bush, Greek and Latin translation by Alistair Jackson (Manchester: Clinamen, 1999)

Système de la nature (The System of Nature) *from the original French of M. de Mirabaud (or, rather, Baron P. H. D. von Holbach)*, A new edition of the translation by Samuel Wilkinson by B.D. Cousins (London: 1839)

Books in French with Substantial References to d'Holbach

Barbier, Antoine–Alexandre, *Dictionnaire des ouvrages anonymes et pseudonymes* (Paris: 1806—1809, and several other editions)

Bergier, M., *Apologie de la Religion Chrétienne Contre l'Auteur du Christianisme dévoilé et contre quelques autres Critiques*, 2 vols (Paris: Humblot, MDCCLXIX)

Damiron, Ph., *Mémoires pour Servir à l'Histoire de la Philosophie au XVIII–e siècle* (Paris: 1858)

Delvaille, Jules, *Essai sur l'Histoire de l'Idée de Progrès jusqu'à la fin du XVIII–e Siècle* (Paris: Allcan et Guillaumin Réunies, 1910)

Diderot, *Correspondance*, ed. by G. Roth, et al., 12 vols (Paris, 1955—1970) [vols VIII, XII, XVIII are the most useful]

Marmontel, Jean–François, *Mémoires d'un Père pour servir à l'instruction de ses enfants* (Paris: 1804)

Morellet, André, *Mémoires sur le 18e siècle et sur la Révolution* (Paris: Librairie française de Ladvocat, 1821), reprinted and published in Paris (Mercure de France, 1988)

Epinay, Mme. D', *Mémoires et Correspondance de Madame D'Epinay*, 3 vols (Paris: 1818)

Fabre, Joseph, *Les Pères de la Révolution: de Bayle à Condorcet* (Paris: 1910)

Galiani, Abbé, *Correspondance inédite de l'Abbé F. Galiani pendant les années 1765 à 1783 avec Mme d'Epinay, Le Baron d'Holbach etc.*, 2 vols (Paris: 1818)

Garat, D.J., *Mémoires historiques sur la vie de Monsieur Suard, sur ses écrits, et sur le 18e siècle* (Paris, 1820)

Genlis, Contesse de, *Les Diners du Baron D'Holbach* (Paris, 1822)

Grimm, Frédéric (Friedrich) Melchior, von Baron (1723—1807) *Correspondance littéraire, philosophique et critique addressée à un souverain d'Allemagne, 1753—1789*, 16 vols (Paris: Lonchamps, 1813) [vols. V, VII & XIV are the most useful]

Hubert, *D'Holbach et ses Amis* (Paris: André Delpeuch, 1928)

Morellet, *Mémoires sur le 18ème siècle et sur la Révolution* (1921)

Plékhanov, Georgy Valentinovich, *Essais sur l'histoire du matérialisme: D'Holbach, Helvétius, Marx* (Paris:1957)

Vercruysse, *Bibliographie Descriptive des Ecrits du Baron d'Holbach* (Paris: Minard, 1971)

Voltaire, *Œuvres Complètes*, (Paris: Garnier, 1881), XLIV, pp. 534—535, 'Lettre à Mme De Saint–Julien'

Books on d'Holbach in English

Cushing, Max Pearson, *Baron d'Holbach: A Study of Eighteenth Century Radicalism in France* (N.Y.: 1914), available as print–on–demand edition through Kessinger Publishing Reprints

Hibbert, Julian, *A Brief Sketch of the Life and Writings of Baron D'Holbach* (London: Watson, 1834)

Topazio, Virgil W., *D'Holbach's Moral Philosophy. Its background and development* (Genève [Geneva], 1956)

Wickwar, W.H., *Baron D'Holbach: A Prelude to the French Revolution* (London: Allen and Unwin, 1935)

Other Works in English with Substantial References to d'Holbach

Beach, Joseph Warren, *The Concept of Nature in Nineteenth–Century English Poetry* (N.Y.: Macmillan, 1936)

Boas, George, *Dominant Themes of Modern Philosophy: A History* (N.Y.: Ronald Press, 1957)

Cobban, *In Search of Humanity: The Role of the Enlightenment in Modern History* (N.Y.: George Braziller, 1960)

Cunningham, Peter, ed., *Letters* [of Horace Walpole], 9 vols (London: 1880)

Gellner, Ernest, *Selected Philosophical Themes: Volume III: The Devil in Modern Philosophy* (N.Y.: Routledge, 2003)

Grieg, J.Y.T., ed., *The Letters of David Hume*, 2 vols (Oxford: Clarendon Press, 1932)

Hancock, Albert Elmer, *The French Revolution and the English Poets: A Study in Historical Criticism* (N.Y.: Holt and Co., 1899)

Herrick, Jim, *Against Faith: Essays on Deists, Skeptics, and Atheists* (N.Y.: Prometheus Books, 1985)

Kors, Alan Charles, *D'Holbach's Coterie: An Enlightenment in Paris* (Princeton, New Jersey; Princeton U.P., 1976)

Romilly, S., *Memoirs of the Life of Sir Samuel Romilly:with a selection from his correspondence, edited by his sons*, 3 vols (London: John Murray, 1840)

Rousseau, Jean–Jacques, *The Confessions*, gen. ed. Tom Griffith, intro. by Derek Matravers, no named translator (London: Wordsworth Classics of World Literature, 1996)

Tallentyre, Stephen G., *The Friends of Voltaire* (London: Smith, Elder, 1906)

Wattles, G., *Atheism in the Philosophe Movement from 1750—1775, with particular reference to Buffon, D'Alembert, Helvétius, D'Holbach and Diderot*, unpublished PhD thesis (University of Oxford, 1986)

Walpole, Horace, *Letters*, ed. by Toynbee, 16 vols (Oxford: Clarendon Press, 1903—1905) [vols VI & XVI are the most useful]

General Books on the Enlightenment in English

Freeman, Charles, *The Closing of the Western Mind: The Rise of Faith and the Fall of Reason* (London: Pimlico, 2003)

Porter, Roy, *The Enlightenment* (Studies in European History series) (Basingstoke: Palgrave, 2001)

Porter, Roy, *Enlightenment: Britain and the Creation of the Modern World* (London: Penguin Books, 2000)

Israel, Jonathan, *Radical Enlightenment:Philosophy and the Making of Modernity 1650—1750* (Oxford: OUP, 2002)

——, *Enlightenment Contested: Philosophy, Modernity, and the Emancipation of Man 1670—1752* (Oxford: OUP, 2006)

Other Works in Various Languages

English translations of the rarer and more difficult works obtainable have been noted where possible. The British Library holds all the items below. The fullest possible information has been noted: frequently old editions do not state a particular publisher—just a place and date. Some works were actually printed in London, but record another place, such as Paris: where this is the case, the true place of publication has been noted, as well as the putative location. Where multiple copies and editions are available, I have generally noted the easiest to obtain.

Websites come and go, so only reliable and authoritative internet sources have been noted, but the reader is encouraged to search for others: there are many rare works of the classics and Church Fathers on the internet.

In a very few instances it has not been possible to trace an extant edition of a work mentioned by d'Holbach or Bergier in U.K libraries: foreign holdings have not been noted.

Acharya, S., *The Christ Conspiracy: The Greatest Story Ever Sold* (Kempton, Illinois: Adventures Unlimited, 1999)

Acosta, Father Joseph de, *Historia natural y moral de la Indias* (Barcelona: L Marini, 1591)

——, *The Natural History of the Spanish Indies in general. The Civil and Moral History of the Spanish West Indies*, trans. John Harris, D.D., F.R.S. (1705)

Akenside, Mark, *The Complete Poetical Works of Mark Akenside with a biographical sketch of the author* (London: Knight and Son, *c.* 1855)

Ambrose, St, *De officiis* [*On the Offices of Ministers*], ed. with an intro., trans. and commentary by Ivor J. Davidson (Oxford: OUP, 2001)

——, *On Belief in the Resurrection*— available on the internet at http://www.monachos.net/library/Ambrose_of_Milan%2C_On_Belief_in _the_Resurrection)

Annet, Peter, *A Collection of the Tracts of a Certain Free Enquirer (Peter Annet)*, with a new introduction by John Vladimir Price (London: Routledge/Thoemmes, 1995)

Antony, Louise M., ed., *Philosophers without Gods: Meditations on Atheism and the Secular Life* (Oxford: OUP, 2007)

Aquinas, Thomas, St, *Summa Theologiae*, 5 vols (Christian Classics, 1981)

Aristotle, *Poetics*, trans. Stephen Halliwell, with Longinus, *On the Sublime*, trans. W.H. Fyfe, revised by Donald Russell, with Demetrius, *On Style*, trans. Doreen C. Innes based on W. Rhys Roberts (Harvard: Harvard University Press/Loeb Classical Library, 1995, reprinted with corrections 1999)

——, *Politics*, trans. H. Rackham (Harvard: Harvard University Press/Loeb Classical Library, 1932)

Arnauld, Antoine, *De la fréquente communion Où les sentimens des Pères, des papes, et des Conciles, touchant l'usage des sacremens de Pénitence & d'Eucharistie* (Paris: A. Vitré, 1644)

Athanasius, *The Life of St Anthony* in *Early Christian Lives* (Penguin Classics) (London: Penguin, 1998)

Athanasius—see also Schaff, Philip, *Select Library of Nicene and Post–Nicene Fathers of the Christian Church*

Augustin, St, *City of God*, 7 vols; vol I trans. G. E. McCracken; vols II, VI & VII trans. W. M. Green; vol III trans. David S. Wiesen; vol IV trans. Philip Levine; vol VI trans. Eva M. Sanford & W. M. Green (Harvard: Harvard University Press/Loeb Classical Library, 1957—89)

——, *Confessions*, trans. W. Watts, 2 vols (Harvard: Harvard University Press/Loeb Classical Library, 1989)

——, *Select Letters*, trans. J.H. Baxter, revised edn (Harvard: Harvard University Press/Loeb Classical Library, 1989)

——, a number of his works are available on the internet as part of the Project Gutenberg at http://www.gutenberg.org/wiki/Main_Page

Bayle, Pierre, *Continuation des Pensées diverses écrites à un Docteur de Sorbonne, à l'occasion de la Comète qui parut au mois de Décembre 1680, ou réponse à plusieurs difficultez que Monsieur *** a proposées à l'auteur* (Rotterdam: 1721)

——, *Various thoughts on the occasion of a comet*, trans. with notes and an interpretative essay by Robert C. Bartlett (N.Y.: State University of New York Press, 2000)

Bellarmine, Robert, *Spiritual Writings*, trans. with an intro. by John Patrick Donnelly and Roland J. Teske, preface by John W. O'Malley (N.Y.: Paulist Press, c.1989)

Bergier, Abbé, *La certitude des Preuves du Christianisme* (Paris: 1771)

——, *Le Déism refuté par lui–même* (Paris: Humblot, 1766)

Bernard, Jean Frédéric, *Le monde, son origine, et son antiquité. Première partie. De l'âme, et de son immortalité. Seconde partie. Essai sur la chronologie* [Anonymous: *Premiere partie* is attributed to J.–F. Bernard and *Seconde partie* is attributed to J.–B. Mirabaud (Londres [i.e., Paris], 1751)

Bernard, St, of Clairvaux, *On the Song of Songs* [also referred to as *Sermon on the Canticle of Canticles*], 4 vols (Cistercian Publications Inc.,U.S., 1989—2004)

Bingham, Alfred J., 'The Abbé Bergier: An Eighteenth–Century Catholic Apologist' in *Modern Language Review*, 3 (July) 1959, pp. 337—350

Bolingbroke, Lord—see Pope, Alexander

Boulainvilliers, Henri de, comte de Saint–Saire, *Œuvres philosophiques*, ed. Renée Simon (La Haye: Martinus Nijhoff, 1973)

Boulanger, Nicolas–Antoine, *Antiquité dévoilée par ses usages* (Paris: Les Belles Lettres, 1978)

——, *Recherches sur l'origine du despotisme oriental* (1773)

Bullet, Jean–Baptiste, *Histoire de l'établissement du christianisme, tirée des seuls auteurs juifs et païens, où l'on trouve une preuve solide de la vérité de cette religion* (Paris: 1764)

——, *The History of the Establishment of Christianity, compiled from Jewish and heathen authors only; exhibiting a substantial proof of the truth of this religion. Translated by William Salisbury with notes by the translater, and some strictures on Mr. Gibbon's account of Christianity and its first teachers* (London: Charles Bathurst, 1776)

Calmet, Dom Augustin, *Commentaire littéral sur tous les livres de l'Ancien et du Nouveau Testament* (Paris: 1707)

——, *Treatise on vampires & revenants : the phantom world : dissertation on those persons who return to earth bodily, the excommunicated, the oupires or vampires, vroucolacas, &c.*, trans. Henry Christmas, ed. Clive Leatherdale (Brighton: Desert Island, 1993)

Catullus poetry with Tibullus, *Pervigilium Veneris*, trans. by F.W. Cornish, J.P. Postgate and J.W. Mackail, revised by J.P. Goold (Harvard: Harvard University Press/Loeb Classical Library, 1989)

Chrysostom, St John, *Discourses*, 5 vols; vols I & II trans. by J. W. Cohoon; vols III-V trans. by H. Lamar Crosby (Harvard: Harvard University Press/Loeb Classical Library, 1932)

Cicero, *Tusculan Disputations*, trans. by J. E. King (Harvard: Harvard University Press/Loeb Classical Library, 1960)

——, *On the Nature of the Gods. Academics,* trans. by H. Rackham, revised edn. (1951) (Harvard: Harvard University Press/Loeb Classical Library, reprinted 2000)

——, *On Old Age. On Friendship. On Divination*, trans. by W.A. Falconer (Harvard: Harvard University Press/Loeb Classical Library, 1923)

——, *On the Republic & On Laws*, trans. by Clinton W. Keys [vol XVI Cicero *Philosophical Treatises* in the Loeb Classical Library] (Harvard: Harvard University Press/Loeb Classical Library, 1989)

Clanchy, M.T., *Early Medieval England* (London: The Folio Society, 1997)

Clark Kee, Howard, ed., *Cambridge Annotated Study Apocrypha* (Cambridge: CUP, 1989)

Clarke, Samuel, *A Demonstration of the Being and Attributes of God: more particularly in answer to Mr. Hobbs, Spinoza, and their followers. Wherein the notion of liberty is stated, and the possibility and certainty of it proved, in opposition to necessity and fate. Being the substance of eight sermons preach'd in the year 1704 at the Lecture founded by the Honourable Robert Boyle, Esq* (London: James Knapton, 1705)

Clarke, Samuel, *The Scripture–Doctrine of the Trinity ... Wherein all the texts in the New Testament relating to that doctrine, and the principal passages in the Liturgy of the Church of England, are collected, compared, and explained* (London: George Strahan, 1713)

——, *The Works of Samuel Clarke*, 4 vols (N.Y./London: Garland, 1978)

Collins, Anthony—see Skelton, Philip, *Deism Revealed...*

Cornford, Francis M., *Plato's Cosmology: The* Timaeus *of Plato* (Cambridge: Hackett Publishing Company, 1997)

Coyer, Gabriel François, *Lettre au R.P. Berthier sur le matérialisme* (Geneva, 1759) also attributed to Diderot and found in his *Œuvres complètes* (1773), IV

Cudworth, Ralph, Dr., *The True Intellectual System of the Universe wherein all the Reason and Philosophy of Atheism is Confuted and its Impossibility Demonstrated, with a Treatise concerning Eternal and Immutable Morality*, with notes and a dissertation by Dr J.L. Mosheim, trans. by John Harrison (London: 1845)

Dawkins, Richard, *The Selfish Gene* (Oxford: OUP, 1976), second edn. (1989), 30th anniversary edn. (2006)

——, *The Blind Watchmaker* (London: Penguin, 2006)

——, *The God Delusion* (London: Transworld Publishers/Bantam Press, 2006)

Dante Alighieri, *The Divine Comedy*, trans. by Robin Kirkpatrick, 3 vols (London: Penguin Classics, 2006—7)

Dennett, Daniel C., *Breaking the Spell: Religion as a Natural Phenomenon* (London: Allen Lane/Penguin Books, 2006)

Deruette, Serge, *Lire Jean Meslier: Curé, Athée Révolutionnaire*, preface by Roland Desné (Brussels: Les Éditions Aden, 2008)

Descartes, René, *Discourse on Method and Related Writings*, trans. with an intro. by Desmond M. Clarke (London: Penguin Books, 1999)

Diderot, Denis and Jean le Rond d'Alembert *Encyclopédie, ou Dictionnaire Raisonné des Sciences, des Arts et des Métiers*, several editions, XVII vols of text and XI vols of plates (Paris: 1751—1772) & Panckoucke's 4–vol *Supplément à l'Encyclopédie*—all these works can be accessed on the internet via the University of Chicago ARTFL Project at http://www.lib.uchicago.edu/efts/ARTFL/projects/encyc/

Diderot, Denis, *The Nun*, trans. by Russell Gouldbourne (Oxford: OUP, 2005)

Diodorus Siculus, *Library of History*, 12 vols; vols I-VI trans. by C.H. Oldfather; vol VII trans. by C.L. Sherman; vol VIII trans. by C. Bradford Wells; vols IX & X trans. by Russel M. Geer; vols XI & XII trans. by Francis R. Walton (Harvard: Harvard University Press/Loeb Classical Library, 1935—1989)

Diogenes Laertius, *The Lives of Eminent Philosophers* [*Vitae philosophorum*], trans. by R. D. Hicks, 2 vols (Harvard: Harvard University Press/Loeb Classical Library, 1925)

Ditton, Humphry, *A discourse concerning the resurrection of Jesus Christ ... Together with an appendix concerning the impossible production of Thought from matter and motion: the nature of humane souls and of brutes: the Anima Mundi, and the hypothesis of the το παν, etc.* (London, 1712 edition & 1714)

Dodwell, Henry, *De Jure Laicorum Sacerdotali, ex sententia Tertulliani aliorumque Veterum Dissertatio. Adversus anonymum Dissertatorem, De Cœnæ Administratione, ubi Pastores non sunt...* (c. 1685)

Dodwell, Henry, The Elder, *The doctrine of the Church of England, concerning the independency of the clergy on the lay–power...* (London, 1697)

Dodwell, Henry—see also Skelton, Philip, *Deism Revealed...*

Dostoevsky, Fyodor, *The Brothers Karamazov*, trans. by Richard Pevear and Larissa Volkhonsky, intro. by Malcolm V. Jones (N.Y., London: Everyman's Library, 1990)

Ellerbe, Helen, *The Dark Side of Christian History* (Windermere, Florida: Morningstar and Lark, 2004)

Epictetus, *Discourses*, trans. by W.A. Oldfather, 2 vols (Harvard: Harvard University Press/Loeb Classical Library, 1989)

Epicurus, *Works*, trans. by Cyril Bailey, intro. by Irwin Edwin (N.Y.: Limited Editions Club, 1947)

Epiphanius, *Adversus Haereses* (*Against Heresies*) or *The Panarion*, trans. by Frank Williams (Leiden: Brill, 1987—94)— some extracts are on the internet at http://www.tertullian.org/rpearse/epiphanius.html

Ehrman, Bart D., *Lost Christianities: The Battles for Scripture and the Faiths We Never Knew* (Oxford: OUP, 2003)

——, *Lost Scriptures: Books that Did Not Make It into the New Testament* (Oxford: OUP, 2003)

——, *Misquoting Jesus: The Story Behind Who Changed the Bible and Why* (N.Y.: HarperOne/HarperCollins, 2005)

Eusebius, *Ecclesiastical History*, 2 vols; vol I (Books 1—5) trans. by Kirsopp Lake, and vol II (Books 6—10) trans. by J.E.L. Oulton (Harvard: Harvard University Press, 1973 & 1926)—some parts available on the internet at http://www.ccel.org/

Fontenelle, (Bernard Le Bovier de) (1657—1757), *Œuvres complètes*, ed. by Alain Niderst, 3 vols (Tours: Fayard, 1989—1991) [further volumes are planned]

Fréret, Nicolas, *Examen critique des apologistes de la religion chrétienne*, (1767) [also attributed to J. Levesque de Burigny]

——, *A preservative against religious prejudices. (The Moseiade.) Originally written in French by N. F.,* trans. into English by D. I. Eaton (London: 1812)

——, *Lettre de Thrasybule à Leucippe*: Edizione critica, introduzione e commento a cura di S. Landucci (Firenze/Florence: Olschki, 1986)

——, *Lettre de Thrasybule à Leucippe—A Letter from Thrasybulus to Leucippe. (On natural and revealed religion). By M. Fréret (or rather, by Baron P. H. D. von Holbach, J. A. Naigeon and N. de la Grange)* (London: Robert Carlile, 1826)

——, *Œuvres de Fréret*, 4 vols (BookSurge Publishing, 2001)—a facsimilie reprint of a 1792 edn. by Jean Servière (J.–F. Bastien, Paris)

Friedman, Richard Elliott, *Who Wrote the Bible?* (San Francisco: Harper, 1997)

Gibbon, Edward, *The History of the Decline and Fall of the Roman Empire*, 3 vols (Everyman's Library Classics, 1994)

Gobien, Charles le, *Lettres édifiantes et curieuses écrites de la Chine, etc.* (1702)

——, *Edifying and curious letters ... (translation of part of the collection entitled: "Lettres édifiantes et curieuses," etc.), translated by the Jesuits* (1707)

Graille, Patrick and Kozul, Mladen, *Discours Antireligieux Français du Dix–Huitième Siècle du Curé Meslier au Marquis de Sade* (Paris: l'Harmattan et les Presses de l'Université Laval, 2003

Greenberg, Gary, *Myths of the Bible: How Ancient Scribes Invented Biblical History* (Naperville, Illinois: Sourcebooks, Inc., 2002)

Harris, Sam, *The End of Faith: Religion, Terror, and the Future of Reason* (London: The Free Press/Simon & Schuster, 2005)

——, *Letter to a Christian Nation* (N.Y.: Alfred A. Knopf, 2006)

Helvétius, Claude–Adrien, *De l'Esprit or Essays on the Mind...* (London, 1807)

Herbert, Lord—see Skelton, Philip, *Deism Revealed...*

Hitchens, Christopher, *The Portable Atheist: Essential Readings for the Nonbeliever* (Philadelphia: Da Capo Press, 2007)

Hobbes, Thomas, *Leviathan, with selected variants from the Latin edition of 1668*, ed. with intro. by Edwin Curley (Indianapolis, Indiana: Hackett Publishing Company, Inc., 1994)

——, see also Skelton, Philip, *Deism Revealed...*

Horace, *Odes and Epodes*, ed. and trans. by Niall Rudd (Harvard: Harvard University Press/Loeb Classical Library, 2004)

Huberman, Jack, *The Quotable Atheist: Ammunition for Nonbelievers, Political Junkies, Gadflies, and Those Generally Hell–Bound* (N.Y.: Nation Books, 2007)

Hume, David, Dialogues Concerning Natural Religion and The Natural History of Religion (Oxford: Oxford World Classics/Paperbacks, 1998)

——, *A Treatise on Human Nature: Being an Attempt to Introduce the Experimental Method of Reasoning into Moral Subjects* (London: Penguin Classics, 1985)

——, *Four Dissertations and Essays on Suicide and the Immortality of the Soul*, intro. by John Immerwahr & John Vladimir Price, pref. by James Fieser (St Augustine's Press, 2001)

Iamblichus, *On the Mysteries* (*Writings from the Greco–Roman World*, Vol 4), bilingual edn., trans., intro. and notes by Emma C. Clarke, John M. Dillon, Jackson P. Hershbell (Atlanta, USA: Society of Biblical Literature, 2003)

Jacobs, Alan, *The Essential Gnostic Gospels: Including the Gospel of Thomas and The Gospel of Mary Magdalene* (London: Watkins Publishing, 2006)

Jerome, St, *Select Letters*, trans. by F.A. Wright (Harvard: Harvard University Press/Loeb Classical Library, 1933)—also available on the internet at http://www.earlychurch.org.uk/lactantius.php

Joinville, Jean de, *Expedition of Saint Lewis in Egypt, extracted from Joinville "Histoire de Saint Louis"...* (1787)

Jordan, Michael, *In the Name of God: Violence and Destruction in the World's Religions* (Stroud, Gloucestershire: Sutton Publishing, 2006)

Josephus, Flavius, *Jewish Antiquities*, 9 vols; Books I–VI (2 vols) trans. by H. St. J. Thackeray; Books VII-XIII trans. by Ralph Marcus; Books XIV-VII trans. by Ralph Marcus and Allen Wikgren; Books XVIII-XX trans. by Louis H. Feldman (Harvard: Harvard University Press/Loeb Classical Library, reprinted 1998)

——, *The Jewish War*, trans. by H. St. J. Thackeray, 3 vols (Harvard: Harvard University Press/Loeb Classical Library, reprinted 1997)

Justin, Martyr, Saint, *Dialogue with Trypho*, trans. by Thomas B. Falls, revised, new intro. by Thomas P. Halton, ed. Michael Slusser (Washington, D.C.: Catholic University of America Press, 2003)

Kasser, R., M. Meyer, and G. Wurst, with additional commentary by Bart D. Ehrman, *The Gospel of Judas* (Washington, D.C.: National Geographic Society, 2006)

Lactantius, *The Divine Institutes*, 2 vols (The Catholic University of America Press: 1992)—also available on the internet at http://www.ccel.org/ccel/schaff/anf07.toc.html

La Fontaine, Jean de, *Œuvres complètes*, 2 vols (Paris: Gallimard, 1978—79)

——, *The Complete Fables of Jean De La Fontaine* (U.S.: Northwestern University Press, 1988)

Longinus—see Aristotle, *Poetics*

Lucretius *On the things of Nature* (*De rerum natura*), trans. by W.H.D. Rouse, revised by Martin F. Smith (Harvard: Harvard University Press/Loeb Classical Library, 1992)

Macrobius, Ambrosius Theodosius, *Saturnalia*, trans., notes and intro. by Percival Vaughan Davies (N.Y. & London: Columbia University Press, 1969)

Magill, Frank N., *Dictionary of World Biography: The Ancient World Vol 1* (Fitzroy Dearborn, 1998)

Marcellinus, Ammianus, *History*, trans. by John C. Rolfe, 3 vols (Harvard: Harvard University Press/Loeb Classical Library, reprinted 2005—2006)

Maréchal, Pierre–Sylvain, *Livre échappé au Déluge ou Pseaumes nouvellement decouvertes* (Paris: 1784)

——, *Dictionnaire des athées anciens et modernes* (Bruxelles, 1883)

McGrath, Alister, *The Twilight of Atheism: The Rise and Fall of Disbelief in the Modern World* (London: Rider, 2004 and 2005)

Menander, *Aspis. Georgos. Dis Exapaton. Dyskolos. Encheiridion. Epitrepontes*, trans. W.G. Arnott (Harvard: Harvard University Press/Loeb Classical Library, 1989)

Menander, *Heros. Theophoroumene. Karchedonios. Kitharistes. Kolax. Koneiazomenai. Leukadia. Misoumenos. Perikeiromene. Perinthia* (Harvard: Harvard University Press/Loeb Classical Library, 1996)

——, *Samia. Sikyonioi. Synaristosai. Phasma. Unidentified Fragments* (Harvard: Harvard University Press/Loeb Classical Library, 2000)

Meslier, Jean, Curé d'Etrépigny, *Mémoire contre la religion*, text prepared and ed. by Jean–Pierre Jackson and Alain Toupin with notes by Jean–Pierre Jackson (Éditions Coda, 2007)

Mirabaud, Jean–Baptiste de, *Le Monde, son origine et son antiquité*—see Bernard, Jean Frédéric

Montesquieu, Charles, *Persian Letters*, trans. By C.J. Betts (London: Penguin, Penguin Classics, 1973)

———, *The Spirit of the Laws* (Cambridge: CUP Cambridge, *Texts in the History of Political Thought*, 1989)

Naigeon, Jacques–André, *Philosophie ancienne et modern*, 3 vols (Paris: 1791—94)

———, *Le militaire filosophe, ou Difficultés sur la religion proposées au R. P. Malebranche par un ancien officer. (Abridged by J. A. Naigeon, with a contribution by Baron von Holbach.)*, nouvelle édition (Londres, 1770)

Nicole, Pierre, and Antoine Arnauld, *La Logique, ou L'art de Penser* (Paris, 1662)

Onfray, Michel, *Atheist Manifesto: The Case Against Christianity, Judaism, and Islam*, trans. by Jeremy Leggatt (N.Y.: Arcade Publishing, 2007)

Origen, *Against Celsus*, trans. from the original into English by James Bellamy (London: *c.* 1680)—available as a Kessinger Publishing print–on–demand edition and on the internet http://www.ccel.org/

Paine, Thomas, *The Age of Reason: Being an Investigation of True and Fabulous Theology*, ed. by Moncure Daniel Conway (N.Y.: Dover Publications, Inc., 2004)

Pascal, Blaise, *Pensées*, trans. by A.J. Krailsheimer (London: Penguin, Penguin Classics, 1995)

Philostratus, *Life of Apollonius of Tyana*, 3 vols, ed. and trans. by Christopher P. Jones (Harvard: Harvard University Press/Loeb Classical Library, 2005/6)

———, *Lives of the Sophists*, ed. and trans. by Wilmer C. Wright (Harvard: Harvard University Press/Loeb Classical Library, 1989)

Phlegon of Tralles, *De mirabilibus et longævis libellus. Eiusdem de Olympijs fragmentum in Greek and Latin* (1568)

———, *Book of Marvels*, trans. by William F. Hansen (Exeter: University of Exeter Press, Exeter Studies in History, 1997)

Pliny (The Elder), *Natural History*, vols I-V and IX ed. and trans. by H. Rackham; vols VI-VIII, ed. and trans. by W.H.S. Jones; vol X ed. and trans. by D. E. Eichholz (Harvard: Harvard University Press/Loeb Classical Library, 1979—89)

Pliny (The Younger), *Letters*, 2 vols, ed. and trans. by Betty Radice, vol I Books 1—7, vol II *Letters* Books VIII-X & *Panegyricus* (Harvard: Harvard University Press/Loeb Classical Library, 1989 & 2004)

Plato, *The Republic*, trans. by A.D. Lindsay (Everyman's Library, new edition 1976, with intro., Bibliography, Chronology and Notes [London: Random House and David Campbell Publishers, Ltd., 1992])

——, *The Trial and Death of Socrates: Four Dialogues*, trans. from the Greek by Benjamin Jowett, gen. series editor Stanley Appelbaum (N.Y.: Dover Thrift Editions, 1992)

Plutarch, *Reply to Colotes* in *Moralia*, Volume XIV, trans. by B. Einarson & P.H. De Lacy (Harvard: Harvard UniversityPress/Loeb Classical Library, 2004)

Pomponazzi, Pietro—see Pomponatius, Petrus

Pomponatius, Petrus, *Apologia P. Pomponatii Mantuani Tractatus de immortalitate animæ*, 2 vols (Justinianus Leonardus Ruberiensis: Bononiæ, 1518)

Pope, Alexander, *Letters from Alexander Pope, Esq; and the Right Hon. the Lord Bolingbroke, to the Reverend Dr. Swift, D.S.P.D. To which is added Almahide, a poem by the Lord Bolingbroke* (London printed; Dublin: reprinted by and for George Faulkner, 1737)

Porphyry, *Arguments of Celsus, Porphyry, and the Emperor Julian against the Christians; also extracts from Diodorus Siculus, Josephus and Tacitus, relating to the Jews. Together with an appendix containing the oration of Libanius in defence of the temples of the heathens*, trans. by Dr. Lardner, etc. (London: Thomas Rodd, 1830)

Quintilian's *Institutio Oratoria*, available in English as *Training of an Orator*, or *The Orator's Education*, 5 vols, trans. and ed. by Donald A. Russell (Harvard: Harvard University Press/Loeb Classical Library, 2001) (see Vol I [Book III] in particular)

Rauschning, H. *The Voice of Destruction* (New York: Puttnam, 1940) first published in England as *Hitler Speaks: Interviews with Hitler*, (London: Thorton Butterworth, 1939)

Raynal, Guillaume—Thomas, abbé de, *Histoire philosophique et politique des établissemens & du commerce des Européens dans les deux Indes*, 6 vols (Amsterdam, 1770)

——, *A history of the two Indies : a translated selection of writings from Raynal's Histoire philosophique et politique des établisments des Européans dans les des deux Indes*, ed. Peter Jimack (Aldershot: Ashgate, 2006)

Riquetti, Victor, Marquis de Mirabeau, *L'Ami des Hommes ou Traité de la population* (Avignon, 1756)

Rivers, Christopher, 'Safe Sex: The Prophylactic Walls of the Cloister in the French Libertine Convent Novel of the Eighteenth Century' in *Journal of the History of Sexuality*, 5, Issue: 3, 1995, pp. 381—403

Robertson, J.M., *Christianity and Mythology* [1900], in T.J. Thorburn, *The Mythical Interpretation of the Gospels: Critical Studies in the Historic Narratives* [N.Y.: Charles Scribner's Sons, 1916]

Rousseau, Jean–Jacques, *Emile*, no named translator (N.Y./London: Everyman Library, 1993)

——, *Lettres écrites de la montagne* (Amsterdam: Marc Michel Rey, 1764)

Schaff, Philip, *Select Library of Nicene and Post–Nicene Fathers of the Christian Church*, 10 vols (Edinburgh: T&T Clark, 1989)

——, *Select Library of Nicene and Post–Nicene Fathers of the Christian Church*, 14 vols, second series (Eerdmans, 1980—86)

Seneca, *Moral Essays*, trans. by John W. Basore, 3 vols (Harvard: Harvard Universtiy Press/Loeb Classical Library, 1989—2001)

Servetus, Michael, *De Trinitatis erroribus libri septem* (J. Secerius, Haguenau, 1531)

——, *Michael Servetus: A translation of his geographical, medical and astrological writings* with introductions and notes by Charles Donald O'Malley (Philadelphia, 1953)

Shaftesbury, Lord—see Skelton, Philip, *Deism Revealed...*

Siculus, Diodorus—see Diodorus Siculus

Skelton, Philip, *Deism revealed. Or the attack on Christianity candidly reviewed in its real merits, as they stand in the celebrated writings of Lord Herbert, Lord Shaftesbury, Hobbes, Toland, Tindal, Collins, Mandeville, Dodwell, Woolston, Morgan, Chubb, and others*, 2nd edn., 2 vols (London: A. Millar, 1751)

Smith, George H., *Atheism: The Case Against God* (N.Y.: Prometheus Books, 1989)

Spinoza, *Theological–Political Treatise*, ed. Jonathan Israel, (Cambridge: CUP., Cambridge Texts in the History of Philosophy, 2007)

——, *A Theologico–Political Treatise* and *A Political Treatise*, trans. with intro. by R.H.M. Elwes (N.Y.: Dover Publications, Inc., 2004)

Strabo, *Geography*, trans. by Horace Leonard Jones, 8 vols (Harvard: Harvard University Press/Loeb Classical Library, reprinted 2005)

Suetonius, *The Lives of the Cæsars*, ed. and trans. by J.C. Rolfe, 2 vols (Harvard: Harvard Universtiy Press/Loeb Classical Library, 1914, reprinted 1989)

Tachard, Gui, *Relacion del reyno de Siam* in Fernandez de Medrano (S.) *Relaciones modernas*, etc. (1701)

——, *A relation of the voyage to Siam, performed by six Jesuits sent by the French king to the Indies and China in the year 1685 : with their astrological observations and their remarks of natural philosophy, geography, hydrography and history* (London: Printed by T.B. for J. Robinson and A. Churchil, 1688)

Tacitus,Cornelius, *Histories*, vol I trans. Clifford H. Moore, vol II trans. Clifford H. Moore and John Jackson (Harvard: Harvard University Press/Loeb Classical Library, 1989)

——, *Annals*, translated by John Jackson, 3 vols (Harvard: Harvard University Press/Loeb Classical Library, 1937)

Tertullian, *Apology and De Spectaculis. Octavius*, trans. T.R. Glover and G.H. Rendall (Harvard: Harvard University Press/Loeb Classical Library, 1966)

The Essential Epicurus, trans. with intro. by Eugene O'Connor (N.Y.: Prometheus Books. 1993)

The Qur'an: A New Translation, M.A.S. Abdel Haleem (Oxford: OUP, 2004)

Tibullus—see Catullus

Tillemont, Louis Sébastien, Le Nain de, *Mémoires pour servir à l'histoire ecclésiastique des six premiers siècles justifiez par les citations des auteurs originaux; avec une chronologie où l'on fait un abrégé de l'histoire ecclésiastique*, 16 vols (Paris, 1701—1712)

——, *Ecclesiastical Memoirs of the First Six Centuries*, trans. by T. Deacon, Nonjuring Bishop of Manchester, 2 vols (London, 1733—35)

Tindal, Matthew—see Skelton, Philip, *Deism Revealed...*

Toland, John, *Christianity Not Mysterious: or a Treatise Shewing That There is Nothing in the Gospel Contrary to Reason, Nor above It* (London: Sam Buckley, 1696)

Toland, John—see also Skelton, Philip, *Deism Revealed...*

Traité des trios imposteurs—Moïse, Jésus, Mahomet (Paris: Max Milo Editions, 2002)

Trenchard, John, *The Natural History of Superstition* (London, 1709)

Vallée, Geoffroy, *La Béatitude des Chrétiens, ou le Fléau de la foi*, 1573, text prepared and ed. Alain Mothu with Patrick Graille (Orléans: Les Editions Demeter, 2005)

Vaneigem, Raoul, ed., *L'Art de ne croire en rien suivi de Livre des trios imposteurs* (Paris: Éditions Payot et Rivages, 2002)

Virgil, *Eclogues, Georgics, Aeneid*, I—VI in vol I; Books VII—XII and *Appendix Vergiliana* in vol II, trans. by H.R. Fairclough, revised by G.P. Goold (Harvard: Harvard Universtiy Press/Loeb Classical Library, first published 1916 [vol I] and 1918 [vol II], revised edition 1999 [vol I] and 2000 [vol II], reprinted 2002 & 2006)

Voltaire, *Œuvres Complètes* (Paris: Garnier, 1881)

——, *Cabales*, X

——, *Candide*, XXI

——, *Dictionnaire philosophique portatif*, XVII–XX

——, *Examen Important de Milord Bolingbroke*, XXVI

——, *Homme aux quarante écus*, XXI

——, *Le Dîner du Comte Boulainvilliers*, XXVI

——, *Questions sur les Miracles*, XXV

——, *Traité sur la tolérance à l'occasion de la mort de Jean Calas*, XXV

Wade, Ira Owen, *The Clandestine Organization and Diffusion of Philosophic Ideas in France from 1700 to 1750* (Princeton, New Jersey: Princeton U.P., 1938)

Warburton, William, Bishop of Gloucester, *Remarks on several occasional reflections: in answer to ... Doctors Stebbing and Sykes. Serving to explain ... the two dissertations in The Divine Legation, concerning the command to Abraham to offer up his son; and the nature of the Jewish Theocracy; objected to by those ... writers. Pt. II* (London: 1745)

Wheless, Joseph, *Forgery in Christianity: A Documented Record of the Foundations of the Christian Religion* (USA: Filiquarian Publishing, LLC, 2007)

Woolston, Thomas—see Skelton, Philip, *Deism Revealed...*

Xenophon, *Memorabilia, Oeconomicus, Symposium, Apology*, trans. E.C. Marchant and O.J. Todd (Harvard: Harvard Universtiy Press/Loeb Classical Library, first published 1923, reprinted 2002)

Figure 91: *The Next Refugee. Punch, or the London Charivari*, 3 December 1859.

Lightning Source UK Ltd.
Milton Keynes UK
12 October 2009

144831UK00001B/2/P